Lecture Notes in Computer Science 5673

Commenced Publication in 1973
Founding and Former Series Editors:
Gerhard Goos, Juris Hartmanis, and Jan van Leeuwen

Jens Palsberg   Zhendong Su (Eds.)

Static Analysis

16th International Symposium, SAS 2009
Los Angeles, CA, USA, August 9-11, 2009
Proceedings

 Springer

Volume Editors

Jens Palsberg
University of California, Department of Computer Science
4531K Boelter Hall, Los Angeles, CA 90095-1596, USA
E-mail: palsberg@cs.ucla.edu

Zhendong Su
University of California, Department of Computer Science
1 Shields Avenue, Davis, CA 95616, USA
E-mail: su@cs.ucdavis.edu

Library of Congress Control Number: 2009930752

CR Subject Classification (1998): D.3, F.3.1-2, I.2.2, F.4.2, B.8.1, D.1

LNCS Sublibrary: SL 2 – Programming and Software Engineering

ISSN   0302-9743
ISBN-10   3-642-03236-2 Springer Berlin Heidelberg New York
ISBN-13   978-3-642-03236-3 Springer Berlin Heidelberg New York

springer.com

© Springer-Verlag Berlin Heidelberg 2009
Printed in Germany

Typesetting: Camera-ready by author, data conversion by Scientific Publishing Services, Chennai, India
Printed on acid-free paper   SPIN: 12721160   06/3180   5 4 3 2 1 0

Preface

Static analysis is increasingly recognized as a fundamental tool for program verification, bug detection, compiler optimization, program understanding, and software maintenance. The series of Static Analysis Symposia has served as the primary venue for presentation of theoretical, practical, and application advances in the area.

This volume contains the proceedings of the 16th International Static Analysis Symposium (SAS 2009), which was held August 9–11, 2009 at UCLA, University of California, Los Angeles, USA. The previous SAS conferences were held in Valencia, Spain (2008); Kongens Lyngby, Denmark (2007); Seoul, South Korea (2006); London, UK (2005); Verona, Italy (2004); San Diego, USA (2003); Madrid, Spain (2002); Paris, France (2001); Santa Barbara, USA (2000); Venice, Italy (1999); Pisa, Italy (1998); Paris, France (1997); Aachen, Germany (1996); Glasgow, UK (1995); and Namur, Belgium (1994).

In response to the call for papers, a total of 52 contributions were submitted to the symposium. After a five-week paper review period and a subsequent two-week online discussion, the Program Committee selected 21 papers for presentation at the symposium and inclusion in this volume. The selection was based on scientific quality, originality, and relevance to the symposium. Each submission was reviewed by four (or more) Program Committee members with the help of external reviewers.

In addition to the 21 accepted papers, this volume also contains abstracts of talks given by two invited speakers: Rastislav Bodik (University of California, Berkeley) and Shaz Qadeer (Microsoft).

SAS 2009 was co-located with LICS 2009, the 24th IEEE Symposium on Logic in Computer Science. SAS and LICS had a day with shared sessions, including an invited speaker: Edmund M. Clarke (Carnegie Mellon University, USA). Last time SAS and LICS were co-located was in 2000 in Santa Barbara, USA.

We would like to thank members of the Program Committee for their thorough reviews and dedicated involvement during the paper selection process. On behalf of the Program Committee, we would like to express our gratitude to all the authors who submitted papers and all the external reviewers for their invaluable contributions. We would also like to thank the Steering Committee for their help and advice, and Andrei Voronkov for making EasyChair available to us. Finally, we gratefully acknowledge the institution that sponsored this event: UCLA, University of California, Los Angeles, USA.

August 2009

Jens Palsberg
Zhendong Su

Organization

Program Chairs

Jens Palsberg   University of California, Los Angeles, USA
Zhendong Su   University of California, Davis, USA

Program Committee

Alex Aiken   Stanford University, USA
María Alpuente   Technical University of Valencia, Spain
Radhia Cousot   CNRS/École Polytechnique, France
Sumit Gulwani   Microsoft Research, USA
Chris Hankin   Imperial College, UK
Joxan Jaffar   National University of Singapore, Singapore
Suresh Jagannathan   Purdue University, USA
Naoki Kobayashi   Tohoku University, Japan
Viktor Kuncak   Swiss Federal Institute of Technology,
                                     Switzerland
Ana Milanova   Rensselaer Polytechnic Institute, USA
Anders Møller   BRICS, University of Aarhus, Denmark
Aditya Nori   Microsoft Research, India
Andreas Podelski   University of Freiburg, Germany
Jakob Rehof   University of Dortmund, Germany
Thomas Reps   University of Wisconsin-Madison, USA
Harald Søndergaard   University of Melbourne, Australia
Eran Yahav   IBM T.J. Watson Research Center, USA
Kwangkeun Yi   Seoul National University, Korea

Steering Committee

Patrick Cousot   École Normale Supérieure, France
Radhia Cousot   CNRS/École Polytechnique, France
Roberto Giacobazzi   Università degli Studi di Verona, Italy
Gilberto Filé   Università di Padova, Italy
David Schmidt   Kansas State University, USA

External Reviewers

Gogul Balakrishnan
Demis Ballis
Gregory Batt
Ralph Becket
Julien Bertrane
Bruno Blanchet
Wei-Ngan Chin
Duc Hiep Chu
Marco Comini
Vijay D'Silva
Julian Dolby
Santiago Escobar
Jérôme Feret
Stephen Fink
Martin Fränzle
Pierre Ganty
Matt Giuca
Trevor Hansen
Martin Henz
Jose Hernandez-Orallo
Jose Iborra
Kazuhiro Inaba
Christophe Joubert
Siau-Cheng Khoo
William Klieber
Soonho Kong
Laura Kovacs
Oukseh Lee
Zhenkai Liang
Yin Liu
Benjamin Livshits
Francesco Logozzo
Salvador Lucas
Michael Maher
Roman Manevich
Matthieu Martel
Damien Massé

Laurent Mauborgne
Jan Midtgaard
Yasuhiko Minamide
Antoine Miné
Jorge Navas
Hakjoo Oh
Sungwoo Park
Ruzica Piskac
Bernie Pope
Shaz Qadeer
Sriram Rajamani
G. Ramalingam
Xavier Rival
Andrey Rybalchenko
Andrew Santosa
Ryosuke Sato
Peter Schachte
Sharon Shoham
Saurabh Srivastava
Peter Stuckey
Kohei Suenaga
Philippe Suter
Carolyn Talcott
Tachio Terauchi
Ashish Tiwari
Takeshi Tsukada
Hiroshi Unno
Kapil Vaswani
Martin Vechev
Ramarathnam Venkatesan
Alicia Villanueva
Razvan Voicu
Tanja Vos
Thomas Wies
Hongseok Yang
Greta Yorsh

Sponsoring Institutions

University of California, Los Angeles, USA

Table of Contents

Invited Talks

Contributed Papers

Algorithmic Program Synthesis with Partial Programs and Decision Procedures

Rastislav Bodik

University of California, Berkeley

Abstract. Program synthesizer can derive programs that are efficient, even surprising, but it must be first "programmed" with human insights about the domain and its implementation tricks. In deductive synthesis, the insights are captured by domain theories, often elusive and always requiring formal expertise. To bring synthesis to everyday programmers, we have been exploring algorithmic synthesis, which is to deductive synthesis what model checking is to deductive verification: Rather than deducing a program with a theorem prover, algorithmic synthesis systematically finds the program in a space of candidate implementations. If we help programmers turn their insights into descriptions of candidates, we have a chance for a practical synthesizer.

I will show how sketches-partial programs that syntactically define the candidate space-allow programmers to express their insight while eliding tedious code fragments. These fragments are filled in by CEGIS, our counterexample-guided inductive synthesis algorithm that exploits recent advances in automated decision procedures. I will also show how these decision procedures allow us to implement an oracle that helps the programmer refine and formalize his insight about a problem. Finally, I will describe the linguistic support for synthesis in our SKETCH language and show how we synthesized complex implementations of ciphers, scientific codes, and concurrent lock-free data-structures.

J. Palsberg and Z. Su (Eds.): SAS 2009, LNCS 5673, p. 1, 2009.

Algorithmic Verification of Systems Software Using SMT Solvers

Shaz Qadeer

Microsoft Research, Redmond

Abstract. Program verification is an undecidable problem; all program verifiers must make a tradeoff between precision and scalability. Over the past decade, a variety of scalable program analysis tools have been developed. These tools, based primarily on techniques such as type systems and dataflow analysis, scale to large and realistic programs. However, to achieve scalability they sacrifice precision, resulting in a significant number of false error reports and adversely affecting the usability of the tool.

In this talk, I will present a different approach to program verification realized in the HAVOC verifier for low-level systems software. HAVOC works directly on the operational semantics of C programs based on a physical model of memory that allows precise modeling of pointer arithmetic and other unsafe operations prevalent in low-level software. To achieve scalability, HAVOC performs modular verification using contracts in an expressive assertion language that includes propositional logic, arithmetic, and quantified type and data-structure invariants. The assertion logic is closed under weakest precondition, thereby guaranteeing precise verification for loop-free and call-free code fragments. To reduce the effort of writing contracts, HAVOC provides a mechanism to infer them automatically. It allows the user to populate the code with candidate contracts and then searches efficiently through the candidate set for a subset of consistent contracts.

The expressive contract language in HAVOC has two important benefits. First, it allows the documentation and verification of properties and invariants specific to a particular software system. Second, it allows a user to systematically achieve the ideal of precise verification (with no false alarms) by interacting with the verifier and providing key contracts that could not be inferred automatically.

HAVOC has been implemented using the Boogie verification-condition generator and the Z3 solver for Satisfiability-Modulo-Theories. I will describe the design and implementation of HAVOC and our experience applying it to verify typestate assertions on medium-sized device drivers with zero false alarms. I will conclude with a discussion of remaining challenges and directions for future work.

J. Palsberg and Z. Su (Eds.): SAS 2009, LNCS 5673, p. 2, 2009.
© Springer-Verlag Berlin Heidelberg 2009

Abstraction Refinement for Quantified Array Assertions

Mohamed Nassim Seghir[1,*], Andreas Podelski[1], and Thomas Wies[1,2]

[1] University of Freiburg, Germany
[2] EPFL, Switzerland

Abstract. We present an abstraction refinement technique for the verification of universally quantified array assertions such as *"all elements in the array are sorted"*. Our technique can be seamlessly combined with existing software model checking algorithms. We implemented our technique in the ACSAR software model checker and successfully verified quantified array assertions for both text book examples and real-life examples taken from the Linux operating system kernel.

1 Introduction

Among the most promising approaches to the verification of software systems is the combination of predicate abstraction [10] with automated abstraction refinement [6]. This approach is commonly referred to as software model checking. Software model checking offers a high degree of automation and has been successfully applied to non-trivial programs such as device drivers. Existing software model checkers (e.g., SLAM [2], BLAST [13], MAGIC [5], and ARMC [21]) have shown to be suitable for the verification of control-oriented properties, but they are limited when it comes to richer properties that involve data structures. A prominent class of such properties are universally quantified assertions over arrays (e.g., sortedness). We show that careful adaptation of existing software model checking techniques is sufficient to verify many interesting programs over arrays.

In order to verify quantified assertions, a program analysis needs to infer inductive invariants that are itself quantified. This contradicts the basic idea of predicate abstraction which is to construct an invariant from small pieces, since quantified assertions cannot be easily split into simpler predicates. In other words, finding the right predicates for verifying quantified assertions becomes as difficult as finding an inductive invariant. Recently, various techniques have been developed that either generalize or extend existing abstract domains (including the predicate abstraction domain) to abstract domains that can express quantified properties [3,11,25,17,22]. However, none of these approaches can be easily

---

* The first author was supported in part by the German Federal Ministry of Education and Research (BMBF) in the framework of the VerisoftXT project under grant 01 IS 07 008.

J. Palsberg and Z. Su (Eds.): SAS 2009, LNCS 5673, pp. 3–18, 2009.
© Springer-Verlag Berlin Heidelberg 2009

integrated into existing software model checkers without major changes to the underlying implementation or making the analysis less scalable.

A simpler approach towards verification of quantified assertions is due to Flanagan and Qadeer [8] and based on *ghost variables*. A ghost variable is an auxiliary program variable that is never modified by the program. It is only used for the purpose of verification. The idea in [8] is to replace each quantified variable in an assertion by a ghost variable. Thus, the ghost variables fix one instantiation for each quantified variable throughout the whole execution of the program. The transformed program can be analyzed using standard predicate abstraction and the inferred inductive invariant is implicitly universally quantified. While this approach is strictly weaker than an approach based on quantified abstract domains, it has shown to be suitable for verifying quantified array assertions with vanilla predicate abstraction, i.e., where all predicates have been provided by the user [8].

Problems arise when this approach is used together with automated abstraction refinement. Standard techniques for extracting predicates from spurious counterexamples such as (weakest) preconditions [6, 1] and interpolants [12] are insufficient. The reason is that these techniques do not infer predicates that allow the analysis to perform the necessary widening, i.e., to compute an invariant that states properties of unbounded intervals in the array. Therefore, the refinement loop often diverges, establishing the invariant, one by one, for all the individual entries in the unbounded intervals.

We adapt an existing abstraction refinement method to handle universally quantified assertions over arrays. Our technique is based on the idea of using ghost variables to eliminate universal quantifiers in assertions, but overcomes the limitation of standard abstraction refinement techniques described above. The technique is tailored towards assertions that quantify over index variables of arrays. It uses a theorem prover to derive consequences from spurious error paths. These consequences determine entries in the array that violate the target property. From these consequences our technique derives predicates that describe unbounded intervals in the array. These predicates enable the analysis to perform the necessary widening that results in a sufficiently strong inductive invariant.

Despite its simplicity our technique is surprisingly effective. We have implemented our technique in the ACSAR software model checker [24]. Using our implementation we successfully verified quantified array assertions for both text book examples such as sorting algorithms and real-life examples taken from the Linux operating system kernel and the Xen hypervisor.

2   Related Work

There have been various attempts to account for the verification of quantified properties including approaches based on predicate abstraction [8, 17, 14], first-order theorem provers [20, 15], templates [3, 11, 25], and shape analysis [9, 22]. Our approach is able to handle all array related examples that have been analyzed in [8, 17, 14, 20, 3, 11, 9]. Some of the examples in [25, 15] involve properties with alternating universal and existential quantifiers such as permutation of arrays. These properties are outside the scope of our approach. In the following, we make a more detailed comparison.

Range predicates [14] describe properties of unbounded array segments which enables the verification of universally quantified array assertions using predicate abstraction with abstraction refinement. In the refinement phase, an axiom-based algorithm is applied to infer new range predicates as Craig interpolants for the spurious counterexample. Range predicates refer to an implicitly quantified variable that ranges over array indices. However, this approach does not handle properties that require quantification over more than one variable, such as properties of multidimensional arrays. Our approach does not have these restrictions.

Lahiri and Bryant proposed an extension of predicate abstraction to infer universally quantified invariants [17]. Their technique is based on index predicates which are predicates that contain free index variables. These index variables are implicitly universally quantified at each program location. Heuristics for inferring index predicates based on counterexample-guided abstraction refinement are described in [18]. This approach is more general than an approach based on ghost variables because the index variables occuring in the computed invariant are quantified per program location rather than globally for the entire program. However, the computation of abstract transformers is more involved than in classical predicate abstraction and requires theorem provers that can effectively deal with quantified formulas.

Several template-based techniques for the generation of quantified invariants have been developed recently [3, 11, 25]. The common idea behind these approaches is that the user provides templates that fix the structure of potential invariants. The analysis then searches for an invariant that instantiates the template parameters. These techniques can handle more complex properties than our approach. In particular, Srivastava and Gulwani [25] have used their approach to verify properties of arrays with alternating quantifiers. On the other hand, techniques that can effectively compute these templates and thus provide the same degree of automation as predicate abstraction refinement have not yet been developed.

Another interesting direction is the recent deployment of resolution-based first-order theorem provers for inferring quantified invariants over arrays. Existing approaches include [20] and [15]. McMillan's approach is based on the computation of quantified interpolants. The idea in [15] is to generate a set of clauses from quantified formulas that encode changes to arrays in the analyzed program, saturate the set under resolution, and then mine the saturated set for interesting quantified invariants. Currently these approaches are still limited due to the missing inbuilt support for arithmetic theories in the underlying theorem provers.

Abstract domains that are used in shape analyses such as in three-valued shape analysis [23] and Boolean heaps [22] can express quantified properties of unbounded data structures (namely, shape analysis constraints [16, 26] in the case of [23] and their universal fragment in the case of [22]). In particular, Gopan *et al.* [9] have used three-valued shape analysis to verify properties of arrays. However, the abstract domains in these shape analyses are exponentially more succinct than the one used in predicate abstraction [19]. While this additional precision is needed for the analysis of programs manipulating linked data structures, our experience shows that it is not necessarily required for the verification of array related properties.

3   Experimental Results

Our work gives a positive answer to the question whether existing software model checking technology can be adapted to effectively verify quantified assertions over arrays and whether such an approach works well in practice. The most important contribution of our work are the experimental results confirming this answer. We start by presenting these results.

Implementation. We integrated our technique into the ACSAR software model checker [24]. The system implements a backward reachability analysis based on predicate abstraction refinement with lazy abstraction [13]. The implementation is done in C++. We performed tests using an X41 Thinkpad laptop with 1 GB of RAM and a 1.6 GHz CPU, running Linux. ACSAR uses the Yices theorem prover [7] for computing the abstraction and analyzing spurious counterexamples. The communication with Yices is performed through its API Lite. The input to ACSAR is a C program annotated with assertions to be verified. The output is either an invariant that implies the correctness of the annotated assertions or a counterexample trace.

Experiments. The results of our experiments are illustrated in Table 1. The column "Property" contains an informal description of the universally quantified assertion that we verified. Column "Iter" refers to the number of refinement steps performed until a safe invariant is computed. Finally, column "Pred" refers to the number of inferred predicates. Our tool is based on lazy abstraction [13], we therefore provide the average number of predicates per location instead of the total number of predicates. The size of examples varies from 10 to 200 lines of code. Although scalability is an important issue, the decisive factor here is the complexity of the property of interest.

Out of all examples, only find, cyber_init, perfect_copy_info, do_enoprof_op and selection_sort take more than 4 seconds verification time. The time includes all verification phases (parsing, theorem prover requests, etc.). The checked assertion for cyber_init is a conjunction of four assertions. The average time for checking each individual assertion is less than 4 seconds.

We divide our tests into two classes. The first class concerns academic examples taken from literature, their names appear without superscript. The example find was proposed by Qadeer and Flanagan [8]. Our tool automatically proves the postcondition specified in their paper. The example array_init is a simple

Table 1. Experimental results for academic and industrial examples. The upper half of the table refers to examples taken from literature. The lower half refers to examples taken from system code. Examples marked with superscript * are from the Linux kernel and driver code. Examples marked with ** are taken from the Xen hypervisor code.

Program	Property	Iter.	Pred.	Time (s)
string_copy	0 terminal string s_1 is copied to s_2	2	4	0.63
scan	array entries before actual entry are not null	3	3	0.54
array_init	array entries are initialized	3	6	0.83
loop1	each array entry is initialized with its index	3	5	0.71
copy1	array a is copied to array b	2	6	0.84
partition	array a contains positive entries and array b contains negative ones	8	7	1.94
num_index	for every array entry i of array a we have $a[i] = 2 * i + 3$	2	6	0.89
part_init	all array entries are initialized to values between 0 and $n - 1$	5	9	3.17
find	every array entry whose index is less than the returned value contains false	8	13	8.81
insertion_sort (inner loop)	entry $a[j]$ is less or equal than all entries of the segment $a[j \ldots i]$	2	14	2.45
selection_sort	array is sorted	3	39	409.87
cyber_init*	for every i, if i modulo 4 is equal to 0, 1, 2 or 3 then $a[i]$ is initialized to v_0, v_1, v_2 or v_3 respectively	8	13	10.36
i2o_device_parse_lct*	entries preceding the actual entry are different from a given value	5	4	1.64
ixj_pad_fsk*	after the execution of 2 loops entries in a given range are initialized	6	7	1.53
ixj_daa_cid_read*	all entries with odd index are equal to v_1 all entries with even index are equal to v_2	5	14	3.81
snd_atiixp_mixer_new*	entries having property p in their pre-state are set to NULL	3	4	1.25
dvb_net_feed_stop*	entries different from 0 in their pre-state are set to 0	3	7	3.41
perfc_copy_info**	for each entry i of array a if $a[i]$ has some property then $b[i]$ and $c[i]$ should be equal	4	12	10.57
do_enoprof_op**	if variable op has value v_1 and variable s has value v_2 then array a is copied to array b	26	3	34.17

array initialization program which is considered in most papers on array verification [14, 11, 3]. Programs num_index and part_init were proposed by Gopan *et al.* [9]. The first one illustrates numeric constraints on the value of array elements. The second one aims to show the handling of multiple arrays as well as partial array initialization. Finally, partition was proposed by Henzinger *et al* [4]. It partitions a given array into two arrays a and b by copying the positive array entries into a and negative ones into b.

The second class of examples covers typical uses of arrays in real world system code. The programs are code fragments taken from the Linux kernel and driver code as well as the Xen hypervisor[1] code.

Selection sort. The most challenging benchmark that we considered is the selection sort example. We refer to Section 4.2, for the source code and a detailed description of this example. We verified that upon termination the array a is sorted in ascending order. The sortedness property was stated in the form

$$\forall x, y \in [0, n-1].\ x < y \Rightarrow a[x] \leq a[y]$$

ACSAR successfully verifies this property. The verification time is significantly larger than in our remaining benchmarks ($\sim$7 minutes). Inspection of the generated predicates revealed that the refinement loop generates many redundant predicates. We therefore believe that the verification time can be significantly reduced by implementing certain redundancy checks.

4   Examples

We now explain our approach and discuss two of the examples from the previous section in more detail: array initialization and selection sort. The first example illustrates the basic idea of our approach. The second example shows that it also works for challenging examples.

4.1   Array Initialization

Our first example is the simple procedure array_init shown in Figure 1. The procedure takes two arguments, an integer array a and an integer n denoting the length of a. The procedure initializes all entries of a to 0. We prove the assertion stating that after termination of the loop all array entries are indeed properly initialized. We use standard notation and formally represent programs in terms of transition constraints over primed and unprimed program variables. Figure 2 shows the corresponding transition constraints for procedure array_init. The program counter is modeled explicitly using the variable pc that ranges over control locations (ℓ_0 stands for the initial location and ℓ_E for the error location). Array a is represented by an uninterpreted function symbol. The notation

---

[1] A hypervisor is a software that permits hardware virtualization. It allows multiple operating systems to run in parallel on a computer. The Xen hypervisor is available at http://www.xen.org/

```
              void array_init (int a[], int n)
              {
                  int i;
ℓ0:
ℓ1:           for(i = 0; i < n; ++i)
              {
                  a[i] = 0;
              }

ℓ2:           assert(∀ x. x ≥ 0 ∧ x < n ⇒ a[x] = 0);
              }
```

Fig. 1. Array initialization

$a[x := e]$ stands for a function update. The set of initial states of the program is described by the formula $pc = \ell_0$ and the set of error locations by the formula $pc = \ell_E$.

$$\tau_0 : pc = \ell_0 \wedge pc' = \ell_1 \wedge a' = a \wedge i' = 0 \wedge k' = k$$
$$\tau_1 : pc = \ell_1 \wedge i < n \wedge pc' = \ell_1 \wedge a' = a[i := 0] \wedge i' = i + 1 \wedge k' = k$$
$$\tau_2 : pc = \ell_1 \wedge i \geq n \wedge pc' = \ell_2 \wedge a' = a \wedge i' = i \wedge k' = k$$
$$\tau_3 : pc = \ell_2 \wedge 0 \leq k \wedge k < n \wedge a(k) \neq 0 \wedge pc' = \ell_E \wedge a' = a \wedge i' = i \wedge k' = k$$

Fig. 2. Transition constraints for array initialization

Transition τ_0 models the initialization of the loop counter in the for loop of procedure array_init, transition τ_1 models the loop body, and τ_2 the loop exit. The assert statement is reflected by transition τ_3 that goes from the loop exit location ℓ_2 to the error location ℓ_E. We use the idea from [8] and replace the quantified variable x in the original assertion by a ghost variable k. Our goal is to prove that the program represented by the transition constraints is safe, i.e., that no error state is reachable from an initial state by consecutive execution of the transitions represented by the transition constraints. If no error state is reachable then the assertion in procedure array_init is never violated.

Our algorithm performs a backward reachability analysis starting from the error states and computes an inductive backward invariant, i.e., an overapproximation of the set of states that are backward-reachable from an error state. If the computed invariant is disjoint from the initial states then the program is safe. An inductive backward invariant for the array initialization program that is disjoint from the initial states is given by the following formula φ:

$$\varphi \stackrel{\text{def}}{=} pc \neq \ell_0 \wedge (pc = \ell_1 \Rightarrow 0 \leq k \wedge k < n \wedge a(k) \neq 0 \wedge k < i)$$

Note that due to the fact that φ is a backward invariant the ghost variable k is implicitly *existentially* quantified. Our analysis is based on predicate abstraction with counterexample guided abstraction refinement. Thus, if the refinement loop is able to infer predicates whose Boolean combination can express φ then the backward analysis will construct a sufficiently strong invariant.

The basis of our refinement procedure is a predicate extraction function that syntactically extracts predicates from preconditions that are computed from spurious error paths. For instance, if we start with an empty set of predicates then the first iteration of the refinement process that goes through the program loop produces the spurious error path $\tau_0; \tau_1; \tau_2; \tau_3$. It then extracts all atomic subformulas from the precondition of the feasible part of the error path: $\mathsf{pre}(\tau_1; \tau_2; \tau_3, pc = \ell_E)$. This formula is given by

$$pc = \ell_1 \wedge 0 \leq k \wedge k < n \wedge a[i := 0](k) \neq 0 \wedge i < n \wedge i + 1 \geq n \qquad (1)$$

Note that function updates such as $a[x := 0]$ can be eliminated via case splits. If we only extracted atomic formulas from preconditions then the analysis would unroll the loop in procedure `array_init` and enumerate all predicates that occur in preconditions of the form

$$\mathsf{pre}((\tau_1)^+; \tau_2; \tau_3, pc = \ell_E)$$

but never infer the predicate $k < i$. The refinement would fail to perform the necessary widening that ensures termination of the analysis. We developed a simple technique that realizes this kind of widening.

First, our technique extracts all ghost variables and index expressions that occur as indices of arrays in the precondition (1) of the counterexample path. Then it determines all disjunctions of inequalities $s_i \neq t_i$ over pairs (s_i, t_i) of index expressions that are consequences of the formula (1). The individual disjuncts $s_i \neq t_i$ of such consequences are then split into inequalities $s_i < t_i$, $s_i > t_i$ and added as additional abstraction predicates. The intuition behind this technique is that the considered disequalities determine the boundaries of intervals in the array that violate the target property. Splitting the disequality into inequalities allows the analysis to perform the necessary widening to infer a sufficiently strong invariant.

In our example the only candidate disequality is given by $k \neq i$ which is indeed a consequence of the formula (1). We therefore add the inequalities $k < i$ and $k > i$ to the set of abstraction predicates which ensures that the refinement loop terminates.

4.2   Selection Sort

Our second example is the procedure `selection_sort` shown in Figure 3. This example is more challenging because it has the so-called *write-many* property, i.e., an array entry can be updated more than once. We show that upon termination of the outer loop, all elements of array a are sorted in ascending order.

The set of transition constraints encoding procedure `selection_sort` is given in Figure 4. Constraint τ_0 models the initialization of the outer **for** loop, τ_1 models the statement before location ℓ_2 and the initialization of the inner **for**

```
void selection_sort (int a[], int n)
{
    int i, j, s;
ℓ₀:
ℓ₁:     for(i = 0; i < n; ++i)
        {
            s = i;
ℓ₂:         for(j = i+1; j < n; ++j)
            {
                if(a[j] < a[s])
                {
                    s = j;
                }
            }
            t = a[i];
            a[i] = a[s];
            a[s] = t;
        }

ℓ₃:     assert(∀ x y. 0 ≤ x < n ∧ 0 ≤ y < n ∧ x < y ⇒ a[x] ≤ a[y]);
}
```

Fig. 3. Selection sort

$\tau_0 : pc = \ell_0 \wedge pc' = \ell_1 \wedge i' = 0 \wedge j' = j \wedge s' = s \wedge k' = k$

$\tau_1 : pc = \ell_1 \wedge i < n \wedge pc' = \ell_2 \wedge s' = i \wedge j' = i+1 \wedge i' = i \wedge k' = k$

$\tau_2 : pc = \ell_2 \wedge j < n \wedge a(j) \geq a(s) \wedge pc' = \ell_2 \wedge a' = a \wedge i' = i \wedge j' = j+1 \wedge s' = s \wedge k' = k$

$\tau_3 : pc = \ell_2 \wedge j < n \wedge a(j) < a(s) \wedge pc' = \ell_2 \wedge a' = a \wedge i' = i \wedge j' = j+1 \wedge s' = j \wedge k' = k$

$\tau_4 : pc = \ell_2 \wedge j \geq n \wedge pc' = \ell_1 \wedge a' = a[i := a(s), s := a(i)] \wedge i' = i+1 \wedge k' = k$

$\tau_5 : pc = \ell_1 \wedge i \geq n \wedge pc' = \ell_3 \wedge a' = a \wedge k' = k$

$\tau_6 : pc = \ell_3 \wedge 0 \leq k < n \wedge 0 \leq l < n \wedge l < k \wedge a(k) < a(l) \wedge pc' = \ell_E \wedge a' = a \wedge k' = k$

Fig. 4. Transition constraints for selection sort

loop, τ_2 and τ_3 model the body of the inner loop, τ_4 the exit of the inner loop and the remaining body of the outer loop, and τ_5 the exit of the outer loop. The assert statement checking the sortedness property in the original program is modeled by τ_6. We introduce the two ghost variables k and l for the universally quantified variables x and y in the original assertion. The following formula shows one of the disjuncts of a safe inductive backward invariant. The shown disjunct covers all backward-reachable states at program location ℓ_1, i.e., the loop cut point of the outer loop in procedure selection_sort:

$$pc = \ell_1 \wedge 0 \leq l \wedge l < i \wedge l < k \wedge k < n \wedge a(k) < a(l)$$

We sketch how the analysis infers the predicate $l < i$. After several iterations our analysis returns the spurious counterexample $\tau_0; \pi$ where

$$\pi \overset{\text{def}}{=} \tau_1; \tau_2; \tau_4; \tau_1; \tau_4; \tau_5; \tau_6$$

Again we extract atomic predicates from the preconditions of the error path and infer additional predicates by checking disequalities that are implied by preconditions of the feasible part of the counterexample. For instance, consider the precondition $\mathsf{pre}(\pi, pc = \ell_E)$ which is given by

$$0 \leq k < n \wedge 0 \leq l < n \wedge l < k \wedge i+1 < n \wedge a(i) \leq a(i+1) \wedge \qquad (2)$$
$$n \leq i+2 \wedge a[i := a(i), i := a(i)](k) < a[i := a(i), i := a(i)](l)$$

Note that the updated function $a[i := a(i), i := a(i)]$ is equal to a. Furthermore, it is easy to see that the implication

$$k = i+1 \wedge l = i \;\Rightarrow\; a(i) > a(i+1) \vee a(k) \geq a(l)$$

is valid. Thus, by contraposition (2) implies the disjunction of inequalities

$$k \neq i+1 \vee l \neq i$$

From this disjunction we extract the predicates

$$l < i, \; l > i, \; i+1 > k, \;\text{ and } i+1 < k \; .$$

5   Predicate Abstraction Refinement

In this section, we describe the by now classical setting of predicate abstraction refinement. The method is parameterized by the procedure **extract** that takes a formula and returns a set of *predicates*. We use a minimal notational setting (following, e.g., [1]) and ignore details (in particular, the concrete programming language and the use of concrete counterexamples for refinement). These details are irrelevant for our main purpose, which is to introduce the specific procedure **extract** used in our analysis of array programs (in the next section). Everything in this setting is standard up to the syntax of the formulas that we use to denote sets of states, in the concrete as well as in the abstract domain.

Concrete domain of formulas. We assume a (generally infinite) set of quantifier-free formulas which we call *base formulas*. We represent an (in general infinite) set of states by a first-order formula φ built up from such base formulas. In our setting, φ is of the form

$$\varphi \equiv \bigvee_{i \in I} \bigwedge_{j \in J_i} \varphi_{ij} \qquad (3)$$

where the φ_{ij}'s are base formulas.

We assume a partial order on formulas $\varphi' \leq \varphi$. The partial order is usually a sound but possibly incomplete implementation (by a theorem prover) of the test of validity of implication.

Pre. A program is a set $\mathcal{P}$ of statements st. For the purpose of the formal presentation, we assume that a statement comes as a transition constraint

$$\mathit{st} \equiv \psi \wedge x_1' = e_1 \wedge \ldots \wedge x_m' = e_m$$

where $x_1, x_2, \ldots, x_m$ are variables (including a program counter pc); as usual, the variable x' stands for the value of x in the successor state. The guard ψ is a conjunction of base formulas. The update formula comes as a conjunction of logical equalities between primed variables and expressions over unprimed variables.

For a statement st, the application of the operator $\mathsf{pre}_{\mathit{st}}$ on a formula φ returns a formula representing the set of all predecessor states of φ under the statement st. The definition extends canonically to a sequence of statements. For a statement st as above, the application of the operator $\mathsf{pre}_{\mathit{st}}$ to the formula φ is implemented by the projection (on unprimed variables) of the conjunction of the transition constraint with the renaming of φ (from unprimed to primed variables). The operator pre for a program (a set of statements) is simply the disjunction of the $\mathsf{pre}_{\mathit{st}}$ over all statements.

$$\mathsf{pre}_{\mathit{st}}(\varphi) \equiv \exists x_1' \ldots \exists x_m' (\varphi[x_1'/x_1, \ldots, x_m'/x_m] \wedge \psi \wedge x_1' = e_1 \wedge \ldots \wedge x_m' = e_m)$$
$$\mathsf{pre}(\varphi) \equiv \bigvee_{\mathit{st} \in \mathcal{P}} \mathsf{pre}_c(\varphi)$$

Invariants. In order to specify correctness, we fix formulas nonInit and unsafe denoting the complement of the set of *initial* and *safe* states, respectively. We define the given program to be *correct* if no unsafe state is reachable from an initial state. In our setting, nonInit is quantifier-free (but unsafe is not).

The correctness can be proven by showing the condition below. Here, $\mathsf{lfp}(\mathsf{pre}, \varphi)$ stands for the least fixpoint of the operator pre above φ.

$$\mathsf{lfp}(\mathsf{pre}, \mathsf{unsafe}) \leq \mathsf{nonInit}$$

A *backward invariant* is an invariant that is *inductive* under pre and implies nonInit, i.e. a formula ψ such that

- unsafe $\leq \psi$,
- $\mathsf{pre}(\psi) \leq \psi$,
- $\psi \leq$ nonInit.

Predicate abstraction. A possible approach to establish correctness is to find an upper abstraction $\mathsf{pre}^{\#}$ of the operator pre (i.e. where $\mathsf{pre}(\varphi) \leq \mathsf{pre}^{\#}(\varphi)$ holds for all formulas φ) such that $\mathsf{lfp}(\mathsf{pre}^{\#}, \mathsf{unsafe})$, the least fixpoint of $\mathsf{pre}^{\#}$ above unsafe, can be computed and is contained in nonInit. Then, $\mathsf{lfp}(\mathsf{pre}^{\#}, \mathsf{unsafe})$ is a backward invariant because of the simple fact that $\mathsf{pre}^{\#}(\varphi) \leq \varphi$ entails $\mathsf{pre}(\varphi) \leq \varphi$. We use predicate abstraction with abstraction refinement to find such an upper abstraction $\mathsf{pre}^{\#}$.

The method generates a sequence of finite sets $\mathcal{P}_n$ of predicates over states (for $n = 0, 1, \ldots$). Since we identify a predicate with the base formula φ defining it, we have that $\mathcal{P}_n$ is a *finite* subset of the given set of base formulas.

We write $\mathcal{L}(\mathcal{P}_n)$ for the (finite!) sublattice of $\mathcal{L}$ that is generated by the set of predicates $\mathcal{P}_n$. We sometimes refer to conjunctions of predicates as "abstract states" (thus, abstract states are exactly the symbolic states in $\mathcal{L}(\mathcal{P}_n)$). We have that $\mathcal{L}(\mathcal{P}_n)$ contains unsafe, but generally $\mathcal{L}(\mathcal{P}_n)$ is not closed with respect to the operator pre. We define the operator $\mathsf{pre}_n^{\#}$ over $\mathcal{L}(\mathcal{P}_n)$ as an abstraction of pre.

The 'best' abstraction $\mathsf{pre}_n^{\#}$ of pre with respect to $\mathcal{P}_n$ is defined in terms of a Galois connection,

$$\mathsf{pre}_n^{\#} \equiv \alpha_n \circ \mathsf{pre} \circ \gamma$$

where the composition $f \circ g$ of two functions f and g is defined from right to left: $f \circ g(x) = f(g(x))$. The abstraction function α_n maps a formula φ to the smallest formula φ' in $\mathcal{L}(\mathcal{P}_n)$ that is larger (wrt. "$\leq$") than φ, formally

$$\alpha_n(\varphi) \equiv \mu\varphi' \in \mathcal{L}(\mathcal{P}_n)^{\sqsubseteq}. \varphi \leq \varphi'.$$

The meaning function γ is the identity.

The construction of the best abstraction is not practical. Hence, one uses a weaker abstraction of pre and one defines $\mathsf{pre}_n^{\#}$ not as the function above but, instead, as follows.

$$\mathsf{pre}_n^{\#}\left(\bigvee_{i \in I} \bigwedge_{j \in J_i} \varphi_{ij}\right) = \bigvee_{i \in I} \mathsf{pre}_n^{\#}\left(\bigwedge_{j \in J_i} \varphi_{ij}\right)$$

and

$$\mathsf{pre}_n^{\#}\left(\bigwedge_{j \in J_i} \varphi_{ij}\right) = \bigwedge\{p \in \mathcal{P}_n \mid \mathsf{pre}(\bigwedge_{j \in J_i} \varphi_{ij}) \leq p\}.$$

Thus, the image of an abstract state (i.e., a conjunction of predicates) under $\mathsf{pre}_n^{\#}$ yields the smallest abstract state above its image under pre.

We will have that $\mathcal{P}_0 \subset \mathcal{P}_1 \subset \ldots$ and hence $\mathcal{L}(\mathcal{P}_0) \subset \mathcal{L}(\mathcal{P}_1) \subset \ldots$ which means an increasing precision of the abstraction α_n for increasing n.

The iterative abstraction refinement method. The method in Figure 5 is parameterized by the refinement procedure extract which takes a formula and returns a finite set of base formulas ("the new predicates"). In each iteration, the method

- constructs the abstract operator $\mathsf{pre}_n^{\#}$ defined by $\mathcal{P}_n$,
- computes the abstract fixpoint $\mathsf{lfp}(\mathsf{pre}_n^{\#}, \mathsf{start})$,
- generates a new set of predicates $\mathcal{P}_{n+1}$

until the abstract proof succeeds, i.e., $\mathsf{lfp}(\mathsf{pre}_n^{\#}, \mathsf{unsafe}) \leq \mathsf{nonInit}$ for some n.

If the method terminates for some n, then $\mathsf{lfp}(\mathsf{pre}_n^{\#}, \mathsf{unsafe})$ is a backward invariant computed over a finite lattice.

```
φ₀ := unsafe
n := 0
loop
    𝒫ₙ := extract(φₙ)
    construct abstract operator preₙ# defined by 𝒫ₙ
    ψ := lfp(preₙ#, unsafe)
    if (ψ ≤ nonInit) then
        STOP with "Success"
    φₙ₊₁ := φₙ ∨ pre(φₙ)
    n := n+1
endloop
```

Fig. 5. Abstract fixpoint checking with iterative abstraction refinement, where extract is a parameterized procedure that infers a finite set of predicates from a formula and $\mathsf{pre}_n^\#$ is a predicate abstraction of pre for the set of predicates $\mathcal{P}_n$

6   Refinement for Arrays

The refinement scheme defined in Figure 5 is parameterized by the procedure extract. This procedure takes a conjunction φ of base formulas and returns a set of base formulas (which are then used to define a set of new predicates). In its most basic version, the procedure $\mathsf{extract}_0$ returns the set of conjuncts.

$$\mathsf{extract}_0(\varphi_1 \wedge \ldots \wedge \varphi_n) = \{\varphi_1, \ldots, \varphi_n\}$$

The rationale for our extension of the procedure $\mathsf{extract}_0$ stems from a result in [1]. This result formally evaluates the power of the refinement scheme with the procedure $\mathsf{extract}_0$ above (the power as a proof method for program correctness). The evaluation uses an idealized oracle-based proof method for comparison. This method works by backward iteration of the (concrete) *pre* operator; i.e., it starts with the formula unsafe and iteratively applies the operator pre. In order to accelerate the convergence towards a fixpoint, it judiciously applies a *syntactic widening* on the formula obtained. The syntactic widening applied to a conjunction φ drops one or more of its conjuncts in φ (for example, applied to the interval constraint $0 < x \wedge x < 1$ it may result in $0 < x$). It is the oracle which judiciously chooses what conjuncts to drop and what conjuncts to keep. The result in [1] states that the (realistic) refinement scheme with the procedure $\mathsf{extract}_0$ achieves the same power as the idealized oracle-based method with syntactic widening.

In our setting, with programs over arrays, the backward invariants used in correctness proofs contain conjuncts that do not syntactically appear in the iterates of the backward iteration procedure. This means that the syntactic widening is not sufficient (even in the idealized proof method above); we need to combine it with a semantic analysis in order to obtain a greater choice for the possible widening results. The *semantic widening* applied to a conjunction φ first *saturates* the conjunction, i.e., adds redundant conjuncts (logical consequences of a certain form), and then applies the syntactic widening to the resulting conjunction.

The saturation consists of adding each disjunction of strict inequalities between index variables x_i and y_i that is entailed (in the theory of linear arithmetic with uninterpreted function symbols) by φ.

$$\mathsf{saturate}(\varphi) = \varphi \wedge \bigwedge \{ \bigvee_{i \in I} x_i < y_i \mid \varphi \models \bigvee_{i \in I} x_i < y_i \}$$

If a disjunction of disequalities $\bigvee_{i \in I} x_i \neq y_i$ is entailed by φ, as, for example, in

$$a[x] > a[y] \wedge a[z] > a[t] \models (x \neq t) \vee (z \neq y)$$

then one obtains the corresponding entailed disjunction of inequalities by replacing each of the disequalities by the disjunction of the two corresponding inequalities.

This leads us to define the predicate extraction procedure $\mathsf{extract}_1$ as the composition of the saturation with the syntactic widening.

$$\mathsf{extract}_1(\varphi) = \mathsf{extract}_0(\mathsf{saturate}(\varphi))$$

Our proof method is the instantiation of the refinement scheme of Figure 5 with the predicate extraction procedure $\mathsf{extract}_1$. By the above-mentioned result in [1], this proof method has the same power as the idealized oracle-based method with semantic widening. I.e., if the unrealistic oracle-based method succeeds in proving that a program is correct, then so does our method.

Practical optimizations. A naive implementation of the procedure $\mathsf{saturate}$, which consists of enumerating all possible disjunctions of inequalities over all index expressions, requires exponentially many (in the number of occuring index expressions) theorem prover queries. In practice we can impose a polynomial bound by considering only disjunctions up to a fixed length. For further optimization, we only consider inequalities between index expressions associated with the same array (not blindly any pair of index expressions). Finally, we construct the checked disjunctions incrementally starting from disjunctions of length one and if a disjunction is entailed, do not check any longer disjunction that includes it.

7 Conclusion

We presented an abstraction refinement technique for verifying quantified assertions over arrays that can be easily integrated into existing software model checkers. Using this technique we were able to verify almost all array related examples in the literature that have been verified using quantified abstract domains. Furthermore, we were able to verify various real-life examples taken from system code. Our results indicate that, at least for quantified assertions over arrays, the use of sophisticated techniques for dealing with quantified assertions can often be avoided if one instead carefully adapts existing techniques for quantifier-free assertions by using domain specific knowledge.

References

1. Ball, T., Podelski, A., Rajamani, S.K.: Relative completeness of abstraction refinement for software model checking. In: Katoen, J.-P., Stevens, P. (eds.) TACAS 2002. LNCS, vol. 2280, pp. 158–172. Springer, Heidelberg (2002)
2. Ball, T., Rajamani, S.K.: The SLAM project: debugging system software via static analysis. In: POPL, pp. 1–3 (2002)
3. Beyer, D., Henzinger, T.A., Majumdar, R., Rybalchenko, A.: Invariant synthesis for combined theories. In: Cook, B., Podelski, A. (eds.) VMCAI 2007. LNCS, vol. 4349, pp. 378–394. Springer, Heidelberg (2007)
4. Beyer, D., Henzinger, T.A., Majumdar, R., Rybalchenko, A.: Path invariants. In: PLDI, pp. 300–309 (2007)
5. Chaki, S., Clarke, E.M., Groce, A., Jha, S., Veith, H.: Modular verification of software components in C. In: ICSE, pp. 385–395 (2003)
6. Clarke, E.M., Grumberg, O., Jha, S., Lu, Y., Veith, H.: Counterexample-guided abstraction refinement. In: Emerson, E.A., Sistla, A.P. (eds.) CAV 2000. LNCS, vol. 1855, pp. 154–169. Springer, Heidelberg (2000)
7. Dutertre, B., de Moura, L.M.: A fast linear-arithmetic solver for DPLL(T). In: Ball, T., Jones, R.B. (eds.) CAV 2006. LNCS, vol. 4144, pp. 81–94. Springer, Heidelberg (2006)
8. Flanagan, C., Qadeer, S.: Predicate abstraction for software verification. In: POPL, pp. 191–202 (2002)
9. Gopan, D., Reps, T.W., Sagiv, S.: A framework for numeric analysis of array operations. In: POPL, pp. 338–350 (2005)
10. Graf, S., Saïdi, H.: Construction of abstract state graphs with PVS. In: Grumberg, O. (ed.) CAV 1997. LNCS, vol. 1254, pp. 72–83. Springer, Heidelberg (1997)
11. Gulwani, S., McCloskey, B., Tiwari, A.: Lifting abstract interpreters to quantified logical domains. In: POPL, pp. 235–246 (2008)
12. Henzinger, T.A., Jhala, R., Majumdar, R., McMillan, K.L.: Abstractions from proofs. In: POPL, pp. 232–244 (2004)
13. Henzinger, T.A., Jhala, R., Majumdar, R., Sutre, G.: Lazy abstraction. In: POPL, pp. 58–70 (2002)
14. Jhala, R., McMillan, K.L.: Array abstractions from proofs. In: Damm, W., Hermanns, H. (eds.) CAV 2007. LNCS, vol. 4590, pp. 193–206. Springer, Heidelberg (2007)
15. Kovacs, L., Voronkov, A.: Finding loop invariants for programs over arrays using a theorem prover. In: Chechik, M., Wirsing, M. (eds.) FASE 2009. LNCS, vol. 5503, pp. 470–486. Springer, Heidelberg (2009)
16. Kuncak, V., Rinard, M.: Boolean Algebra of Shape Analysis Constraints. In: Steffen, B., Levi, G. (eds.) VMCAI 2004. LNCS, vol. 2937, pp. 59–72. Springer, Heidelberg (2004)
17. Lahiri, S.K., Bryant, R.E.: Constructing quantified invariants via predicate abstraction. In: Steffen, B., Levi, G. (eds.) VMCAI 2004. LNCS, vol. 2937, pp. 267–281. Springer, Heidelberg (2004)

18. Lahiri, S.K., Bryant, R.E.: Indexed predicate discovery for unbounded system verification. In: Alur, R., Peled, D.A. (eds.) CAV 2004. LNCS, vol. 3114, pp. 135–147. Springer, Heidelberg (2004)
19. Manevich, R., Yahav, E., Ramalingam, G., Sagiv, M.: Predicate Abstraction and Canonical Abstraction for Singly-Linked Lists. In: Cousot, R. (ed.) VMCAI 2005. LNCS, vol. 3385, pp. 181–198. Springer, Heidelberg (2005)
20. McMillan, K.L.: Quantified invariant generation using an interpolating saturation prover. In: Ramakrishnan, C.R., Rehof, J. (eds.) TACAS 2008. LNCS, vol. 4963, pp. 413–427. Springer, Heidelberg (2008)
21. Podelski, A., Rybalchenko, A.: ARMC: the logical choice for software model checking with abstraction refinement. In: Hanus, M. (ed.) PADL 2007. LNCS, vol. 4354, pp. 245–259. Springer, Heidelberg (2006)
22. Podelski, A., Wies, T.: Boolean heaps. In: Hankin, C., Siveroni, I. (eds.) SAS 2005. LNCS, vol. 3672, pp. 268–283. Springer, Heidelberg (2005)
23. Sagiv, M., Reps, T., Wilhelm, R.: Parametric shape analysis via 3-valued logic. ACM TOPLAS (2002)
24. Seghir, M.N., Podelski, A.: ACSAR: Software model checking with transfinite refinement. In: SPIN, pp. 274–278 (2007)
25. Srivastava, S., Gulwani, S.: Program verification using templates over predicate abstraction. In: PLDI (to appear, 2009)
26. Yorsh, G., Reps, T.W., Sagiv, M., Wilhelm, R.: Logical Characterizations of Heap Abstractions. ACM Transactions on Computational Logic 8(1) (2007)

Inferring Dataflow Properties of User Defined Table Processors

Songtao Xia, Manuel Fähndrich, and Francesco Logozzo

Microsoft Research, Redmond, WA (USA)
{sxia,maf,logozzo}@microsoft.com

Abstract. In SCOPE, a SQL style cloud-level data-mining scripting language, table processing capabilities are often provided by user defined .NET methods. The SCOPE compiler can optimize a query plan if it knows certain dataflow relations between the input and output tables, such as column independence, column equality, or that a column's values are non-null. This paper presents an automated analysis for inferring such relations from implementations of SCOPE table processing methods. Since most table processing methods are written as .NET iterators, our analysis must accurately deal with the resulting state-machine implementing such iterators. Other complications addressed are naming and estimating column numbers, aliasing and escaping, and the inference of universally quantified loop invariants.

We prototyped the analysis as Scooby, a static analyzer for .NET iterators. Scooby is able to discover useful properties for typical SCOPE programs automatically and efficiently.

1 Introduction

SCOPE [7] is an extensible language used by Live Search for cloud-scale data mining, where peta-byte data files are stored over thousands of distributed servers. A SCOPE script contains declarative table processing commands and procedural assignments to variables that hold intermediate tables. In a table processing command, SCOPE allows user defined table operators, which are implemented as .NET methods, to be used alongside system-provided ones. The SCOPE compiler will transform both the script and the .NET assemblies into efficient, parallel execution plans that will be executed on a cloud-scale storage and job execution environment called Cosmos [7,18] so that programmers can focus on data-mining tasks without worrying about parallel computing details.

Because the amount of computational resources required to execute a SCOPE job is huge, and because SCOPE scripts are used by Live Search on a daily basis, optimization is unquestionably important. There are many optimization opportunities that hinge on knowing domain specific dataflow properties of the .NET methods. For example, if the SCOPE compiler knows that a certain table column is not used by the user-defined operator in generating its output, then there is a chance that the column can be removed. Our goal is to provide a static analyzer whose output informs the SCOPE compiler about optimization

J. Palsberg and Z. Su (Eds.): SAS 2009, LNCS 5673, pp. 19–35, 2009.

opportunities. In particular, the analyzer produces: (1) a dependence relation that describes which output columns (may) depend on which input columns, (2) a non-null relation that describes which output columns are (definitely) non-null, and (3) an equality relation that describes which output column equals (in a sense that will be explained later) which input column.

In writing this dataflow analyzer, we faced many technical challenges. First, all these user-defined operators are methods that return an IEnumerable<Row> object (called an iterator method). C# compilers compile an iterator method into a closure class. Since source code is not always available to SCOPE's optimizer, we have to analyze compiled code. An ordinary analysis is imprecise and in general useless on a closure class method, since such methods implement state machines. Second, designing a sound and accurate dependence analysis is challenging. We not only need an accurate way to estimate which input columns are involved, but also have to consider aliasing between references and side effects of method calls. Thirdly, if the method of interest has a loop which sets consecutive output columns to consecutive input columns, the equality analysis has to infer a universally quantified loop invariant [16,15], which is a hard problem. The technical contributions of this paper are in the answers to these challenges:

- In Section 4, we show how we extend the existing analysis infrastructure [21] from the Clousot [22] project so that an analysis designed for a normal .NET method can be easily transformed into one that handles an iterator method with little or no change. Such a semi-automatic transformation is new.
- In Section 6, we describe in detail how we compute a conservative yet relatively accurate dependence relation. The approach involves an escape analysis that traces aliasing and side effects and a numerical domain to estimate the range of variables that denote column numbers.
- In Section 7, we describe how we use a reduced product [9] of a symbolic range domain, a numerical domain, and a index set domain to infer a restricted form of quantified invariants in typical user defined table operations. This is a new application of the state-of-the-art quantified invariants inference approaches[16,15] augmented with a novel index set abstraction.

We prototyped our analysis as Scooby: a static analyzer that infers useful properties automatically from .NET assemblies. It does so accurately (able to give best or near best possible answers for over 100 test cases and real-life examples) and efficiently (finishing in at most a few seconds for real life examples). We report our experience in developing and applying Scooby in Section 8.

2   Motivation: SCOPE and Its Optimization

A SCOPE script describes queries over cloud-level databases. Its syntax is a mixture of SQL and procedural statements. The result of a select operation can be assigned to a table variable and referred to later, as shown in Listing 1.1.

At one step of table processing, a SCOPE programmer can use select and join operations provided by SCOPE, or custom defined table operations. In this

```
1 T1 = extract * from
2      "clicktimes.log"
3      using MyExtractor
4
5 T2 = select sum from
6      process T1
7      using MyProcessor;
```

Listing 1.1: SCOPE
script with a
user-defined processor

```
1 public override IEnumerable<Row> Process
2    (IEnumerable<Row> input, Row outputRow) {
3    foreach (Row row in input) {
4      int sum =0;
5      for (int i =0; i<5; i++) sum += row[i];
6      outputRow[0].Set(sum);
7      yield return outputRow;
8    }
9 }
```

Listing 1.2: Process method for MyProcessor

paper we look at three forms of user defined operations: (1) processors, which transform one table into another; (2) reducers, which transform a sub-table (typically from a group-by operation) into another sub-table; or (3) combiners, which combine two sub-tables into one. To SCOPE, these operations are .NET methods stored in a .NET assembly, though programmers typically use C# to define these operators. The code snippet in Listing 1.2 is the C# code for the Process method of the MyProcessor class, which is used in the process command in Listing 1.1. The C# statement **yield return** returns one element in the resulting IEnumerable<Row> collection. The elements of a collection are accessed through a **foreach** statement. The SCOPE compiler is targeting the following optimizations:

- Removal of unnecessary columns: An input column is unnecessary if no output table of the script relies on this column.
- Elimination of redundant selection conditions: When the values of an output column are a subset of an input column, then any constraint satisfied by the input column is also satisfied by the output column.
- Elimination of unnecessary runtime non-null checks: If a column is known to be non-null, then code inserted to check non-nullness may be skipped.

The next section describes what analysis problems need to be solved to enable each of these optimizations.

3   Problem Description

For the methods of interest, i.e., processors, reducers and combiners, we know which parameters represent which input tables and their respective schemas. We refer to an input table as I and its schema S_I, with O and S_O for an output table and its schema, respectively. For a schema S, S.Count is the number of its columns. A table is viewed as a sequence of rows. We use r for a row and r_T for a row from table T. The i-th column of row r is $r[i]$. For a table T, we write $T[i]$ for the projection of T onto the i-th column, which is interpreted as a table of one column.

Corresponding to the optimization opportunities listed previously, we are interested in the following analyses.

- *Column-column (in)dependence:* Suppose that $O[i] = f(I[1], ..., I[n])$ for some function f. If $f(...I^1[j], ...) = f(...I^2[j]...)$, for any two possible values of the j-th column in the input, $I^1[j]$ and $I^2[j]$, we say $\texttt{Ind}(i,j)$, meaning that the i-th column of output does not depend on the j-th column of input. In this paper, we conservatively compute a may-depend-on relation with $\texttt{Ind}$ its negation.

- *(Existential) equality:* $\texttt{Eq}(i,I,j)$ is defined as $\forall r_O \in O . \exists r_I \in I . r_O[i] = r_I[j]$. Intuitively, this means that every value of the i-th output column equals some value from the j-th input column of input table I.
- *Non-null columns*: For an output table column i this property is defined as: $\forall r_O \in O . r_O[i] \neq \texttt{null}$.

In order to use our analyses as optimization enablers, they must be conservative, meaning the dependence analysis must overestimate dependencies, the equality analysis must underapproximate equalities, and the non-null analysis must underapproximate non-nullness. The next subsections describe challenges our analyses must address.

3.1   Challenge 1: Analyzing .NET Iterators

The SCOPE optimizer has only access to the compiled (.NET) version of user-defined operators. Thus, we analyze the .NET MSIL (intermediate language) instead of source code. The way an iterator method is compiled to the .NET platform constitutes a major challenge for the analyzer.

Compilation of an iterator method is best explained by how the elements of an IEnumerable collection are accessed. In C#, one uses a **foreach** statement (see the comments in Listing 1.3). The **foreach** statement is compiled to the pseudo code in Listing 1.3, where the MoveNext method will be called repeatedly to test if the iterator has any element left. If so, the current element can be fetched.

An iterator method is compiled to a closure class implementing IEnumerator. Parameters of the iterator method and local variables become fields of the closure class. The closure class implements the MoveNext method, which contains the iterator method code interspersed with state machine management code. There is one initial state (when MoveNext has not been called), possibly several continuing states (when there are some items remaining), and one end state (when no item is left). In the remaining part of the paper, we will refer to these states as M−states. If a call to MoveNext returns **true**, then the next call to MoveNext will resume from a continuing state: the control jumps right back to where the computation paused last time (Line 19 in Listing 1.4).

An ordinary analyzer is ineffective if applied directly to a MoveNext method, as the analyzer has no knowledge of the state machine. For example, going through lines 2-6-19-16 in Listing 1.4, the analyzer does not know any of the dataflow facts (such as "var itor is an iterator of the input table") that hold before the return on Line 15. It does not know that this path is handling a continuing state, where ideally we should inherit knowledge from the previous return. In Section 4, we present a way to transform an ordinary analysis into one that works for iterators.

```
1 // foreach Row r in p.Process(input, outputRow) {
2 it = p.Process(input, outputRow).GetEnumerator();
3 while ( it . MoveNext()) {
4   //    Console.WriteLine(r );
5   t = it . Current;
6   Console.WriteLine(r);
7 //}
8 }
```

Listing 1.3: Using foreach

```
1 class closure_C {
2   C _this ;    IEnumerable<Row> _input;
3   Row current; Row _outputRow;
4   Row _row; int _sum;
5   IEnumerator<Row> _itor;
6   bool MoveNext() {
7     switch (state) {
8       case Initial :
9         _itor = _input. GetEnumerator();
10        while ( _itor . MoveNext()) {
11          _row = _itor . Current;
12          for ( int i=0; i<5; i++)
13            _sum += _row[i];
14          _outputRow[0].Set(_sum);
15          current = _outputRow;
16          state = Continuing_1;
17          return true;
18          Resume_Point1:
19        }
20        state = End; return false ;
21      case Continuing_1:
22        goto Resume_Point1;
23      default: return false ;
24   }
25 }
```

Listing 1.4: Closure Class

```
1  ...
2  // sv0 is this . input
3  // sv100 is this.
4  // [ itor = input. GetEnumerator]
5  sv1 := call  GetEnumerator sv0;
6  stfld sv100 itor sv1;
7
8  // [while ( itor . MoveNext())]
9  sv2 := call  MoveNext sv1;
10 goto L1 L2;
11
12 L1: assume (sv2);
13 // [row = itor . Current]
14 sv8:= ldfld sv100 itor ;
15 sv9:= call  getCurrent sv8;
16 stfld sv100 row sv9;
17 ...
18 // [sum += row[i]]
19 sv10 := ldfld sv100 row
20 sv12 := ldfld sv100 i
21 sv11 := call  GetItem sv10 sv12
22 sv14 := ldfld sv100 sum
23 sv13 := add sv14 sv11
24 stfld sv100 sum sv13
25 ...
26 sv16:= ldfld sv100 sum
27 sv18:= call  Column.Set sv17 sv16; //
28
29 L2: assume (!sv2);
```

Listing 1.5: Compiled MoveNext
Fragments

Fig. 1. Compilation of .NET Iterators

3.2   Challenge 2: Accurate and Conservative Dependence Analysis

The dependence analysis needs to be both conservative and accurate. For accuracy, there are two issues. First, we need a finer distinction between different parts of the input table. A naive approach introduces too many dependencies. For example, if we use the standard control dependence computation [24] for lines 9 to 16 of Listing 1.4, then every output column depends on the input table itself, due to the call to itor .MoveNext on line 10. Depending on the input table itself implies depending on every column of it, which is overly inaccurate.

Second, to perform unused column elimination transitively (columns solely used to compute other unused column are also unused) we want to compute precisely which input column (represented by its number) a particular output column depends on. When the input column number of concern is a variable, we estimate the set of its possible values. A convenient way is to compute the upper and lower bounds of variables. For example, in Listing 1.2, output column 0 depends on input column 0 (the lower bound of i) to 4 (the upper bound).

Aliasing and side effects are a major concern to a conservative analysis. When we store a value from the input table to a field of an object, we want to know if other objects will be affected as well. When we call a method, we want to know if the result will in addition depend on a column of the input that may have been previously stored and referenced by the method body. In general, aggressive and accurate aliasing analysis is expensive. But in the user defined operators, there is no input aliasing (that is, the input tables and the fields in the classes that implement the operations are not aliased). This fact allows us to have a coarse grained, inexpensive alias analysis.

3.3 Challenge 3: Quantified Invariants for Equality Analysis

To infer equalities between input and output columns when columns are indexed by loop variables, our analysis has to compute quantified invariants, as shown by the examples below. For both examples, we would like to say that output columns

```
1 for (int i=0; i<6; i++)
2   orow[i] = irow[i];
```

```
1 int i = 0;
2 while (i<6) {
3   if (*) { i++; orow[i−1] = irow[i−1];}
4   else { orow[i] = irow[i]; i++; }
5 }
```

Fig. 2. Copying multiple input columns into the output

0 to 5 equal to the input columns 0 to 5, respectively. This requires us to infer formulas of the form: $\forall j \in [0, i), r_O[j] = r_I[j]$ as a loop invariant. In Section 7, we will describe a simple approach to generate such loop invariants. It applies well to typical SCOPE programs. In addition, we shall handle the general case when the loop increment is not necessarily 1, or the assignment happens possibly on different indices in different paths through the loop body, as shown by the example on the right side of the code snippet above. Our proposed solution is to determine a range $[i, i+k)$ of indices such that $r_O[j] = r_I[j]$ holds $\forall j \in [i, i+k)$ along all paths through the loop body. If k is the loop increment, then this constitutes a proof of the induction step for proving the invariant.

Deciding whether two instances (of indices) are the same (used at the join point), whether an instance is in between i and $i+k$, or whether two instances are distinct, all need reasoning about integer (in)equality. We use a numerical abstract domain for this reasoning. In Section 7, we describe a quantified invariant inference approach that combines an index set and a numerical domain, based on the intuition introduced above.

4   Analysis Infrastructure

We built our analyzer on top of a generic abstract interpretation based analysis infrastructure [22]. This infrastructure reads MSIL instructions of a .NET assembly and transforms them to a form that is suitable for static analysis. In this section, we first give basic definitions of abstract interpretation, then we describe the program representation provided by the infrastructure.

4.1   Abstract Interpretation

An abstract domain D is $(E, \leq, \sqcup, \sqcap, \nabla)$, where E is a partial order set of abstract values, $\leq$ is the partial order, and $\sqcup, \sqcap$ and ∇ are the join, meet and widening operators, respectively.

A transfer function $F : \mathcal{I} \times E \to E$, where $\mathcal{I}$ is the instruction set, defines the abstract transfer for an instruction. The infrastructure provides an analysis driver δ, which, when given a transfer function F, returns a method analysis that yields an abstract state for every program location in the method. In other words, $\delta(D, F)(m : M, e : E) : L \to E$, where L is the set of program locations in m, and e is the initial abstract state.

Clousot, a contract checker for .NET programs, includes a library of abstract domains. Of interest are several numerical domains, such as Linear (in)equality [19], Octagon[23], Polyhedra[10], SubPolyhedra[22], etc. Details of these domains are beyond the scope of this paper. It suffices to know that they support the following operations: (1) testing of predicates, for which we write $n \vdash P$ for the numerical domain n and a predicate P; (2) finding the lower and upper bounds of a variable. We write lb for the lower bound and ub for the upper bound; and (3) adding facts: we will write $n; v$ for adding the condition represented by symbolic value v to the domain.

4.2   Program Representation

A program is a control flow graph of basic blocks connected with edges. A basic block has a single entrance and a single exit and is made up of instructions. A basic block has multiple successors when it ends with a conditional jump. An assume statement is introduced at the targets of the conditional jump so that we can handle conditional jumps as ordinary control transfers. The infrastructure labels back edges to identify loops.

Inside a basic block, the (pseudo) instructions are similar to Single Statement Assignment (SSA). The infrastructure abstracts the heap into a correspondence between *symbolic values* and *access paths*. An access path, which represents heap locations, can be viewed as an expression formed by either a parameter or a local variable, or operations such as field access on another access path, for example, this . f. We refer to the set of heap locations as Mloc. At any given program point, a symbolic value is used to denote the content of an access path. Function $ap(v, pc)$ returns an access path that holds symbolic value v at program point pc. Instructions make the symbolic value representing the result explicit. For example, a load constant instruction is represented as $sv_{100} :=$ ldconst 1. In a sense, this is equivalent to $assume(sv_{100} == 1)$. An abstract domain used with this infrastructure refers to symbolic values instead of program variables.

At join points of the control flow, the set of symbolic values used on the incoming branches must be normalized to a common set (similar to SSA phi-nodes) [14,20]. For this reason, the infrastructure inserts explicit rebinding operations rebind(f) on branches to join points. The rebinding function $f : SV \to SV$ represents the following parallel assignments $\{sv := f(sv) \mid sv \in \text{dom}(f)\}$[1]. To handle rebinding, an abstract domain must provide a rebinding operation $\beta : E \times (SV \to SV) \to E$ which computes the abstraction value under the new binding. For example, if sv_1 is assigned to sv_0, and $sv_1 > 0$ is part of the abstract state, the new abstract state should contain $sv_0 > 0$.

The instructions used in this paper, together with rebind and assume, are listed in Figure 3. In Listing 1.5, we list the pseudo code fragments that represent the IL form for several important statements from Listing 1.4.

Instruction	Comment
v := ldconst c	load const
v_1 := ldfld v_2 field	load a field
stfld v_1 field v_2	store v_2 to v_1.f
v_0 = call m $(v_1, \ldots, v_n)$	method call, v_1 is receiver if not static
v_0 := bop v_1 v_2	binary operation
assume(v)	assume statement
rebind (f)	rebinding, where $f : SV \to SV$.

Fig. 3. Pseudo-instructions provided by the infrastructure

5   Iterator Analysis

In this section, we show how to automatically turn an ordinary method abstract interpretation $A = (e, D, F)$ into an iterator analysis $A_I = (e_I, D_I, F_I)$ that works on an iterator method, such as MoveNext. The main idea is to split the abstract states computed by A based on the M-state and to compute an iterator invariant that holds between iterator invocations. We can abstract from the exact M-state as we only need to know if the iterator is in the initial state (class 0), the final state (class 2), or any other state where there is a valid current element (class 1).

Thus, if $D = (E, \leq, \sqcup, \sqcap, \nabla)$, the domain of the iterator analysis is $E_I = S \to N \times E$, where $S = \{0, 1, 2\}$ is the iterator state abstraction. For each iterator

---

[1] It is important to view these assignments as a parallel assignment, for on back-edges, the same symbolic value may appear on both sides of the assignments.

state class, we form a product domain consisting of a numerical domain N (e.g. intervals) and the original domain D. We use N to constrain the actual iterator state variable this.istate to the proper class.[2] The operations $\leq_I$, $\sqcup_I$, $\sqcap_I$ and ∇_I over E_I are simply extending $\leq$, $\sqcup$, $\sqcap$ and ∇ in the codomain of E_I in the natural way.

Abstract states e_I in E_I maintain the invariant that $e_I(s) \vdash$ this.istate $\in$ class(s) where class(s) is simply the set of iterator states in our abstract iterator state class s. Thus, at program points where the iterator state definitely falls into one particular class, the other classes map to $\perp$. At program points where the iterator state is ambiguous, the classes map to the program state that is known to hold, provided the actual iterator state falls into a particular class.

The transfer function F_I operating over E_I is defined as follows:

$$F_I(i, e_I)(s) = \bigsqcup_{j=0,1,2} F(i, e_I(j)) \sqcap \text{this.istate} \in \text{class}(s)$$

The transfer function applies the effect of instruction i to each class and then redistributes the results among the classes while filtering for the proper iterator state. The redistribution is necessary when i is updating the iterator state.

To compute the iterator invariant that holds between invocations, we compute the minimal fixpoint of the sequence of method start states

$$e_{Ik+1} = e_{Ik} \nabla_I \beta(\delta(D_I, F_I)(m, e_{Ik})(l_{exit}), \text{Mp})$$

starting with the initial state

$$e_{I0}(s) = \begin{cases} e \sqcap \text{this.istate} = 0 & \text{if } s = 0 \\ \perp & \text{otherwise} \end{cases}$$

We assume that there is only one exit point in the method, l_{exit}. The parallel assignment operation based on Mp translates the symbolic variables representing the state on exit of the method back to the symbolic variables representing the state on entry to the method: $\text{Mp}(v_1) = \{v | \text{ap}(v) = \text{ap}(v_1)\}$.

Since we are effectively analyzing a loop, we need to use widening ∇_I to guarantee that the sequence converges.

Using this approach, we can transform the non-null analysis (based on [12]) implemented by Clousot to one that can analyze iterators. The only change we had to make to the original non-null analysis is to encode the fact that the field of the closure class that corresponds to "this" in the original method is non-null (the field _this at Line 2, Listing 1.4).

For the dependence and equality analyses, we only present the ordinary abstract interpretation, with the understanding that the analyses performed by Scooby are iterator analyses, obtained using the approach described in this section.

---

[2] If D is able to handle numerical constraints, then the produce with N could be avoided as an optimization.

6   Dependence Analysis

Our dependence analysis is performed in two stages: first, a symbolic dependence analysis computes dependence between column numbers represented as symbolic expressions. Second, based on a numerical analysis, an estimation stage further approximates the symbolic dependence with a relation over integer column numbers.

6.1   Symbolic Dependence Analysis

The goal of the dependence analysis is to compute for each output column $O[v]$, which parts of the input tables it depends on.

Traceables. We express dependencies in terms of a set of *traceables* $tr \in \mathtt{Tr}$. A traceable is a symbolic representation of a part of an input table. A *table traceable* $\mathtt{Table}(i)$ represents an entire input table corresponding to a method parameter i. A *column traceable* $\mathtt{Col}(i, v)$ represents a column of input table i, where the symbolic value v is the column index. Finally, a *row count* traceable $\mathtt{RC}(i)$ refers to the number of rows in table i. If the output row depends only on the row count of input table i but not any other part of the table, then the input table can be optimized to have just the right number of rows, but no data.

Overview. We track the set of traceables stored in a set of non-aliased locations CF, consisting of the iterator closure fields corresponding to the original iterator method locals (all remaining local loads and stores are eliminated in our SSA form). Traceables stored to any other location are considered escaping. For method calls, we distinguish three groups: 1) pure methods, 2) well-known methods operating on the tables and rows, and 3) unknown methods. Traceables passed to unknown methods are considered escaped. The well-known methods consist of

GetRows	called on a table to get an IEnumerable<Row>
GetEnumerator	called on an IEnumerable to get an IEnumerator
GetCurrent	called on an IEnumerator to get the current enumeration value
GetItem	called on a Row to index into a particular column
MoveNext	called on an IEnumerator to advance it and test if exhausted
Column.Set	called to assign an output row column at a particular index

A standard fixpoint computes data dependencies between all symbolic variables appearing in the method and the set of traceables, as well as the set of escaped values.

After computing the direct dependencies of each output column, we add all escaped traceables to all output columns to obtain a conservative analysis result.

Control Dependencies. Besides data dependencies, we have to worry about control dependencies as well. For example, a processor that counts the number of rows in an input table does not have any direct data dependencies on any input columns, yet depends on the number of rows passed in. Such dependencies only show up as control dependencies on the enumerator enumerating through the table rows. We thus need to compute a control dependence between program points as well as the symbolic value representing the conditions. The former is a textbook exercise of computing the dominance frontier on a reversed control flow graph [24]. The later is readily available from the infrastructure. Thus, given a program point p, we have a set of symbolic values $C(p)$ for the conditions that may affect the program control leading to p. Note that we don't include control dependencies on entire $\texttt{Table}(i)$ traceables as these represent false dependencies arising from testing if the input table is null or if an iterator over an input table is null. We will omit further details of including these control dependencies in the transfer functions below.

Abstract Domain. We use an abstract domain (A_1, A_2, A_3, A_4) consisting of: $A_1 = 2^{\mathsf{Tr}}$ is the set of escaped traceables, $A_2 = \mathsf{SV} \rightarrow 2^{\mathsf{Tr}}$ tracks the set of traceables a symbolic variable depends on, $A_3 = \mathsf{CF} \rightarrow 2^{\mathsf{Tr}}$ tracks the dependencies of the contents of the closure fields, and $A_4 = \mathsf{SV} \rightarrow 2^{\mathsf{Tr}}$ keeps track of which output columns were assigned which dependencies. The domain operations are component-wise and standard, so we omit them.

The initial state for the analysis is $(\emptyset, \emptyset, tpar, \emptyset)$, where $tpar$ primes the closure fields corresponding to the original table input parameters $tpar(\text{loc}(this.\_I)) = \{\texttt{Table}(I)\}$ for all table input parameters I.

Transfer Function. The transfer function is defined in Figure 4 for all relevant instructions. The auxiliary function $\mathsf{InOut}(a_2, args, m)$ is used to compute the union of all dependencies carried by m's input parameters and to assign them to all of m's outputs.

Instruction	Next State (Pre-State:(a_1, a_2, a_3, a_4))
v=ldfld o f	$a_2 := \begin{cases} a_2[v := a_2[o] \cup a_3[\text{loc}(o.f)]] & \text{if } \text{loc}(o.f) \in \mathsf{CF} \\ a_2[v := a_2[o]] & \text{otherwise} \end{cases}$
stfld o f v	$a_3 := a_3[\text{loc}(o.f) := a_2[v]]$ if $\text{loc}(o.f) \in \mathsf{CF}$.
v=op v1 v2	$a_2 := a_2[v := a_2[v1] \cup a_2[v2]]$
v=call m args	$a_2 := \mathsf{InOut}(a_2, args, m)$ if m is a pure method
	$a_2 := a_2[v := a_2[args[0]]]$ if m is GetRows or GetEnumerator
	$a_2 := a_2[v := \texttt{Table}(i)]$ if m is GetCurrent and $\texttt{Table}(i) \in a_2[args[0]]$
	$a_2 := a_2[v := \texttt{Col}(i, args[1])]$ if m is GetItem and $\texttt{Table}(i) \in a_2[args[0]]$
	$a_2 := a_2[v := \texttt{RC}(i)]$ if m is MoveNext and $\texttt{Table}(i) \in a_2[args[0]]$
	$a_4 := a_4[args[0] := a_4[args[0]] \cup a_2[args[1]]]$ if m is Column.Set
	$a_1 := a_1 \bigcup_j a_2[args[j]]$ otherwise

Fig. 4. Transfer function for dependency analysis. Control dependences omitted.

6.2 Estimation

The iterator analysis applied to the dependence analysis of the previous section produces a fixpoint (a_1, a_2, a_3, a_4) from which we extract the final column dependencies as follows. We use the numeric domain of the iterator analysis to compute lower $\mathtt{lb}(v)$ and upper $\mathtt{ub}(v)$ bounds for any symbolic variable v. Then $O[i]$ depends on $I[j]$, provided

$$\exists v \in \mathsf{dom}(a_4) \text{ such that } \mathtt{lb}(v) \leq i \wedge i \leq \mathtt{ub}(v) \text{ and } j \in \mathtt{allcols}(I, a_4[v] \cup a_1)$$

Auxiliary function $\mathtt{allcols}(I, T)$ is the set of column indices of input table I included in the set of traceables T:

- If $\mathsf{Table}(I) \in T$, then the set of all column numbers in the table $[0, S_I.\mathsf{Count})$ is in $\mathtt{allcols}(I, T)$, where S_I is the schema for I.
- If $\mathsf{Col}(I, v) \in T$, then the set of all column numbers $[\mathtt{lb}(v), \mathtt{ub}(v)]$ is in $\mathtt{allcols}(I, T)$.

Example. In Listing 1.5, we find that sv_1 depends on $\mathsf{Table}(\mathsf{input})$, sv_2 depends on $\mathsf{RC}(\mathsf{input})$; this dependence is control-dependent on in the loop body and does not introduce column-column dependency on the final output. Inside the loop, sv_8 depends on $\mathsf{Table}(\mathsf{input})$ via itor's dependence; sv_9 depends on $\mathsf{Table}(\mathsf{input})$ via GetCurrent, which is propagated to sv_{10} via closure field row. sv_{11} depends on $\mathsf{Col}(\mathsf{input}, sv_{12})$, where sv_{12} is the symbolic value for i at line 20. sv_{13} and sum all inherit the same dependence $\mathsf{Col}(\mathsf{input}, sv_{12})$ and propagate it to the output column index sv_{17}. Our implementation is able to figure out sv_{17} is output column number 0 (not shown). The estimation stage further finds the bounds for sv_{12} to be $[0, 4]$.

7   Equality Analysis

The goal of the equality analysis is to find relations $\mathsf{Eq}(i, I, j)$, stating that all elements in column i of the output are equal to some value of column j of input table I.

If the user defined code sets output columns to input columns using constant indices, such relations are not difficult to discover. This section deals only with the more difficult case where the user code consists of a loop, copying several input columns to several output columns, and the column indices are symbolic (see Fig 2).

We use a "guess and verify" approach by finding a candidate loop and a guessed invariant and checking that the invariant holds by performing an abstract interpretation over the loop body. A candidate loop satisfies the following conditions:

- The loop variable v ranges over $[i, j)$
- The loop increment is a constant k
- All output row assignment in the loop body are semantically of the form $\mathsf{orow}[v + e] = \mathsf{inputrow}[v + e + o]$, where o is a loop constant
- All output row assignments after the loop are to indices provably disjoint from $[i, j)$.

Such loops are identified by using a numerical analysis N and custom code to identify the output row assignments. If we find such a loop, we try to prove the following loop invariant $\forall l \in [i, v).\mathsf{orow}[l] = \mathsf{inputrow}[l + o]$ which is equivalent to $\mathsf{Eq}(l, \mathsf{input}, l + o)$ for $l \in [i, v)$.

We analyze the loop body using an abstract domain (N, C), where N is a numeric domain we use to answer questions about index (in)equality, and $C = 2^{\mathsf{SV}}$ is an index set of symbolic variables. An abstract state (n, c) satisfies the following invariant at every program point:

$$\forall sv \in c. \; n \vdash v \leq sv < v + k \quad \wedge \quad \forall sv' \in c. \; sv \neq sv' \Rightarrow n \vdash sv \neq sv'$$

In words, this means that the set of indices in the index set are semantically disjoint in the range $[v, v + k)$. The transfer function makes sure that this invariant is maintained, or it sets the index set to the empty set. An abstract state (n, c) models the following set of equalities:

$$\forall l.(i \leq l \wedge n \vdash l < v \vee \exists sv \in c. \; n \vdash sv = l) \Rightarrow \mathsf{orow}[l] = \mathsf{inputrow}[l + o]$$

which extends the range $[i, v)$ of equalities with the discrete indices in the index set. The initial abstract value entering the loop is $(n, \emptyset)$, where n is obtained from any prior computed numeric analysis over the code. This abstract state is trivially true on loop entry, as the index variable v must start at i and thus represents the empty set of equalities.

At loop back edges, we check that the cardinality of the index set c is equal to the loop increment k. If it holds, then we prove the loop invariant, otherwise, we reject the candidate equality relation.

An interesting problem is how to compute the join of index sets. Given (n_1, c_1) and (n_2, c_2), the join is (n, c), where $n = n_1 \sqcup n_2$, and $c = \{v_1 | v_1 \in c_1 \wedge (\exists v_2.v_2 \in c_2 \wedge n \vdash v_1 = v_2)\}$. In words, we perform a semantic intersection of indices based on the knowledge that they are all disjoint.

We summarize the analysis by showing the relevant part of the transfer function:

Instruction	Condition	New Abstract State Old state is (n, c)
Rebind(f)	enter loop	$(\beta(n, f), \{\})$
	loop back edge	$(\beta(n, f), \{\})$ if $|c| = k$ and $n \vdash f(v) = v + k$ reject candidate otherwise
oRow[v1] := inputRow[v2]		$(n, c \cup \{v1\})$ if $n \vdash v1 = v + e$ and $n \vdash v2 = v + e + o$ and $n \vdash 0 \leq e < k$ and $\forall sv \in c.n \vdash sv \neq v1$

8 Implementation

We implemented the analyses described in this paper as part of Scooby using C# (about 10 KLocs). Scooby can be used as both a standalone tool and a library. It has been tested using more than 100 test cases and examples. The effectiveness of Scooby is demonstrated by the accuracy with which it infers dependency and equality relations for real, practical examples. These examples are from programs that are run by the Live Search team on a daily basis. We compared the results of Scooby against the dependence/equality relation discovered manually.

In the table below, we show measurements of Scooby's analysis accuracy for some representative examples. The core processing methods of these examples range from dozens to hundreds lines of C# code. We also list the number of symbolic values involved in the analysis: we can handle with no difficulty hundreds of symbolic values. The execution time is typically below one second, though there are cases a few seconds are recorded. Since such execution time is already satisfactory, and our tool is not specially optimized for efficiency, execution time is not listed in the table. For all the examples, the analyses results are correct, meaning that no dependence pairs are missed, or false equality pairs are reported. We measure the accuracy of dependence analysis by counting the number of total necessary dependence pairs and the number of false dependence pairs reported by our analysis. The accuracy of equality analysis is measured by counting the total number of actual equalities and the number of equality pairs missed by our analysis. Missing equality is rare but there are a small number of false dependencies, mainly due to false escaped values. For example, the link-data and clickboost examples below report escaped values, one due to storing into an array and the other due to a function call that is not recognized to be pure. In linkdata, the false escaped value does not matter because the equality analysis results supersede the dependence analysis. In the clickboost example however, the inaccuracy causes every output column to depend on one extra input column. Often, we can improve accuracy by detecting the purity of library methods. We are automating this detection using a purity checker based on [5].

Program	Loc	#SV	Escaped Value		Dependencies			Equalities	
			Kind	Cause	Total	False	Cause	Total	Missed
multivalue	24	80	n/a	n/a	14	182	Numerical	14	0
multiedits	80	257	n/a	n/a	10	0	n/a	0	0
linkdata	85	225	Col	Array	6	78	Escaped val.	6	0
urlpairs	101	269	n/a	n/a	9	0	n/a	0	0
querypairs	175	326	n/a	n/a	36	0	n/a	0	0
clickboost	249	720	Col	Call	50	6	Escaped val	1	0

Apart from the experiments above, we designed many test cases to expose inaccuracies in our analysis. The common sources of inaccuracy are: (1) we analyze only the method that implements the user defined operator; (2) our handling of aliasing and side effects is coarse-grained; (3) disjunctive loop invariants are required; (4) more complicated loop patterns than we discussed in the paper are used, and (5) limitations of our numerical domains.

9   Related Work

The dependence analysis discussed in this paper is a unique problem. It is different than the functional dependency concept in relational databases [8], which talks about attributes in one relation. The dependence analysis is close to the control and data dependence studied by the compiler optimization community [2,24], particularly for vector optimization (for example [3]). Yet our problem requires a much refined analysis on the input table columns, which involves reasoning about numerical (in)equalities. In many ways, our analysis resembles analyses that monitor information flow in computer security (for example [1,29,25]).

Customer defined type systems/analyses are used to assist in the correctness of cluster scale distributed system (for example [28]). It is possible to use or extend our analyses for static correctness guarantees, non-null analysis being one such example. There are several works on inferring loop invariants (for example [13,11]).

The escape analysis used here is a simple one, but sufficient for our purposes. Much work on points-to/alias/escape analyses (for example [30,6]) exists in the literature. In comparison, those analyses provide more accurate answers to more challenging questions. As mentioned, automatic purity checking is part of our future work.

10   Conclusion

This paper investigates a number of analyses for embedded .NET programs in the context of database table processing. We designed and implemented novel algorithms to compute input-output column dependencies and equalities. Since we had to analyze .NET iterators, we also produced an automated way to transform an ordinary method abstract interpretation into one that computes invariants for .NET iterators. We adopt numerical domains to reason about the column numbers and we extend quantified loop invariant inference techniques with index sets. All these are implemented in Scooby. Although there is room for improvement, especially in the area of automatic purity checking, Scooby has been proven effective in practice. Ideas introduced in this paper, in particular the analysis of iterators and the use of index sets in quantified invariant inference, should be useful in other settings.

References

1. Abadi, M., Banerjee, A., Heintze, N., Riecke, J.G.: A core calculus of dependency. In: Proc. 26th ACM Symp. on Principles of Programming Languages (POPL), pp. 147–160. ACM Press, New York (1999)
2. Aho, A.V., Sethi, R., Ullman, J.D.: Compilers: Principles, Techniques, and Tools. Addison Wesley, Reading (1986)
3. Allen, R., Kennedy, K.: Compiler Optimization for Modern Architectures: a Dependence-based Approach. Morgan Kaufmann, San Francisco (2001)

4. Ball, T., Rajamani, S.K.: The slam project: debugging system software via static analysis. In: POPL 2002: Proceedings of the 29th ACM SIGPLAN-SIGACT symposium on Principles of programming languages, pp. 1–3. ACM, New York (2002)
5. Barnett, M., Fändrich, M., Garbervetsky, D., Logozzo, F.: Annotations for (more) precise points-to analysis. In: IWACO 2007: ECOOP International Workshop on Aliasing, Confinement and Ownership in object-oriented programming (July 2007)
6. Blanchet, B.: Escape analysis: correctness proof, implementation and experimental results. In: POPL 1998: Proceedings of the 25th ACM SIGPLAN-SIGACT symposium on Principles of programming languages, pp. 25–37. ACM, New York (1998)
7. Chaiken, R., Jenkins, B., Larson, P., Ramsey, B., Shakib, D., Weaver, S., Zhou, J.: Scope: easy and efficient parallel processing of massive data sets. PVLDB 1(2), 1265–1276 (2008)
8. Codd, E.F.: A relational model of data for large shared data banks. Commun. ACM 26(1), 64–69 (1983)
9. Cousot, P., Cousot, R.: Systematic design of program analysis frameworks. In: Proceedings of POPL 1979 (1979)
10. Cousot, P., Halbwachs, N.: Automatic discovery of linear restraints among variables of a program. In: POPL 1978 (1978)
11. Ernst, M.D.: Dynamically Discovering Likely Program Invariants. Ph.D thesis, University of Washington (2000)
12. Fähndrich, M.A., Leino, K.R.M.: Declaring and checking non-null types in an Object-Oriented language. In: OOPSLA 2003, pp. 302–312. ACM Press, New York (2003)
13. Flanagan, C., Leino, K.R.M.: Houdini, an annotation assistant for ESC/Java. In: Oliveira, J.N., Zave, P. (eds.) FME 2001. LNCS, vol. 2021, pp. 500–517. Springer, Heidelberg (2001)
14. Flanagan, C., Saxe, J.B.: Avoiding exponential explosion: generating compact verification conditions. In: Proceedings of POPL 2001, pp. 193–205. ACM, New York (2001)
15. Gulwani, S., McCloskey, B., Tiwari, A.: Lifting abstract interpreters to quantified logical domains. In: POPL 2008. ACM Press, New York (2008)
16. Halbwachs, N., Péron, M.: Discovering properties about arrays in simple programs. SIGPLAN Not. 43(6), 339–348 (2008)
17. ECMA Int. Standard ECMA-355, Common Language Infrastructure (June 2006)
18. Isard, M., Budiu, M., Yu, Y., Birrell, A., Fetterly, D.: Dryad: Distributed data-parallel programs from sequential building blocks. In: European Conference on Computer Systems (EuroSys), Lisbon, Portugal, March 21-23. Microsoft Research, Silicon Valley (2007)
19. Karr, M.: On affine relationships among variables of a program. Acta Informatica 6(2), 133–151 (1976)
20. Rustan, K., Leino, M.: Efficient weakest preconditions. Inf. Process. Lett. 93(6), 281–288 (2005)
21. Logozzo, F., Fähndrich, M.A.: On the relative completeness of bytecode analysis versus source code analysis. In: Hendren, L. (ed.) CC 2008. LNCS, vol. 4959, pp. 197–212. Springer, Heidelberg (2008)
22. Logozzo, F., Fähndrich, M.A.: Pentagons: A weakly relational abstract domain for the efficient validation of array accesses. In: SAC 2008 (2008)
23. Miné, A.: Weakly Relational Numerical Abstract Domains. Ph.D thesis, École Polythechnique (2004)
24. Muchnick, S.S.: Advanced Compiler Design and Implementation. Morgan Kaufmann, San Francisco (1997)

25. Myers, A.C.: Jflow: practical mostly-static information flow control. In: POPL 1999: Proceedings of the 26th ACM SIGPLAN-SIGACT symposium on Principles of programming languages, pp. 228–241. ACM, New York (1999)
26. Pnueli, A., Xu, J., Zuck, L.: Liveness with (0, 1, infty)-counter abstraction. In: Brinksma, E., Larsen, K.G. (eds.) CAV 2002. LNCS, vol. 2404, pp. 107–122. Springer, Heidelberg (2002)
27. Sankaranarayanan, S., Ivancic, F., Gupta, A.: Program analysis using symbolic ranges. In: Riis Nielson, H., Filé, G. (eds.) SAS 2007. LNCS, vol. 4634, pp. 366–383. Springer, Heidelberg (2007)
28. Saraswat, V., Nystrom, N., Palsberg, J., Grothoff, C.: Constraint types for object oriented languages. In: Proceedings of of OOPSLA 2008, ACM SIGPLAN Conference on Object-Oriented Programming Systems, Languages and Applications (2008)
29. Smith, G.: A new type system for secure information flow. In: CSFW14, pp. 115–125. IEEE Computer Society Press, Los Alamitos (2001)
30. Steensgaard, B.: Points-to analysis in almost linear time. In: POPL 1996: Proceedings of the 23rd ACM SIGPLAN-SIGACT symposium on Principles of programming languages, pp. 32–41. ACM, New York (1996)

Polymorphic Fractional Capabilities

Hirotoshi Yasuoka and Tachio Terauchi

Tohoku University
{yasuoka,terauchi}@kb.ecei.tohoku.ac.jp

Abstract. The capability calculus is a framework for statically reasoning about program resources such as deallocatable memory regions. Fractional capabilities, originally proposed by Boyland for checking the determinism of parallel reads in multi-thread programs, extend the capability calculus by extending the capabilities to range over the rational numbers. Fractional capabilities have since found numerous applications, including race detection, buffer bound inference, security analyses, and separation logic. However, previous work on fractional capability systems either lacked polymorphism or lacked an efficient inference procedure. Automated inference is important for the application of the calculus to static analysis. This paper addresses the issue by presenting a polymorphic fractional capability calculus that allows polynomial-time inference via a reduction to rational linear programming.

1 Introduction

The capability calculus [5] was originally proposed as a framework for region-based memory management, that is, a system for guaranteeing that a deallocated region is never accessed. The capability calculus is a good framework for statically reasoning about properties of general program resources such as memory regions [5], reference cells [4], and communication channels [14]. Researchers [4,13] extended the framework to *fractional capabilities* ([4] called them *fractional permissions*), allowing **(1)** more flexibility by letting the capabilities range over rational numbers, which allows reasoning about concurrent reads and writes, and **(2)** efficient inference via a reduction to (rational) linear programming, whereas no efficient inference is known for the non-fractional calculi[1]. Fractional capabilities have found applications in many areas of program verification and program logic, including determinism checking [4,12,13], separation logic [3], security protocol analysis [2,7], buffer bound inference [14], race detection [10], and secure information flow [11].

Previous work on capability calculus either lacked parametric polymorphism [14,10,11] or lacked an efficient inference procedure [4,3]. By parametric polymorphism, we mean allowing capabilities appearing in the function types to be parametrized by *resource variables*[2]. The issue turns out to be surprisingly non-trivial as "obvious" approaches result in an overly conservative system.

---

[1] Indeed, some of them are proven to be NP-hard [13,7].

[2] Resource variables range over program resources to be reasoned by the calculus such as memory locations or communication channels, depending on the application.

J. Palsberg and Z. Su (Eds.): SAS 2009, LNCS 5673, pp. 36–51, 2009.

The rest of the paper is organized as follows. In the next section, we give an overview of the main issues, highlighting the problems with naive approaches, and presenting our solution informally. Section 3 formally presents the solution and proves its soundness. Section 4 shows the type inference algorithm. The inference algorithm utilizes linear programming and runs in time polynomial in the size of the underlying Hindley-Milner types. To present the idea assuming little prior background in fractional capabilities, we focus on the application of the capability calculus to the problem of region-based memory management [5]. But, our idea can also be applied to other fractional capability calculi. Section 5 discusses how the idea can be transferred to the capability calculus for race detection [10]. Section 6 discusses related work and concludes. The proofs and the figures omitted from the main body of the paper are in the long version [16].

2   Informal Overview

We informally present the idea by showing how the capability calculus guarantees region-based memory safety. A program is said to be *memory safe* if it does not access a deleted region. Consider the following program fragment.

$$\begin{aligned}
&\texttt{let } a = \texttt{ref } 0@\rho_a \texttt{ in}\\
&\texttt{let } b = \texttt{ref } 0@\rho_b \texttt{ in}\\
&\texttt{let } f = \texttt{fun } f[\rho] \ (x : \mathit{ref}(\mathit{int})@\rho) \ = \ !x; \texttt{free } \rho \texttt{ in}\\
&\quad f[\rho_a] \ (a); f[\rho_b] \ (b)
\end{aligned}$$

The program allocates two reference cells a and b, hopefully in separate regions ρ_a and ρ_b. The function f is called with each cell, dereferencing the given cell and deleting its region. Here, ρ is a region parameter that is passed from the caller. Unlike in the traditional stack-discipline of the Tofte-Talpin region calculus [15], the capability calculus allows non-scoped region deletion, which introduces more opportunities for dangling pointers. Here, ; is the sequential composition, $!e$ reads the reference cell e, and **free** ρ deletes the region ρ.

Note that we need f to be polymorphic in ρ because otherwise, the regions ρ_a and ρ_b would be equated, and so the program becomes memory unsafe (as the second call to f would try to read from the deleted region). Therefore, we would like to assign f the following polymorphic type.

$$\forall \rho.(\{\rho \mapsto 1\}, \mathit{ref}(\mathit{int})@\rho) \to (\{\rho \mapsto 0\}, \mathit{int})$$

The type says that the function takes a region ρ and an argument of the type $\mathit{ref}(\mathit{int})@\rho$ (i.e., an integer reference allocated in the region ρ) and returns an integer. It also says that the caller is required to have the *capability* $\{\rho \mapsto 1\}$. (Any capability greater than 0 is sufficient for dereferencing or writing to the region whereas the capability greater than or equal to 1 is needed to delete the region). The function returns to the caller the capability $\{\rho \mapsto 0\}$ indicating that ρ is deleted and cannot be accessed or deleted after the call.

```
letreg ρₐ in
  let a = ref 0@ρₐ in
  let f = fun f[ρₓ, ρᵧ] (x : ref(int)@ρₓ, y : ref(int)@ρᵧ) = !x; free ρₓ; !y
  in
  f[ρₐ, ρₐ] (a, a)
```

Fig. 1. A memory unsafe program

Instantiating the polymorphic type at the calls, we get the types

$$(\{\rho_a \mapsto 1\}, ref(int)@\rho_a) \to (\{\rho_a \mapsto 0\}, int)$$
$$(\{\rho_b \mapsto 1\}, ref(int)@\rho_b) \to (\{\rho_b \mapsto 0\}, int)$$

and we are able to type check the program as memory safe, assuming that the capability before the code fragment is $\{\rho_a \mapsto 1, \rho_b \mapsto 1\}$, indicating that the code may access and delete the regions ρ_a and ρ_b. The capability for a region ρ is initialized to 1 when the region is created.

Formally, a capability is a mapping from region variables (ρ's) to non-negative rationals $[0, \infty)$ (e.g., $\{\rho_a \mapsto 1\}$ is a shorthand for a function that maps ρ_a to 1 and all other region variables to 0). Note that instantiating the type of f by ρ_a and ρ_b involve substitutions $\{\rho \mapsto 1\}[\rho_a/\rho] = \{\rho_a \mapsto 1\}$ and $\{\rho \mapsto 1\}[\rho_b/\rho] = \{\rho_b \mapsto 1\}$. Given a capability Ψ, the *naive instantiation* $\Psi[\rho_1/\rho_2]$ syntactically replaces ρ_2 in the capability Ψ by ρ_1.

2.1   Additive Instantiation

Unfortunately, the naive instantiation is inadequate. Consider the program shown in Figure 1. Now, f takes two cells, x and y, accesses x, deletes the region in which x is allocated (i.e., ρ_x), and then accesses y. Here, letreg ρ_a allocates a new region named ρ_a. Note that the program is unsafe because f is called with both arguments set to a, and therefore, deletes the region where a is allocated (i.e., ρ_a) before accessing a for the second time.

The function f can be given the type

$$\forall \rho_x.\forall \rho_y.(\Psi_{in}, ref(int)@\rho_x, ref(int)@\rho_y) \to (\Psi_{out}, int)$$

where $\Psi_{in} = \{\rho_x \mapsto 1, \rho_y \mapsto q\}$ and $\Psi_{out} = \{\rho_x \mapsto 0, \rho_y \mapsto q\}$ for some $q > 0$. When we instantiate the type via the substitution $\theta = [\rho_a/\rho_x][\rho_a/\rho_y]$ naively, the capability required before the call is $\Psi_{in}\theta = \{\rho_a \mapsto 1, \rho_a \mapsto q\}$ and the capability required after the call is $\Psi_{out}\theta = \{\rho_a \mapsto 0, \rho_a \mapsto q\}$. The capabilities are not mappings. To overcome the issue, the existing polymorphic fractional capability calculi (e.g. [4]) performs *additive instantiation*, defined as follows.

$$\Psi[\rho_1/\rho_2]_\oplus = \{\rho_1 \mapsto \Psi(\rho_2) + \Psi(\rho_1)\} \cup \{\rho_2 \mapsto 0\} \cup \{\rho \mapsto \Psi(\rho) \mid \rho \notin \{\rho_1, \rho_2\}\}$$

Then,

$$\Psi_{in}[\rho_a/\rho_x]_\oplus[\rho_a/\rho_y]_\oplus = \{\rho_a \mapsto 1, \rho_y \mapsto q\}[\rho_a/\rho_y]_\oplus = \{\rho_a \mapsto 1 + q\}$$

With this instantiation scheme, we are able to safely reject the program in Figure 1, because now the call $f[\rho_a, \rho_a](a, a)$ requires $\{\rho_a \mapsto 1 + q\}$ where $q > 0$, but the caller only has $\{\rho_a \mapsto 1\}$.

2.2 Down Instantiation

The additive instantiation scheme discussed above, while sound, is somewhat conservative in the presence of recursive calls. Consider the following program.

```
letreg ρₐ in
   let a = ref 0@ρₐ in
   let f =
        fun f[ρₓ, ρᵧ] (x : ref(int)@ρₓ, y : ref(int)@ρᵧ) = !x; !y; f[ρₓ, ρₓ] (x, x)
   in  f[ρₐ, ρₐ] (a, a)
```

This program is obviously safe (because no region is deleted). However it is not typable with the additive instantiation scheme. To see this, note that f must have a type of form $\forall \rho_x, \rho_y.(\Psi_{in}, ref(int)@\rho_x, ref(int)@\rho_y) \rightarrow (\Psi_{out}, int)$ with $\Psi_{in}(\rho_x) > 0$ and $\Psi_{in}(\rho_y) > 0$ because f accesses both x and y. But, the capability

$$\Psi_{rec} = \Psi_{in}[\rho_x/\rho_x]_\oplus[\rho_y/\rho_x]_\oplus = \Psi_{in}[\rho_y/\rho_x]_\oplus$$

is required before the recursive call $f[\rho_x, \rho_x](x, x)$. Thus, $\Psi_{rec}(\rho_x) = \Psi_{in}(\rho_x) + \Psi_{in}(\rho_y)$. But because $\Psi_{in} = \Psi_{rec}$ (or $\Psi_{in} \geq \Psi_{rec}$[3]), we have

$$\Psi_{in}(\rho_x) \geq \Psi_{in}(\rho_x) + \Psi_{in}(\rho_y) \quad \Psi_{in}(\rho_x) > 0 \quad \Psi_{in}(\rho_y) > 0$$

It is easy to see that there exists no non-negative rational number that can be assigned to $\Psi_{in}(\rho_x)$ to satisfy these inequalities. Therefore, the type system rejects the program as untypable.

One way to overcome the issue is to allow polymorphism over the fractions as done in some fractional capability calculi [4,3]. Unfortunately, it is unclear whether an efficient inference exists for such systems.

Instead, we propose to relax the caller's requirement when the function does not delete the region. Specifically, when a function requests a positive capability for some ρ, we allow a call to the function to be type checked with a positive capability for ρ that is lower than the actual capability requested by the callee, provided that the call does not delete ρ. The rationale for this is that any positive capability is sufficient for a region access (but not region deletion). To this end, we introduce a new instantiation scheme called *down instantiation*, defined as follows.

$$\Psi[\rho_1/\rho_2]_\Downarrow = \{\rho_1 \mapsto \frac{1}{2}(\Psi(\rho_2) + \Psi(\rho_1))\} \cup \{\rho \mapsto \Psi(\rho) \mid \rho \notin \{\rho_1, \rho_2\}\}$$

Note that the down instantiation *lowers* the capability by one half for the region being instantiated.

---

[3] This constraint is from the fact that a sequential composition passes capabilities along the sequence.

$\rho \in \mathbf{Regvar}$
$\Psi \in \mathbf{Regvar} \rightarrow [0, \infty)$
$L ::= \emptyset \mid L \cup \{\rho\}$
$\tau ::= int \mid ref\,(\tau)@\rho \mid (\Psi_{in}, \tau_{in}) \xrightarrow{L} (\Psi_{out}, \tau_{out}) \mid \forall \rho.\tau$

$v ::= \lambda x : \tau.e \mid \Lambda \rho.v$
$e ::= n \mid x \mid v \mid \mathbf{fix}\, x : \tau.v \mid e\,(e') \mid e[\rho]$
$\quad \mid \mathbf{ref}\, e@\rho \mid\, !e \mid e := e' \mid \mathbf{letreg}\, \rho\, \mathbf{in}\, e \mid \mathbf{free}\, \rho$

Fig. 2. The syntax of the region language

Using the down instantiation in the running example, linear inequalities to be solved becomes as follows.

$$\Psi_{in}(\rho_x) \geq \frac{1}{2}(\Psi_{in}(\rho_x) + \Psi_{in}(\rho_y)) \quad \Psi_{in}(\rho_x) > 0 \quad \Psi_{in}(\rho_y) > 0$$

These inequalities are solvable (e.g., by assigning 1 to both $\Psi_{in}(\rho_x)$ and $\Psi_{in}(\rho_y)$), and hence, the program becomes typable.

For soundness, we may only apply the down instantiation to regions that are not deleted by the call because it would be unsafe to lower a capability required for a region deletion to some positive number less than 1. Therefore, we select the instantiation scheme based on which region a function call may delete. We use the additive instantiation when instantiating regions that are deleted, and use the down instantiation for those that are not. We use *effects* to infer the deleted regions. In the example above, the effect analysis detects that f frees neither ρ_x nor ρ_y, and therefore, that the down instantiation can be used for ρ_x and ρ_y.

3   Polymorphic Fractional Capability Calculus

We now formally define the polymorphic fractional capability calculus. We focus on the simple region language shown in Figure 2. The language is essentially the standard Tofte-Talpin region language [15] extended with **free** ρ and function types containing capabilities. Note that **free** ρ can be used to free a region before its scope expires (i.e., before e is fully evaluated in **letreg** ρ **in** e), thus possibly creating a dangling pointer.

We briefly describe the syntax of expressions (e). Expressions include integer constants n, variables x, functions $\lambda x : \tau.e$, region variable abstractions $\Lambda \rho.v$, recursive definitions $\mathbf{fix}\, x : \tau.v$, function applications $e\,(e')$, region applications $e[\rho]$, reference allocations $\mathbf{ref}\, e@\rho$, reference reads $!e$, reference writes $e := e'$, region allocations $\mathbf{letreg}\, \rho\, \mathbf{in}\, e$, and region deallocations $\mathbf{free}\, \rho$. Region abstraction and recursive definition are restricted to *values* v, which, for now, are just functions (and their region abstractions). For simplicity, the region language only allocates reference cells in regions, but it is easy to extend the language so that function closures are also allocated in regions. We write $\mathbf{let}\, x : \tau = e_1 \,\mathbf{in}\, e_2$ for $(\lambda x : \tau.e_2)\,(e_1)$, and $e_1; e_2$ for $\mathbf{let}\, x : \tau = e_1 \,\mathbf{in}\, e_2$ where x is not free in e_2.

Each function takes a single argument, but a multi-argument function can be encoded via currying. Instead of letting functions directly take region arguments as in Section 2, we use separate syntax for region variable abstraction and region instantiation. We also use separate syntax for recursive definition. For example, fun $f[\rho]$ $(x : \tau) = e$ from Section 2 can be expressed as fix $f : \tau'.\Lambda\rho.\lambda x : \tau.e$. Multi-region arguments can also be encoded by currying.

Next, we describe the grammar of the types. The types include integer types int, reference types $ref(\tau)@\rho$, region polymorphic types $\forall\rho.\tau$, and function types $(\Psi_{in}, \tau_{in}) \xrightarrow{L} (\Psi_{out}, \tau_{out})$ where L denotes the latent effect. Unlike in the Tofte-Talpin region system, we do not use effects to control the access to regions. As explained in Section 2, the latent effect overapproximates the regions that may be deleted by calling the function.

Ψ denotes a *capability*, which as discussed above, is a function from region variables **Regvar** to non-negative rational numbers in the range $[0, \infty)$. As discussed in Section 2, a capability represents the access rights over the regions. Informally, having Ψ such that $\Psi(\rho) > 0$ means that the region ρ can be accessed (i.e., allocated, read, or written). In addition, $\Psi(\rho) \geq 1$ means that the region ρ can also be deleted. Deleting a region *consumes* the capability, that is, the capability for ρ after free ρ becomes 0. The capability for a region is initialized to 1 when the region is created.

3.1 Dynamic Semantics

We define the operational semantics of the region language. The semantics is defined as small step reductions from states to states, where a *state* is a triple (R, h, e) consisting of a *region environment* R, a *store* h, and a *run-time expression* e. A region environment maps region variables to $\{0, 1\}$ where 0 indicates that the region has been deleted, and 1 indicates that the region is alive. A store is a mapping from *locations* ℓ to values. We extend values to include integers and locations as follows: $v ::= \cdots \mid n \mid \ell@\rho$.

Here, $\ell@\rho$ is a location ℓ allocated in the region ρ. The semantics trivially guarantees that for any ℓ, there is a unique ρ such that $\ell@\rho$ appears as a value in the semantics. Also, the semantics guarantees that if $\ell@\rho$ appears somewhere in the reduction, then $\rho \in dom(R)$ at that point, and that ℓ in $dom(h)$. However, it does not guarantee that $R(\rho) = 1$ at such a point, which, importantly, allows dangling pointers, and therefore, memory unsafe programs. It is the job of the static system to reject such unsafe programs (cf. Section 3.2).

Figure 3 shows a few representative reduction rules (see the long version [16] for the complete set of rules). **App** handles function calls and **TyApp** handles region parameter passing. Here, the substitution $e[\rho_1/\rho_2]$ is defined in the standard capture-avoiding way. We defer the definition of substitution for types $\tau[\rho_1/\rho_2]$ to Section 3.2, which is also capture avoiding. We let expressions and types equivalent up to renaming of bound variables and region variables.

Ref handles reference allocations, and requires the region where the reference is allocated to be alive. The reduction gets stuck when trying to access a deleted region. The reduction rules for other reference accesses (i.e., reads and writes)

$$(R, h, (\lambda x : \tau.e) \, (v)) \rightarrow (R, h, e[v/x]) \quad \textbf{App}$$

$$(R, h, (\Lambda \rho.v)[\rho']) \rightarrow (R, h, v[\rho'/\rho]) \quad \textbf{TyApp}$$

$$\frac{R(\rho) = 1 \quad \ell \notin dom(h)}{(R, h, \textbf{ref } v@\rho) \rightarrow (R, h[\ell \mapsto v], \ell@\rho)} \quad \textbf{Ref}$$

$$\frac{\rho \notin dom(R)}{(R, h, \textbf{letreg } \rho \textbf{ in } e) \rightarrow (R[\rho \mapsto 1], h, e)} \quad \textbf{Letreg}$$

$$\frac{R(\rho) = 1}{(R, h, \textbf{free } \rho) \rightarrow (R[\rho \mapsto 0], h, 0)} \quad \textbf{Free}$$

$$\frac{e \rightarrow e'}{E[e] \rightarrow E[e']} \quad \textbf{Context}$$

Fig. 3. Representative reduction rules

are similar. Here, the notation $f[u \mapsto v]$ denotes the extension of f by u mapping to v. That is, $f[u \mapsto v] = f \cup \{u \mapsto v\}$ for $u \notin dom(f)$. **Letreg** creates a fresh region, and **Free** frees a live region. Reduction gets stuck when trying to free an already freed region. **Context** is the usual rule to allow reduction in an evaluation context. The evaluation contexts are defined as follows.

$$E ::= [\,] \mid E \, (e) \mid v \, (E) \mid E[\rho] \mid \textbf{ref } E@\rho \mid E := e \mid v := E \mid !E$$

Let us write $(R, h, e) \rightarrow^* (R', h', e')$ for zero or more reduction steps from the state (R, h, e) to (R', h', e'). We say that the program e is memory safe if reducing from the initial state $(\emptyset, \emptyset, e)$ does not get stuck. More formally,

Definition 1 (Safety). *We say that e is memory safe if for any state (R_1, h_1, e_1) such that $(\emptyset, \emptyset, e) \rightarrow^* (R_1, h_1, e_1)$, either e_1 is a value or there exists a state (R_2, h_2, e_2) such that $(R_1, h_1, e_1) \rightarrow (R_2, h_2, e_2)$.*

3.2   Static Semantics

A capability calculus is a type system, and consists of a set of deductive typing rules. We present the polymorphic fractional capability calculus that guarantees that a typable program is memory safe.

Figure 4 presents the typing rules. The typing judgements are of the form $\Gamma, \Psi \vdash e : \tau, \Psi', L$. Here, the *type environment* Γ maps variables to types, *pre-capability* Ψ is the capability of the program before the evaluation of e, *post-capability* Ψ' is the capability after evaluating e, τ is the type of e, and L is the effect of e.

We briefly describe the typing rules. *Int* and *Var* are self-explanatory. In *Fun*, we type check the body starting with the pre-capability of the function

$$\frac{}{\Gamma,\Psi \vdash n : int, \Psi, \emptyset} \ \textbf{Int} \qquad \frac{}{\Gamma,\Psi \vdash x : \Gamma(x), \Psi, \emptyset} \ \textbf{Var}$$

$$\frac{\Gamma[x \mapsto \tau_{in}], \Psi_{in} \vdash e : \tau_{out}, \Psi_{out}, L \quad \forall \rho \notin L.\Psi_{in}(\rho) = \Psi_{out}(\rho)}{\Gamma,\Psi \vdash \lambda x : \tau_{in}.e : (\Psi_{in}, \tau_{in}) \xrightarrow{L} (\Psi_{out}, \tau_{out}), \Psi, \emptyset} \ \textbf{Fun}$$

$$\frac{}{\Gamma,\Psi \vdash \ell @ \rho : ref(\Gamma(\ell)) @ \rho, \Psi, \emptyset} \ \textbf{Loc} \qquad \frac{\Gamma[x \mapsto \tau], \Psi \vdash v : \tau, \Psi, \emptyset}{\Gamma,\Psi \vdash \texttt{fix}\ x : \tau.v : \tau, \Psi, \emptyset} \ \textbf{Fix}$$

$$\frac{\Gamma,\Psi \vdash e_1 : (\Psi_{in}, \tau_{in}) \xrightarrow{L} (\Psi_{out}, \tau_{out}), \Psi_1, L_1 \quad \Gamma,\Psi_1 \vdash e_2 : \tau_{in}, \Psi_{keep} + \Psi_{in}, L_2}{\Gamma,\Psi \vdash e_1(e_2) : \tau_{out}, \Psi_{keep} + \Psi_{out}, L_1 \cup L_2 \cup L} \ \textbf{App}$$

$$\frac{\Gamma,\Psi \vdash v : \tau, \Psi', \emptyset \quad \rho \notin free(\Gamma)}{\Gamma,\Psi \vdash \Lambda\rho.v : \forall \rho.\tau, \Psi', \emptyset} \ \textbf{RegAbs} \qquad \frac{\Gamma,\Psi \vdash e : \forall \rho.\tau, \Psi', L}{\Gamma,\Psi \vdash e[\rho'] : \tau[\rho'/\rho], \Psi', L} \ \textbf{TyApp}$$

$$\frac{\Gamma,\Psi \vdash e : \tau, \Psi', L \quad \Psi'(\rho) > 0}{\Gamma,\Psi \vdash \texttt{ref}\ e @ \rho : ref(\tau) @ \rho, \Psi', L} \ \textbf{Ref} \qquad \frac{\Gamma,\Psi \vdash e : ref(\tau) @ \rho, \Psi', L \quad \Psi'(\rho) > 0}{\Gamma,\Psi \vdash\ !e : \tau, \Psi', L} \ \textbf{Deref}$$

$$\frac{\Gamma,\Psi \vdash e : ref(\tau) @ \rho, \Psi_1, L_1 \quad \Gamma,\Psi_1 \vdash e' : \tau, \Psi', L_2 \quad \Psi'(\rho) > 0}{\Gamma,\Psi \vdash e := e' : int, \Psi', L_1 \cup L_2} \ \textbf{Write}$$

$$\frac{\Gamma,\Psi + \{\rho \mapsto 1\} \vdash e : \tau, \Psi', L \quad \rho \notin free(\Gamma) \cup free(\tau) \quad \Psi(\rho) = \Psi'(\rho) = 0}{\Gamma,\Psi \vdash \texttt{letreg}\ \rho\ \texttt{in}\ e : \tau, \Psi', L \setminus \{\rho\}} \ \textbf{Letreg}$$

$$\frac{}{\Gamma,\Psi + \{\rho \mapsto 1\} \vdash \texttt{free}\ \rho : int, \Psi, \{\rho\}} \ \textbf{Free}$$

Fig. 4. The type checking rules

Ψ_{in} and ending in the post-capability Ψ_{out}. We also record L as the latent effect of the function. The condition $\forall \rho \notin L.\Psi_{in}(\rho) = \Psi_{out}(\rho)$ becomes handy when proving the soundness of the type system[4].

RegAbs, **Fix**, and **Loc** are self-explanatory. Here, $free(\Gamma)$ is defined to be $\{free(\tau) \mid \tau \in ran(\Gamma)\}$ where $free(\tau)$ is defined as follows.

$$free(int) = \emptyset$$
$$free(ref(\tau)@\rho) = free(\tau) \cup \{\rho\}$$
$$free((\Psi_{in}, \tau_{in}) \xrightarrow{L} (\Psi_{out}, \tau_{out})) = free(\tau_{in}) \cup free(\tau_{out}) \cup L$$
$$free(\forall \rho.\tau) = free(\tau) \setminus \{\rho\}$$

App types function applications. The rule takes care of the left-to-write reduction order by connecting the post-capability of e_1 (i.e., Ψ_1) to the pre-capability of e_2. Here the capability addition $\Psi_1 + \Psi_2$ is defined point-wise as $\lambda \rho.\Psi_1(\rho) + \Psi_2(\rho)$. Note that the post-capability of e_2, is "split" into Ψ_{keep} and Ψ_{in} so that only Ψ_{in} needs to be given to the function and Ψ_{keep} is kept by the caller and combined

---

[4] It is actually redundant for closed programs as it can be derived as a lemma.

$$int[\rho_1/\rho_2] = int$$

$$(ref(\tau)@\rho_1')[\rho_1/\rho_2] = ref(\tau[\rho_1/\rho_2])@\rho_1'[\rho_1/\rho_2]$$

$$(\forall\rho_1'.\tau)[\rho_1/\rho_2] = \forall\rho_1'.(\tau[\rho_1/\rho_2]) \quad \text{where } \rho_1' \neq \rho_2$$

$$((\Psi_{in},\tau) \xrightarrow{L} (\Psi_{out},\tau'))[\rho_1/\rho_2] =$$
$$(\Psi_{in}[\rho_1/\rho_2]^L, \tau[\rho_1/\rho_2]) \xrightarrow{L[\rho_1/\rho_2]} (\Psi_{out}[\rho_1/\rho_2]^L, \tau'[\rho_1/\rho_2])$$

Fig. 5. $\tau[\rho_1/\rho_2]$

$$\Psi[\rho_1/\rho_2]^L = \begin{cases} \Psi[\rho_1/\rho_2]_\Downarrow & \text{if } \rho_1 \notin L[\rho_1/\rho_2] \\ \Psi[\rho_1/\rho_2]_\oplus & \text{if } \rho_1 \in L[\rho_1/\rho_2] \end{cases}$$

Fig. 6. $\Psi[\rho_1/\rho_2]^L$ (see Section 2 for the definitions of $\Psi[\rho_1/\rho_2]_\oplus$ and $\Psi[\rho_1/\rho_2]_\Downarrow$)

with the post-capability of the function. This capability "flow around" technique provides context sensitivity as each call site can use a different Ψ_{keep} to avoid conflating capabilities. (Note, however, that this context sensitivity is orthogonal to parametric region polymorphism.) The flow around technique is inspired by similar ideas used in Cqual [6] and Locksmith [8], and has also been used in the fractional capability calculus for race detection [10].

TyApp handles region instantiation. The type substitution $\tau[\rho'/\rho]$ is non-standard and is defined in Figure 5. The substitution rules for integer types, reference types, and region polymorphic types are self-explanatory (recall that the substitution is capture avoiding). For function types, we instantiate its pre-capability and the post-capability via the special substitution of the form $\Psi[\rho_1/\rho_2]^L$. Figure 6 defines the substitution. Note that it only does the additive instantiation for region variables in L, and does the down instantiation for other regions. This formally implements the controlled additive instantiation discussed in Section 2. We explain the down instantiation in further detail. The down instantiation is applied for regions that are only accessed but not deleted in the function. Since accessing these regions needs capabilities greater than 0, a function caller needs a capability that satisfies the constraint

$$\Psi_{\text{caller}}(\rho) > 0 \text{ if } \Psi_{\text{pre}}(\rho) > 0$$

where Ψ_{caller} is the capability necessary to call the function, and Ψ_{pre} is the pre-capability of the function. However, because linear programming cannot deal with the logical implication, we transform the constraint into the following constraint[5]:

$$\Psi_{\text{caller}}(\rho) \geq \tfrac{1}{2}\Psi_{\text{pre}}(\rho)$$

---

[5] Dividing capabilities by a number greater than 2 is still sound. For now, we adopt 2, because choosing a greater number does not contribute to the precision of the analysis.

Ref, **Deref**, and **Write** type check reference accesses by checking that the program has enough capability for the accesses. Unlike in the usual effect-based region calculus, the rules do not add the accessed regions to the effect.

Letreg creates a new region and adds the capability to access the region to the pre-capability of e. **Free** frees a region. Note that the pre-capability is required to have the full capability to access the region and deletes it from the post-capability. **Free** also adds ρ to the effect to record that the expression deletes ρ.

Next, we define the notion of a well-typed state. Let $0 = \lambda\rho.0$, that is, a capability that maps all regions to 0. We write $\Gamma \vdash h$ if for each $\ell \in dom(h)$, $\Gamma, 0 \vdash h(\ell) : \Gamma(\ell), 0, \emptyset$. We write $\vdash \Gamma$ if for all function types $(\tau, \Psi_{in}) \rightarrow^L (\tau', \Psi_{out})$ appearing in Γ, $\rho \notin L$ implies $\Psi_{in}(\rho) = \Psi_{out}(\rho)$.

Definition 2 (Well-typed State). *We write $\Gamma \vdash (R, h, e, \tau, \Psi')$ if there exist Ψ and L such that (1) $\Gamma \vdash h$, (2) $\Gamma, \Psi \vdash e : \tau, \Psi', L$, (3) $R(\rho) \geq \Psi(\rho)$ for all $\rho \in dom(R)$, and (4) $\vdash \Gamma$.*

We prove that typability is preserved under region instantiations, with a "large enough" effect. The proofs appear in the long version [16].

Lemma 1 (Region Variable Substitution). *Suppose $\Gamma, \Psi \vdash e : \tau, \Psi', L'$ and $L' \subseteq L$. Then, $\Gamma[\rho'/\rho], \Psi[\rho'/\rho]^L \vdash e[\rho'/\rho] : \tau[\rho'/\rho], \Psi'[\rho'/\rho]^L, L'[\rho'/\rho]$.*

Using the lemma, we show that typability is preserved across reductions.

Lemma 2 (Preservation). *Suppose $\Gamma \vdash (R, h, e, \tau, \Psi')$ and $(R, h, e) \rightarrow (R', h', e')$. Then, there exists $\Gamma' \supseteq \Gamma$ such that $\Gamma' \vdash (R', h', e', \tau, \Psi')$.*

Lemma 3 (Progress). *Suppose $\Gamma \vdash (R, h, e, \tau, \Psi')$ and e is a closed term. Then, either e is a value or there exist R', h', and e' such that $(R, h, e) \rightarrow (R', h', e')$.*

From Lemma 2 and Lemma 3, it follows that if e is well-typed then e is memory safe.

Theorem 1. *Suppose $\emptyset \vdash (\emptyset, \emptyset, e, \tau, \Psi')$. Then, e is memory safe.*

4   Capability Inference

We now give a polynomial time capability inference algorithm for the capability calculus. Note that the focus of the paper is not region inference, and therefore, the input program is an expression in the source syntax (cf. Figure 2) that already contains region commands (i.e., region creations, region deletions, and region abstractions). In addition, the algorithm assumes that it is given types for the bound variables, including the effects, except for the capabilities (i.e., Ψ's). Such region and effect annotations may be provided externally as in the original capability calculus [5], or inferred by known techniques [15,9]. We note that there can be more than one valid region and effect annotations for a program. For example, using [9], polymorphism is restricted to only over `let` and `fix` bound variables (i.e., not λ-bound variables). But, our algorithm can infer capabilities given any valid annotation, in time polynomial in the size of the annotation.

More formally, we assume that every variable binding in the program is annotated by the following signature σ.

$$\psi \in \mathbf{Capvar}$$
$$\varphi ::= \psi \mid \varphi[\rho'/\rho]^L$$
$$\sigma ::= int \mid ref(\sigma)@\rho \mid (\varphi_{in}, \sigma_{in}) \xrightarrow{L} (\varphi_{out}, \sigma_{out}) \mid \forall \rho.\sigma$$

Here, *capability variables* ψ are place holders for the actual capabilities to be inferred by the algorithm (we use the lower-case "psi" for the variables). Each φ appearing in the annotation is a distinct capability variable (i.e., some ψ). The form $\varphi[\rho'/\rho]^L$ appears during the constraint generation. Unless specified otherwise, we overload e to expressions with σ annotations. Without loss of generality, we assume that bound variables and region variables are distinct in the given program.

The inference judgements are of the form $\Delta, \psi \vdash e : \sigma, \psi', L \Rightarrow C$, which is read "given environment Δ, e is inferred to have the signature σ, the pre-capability variable ψ, the post-capability variable ψ', and the effect L with the set of *capability constraints* C". A capability constraint is of the following forms.

$$\psi(\rho) = \psi'(\rho) \quad \psi(\rho) > 0 \quad \varphi = \varphi'$$
$$\psi = \psi' + \{\rho \mapsto 1\} \quad \psi(\rho) = 0 \quad \varphi_0 = \varphi_1 + \varphi_2$$

To generate constraints, we initialize Δ such that for each variable x, $\Delta(x) = \sigma$ where σ is the signature of x given in the annotation, that is, either `fix` $x : \sigma.v$ or $\lambda x : \sigma.e$ appears in the program (recall that bound variables are distinct). We also pick distinct capability variables ψ_{start} and ψ_{end}, and we generate constraints C by $\Delta, \psi_{start} \vdash e : \sigma, \psi_{end}, L \Rightarrow C$ where e is the input program, and ψ_{start}, ψ_{end} are distinct capability variables.

Figure 7 shows a few representative constraint generation rules (see the long version [16] for the complete set of rules). Each rule is a straightforward syntax-directed constraint generation rule for the type checking rules from Figure 4. The rules use the relation $\vdash \sigma =_u \sigma' \Rightarrow C$ to generate capability equality constraints of the form $\varphi = \varphi'$. The relation is defined inductively on the structure of the types, and is straightforward (see the long version [16]). We assume that the type annotations in the input program are correct in the sense that the instances of the rules are all well-defined in the constraint generation.

The substitution $\sigma[\rho'/\rho]$ is defined exactly like $\tau[\rho'/\rho]$ from Figure 5 (i.e., inductively on the structure of σ) with the substitution $\varphi[\rho'/\rho]^L$ just interpreted syntactically.

Let $\mathfrak{L}$ be the set of regions occurring in the program. For each capability variable ψ and a region $\rho \in \mathfrak{L}$, we associate a distinct linear programming variable

$$\frac{\psi \text{ fresh} \qquad \Delta, \psi_{in} \vdash e : \sigma_{out}, \psi_{out}, L \Rightarrow C}{\Delta, \psi \vdash (\lambda x : \sigma_{in}.e) : (\psi_{in}, \sigma_{in}) \xrightarrow{L} (\psi_{out}, \sigma_{out}), \psi, \emptyset \Rightarrow \\ C \cup \{\psi_{in}(\rho) = \psi_{out}(\rho) \mid \rho \in \mathfrak{L} \setminus L\}} \text{ cFun}$$

$$\frac{\psi, \psi' \text{ fresh}}{\Delta, \psi \vdash \textbf{free } \rho : int, \psi', \{\rho\} \Rightarrow \{\psi = \psi' + \{\rho \mapsto 1\}\}} \text{ cFree}$$

$$\frac{\Delta, \psi \vdash e_1 : (\varphi_{in}, \sigma_{in}) \xrightarrow{L} (\varphi_{out}, \sigma_{out}), \psi_1, L_1 \Rightarrow C_1 \\ \Delta, \psi_2 \vdash e_3 : \sigma', \psi_3, L_2 \Rightarrow C_2 \qquad \vdash \sigma_{in} =_u \sigma' \Rightarrow C_3 \qquad \psi_{keep} \text{ fresh}}{\Delta, \psi \vdash e_1 (e_2) : \sigma_{out}, \psi', L_1 \cup L_2 \cup L \Rightarrow \\ C_1 \cup C_2 \cup C_3 \cup \{\psi_1 = \psi_2, \psi_3 = \varphi_{in} + \psi_{keep}, \psi' = \psi_{keep} + \varphi_{out}\}} \text{ cApp}$$

Fig. 7. Representative constraint generation rules

$\xi_{\psi,\rho}$ to denote $\psi(\rho)$. We reduce the capability constraints to linear inequality constraints by applying the following rules.

$$
\begin{aligned}
\psi(\rho) = \psi'(\rho) &\Rightarrow & \{\xi_{\psi,\rho} = \xi_{\psi',\rho}\} \\
\psi(\rho) > 0 &\Rightarrow & \{\xi_{\psi,\rho} > 0\} \\
\varphi = \varphi' &\Rightarrow & \{S(\varphi,\rho) = S(\varphi',\rho) \mid \rho \in \mathfrak{L}\} \\
\psi = \psi' + \{\rho_f \mapsto 1\} &\Rightarrow & \{\xi_{\psi,\rho} = \xi_{\psi',\rho} \mid \rho \in \mathfrak{L} \setminus \{\rho_f\}\} \cup \{\xi_{\psi,\rho_f} = \xi_{\psi',\rho_f} + 1\} \\
\psi(\rho) = 0 &\Rightarrow & \{\xi_{\psi,\rho} = 0\} \\
\varphi_0 = \varphi_1 + \varphi_2 &\Rightarrow & \{S(\varphi_0,\rho) = S(\varphi_1,\rho) + S(\varphi_2,\rho) \mid \rho \in \mathfrak{L}\}
\end{aligned}
$$

where $S(\varphi, \rho)$ is defined as follows.

$$
\begin{aligned}
S(\psi, \rho) &= \xi_{\psi,\rho} \\
S(\varphi[\rho_a/\rho_x]^L, \rho) &= \text{if } \rho = \rho_x \text{ then } 0 \\
&\quad \text{else if } \rho \neq \rho_a \text{ then } S(\varphi, \rho) \\
&\quad \text{else if } \rho_x \notin L \text{ then } \tfrac{1}{2}(S(\varphi, \rho_x) + S(\varphi, \rho_a)) \\
&\quad \text{else } S(\varphi, \rho_x) + S(\varphi, \rho_a)
\end{aligned}
$$

We also add the inequality $\xi_{\psi,\rho} \geq 0$ for each $\xi_{\psi,\rho}$ to ensure that capabilities are within the range $[0, \infty)$. Then, we check whether there exists a solution to the set of these inequalities, and if so, we accept the program as safe, and otherwise, we reject the program.

To apply linear programing algorithms that can only take non-strict inequalities such as GLPK [1], we add a fresh linear programming variable ξ_s and replace each $\xi_{\psi,\rho} > 0$ with $\xi_{\psi,\rho} \geq \xi_s$, and set the objective function to be ξ_s. We then ask the linear programming solver to find a solution that maximizes ξ_s and accept if and only if the solver returns a solution with $\xi_s > 0$.

The soundness and the completeness of the inference is stated and proven in the long version [16].

4.1 Time Complexity

We discuss the time complexity of the capability inference algorithm. Recall that we assume that region and effect annotations are provided[6]. The complexity of the constraint generation is polynomial in the size of the given region and effect annotations, and so is the size of the generated set of linear inequalities. The complexity of (rational) linear programming is polynomial in the size of the linear inequalities. Therefore, the complexity of our inference algorithm is polynomial in the size of the provided types.

NP-hardness of non-fractional capability calculus: It is possible to show that restricting capabilities to range only over the set $\{0, 1\}$ instead of the range $[0, \infty)$ renders the capability inference NP-hard, even without polymorphism [13,7]. Therefore, not only is the fractional capability calculus able to prove more programs memory safe than the non-fractional variant, it is actually more computationally tractable, assuming that $P \neq NP$.

5 Adding Polymorphism to Other Fractional Capability Calculi

Our approach can be used to add parametric polymorphism to other fractional capability calculus applications. We take race detection [10] for instance and discuss the methodology.

Recall that, for the region calculus, we may use the down instantiation for regions that are only accessed (i.e., read, written, or allocated) but not deleted in the function. Because the race detection calculus needs to distinguish reads from writes[7], we use the down instantiation for abstract locations[8] that are only read but not written. In the race calculus, writes and reads are distinguished by requiring the capability greater or equal to 1 for writes and capability greater than 0 for reads. We define a new instantiation scheme, called *1-instantiation*, to instantiate abstract locations that may be written in functions:

$$\Psi[\rho_1/\rho_2]_1 = \{\rho_1 \mapsto 1\} \cup \{\rho \mapsto \Psi(\rho) \mid \rho \notin \{\rho_1, \rho_2\}\}$$

Note that this scheme lowers the capability for ρ_2 to 1. We use effects to track the abstract locations that may be written.

To prove Lemma 1, it is important that the effect L contains the regions where pre-capability (i.e., Ψ) and post-capability (i.e., Ψ') are different (cf. proof in the long version [16]). For the region calculus, this occurs only when the **Free**

---

[6] They may be inferred in time polynomial in the size of the underlying Hindley-Milner type under certain restrictions (e.g., rank-1 restriction) via methods like [9].

[7] Formally, a race occurs when two accesses to a memory location happens concurrently such that one of them is a write, and so a concurrent read is not a race.

[8] Abstract locations soundly approximates the actual locations. They serve the role similar to region variables in the region calculus, and we overload ρ to range over abstract locations in this section.

$$\frac{\Gamma, \Psi \vdash e_1 : ref(\tau)@\rho, \Psi_1, L_1, L_2 \quad \Gamma, \Psi_1 \vdash e_2 : \tau, \Psi_2, L_1', L_2' \quad \Psi_2(\rho) \geq 1}{\Gamma, \Psi \vdash e_1 := e_2 : int, \Psi_2, L_1 \cup L_1', L_2 \cup L_2' \cup \{\rho\}} \text{ WRITE}$$

$$\frac{}{\Gamma, \Psi + \Psi_1 \vdash \text{newlock} : \text{lock}(\Psi_1), \Psi, positive(\Psi_1), \emptyset} \text{ NEWL}$$

$$\text{where } positive(\Psi) = \{\rho \in dom(\Psi) \mid \Psi(\rho) > 0\}$$

Fig. 8. Representative polymorphic fractional race typing rules

type rule is applied (see Figure 4). In the race detection calculus, this occurs when capabilities are passed across threads via operations like lock creation, lock acquisition, and lock release. For example, the following rule is applied for lock creation.

$$\frac{}{\Gamma, \Psi + \Psi_1 \vdash \text{newlock} : \text{lock}(\Psi_1), \Psi}$$

Note that pre-capability, $\Psi + \Psi_1$, may differ from the post-capability, Ψ, and so we need to track the abstract locations where the capabilities differ as effects. Like in the region calculus, we use additive instantiation for such abstraction locations.

To summarize, we have three instantiation schemes for the race detection calculus: the down instantiation for read-only locations, 1-instantiation for read-or-write-only locations, and the additive instantiation for the rest (i.e., ones that may be possibly passed across threads).

As in the region calculus, we use effects to select the instantiation schemes. We now have two kinds of effects, one for abstract locations that change their capabilities (L_1 in the definition below), and one for abstract locations that are written (L_2 in the definition below). The new instantiation rule is defined as follows.

$$\Psi[\rho_1/\rho_2]^{L_1, L_2} = \begin{cases} \Psi[\rho_1/\rho_2]_\Downarrow & \text{if } \rho_1 \notin (L_1 \cup L_2)[\rho_1/\rho_2] \\ \Psi[\rho_1/\rho_2]_\oplus & \text{if } \rho_1 \in L_1[\rho_1/\rho_2] \\ \Psi[\rho_1/\rho_2]_1 & \text{if } \rho_1 \in (L_2 \setminus L_1)[\rho_1/\rho_2] \end{cases}$$

We modify the type checking rules to track effects. Judgements are of the form $\Gamma, \Psi \vdash e : \tau, \Psi', L_1, L_2$ where L_1 overapproximates abstract locations that may change in e, and L_2 overapproximates abstract locations that are written in e.

Figure 8 shows a few representative type checking rules. **WRITE** rule adds the written abstract location in the effect L_2. In **NEWL** rule, we add the abstract locations that are passed by the lock creation, that is, $positive(\Psi_1)$. Inferring $positive(\Psi_1)$ requires solving linear inequalities, inducing cyclic dependencies between capability constraint generation and capability constraint solving. Fortunately, it is sound to overapproximate effects, and so a tractable approach is to use all abstract locations (i.e., $\mathfrak{L}$) in place of $positive(\Psi_1)$ at **NEWL** (and other type rules that also change capabilities). By an argument analogous to the one in Section 4.1, it can be shown that the capability inference for such a system is polynomial time computable.

6   Related Work and Conclusion

Fractional capabilities were originally proposed by Boyland to guarantee determinism of multi-thread programs while permitting parallel reads [4]. For the monomorphic fragment, it has been shown that the type inference can be solved efficiently by a reduction to linear programming [12,13], and later work has exploited this observation to create efficient fractional-capability-based program analyses, ranging from race detection to security analyses [7,14,10,11].

While extending these calculi to parametric polymorphism is discussed in some of the papers (e.g., [4,13,10]), none has shown how to do type inference efficiently in the presence of polymorphism. This paper addresses the issue by presenting a general methodology to extend a fractional capability calculus to parametric polymorphism while preserving soundness and the ability to do efficient type inference.

Acknowledgement

We would like to thank Naoki Kobayashi and anonymous reviewers for useful comments.

References

1. GNU Linear Programming Kit, http://www.gnu.org/software/glpk/glpk.html
2. Bierhoff, K., Aldrich, J.: Modular typestate checking of aliased objects. In: Proceedings of the 22nd Annual ACM SIGPLAN Conference on Object-Oriented Programming, Systems, Languages, and Applications, OOPSLA, pp. 301–320 (2007)
3. Bornat, R., Calcagno, C., O'Hearn, P., Parkinson, M.: Permission accounting in separation logic. In: Proceedings of the 32nd ACM SIGPLAN-SIGACT Symposium on Principles of Programming Languages, POPL, pp. 259–270 (2005)
4. Boyland, J.: Checking interference with fractional permissions. In: Cousot, R. (ed.) SAS 2003. LNCS, vol. 2694, pp. 55–72. Springer, Heidelberg (2003)
5. Crary, K., Walker, D., Morrisett, G.: Typed memory management in a calculus of capabilities. In: Proceedings of the 26th ACM SIGPLAN-SIGACT Symposium on Principles of Programming Languages, POPL, pp. 262–275 (1999)
6. Foster, J.S., Terauchi, T., Aiken, A.: Flow-sensitive type qualifiers. In: Proceedings of the ACM SIGPLAN Conference on Programming Language Design and Implementation, PLDI, pp. 1–12 (2002)
7. Kikuchi, D., Kobayashi, N.: Type-based verification of correspondence assertions for communication protocols. In: Shao, Z. (ed.) APLAS 2007. LNCS, vol. 4807, pp. 191–205. Springer, Heidelberg (2007)
8. Pratikakis, P., Foster, J.S., Hicks, M.: Locksmith: context-sensitive correlation analysis for race detection. In: Proceedings of the ACM SIGPLAN Conference on Programming Language Design and Implementation, PLDI, pp. 320–331 (2006)
9. Rehof, J., Fähndrich, M.: Type-base flow analysis: from polymorphic subtyping to cfl-reachability. In: Proceedings of the 23th ACM SIGPLAN-SIGACT Symposium on Principles of Programming Languages, POPL, pp. 54–66 (2001)

10. Terauchi, T.: Checking race freedom via linear programming. In: Proceedings of the ACM SIGPLAN Conference on Programming Language Design and Implementation, PLDI, pp. 1–10 (2008)
11. Terauchi, T.: A type system for observational determinism. In: Proceedings of the 21st IEEE Computer Security Foundations Symposium, CSF, pp. 287–300 (2008)
12. Terauchi, T., Aiken, A.: Witnessing side-effects. In: Proceedings of the 10th ACM SIGPLAN International Conference on Functional Programming, ICFP, pp. 105–115 (2005)
13. Terauchi, T., Aiken, A.: A capability calculus for concurrency and determinism. ACM Trans. Program. Lang. Syst. (2008)
14. Terauchi, T., Megacz, A.: Inferring channel buffer bounds via linear programming. In: Drossopoulou, S. (ed.) ESOP 2008. LNCS, vol. 4960, pp. 284–298. Springer, Heidelberg (2008)
15. Tofte, M., Talpin, J.P.: Implementation of the typed call-by-value λ-calculus using a stack of regions. In: Proceedings of the 21st ACM SIGPLAN-SIGACT Symposium on Principles of Programming Languages, POPL, pp. 188–201 (1994)
16. Yasuoka, H., Terauchi, T.: Polymorphic fractional capabilities(long version) (2008), http://www.kb.ecei.tohoku.ac.jp/~yasuoka/papers/polyfrac.pdf

Automatic Parallelization and Optimization of Programs by Proof Rewriting

Clément Hurlin

INRIA Sophia Antipolis – Méditerranée and University of Twente

Abstract. We show how, given a program and its separation logic proof, one can parallelize and optimize this program and transform its proof simultaneously to obtain a proven parallelized and optimized program. To achieve this goal, we present new proof rules for generating proof trees and a rewrite system on proof trees.

1 Introduction

As the trend towards multi-core processors is growing, software developers must write parallel code. Because writing parallel software is notoriously harder than writing sequential software, inferring parallelism automatically is a possible solution to the challenges faced by software developers. A well-known technique for inferring parallelism is to detect pieces of programs that access disjoint parts of the heap. Previously [19,21,24], various pointer analysis have been used to achieve this goal for programs manipulating simple data structures and arrays.

In this paper, we describe a new technique to infer parallelism from proven programs. Instead of designing ad-hoc analysis techniques, we use separation logic [34] to analyze programs before parallelizing them. We use separation logic's $\star$ operator – which expresses disjointness of parts of the heap – to detect potential parallelism. Compared to [19,21,24], using the $\star$ operator avoids relying on reachability properties. This permits to discover disjointness of arbitrary data structures, paving the way to parallelize and optimize object-oriented programs proven with separation logic [32].

Contrary to most previous works that manipulate proofs [5,29,33], our algorithms manipulate proof trees representing derivations of Hoare triplets. The overall procedure is as follows: we generate a proof tree $\mathcal{P}$ of a program C, then we rewrite $\mathcal{P}, C$ into $\mathcal{P}', C'$ such that $\mathcal{P}'$ is a proof of C' and C' is a parallelized and optimized version of C. The generation of proof trees is done with a modified version of smallfoot [8] and the rewrite system is implemented in tom [4].

Our algorithm for rewriting proof trees focuses on two rules of separation logic: the (Frame) and the (Parallel) rules. First, the (Frame) rule [34] allows reasoning about a program in isolation from its environment, by focusing only on the part of the heap that this program accesses. Second, the (Parallel) rule [30] allows reasoning about parallel programs that access disjoint parts of the heap.

$$\frac{\{\Xi\}C\{\Xi'\}}{\{\Xi \star \Theta\}C\{\Xi' \star \Theta\}} \text{ (Frame)} \qquad \frac{\{\Xi\}C\{\Theta\} \quad \{\Xi'\}C'\{\Theta'\}}{\{\Xi \star \Xi'\}C\|C'\{\Theta \star \Theta'\}} \text{ (Parallel)}$$

J. Palsberg and Z. Su (Eds.): SAS 2009, LNCS 5673, pp. 52–68, 2009.

The basic idea of our reasoning is depicted by the following rewrite rule:

$$\frac{\dfrac{\{\varXi\}C\{\varTheta\}}{\{\varXi\star\varXi'\}C\{\varTheta\star\varXi'\}}\;(\text{Frame})\quad\dfrac{\{\varXi'\}C'\{\varTheta'\}}{\{\varTheta\star\varXi'\}C'\{\varTheta\star\varTheta'\}}\;(\text{Frame})}{\{\varXi\star\varXi'\}C;\,C'\{\varTheta\star\varTheta'\}}\;(\text{Seq})$$

$$\downarrow\text{Parallelize}^1$$

$$\frac{\{\varXi\}C\{\varTheta\}\quad\{\varXi'\}C'\{\varTheta'\}}{\{\varXi\star\varXi'\}C\|C'\{\varTheta\star\varTheta'\}}\;(\text{Parallel})$$

The diagram above should be read as follows: Given a proof of the sequential program C; C' we rewrite this proof into a proof of the parallel program $C\|C'$. If the initial proof tree is valid, this rewriting yields a valid proof tree because the leaves of the rewritten proof tree are included in the leaves of the initial proof tree.

Our procedure differs from recent and concurrent work [33] on three main points: *(1)* instead of attaching labels to heaps, we use the (Frame) rule to statically detect independent parts of the program, leading to a technically simpler procedure; *(2)* we express optimizations by rewrite rules on proof trees, allowing us to feature other optimizations than parallelization and to use different optimization strategies; and *(3)* we have an implementation. Having said these differences, both our work and Raza et al.'s work [33] build upon the insight that separation logic proofs are a convenient tool to detect parallelism.

Contributions. We present the careful design of proof rules adapted for our rewrite rules (Section 3). These proof rules are derived from [8]'s proof rules. We present sound rewrite rules from proof trees to proof trees that yield optimized programs (Section 4). Considered optimizations are parallelization, early disposal, late allocation, early lock releasing, and late lock acquirement. We present an implementation of our algorithms that uses smallfoot [7] as the proof tree generator and tom [4] as the rewrite engine (Section 5). We illustrate our algorithms by two examples (Section 6).

Outline. The rest of the paper is organized as follows: we present the formal language we use throughout the paper in Section 2, we show how our technique will benefit from the recent advances of separation logic in Section 7, we discuss related work in Section 8, and we conclude in Section 9.

2 Background

This section recalls the relevant parts of [8]'s framework that we use in our work.

Our assertion language distinguishes between pure (heap independent) and spatial (heap dependent) assertions:

---

[1] To disambiguate between Hoare rules (enclosed in parentheses) and rewrite rules, we underline rewrite rules.

$$
\begin{array}{rll}
x, y, z & \in\ \mathsf{Var} & \text{variables}\\
E, F, G & ::=\ \mathtt{nil}\mid x & \text{expressions}\\
b & ::=\ E = E \mid E \neq E & \text{boolean expressions}\\
\Pi & ::=\ b \mid \Pi \wedge \Pi & \text{pure formulas}\\
f, g, f_i, l, r, \ldots & \in\ \mathsf{Fields} & \text{fields}\\
\rho & ::=\ f_1 : E_1, \ldots, f_n : E_n & \text{record expressions}\\
S & ::=\ E \mapsto [\rho] \mid \mathtt{ls}(E, F) \mid \mathtt{tree}(E) & \text{simple spatial formulas}\\
\Sigma & ::=\ \mathtt{emp} \mid S \mid \Sigma \star \Sigma & \text{spatial formulas}\\
\Xi, \Theta & \in\ \Pi \mathbin{\vert} \Sigma & \text{formulas}
\end{array}
$$

The meaning of simple spatial formulas is as follows: $E \mapsto [\rho]$ represents a heap containing one cell at address E with content ρ, $\mathtt{ls}(E, F)$ represents a heap containing a linked list segment from address E to address F, and $\mathtt{tree}(E)$ represents a heap containing a tree whose root is at address E and whose left and right subtrees can be dereferenced with fields l and r. The formula $E \mapsto [\rho]$ can mention any number of fields in ρ: the values of omitted fields are implicitly existentially quantified. Top-level formulas are pairs $\Pi \mathbin{\vert} \Sigma$ where Π is a $\wedge$-separated sequence of pure formulas (indicating equalities/inequalities between expressions) and Σ is a $\star$-separated sequence of spatial formulas (indicating facts about the heap). The semantics of formulas is omitted and can be found in [8].

Entailment between formulas is written $\Xi \vdash \Theta$. We lift $\vdash$ to pure formulas and $\star$ to formulas (note that $\mathbin{\vert}$ binds tighter than $\star$) as follows:

$$
\Pi \vdash \Pi' \ \triangleq\ \Pi \mathbin{\vert} \mathtt{emp} \vdash \Pi' \mathbin{\vert} \mathtt{emp} \qquad \Pi \mathbin{\vert} \Sigma \star \Pi' \mathbin{\vert} \Sigma' \ \triangleq\ (\Pi \wedge \Pi') \mathbin{\vert} (\Sigma \star \Sigma')
$$

We use σ to range over substitutions of the form $x_0/y_0, \ldots, x_n/y_n$. Below we abusively write $\Pi \vdash x_0/y_0, \ldots, x_n/y_n$ to denote $\Pi \vdash x_0 = y_0 \wedge \cdots \wedge x_n = y_n$. We define a syntactical equivalence relation between formulas as follows:

$$
\Pi \mathbin{\vert} \Sigma \Leftrightarrow \Pi' \mathbin{\vert} \Sigma' \text{ iff } \begin{cases} \Pi \text{ is a permutation of } \Pi'\\ \exists \sigma, \Pi \vdash \sigma \text{ and } \Sigma[\sigma] \text{ is a permutation of } \Sigma' \end{cases}
$$

Hoare triplets have the form $\{\Xi\}C\{\Theta\}$ where C is a command. Atomic commands A and commands C are defined by the following grammar (where p ranges over procedure names):

$$
\begin{array}{rl}
A & ::=\ x := E \mid x := E \to f \mid E \to f := F \mid x := \mathtt{new}() \mid \mathtt{dispose}(E)\\
C & ::=\ A \mid \mathtt{empty} \mid \mathtt{if}\ b\ \mathtt{then}\ C\ \mathtt{else}\ C \mid \mathtt{while}(b)\{C\}\\
& \mid\ \mathtt{lock}(r) \mid \mathtt{unlock}(r) \mid p(\overline{E_1}; \overline{E_2}) \mid C;\ C \mid C \| C'
\end{array}
$$

Atomic command $x := E \to f$ looks up the content of field f of cell at address E, while $E \to f := F$ mutates the content of field f of cell at address E. In $\mathtt{lock}(r)$ and $\mathtt{unlock}(r)^2$, r is a lock or a *resource* [30]. Resources are declared

---

[2] To smallfoot's experts: smallfoot uses conditional critical regions `with do endwith` instead of `lock/unlock` commands. However, because smallfoot generates *verification conditions* [8], conditional critical regions are treated like `lock/unlock` commands in smallfoot's implementation. That is why we use `lock/unlock` commands.

in the (omitted) program's header and come with a *resource invariant*, i.e., a formula describing the part of the heap guarded by the resource. Intuitively, when a resource is locked by a process, the resource's invariant is transferred to the process; while when a resource is unlocked, the resource's invariant is transferred from the process back to the resource. In procedure calls $p(\overline{E_1}; \overline{E_2})$, $\overline{E_1}$ are the parameters that are unchanged in p's body, while $\overline{E_2}$ are the parameters that are assigned in p's body.

To mutate and lookup the content of records, we use the following notations:

$$\mathsf{mutate}(\rho, f, F) = \begin{cases} f : F, \rho' \text{ if } \rho = f : E, \rho' \\ f : F, \rho \text{ if } f \notin \rho \end{cases} \quad \mathsf{lkp}(\rho, f) = \begin{cases} E & \text{if } \rho = f : E, \rho' \\ x \text{ fresh} & \text{if } f \notin \rho \end{cases}$$

3 Derived Rules with Explicit Antiframes and Frames

In this section we show how to generate proof trees where *antiframes* [13] (portions of the state needed to execute a command) and frames (portions of the state useless to execute a command) are made explicit. Making antiframes and frames explicit will be needed in Section 4 for our rewrite rules to work.

The (Frame) rule is one of the central ingredients of separation logic's success. It allows reasoning with *small axioms* [31] about atomic commands. In practice, however, the small axioms are not used and frames are not computed at each atomic command. Consider, for example, the rule for field lookup used in [8][3]:

$$\frac{\Pi \vdash F = E \qquad x' \text{ fresh} \qquad \mathsf{lkp}(\rho, f) = G}{\{\Pi \mid \Sigma \star F \mapsto [\rho]\}x := E \to f\{x = G[x'/x] \wedge \Pi[x'/x] \mid (\Sigma \star F \mapsto [\rho])[x'/x]\}}$$

This rule does not frame the precondition: the whole pure part of the precondition (Π) is used to show $F = E$ and the substitution x'/x is applied to the whole precondition ($\Pi \mid \Sigma \star F \mapsto [\rho]$). In other words, this rule does not exhibit the part of the precondition that is framed i.e., *(1)* the pure part of the precondition that is useless to show $F = E$ and *(2)* the part of the precondition that is left unaffected by the substitution x'/x.

Fig. 1 shows rules (derived from [8]) for each atomic command where antiframes and frames are made explicit. In these rules, we subscript formulas representing antiframes by a and formulas representing frames by f. We indicate on the right-hand side of applications of (Frame) the formula being framed. Finally, extra side conditions of (Frame) are indicated as additional premises.

To help the reader understand these rules, we detail the rule exhibiting the antiframe and frame at a field lookup command (the second rule). The antiframe consists of *(1)* the pure part of the precondition which is necessary to show $F = E$: it is Π_a and of *(2)* the spatial part of the precondition asserting that the cell at E exists ($F \mapsto [\rho]$) and the spatial part of the precondition affected by the substitution x'/x (Σ_a). The frame is the antiframe's complement (Ξ_f).

---

[3] Where, for clarity, we do the following modifications to [8]'s presentation: we include the "rearrangement" step and we omit the continuation.

$$\dfrac{x'\ \text{fresh}}{\{\Xi_a\}x := E\{\Xi_a[x'/x]\}}\ (\text{Assign})\qquad x \notin \Xi_f}{\{\Xi_a \star \Xi_f\}x := E\{\Xi_a[x'/x] \star \Xi_f\}}\ (\text{Frame } \Xi_f)$$

$$\dfrac{\dfrac{\Pi_a \vdash F = E \quad x'\ \text{fresh} \quad \mathsf{lkp}(\rho, f) = G}{\Xi = \Pi_a[x'/x] \wedge x = G[x'/x] \mid (\Sigma_a \star F \mapsto [\rho])[x'/x]}}{\{\Pi_a \mid \Sigma_a \star F \mapsto [\rho]\}x := E \to f\{\Xi\}}\ (\text{Lookup})\qquad x \notin \Xi_f}{\{(\Pi_a \mid \Sigma_a \star F \mapsto [\rho]) \star \Xi_f\}x := E \to f\{\Xi \star \Xi_f\}}\ (\text{Frame } \Xi_f)$$

$$\dfrac{\dfrac{\Pi_a \vdash F = E \quad \mathsf{mutate}(\rho, f, G) = \rho'}{\{\Pi_a \mid F \mapsto [\rho]\}E \to f := G\{\Pi_a \mid F \mapsto [\rho']\}}\ (\text{Mutate})}{\{\Pi_a \mid F \mapsto [\rho] \star \Xi_f\}E \to f := G\{\Pi_a \mid F \mapsto [\rho'] \star \Xi_f\}}\ (\text{Frame } \Xi_f)$$

$$\dfrac{\dfrac{x'\ \text{fresh}}{\{\Xi_a\}x := \mathbf{new}()\{\Xi_a[x'/x] \star x \mapsto []\}}\ (\text{New})\qquad x \notin \Xi_f}{\{\Xi_a \star \Xi_f\}x := \mathbf{new}()\{\Xi_a[x'/x] \star x \mapsto [] \star \Xi_f\}}\ (\text{Frame } \Xi_f)$$

$$\dfrac{\dfrac{\Pi_a \vdash F = E}{\{\Pi_a \mid F \mapsto [\rho]\}\mathbf{dispose}(E)\{\Pi_a \mid \mathbf{emp}\}}\ (\text{Dispose})}{\{\Pi_a \mid F \mapsto [\rho] \star \Xi_f\}\mathbf{dispose}(E)\{\Pi_a \mid \mathbf{emp} \star \Xi_f\}}\ (\text{Frame } \Xi_f)$$

Fig. 1. Derived rules for atomic commands with explicit antiframes and frames

Theorem 1. *The rules in Fig. 1 are sound.*

Sketch of the proof. Observe that the restrictions imposed on explicit frames ($x \notin \Xi_f$) make explicit frames immune to substitutions x'/x (cases (Assign), (Lookup), and (New)). Then, further observe that these rules derive from [8]'s rules (which are sound). □

We have not discussed the rule for method calls. That is intentional: existing proof rules for method calls [34,7] already compute frames and antiframes at procedure calls. Similarly, we use standard rules for loops and conditionals. There is a caveat though: because smallfoot generates verification conditions [7], proofs for while loops are "separated" from the enclosing method. This forbids to move code from within a loop outside of the loop (and conversely).

4   Automatic Optimizations by Proof Rewriting

In this section, we show rewrite rules for proof trees (ranged over by the meta-variable $\mathcal{P}$). The proof trees we consider are built using [8]'s framework but we use Fig. 1's rules for atomic commands. This is crucial because all our rewrite rules mention the (Frame) rule on their left hand side i.e., they cannot fire if frames are not explicit.

$$\cfrac{\cfrac{\qquad}{\{\Lambda_x^-\}x\to f := E\{\Lambda_x^E\}}\text{(Mutate)}}{\{\Lambda_{x,y,z}^{-,-,-}\}x\to f := E\{\Lambda_{x,y,z}^{E,-,-}\}}\text{(Fr }\Lambda_{y,z}^{-,-})\quad\cfrac{\cfrac{\cfrac{\{\Lambda_y^-\}y\to f := F\{\Lambda_y^F\}}{\{\Lambda_{x,y,z}^{E,-,-}\}y\to f := F\{\Lambda_{x,y,z}^{E,F,-}\}}}{\text{(Mutate)}}\text{(Fr }\Lambda_{x,z}^{E,-})\quad\cfrac{\cfrac{\{\Lambda_z^-\}z\to f := G\{\Lambda_z^G\}}{\{\Lambda_{x,y,z}^{E,F,-}\}z\to f := G\{\Lambda_{x,y,z}^{E,F,G}\}}}{\text{(Mutate)}}\text{(Fr }\Lambda_{x,y}^{E,F})}{\{\Lambda_{x,y,z}^{E,-,-}\}y\to f := F;\; z\to f := G\{\Lambda_{x,y,z}^{E,F,G}\}}\text{(Seq)}}{\{\Lambda_{x,y,z}^{-,-,-}\}x\to f := E;\; y\to f := F;\; z\to f := G\{\Lambda_{x,y,z}^{E,F,G}\}}\text{(Seq)}$$

Fig. 2. A proof tree obtained by applying Fig. 1's rules

A proof tree is *valid* if each inference is an instance of the proof rules. A rewrite rule $\mathcal{P}\to\mathcal{P}'$ takes an input proof tree $\mathcal{P}$ and yields an output proof tree $\mathcal{P}'$.

Definition 1. *A rewrite rule $\to$ is* sound *iff for all valid proof trees $\mathcal{P}$ such that $\mathcal{P}\to\mathcal{P}'$, $\mathcal{P}'$ is valid.*

The rewrite rules we present in the paper satisfy the following properties: *(1)* the rewrite rules are sound and *(2)* the rewrite rules preserve specifications i.e., given a proof tree whose root is $\{\Xi\}_-\{\Theta\}$, any tree returned by the rewrite system will have $\{\Xi\}_-\{\Theta\}$ as its root. This holds simply because all our rewrite rules leave the pre/postcondition of the root of the input proof tree untouched.

We conjecture that our rewrite system actually provides a stronger guarantee than preserving specifications. Plausibly, the set of final states of an input program and the set of final states of the corresponding optimized program are related. We leave this study, however, as future work.

4.1   Generated Proof Trees Have a Particular Shape

Most proof trees generated by Fig. 1's rules do not match the left-hand side of the rewrite rule <u>Parallelize</u> shown in the introduction. To exemplify this statement, we define the following abbreviation:

$$\Lambda_{x_0,\ldots,x_m}^{E_0,\ldots,E_m} \triangleq x_0 \mapsto [f : E_0] \star \cdots \star x_m \mapsto [f : E_m]$$

Note that this abbreviation enjoys the following equivalence:

$$\Lambda_{x_0,\ldots,x_m,x_{m+1},\ldots,x_{m+k}}^{E_0,\ldots,E_m,E_{m+1},\ldots,E_{m+k}} \Leftrightarrow \Lambda_{x_0,\ldots,x_m}^{E_0,\ldots,E_m} \star \Lambda_{x_{m+1},\ldots,x_{m+k}}^{E_{m+1},\ldots,E_{m+k}}$$

Now, to see why proof trees generated by Fig. 1's rules do not match the left-hand side of the rewrite rule <u>Parallelize</u>, consider the proof tree shown in Fig. 2 (where pure formulas are omitted, (Fr) abbreviates (Frame), and _ denotes existentially quantified values). The rewrite rule <u>Parallelize</u> cannot fire on Fig. 2's proof tree because this proof tree contains applications of (Frame) at each atomic command. Generally, given a program $A_0; A_1; \ldots$, the proof rules with explicit frames generate a proof tree with the following shape:

$$\cfrac{\cfrac{\cdots}{\{\ldots\}A_0\{\ldots\}}\text{(Frame)}\quad\cfrac{\cfrac{\cdots}{\{\ldots\}A_1\{\ldots\}}\text{(Frame)}\quad\cdots}{\{\ldots\}A_1;\ldots\{\ldots\}}\text{(Seq)}}{\{\ldots\}A_0; A_1;\ldots\{\ldots\}}\text{(Seq)}$$

Proof trees with the shape above are inappropriate for the rewrite rule Parallelize. Intuitively, the problem lies in the successive applications of (Frame) being redundant: the same formula is framed multiple times. For example, in the proof tree shown in Fig. 2, the formula Λ_x^E is framed twice: once in the center (Frame) and once in the right (Frame).

More generally, the presence of redundant frames means that applications of (Frame) are on *short* commands. However, as the left-hand side of the rewrite rule for parallelization described in the introduction shows, to parallelize *long* commands, applications of (Frame) have to be on long commands. Hence, removing redundant frames is a mandatory step before parallelizing. The next section shows how to remove redundancy by inferring applications of (Frame) on long commands from application of (Frame) on short commands.

4.2   Removing Redundancy in Frames

The redundancy in applications of (Frame) originally comes from the symbolic execution algorithm. Because symbolic execution mimics an operational update of the state at each atomic command, it cannot reason about a succession of commands: each atomic command is treated independently. To fix this issue, two solutions are available. The first solution is to build a new program verifier that infers frames for non-atomic commands. We think this solution is inadequate because it requires to design a program verifier with proof rewriting in mind (breaking separation of concerns). The second solution, chosen in this paper, is to minimize the modifications of the program verifier and to do as much work as possible on the proof rewriting side.

$$\dfrac{\{\Xi_a\}C\{\Xi_p\}}{\{\Xi_a \star \Xi_f\}C\{\Xi_p \star \Xi_f\}}\text{ (Frame }\Xi_f)\quad \dfrac{\dfrac{\dfrac{\{\Theta_a\}C'\{\Theta_p\}}{\{\Theta_a \star \Theta_f\}C'\{\Theta_p \star \Theta_f\}}\text{ (Frame }\Theta_f)\quad \{\Theta_p \star \Theta_f\}C''\{\Xi'\}}{\{\Theta_a \star \Theta_f\}C';\,C''\{\Xi'\}}\text{ (Seq)}}{\{\Xi_a \star \Xi_f\}C;\,C';\,C''\{\Xi'\}}\text{ (Seq)}$$

$$\downarrow \text{FactorizeFrames}$$

$$\dfrac{\dfrac{\{\Xi_a\}C\{\Xi_p\}}{\{\Xi_a \star \Xi_{f_0}\}C\{\Xi_p \star \Xi_{f_0}\}}\text{ (Frame }\Xi_{f_0})\quad \dfrac{\dfrac{\{\Theta_a\}C'\{\Theta_p\}}{\{\Theta_a \star \Theta_{f_0}\}C'\{\Theta_p \star \Theta_{f_0}\}}\text{ (Frame }\Theta_{f_0})}{\dfrac{\{\Xi_a \star \Xi_{f_0}\}C;\,C'\{\Theta_p \star \Theta_{f_0}\}}{\{\Xi_a \star \Xi_f\}C;\,C'\{\Theta_p \star \Theta_f\}}\text{ (Frame }\Xi_c)}\text{ (Seq)}\quad \{\Theta_p \star \Theta_f\}C''\{\Xi'\}}{\{\Xi_a \star \Xi_f\}C;\,C';\,C''\{\Xi'\}}\text{ (Seq)}$$

Guard: $\Xi_f \Leftrightarrow \Xi_{f_0} \star \Xi_c$ and $\Theta_f \Leftrightarrow \Theta_{f_0} \star \Xi_c$

Fig. 3. Rewrite rule to factorize applications of (Frame)

Fig. 3 shows the rewrite rule FactorizeFrames that removes redundancy in applications of (Frame). FactorizeFrames fires if C and C' are two consecutive commands that both frame a part of the state (Ξ_f and Θ_f respectively) such that the two parts of the state share a common part (Ξ_c as imposed by the guard). In FactorizeFrames's right-hand side, the common part of the state is framed *once*, below the application of (Seq).

Both the left-hand side of FactorizeFrames (abbreviated by lhs below) and the right-hand side of FactorizeFrames (abbreviated by rhs below) include the proof tree of the triplet $\{\Theta_p \star \Theta_f\}C''\{\Xi'\}$. We need to include such a proof tree to match two possible cases: C'' can be a dummy "continuation" (represented by the **empty** command) or a "normal" continuation. In the implementation, all rewrite rules use this "possible continuation" trick.

Fig. 4 exemplifies an application of FactorizeFrames to Fig. 2's proof tree: the redundancy of Λ_x^E in the center and the right (Frame)s is factorized in a single (Frame).

$$\cfrac{\cfrac{}{\{\Lambda_x^-\}x \to f := E\{\Lambda_x^E\}}\text{(Mutate)}}{\cfrac{}{\{\Lambda_{x,y,z}^{--}\}x \to f := E\{\Lambda_{x,y,z}^{E,--}\}}\text{(Fr }\Lambda_{y,z}^{--})} \quad \cfrac{\cfrac{\cfrac{}{\{\Lambda_y^-\}y \to f := F\{\Lambda_y^F\}}\text{(Mutate)}}{\{\Lambda_{y,z}^{--}\}y \to f := F\{\Lambda_{y,z}^{F,-}\}}\text{(Fr }\Lambda_z^-) \quad \cfrac{\cfrac{}{\{\Lambda_z^-\}z \to f := G\{\Lambda_z^G\}}\text{(Mutate)}}{\{\Lambda_{y,z}^{F,-}\}z \to f := G\{\Lambda_{y,z}^{F,G}\}}\text{(Fr }\Lambda_y^F)}{\cfrac{\cfrac{\{\Lambda_{y,z}^{--}\}y \to f := F; z \to f := G\{\Lambda_{y,z}^{F,G}\}}{\{\Lambda_{x,y,z}^{E,--}\}y \to f := F; z \to f := G\{\Lambda_{x,y,z}^{E,F,G}\}}\text{(Fr }\Lambda_x^E)}{}\text{(Seq)}}$$
$$\overline{\{\Lambda_{x,y,z}^{--}\}x \to f := E; y \to f := F; z \to f := G\{\Lambda_{x,y,z}^{E,F,G}\}}\text{(Seq)}$$

Fig. 4. Fig. 2's proof tree after applying FactorizeFrames once

Theorem 2. *The rewrite rule FactorizeFrames is sound.*

Proof. Suppose the left-hand side of FactorizeFrames is valid. The goal is to show that the right-hand side of FactorizeFrames rhs is valid.

For the application of (Frame Ξ_c) to be valid, we must show the two following equivalences: $\Xi_a \star \Xi_f \Leftrightarrow \Xi_a \star \Xi_{f_0} \star \Xi_c$ and $\Theta_p \star \Theta_f \Leftrightarrow \Theta_p \star \Theta_{f_0} \star \Xi_c$. But these two equivalences follow directly from FactorizeFrames's guard.

For the application of (Frame Θ_{f_0}) to be valid, we must show the following equivalence:

$$\Xi_p \star \Xi_{f_0} \Leftrightarrow \Theta_a \star \Theta_{f_0} \tag{goal}$$

From FactorizeFrames's first guard, we obtain:

$$\Xi_p \star \Xi_f \Leftrightarrow \Xi_p \star \Xi_{f_0} \star \Xi_c \tag{1}$$

From the validity of the application of (Seq) in FactorizeFrames's lhs, we obtain: $\Xi_p \star \Xi_f \Leftrightarrow \Theta_a \star \Theta_f$. Then, from FactorizeFrames's second guard, we obtain:

$$\Xi_p \star \Xi_f \Leftrightarrow \Theta_a \star \Theta_{f_0} \star \Xi_c \tag{2}$$

By simplifying Ξ_c on the right hand sides of (1) and (2), we obtain the desired goal. Now FactorizeFrames's validity is deduced as follows: *(1)* each inference in FactorizeFrames's rhs is a valid instance of the proof rules and *(2)* the leaves of FactorizeFrames's rhs are identical to the leaves of FactorizeFrames's lhs (which are valid by hypothesis). □

Because FactorizeFrames's guard uses the syntactical equivalence $\Leftrightarrow$, it might miss some semantical equivalences. Using an entailment relation $\vdash$ would be more powerful. However, we leave open the problem of finding common frames with a semantical equivalence for the following reason: finding a common frame (i.e., given Ξ and Θ; find Ξ_c, Ξ_r, and Θ_r such that $\Xi \vdash \Xi_r \star \Xi_c$ and $\Theta \vdash \Theta_r \star \Xi_c$) cannot be expressed efficiently in terms of known problems; such as a frame problem [8] (given Ξ and Θ, find Ξ_f such that $\Xi \vdash \Xi_f \star \Theta$), or a bi-abduction problem [13] (given Ξ and Θ, find Ξ_a and Θ_f such that $\Xi \star \Xi_a \vdash \Theta \star \Theta_f$).

4.3 Parallelization

In practice, factorizing frames is a mandatory step before applying the Parallelize rewrite rule shown in the introduction. For example, applying Parallelize to the proof tree shown in Fig. 4 yields a proof of the following Hoare triplet:

$$\{\Lambda_{x,y,z}^{-,-,-}\}x{\rightarrow}f := E \parallel (y{\rightarrow}f := F \parallel z{\rightarrow}f := G)\{\Lambda_{x,y,z}^{E,F,G}\}$$

For the Parallelize rewrite rule to be sound, we add the guard that C does not modify variables in Ξ', C', and Θ' (and conversely). Note that, for clarity of presentation, the Parallelize rule shown in the introduction does not include the "possible continuation" trick mentioned above. We refer the interested reader to our companion report [25] for the complete rule.

4.4 Generic Optimizations

In this subsection, we present an optimization that changes the program's execution order. This optimization has four concrete applications: *(1)* dispose memory as soon as possible to avoid out of memory errors, *(2)* allocate memory as late as possible to leave more allocatable memory, *(3)* release locks as soon as possible to increase parallelism, and *(4)* acquire locks as late as possible to increase parallelism. Fig. 5 shows the rewrite rule for changing the program's execution order.

GenericOptimization fires if the program has the shape $C; C'; C''$ such that C' frames the postcondition of C (as imposed by the guard). Then, the program's order is changed so that C' executes before C. It should be noted that this rule imposes that C frames the precondition of C' by the following reasoning: for the first application of (Seq) to be valid in GenericOptimizations's lhs, we have $\Xi_p \star \Xi_f \Leftrightarrow \Theta_a \star \Theta_f$. From the guard, it follows that $\Xi_p \star \Xi_f \Leftrightarrow \Theta_a \star \Xi_p \star \Xi_r$. By simplifying Ξ_p on both sides, we obtain: $\Xi_f \Leftrightarrow \Theta_a \star \Xi_r$. We can conclude that C frames the precondition of C' (Θ_a).

We now detail GenericOptimization's four concrete applications. *(1)* If C' is a dispose command, because C frames the precondition of C', it means that C does not access the state disposed by C': better execute C' first to dispose memory as soon as possible. *(2)* If C is a new command, because C' frames the postcondition of C, it means that C' does not access the state allocated by C: better execute C after C' to leave C' more allocatable memory. *(3)* If C' is an unlock command, because C frames the precondition of C' (i.e. the lock's resource invariant), it means that C does not access the part of the heap represented by the lock's resource invariant: better execute C' to release the lock

$$\cfrac{\cfrac{\{\Xi_a\}C\{\Xi_p\}}{\{\Xi_a * \Xi_f\}C\{\Xi_p * \Xi_f\}}\ (\text{Fr}\ \Xi_f) \quad \cfrac{\cfrac{\{\Theta_a\}C'\{\Theta_p\}}{\{\Theta_a * \Theta_f\}C'\{\Theta_p * \Theta_f\}}\ (\text{Fr}\ \Theta_f) \quad \{\Theta_p * \Theta_f\}C''\{\Xi'\}}{\{\Theta_a * \Theta_f\}C';\ C''\{\Xi'\}}\ (\text{Seq})}{\{\Xi_a * \Xi_f\}C;\ C';\ C''\{\Xi'\}}\ (\text{Seq})$$

$$\downarrow \text{GenericOptimization}$$

$$\cfrac{\cfrac{\{\Theta_a\}C'\{\Theta_p\}}{\{\Xi_a * \Theta_a * \Xi_r\}C'\{\Xi_a * \Theta_p * \Xi_r\}}\ (\text{Fr}\ \Xi_r * \Xi_a) \quad \cfrac{\cfrac{\{\Xi_a\}C\{\Xi_p\}}{\{\Xi_a * \Theta_p * \Xi_r\}C\{\Xi_p * \Theta_p * \Xi_r\}}\ (\text{Fr}\ \Theta_p * \Xi_r) \quad \{\Xi_p * \Theta_p * \Xi_r\}C''\{\Xi'\}}{\{\Xi_a * \Theta_p * \Xi_r\}C;\ C''\{\Xi'\}}\ (\text{Seq})}{\{\Xi_a * \Xi_f\}C';\ C;\ C''\{\Xi'\}}$$

$$\text{Guard: } \Theta_f \Leftrightarrow \Xi_p * \Xi_r$$

Fig. 5. Rewrite rule to change the program's execution order

first. *(4)* If C is a `lock` command, because C' frames the postcondition of C (i.e. the lock's resource invariant), it means that C' does not access the part of the heap represented by the lock's resource invariant: better execute C after C' to acquire the lock as late as possible.

Theorem 3. *The rewrite rule* GenericOptimization *is sound.*

Proof. Apply the guard's equivalence in the right places and observe that *(1)* each inference in GenericOptimization's rhs is a valid instance of the proof rules and *(2)* the leaves of GenericOptimization's rhs are identical to the leaves of GenericOptimization's lhs (which are valid by hypothesis). □

5   Implementation

The techniques described in the previous sections have been implemented in a tool called *éterlou*. Éterlou consists of two distinct modules:

A proof tree generator which is an extended version of smallfoot [7]. The proof tree generator generates proof trees using Fig. 1's rules. Our extension does not interfere with the algorithms already present in smallfoot: it only computes antiframes and frames at each atomic command (by using both smallfoot's built-in algorithms and dedicated algorithms).

Because the (Frame) rule is the central ingredient of our procedure, it is crucial that the implementation of Fig 1's rules computes the *biggest frames* (formulas Ξ_f) possible. As an example, our implementation of the rule for field lookup (Fig 1's second rule) computes the smallest antiframe Π_a that suffices to show $F = E$. By computing the smallest antiframes, our implementation also computes the biggest frames.

A proof tree rewriter which implements the various rewrite rules shown in this paper. The proof tree rewriter is written in tom [4], an extension of Java that adds constructs for pattern matching. We make extensive use of tom's mapping facility to pattern match against user-defined Java objects. Another crucial feature is the possibility to define rewriting strategies.

All the examples of this paper have been generated with éterlou. We have tested éterlou against several example programs provided in smallfoot's distribution and pointer programs of our own. Our experiments revealed that to obtain the best optimizations possible, the rewrite rules must usually be applied in a given order and/or with specific strategies. For example, FactorizeFrames must be applied before Parallelize for the latter rewrite rule to fire. In addition, applying rewrite rules from top to bottom (i.e., rewriting at the root before trying to rewrite in subtrees) generally yields programs where parallelized commands are longer (compared to other strategies such as bottom to top).

6 Examples

Fig. 6 shows procedure *rotate_tree* (borrowed from [33]) that takes a tree at x and rotates it by recursively swapping its left and right subtrees. Applying FactorizeFrames and Parallelize to *rotate_tree* yields a program where the field assignments and the recursive calls are executed in parallel. We achieve better parallelism than [33] by parallelizing the field assignments and the recursive calls.

```
requires tree(x);
ensures  tree(x);                     requires tree(x);
rotate_tree(x; ){                     ensures  tree(x);
  local x1, x2;                       rotate_tree(x; ){
  if(x = nil){}                         local x1, x2;
  else{                                 if(x = nil){}
    x1 := x→l;            →            else{
    x2 := x→r;                           x1 := x→l;
    x→l := x2;                           x2 := x→r;
    x→r := x1;                           (x→l := x2; x→r := x1) ||
    rotate_tree(x1; );                   rotate_tree(x1; ) || rotate_tree(x2; ); }}
    rotate_tree(x2; ); }}
```

Fig. 6. Parallelization of a recursive procedure

```
requires x ↦ [val : _];              requires x ↦ [val : _];
ensures  emp;                        ensures  emp;
copy_and_dispose(x; ){               copy_and_dispose(x; ){
  local v;                             local v;
  lock(r_c↦[val:_]);       →          v := x→val;
  v := x→val;                          dispose(x);
  c→val := v;                          lock(r_c↦[val:_]);
  dispose(x);                          c→val := v;
  unlock(r_c↦[val:_]); }              unlock(r_c↦[val:_]); }
```

Fig. 7. Optimization of a critical region

Fig. 7 shows procedure *copy_and_dispose* (where resource r is subscripted by its invariant) that copies the content of field *val* of cell x to field *val* of cell c (r's resource invariant). Applying GenericOptimization optimizes *copy_and_dispose* in two ways: the critical region is shortened and cell x is disposed earlier.

The proof trees corresponding to Fig. 6 and Fig. 7's transformations as well as éterlou's implementation are available [1].

7 Benefits from Separation Logic's Advances

In this section, we review advances of separation logic that have not been implemented in smallfoot and we describe how our technique would benefit from these advances. As we use features from other papers, we are sometimes sloppy on definitions and appeal to the reader's intuition to understand the notations.

7.1 Object-Orientation

[32] applied separation logic to object-oriented programs. In Parkinson's work, separation logic's $\star$ splits objects per field. With our notations, this means that $p \mapsto [x : \_] \star p \mapsto [y : \_]$ represents a point with two fields x and y (and omitted fields are *not* existentially quantified). Splitting on a per-field basis provides fine-grained parallelism which allows to build such a proof:

$$\{p \mapsto [x : \_] \star p \mapsto [y : \_]\}$$
$$p \to x := E \parallel p \to y := F$$
$$\{p \mapsto [x : E] \star p \mapsto [y : F]\}$$

Integrating Parkinson's semantics of $\star$ in the proof tree generator would allow Parallelize to fire more often. For example, in *rotate_tree*, $x \to l := x_2; x \to r := x_1$ would be parallelized to $x \to l := x_2 \parallel x \to r := x_1$.

In addition, we highlight that lifting our technique to object-oriented programs is straightforward since our procedure's key mechanism is the (Frame) rule which is supported by object-oriented separation logic [32,23,22].

7.2 Permission Accounting

[10][4] gave an alternative reading of the points-to predicate $\mapsto$ by adding an extra parameter (called a *permission* π) to it. Permissions are fractions in $(0, 1]$. Now, the points-to predicate $x \overset{\pi}{\mapsto} [\rho]$ has the following meaning: *(1)* it asserts that x points to the record ρ and *(2)* if $\pi = 1$, it asserts write and read permission to the record pointed to by x; if $\pi < 1$, it asserts readonly permission to the record pointed to by x. The following property holds:

$$x \overset{\pi}{\mapsto} [\rho] \Leftrightarrow x \overset{\frac{\pi}{2}}{\mapsto} [\rho] \star x \overset{\frac{\pi}{2}}{\mapsto} [\rho]$$

Integrating permission accounting in the proof tree generator would allow Parallelize to fire more often.

---

[4] In this paragraph, we consider only fractional permissions [12] but our remarks also apply for the counting model and the combined model.

7.3 Fork/Join Parallelism

[23,20] lifted the (Parallel) rule to Java's fork/join style of parallelism. Calling fork(t) starts a new thread t that executes in parallel with the rest of the program. Calling join(t) stops the calling thread until thread t finishes: when t finishes the calling thread is resumed.

When a parent thread forks a new thread, a part of the parent's state is transferred to the new thread. This is formalized by the following rule:

$$\frac{\varXi \text{ is } t\text{'s precondition}}{\{\varXi\}\texttt{fork}(t)\{\texttt{emp}\}} \text{ (Fork)}$$

Dually, when a thread joins another thread, the former "takes back" a part of the latter's state. To formalize this behavior, [23]'s assertion language contains a new predicate Join(t, π) which asserts that the thread in which it appears can take back part π of thread t's state (like in Bornat's work, π is a permission). In addition, the assertion language allows to multiply formulas by a permission, written $\pi \cdot \varXi$. To give the reader an intuition of the meaning of multiplication, we note that integrating multiplication in our framework would make the following property true:

$$\pi \cdot (\varPi \mid x \overset{1}{\mapsto} [\rho]) \Leftrightarrow \varPi \mid x \overset{\pi}{\mapsto} [\rho]$$

With the Join predicate and formula multiplication, one can formalize join's behavior. The rule below expresses that a thread joining another thread t can take back a part of t's state:

$$\frac{\varXi \text{ is } t\text{'s postcondition}}{\{\texttt{Join}(t, \pi)\}\texttt{join}(t)\{\pi \cdot \varXi\}} \text{ (Join)}$$

Integrating (Fork) and (Join) in our framework would add two concrete applications to the rewrite rule GenericOptimization. *(1)* If C' is a fork command, GenericOptimization would rewrite proofs so that new threads are forked as soon as possible (increasing parallelism). *(2)* If C is a join command, GenericOptimization would rewrite proofs so that threads join other processes as late as possible (increasing parallelism and reducing joining time).

7.4 Variable as Resources

[10] showed how to treat variables like resources (heap cells in our terminology). This allows to get rid of the side condition in the (Parallel) rule resulting in a more uniform proof system. The assertion language contains a new predicate $\texttt{Own}_\pi(x)$ that asserts ownership π of variable x.

Roughly, writing a variable requires permission 1 while reading a variable requires some permission π (in analogy with the permission-accounting model). This rules out programs with races on shared variables:

$$\{\texttt{Own}_1(x) \star ?\}$$
$$x = y \parallel x = z$$

Above, ? cannot be filled with a predicate asserting ownership of x (needed for verifying the parallel statement's rhs) because $\texttt{Own}_1(x)$ is already needed to verify the parallel statement's lhs (and $\texttt{Own}_1(x)$ cannot be $\star$-combined with $\texttt{Own}_\pi(x)$ for any π).

The variable as resources technique would fit perfectly in our framework because variables that are not accessed by commands would be made explicit: $\texttt{Own}_\pi(\_)$ predicates would appear in frames. In other words, program verifiers implementing the variable as resources technique would compute explicit frames and antiframes for atomic commands like Fig. 1's rules do.

8   Related Work

Separation logic was discovered by Reynolds [34]. O'Hearn [30] extended separation logic to deal with disjoint and lock-based concurrency. Parkinson [32] adapted separation logic to object-oriented programs. Program verifiers in separation logic include smallfoot [7], a tool for C [26], and tools for object-oriented programs [17,14].

The closest (and concurrent) related work is [33] which uses separation logic to parallelize programs. Our work differs in four ways: *(1)* [33] attaches labels to heaps and uses disjointness of labels to detect possible parallelism, while we use the (Frame) rule to statically detect possible parallelism, leading to a technically simpler procedure; *(2)* we express optimizations by rewrite rules on proof trees, allowing us to feature other optimizations than parallelization and to use different optimization strategies; *(3)* [33] is applied after a shape analysis [16,6], while our analysis is applied after verification with a program verifier; and *(4)* contrary to [33], we have an implementation.

Practical approaches for parallelizing programs include parallelizing compilers [9,3]. Parallelizing compilers focuses on loop parallelization and do not consider arbitrary pieces of code. Parallelizing compilers can yield code that executes an order of magnitude faster than classical compilers. Loop parallelization has been actively studied [27,2,36].

Formal approaches for optimizing programs include certified compilers [35,28] and certifying compilers [5,29]. Certified compilers include optimizations that we do not consider and provide fully machine-checked proofs. Certifying compilers manipulate formulas representing proof obligations whereas we manipulate proof trees representing derivation of Hoare triplets. For this reason, we can consider high-level optimizations such as parallelization whereas we cannot consider the low-level optimizations described in [5,29].

Techniques to dispose memory as soon as possible have been studied for machine registers [18] where the goal is to use as few registers as possible. Works on atomicity [15,11] include techniques to release locks as soon as possible.

9   Conclusion and Future Work

We show a new technique to optimize programs proven correct in separation logic. Optimizations are done by rewriting proofs represented as derivation of Hoare triplets. The core of the procedure uses separation logic's (Frame) rule to statically detect parts of the state which are useless for a command to execute. Considered optimizations are parallelization, early disposal, late allocation, early lock releasing, and late lock acquirement. Optimizations are expressed as rewrite rules between proof trees and are performed automatically.

The procedure has been implemented in the éterlou tool. Éterlou consists of a proof tree generator (a modified version of the smallfoot program verifier [7]) and a proof tree rewriter written in tom [4]. Small-scale experiments show that the approach is practical.

Future work includes extension to permission-accounting separation logic and object-oriented programs. The extension to permission-accounting is expected to increase the efficiency of the Parallelize rewrite rule. The extension to object-oriented programs will allow us to do larger scale experiments and to study how abstraction [32] behaves w.r.t. to our technique. For this, we plan to use recent implementations of program verifiers for object-oriented programs annotated with separation logic [17,14]. On a practical side, future work includes study of the different rewriting strategies and their impact on the efficiency of optimizations.

Acknowledgments. I thank Gilles Barthe, Radu Grigore, Christian Haack, Marieke Huisman, and Tamara Rezk for their very useful comments that helped crafting this paper. I have been supported in part by IST-FET-2005-015905 Mobius project and in part by ANR-06-SETIN-010 ParSec project.

References

1. Proof trees of the examples, additional examples, and open source implementation, http://www-sop.inria.fr/everest/Clement.Hurlin/eterlou/eterlou.shtml
2. Aiken, A., Nicolau, A.: Optimal loop parallelization. ACM SIGPLAN Notices 23(7) (1988)
3. Artigas, P., Gupta, M., Midkiff, S., Moreira, J.: Automatic loop transformations and parallelization for Java. In: International Conference on Supercomputing. ACM Press, New York (2000)
4. Balland, E., Brauner, P., Kopetz, R., Moreau, P.-E., Reilles, A.: Tom: Piggybacking rewriting on Java. In: Baader, F. (ed.) RTA 2007. LNCS, vol. 4533, pp. 36–47. Springer, Heidelberg (2007)
5. Barthe, G., Grégoire, B., Kunz, C., Rezk, T.: Certificate translation for optimizing compilers. In: Yi, K. (ed.) SAS 2006. LNCS, vol. 4134, pp. 301–317. Springer, Heidelberg (2006)
6. Berdine, J., Calcagno, C., Cook, B., Distefano, D., O'Hearn, P.W., Wies, T., Yang, H.: Shape analysis for composite data structures. In: Damm, W., Hermanns, H. (eds.) CAV 2007. LNCS, vol. 4590, pp. 178–192. Springer, Heidelberg (2007)

7. Berdine, J., Calcagno, C., O'Hearn, P.W.: Smallfoot: Modular automatic assertion checking with separation logic. In: de Boer, F.S., Bonsangue, M.M., Graf, S., de Roever, W.-P. (eds.) FMCO 2005. LNCS, vol. 4111. Springer, Heidelberg (2006)

8. Berdine, J., Calcagno, C., O'Hearn, P.W.: Symbolic execution with separation logic. In: Yi, K. (ed.) APLAS 2005. LNCS, vol. 3780, pp. 52–68. Springer, Heidelberg (2005)

9. Bik, A., Gannon, D.: Automatically exploiting implicit parallelism in Java. Concurrency: Practice and Experience 9 (1997)

10. Bornat, R., Calcagno, C., Yang, H.: Variables as resource in separation logic. In: Mathematical Foundations of Programming Semantics. Electronic Notes in Theoretical Computer Science, vol. 155. Elsevier, Amsterdam (2005)

11. Boyapati, C., Lee, R., Rinard, M.: Ownership types for safe programming: Preventing data races and deadlocks. In: ACM Conference on Object-Oriented Programming Systems, Languages, and Applications. ACM Press, New York (2002)

12. Boyland, J.: Checking interference with fractional permissions. In: Cousot, R. (ed.) SAS 2003. LNCS, vol. 2694. Springer, Heidelberg (2003)

13. Calcagno, C., Distefano, D., OHearn, P., Yang, H.: Compositional shape analysis by means of bi-abduction. In: Shao, Z., Pierce, B.C. (eds.) Principles of Programming Languages. ACM Press, New York (to appear, 2009)

14. Chin, W., David, C., Nguyen, H., Qin, S.: Enhancing modular OO verification with separation logic. In: Necula, G.C., Wadler, P. (eds.) Principles of Programming Languages. ACM Press, New York (2008)

15. Cunningham, D., Gudka, K., Eisenbach, S.: Keep off the grass: Locking the right path for atomicity. In: Hendren, L. (ed.) CC 2008. LNCS, vol. 4959, pp. 276–290. Springer, Heidelberg (2008)

16. Distefano, D., O'Hearn, P.W., Yang, H.: A local shape analysis based on separation logic. In: Hermanns, H., Palsberg, J. (eds.) TACAS 2006. LNCS, vol. 3920, pp. 287–302. Springer, Heidelberg (2006)

17. DiStefano, D., Parkinson, M.: jStar: Towards practical verification for Java. In: ACM Conference on Object-Oriented Programming Systems, Languages, and Applications, vol. 43. ACM Press, New York (2008)

18. Ergin, O., Balkan, D., Ponomarev, D., Ghose, K.: Early register deallocation mechanisms using checkpointed register files. IEEE Computer 55 (2006)

19. Ghiya, R., Hendren, L.J., Zhu, Y.: Detecting parallelism in c programs with recursive data structures. In: Koskimies, K. (ed.) CC 1998, vol. 1383. Springer, Heidelberg (1998)

20. Gotsman, A., Berdine, J., Cook, B., Rinetzky, N., Sagiv, M.: Local reasoning for storable locks and threads. In: Shao, Z. (ed.) APLAS 2007. LNCS, vol. 4807, pp. 19–37. Springer, Heidelberg (2007)

21. Gupta, R., Pande, S., Psarris, K., Sarkar, V.: Compilation techniques for parallel systems. Parallel Computing 25(13) (1999)

22. Haack, C., Huisman, M., Hurlin, C.: Reasoning about Java's reentrant locks. In: Ramalingam, G. (ed.) APLAS 2008. LNCS, vol. 5356, pp. 171–187. Springer, Heidelberg (2008)

23. Haack, C., Hurlin, C.: Separation logic contracts for a Java-like language with fork/join. In: Meseguer, J., Rosu, G. (eds.) AMAST 2008. LNCS, vol. 5140, pp. 199–215. Springer, Heidelberg (2008)

24. Hendren, L.J., Nicolau, A.: Parallelizing programs with recursive data structures. IEEE Transactions on Parallel and Distributed Systems 1 (1990)

25. Hurlin, C.: Automatic parallelization and optimization of programs by proof rewriting. Technical Report 6806, INRIA. Initial version: January 2009, revised version: April 2009
26. Jacobs, B., Piessens, F.: The verifast program verifier. Technical Report CW520, Katholieke Universiteit Leuven (2008)
27. Lamport, L.: The parallel execution of do loops. Communications of the ACM 17(2) (1974)
28. Leroy, X.: Formal certification of a compiler back-end or: programming a compiler with a proof assistant. In: Morrisett, J.G., Jones, S.L.P. (eds.) Principles of Programming Languages. ACM Press, New York (2006)
29. Necula, G.C.: Translation validation for an optimizing compiler. ACM SIGPLAN Notices 35(5) (2000)
30. O'Hearn, P.W.: Resources, concurrency and local reasoning. Theoretical Computer Science 375(1-3) (2007)
31. O'Hearn, P.W., Reynolds, J., Yang, H.: Local reasoning about programs that alter data structures. In: Fribourg, L. (ed.) CSL 2001 and EACSL 2001. LNCS, vol. 2142, p. 1. Springer, Heidelberg (2001) (invited paper)
32. Parkinson, M.: Local Reasoning for Java. Ph.D thesis, University of Cambridge (2005)
33. Raza, M., Calcagno, C., Gardner, P.: Automatic parallelization with separation logic. In: European Symposium on Programming (to appear, 2009)
34. Reynolds, J.C.: Separation logic: A logic for shared mutable data structures. In: Logic in Computer Science. IEEE Press, Los Alamitos (2002)
35. Strecker, M.: Formal Verification of a Java Compiler in Isabelle. In: Voronkov, A. (ed.) CADE 2002. LNCS, vol. 2392, p. 63. Springer, Heidelberg (2002)
36. Xue, C., Shao, Z., Sha, E.-M.: Maximize parallelism minimize overhead for nested loops via loop striping. Journal of VLSI Signal Processing Systems 47(2) (2007)

Refinement of Trace Abstraction

Matthias Heizmann, Jochen Hoenicke, and Andreas Podelski

University of Freiburg, Germany

Abstract. We present a new counterexample-guided abstraction refinement scheme. The scheme refines an over-approximation of the set of possible traces. Each refinement step introduces a *finite automaton* that recognizes a set of infeasible traces. A central idea enabling our approach is to use *interpolants* (assertions generated, e.g., by the infeasibility proof for an error trace) in order to automatically construct such an automaton. A data base of *interpolant automata* has an interesting potential for reuse of theorem proving work (from one program to another).

1 Introduction

The automatic refinement of abstraction is an active research topic in static analysis [1,3,4,5,6,7,8,9,10,11,13,12,15,16,18]. It is widely agreed that the calls to a theorem prover, as used in existing methods for the construction of a sequence of increasingly precise abstractions, represent an obstacle to scalability. The problem is accentuated when costly decision procedures are employed to deal with arrays and heaps [19,20,23]. One way to address this obstacle is to increase the reuse of theorem work [11,13,12,18]. The question is in what form one should combine the results of theorem prover calls, and in what form they should be presented and stored.

Let us informally investigate the shortcomings inherent to the usage of theorem provers in the classical counterexample-guided abstraction refinement scheme (as, e.g., in [1,2,5,12,13,15]).

- In a first step, the theorem prover is called to prove the infeasibility of an error trace (in case it is a spurious counterexample). The corresponding unsatisfiability proof is then used for nothing but *guessing* the constituents of the new abstraction. If, as in [12,15], the unsatisfiability proof is used to generate interpolants which contain valuable information about the reason of infeasibility, then these are *cannibalized* for their atomic conjuncts.
- In a second step, the theorem prover is called to construct the transformer for the new abstraction; this step does not exploit the theorem proving work invested in the first step; in fact, the subsequent analysis of the new abstraction realizes a second proof of the infeasibility of the previous error trace.
- The theorem prover constructs the transformer for each new abstraction from scratch (at least on the part of the transformer's domain that has changed).
- The theorem proving work starts for each new program from scratch. This means all theorem proving work is done on-line, whereas ideally, most if not all of it should be done off-line, i.e., in a pre-processing step.

J. Palsberg and Z. Su (Eds.): SAS 2009, LNCS 5673, pp. 69–85, 2009.

In this paper, we present a new counterexample-guided abstraction refinement scheme. The scheme refines an over-approximation of the set of possible traces (in contrast to existing schemes which refine an over-approximation of the set of possible states). Each refinement step introduces a *finite automaton* that recognizes a set of infeasible traces. Such a *trace automaton* uses the *alphabet of statements*; each word over this alphabet is a trace. A central idea enabling our approach is to use *interpolants* (assertions generated, e.g., by the infeasibility proof for an error trace) in order to automatically construct such an automaton. The resulting *interpolant automaton* accepts not only the given error trace but many other (in general infinitely many) infeasible traces of varying shape and length.

The idea of using interpolants for the construction of an automaton overcomes a major difficulty in the construction of automata for the approximation of possible traces. Existing constructions (e.g., in [14,21] for hybrid systems) are based on ad hoc criteria; while the resulting methods succeed on several interesting examples, they are not general or complete. We also note a difference in the kind of alphabets used. In [14,21], the alphabet consists of action labels (or edge labels) defined by the input program (hybrid system), and the infeasibility property is specific to that program. In contrast, our notion of infeasibility depends solely on the programming language semantics.

One perspective opened by our work is a refinement loop that queries a database of interpolant automata; if there exists one that accepts the submitted error trace (which means that the error trace is not feasible), then the interpolant automaton gets added as another component to the trace abstraction. In this scenario, the interpolant automata can be constructed off-line (automatically, or manually using interactive verification methods).

2   Example

The correctness of the annotated program $\mathcal{P}$ in Fig. 1 is defined by the validity of its assertions. The correctness can be stated equivalently with the help of the automaton $\mathcal{A}_\mathcal{P}$ depicted in Fig. 2, the so-called program automaton. The transition graph of $\mathcal{A}_\mathcal{P}$ is the control flow graph of $\mathcal{P}$ where assertions are translated to edges to an error state.

The program automaton recognizes a set of words over the alphabet of statements (statements are framed in order to stress that they are used as letters of an alphabet). Each accepted word is a trace along a path in the control flow graph. The correctness of the annotated program $\mathcal{P}$ is expressed by the fact that all such traces are infeasible (which means that there is no valid execution leading from the initial location to the error location).

We next describe how our refinement scheme will generate a sequence of *trace abstractions* and, finally, prove the correctness of $\mathcal{P}$. Generally, each trace abstraction is a tuple of automata $(\mathcal{A}_1 \ldots \mathcal{A}_n)$ over the alphabet of statements. An automaton in the tuple recognizes a subset of infeasible traces. This subset is used to restrict the set of traces recognized by the program automaton.

```
ℓ₀: x=0
ℓ₁: y=0
ℓ₂: while(nondet) {x++}
    assert(x!=-1)
    assert(y!=-1)
```

Fig. 1. Annotated program $\mathcal{P}$. The program $\mathcal{P}$ is correct if the assertions are valid.

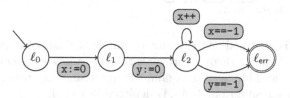

Fig. 2. Program automaton $\mathcal{A}_{\mathcal{P}}$ encoding the correctness of $\mathcal{P}$. The program $\mathcal{P}$ is correct iff every word accepted by $\mathcal{A}_{\mathcal{P}}$ is an infeasible trace.

First Iteration of Refinement Loop. The initial trace abstraction (for the first iteration of the refinement loop) is the empty tuple. The resulting restriction of the program automaton is the program automaton itself. In our example, the program automaton is not empty; it accepts, e.g., the trace π_1.

$$\pi_1 = \boxed{\texttt{x:=0}}.\boxed{\texttt{y:=0}}.\boxed{\texttt{x++}}.\boxed{\texttt{y==-1}}$$

The trace π_1 is returned as the counterexample of the first iteration of the refinement loop. A theorem prover is called to analyze the counterexample. The trace π_1 is infeasible. The unsatisfiability proof showing this, is used to construct the automaton $\mathcal{A}_1$ depicted in Fig. 3. This automaton accepts not only the trace π_1 but all traces that are infeasible for the same reason as π_1. In more detail: the unsatisfiability proof returns a sequence of *interpolants*. Each trace accepted by $\mathcal{A}_1$ has the same sequence of interpolants as π_1, up to repetition of subsequences of interpolants, and it is in this precise sense that it has the same "reason of infeasibility" as π_1. As explained later, the states q_i are in bijection with interpolants in the sequence, which is why we call $\mathcal{A}_1$ an *interpolant automaton*.

Second Iteration of Refinement Loop. The second abstraction (obtained from refining the initial abstraction) is the tuple $(\mathcal{A}_1)$ consisting of one component, the automaton derived in the previous refinement. The resulting restriction of the program automaton is the intersection of the program automaton with the complement of $\mathcal{A}_1$. In our example, the resulting automaton does not accept the trace π_1, the counterexample in the first refinement. Still, it is not empty; it accepts, e.g., the trace π_2.

$$\pi_2 = \boxed{\texttt{x:=0}}.\boxed{\texttt{y:=0}}.\boxed{\texttt{x++}}.\boxed{\texttt{x==-1}}$$

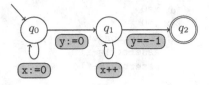

Fig. 3. Interpolant automaton $\mathcal{A}_1$, constructed from the unsatisfiability proof for the error trace $\pi_1 = \boxed{\texttt{x:=0}}.\boxed{\texttt{y:=0}}.\boxed{\texttt{x++}}.\boxed{\texttt{y==-1}}$. It recognizes the set of traces that are infeasible for the same reason as π_1.

The trace π_2 is returned as the counterexample of the second iteration of the refinement loop. Again, a theorem prover is called to analyze the counterexample. The trace π_2 is infeasible as well. Again, the unsatisfiability proof showing this, is used to construct an automaton, $\mathcal{A}_2$ depicted in Fig. 4.

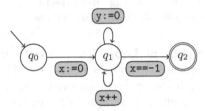

Fig. 4. Interpolant automaton $\mathcal{A}_2$ which is constructed from the unsatisfiability proof for the counterexample $\pi_2 = \boxed{\texttt{x:=0}}.\boxed{\texttt{y:=0}}.\boxed{\texttt{x++}}.\boxed{\texttt{x==-1}}$

Third and Final Iteration of the Refinement Loop. The third abstraction (obtained from refining the second abstraction) is the tuple $(\mathcal{A}_1, \mathcal{A}_2)$ constructed by extending the previous tuple with another component, the automaton derived in the previous refinement. The resulting restriction of the program automaton is the intersection of the program automaton with the complement of $\mathcal{A}_1$ and with the complement of $\mathcal{A}_2$. In our example, the resulting automaton $\mathcal{A}_\mathcal{P} \cap \overline{\mathcal{A}_1} \cap \overline{\mathcal{A}_2}$ does not accept the trace π_2, the counterexample in the first refinement. In fact, it does not accept any word; it is empty. The emptiness of $\mathcal{A}_\mathcal{P} \cap \overline{\mathcal{A}_1} \cap \overline{\mathcal{A}_2}$ proves the correctness of the annotated program $\mathcal{P}$.

3   Traces

We assume a fixed set of statements Σ. We will consider Σ as an alphabet and statements as its letters. A trace $\pi = st_1 \ldots st_n$ is a word over this alphabet; i.e., $\pi \in \Sigma^*$.

It is important to realize that the notion of a trace is independent of a program (a trace may not correspond to a path in the program's control flow graph) and independent of the programming language semantics (a trace may not correspond to any possible execution). In order to stress the usage of statements as letters of an alphabet, we sometimes frame each statement/letter. For example, we can write the alphabet of the example program in Section 2 as

$$\Sigma_{ex} = \{\boxed{\texttt{x:=0}}, \boxed{\texttt{y:=0}}, \boxed{\texttt{x++}}, \boxed{\texttt{x==-1}}, \boxed{\texttt{y==-1}}\}$$

and

$$\pi = \boxed{\texttt{x++}}.\boxed{\texttt{x:=0}}.\boxed{\texttt{x:=0}}.\boxed{\texttt{y==-1}}.\boxed{\texttt{x==-1}}$$

is a possible trace. All automata that we consider in this work are automata over the given alphabet Σ; i.e., they recognize sets of traces.

Program Automaton $\mathcal{A_P}$. We present an annotated program $\mathcal{P}$ directly as a trace automaton $\mathcal{A_P}$ which we call the *program automaton*. We can obtain the program automaton in two ways. If we start with an annotated program as in Fig. 1 then we translate the assertions to edges to an error location in the control flow graph. In the resulting program automaton

$$\mathcal{A_P} = \langle LOC, \delta_\mathcal{P}, \{\ell_{\text{init}}\}, \{\ell_{\text{err}}\}\rangle,$$

- the automaton states are program locations,
- the transition relation $\delta_\mathcal{P}$ contains exactly the edges $(\ell, \textit{st}, \ell')$ of the control flow graph,
- the (unique) initial state is the (unique) initial location,
- the (unique) final state is the (unique) error location.

Alternatively, we may follow the automata-theoretic approach to program verification [22]. We use an LTL formula φ to specify a safety property (e.g., a second *lock* statement is not executed before an *unlock* statement). Let $\mathcal{A_{\neg\varphi}}$ be the automaton that accepts all *bad prefixes*, i.e., traces that witness the violation of the safety property specified by φ. Let $\mathcal{A_{CFG}}$ be the automaton whose states are the program locations of $\mathcal{P}$, whose transition graph is the control flow graph of $\mathcal{P}$, and each state is accepting. We construct the program automaton $\mathcal{A_P}$ as the intersection of $\mathcal{A_{CFG}}$ and $\mathcal{A_{\neg\varphi}}$. It accepts all traces that violate the safety property φ and follow a path in the control flow graph of $\mathcal{P}$.

Error Trace. We call a trace accepted by the program automaton $\mathcal{A_P}$ an error trace. An error trace corresponds to a path from the initial location to the error location. In order to determine if such a path corresponds to a possible execution, the semantics of the statements has to be taken into account.

Infeasibility. We assume that the semantics of statements is given by the (strongest) postcondition operator *post*. The predicate $post(\textit{st}, \varphi)$ is the *(strongest) postcondition* of the predicate φ under the statement *st*. The extension of the postcondition from a statement to a trace is straightforward. We define that the trace $\pi = \textit{st}_1 \ldots \textit{st}_n$ is *infeasible* if

$$post(\pi, \top) \subseteq \bot$$

which expresses that the trace π has no possible execution.

Alternatively, infeasibility can be stated in terms of the (weakest) precondition operator. We use $wp(\mathit{st}, \varphi)$ to denote the *(weakest) precondition* of the predicate φ under the statement st. A trace π is infeasible if

$$\top \subseteq wp(\pi, \bot)$$

It is important to realize that the notion of feasibility is independent from the control flow graph (i.e., a feasible trace may not correspond to any path in the control flow graph).

Correctness. Having defined the notion of infeasibility, we can use the program automaton $\mathcal{A}_\mathcal{P}$ to define correctness. The annotated program $\mathcal{P}$ is correct if every trace accepted by $\mathcal{A}_\mathcal{P}$ is infeasible, formally

$$\mathcal{L}(\mathcal{A}_\mathcal{P}) \subseteq \textsf{Infeasible}.$$

4   Trace Abstraction

The program automaton $\mathcal{A}_\mathcal{P}$ encodes what trace is a path according to the control flow graph of the program. We will use a trace abstraction to encode a sufficient condition for when a trace is infeasible according to the semantics of the programming language.

Definition 1 (Trace Abstraction $(\mathcal{A}_1, \ldots, \mathcal{A}_n)$). *A trace abstraction is given by a tuple of automata $(\mathcal{A}_1, \ldots, \mathcal{A}_n)$ such that each $\mathcal{A}_i$ recognizes a subset of infeasible traces, for $i = 1 \ldots n$.*

Having separated the program-specific information and the programming language-specific information by the program automaton $\mathcal{A}_\mathcal{P}$ and a trace abstraction $(\mathcal{A}_1, \ldots, \mathcal{A}_n)$, we need to combine the two in order to reason about correctness. This combination comes again in the form of an automaton; we define it as the intersection of the program automaton with the complements of $\mathcal{A}_1, \ldots, \mathcal{A}_n$, which we write

$$\mathcal{A}_\mathcal{P} \cap \overline{\mathcal{A}_1} \cap \ldots \cap \overline{\mathcal{A}_n}$$

where we use the symbol $\cap$ for the intersection of automata and $\overline{\mathcal{A}}$ for the complement of the automaton $\mathcal{A}$ (and assume that these two operations on automata implement the corresponding two operations on the recognized languages).

Proof Method Based on Trace Abstraction. Given the program automaton $\mathcal{A}_\mathcal{P}$, we say that *the trace abstraction $(A_1, \ldots, A_n)$ does not admit an error trace* if the language recognized by the automaton $\mathcal{A}_\mathcal{P} \cap \overline{\mathcal{A}_1} \cap \ldots \cap \overline{\mathcal{A}_n}$ is empty.

$$\mathcal{L}(\mathcal{A}_\mathcal{P} \cap \overline{\mathcal{A}_1} \cap \ldots \cap \overline{\mathcal{A}_n}) = \emptyset$$

In this presentation we do not investigate how one can implement the emptiness test efficiently. Let us mention however, that the emptiness test can be done on the fly; only the reachable part of this abstraction has to be computed and not all components q_i in a state of the product $(q_1, \ldots q_n)$ have to be made explicit.

The next two theorems state that a sound and complete proof method can be based on trace abstraction. By the algebraic properties of the intersection operation, the proof method based on trace abstraction is modular; i.e., the components $\mathcal{A}_i$ can be constructed independently one from another and their order does not matter.

Theorem 1 (Soundness). *If a trace abstraction $(\mathcal{A}_1, \ldots, \mathcal{A}_n)$ does not admit an error trace, i.e., $\mathcal{L}(\mathcal{A}_\mathcal{P} \cap \overline{\mathcal{A}_1} \cap \ldots \cap \overline{\mathcal{A}_n}) = \emptyset$, then the program $\mathcal{P}$ is correct.*

Proof. The assumption $\mathcal{L}(\mathcal{A}_\mathcal{P} \cap \overline{\mathcal{A}_1} \cap \ldots \cap \overline{\mathcal{A}_n}) = \emptyset$ means that every trace accepted by $\mathcal{A}_\mathcal{P}$ is accepted by one of $\mathcal{A}_1, \ldots, \mathcal{A}_n$.

$$\mathcal{L}(\mathcal{A}_\mathcal{P}) \subseteq \mathcal{L}(\mathcal{A}_1) \cup \cdots \cup \mathcal{L}(\mathcal{A}_n)$$

By definition of trace abstraction, each $\mathcal{A}_i$ recognizes a subset of infeasible traces.

$$\mathcal{L}(\mathcal{A}_1) \cup \cdots \cup \mathcal{L}(\mathcal{A}_n) \subseteq \text{INFEASIBLE}$$

Hence, every trace accepted by $\mathcal{A}_\mathcal{P}$ is infeasible, which is how the correctness of the program $\mathcal{P}$ is defined. $\square$

According to folklore wisdom, if completeness holds, then it does for a trivial reason which does not provide any further insight. The proof method based on trace abstraction is no exception.

Theorem 2 (Completeness). *If the program $\mathcal{P}$ is correct, then there exists a trace abstraction $(\mathcal{A}_1, \ldots, \mathcal{A}_n)$ that does not admit an error trace, i.e., $\mathcal{L}(\mathcal{A}_\mathcal{P} \cap \overline{\mathcal{A}_1} \cap \ldots \cap \overline{\mathcal{A}_n}) = \emptyset$.*

Proof. Assume $\mathcal{P}$ is correct. Then, by definition, $\mathcal{A}_\mathcal{P}$ does not accept any trace, which is equivalent to $\mathcal{L}(\mathcal{A}_\mathcal{P}) \subseteq \text{INFEASIBLE}$. We set $n = 1$ and choose the trace abstraction $(\mathcal{A}_1)$ where $\mathcal{A}_1 = \mathcal{A}_\mathcal{P}$. If we "implement" this abstraction we get the automaton $\mathcal{A}_\mathcal{P} \cap \overline{\mathcal{A}_\mathcal{P}}$ which recognizes the empty set. Hence $(\mathcal{A}_1)$ does not admit an error trace. $\square$

5   CEGAR for Trace Abstraction

In the iterated refinement scheme depicted in Fig. 5, we transfer the classical check-analyze-refine loop to trace abstraction. The initial trace abstraction is the empty tuple of automata $(n = 0)$. If the trace abstraction $(\mathcal{A}_1, \ldots, \mathcal{A}_n)$ admits an error trace, say π, we check whether π is infeasible. If this is the case, we extend the trace abstraction with an automaton $\mathcal{A}_{n+1}$ that accepts (at least) the infeasible trace π.

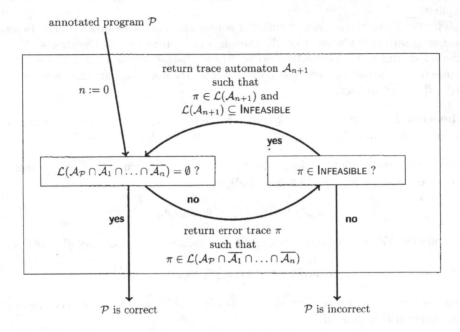

Fig. 5. Counterexample-guided abstraction refinement scheme for trace abstraction. The program $\mathcal{P}$ is correct if $\mathcal{L}(\mathcal{A}_\mathcal{P}) \subseteq \text{INFEASIBLE}$.

Incrementality. If the trace abstraction $(\mathcal{A}_1, \ldots, \mathcal{A}_n)$ does not admit an error trace then it still does not when we add any number of components to the tuple. As a consequence, in a series of successive refinements, one never has to withdraw a previously added component ("superfluous components in a tuple do not hurt").

Progress. The infeasible error trace π returned in the n-th iteration of the refinement loop gets eliminated by the refined abstraction; i.e., the trace abstraction $(\mathcal{A}_1, \ldots, \mathcal{A}_n, \mathcal{A}_{n+1})$ does not admit the error trace π.

6   Interpolant Automata

In the setting of iterated refinement for trace abstraction (Fig. 5) in the previous section, it is trivial to construct an automaton $\mathcal{A}_{n+1}$ that accepts exactly the infeasible error trace π. The corresponding trivial refinement excludes one and only one infeasible error trace. The question is how one can generalize the counterexample, i.e., construct an automaton $\mathcal{A}_{n+1}$ that recognizes a set consisting of π and more infeasible traces. Ideally, those traces share with π the 'reason of infeasibility'.

An immediate idea is to augment the trivial automaton (which accepts exactly the infeasible error trace π) with transitions that are labeled by "irrelevant statements" and that are self-loops (transitions from and to the same automaton state). A statement is irrelevant if it does not modify a variable whose value determines the infeasibility. In our example from Section 2, in the construction of the automaton $\mathcal{A}_1$ for the error trace π_1 (see Fig. 3), one would thus obtain the self-loop labeled (x++). One would, however, fail to add the self-loop labeled (x++) in the construction of the automaton $\mathcal{A}_2$. One would also fail to introduce general loops in the construction of the automaton.

The first step towards a generally applicable construction is to consider a *sequence of predicates* $I_0, I_1, \ldots, I_n$ (to which we refer as interpolants for reasons that will become apparent later). In many settings that we consider, this sequence is related to the error trace π; it may be generated, for example, by the proof of the infeasibility of π.

The general notion of an *interpolant automaton* that we introduce below, however, does not refer to an error trace. It refers to an arbitrary sequence of predicates $I_0, I_1, \ldots, I_n$. Given such a sequence, we will associate each predicate I_i with an automaton state q_i. The automaton states are not necessarily pairwise distinct; i.e., we may associate two different predicates I_i and I_j with the same automaton state, and we may associate the same predicate with two different states (i.e., we may have $I_i \neq I_j, q_i = q_j$ and we may have $I_i = I_j, q_i \neq q_j$). The non-constructive definition below accommodates a wide range of possible constructions. The definition of a *canonical interpolant automaton* further below is constructive.

Definition 2 (Interpolant Automaton $\mathcal{A}_\mathcal{I}$). *Given a sequence of predicates* $\mathcal{I} = I_0, I_1, \ldots, I_n$ *(to which we will refer as "interpolants"), we call a trace automaton*

$$\mathcal{A}_\mathcal{I} = \langle Q_\mathcal{I}, \delta_\mathcal{I}, Q_\mathcal{I}^{\text{init}}, Q_\mathcal{I}^{\text{fin}} \rangle$$

an interpolant automaton *if we can index its set of states* $Q_\mathcal{I}$ *with the set of indices of the sequence* $\{0, \ldots, n\}$,

$$Q_\mathcal{I} = \{q_0, \ldots, q_n\}$$

and thus associate each interpolant I_i *with a state* q_i, *such that the following three conditions hold.*

- *Each pair of interpolants associated with a state transition is inductive.*

$$(q_i, \mathit{st}, q_j) \in \delta_\mathcal{I} \quad \text{implies} \quad post(\mathit{st}, I_i) \subseteq I_j$$

- *Each interpolant associated with an initial state is the* true *predicate.*

$$q_i \in Q_\mathcal{I}^{\text{init}} \quad \text{implies} \quad I_i = \top$$

- *Each interpolant associated with a final state is the* false *predicate.*

$$q_i \in Q_\mathcal{I}^{\text{fin}} \quad \text{implies} \quad I_i = \bot$$

Theorem 3. *An interpolant automaton $\mathcal{A}_\mathcal{I}$ recognizes a subset of infeasible traces.*

$$\mathcal{L}(\mathcal{A}_\mathcal{I}) \subseteq \textsf{INFEASIBLE}$$

Proof. We show (by induction on the length of a trace π) that if $q_j \in \delta(\pi, q_i)$ then the inclusion $post(\pi, I_i) \subseteq I_j$ holds. Thus, for every trace π accepted by $\mathcal{A}_\mathcal{I}$ the inclusion

$$post(\pi, \top) \subseteq \bot,$$

holds, which means that π is infeasible. □

Completeness. We may ask whether a proof method based on trace abstraction is still complete if the automata $\mathcal{A}_i$ of a trace abstraction $(\mathcal{A}_1, \ldots, \mathcal{A}_n)$ are restricted to be interpolant automata. Again, the completeness argument is disappointingly simple. If the program is correct, the program automaton $\mathcal{A}_\mathcal{P}$ is an interpolant automaton. To see this, define I_i to be the set of states at the location ℓ_i reachable from any state at location ℓ_0 (assuming the locations of the program automaton $\mathcal{A}_\mathcal{P}$ are exactly $\ell_0, \ldots, \ell_n$). We associate I_i with the state ℓ_i of the program automaton. Since we assume that the program is correct, we know that the interpolant associated with the error location $\ell_{\textsf{err}}$ is the *false* predicate $\bot$.

Interpolant Automata and Floyd-Hoare style Proofs of Program Correctness. In the discussion of completeness above, we can more generally define I_i to be any invariant assertion associated with the location ℓ_i in a Floyd-Hoare style proof of the partial correctness of the program $\mathcal{P}$. This is because, when we transfer the partial-correctness statement to the control flow graph with the error location $\ell_{\textsf{err}}$, we will label the error location $\ell_{\textsf{err}}$ with the *false* predicate $\bot$. The condition on each pair of interpolants associated with a transition (in Definition 2) is exactly the inductiveness of the invariant assertions in the Floyd-Hoare style proof.

The proof of partial-correctness may refer to the full program or just a program fragment, constituted, e.g., by the *slice* of the control flow graph which is executed by the error trace π. In a concrete setting, there are many ways in which one may obtain such a proof: manually, or by a constraint solving method as, e.g., in [3], or by one of the methods based on (counterexample-guided abstraction refinement of) state abstraction, e.g., [1,3,4,11,13,15,18].

Once the interpolant automaton is formed, it no longer carries any reference to program states (or invariant assertions and such). A trace automaton is a graph; it is detached from both the original program and the semantics of statements (as predicate transformers). As a consequence, refinement of trace abstraction does not involve logical conjunction and theorem prover calls; it is a graph operation.

Determinism. The general setting of non-deterministic trace automata is potentially useful for a compact representation of infeasibility. If the trace automaton is deterministic then its complement can have the same transition graph (up to *sink states* which are introduced to obtain a total transition relation). This is the case, e.g., when the trace automaton is the program automaton $\mathcal{A}_{\mathcal{P}}$ or, more generally, when the transition graph of the trace automaton is a subgraph of the (possibly partially unfolded) control flow graph (since a statement cannot lead to different locations).

Canonical Interpolant Automaton. Next, we will introduce the notion of a *sequence of interpolants* for the error trace π and use it to give a constructive definition of a special case of an interpolant automaton.

Sequence of Interpolants for an Error Trace. Given an infeasible error trace $\pi = st_1, \ldots, st_n$, we call a sequence of predicates $\mathcal{I} = I_0, I_1, \ldots, I_n$ a *corresponding sequence of interpolants* (corresponding to π) if the following conditions hold (where $\top$ is the *true* predicate and $\bot$ is the *false* predicate).

- $I_0 = \top$

- $post(st_{i+1}, I_i) \subseteq I_{i+1}$, for $i = 0 \ldots n - 1$

- $I_n = \bot$

If we split the trace π at any position i into a prefix $st_1 \ldots st_i$ and suffix $st_{i+1} \ldots st_n$ then every state reached under a possible execution of the prefix $st_1 \ldots st_i$ satisfies I_i and no state satisfying I_i has a possible execution under the suffix $st_{i+1} \ldots st_n$. In other words, the interpolant I_i is an overapproximation of the postcondition of *true* under the prefix and an underapproximation of the weakest precondition *false* under the suffix, formally

$$post(st_1 \ldots st_i, \top) \subseteq I_i \subseteq wp(st_{i+1} \ldots st_n, \bot).$$

A sequence of interpolants may be, but is not necessarily a sequence of Craig interpolants generated from the proof of infeasibility of a counterexample (in the spirit of [13,15,17,18]). A sequence of interpolants may also arise as the sequence of invariant assertions along the sequence of program locations in a Hoare-style proof (for the correctness of the program fragment corresponding to the spurious counterexample).

In order to motivate the definition of the canonical interpolant automaton, we will give a schematic example of its construction.

Example. In the schematic setting depicted in Fig. 6, we assume that

- $\pi = st_1 \ldots st_n$ is an infeasible error trace along the locations $\ell_0, \ldots, \ell_n$,
- $\mathcal{I} = I_0, \ldots, I_n$ is a corresponding sequence of interpolants,
- i and j are two positions such that $j < i$, $\ell_i = \ell_j$, and $post(st_{j+1}, I_i) \subseteq I_{j+1}$.

To make the example simple, let us assume that ℓ_j is the only repeated location in π. The assumption that ℓ_i is the same location as ℓ_j implies the existence of a loop in the control flow graph that goes from ℓ_j via $\ell_{j+1} \ldots \ell_{i-1}$ back to ℓ_j. The error trace π executes this loop exactly once.

We now construct the automaton $\mathcal{A}_{\mathcal{I}}^{\pi}$ depicted in Fig. 6 by taking the trivial automaton (which accepts exactly only the one infeasible error trace π) and add exactly one 'back edge', namely the transition (q_i, st_{j+1}, q_j). The automaton $\mathcal{A}_{\mathcal{I}}^{\pi}$ accepts all traces that follow the same path in the control flow graph as π (and that execute the loop through ℓ_j at least once).

$$\mathcal{L}(\mathcal{A}_{\mathcal{I}}^{\pi}) = st_1 \ldots st_j st_{j+1} \ldots st_i (st_{j+1} \ldots st_i)^* st_{i+1} \ldots st_n$$

To see that the trace $\pi_k = st_1 \ldots st_j st_{j+1} \ldots st_i (st_{j+1} \ldots st_i)^k st_{i+1} \ldots st_n$ is infeasible for $k \geq 0$, we first observe that the inclusion $post(st_{j+2} \ldots st_i, I_{j+1}) \subseteq I_i$ holds by the definition of a sequence of interpolants for π. This together with the assumption $post(st_{j+1}, I_i) \subseteq I_{j+1}$ implies $post(st_{j+1} \ldots st_i, I_i) \subseteq I_i$. Thus, the inclusion

$$post(st_{j+1} \ldots st_i (st_{j+1} \ldots st_i)^k, I_j) \subseteq I_i$$

holds for $k \geq 0$. This implies $post(\pi_k, \top) \subseteq \bot$, the infeasibility of π_k. $\square$

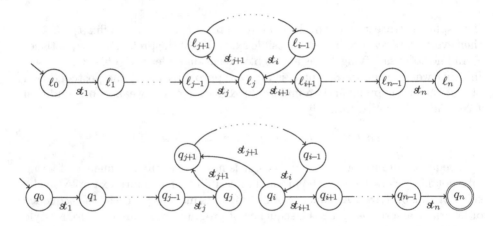

Fig. 6. The infeasible error trace $\pi = st_1 \ldots st_n$ follows the path with the locations $\ell_0, \ldots, \ell_n$ in the control flow with a loop through ℓ_j ($\ell_i = \ell_j$). We assume that $\mathcal{I} = I_0, \ldots, I_n$ is a corresponding sequence of interpolants with $post(st_{j+1}, I_i) \subseteq I_{j+1}$. Adding the transition (q_i, st_{j+1}, q_j) to the trivial automaton (which accepts only π) results in the automaton $\mathcal{A}_{\mathcal{I}}^{\pi}$.

Definition 3 (Canonical Interpolant Automaton $\mathcal{A}_{\mathcal{I}}^{\pi}$). *Given a sequence of interpolants* $\mathcal{I} = I_0, I_1, \ldots, I_n$ *corresponding to the infeasible error trace* $\pi = st_1, \ldots, st_n$ *along the sequence of locations* $\ell_0, \ldots, \ell_n$, *we introduce pairwise different states* $q_0, \ldots, q_n$ *and define the canonical interpolant automaton* $\mathcal{A}_{\mathcal{I}}^{\pi}$ *for* π *and* $\mathcal{I}$ *as follows.*

$$\mathcal{A}_{\mathcal{I}}^{\pi} = \langle Q_{\mathcal{I}}, \delta_{\mathcal{I}}, Q_{\mathcal{I}}^{\mathsf{init}}, Q_{\mathcal{I}}^{\mathsf{fin}} \rangle$$

- $Q_\mathcal{I} = \{q_0, \ldots, q_n\}$

- $\delta_\mathcal{I} = \{(q_i, \mathit{st}_{j+1}, q_{j+1}) \mid i, j = 0, \ldots, n-1,\ j \leq i,\ \ell_i = \ell_j,$
$$post(\mathit{st}_{j+1}, I_i) \subseteq I_{j+1}\}$$

- $Q_\mathcal{I}^{\mathrm{init}} = \{q_0\}$

- $Q_\mathcal{I}^{\mathrm{fin}} = \{q_n\}$

The canonical interpolant automaton $\mathcal{A}_\mathcal{I}^\pi$ accepts the error trace π. This follows from the definition of the sequence of interpolants. In general $\mathcal{A}_\mathcal{I}^\pi$ accepts an infinite set of traces. In a sense, $\mathcal{A}_\mathcal{I}^\pi$ accepts exactly the traces that are infeasible for the same reason as π. More precisely, in order to prove the infeasibility of a trace accepted by $\mathcal{A}_\mathcal{I}^\pi$, we can use the same sequence of interpolants (up to repetition of subsequences) as in the proof of infeasibility of π.

The inclusions $post(\mathit{st}_{i+1}, I_i) \subseteq I_{i+1}$ hold by the definition of sequence of interpolants. Thus, after having generated the sequence of interpolants $\mathcal{I}$ (for the proof of the infeasibility of the trace π), one needs additional theorem prover calls only for each inclusion $post(\mathit{st}_{j+1}, I_i) \subseteq I_{j+1}$ where $j < i$ and $\ell_i = \ell_j$. Thus, the number of additional theorem prover calls is bounded by the number of repeated locations in the sequence of locations along the error trace π.

Speculative Computation of Infeasibility. The general definition of interpolant automata accommodates optimizations where one invests theorem proving work speculatively. That is, one checks the validity of inclusion other than the ones required in the construction of the canonical interpolant automaton. The goal is to add more edges to the transition graph, and thus obtain an interpolant automaton that recognizes a larger set of infeasible traces. One possibility is to remove the side-condition for i, j from the definition of $\delta_\mathcal{I}$, i.e., one checks the inclusions $post(\mathit{st}_{j+1}, I_i) \subseteq I_{j+1}$ for all pairs of locations. If the interpolant I_i is subsumed by the interpolant I_j we may add a transition (q, st, q_j) to the state q_j if the corresponding transition (q, st, q_i) to the state q_i exists. Yet another possibility is to check the validity of inclusions $post(\mathit{st}, I_i) \subseteq I_j$ where st is not necessarily a statement in the error trace π. This leads to, e.g., exploring both branches of a conditional statement and thus adding a branching structure to the interpolant automaton.

Caching Infeasibility. When verifying many programs or program parts, similar patterns of infeasible error traces may occur several times. Our notion of infeasibility is independent of a particular program. It allows the reuse of interpolant automata for the verification of other programs. One can imagine a refinement scheme based on a database of interpolant automata. If the trace abstraction $(\mathcal{A}_1, \ldots, \mathcal{A}_n)$ admits an error trace π then the database can be queried for an automaton that accepts π (modulo variable renaming). If such an automaton exists, then π is infeasible and the abstraction is refined to $(\mathcal{A}_1, \ldots, \mathcal{A}_n, \mathcal{A}_{n+1})$ by adding the new automaton to the tuple.

Example. Reconsider the example of Section 2. The automata $\mathcal{A}_1$ (depicted in Fig. 3) and $\mathcal{A}_2$ (depicted in Fig. 4) are interpolant automata resulting from a construction similar to the canonical interpolant automaton where states q_i and q_j are merged if the interpolants I_i and I_j are equal. (The test of equality of predicates requires in general a call to the theorem prover.)

The automaton $\mathcal{A}_1$ is obtained from the corresponding sequence of interpolants

$$\top, \quad \top, \quad y = 0, \quad y = 0, \quad \bot$$

given the error trace

$$\pi_1 = \boxed{\texttt{x:=0}} . \boxed{\texttt{y:=0}} . \boxed{\texttt{x++}} . \boxed{\texttt{y==-1}} .$$

The automaton $\mathcal{A}_2$ is obtained from the corresponding sequence of interpolants

$$\top, \quad x \geq 0, \quad x \geq 0, \quad x \geq 0, \quad \bot$$

given the error trace

$$\pi_2 = \boxed{\texttt{x:=0}} . \boxed{\texttt{y:=0}} . \boxed{\texttt{x++}} . \boxed{\texttt{x==-1}} . \qquad \square$$

7   Predicate Abstraction

In this section we compare predicate abstraction as in [1,3,4,5,13,12,15,16]) with trace abstraction. We start by formalizing predicate abstraction. Given a finite set of predicates, say

$$\mathsf{Pred} = \{p_1, \ldots, p_m\}$$

we call an m-tuple $\langle b_1, ..., b_m \rangle$ of possibly negated predicates a a *bitvector* (we assume a fixed order on the predicates).

$$\langle b_1, ..., b_m \rangle \text{ where } b_j \text{ is either } p_j \text{ for } \neg p_j, \text{ for } j = 1, \ldots, m$$

Given a program $\mathcal{P}$ with the post operator *post*, we construct the relation $\delta_\#$ between bitvectors (in principle by calling a theorem prover for each pair of bitvectors and each statement).

$$\delta_\# = \{(\langle b_1, ..., b_m \rangle, \mathit{st}, \langle b'_1, ..., b'_m \rangle) \mid post(\mathit{st}, b_1 \wedge ... \wedge b_m) \cap b'_1 \wedge ... \wedge b'_m \neq \bot\}$$

The predicate abstraction of the program $\mathcal{P}$ wrt. Pred can be defined as the finite-state abstract program $\mathcal{P}^\#_{\mathsf{Pred}}$, whose states are pairs of a program location and a bitvector, and whose transitions are induced by the relation $\delta_\#$ between bitvectors.

Theorem 4. *Predicate abstraction is a special case of trace abstraction: the abstraction defined by a tuple of predicates can be expressed by a tuple consisting of one single trace automaton.*

Proof. We define the trace automaton $\mathcal{A}_\#$ whose states are the bitvectors, the transition relation is $\delta_\#$, and each state is an initial and a final state.

$$\mathcal{A}_\# = \langle Q_\#, \delta_\#, Q_\#, Q_\# \rangle$$

This automaton recognizes a superset of *all* feasible traces (and *not* just feasible traces of $\mathcal{A}_\mathcal{P}$; note that the transition relation $\delta_\#$ is total). We define the automaton $\mathcal{A}_{\mathsf{Pred}}$ as the complement of $\mathcal{A}_\#$. Since $\mathcal{A}_{\mathsf{Pred}}$ recognizes a subset of infeasible traces, the 1-tuple $(\mathcal{A}_{\mathsf{Pred}})$ is a trace abstraction.

$$\mathcal{A}_{\mathsf{Pred}} = \overline{\mathcal{A}_\#}$$

The product of the program automaton $\mathcal{A}_\mathcal{P}$ with the complement of $\mathcal{A}_{\mathsf{Pred}}$, i.e., with $\mathcal{A}_\#$, is exactly the abstract program $\mathcal{P}^\#_{\mathsf{Pred}}$, the predicate abstraction of the concrete annotated program $\mathcal{P}$ wrt. the set of predicates Pred.

$$\mathcal{P}^\#_{\mathsf{Pred}} = \mathcal{A}_\mathcal{P} \cap \overline{\mathcal{A}_{\mathsf{Pred}}}$$

Thus, the trace abstraction $(\mathcal{A}_{\mathsf{Pred}})$ expresses the predicate abstraction of the program $\mathcal{P}$ wrt. Pred.   □

Trace abstraction is strictly more expressive than predicate abstraction, since it is not possible to derive predicates from trace automata (as explained above, a trace automaton is detached from the original program and in particular it does not convey the semantics of its statements as predicate transformers).

Refinement, Combination of Abstractions. Trace abstraction allows one to combine abstractions with a minimal investment of theorem proving work. In order to explicate this point, we will build on the fact (established above) that one can use predicate abstraction to construct one or more of the component automata $\mathcal{A}_i$ in a trace abstraction $(\mathcal{A}_1, \ldots, \mathcal{A}_n)$.

We now consider the combination of the two predicate abstractions defined by the sets of predicates Pred_1 and Pred_2, once as the trace abstraction defined by the 2-tuple of the two predicate abstractions, i.e.,

$$(\mathcal{A}_{\mathsf{Pred}_1}, \mathcal{A}_{\mathsf{Pred}_2}),$$

and once as the predicate abstraction for the set of predicates Pred defined by the union of the two sets of predicates, $\mathsf{Pred} = \mathsf{Pred}_1 \cup \mathsf{Pred}_2$. As seen above, this predicate abstraction can be expressed equivalently as the trace abstraction defined by the 1-tuple with the automaton $\mathcal{A}_{\mathsf{Pred}}$, i.e.,

$$(\mathcal{A}_{\mathsf{Pred}_1 \cup \mathsf{Pred}_2}).$$

The combination as a trace abstraction $(\mathcal{A}_{\mathsf{Pred}_1}, \mathcal{A}_{\mathsf{Pred}_2})$ is coarser (in general strictly coarser) than the combination as a predicate abstraction $(\mathcal{A}_{\mathsf{Pred}_1 \cup \mathsf{Pred}_2})$, but it can be computed without additional theorem proving work. It is possible to formally account for this phenomenon in terms of *products of abstract domains* [6,7].

8   Conclusion

We have presented a refinement scheme whose novelty lies in the following points.

- Trace abstraction instead of state abstraction. The goal of the iterated refinement is the successive restriction of the approximation of the set of execution traces (and not of the set of reachable states).
- Compositionality of refinement. The refinement is decomposed into independent steps (the construction of one automaton does not build on another automaton). The results of the individual steps are composed by a graph operation (the intersection of automata).
- Interpolant automata. We use interpolants in order to construct an automaton (which recognizes a set of infeasible traces). Interpolants can be Craig interpolants, or any other inductive assertions in a Floyd-Hoare style proof.
- Coarse-grained caching. Each trace automaton represents the *macro* result of a coherent set of theorem prover calls.
- Reuse from one program to another. The notion of an infeasible trace refers to the programming language semantics. The refinement through an automaton is applicable beyond one specific program.

The scope of this paper is to introduce the principles of the refinement scheme for trace abstraction. Hence, we have aimed at the most general formulation possible. The question of the most practical instantiation of the refinement scheme remains a topic of future work. In particular, the realization of a data base of interpolant automata which accounts for common programming patterns raises a number of interesting research issues.

Acknowledgements. We thank Ahmed Bouajjani, Ken McMillan, Natarajan Shankar, and Ashish Tiwari for fruitful discussions. This work was partly supported in part by the German Research Foundation (DFG) as part of the Transregional Collaborative Research Center "Automatic Verification and Analysis of Complex Systems" (SFB/TR 14 AVACS) and by NSF grant CNS-0749931 while the third author visited SRI International.

References

1. Ball, T., Podelski, A., Rajamani, S.K.: Relative completeness of abstraction refinement for software model checking. In: Katoen, J.-P., Stevens, P. (eds.) TACAS 2002. LNCS, vol. 2280, pp. 158–172. Springer, Heidelberg (2002)
2. Ball, T., Rajamani, S.K.: The SLAM project: debugging system software via static analysis. In: POPL 2002, pp. 1–3. ACM, New York (2002)
3. Beyer, D., Henzinger, T.A., Majumdar, R., Rybalchenko, A.: Path invariants. In: PLDI 2007, pp. 300–309. ACM, New York (2007)
4. Brückner, I., Dräger, K., Finkbeiner, B., Wehrheim, H.: Slicing abstractions. In: Arbab, F., Sirjani, M. (eds.) FSEN 2007. LNCS, vol. 4767, pp. 17–32. Springer, Heidelberg (2007)

5. Clarke, E.M., Grumberg, O., Jha, S., Lu, Y., Veith, H.: Counterexample-guided abstraction refinement. In: Emerson, E.A., Sistla, A.P. (eds.) CAV 2000. LNCS, vol. 1855, pp. 154–169. Springer, Heidelberg (2000)
6. Cousot, P.: Méthodes itératives de construction et d'approximation de points fixes d'opérateurs monotones sur un treillis, analyse sémantique de programmes (in French). Thèse d'État ès sciences mathématiques, Université Joseph Fourier, Grenoble, France, March 21 (1978)
7. Cousot, P.: Semantic foundations of program analysis. In: Muchnick, S., Jones, N. (eds.) Program Flow Analysis: Theory and Applications, ch. 10, pp. 303–342. Prentice-Hall, Englewood Cliffs (1981)
8. Cousot, P., Cousot, R.: Abstract interpretation: a unified lattice model for static analysis of programs by construction or approximation of fixpoints. In: POPL 1977, pp. 238–252. ACM, New York (1977)
9. Cousot, P., Cousot, R.: Refining model checking by abstract interpretation. Automated Software Engineering 6(1), 69–95 (1999)
10. Giacobazzi, R., Quintarelli, E.: Incompleteness, counterexamples, and refinements in abstract model-checking. In: Cousot, P. (ed.) SAS 2001. LNCS, vol. 2126, pp. 356–373. Springer, Heidelberg (2001)
11. Gulavani, B.S., Chakraborty, S., Nori, A.V., Rajamani, S.K.: Automatically refining abstract interpretations. In: Ramakrishnan, C.R., Rehof, J. (eds.) TACAS 2008. LNCS, vol. 4963, pp. 443–458. Springer, Heidelberg (2008)
12. Henzinger, T.A., Jhala, R., Majumdar, R., McMillan, K.L.: Abstractions from proofs. In: POPL 2004, pp. 232–244. ACM, New York (2004)
13. Henzinger, T.A., Jhala, R., Majumdar, R., Sutre, G.: Lazy abstraction. In: POPL 2002, pp. 58–70. ACM, New York (2002)
14. Jha, S.K., Krogh, B.H., Weimer, J.E., Clarke, E.M.: Reachability for linear hybrid automata using iterative relaxation abstraction. In: Bemporad, A., Bicchi, A., Buttazzo, G. (eds.) HSCC 2007. LNCS, vol. 4416, pp. 287–300. Springer, Heidelberg (2007)
15. Jhala, R., McMillan, K.L.: A practical and complete approach to predicate refinement. In: Hermanns, H., Palsberg, J. (eds.) TACAS 2006. LNCS, vol. 3920, pp. 459–473. Springer, Heidelberg (2006)
16. Lakhnech, Y., Bensalem, S., Berezin, S., Owre, S.: Incremental verification by abstraction. In: Margaria, T., Yi, W. (eds.) TACAS 2001. LNCS, vol. 2031, pp. 98–112. Springer, Heidelberg (2001)
17. McMillan, K.L.: Interpolation and sat-based model checking. In: Hunt Jr., W.A., Somenzi, F. (eds.) CAV 2003. LNCS, vol. 2725, pp. 1–13. Springer, Heidelberg (2003)
18. McMillan, K.L.: Lazy abstraction with interpolants. In: Ball, T., Jones, R.B. (eds.) CAV 2006. LNCS, vol. 4144, pp. 123–136. Springer, Heidelberg (2006)
19. McMillan, K.L.: Quantified invariant generation using an interpolating saturation prover. In: Ramakrishnan, C.R., Rehof, J. (eds.) TACAS 2008. LNCS, vol. 4963, pp. 413–427. Springer, Heidelberg (2008)
20. Podelski, A., Wies, T.: Boolean heaps. In: Hankin, C., Siveroni, I. (eds.) SAS 2005. LNCS, vol. 3672, pp. 268–283. Springer, Heidelberg (2005)
21. Segelken, M.: Abstraction and counterexample-guided construction of omega - automata for model checking of step-discrete linear hybrid models. In: Damm, W., Hermanns, H. (eds.) CAV 2007. LNCS, vol. 4590, pp. 433–448. Springer, Heidelberg (2007)
22. Vardi, M.Y., Wolper, P.: An automata-theoretic approach to automatic program verification. In: LICS 1986, pp. 332–344. IEEE Computer Society, Los Alamitos (1986)
23. Wies, T.: Symbolic Shape Analysis. Ph.D Thesis, Albert-Ludwigs-Universität, Freiburg, Germany (2009)

The Causal Graph Revisited
for Directed Model Checking

Martin Wehrle and Malte Helmert

University of Freiburg, Germany
{mwehrle,helmert}@informatik.uni-freiburg.de

Abstract. Directed model checking is a well-established technique to tackle the state explosion problem when the aim is to find error states in large systems. In this approach, the state space traversal is guided through a function that estimates the distance to nearest error states. States with lower estimates are preferably expanded during the search. Obviously, the challenge is to develop distance functions that are efficiently computable on the one hand and as informative as possible on the other hand. In this paper, we introduce the *causal graph* structure to the context of directed model checking. Based on causal graph analysis, we first adapt a distance estimation function from AI planning to directed model checking. Furthermore, we investigate an abstraction that is guaranteed to preserve error states. The experimental evaluation shows the practical potential of these techniques.

1 Introduction

Directed model checking is a well-established technique to efficiently detect error states in large systems. In this approach, a distance heuristic is used to estimate the distance of each state encountered during the state space traversal to a nearest error state. The search then prefers states with lower estimated error distance. Obviously, the success of this approach crucially depends on the quality of this distance function. On the one hand, it should be as informative as possible to only explore a relatively low number of states until an error state is found. On the other hand, it should also be efficient to compute such that the overall performance of the model checking process is increased.

The area of directed model checking has recently found much attention, and various distance estimation functions have been proposed in this context [4,6,10,13,14,18]. The basic principle to construct such functions is to first *abstract* the system under consideration, and then to use the length of an abstract error trace in this abstraction as an estimation for the actual length in the concrete. There are different strategies to define such distance functions. One way is to define abstractions that are coarse enough to find shortest abstract error traces in polynomial time (see, e. g., [4]). A different strategy is to choose an abstraction that is more fine-grained and does not admit polynomial algorithms for computing shortest abstract error traces. The distance estimate is then computed by *approximating* such error traces (see, e. g., [13]). Both strategies have proved to be successful for directed model checking.

In this paper, we introduce the *causal graph* structure to the context of directed model checking. For a given system Ξ, the causal graph is a dependency graph on the component processes of Ξ that reflects how state changes in certain processes depend on state

J. Palsberg and Z. Su (Eds.): SAS 2009, LNCS 5673, pp. 86–101, 2009.

changes in others. Based on causal graph analysis, we first propose an adaptation of a distance function that has originally been introduced in the area of AI planning [7,8]. We will see that this distance function follows the second strategy as outlined above. Furthermore, we propose a simple abstraction based on causal graph properties called *safe abstraction*, which is guaranteed not to introduce spurious error states (i. e., error traces found in this abstraction are guaranteed to correspond to error traces in the concrete system). We demonstrate that error detection is often significantly easier in this abstraction compared to the original system.

The structure of this paper is as follows. In Section 2, we give the basic notations and background needed for this work. Our contributions based on the causal graph are given in Sections 3 and 4, followed by an empirical experimental evaluation in Section 5. We conclude the paper and give an outlook on future work in Section 6.

2 Preliminaries

In this section, we define the notation and semantics for the systems considered in this paper, followed by an introduction to directed model checking.

2.1 Processes and Systems

We model systems as parallel processes running in lockstep using global synchronization labels. Throughout the paper, let Σ be a finite set of synchronization labels (symbols). To distinguish between local states of an atomic process and the global state of the overall system, we use the term *location* for the former and *state* for the latter.

Definition 1 (process). *A process p is a labeled directed graph (L, T), where $L \neq \emptyset$ is the finite set of locations of p and $T \subseteq L \times \Sigma \times L$ is the set of local transitions of p.*

Whenever a given process performs a local transition from location l to l' with associated label $a \in \Sigma$, then all other processes must simultaneously perform a local transition with the same label a, or else the transition is not permitted. This gives rise to the following definition of the parallel composition of two processes. Parallel composition is an associative and commutative operation, up to isomorphism. For example, we can obtain $p_2 \parallel p_1$ from $p_1 \parallel p_2$ by renaming locations (l_1, l_2) to (l_2, l_1).

Definition 2 (parallel composition). *Let $p_1 = (L_1, T_1)$ and $p_2 = (L_2, T_2)$ be processes. The parallel composition of $p_1 \parallel p_2$ of p_1 and p_2 is the process (L, T) with $L = L_1 \times L_2$ and $T = \{((l_1, l_2), a, (l_1', l_2')) \mid (l_1, a, l_1') \in T_1 \wedge (l_2, a, l_2') \in T_2\}$.*

A *system* is simply the parallel composition of one or more processes. We choose this particular system model for ease of presentation; our basic ideas equally apply to other process models, such as ones involving internal transitions of processes or binary (rather than global) synchronization. Alternatively, such synchronization behaviour can also be modelled directly with our semantics. For example, to model asynchronous internal transitions of a process p, we can use a dedicated synchronization label $a_p \in \Sigma$ such that all internal transitions of p are labeled with a_p and all locations l of all other processes have transitions looping from l to l labeled with a_p. (More generally, such sets of loops can be used to model synchronization labels irrelevant to certain processes.)

Definition 3 (system). *A system is a pair* $\Xi = ((p_1, \ldots, p_n), s_0)$*, where* $p_1, \ldots, p_n$
($n \geq 1$*) are processes called the components of* Ξ*. The parallel composition* $P(\Xi) =$
$p_1 \parallel \ldots \parallel p_n$ *of the components is called the composite process of* Ξ*. Locations of*
$P(\Xi)$ *are called states; we denote the states and transitions of* $P(\Xi)$ *by* $S(\Xi)$ *and*
$T(\Xi)$*, respectively. The state* $s_0 \in S(\Xi)$ *is called the initial state of the system.*

A trace $\pi = s_0, a_0, s_1, a_1, \ldots, a_{n-1}, s_n$ *of* Ξ *is an alternating sequence of states and*
synchronization labels starting from the initial state such that $(s_{i-1}, a_{i-1}, s_i) \in T(\Xi)$
for all $i \in \{1, \ldots, n\}$*. The length of a trace,* $|\pi|$*, is its number of transitions, i.e.,*
$|\pi| = n$ *for the given trace.*

The problem we address in this paper, as in most work on directed model checking,
is the *detection of error states* of a system, i.e., states reachable from the initial state
which have an undesirable property. In CTL terms, this corresponds to proving the
formula $\mathrm{E\,F}\,\varphi$ where φ is a non-temporal formula that describes undesirable states.
This is equivalent to the *falsification of invariants* of a system, i.e., to disproving the
CTL formula $\mathrm{A\,G}\,\neg\varphi$. In this paper, we consider the common situation where $\varphi =$
$\varphi_1 \wedge \cdots \wedge \varphi_n$ is a conjunction of formulae where each formula φ_i describes properties
of an individual component process p_i of the system. In this case, we can represent each
conjunct φ_i by the set of locations of p_i that satisfy it.

Definition 4 (model checking task). *A model checking task is a pair* $\Theta = (\Xi, L^*)$*,*
where $\Xi = (((L_1, T_1), \ldots, (L_n, T_n)), s_0)$ *is a system and* $L^* = (L_1^*, \ldots, L_n^*)$ *with*
$L_i^* \subseteq L_i$ *for all* $i \in \{1, \ldots, n\}$ *denotes the target locations for each process of* Ξ*.*

An error trace of Θ *is a trace of* Ξ *that ends in a state* $s \in L_1^* \times \cdots \times L_n^*$*.*

To conclude this background section, we briefly remark that there is a close correspondence between finding error traces in our process model on the one hand and the
nonemptiness problem for intersections of regular automata on the other hand. In this
view, processes correspond to regular automata, the L_i^* sets correspond to accepting
states, and parallel composition corresponds to language intersection. While this view
is not necessarily useful for efficiently determining error traces in practical systems, it
does show that deciding existence of error traces in a system is PSPACE-complete [11].

2.2 Directed Model Checking

Directed model checking is the approach of finding error states through an explicit state-
space traversal guided by a distance estimation function $d^\#$. This function is computed
fully automatically based on the declarative description of the system. In a nutshell, $d^\#$
is a function that maps states to natural numbers, reflecting an estimate of the shortest
error distance. Typically, this estimate is the length of a corresponding abstract error
trace. Each state encountered during a forward state-space traversal starting from the
initial state is evaluated with $d^\#$, and states with lower values are preferred. Note that
abstract distance functions only influence the *order* in which the states are explored,
and hence completeness is *not* affected. On the one hand, it is desirable to have distance
functions that are as informative as possible, so that only few states need to be explored
until an error state is found. On the other hand, the computation of the distance estimate
must not be too expensive.

```
1  function verify(Ξ, L*, d#):
2      s₀ = initial state of Ξ
3      open = empty priority queue
4      closed = ∅
5      priority = d#(s₀)
6      open.insert(s₀, priority)
7      while open is not empty:
8          s = open.pop-minimum()
9          if s satisfies φ(L*):
10             return False
11         closed = closed ∪ {s}
12         for each transition (s, a, s') ∈ T(Ξ):
13             if s' ∉ closed and s' ∉ open:
14                 priority = d#(s')
15                 open.insert(s', priority)
16     return True
```

Fig. 1. A basic directed model checking algorithm

Figure 1 shows a basic directed model checking algorithm. Given a model checking task (Ξ, L^*) and distance function $d^\#$, the algorithm returns *False* if there is a state that satisfies the error condition represented by L^*; otherwise it returns *True*. The initial state of Ξ is s_0. The algorithm maintains a priority queue *open* which contains visited, but not yet explored states. Through the method *open.pop-minimum*, the algorithm determines one such state s with minimum priority value (i. e., minimum estimated error distance) and removes it from the priority queue. This state s is then *expanded*, which is a three-step process. First, check if it is an error state; if so, we are done. Second, mark the state as explored by adding it to the *closed* set, so it will not be considered again later. Finally, determine the successor states of s and add them to the priority queue unless they have been encountered before. After expanding s, the process iterates with the new minimal element of *open*, until an error state is encountered or there remain no further states to check, at which point we can conclude that no error state can be reached.

This algorithm is known as *greedy search* (there are other algorithms like A^* for *optimal* search [17]; these are not considered in this paper). In a practical implementation of the algorithm, every state additionally stores information about how it has been reached, i. e., its immediate predecessor state and synchronization label at the time it was added to *open*. Therefore, if an error state s is finally reached, an error trace can be generated by back-tracing from s. Clearly, the efficiency of greedy search crucially depends on the quality of the estimates provided by $d^\#$. If these are perfect, the number of expansion steps of the algorithm is $n + 1$ where n is the length of the shortest error trace. On the other hand, if the estimates are completely uninformative, the algorithm degenerates to an unguided search algorithm such as depth-first search.

3   The Causal Graph

In this section, we introduce the central concepts of the causal graph heuristic, namely the *causal graph* and the *local subsystems* it induces. To provide some intuition for our

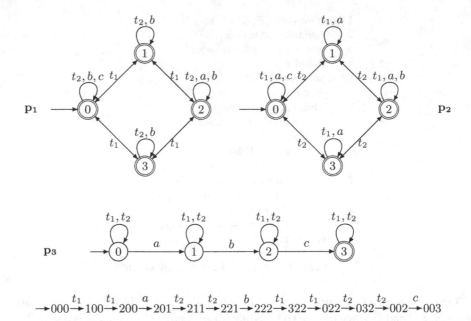

Fig. 2. An example system with three processes and a corresponding error trace. A transition with more than one label is an abbreviation for several parallel transitions, one for each label.

definitions, we illustrate them with a running example (Fig. 2). The example system consists of three processes p_1, p_2 and p_3, each with locations $\{0, 1, 2, 3\}$ and transitions as shown in the figure. We assume that all processes are initially in location 0 and that we consider a state to be an error state iff process p_3 is in location 3 (i.e., $L_1^* = L_2^* = \{0, 1, 2, 3\}$ and $L_3^* = \{3\}$). The shortest error traces for this example have length 11 (one such error trace is also shown in Fig. 2), and indeed this is the distance estimate that the causal graph heuristic will assign in this case. However, other distance estimators considered in the directed model checking literature underestimate the true error distance:

- The d^L and d^U estimators [6,5] measure the graph-theoretic distance to the nearest location L_i^* in each automaton p_i without taking into account synchronization labels. The d^L estimator maximizes over the individual distances, whereas d^U sums these values. In this case, we obtain $d^L(s_0) = \max\{0, 0, 3\} = 3$ and $d^U(s_0) = 0 + 0 + 3 = 3$ because only p_3 needs to move to a different location (3), which can be reached from location 0 in three steps.
- The h^L and h^U estimators [13] compute abstract error traces under the *monotonicity abstraction*. In the context of our running example, h^U considers an abstracted problem where each process can "jump back to" a previously visited location at every step free of cost. In this case, we obtain $h^U(s_0) = 7$ because h^U fails to take into account that processes p_1 and p_2 must return to location 0 from location 2 in order to support the transition of p_3 from 2 to 3 via synchronization label c. The h^L estimator has the same weakness as h^U but additionally assumes in its abstraction that

the required transitions of p_1 and p_2 from 0 to 2 can be performed simultaneously, leading to an estimate of $h^L(s_0) = 5$.

A common weakness of all these estimators, which causes the imperfect distance estimates, is that they fail to take into account that reaching a certain location of p_3 has a *side effect* on p_1 and p_2. In particular, they assume that as soon as p_3 has reached location 2, the error location 3 can be reached immediately in a single transition. The transition of p_3 from 2 to 3 requires p_1 and p_2 to follow a transition with label c, and the initial locations of p_1 and p_2 have outgoing transitions with this label from their locations in s_0, which is good enough for h^U and h^L (d^L and d^U do not care about synchronization at all). The estimators do not recognize that p_1 and p_2 must initially *move away* from location 0 (to location 2) before p_3 reaches location 2 in order to synchronize on the labels a (for p_1) and b (for p_2).

The causal graph heuristic overcomes this limitation by finding error traces in simple cases like this example *directly*, without further abstraction, while distances in "larger" systems are computed by combining information from smaller subsystems. To make this more precise, we must introduce the notion of causal graph. To motivate the following definition, observe that the labels $\{t_1, t_2, a, b, c\}$ play very different roles for the three processes in the example system:

- Label t_1 is very important for process p_1 because all proper (non-looping) transitions between locations of p_1 must synchronize on this label. We say that a label $a \in \Sigma$ *affects* a process (L, T) if $(l, a, l') \in T$ for some $l \neq l'$. In the example, t_1 affects p_1, t_2 affects p_2 and a, b and c affect p_3.
- Labels a and c do not cause non-looping transitions in p_1, but they are still relevant for the process because the current location of p_1 influences whether or not the overall system can synchronize on these labels. For example, the system cannot synchronize on a unless p_1 is in location 2. We say that a label $a \in \Sigma$ *restricts* a process (L, T) if there exists a location $l \in L$ such that for all $l' \in L$, $(l, a, l') \notin T$. In the example, a restricts p_1 and p_3, b restricts p_2 and p_3, and c restricts all processes.
- Finally, labels t_2 and b are completely irrelevant for process p_1: no matter in which location the process is, it can synchronize on these labels, and they cannot cause a change in location. We say that a label $a \in \Sigma$ is *irrelevant* for a process (L, T) if it does not affect or restrict the process. In the example, t_1 is irrelevant for p_2 and p_3, t_2 is irrelevant for p_1 and p_3, a is irrelevant for p_2, and b is irrelevant for p_1.

Using these different roles for labels and processes, we define the *causal graph* of a system Ξ as follows.

Definition 5 (causal graph). *The causal graph $CG(\Xi)$ of a system Ξ is the directed graph whose vertices are the component processes $p_1, \ldots, p_n$ of Ξ and which contains an arc from p_i to p_j iff $i \neq j$ and there exists a label $a \in \Sigma$ that restricts or affects p_i and affects p_j.*

The causal graph of the running example is shown in Fig. 3. Intuitively, the causal graph contains an arc from process p_i to p_j if there may be a need to change the location of p_i in order to change the location of p_j. To translate this intuition into a formal result, we first introduce the notion of *subsystems*.

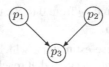

Fig. 3. The causal graph for the running example system

Definition 6 (subsystem). *Let $\Xi = ((p_1, \ldots, p_n), s_0)$ be a system, let $\Theta = (\Xi, (L_1^*, \ldots, L_n^*))$ be a model checking task for Ξ, and let $P = \{p_{i_1}, \ldots, p_{i_k}\}, 1 \leq i_1 < \cdots < i_k \leq n$ be a subset of the component processes of Ξ.*

The system $\Xi[P] := ((p_{i_1}, \ldots, p_{i_k}), (s_{0i_1}, \ldots, s_{0i_k}))$ is called the subsystem of Ξ induced by P, and the model checking task $\Theta[P] := (\Xi[P], (L_{i_1}^*, \ldots, L_{i_k}^*))$ is called the subtask of Θ induced by P.

It is easy to see that for any choice of P, $\Xi[P]$ is an *over-approximation* of Ξ: every trace π of Ξ induces a corresponding trace of $\Xi[P]$, which can be obtained from π by projecting all states to the components in P. Moreover, every error trace for Θ is an error trace for $\Theta[P]$. Of course, the converse is not true in general, and the existence of error traces for $\Theta[P]$ does not imply that there are error traces for Θ. However, there is a simple sufficient criterion under which all error traces of $\Theta[P]$ *do* correspond to error traces of Θ with the same synchronization sequence: namely, if P includes all processes with a non-trivial target location set (i. e., processes p_i for which not all locations are in the set L_i^*), as well as all causal graph *ancestors* of such processes. This is essentially the idea of *cone-of-influence reduction* [2].

In fact, cone-of-influence reduction is still error-preserving if we consider an alternative definition of causal graphs where we only introduce an arc from p_i to p_j if some label *restricts* p_i and affects p_j. The reason why we also include arcs from p_i to p_j if some common label *affects* both of them is that this gives an additional decomposition result, which we will discuss in Section 4.1.

As a side remark, under our definition, if the causal graph consists of more than one weakly connected component, then there exists an error trace iff each subtask induced by a weakly connected component has an error trace. (The overall error trace is then essentially the concatenation of these "subtraces".) The intuitive reason for this property is that if two sets of processes P and P' are causally disconnected, then all state transitions that affect the locations of processes in P are not restricted by or affect the locations of processes in P' (and vice versa), and hence the corresponding subtasks can be addressed independently. A similar decomposition result does not hold under the alternative definition of causal graphs, where traces that affect the processes P are not restricted by the processes P', but can still change the locations of P' as a side effect.

4   The Causal Graph Heuristic

The causal graph heuristic estimates the cost of reaching an error state by computing distance estimates for a number of subtasks which are derived by looking at small "windows" of the causal graph. In this section, we describe this procedure conceptually as a bottom-up computation along a topological sorting of the causal graph. (In a practical implementation, a top-down implementation is more efficient, but both approaches lead to the same distance estimates.) Since we require a topological sorting of the causal graph, the procedure only works for acyclic causal graphs; we will later explain how to deal with the cyclic case. For now, let us just remark that deciding the existence of error traces is already PSPACE-complete for systems with acyclic causal graphs, even under the further restriction that all processes have only two locations [1].

Throughout this section, we assume that we are given a model checking task $\Theta = (\Xi, (L_1^*, \ldots, L_n^*))$ for a system $\Xi = ((p_1, \ldots, p_n), s_0)$, and that our objective is to compute a distance estimate for a given state s of Ξ, which we denote as $h^{CG}(s)$. For each process $p_i = (L_i, T_i)$ and each pair of locations $l_i, l_i' \in L_i$, the causal graph heuristic computes a distance estimate $cost_{p_i}(l_i, l_i')$ for the cost of changing the location of p_i from l_i to l_i'. The overall distance estimate of s is then defined as the sum of the costs of reaching the nearest error location in each process, i.e., $h^{CG}(s) = \sum_{i=1}^{n} \min_{l_i^* \in L_i^*} cost_{p_i}(l_i, l_i^*)$ for $s = (l_1, \ldots, l_n)$. Note that the d^U estimate, due to Edelkamp et al. [6,5], is defined by the same equation, but using a different estimate for $cost_{p_i}(l_i, l_i^*)$, which is simply the graph-theoretic distance from l_i to l_i^*. In contrast, the cost estimates for h^{CG} take synchronization labels into account and usually provide larger (and, as we shall see in the experimental evaluation in Section 5, more accurate) estimates than the graph-theoretic distance.

4.1 Independent Processes

In this section and the following, we describe how the $cost_p(l, l')$ estimates are computed. We begin with the case where process p has no predecessors in the causal graph. We call such a process *independent* because (by the definition of causal graphs) it can change location independently of and without affecting the locations of other processes.

Let $p = (L, T)$ be an independent process. In this case, like in the case of the d^U heuristic, we define $cost_p(l, l')$ as the graph-theoretic distance from l to l' in p. For independent processes, this is an appropriate definition because local transitions are not restricted by any other processes. Hence, in any state of the system, a sequence of synchronization labels leading from l to l' does correspond to an executable trace that changes the location of p from l to l', without affecting the locations of other processes.

In our running example, Fig. 3 shows that processes p_1 and p_2 do not have predecessors in the causal graph, and indeed, Fig. 2 shows that these are independent processes, as the only labels affecting them – t_1 for p_1, t_2 for p_2 – are irrelevant for the other processes. Therefore, the cost estimates for these processes equal the graph distances (e.g., $cost_{p_1}(0, 2) = 2$ and $cost_{p_2}(2, 3) = 1$).

Safe Abstraction. For some independent processes, there is actually no need to compute any cost estimates at all. Consider the case where p is independent and all cost estimates for p are finite (or, equivalently, p is strongly connected). Without loss of generality, we assume that

- the target location set for p is not empty (otherwise, trivially there exist no error states, since the error states are formed as the Cartesian product of the target location sets of the processes), and
- each label a that occurs in a transition of any process also occurs in a transition of p (otherwise transitions with label a can never be synchronized, and we can remove all such transitions in a preprocessing step).

In this case, it is possible to separate the local transitions for p from the rest of the model checking task completely. Let $\Xi[P']$ be the subsystem induced by all processes of Ξ except p, i. e., $P' = \{p_1, \ldots, p_n\} \setminus \{p\}$. Given a state s of Ξ and an error trace π' for $\Xi[P']$ that starts in the projection of s to P', we can compute an error trace for Ξ starting from s with a simple polynomial algorithm:

- If $|\pi'| = 0$ (i. e., π' is the empty trace), then s' is already an error state for $\Xi[P']$, and hence all processes except possibly p are in a target location in state s. Because p is strongly connected and has at least one target location, we can find a sequence of local transitions of p that lead from its location in s to a target location of p. Because p is independent, these transitions are not restricted by the other processes and do not affect their locations. By following these local transitions, we can go from state s to a global error state.
- If $|\pi'| = n \geq 1$, then the trace starts with some global transition (s', a, t') of $\Xi[P']$. Because p is strongly connected and has at least one location with an outgoing transition labeled a, we can find a sequence of local transitions of p that lead from its location in s to a location in which p can synchronize on a. Because p is independent, these transitions are not restricted by the other processes and do not affect their locations. By following these local transitions, we can go from state s to a state $\tilde{s}$ whose projection to P' is s' and in which all processes can synchronize on a, and from there to a state t whose projection to P' is t'. Since t' starts an error trace of length $n - 1$ in $\Xi[P']$, we can reach an error state of Ξ from t (and hence, from s) by an inductive argument.

The analysis shows that if the independent process p is strongly connected, there exists a *safe abstraction* of Ξ to P': any error trace of $\Xi[P']$ induces an error trace of Ξ, and of course the converse is also true because subsystems are always over-approximations.

Under these circumstances, we can run the directed model checking algorithm directly on $\Xi[P']$ instead of Ξ, and then apply the above procedure to convert the error trace for the abstracted problem into a concrete one. Of course, the abstraction may cascade, as $\Xi[P']$ may admit further safe abstractions, even for processes that were not originally independent in P. In our experimental analysis (Section 5), we will present results for the causal graph heuristic both with and without safe abstraction.

We briefly remark that in our running example, we could safely abstract away p_1 and p_2 since these processes are independent and strongly connected. However, as we will now turn to the question of computing cost estimates for non-independent processes, we will assume for the rest of this section that safe abstraction is not performed on the running example.

```
 1 function compute-costs(Ξ, s, p, l):
 2     Let pred(p) be the set of immediate predecessors of p in CG(Ξ).
 3     (L, T) := p
 4     cost_p(l, l) := 0
 5     cost_p(l, l') := ∞ for all l' ∈ L \ {l}
 6     context(l, p_i) := location of p_i in s, for all p_i ∈ pred(p)
 7     unreached := L
 8     while unreached contains a location l' ∈ L with cost_p(l, l') < ∞:
 9         Choose such a location l' ∈ unreached minimizing cost_p(l, l').
10         unreached := unreached \ {l'}
11         for each transition (l', a, l'') ∈ T from l' to some l'' ∈ unreached:
12             target-cost := cost_p(l, l') + 1
13             target-context := ∅
14             for each process p_i = (L_i, T_i) ∈ pred(p):
15                 m := context(l', p_i)
16                 Choose (m', m'') ∈ L_i × L_i such that (m', a, m'') ∈ T_i
                       and cost_{p_i}(m, m') is minimized.
17                 target-cost := target-cost + cost_{p_i}(m, m')
18                 target-context(p_i) := m''
19             if target-cost < cost_p(l, l''):
20                 cost_p(l, l'') := target-cost
21                 context(l'', p_i) := target-context(p_i) for all p_i ∈ pred(p)
22     return cost_p(l, l') for all l' ∈ L
```

1 **function** compute-costs(Ξ, s, p, l):

2   Let $pred(p)$ be the set of immediate predecessors of p in $CG(\Xi)$.

3      $(L, T) := p$

4      $cost_p(l, l) := 0$

5      $cost_p(l, l') := \infty$ for all $l' \in L \setminus \{l\}$

6      $context(l, p_i) :=$ location of p_i in s, for all $p_i \in pred(p)$

7      $unreached := L$

8   **while** $unreached$ contains a location $l' \in L$ with $cost_p(l, l') < \infty$:

9   Choose such a location $l' \in unreached$ minimizing $cost_p(l, l')$.

10          $unreached := unreached \setminus \{l'\}$

11   **for each** transition $(l', a, l'') \in T$ from l' to some $l'' \in unreached$:

12             $target\text{-}cost := cost_p(l, l') + 1$

13             $target\text{-}context := \emptyset$

14   **for each** process $p_i = (L_i, T_i) \in pred(p)$:

15                 $m := context(l', p_i)$

16   Choose $(m', m'') \in L_i \times L_i$ such that $(m', a, m'') \in T_i$ and $cost_{p_i}(m, m')$ is minimized.

17                 $target\text{-}cost := target\text{-}cost + cost_{p_i}(m, m')$

18                 $target\text{-}context(p_i) := m''$

19   **if** $target\text{-}cost < cost_p(l, l'')$:

20                 $cost_p(l, l'') := target\text{-}cost$

21                 $context(l'', p_i) := target\text{-}context(p_i)$ for all $p_i \in pred(p)$

22   **return** $cost_p(l, l')$ for all $l' \in L$

Fig. 4. Modified Dijkstra algorithm for computing $cost_p(l, l')$

4.2 Processes with Causal Predecessors

For processes p which do have predecessors in the causal graph, cost estimates are also computed by searching for paths in the labeled directed graph defined by the process. However, here we improve on the d^U approach by taking into account the synchronization labels on the local transitions: in addition to counting the number of local transitions of p required to reach a given location, we also consider the costs for moving the other processes of the system into locations which can synchronize with these transitions. Note that by the definition of causal graphs, the *only* processes which can potentially restrict the non-looping local transitions of p are its causal predecessors, which we denote as $pred(p)$. Because we compute costs in a bottom-up order along a topological sorting of the causal graph, we have already computed all cost estimates for these processes. Hence, the computation of $cost_p(l, l')$ is based on finding traces from l to l' in the subsystem of Ξ induced by $\{p\} \cup pred(p)$, taking into account the known cost estimates for the processes $pred(p)$.

The algorithm for computing the cost values $cost_p(l, l')$ is shown in Fig. 4. It is a modification of Dijkstra's algorithm for finding shortest paths in weighted directed graphs, applied to the process $p = (L, T)$. Like Dijkstra's algorithm, it is a one-to-all procedure, i.e., for a given start location l, it computes $cost_p(l, l')$ for all $l' \in L$. The only difference to Dijkstra's algorithm is that we do not define the cost of a transition $(l', a, l'') \in T$ before applying the algorithm. Instead, the transition cost is computed as soon as location l' is expanded by the algorithm, and it depends on the current locations of $pred(p)$ in the situation where l' is reached.

In detail, the cost of reaching $l'' \in L$ through transition $(l', a, l'') \in T$ is computed as the cost of reaching l' plus the *setup cost* required to take $pred(p)$ into locations that allow synchronization on the label a, plus 1 for taking the actual transition with label a that takes p from l' to l'' (lines 12–18). To estimate the setup cost for each predecessor $p_i \in pred(p)$, we associate each location $l' \in L$ with locations $context(l', p_i)$ for each $p_i \in pred(p)$, with the interpretation that when $l' \in L$ is first reached, we assume that process p_i is in location $m = context(l', p_i)$. The setup cost for a given process is then the cheapest cost, according to the previously computed $cost_{p_i}$ values, for taking process p_i from m to a location m' where it can synchronize on the label a (lines 15–17).

If it turns out that $(l', a, l'') \in T$ reaches l'' more cheaply than the previously considered transitions (line 19), then the cost of l'' is updated accordingly (line 20, as in Dijkstra's algorithm). At the same time, the context of l'' is set so that it reflects the way in which we have reached the location: by performing appropriate setup transitions for $pred(p)$ and then synchronizing on label a (lines 16, 18, 21).

We remark that the algorithm is not guaranteed to find a globally shortest trace in the subsystem induced by $\{p\} \cup pred(p)$. Indeed, it may fail to find *any* path to a given location $l' \in L$ even though it is reachable. The reason for this is that the setup for each transition (l', a, l'') is performed greedily, without backtracking on the choice of *how* to modify the current context in order to allow synchronization on label a: we always pick a *locally cheapest* setup sequence. While it would of course be preferable to guarantee the success of the *compute-costs* algorithm, unfortunately this is not possible to do in polynomial time if $P \neq NP$: if we could, this would decide the existence of error traces in the model checking task induced by $\{p\} \cup pred(p)$. However, it is known that error detection for the subtask induced by a single process and its direct causal graph predecessors is NP-complete [7].

Returning to our running example, the algorithm computes the following cost estimates $cost_{p_3}(0, l')$ for the state $(0, 0, 0)$:

- $cost(p_3)(0, 0) = 0$: This is due to the initialization step (line 4).
- $cost(p_3)(0, 1) = 0 + 1 + 2 = 3$: the three terms correspond to the cost of location 0, the constant term 1, and the setup cost to reach locations of p_1 and p_2 in which we can synchronize on label a. In this case, we need to change p_1 from location 0 to 2, for a setup cost of 2.
- $cost(p_3)(0, 2) = 3 + 1 + 2 = 6$: cost of location 1, constant term 1, setup cost to reach locations of p_1 and p_2 in which we can synchronize on label b. In this case, we need to change p_2 from location 0 to 2, for a setup cost of 2.
- $cost(p_3)(0, 3) = 6 + 1 + 4 = 11$: cost of location 2, constant term 1, setup cost to reach locations of p_1 and p_2 in which we can synchronize on label c. In this case, we need to change both processes from location 2 to 0, for a setup cost of $2 + 2$.

4.3 Causal Graphs with Cycles

Up to this point, we have given a complete description of how to compute $h^{CG}(s)$ for systems with acyclic causal graphs. Unfortunately, many practical systems tend to have causal graphs with cycles. In this work, we use a rather simple idea to extend the definition of the heuristic to the general case (for an alternative approach, see Section 6).

If $CG(\Xi)$ is not acyclic, we impose a total order $p'_1 \prec \cdots \prec p'_n$ on the processes of Ξ. The computation of cost values then proceeds as previously described, except that for process p'_i, the *compute-costs* function does not consider *all* causal predecessors $pred(p'_i)$ of p'_i, but only those which are ordered before p'_i in the ordering. Semantically, this means that we do not consider the synchronization costs for *all* processes, but only a subset of them. Of course, different total orders lead to different synchronization aspects being respected by this abstraction, so in practice one would prefer an order which is "close" to a topological sorting in some sense (e. g., loses as few arcs of the causal graph as possible). In our experiments, we use some simple greedy criteria to compute a reasonable ordering (see Section 5.1).

5 Evaluation

We implemented the causal graph heuristic and the safe abstraction technique from Section 4 in the model checker MCTA [15] and evaluated it on a number of academic and industrial benchmarks. The experimental results were obtained on a system with a 3 GHz Intel Pentium 4 CPU, using a memory bound of 1 GB. We compare h^{CG} with the other distance functions d^L, d^U [6,5], h^L and h^U [13] as implemented in MCTA.

5.1 Implementation Details

Our benchmark models consist of parallel automata with interleaving and binary synchronization semantics. This easily fits into the process model used throughout this paper. In addition, some benchmarks feature bounded integer variables and (unbounded) clock variables. Edges in the automata can be guarded by integer or clock constraints, and edges can also reset clock variables and set integers to new values as effects.

The h^{CG} heuristic as implemented in MCTA directly reflects integer and location variables, whereas clocks are ignored for the distance computation. (In fact, abstracting clocks away is the easiest way to deal with them for the computation of distance functions and has already successfully been done in other approaches [4,13].) Essentially, each automaton and each bounded integer variable is identified with a process p in the sense of Definition 1. Both kinds of processes can be subject to safe abstraction as described in Section 4.1; however, as clocks are ignored by the distance computation, to ensure safety we additionally check that these processes do not affect clock variables.

For systems with cyclic causal graphs, we greedily impose an ordering on the processes such that as much as possible of the important synchronization behaviour is respected. Essentially, arcs in the causal graph are preferably ignored if they are induced by as few system transitions as possible. Furthermore, as processes that correspond to automata play a dedicated role in the system, we order them after processes that correspond to integer variables. In more detail, we require for all processes p, p' that if p corresponds to an automaton and $p \prec p'$, then p' also corresponds to an automaton.

Table 1. Experimental results in terms of number of explored states and search time for the heuristics d^L, d^U, h^L, h^U in comparison to h^{CG} and h^{CG} with safe abstraction (denoted with h^{CG}_{safe}). Dashes indicate exhaustion of memory (> 1 GB).

Inst.	explored states						search time in seconds					
	d^L	d^U	h^L	h^U	h^{CG}	h^{CG}_{safe}	d^L	d^U	h^L	h^U	h^{CG}	h^{CG}_{safe}
C_1	18796	16817	1928	715	5129	5129	0.1	0.1	0.1	0.0	0.5	0.5
C_2	66389	61229	4566	1612	6268	2721	0.4	0.4	0.1	0.1	0.6	0.4
C_3	94536	85332	6002	734	6943	3241	0.6	0.6	0.2	0.1	0.6	0.4
C_4	1.11e+6	1.04e+6	81131	9120	57493	6201	6.8	6.3	1.7	0.3	1.1	0.3
C_5	1.27e+7	1.21e+7	430494	83911	494778	13675	76.3	74.7	9.2	2.1	9.3	0.5
C_6	–	–	4.56e+6	718015	5.54e+6	24125	–	–	83.1	12.4	68.4	0.9
C_7	–	–	–	2.55e+6	–	57595	–	–	–	41.4	–	2.3
C_8	–	–	–	–	–	122880	–	–	–	–	–	6.5
C_9	–	–	–	–	–	379981	–	–	–	–	–	24.2
M_1	12277	185416	4581	7668	6245	6245	0.3	6.1	0.1	0.1	0.1	0.1
M_2	43784	56240	15832	18847	18988	8472	0.6	0.8	0.2	0.2	0.2	0.2
M_3	54742	869159	7655	19597	27365	10632	0.8	398.0	0.1	0.2	0.4	0.2
M_4	202924	726691	71033	46170	96418	18574	3.4	110.5	0.8	0.5	1.4	0.4
N_1	15732	10215	50869	9117	8171	8171	0.4	0.2	2.7	0.1	0.2	0.2
N_2	102909	642660	30476	23462	30540	30540	3.0	239.6	0.6	0.5	0.8	0.8
N_3	131202	1.16e+6	11576	43767	40786	40786	4.1	2342.2	0.2	0.9	1.1	1.1
N_4	551091	330753	100336	152163	252558	252558	24.0	11.7	2.1	3.7	9.5	9.5
F_5^A	271	271	9	9	11	11	0.0	0.0	0.0	0.0	0.0	0.0
F_{10}^A	271	271	9	9	11	11	0.0	0.0	0.0	0.0	0.0	0.0
F_{15}^A	271	271	9	9	11	11	0.0	0.0	0.0	0.0	0.0	0.0
F_5^B	496	9	179	7	9	9	0.0	0.0	0.0	0.0	0.0	0.0
F_{10}^B	–	9	86378	7	9	9	–	0.0	2.1	0.0	0.0	0.0
F_{15}^B	–	9	–	7	9	9	–	0.0	–	0.0	0.0	0.0
A_2	27	23	36	25	13	13	0.0	0.0	0.0	0.0	0.0	0.0
A_3	344	296	206	82	199	199	0.0	0.0	0.0	0.0	0.0	0.0
A_4	38209	19034	76811	39	179	179	0.5	0.3	12.9	0.1	0.1	0.1
A_5	–	–	263346	4027	188499	188499	–	–	90.8	3.1	90.8	90.7
A_6	–	–	–	–	–	–	–	–	–	–	–	–

5.2 Benchmarks

Our benchmarks stem from the AVACS[1] benchmark suite. The M and N examples ("Mutual Exclusion") are industrial benchmarks which come from a case study that models a real-time protocol to ensure mutual exclusion of a state in a distributed system via asynchronous communication. The protocol is described in full detail by Dierks [3]. The C examples ("Single-tracked Line Segment") stem from a case study from an industrial project partner of the UniForM project [12] where the problem is to design a distributed real-time controller for a segment of tracks where trams share a piece of track. For the evaluation of our approach we chose the property that both directions are never given simultaneously permission to enter the shared segment. In both case

---

[1] http://www.avacs.org/

Table 2. Experimental results in terms of error trace length for the heuristics d^L, d^U, h^L, h^U in comparison to h^{CG} and h^{CG} with safe abstraction (denoted with h^{CG}_{safe}). Dashes indicate exhaustion of memory (> 1 GB). Abbreviations: #a: number of parallel automata, #vars: number of integer and clock variables, #safe: number of variables removed by safe abstraction. For h^{CG}_{safe}, trace lengths reported as $x + y$ denote trace length x for the abstract error trace and $x + y$ for the concrete error trace.

Instance	#a	#vars	#safe	d^L	d^U	h^L	h^U	h^{CG}	h^{CG}_{safe}
C_1	5	15	0	1167	1058	100	73	118	118
C_2	6	17	1	1847	1674	132	99	169	118 + 0
C_3	6	18	1	2153	1214	128	86	167	118 + 0
C_4	7	20	2	6805	2949	344	139	354	125 + 5
C_5	8	22	3	35067	11696	1057	300	1034	125 + 9
C_6	9	24	4	–	–	3217	864	4167	132 + 14
C_7	10	26	5	–	–	–	2412	–	139 + 19
C_8	10	27	5	–	–	–	–	–	132 + 16
C_9	10	28	5	–	–	–	–	–	192 + 30
M_1	3	15	0	2779	106224	457	71	231	231
M_2	4	17	1	11739	13952	1124	119	395	240 + 3
M_3	4	17	1	12701	337857	748	124	361	205 + 4
M_4	5	19	2	51402	290937	3381	160	642	219 + 7
N_1	3	18	0	3565	2669	26053	99	243	243
N_2	4	20	0	18180	415585	1679	154	376	376
N_3	4	20	0	20021	262642	799	147	232	232
N_4	5	22	0	90467	51642	2455	314	478	478
F_5^A	6	6	0	218	218	8	8	8	8
F_{10}^A	11	11	0	218	218	8	8	8	8
F_{15}^A	16	16	0	218	218	8	8	8	8
F_5^B	5	6	0	79	6	12	6	6	6
F_{10}^B	10	11	0	–	6	22	6	6	6
F_{15}^B	15	16	0	–	6	–	6	6	6
A_2	8	0	0	22	13	21	21	12	12
A_3	16	0	0	169	39	24	18	24	24
A_4	32	0	0	867	129	42	28	36	36
A_5	64	0	0	–	–	112	47	56	56
A_6	128	0	0	–	–	–	–	–	–

studies, a subtle error has been inserted by manipulating a delay so that the asynchronous communication between these automata is faulty.

The F^A and F^B examples are flawed versions of the *Fischer protocol* for mutual exclusion (cf. [16]). The difference between F^A and F^B is in the way they encode the error condition.

As a final set of benchmarks, we use the *arbiter trees* case study, which models a mutual exclusion protocol based on a tree of binary arbiters [19]. Client processes are situated at the leaves of the tree. The benchmarks A_2–A_6 contain arbiter trees of height 2–6, with an exponentially growing number of processes.

5.3 Results

We compare the h^{CG} heuristic and the safe abstraction technique based on causal graph analysis with the heuristics d^L, d^U [6,5], h^L and h^U [13] as implemented in MCTA. We compare the number of explored states, the search time in seconds (Table 1) and the length of the found error traces (Table 2). Table 2 also gives additional information about the benchmark models, such as the number of parallel processes and the number of processes removed by safe abstraction.

The results show that our distance function is competitive with the previous approaches. In addition, safe abstraction leads to significantly better performance when applicable. We observe that the h^{CG} heuristic is much more accurate than the d^L and d^U heuristics. Due to better guidance, significantly fewer states are explored until an error state is found, leading to much better overall performance in most cases. Moreover, the error traces found by h^{CG} are significantly shorter than those obtained by d^L and d^U. This significant improvement is particularly interesting because of the connection between h^{CG} and d^U (recall that for independent processes, the cost estimates of h^{CG} and d^U are equal). The experimental results further show that h^{CG} is competitive with h^L, although somewhat less informed than h^U.

Considering the results for safe abstraction, we observe that in models that contain independent variables, the model reduction obtained by safe abstraction leads to a significant performance gain with h^{CG}. Moreover, the computational overhead to find such variables is low (a fraction of a second).

6 Conclusions

We have introduced the causal graph structure to directed model checking and demonstrated it to be a useful concept for error detection. We have adapted a distance estimation function from AI planning based on causal graph analysis, which is competitive with other distance heuristics in MCTA. Further, we presented an abstraction with the property that reachable abstract error states are guaranteed to correspond to reachable error states in the original system. We have shown that such safe abstractions can significantly improve the overall performance of a directed model checking algorithm when applicable, while requiring very little preprocessing overhead when not applicable.

In the future, it will be interesting to consider further extensions of the causal graph concept, in particular the question of how to deal with cycles in the causal graph more directly (see also [9]). In contrast to the approach presented in this paper, where cycles are resolved through a statically imposed ordering of processes, this could also be done *dynamically* during search. Furthermore, there seems to be potential to consider "larger" local subproblems than we have done, in order to improve the precision of the h^{CG} estimator. We expect that these approaches will allow further advances in the practical performance of directed model checking approaches.

Acknowledgments

This work was partly supported by the German Research Foundation (DFG) as part of the Transregional Collaborative Research Center "Automatic Verification and Analysis of Complex Systems" (SFB/TR 14 AVACS, http://www.avacs.org/).

References

1. Brafman, R.I., Domshlak, C.: Structure and complexity in planning with unary operators. Journal of Artificial Intelligence Research 18, 315–349 (2003)
2. Clarke, E.M., Grumberg, O., Peled, D.A.: Model Checking. The MIT Press, Cambridge (2000)
3. Dierks, H.: Comparing model-checking and logical reasoning for real-time systems. Formal Aspects of Computing 16(2), 104–120 (2004)
4. Dräger, K., Finkbeiner, B., Podelski, A.: Directed model checking with distance-preserving abstractions. In: Valmari, A. (ed.) SPIN 2006. LNCS, vol. 3925, pp. 19–34. Springer, Heidelberg (2006)
5. Edelkamp, S., Leue, S., Lluch-Lafuente, A.: Directed explicit-state model checking in the validation of communication protocols. International Journal on Software Tools for Technology Transfer 5(2), 247–267 (2004)
6. Edelkamp, S., Lluch-Lafuente, A., Leue, S.: Directed explicit model checking with HSF-SPIN. In: Dwyer, M.B. (ed.) SPIN 2001. LNCS, vol. 2057, pp. 57–79. Springer, Heidelberg (2001)
7. Helmert, M.: A planning heuristic based on causal graph analysis. In: Zilberstein, S., Koehler, J., Koenig, S. (eds.) Proceedings of the 14th International Conference on Automated Planning and Scheduling (ICAPS 2004), pp. 161–170. AAAI Press, Menlo Park (2004)
8. Helmert, M.: The Fast Downward planning system. Journal of Artificial Intelligence Research 26, 191–246 (2006)
9. Helmert, M., Geffner, H.: Unifying the causal graph and additive heuristics. In: Rintanen, J., Nebel, B., Beck, J.C., Hansen, E. (eds.) Proceedings of the 18th International Conference on Automated Planning and Scheduling (ICAPS 2008). AAAI Press, Menlo Park (2008)
10. Hoffmann, J., Smaus, J.-G., Rybalchenko, A., Kupferschmid, S., Podelski, A.: Using predicate abstraction to generate heuristic functions in Uppaal. In: Edelkamp, S., Lomuscio, A. (eds.) MoChArt IV. LNCS, vol. 4428, pp. 51–66. Springer, Heidelberg (2007)
11. Kozen, D.: Lower bounds for natural proof systems. In: Proceedings of the 18th Annual Symposium on Foundations of Computer Science (FOCS 1977), pp. 254–266. IEEE Computer Society, Los Alamitos (1977)
12. Krieg-Brückner, B., Peleska, J., Olderog, E.-R., Baer, A.: The UniForM workbench, a universal development environment for formal methods. In: Woodcock, J.C.P., Davies, J., Wing, J.M. (eds.) FM 1999. LNCS, vol. 1709, pp. 1186–1205. Springer, Heidelberg (1999)
13. Kupferschmid, S., Hoffmann, J., Dierks, H., Behrmann, G.: Adapting an AI planning heuristic for directed model checking. In: Valmari, A. (ed.) SPIN 2006. LNCS, vol. 3925, pp. 35–52. Springer, Heidelberg (2006)
14. Kupferschmid, S., Hoffmann, J., Larsen, K.G.: Fast directed model checking via russian doll abstraction. In: Ramakrishnan, C.R., Rehof, J. (eds.) TACAS 2008. LNCS, vol. 4963, pp. 203–217. Springer, Heidelberg (2008)
15. Kupferschmid, S., Wehrle, M., Nebel, B., Podelski, A.: Faster than UPPAAL? In: Gupta, A., Malik, S. (eds.) CAV 2008. LNCS, vol. 5123, pp. 552–555. Springer, Heidelberg (2008)
16. Lamport, L.: A fast mutual exclusion algorithm. ACM Transactions on Computer Systems 5(1), 1–11 (1987)
17. Pearl, J.: Heuristics: Intelligent search strategies for computer problem solving. Addison-Wesley, Reading (1984)
18. Qian, K., Nymeyer, A.: Guided invariant model checking based on abstraction and symbolic pattern databases. In: Jensen, K., Podelski, A. (eds.) TACAS 2004. LNCS, vol. 2988, pp. 497–511. Springer, Heidelberg (2004)
19. Seitz, C.L.: Ideas about arbiters. Lambda 1, 10–14 (1980)

Proving the Correctness of the Implementation of a Control-Command Algorithm

Olivier Bouissou

CEA LIST, Laboratory of Modelling and Analysis of Systems in Interaction,
Point Courrier 94, Gif-sur-Yvette, F-91191 France
Olivier.Bouissou@cea.fr

Abstract. In this article, we study the interactions between a control-command program and its physical environment via sensors and actuators. We are interested in finding invariants on the continuous trajectories of the physical values that the program is supposed to control. The invariants we are looking for are periodic sequences of intervals that are abstractions of the values read by the program. To compute them, we first build octrees that abstract the impact of the program on its environment. Then, we compute a period of the abstract periodic sequence and we finally define the values of this sequence as the fixpoint of a monotone map. We present a prototype analyzer that computes such invariants for C programs using a simple specification language for describing the continuous environment. It shows good results on classical benchmarks for hybrid systems verification.

1 Introduction

The behavior of an embedded, control-command program depends on both a discrete system (the program) and a continuous system (the physical environment). The program constantly interacts with the environment, picking up physical values by means of sensors and modifying them via actuators. The goal of the program is usually to control its environment, i.e. it must ensure that some physical values remain stable by activating the right actuator at the right time. The correctness of a control-command program thus relies on two properties. First, we must prove that the program does not induce any bad behaviors, i.e. that no bugs were introduced by the developer. Formal methods, and in particular abstract interpretation techniques [8,9], are widely used to prove this for some kinds of bugs (either run-time error [1], errors due to the precision of floating point computations [25] or execution time validation [12]). Then, we must prove that the program correctly controls its environment. This is usually done on high level models like Simulink, via numerical simulations. Sometimes, formal methods are used on equivalent models like hybrid automata [10,17,18], but this has not been done on the program itself. We leave the notion of "a program correctly controlling its environment" voluntarily vague as it may cover many properties. For example, one may want to prove the stability of the continuous trajectories under the influence of the program (which was mainly studied for

J. Palsberg and Z. Su (Eds.): SAS 2009, LNCS 5673, pp. 102–119, 2009.

switched dynamical systems [19,29]), or one may try to prove that some region of the continuous state space is reached (which is the main goal of the existing analysis techniques on hybrid automata or equivalent models [18,23]).

In this article, we focus on proving the correctness of the control-command program, without having a particular property in mind. Actually, we provide an abstract interpretation based method to compute invariants on the trajectories of the continuous environment that are sufficient to check the properties of interest. These invariants, that hold for every execution of the program, are defined in Section 1.2. They allow us to prove that the implementation choices (frequency of the sensors, format of floating point numbers, . . .) do not modify the behavior of the control algorithm. We extend the work from [3], where we considered open loop programs, as we now take into account the action of the program on its environment. In the rest of this introduction, we present an example of the kind of programs that we consider (Section 1.1) and we recall the concrete model that we developed in [4] for such hybrid discrete-continuous systems (Section 1.2).

1.1   Introductory Example

We consider the so-called "two tanks system", well known from the hybrid system community [21]. It consists of two water tanks linked together by an horizontal tube (see Figure 1(a)). There is a constant input of water in the first tank, and a tube at the bottom of the second tank lets the water leave the system. At each instant, a controller monitors the water levels in both tanks and must keep them between safe bounds. To do so, it may act on two valves (v_1 and v_2 on Figure 1(a)) that control the flow of water in the horizontal tubes. The evolution of the water levels is governed by the differential equations of Figure 1(b), where $v_i = 0$ if the valve i is closed, and $v_i = 1$ otherwise.

A controller for this system is a synchronous, control-command program: at each time stamp, it reads values from sensors (the water levels), computes an answer (open or close each valve) and writes this answer to actually modify the physical system. This read-compute-write loop is well cadenced as the program is synchronous. An execution of this system typically runs as follows: the initial state consists of initial water levels in both tanks and an initial mode (open or close) for each valve. After an initialization period in which the system reaches its stable state, we observe a cyclic behavior: the water level in each tank follows a periodic evolution while the decisions made by the program (open or close the valves) are the same from one period to the other. This kind of behavior (an initialization phase followed by a periodic evolution) is typical of control-command systems and it is what we try to automatically exhibit in this article.

1.2   Concrete Model

We consider hybrid systems made of a pair (P, κ) where P is a program written in an extension of an imperative programming language and κ contains a set $\{F_c \ : \ c \in \mathbb{B}^m\}$ of ordinary differential equations (ODEs). Here $\mathbb{B} = \{0, 1\}$ is the concrete domain of boolean values and m is the number of (binary) actuators of

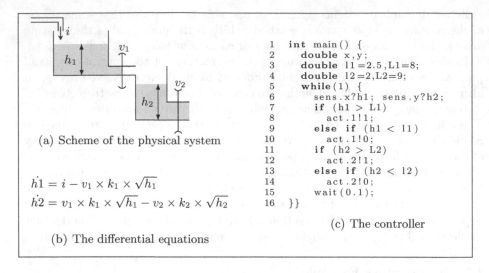

(a) Scheme of the physical system

$$\dot{h1} = i - v_1 \times k_1 \times \sqrt{h_1}$$
$$\dot{h2} = v_1 \times k_1 \times \sqrt{h_1} - v_2 \times k_2 \times \sqrt{h_2}$$

(b) The differential equations

```
1   int main() {
2       double x,y;
3       double l1=2.5,L1=8;
4       double l2=2,L2=9;
5       while(1) {
6           sens.x?h1; sens.y?h2;
7           if (h1 > L1)
8               act.1!1;
9           else if (h1 < l1)
10              act.1!0;
11          if (h2 > L2)
12              act.2!1;
13          else if (h2 < l2)
14              act.2!0;
15          wait(0.1);
16  }}
```

(c) The controller

Fig. 1. The two tanks system

the system. Each $c \in \mathbb{B}^m$ is a continuous mode, one dimension of c indicates the state of one actuator of the system. For each $c \in \mathbb{B}^m$, the function F_c defines an ODE that can govern the way the continuous environment behaves: the program chooses between these continuous modes via the actuators. At each instant, the state of the system thus consists of a state of the program P, a value for each continuous variable and a continuous mode $c \in \mathbb{B}^m$.

The extension of imperative programming languages that is used for P contains standard imperative statements plus three hybrid statements. The *sens.x?y* statement lets the program read values from the environment via sensors: it binds the value of the discrete variable x with the current value of the continuous variable y. The *act.i!b* statement (with $i \in [1, m]$, m being the number of actuators of the system, and $b \in \mathbb{B}$) lets the program change the upcoming continuous mode: it sets the ith dimension of the current continuous mode to b. Finally, the *wait* statement lets the program measure the continuous time.

The execution model is the following. The continuous and the discrete systems are processes that run in parallel and, from time to time, communicate. The time is governed by the program: we assume that all statements except *wait* are instantaneous so that the program computes the execution time. The communication from the environment to the program P is done via the *sens* statement: P reads the values $v \in \mathbb{R}^n$ of the continuous variables[1] at the time t the statement is executed. We write it $v \xrightarrow{t} P$. The communication from P to the environment is done via the *act* statement: P changes the ODE governing the dynamics from the time the statement is executed. When the *act.i!b* statement is executed, the ith dimension of the mode is changed to b, we write that: $P \xrightarrow{t} (i, b)$. The new continuous mode is then $c' \in \mathbb{B}^m$ such that c' is the vector c where the ith

---

[1] In this article, $\mathbb{R}$ (resp. $\mathbb{R}_+$) denotes the set of real (resp. non-negative real) numbers.

coordinate is changed to b. We write that $c' = c \oplus (i, b)$. If we apply various changes at once, we write $c \oplus \{(i_1, b_1), \ldots, (i_j, b_j)\}$. For example, if $c = [0; 1]$ and $c' = c \oplus \{(1, 1), (2, 0)\}$, then $c' = [1; 0]$. This corresponds to executing, at the same time stamp, the lines 8 and 14 of the program of Figure 1(c).

In this article, we are interested in the semantics of the continuous part of a hybrid system (P, κ), we will compute abstractions of it. We note $\llbracket P \rrbracket_c$ its continuous semantics: $\llbracket P \rrbracket_c$ is a function from $\mathbb{R}_+$ to $\mathbb{B}^m \times \mathbb{R}^n$ associating at each instant a continuous mode and a value such that:

$$\forall t \in \mathbb{R}_+, \ \llbracket P \rrbracket_c(t) = \big(c(t), y(t)\big) \text{ with } \dot{y}(t) = F_{c(t)}\big((y(t))\big) .$$

We only consider synchronous control-command programs that read values at the beginning of each cycle and act on its environment at the end of this cycle. If h is the duration of one cycle, we note $F_h : \mathbb{B}^m \times \mathbb{R}^n \to \mathbb{B}^m \times \mathbb{R}^n$ the concrete transition function defined as, with $(c, v) \in \mathbb{B}^m \times \mathbb{R}^n$:

$$F_h(c, v) = (c', v') \ : \ \exists t \in \mathbb{R}_+, \ \llbracket P \rrbracket_c(t) = (c, v) \text{ and } \llbracket P \rrbracket_c(t + h) = (c', v') . \tag{1}$$

In other words, the concrete transition function maps the state of the continuous system at the beginning of a cycle with the state of system at the beginning of the next cycle. On such hybrid systems, we look for invariants that overapproximate the continuous semantics $\llbracket P \rrbracket_c$, as defined in Definition 1. In this definition, as in the rest of this article, $\mathbf{I}$ denotes the complete lattice of n-dimensional boxes.

Definition 1 (Trajectory invariants). *A* trajectory invariant *of a control-command system* (P, κ) *is function* $\phi : \mathbb{R}_+ \to \mathbf{I}$, *such that:*
$\forall t \in \mathbb{R}_+, \ \llbracket P \rrbracket_c(t) = \big(c(t), y(t)\big) \text{ with } y(t) \in \phi(t).$
A discrete trajectory invariant *is a sequence* $\tilde{\phi} : \mathbb{N} \to \mathbf{I}$ *such that, if h is the duration of one cycle of P:* $\forall k \in \mathbb{N}, \ \llbracket P \rrbracket_c(k \times h) = \big(c(k), y(k)\big) \text{ with } y(k) \in \tilde{\phi}(k).$

The main contribution of this paper is to provide a method for computing discrete trajectory invariants for control-command program given in the formalism presented in this section. While existing analysis techniques for hybrid systems are specialized for proving a certain kind of property on high-level models, this work focuses on inferring the most general invariants on code-level models.

Example 1. Figure 1(c) shows a program P for the two-tanks system written in this language. The whole system is then $\big(P, \{F_{0,0}, F_{0,1}, F_{1,0}, F_{1,1}\}\big)$ where $F_{i,j}$ corresponds to the ODE of Figure 1(b) with $v_1 = i$ and $v_2 = j$. For example, line 8 in the program represents the action of opening the valve v_1.

Outline of the paper. In Section 2, we informally explain the main ideas of our analysis. In Section 3, we present the domains that we use and we study their properties. In Sections 4 and 5, we present our three-steps analysis. Section 6 presents our implementation while Section 7 presents concluding remarks.

2   Informal Presentation of the Analysis

We thus consider a control-command program together with a specification of its environment encoded in the model presented in Section 1.2, and try to derive discrete trajectory invariants of it. Our analysis proceeds in three steps. First, we compute an abstraction of F_h. To do that, we use an abstraction of the program (see Section 4) as a set of boolean functions that answer the following questions: given an input v, will the jth act statement be activated ? Then, we look for an overapproximation of the sequence of values read by the program. In order to finitely represent this infinite sequence, we try to exhibit an abstract periodic behavior, i.e. an ultimately periodic sequence of intervals that contains all the values read by the sensors. We first look for a period in this abstract sequence (see Section 5.2). Note that if there is no periodic behavior in the concrete sequence, we will obtain a period of 1 in the abstract sequence, meaning that we only bind the values by an interval. So, our analysis always terminates, even if there is no periodic evolution in the first place. On the other hand, if there is a periodic behavior in the system, we will exhibit it. Once we have the period for the abstract sequence, we compute the values of that sequence (see Section 5.3) as the fixpoint of a monotone map on a complete lattice.

In the rest of the article, n will denote the number of sensors, m the number of binary actuators and h the period of one cycle of the system, i.e. the program reads values at time $t_k = k \times h$, $\forall k \in \mathbb{N}$. We also note m_a the number of act statements in the program, and for each $j \in [1, m_a]$, we note $i_j \in [1, m]$ the dimension and $b_j \in \mathbb{B}$ the boolean value such that the jth act statement is $act.i_j!b_j$. So, for each $j \in [1, m_a]$, if the jth statement is executed at time t_k, we have $P \xrightarrow{t_k} (i_j, b_j)$. For example, if the second act statement in Figure 1(c) is executed, we have $P \xrightarrow{t_k} (1, 0)$. If this comes in response to an input $v \in \mathbb{R}^n$ (i.e. if at time t_k, the program also read v), we write: $(v \xrightarrow{t_k} P) \Rightarrow (P \xrightarrow{t_k} (i_j, b_j))$.

In order to reduce the complexity of defining an abstraction of the transition function F_h, we will assume in the rest of this article that the program is *time-invariant*, i.e. the action it takes in response to a read value v does not depend on the time this value was read. In other words, if at some time t_k the program reads the value v and then activates an act statement, it will activate it again if the same value v is read at time $t_{k'} \neq t_k$. This is formally stated in Definition 2.

Definition 2 (Time-invariant program). *We say that a program P is time-invariant if it holds, for all $v \in \mathbb{R}^n$ and for all $j \in [1, m_a]$, that:*

$$\left(\exists k \in \mathbb{N} : \left(v \xrightarrow{t_k} P \Rightarrow P \xrightarrow{t_k} (i_j, b_j) \right) \right) \implies \left(\forall k' \in \mathbb{N} : \left(v \xrightarrow{t_{k'}} P \Rightarrow P \xrightarrow{t_{k'}} (i_j, b_j) \right) \right).$$

We recall that m_a is the number of act *statements in the program and that for $j \in [1, m_a]$, the jth act statement is $act.i_j!b_j$.*

This assumption may be restrictive as it excludes, for example, a program that integrates its input values and activates the actuators based on this computation. However, many safety critical control-command programs are time-invariant.

3 Domains

The abstract boolean lattice is $\mathbf{B} = \{\perp_{\mathbf{B}}, \mathbf{0}, \mathbf{1}, \top_{\mathbf{B}}\}$, with $\gamma_b : \mathbf{B} \rightarrow \mathcal{P}(\mathbb{B})$ being the canonical concretization. More generally, bold typed symbols represent abstract values while normal symbols represent concrete values. The symbol v (resp. $\mathbf{v}$) refers to the concrete (resp. abstract) state for the continuous variables, i.e. $v \in \mathbb{R}^n$ and $\mathbf{v} \in \mathbf{I}$. The symbol c (resp. $\mathbf{c}$) refers to the concrete (resp. abstract) continuous mode, i.e. $c \in \mathbb{B}^m$ and $\mathbf{c} \in \mathbf{B}^m$.

3.1   Abstract Continuous State

The state of the continuous environment is given by a vector of real values (for the continuous variables) and the continuous mode that governs its evolution. Continuous variables are abstracted by boxes. Continuous modes are elements of $\mathbb{B}^m$, we abstract them by elements of $\mathbf{B}^m$ and define $\mathbf{M} = \mathbf{B}^m$. We note $\gamma_{\mathbf{M}} : \mathbf{M} \to \mathcal{P}(\mathbb{B}^m)$ the canonical concretization function. The set $\mathbf{M}$ is a complete lattice with order $\sqsubseteq_{\mathbf{M}}$, supremum $\top_{\mathbf{M}}$, infimum $\bot_{\mathbf{M}}$, join $\sqcup_{\mathbf{M}}$ and meet $\sqcap_{\mathbf{M}}$.

Definition 3 (Abstract continuous states). *The domain of abstract continuous states is* $\mathbf{S} = \mathbf{M} \times \mathbf{I}$. *The concretization function* $\gamma_{\mathbf{s}}$ *is defined componentwise and the order* $\sqsubseteq_{\mathbf{s}}$ *is defined as:*

$$\forall (\mathbf{c}, \mathbf{v}), (\mathbf{c}', \mathbf{v}') \in \mathbf{S}, (\mathbf{c}, \mathbf{v}) \sqsubseteq_{\mathbf{s}} (\mathbf{c}', \mathbf{v}') \Leftrightarrow ((\mathbf{c} \sqsubseteq_{\mathbf{M}} \mathbf{c}') \wedge (\mathbf{v} \subseteq \mathbf{v})) .$$

We also introduce a notion of distance between abstract states, based on the Hausdorff distance $d_H : \mathbf{I} \times \mathbf{I} \to \mathbb{R}_+$ defined by:

$$d_H(\mathbf{v}, \mathbf{v}') = \max \left(\max_{x \in \mathbf{v}} \left\{ \min_{y \in \mathbf{v}'} |x - y| \right\}, \max_{x \in \mathbf{v}'} \left\{ \min_{y \in \mathbf{v}} |x - y| \right\} \right) .$$

Definition 4 (Distance on continuous states). *The distance between two abstract states* $(\mathbf{c}, \mathbf{v})$ *and* $(\mathbf{c}', \mathbf{v}')$ *is:*

$$d_{\mathbf{s}}((\mathbf{c}, \mathbf{v}), (\mathbf{c}', \mathbf{v}')) = \begin{cases} \infty & \textit{if } \mathbf{c} \not\sqsubseteq_{\mathbf{M}} \mathbf{c}' \textit{ and } \mathbf{c}' \not\sqsubseteq_{\mathbf{M}} \mathbf{c} \\ d_H(\mathbf{v}, \mathbf{v}') & \textit{otherwise} \end{cases} .$$

Intuitively, if two states $(\mathbf{c_1}, \mathbf{v_1})$ and $(\mathbf{c_2}, \mathbf{v_2})$ are close enough, then the possible evolutions of the dynamical system starting from two points within $\gamma_{\mathbf{s}}(\mathbf{c_1}, \mathbf{v_1})$ and $\gamma_{\mathbf{s}}(\mathbf{c_2}, \mathbf{v_2})$ remain close. This is the reason for the first condition in the definition of $d_{\mathbf{s}}$: if two states have incomparable modes, then their future evolution may be completely different, as different modes represent significantly different dynamics (for example, in Figure 1(b), the various modes represent the fact that the two valves are closed or open, leading to an increase or a decrease in the water levels). Their distance is thus set to ∞ to notice that they may lead to significantly different trajectories.

3.2   Cyclic Sequences of States

We abstract infinite sequences of states by *cyclic sequences*. A cyclic sequence is a pair made of a *lasso shaped graph* and a function linking each vertex of the graph to an abstract continuous state. A lasso shaped graph (also used in [16] to prove non-termination of programs) is a finite, directed graph G composed of two linked subgraphs: a *stem* and a *loop*. The *size* of the graph G, noted $|G|$, is the number of vertices. The *loop size* (resp. *stem size*) of the graph is the number of vertices in the loop (resp. stem): we note it $|G|_l$ (resp. $|G|_s$). For a graph G, V_G denotes its vertices and E_g its edges.

Definition 5 (Cyclic sequences). *A cyclic sequence over the domain* $\mathbf{S}$ *is a pair* $\mathbf{s} = (G, f)$ *where* G *is a lasso shaped graph and* $f : V_G \to \mathbf{S}$ *maps vertices of* G *with abstract states. We note* $\mathbf{S}^{\circlearrowleft}$ *the set of all cyclic sequences over* $\mathbf{S}$.

Cyclic sequences are finite representations of infinite sequences of abstract states. Let $\mathbf{s} = (G, f) \in \mathbf{S}^{\circlearrowleft}$, with $V_G = \{w_0, \ldots, w_{p-1}\}$, and let i be the index of the first vertex within the loop: $i = |G|_s$. We note $\hat{\mathbf{s}} : \mathbb{N} \to \mathbf{S}$ the function defined by:

$$\forall k \in \mathbb{N}, \ \hat{\mathbf{s}}(k) = \begin{cases} f(w_k) & \text{if } k < |G| \\ \perp_{\mathbf{s}} & \text{if } k \geq |G| \text{ and } |G|_l = 0 \\ f(w_{(p+(k-i \ \text{mod} \ |G|_l)})) & \text{otherwise} \end{cases} .$$

Example 2. Figure 4 in Section 6 shows an example of a cyclic sequence: it is the invariant computed on the trajectories of the heater problem (see Section 6).

Definition 6 (Order on cyclic sequences). *The order* $\sqsubseteq^{\circlearrowleft}$ *is the point-wise extension of the order on abstract states, if the sequences have the same graph. Formally, we have, for* $\mathbf{s_1} = (G_1, f_1) \in \mathbf{S}^{\circlearrowleft}$ *and* $\mathbf{s_2} = (G_2, f_2) \in \mathbf{S}^{\circlearrowleft}$:

$$\mathbf{s_1} \sqsubseteq^{\circlearrowleft} \mathbf{s_2} \Leftrightarrow G_1 = G_2 \text{ and } \forall w \in G_1, \ f_1(w) \sqsubseteq_{\mathbf{s}} f_2(w) .$$

Note that this definition implies, in particular, that $\forall k \in \mathbb{N}, \ \hat{\mathbf{s}}_1(k) \sqsubseteq_{\mathbf{s}} \hat{\mathbf{s}}_2(k)$. To define the join of two cyclic sequences, we introduce a new element $\top^{\circlearrowleft} \in \mathbf{S}^{\circlearrowleft}$ such that $\forall \mathbf{s} \in \mathbf{S}, \ \mathbf{s} \sqsubseteq^{\circlearrowleft} \top^{\circlearrowleft}$. The join of two cyclic sequences $\mathbf{s_1}, \mathbf{s_2} \in \mathbf{S}^{\circlearrowleft}$ is then defined as follows: if $\mathbf{s_1}$ and $\mathbf{s_2}$ share the same graph, we make the union of the states associated to each vertex, otherwise, we return $\top^{\circlearrowleft}$. Formally we have:

$$\forall \mathbf{s_1}, \mathbf{s_2} \in \mathbf{S}^{\circlearrowleft}, \ \mathbf{s_1} \sqcup^{\circlearrowleft} \mathbf{s_2} = \begin{cases} \top^{\circlearrowleft} & \text{if } G_1 \neq G_2 \\ (G_1, f) : \forall w \in G_1, f(w) = f_1(w) \sqcup_{\mathbf{s}} f_2(w) & \text{otherwise} \end{cases} . \quad (2)$$

Let us remark that if $\mathbf{s} = \mathbf{s_1} \sqcup^{\circlearrowleft} \mathbf{s_2}$, $\mathbf{s} \neq \top^{\circlearrowleft}$, then $\forall k \in \mathbb{N}, \ \hat{\mathbf{s}}(k) = \hat{\mathbf{s}}_1(k) \sqcup_{\mathbf{s}} \hat{\mathbf{s}}_1(k)$. We define in the same way the intersection of $\mathbf{s_1}$ and $\mathbf{s_2}$: if they share the same graph, we compute the meet of the values associated to each vertex. Otherwise, we set the meet to be the $\perp^{\circlearrowleft}$, a new element of $\mathbf{S}^{\circlearrowleft}$ such that $\forall \mathbf{s} \in \mathbf{S}^{\circlearrowleft}, \ \perp^{\circlearrowleft} \sqsubseteq^{\circlearrowleft} \mathbf{s}$.

Property 1. The domain $(\mathbf{S}^{\circlearrowleft}, \sqsubseteq^{\circlearrowleft}, \sqcup^{\circlearrowleft}, \sqcap^{\circlearrowleft})$ is a complete lattice.

Proof. As $\mathbf{S}$ is a complete lattice, so is the domain of functions $V_G \to \mathbf{S}$ for some lasso graph $G = (V_G, E_G)$. As two elements of $\mathbf{S}^{\circlearrowleft}$ are comparable if and only if they share the same graph, this proves that $\mathbf{S}^{\circlearrowleft}$ is a complete lattice. $\square$

Definition 7 (Concretization $\gamma^{\circlearrowleft}$**).** *The concretization* $\gamma^{\circlearrowleft} : \mathbf{S}^{\circlearrowleft} \to \mathcal{P}(\mathbb{N} \to \mathbb{R}^n)$ *maps a cyclic sequence with infinitely many concrete sequences:*

$$\forall \mathbf{s} \in \mathbf{S}^{\circlearrowleft}, \ \gamma^{\circlearrowleft}(\mathbf{s}) = \{s : \mathbb{N} \to \mathbb{R}^n \ : \ \forall k \in \mathbb{N}, \exists b \in \mathbb{B}^m, (b, s(k)) \in \gamma_{\mathbf{s}}(\hat{\mathbf{s}}(k))\} .$$

Property 2. The function $\gamma^{\circlearrowleft}$ is monotone.

4 Abstraction of the Program

We now explain how, with the assumption of Section 2, we compute an abstraction of the program that is sufficient for computing the abstraction of the iteration function. In this way, we split our analysis of the hybrid system in two steps: first (in this section) we focus on the discrete program, then (in Section 5) we use this program abstraction and we focus on the continuous environment.

4.1 Definition of a Program Abstraction

To build the program abstraction, we see a program as a decision function that, given an input (the value read by the sensor), decides whether or not each actuator must be activated. In other words, we are only interested in the impact a program has on its environment and not in its intern evolution. For the jth *act* statement in the program, we consider the boolean function $\Phi_j : \mathbb{R}^n \to \mathbb{B}$ defined by $\Phi_j(v) = 1$ if $\left((v \xrightarrow{t_k} P) \Rightarrow (P \xrightarrow{t_k} (i_j, b_j))\right)$, and $\Phi_j(v) = 0$ otherwise. In other words, Φ_j returns 1 if, when the program reads the value v, it activates the jth *act* statement, and 0 otherwise. A program abstraction (see Definition 8) is a collection of boolean inclusion functions that safely abstract these functions.

Definition 8 (Program abstraction). *Let* (P, κ) *be a system of our concrete model with* m_a *binary actuators. An abstraction of the program consists of* m_a *inclusion boolean functions* $[\Phi_1], \ldots, [\Phi_{m_a}] : \mathbf{I} \to \mathbf{B}$, *such that:*

$$\forall \mathbf{v} \in \mathbf{I},\; j \in [1, m_a], \begin{cases} [\Phi_j](\mathbf{v}) = 1 & if\; (\forall v \in \mathbf{v},\; v \xrightarrow{t_k} P \Rightarrow P \xrightarrow{t_k} (i_j, b_j)) \\ [\Phi_j](\mathbf{v}) = 0 & if\; (\forall v \in \mathbf{v},\; v \xrightarrow{t_k} P \Rightarrow P \xrightarrow{t_k} (i_j, b_j)) \\ [\Phi_j](\mathbf{v}) = \top_B & otherwise \end{cases} \cdot$$

With the assumption that the program is time-invariant (see Section 2), we can compute such program abstractions using standard reachability analysis for imperative programs. It suffices to check if, with an input $\mathbf{v} \in \mathbf{I}$, the program reaches the jth *act* statement (for example, [6,7] or even [5] can be used to do that). We can thus compute, for each *act* statement of the program, the function $[\Phi_j]$. However, the computation of $[\Phi_j](\mathbf{v})$ can be computationally expensive for large programs, and we will need to compute that often. Thus, we chose to partition, for each $j \in [1, m_a]$, the input state space into three regions R_0^j, R_1^j and $R_\top^j$ in such a way that, if $\mathbf{v} \subseteq R_\mathbf{b}^j$, then $[\Phi_j](\mathbf{v}) = \mathbf{b}$ for all $\mathbf{b} \in \mathbf{B}$. These regions serve as a program abstraction: to decide whether an actuator is activated, we just need to check in which region the input lies.

4.2 Representation as Octrees

A n-dimension *octree*[2] is a directed, acyclic graph with a unique root and two kinds of nodes: non terminal nodes $N(\mathbf{v})$, with $\mathbf{v} \in \mathbf{I}$ and terminal nodes $V(\mathbf{b})$

---

[2] The term *octree* is generally used for 3-dimension trees only (i.e. trees with 8 children for each node). We here use it for the more general case of n-dimension trees.

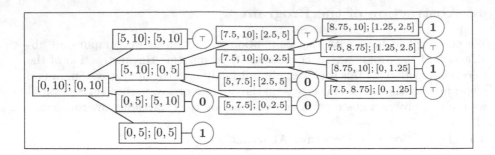

Fig. 2. A 2-dimension octree T with domain $[0, 10] \times [0, 10]$. It verifies $T([1,3];[2;4]) = 1$ and $T([1,3];[4;6])) = \top_{\mathbf{B}}$.

with $\mathbf{b} \in \mathbf{B}$. Each non terminal node $N(\mathbf{v})$ has either one terminal child or 2^n non terminal children $N_i(\mathbf{v_i})$, $i \in [1, 2^n]$, with: $\forall i, j \in [1, 2^n]$, $\mathbf{v_i} \cap \mathbf{v_j} = \emptyset$ and $\bigsqcup_{i \in [1,2^n]} \mathbf{v_i} = \mathbf{v}$. We note $\mathbf{T}$ the set of all n-dimension octrees. The root of an octree T must be a non terminal node $N(\mathbf{v})$, and we say that $\mathbf{v}$ is the domain of T, denoted $\mathbf{v} = dom(T)$. Figure 2 shows an example of a 2-dimension octree.

An octree $T \in \mathbf{T}$ represents a partition of the state space into the three regions R_0, R_1 and $R_\top$ mentioned before. Now, for an input $\mathbf{v} \in dom(T)$, we check efficiently in which region it is included by computing $T(v)$ defined by $T(\mathbf{v}) = \bigsqcup \{\mathbf{b} \ : \ \exists \ N(\mathbf{v'}) \in T, \ \mathbf{v} \cap \mathbf{v'} \neq \emptyset$ and $N(\mathbf{v'})$ has a child $V(\mathbf{b})\}$. The value $T(v)$ is thus the join of all $\mathbf{b} \in \mathbf{B}$ such that $\mathbf{v}$ intersects the region $R_{\mathbf{b}}$.

Property 3. For every octree T, the function $F_T : dom(T) \rightarrow \mathbf{B}$ defined by $\forall \mathbf{v} \in dom(T)$, $F_T(\mathbf{v}) = T(\mathbf{v})$ is monotone.

Proof. Let $\mathbf{v_1}$, $\mathbf{v_2} \in dom(T)$ with $\mathbf{v_1} \subseteq \mathbf{v_2}$. Let S be the set of non terminal nodes $N(\mathbf{v_k})$ of T with a child $V(\mathbf{b_k})$ such that $\mathbf{v_k} \cap \mathbf{v_1} \neq \emptyset$. Then, $T(\mathbf{v_1}) = \sqcup\{\mathbf{b_k} \ : \ N(\mathbf{v_k}) \in S\}$. Let now $N(\mathbf{v_k}) \in S$. As $\mathbf{v_1} \subseteq \mathbf{v_2}$, it holds that $\mathbf{v_k} \cap \mathbf{v_2} \neq \emptyset$, so that $\mathbf{b_k} \sqsubseteq_{\mathbf{B}} T(\mathbf{v_2})$. This implies that $T(\mathbf{v_1}) \sqsubseteq_{\mathbf{B}} T(\mathbf{v_2})$. $\qquad\square$

We use Algorithm 1 to compute an octree that represents the regions R_0, R_1 and $R_\top$ for one *act* statement of the program. Theorem 1 shows that these octrees are sound program abstractions.

Theorem 1. *For every time-invariant program P with m_a act statement, and for every $j \in [1, m_a]$, the octree $T_j = \texttt{BuildOctree}(P, j)$ verifies that:*

$$\forall \mathbf{v} \subseteq dom(T_j), \ \forall v \in \mathbf{v}, \ \Phi_j(v) \in \gamma_b(T_j(\mathbf{v})) \ .$$

We recall that Φ_j is the concrete function deciding whether the jth act statement is activated given some input values, see Section 4.1.

Remark 1. The maximal depth of the octrees computed in Algorithm 1 is a time-precision trade-off: deeper octrees are more precise but the computation time is exponential in this maximal depth.

```
Input: P;                           /* A time-invariant program */
Input: D ∈ I;                       /* Range for the input variables of P */
Input: j, N_max ∈ N;   /* The actuator to reach and the maximal depth */
Result: An octree T of maximal depth N_max

start
    T = N(D);                       /* Initialize the octree and set its root */
    b = [Φ_j](D);
    if b = ⊤_B ∧ N_max ≠ 0 then
        Find v_1, ..., v_{2^n} such that D = v_1 ⊔ v_2 ⊔ ··· ⊔ v_{2^n};
        for every v ∈ {v_1, ..., v_{2^n}} do
            aux = BuildOctree(P, v, j, N_max − 1); Add aux as a child of T;
        done
    else
        Add V(b) as a child of T;
    endif
    return T;
end
```

Algorithm 1. BuildOctree(P,D,j,N_{max}): construction of an octree of domain **D** and depth N_{max} that represents the function [Φ_j]

5 Abstraction of the Continuous Evolution

In this section, we explain how, given an abstraction of the program as a set of octrees, we compute an abstraction of the evolution of the continuous environment as a cyclic sequence (see Section 3). This cyclic sequence is computed in two steps: first, we compute the lasso shaped graph and an initial guess for the values of the vertices, then we compute the values of each vertex of the graph. Both steps are based on an iteration of an *abstract transition function* that overapproximates the concrete transition function (see Section 1.2).

5.1 The Abstract Transition Function

For each continuous mode $c \in \mathbb{B}^m$, the environment evolves according to an ODE $\dot{y} = F_c(y)$ (see Section 1.2). So, if at some time t we have $[\![P]\!]_c(t) = (c, y_t)$ for $c \in \mathbb{B}^m$ and $y_t \in \mathbb{R}^n$, and if the program does not change the continuous mode between t and $t + h$, then we have $[\![P]\!]_c(t + h) = (c, y_\infty(h))$, i.e. $F_h(c, y_t) = (c, y_\infty(h))$, where y_∞ is the solution of the ODE $\dot{y} = F_c(y)$ with initial state $y_\infty(0) = y_t$. The theory of guaranteed integration [24] shows that it is possible to overapproximate y_∞. In particular, the library GRKLib [2] proposes a systematic way to compute a monotone function $[F_c] : I \times \mathbb{R}_+ \to I$ such that[3]:

$$\forall v \in I, \ \forall t, h \in \mathbb{R}_+, \ y_\infty(t) \in v \Rightarrow y_\infty(t + h) \in [F_c](v, h) .$$

Let us now define the abstract transition function $\mathbf{F_h}$ that overapproximates the concrete transition function F_h defined Section 1.2.

---

[3] Remark that there is no limitation on F_c: we consider linear and non-linear dynamics.

Definition 9 (Abstract transition function). *Let (P, κ) be a system of our concrete model, with $\kappa = \{F_c : c \in \mathbb{B}^m\}$, and let m_a be the number of act statements in P. Let $\{T_i : i \in [1, m_a]\}$ be a program abstraction as defined in Section 4. The abstract transition function $\mathbf{F_h}$ is a function between abstract states, $\mathbf{F_h} : \mathbf{S} \to \mathbf{S}$, defined by $\forall (\mathbf{c}, \mathbf{v}) \in \mathbf{S}$, $\mathbf{F_h}(\mathbf{c}, \mathbf{v}) = (\mathbf{c}', \mathbf{v}')$ with:*

$$\begin{cases} \mathbf{v}' = \bigsqcup_I \{[F_c](\mathbf{v}, h) : c \in \gamma_m(\mathbf{c})\} \\ \mathbf{c}' = \mathbf{c} \oplus \{(i_j, b_j) : j \in [1, m_a] \wedge \mathbf{1} \sqsubseteq_\mathbf{B} T_j(\mathbf{v}')\} \end{cases} .$$

We recall (see Section 1.2) that for a continuous mode $c \in \mathbb{B}^m$, an integer $i \in [1, m]$ and a boolean value $b \in \mathbb{B}$, $c \oplus (i, b)$ is the continuous mode c where the ith dimension is set to b. We use the same notation for abstract modes $\mathbf{c} \in \mathbf{M}$.

The abstract transition function $\mathbf{F_h}$ thus transforms an abstract state $(\mathbf{c}, \mathbf{v}) \in \mathbf{S}$ as follows: we compute the effect of every possible continuous modes $c \in \gamma_m(\mathbf{c})$ on $\mathbf{v}$ using the guaranteed integration function $[F_c]$, and then compute the join of all these evolutions to form the new abstract continuous state $\mathbf{v}'$. Then, for each *act* statement (i.e. for each $j \in [1, m_a]$) we check if it is activated under the input $\mathbf{v}'$ by computing $T_j(\mathbf{v}')$. For all those statements that are potentially activated (i.e. such that $\mathbf{1} \sqsubseteq_\mathbf{B} T_j(\mathbf{v}')$), we compute their effect on the continuous mode $\mathbf{c}$ by computing $\mathbf{c} \oplus (i_j, b_j)$.

Property 4. The abstract continuous function $\mathbf{F_h}$ is monotone over the complete lattice of continuous states (its monotonicity relies on the monotonicity of all the functions $[F_c]$ and T_j for $c \in \mathbb{B}^m$ and $j \in [1, m_a]$, see Property 3).

We can now state our main theorem for this section that proves that the abstract transition function is an abstraction of the concrete transition function.

Theorem 2. *Let (P, κ) be a control-command system, and let $\mathbf{F_h}$ be the function given at Definition 9. For all $(\mathbf{c}, \mathbf{v}) \in \mathbf{S}$, it holds that $F_h \circ \gamma_\mathbf{s}(\mathbf{c}, \mathbf{v}) \subseteq \gamma_\mathbf{s} \circ \mathbf{F_h}(\mathbf{c}, \mathbf{v})$.*

5.2   Constructing the Graph

The computation of the cyclic sequence that serves as a discrete trajectory invariant (see Definition 1) requires two steps: first, we need to compute the lasso-shaped graph, and then we need to compute the abstract values associated to each vertex. In this section, we focus on the first task. To build the graph, we use Algorithm 2 that we here explain. Starting from an initial cyclic sequence (G_0, f_0) whose graph contains only one vertex w with $f(w) = \mathbf{s}_0$, where $\mathbf{s}_0$ is the initial abstract continuous state, we iterate the following process. We first compute $\mathbf{s} = \mathbf{F_h}\big(f(v)\big)$, i.e. the abstract continuous state at the next time stamp. If we find a vertex w' in the graph such that $\mathbf{s} \sqsubseteq_\mathbf{s} f(w')$, then we make a loop between w and w' – this case means that the we already overapproximated the evolution of the environment up to $t = \infty$. If there is no such vertex w', then we compute the minimal distance between $\mathbf{s}$ and $f(w')$ for all vertices w'. If this distance is smaller than some threshold α, we make a loop between w and w' – this case means that we have computed the evolution of the continuous system

```
Input: (G₀, f₀),  α ;        /* Initial sequence and distance threshold */
Input: Fₕ ;                          /* Abstract transition function */
Result: A cyclic sequence (G, f)

start
    (G, f) = (G₀, f₀); w = w₀ ; // w is the last added vertex
    while |G|ₗ = 0 do
        s = Fₕ(f(v));
        if ∃w' ∈ V_G : s ⊑ₛ f(w') then
        |   E_g = E_G ∪ {(w, w')}; // The graph now contains a loop
        else
            d = min{dₛ(s, f(w')) : w' ∈ V_g};
            if d > α then
            |   V_G = V_G ∪ {w*} ; // w* is a new, fresh state
            |   f(w*) = s; E_g = E_G ∪ {(w, w*)}; w = w*;
            else
            |   Choose w' ∈ V_G such that dₛ(f(w'), s) < α;
            |   E_g = E_G ∪ {(w, w')}; // The graph now contains a loop
            endif
        endif
    done
    return (G, f);
end
```

Algorithm 2. BuildLassoGraph: construction of the initial lasso graph

from a state "close to" w. Otherwise, we add a new vertex to the graph and start over from this vertex.

Of course, this algorithm may not terminate or take a very long time before creating a loop. We enforce the termination by using a widening strategy on the threshold α: at each iteration (or every K iterations, where K is a predefined number), we increase α to capture more abstract periodic behaviors. The cyclic sequence we compute is always a safe abstraction of the beginning of the continuous evolution, as stated by Theorem 3 (a direct consequence of Theorem 2).

Theorem 3. *Let* $\mathbf{s} = (G, f)$ *be the cyclic sequence returned by the algorithm* $BuildLassoGraph$. *Then for all* $k \in [0, |G| - 1]$, *we have* $[\![P]\!]_c(k \times h) \in \gamma_\mathbf{s}(\hat{\mathbf{s}}(k))$.

Remark 2. At this point, we only have an overapproximation of $[\![P]\!]_c(k \times h)$ for all $k < |G|$ as, when we created the loop, we may have changed the value of one vertex without propagating it to its successors. This is done in Section 5.3.

Remark 3. Parameter α in Algorithm 2 is a time-precision trade-off: the larger α, the faster the algorithm terminates, and the larger the overapproximation is.

5.3   Computing the Values

We now explain how, starting from the initial cyclic sequence $\mathbf{s_o}$ computed by the Algorithm 2, we compute an overapproximation of the continuous evolution up to time ∞. To do so, we see the graph of the cyclic sequence as a control flow graph as used for the static analysis of programs. The transition function between two vertices of the graph is the abstract transition function $\mathbf{F_h}$. Thus, we define the function $\mathbf{F_S} : \mathbf{S}^\circlearrowleft \to \mathbf{S}^\circlearrowleft$ that updates the cyclic sequence as:

$$\mathbf{F_S} : \begin{cases} \mathbf{S}^\circlearrowleft \to \mathbf{S}^\circlearrowleft \\ (G,f) \mapsto (G,f') \text{ with } \forall w \in V_G, \ f'(w) = \bigsqcup_{(w',w) \in E_G} \mathbf{F_h}(f(w')) \end{cases}.$$

Property 5. The function $\mathbf{F_S}$ is monotone over the complete lattice $\mathbf{S}^\circlearrowleft$.

As $\mathbf{F_S}$ is a monotone function over a complete lattice, it has a least fixpoint greater than $\mathbf{s_0}$ (the cyclic sequence computed by Algorithm 2). We can compute it using Kleene's iteration. Theorem 4 shows that this fixpoint is an overapproximation of the concrete sequence of values read by the program.

Theorem 4. *Let* $\mathbf{s} \in \mathbf{S}^\circlearrowleft$ *be the least fixpoint of* $\mathbf{F_S}$ *greater than* $\mathbf{s_0}$, *and let* $[\![P]\!]_c(t) = (c(t), y(t))$ *for all* $t \in \mathbb{R}_+$. *Then, the sequence* $\big(y(k \times h)\big)_{k \in \mathbb{N}}$ *verifies* $\big(y(k \times h)\big)_{k \in \mathbb{N}} \in \gamma^\circlearrowleft(\mathbf{s})$, *i.e. we have:* $\forall k \in \mathbb{N}, \ [\![P]\!]_c(k \times h) \in \gamma_{\mathbf{s}}(\hat{\mathbf{s}}(k))$.

Theorem 4 states that the computed cyclic sequence is a discrete trajectory invariant of the program P, as defined in Definition 1. It may thus be used to prove more complex properties like stability or reachability.

Remark 4. To accelerate Kleene's iteration for computing the fixpoint of $\mathbf{F_S}$, we use standard widening techniques on abstract continuous states. The widening naturally occurs on the first vertex of the loop of the cyclic sequence.

5.4   Discussion about the Method

During the analysis, several operations may lead to a coarse approximation of the continuous trajectory. It is particularly the case if, during the iterations of $\mathbf{F_h}$, we obtain a state with the abstract mode $\top_M$ (or $\top_B$ in some direction). Then, as we don't know the continuous mode of the future evolution, we need to follow several modes. In the case of a control-command program, the different modes correspond to significantly different dynamics, so that following several of them lead to a huge overapproximation. There are various reasons for obtaining an imprecise abstract mode, we now explain them and we give some solutions on how to avoid them. Let thus $(\mathbf{c}, \mathbf{v}) \in \mathbf{S}$ be such that $\mathbf{F_h}(\mathbf{c}, \mathbf{v}) = (\mathbf{c}', \mathbf{v}')$, where $\mathbf{c}'$ contains $\top_B$ in at least one dimension.

Problems due to the program abstraction. We may obtain $\top_B$ because the box $\mathbf{v}'$ lies within the region $R_\top^j$ for some $j \in [1, m_a]$. This means that the program abstraction is too coarse. We can then locally increase the precision of the program abstractions by increasing the maximal depth we allow for the octrees. In this way, we will eventually enter the R_1^j or R_2^j regions. However, we might also enter both, which gives us another issue: if we have $\mathbf{v}' \cap R_1^j \neq \emptyset$ and $\mathbf{v}' \cap R_0^j \neq \emptyset$, then $T_j(v) = \top_B$, so $\mathbf{c}'$ contains $\top_B$ in the jth coordinate. To reduce the loss of precision in this case, we can follow separately the possible dynamics, and try to collect them later. This is very similar to the disjunctive analysis used in the static analysis of programs [27]. We use our notion of distance for joining the different paths. Of course, this technique may lead to a combinatorial explosion in the number of states of the system, so in practice we limit the number of steps we make within each dynamics.

Problems due to the guaranteed integration. Another source of imprecision comes from the overapproximation of the continuous dynamics due to the guaranteed integration, that may compute a too large box $\mathbf{v}'$. To reduce it, a solution consists in using local subdivisions: we split $\mathbf{v}$ into smaller boxes, compute $\mathbf{F_h}$ on each of them and then join the results. This is not guaranteed to reduce the imprecision, but it has good results when the continuous dynamics is stiff.

Some remarks on our notion of distance. The distance d_s indicates how close the evolutions of the system starting from two abstract states will be. Of course, it is difficult to know if two states will remain close with only the information of their distance at some instant t_k. If the states are close to a region where the mode must change, their evolutions might diverge, and we should not merge them. Another heuristic considering more than one time stamp could detect such situations. However, on contracting systems (i.e. systems in which the distance between two trajectories decreases with time), our method has good results.

Comparison with other techniques. Finally, we would like to make an informal comparison between our method for computing invariants on control-command systems and the existing analysis techniques for hybrid systems [13,15,18,26]. First, we consider linear and non-linear dynamics, which is almost never the case for the reachability analysis on hybrid automata. We also consider complicated discrete dynamics, as the only limitation on the program is that it must be time-invariant. Thus, the regions where there is a mode change may be very complicated: for example, in some control-command programs we analyzed, the decision for activating the actuator depends on the result of a Runge-Kutta integration predicting the value of the continuous variables one second later. The regions represented by the octree were then non convex and very irregular. Modeling such systems (frequent in industrial systems) with hybrid automata would be a very difficult task in its own. Finally, as we consider code-level models, we can focus on computing discrete trajectory invariants as the mode changes only occur at time t_k for some $k \in \mathbb{N}$, while analysis techniques on high-level models need to enclose the trajectories for all $t \in \mathbb{R}_+$ to detect the mode changes. Our task is thus simplified because we consider more realistic models. Let us remark that this approach is also used in [28] where the authors start from the very general model of hybrid automata and impose a periodicity condition for the control actions. We, at the opposite, start from a new model which is especially designed for such perdiodically controlled hybrid systems.

6   Experimentation

We implemented the techniques presented in this article in a prototype analyzer named HyPrA (for Hybrid Programs Analyzer). HyPrA is based on Newspeak [20] for parsing the C files and it uses a specification language for specifying the actuators, sensors and continuous modes of the system. The specifications are special C comments understood by Newspeak, so our framework can be easily integrated into a development cycle. The user may provide plugins that compute the overapproximations of the continuous dynamics, or HyPrA may build them automatically using the specifications and an OCAML version of GRKLib.

Problem	Initial state	Width in the loop	Graph size/ Loop size	Computation time (s)
Heater	$[0, 5]$	0.19	11/3	0.071
Navigation	$[3.5, 3.6] \times [3.5, 3.6]$	0.2	16/1	5.456
Two-tanks	$[5, 5] \times [6, 6]$	0.8	96/96	32.9

Fig. 3. Results of HyPrA on classical hybrid systems benchmarks

Fig. 4. Result of HyPrA on the heater problem. The figure shows the computed invariant as a cyclic sequence. In the bolded vertices, the continuous mode is **0**, meaning the heater is off. In the normal vertices, the continuous mode is **1**, meaning the heater is on. The labels represent the value of the continuous variable associated to the vertices of the graph.

We tested our analyzer on various benchmarks from the hybrid systems literature: the two-tanks system, the heater and the navigation problems [11]. In the heater problem, the dynamics are strongly contracting thus making our tool converge quickly. The navigation problem shows that HyPrA can be used to prove reachability of some region: to do that, we associated to this region a special continuous mode where all derivatives are equal to 0: if the trajectory enters this mode, it stops here, and we immediately obtain a loop of size 1 and a fixpoint. Finally the two-tanks problem shows that our tool can deal with non-linear dynamics. The table on Figure 3 shows for each problem the chosen initial state, the size of the computed cyclic sequence, the size of its loop and the computation time. Figure 4 shows the cyclic sequence computed for the heater problem. We also indicate in the table the width of the abstract state of the first vertex within the loop (column "Width in the loop"). Actually, it should be noted that when we find such a loop, not only do we prove that the trajectories starting from the initial state remain within the loop, but also that any trajectory starting from a point within a vertex of the loop remains in the loop. For example, in the two tanks system, we chose a point as initial state, but the width of the first loop vertex is large, thus proving the correctness of the control-command program for a set of initial configurations.

7   Conclusion and Future Works

In this article, we presented a method for the static analysis, using the abstraction interpretation framework, of the physical environment of embedded control-command programs. Using the fact that the program is time-invariant, we transform the control-command system into a system of *switched ordinary differential equations* [22] where the switching function is given by a program abstraction. Then, we look for a discretized overapproximation of the solution of this system as a ultimately periodic sequence of intervals. We use a notion of distance between abstract states to detect the periodic behavior. Our implementation shows that our method is efficient, in particular for non-linear dynamics: we can derive precise invariants on such systems.

Our analysis relies on the domain of intervals: we use them as the abstraction of the physical environment and we use interval analysis techniques for computing the octrees that serve as a program abstraction. Of course, using relational domains can improve the precision of the analysis: we plan to investigate the guaranteed integration of ODEs using zonotopes. They are already used for the verification of hybrid systems [15] and the static analysis of numerical programs [14], we believe they are well suited for our framework. We will also investigate methods to improve the precision of our analysis. For now, we did not implement any of the ideas mentioned in Section 5.4. The disjunctive analysis is probably the best way to improve the precision, and we can control the combinatorial explosion inherent by choosing a large threshold on the minimum distance for joining two states. Finally, removing the time invariant assumption will be a more complex task: defining a safe program abstraction is more complex as the action of the program on its environment depends on all the sensed values. To do so, we would probably need to analyze both the programs and the environment at the same time, and not one after the other as it is the case now.

References

1. Blanchet, B., Cousot, P., Cousot, R., Feret, J., Mauborgne, L., Miné, A., Monniaux, D., Rival, X.: A static analyzer for large safety-critical software. In: PLDI 2003, pp. 196–207. ACM, New York (2003)
2. Bouissou, O., Martel, M.: GRKLib: a guaranteed runge-kutta library. In: Follow-up of International Symposium on Scientific Computing, Computer Arithmetic and Validated Numerics. IEEE Press, Los Alamitos (2007)

3. Bouissou, O., Martel, M.: Abstract interpretation of the physical inputs of embedded programs. In: Logozzo, F., Peled, D.A., Zuck, L.D. (eds.) VMCAI 2008. LNCS, vol. 4905, pp. 37–51. Springer, Heidelberg (2008)
4. Bouissou, O., Martel, M.: A hybrid denotational semantics of hybrid systems. In: Drossopoulou, S. (ed.) ESOP 2008. LNCS, vol. 4960, pp. 63–77. Springer, Heidelberg (2008)
5. Chen, Y., Gansner, E., Koutsofios, E.: A C++ data model supporting reachability analysis and dead code detection. In: Jazayeri, M. (ed.) ESEC 1997 and ESEC-FSE 1997. LNCS, vol. 1301, pp. 414–431. Springer, Heidelberg (1997)
6. Cook, B., Gotsman, A., Podelski, A., Rybalchenko, A., Vardi, M.: Proving that programs eventually do something good. SIGPLAN Notices 42(1), 265–276 (2007)
7. Cook, B., Podelski, A., Rybalchenko, A.: Termination proofs for systems code. In: PLDI 2006, pp. 415–426. ACM, New York (2006)
8. Cousot, P., Cousot, R.: Abstract interpretation: a unified lattice model for static analysis of programs by construction or approximation of fixpoints. In: POPL 1977, pp. 238–252. ACM Press, New York (1977)
9. Cousot, P., Cousot, R.: Abstract interpretation frameworks. Journal of Logic and Computation 2(4), 511–547 (1992)
10. de Oliveira, I.R., Cugnasca, P.S.: Checking safe trajectories of aircraft using hybrid automata. In: SAFECOMPK 2002, pp. 224–235. Springer, Heidelberg (2002)
11. Fehnker, A., Ivancic, F.: Benchmarks for hybrid systems verification. In: Alur, R., Pappas, G.J. (eds.) HSCC 2004. LNCS, vol. 2993, pp. 326–341. Springer, Heidelberg (2004)
12. Ferdinand, C., Heckmann, R., Langenbach, M., Martin, F., Schmidt, M., Theiling, H., Thesing, S., Wilhelm, R.: Reliable and precise WCET determination for a real-life processor. In: Henzinger, T.A., Kirsch, C.M. (eds.) EMSOFT 2001. LNCS, vol. 2211, pp. 469–485. Springer, Heidelberg (2001)
13. Frehse, G.: Phaver: Algorithmic verification of hybrid systems past hytech. In: Morari, M., Thiele, L. (eds.) HSCC 2005. LNCS, vol. 3414, pp. 258–273. Springer, Heidelberg (2005)
14. Goubault, E., Putot, S.: Static analysis of numerical algorithms. In: Yi, K. (ed.) SAS 2006. LNCS, vol. 4134, pp. 18–34. Springer, Heidelberg (2006)
15. Le Guernic, C., Girard, A.: Zonotope-hyperplane intersection for hybrid systems reachability analysis. In: Egerstedt, M., Mishra, B. (eds.) HSCC 2008. LNCS, vol. 4981, pp. 215–228. Springer, Heidelberg (2008)
16. Gupta, A., Henzinger, T., Majumdar, R., Rybalchenko, A., Xu, R.: Proving non-termination. In: POPL 2008, pp. 147–158. ACM Press, New York (2008)
17. Henzinger, T.A.: The theory of hybrid automata. In: Symposium on Logic in Computer Science, pp. 278–292. IEEE Computer Society Press, Los Alamitos (1996)
18. Henzinger, T.A., Rusu, V.: Reachability verification for hybrid automata. In: Henzinger, T.A., Sastry, S.S. (eds.) HSCC 1998. LNCS, vol. 1386, pp. 190–204. Springer, Heidelberg (1998)
19. Hespanha, J.: Uniform stability of switched linear systems: Extensions of LaSalle's invariance principle. IEEETAC 49(4), 470–482 (2004)
20. Hymans, C., Levillain, O.: Newspeak, Doubleplussimple Minilang for Goodthinkful Static Analysis of C. Technical Note 2008-IW-SE-00010-1, EADS IW/SE (2008)
21. Kowalewski, S., Stursberg, O., Fritz, M., Graf, H., Hoffmann, I., Preußig, J., et al.: A case study in tool-aided analysis of discretely controlled continuous systems: the two tanks problem. In: Antsaklis, P.J., Kohn, W., Lemmon, M.D., Nerode, A., Sastry, S.S. (eds.) HS 1997. LNCS, vol. 1567, p. 163. Springer, Heidelberg (1999)

22. Liberzon, D.: Switching in Systems and Control. Birkhäuser, Boston (2003)
23. Ben Makhlouf, I., Kowalewski, S.: An evaluation of two recent reachability analysis tools for hybrid systems. In: Second IFAC Conference on Analysis and Design of Hybrid Systems, pp. 377–382. Elsevier, Amsterdam (2006)
24. Nedialkov, N.S., Jackson, K.R., Corliss, G.F.: Validated solutions of initial value problems for ordinary differential equations. Applied Mathematics and Computation 105(1), 21–68 (1999)
25. Putot, S., Goubault, E., Martel, M.: Static analysis-based validation of floating-point computations. In: Alt, R., Frommer, A., Kearfott, R.B., Luther, W. (eds.) Dagstuhl Seminar 2003. LNCS, vol. 2991, pp. 306–313. Springer, Heidelberg (2004)
26. Ramdani, N., Meslem, N., Candau, Y.: Reachability of uncertain nonlinear systems using a nonlinear hybridization. In: Egerstedt, M., Mishra, B. (eds.) HSCC 2008. LNCS, vol. 4981, pp. 415–428. Springer, Heidelberg (2008)
27. Sankaranarayanan, S., Ivančić, F., Shlyakhter, I., Gupta, A.: Static analysis in disjunctive numerical domains. In: Yi, K. (ed.) SAS 2006. LNCS, vol. 4134, pp. 3–17. Springer, Heidelberg (2006)
28. Wongpiromsarn, T., Mitra, S., Murray, R.M., Lamperski, A.G.: Periodically controlled hybrid systems. In: HSCC 2009. LNCS, vol. 5469, pp. 396–410. Springer, Heidelberg (2009)
29. Yfoulis, C., Shorten, R.: A numerical technique for stability analysis of linear switched systems. In: Alur, R., Pappas, G.J. (eds.) HSCC 2004. LNCS, vol. 2993, pp. 631–645. Springer, Heidelberg (2004)

Abstract Interpretation of FIFO Replacement

Daniel Grund and Jan Reineke

Saarland University, Saarbrücken, Germany

Abstract. In hard real-time systems, the execution time of programs must be bounded by static timing analysis. For today's embedded systems featuring caches, static analyses must predict cache hits and misses with high precision to obtain *useful* bounds. For caches with least-recently-used (LRU) replacement policy, efficient and precise cache analyses exist. However, for other widely-used policies like first-in first-out (FIFO), current cache analyses are much less precise.

This paper discusses challenges in FIFO cache analysis and advances the state of the art. We identify a generic framework for cache analysis that couples may- and must-analyses by means of domain cooperation. Our main contribution is a more precise may-analysis for FIFO. It not only increases the number of predicted misses, but also—due to the domain cooperation—the number of predicted hits. We instantiate the framework with a canonical must-analysis and three different may-analyses, including our new one, and compare the resulting three analyses to the collecting semantics. Our evaluation results characterize the progress achieved by our new may-analysis and reveal room for further improvement.

Keywords: Cache Analysis, FIFO Replacement, Domain Cooperation, May/Must Reasoning.

1   Introduction

In hard real-time systems, one needs to derive off-line guarantees for the timeliness of reactions. Thereby, one fundamental problem is to bound the worst-case execution time (WCET) of programs [1]. To obtain tight and thus useful bounds on the execution times, timing analyses *must* take into account the cache architecture of the employed CPUs. However, developing cache analyses—analyses that statically determine whether a memory access associated with an instruction will always be a hit or a miss—is a challenging problem.

Precise and efficient analyses have been developed for set-associative caches that employ the least-recently-used (LRU) replacement policy [2,3,4,5,6]. Generally, research in the field of embedded real-time systems assumes LRU replacement. In practice however, other policies like first-in first-out (FIFO) or pseudo-LRU (PLRU) are also commonly used, e.g., in the INTEL XSCALE, some ARM9 and ARM11, and the POWERPC 75X series.

As Section 2.3 explains, two kinds of information can be naturally distinguished in cache analysis: must-information that allows for predicting hits, and

J. Palsberg and Z. Su (Eds.): SAS 2009, LNCS 5673, pp. 120–136, 2009.

may-information that allows for predicting misses. Previous work showed that it is inherently more difficult to obtain may-information for FIFO than for LRU; see [7] and Section 3. A first step towards the analysis of those policies was the general concept of relative competitiveness; see [8] and Section 5. Depending on the particular policy, however, a cache analysis based on relative competitiveness may be anything from very precise to ineffective.

In Section 4, we describe a generic policy-independent framework for cache analysis. It allows for cooperation of may- and must-analyses through a minimal interface, which improves their precision.

Then, we present our main contributions: a may- and a must-analysis for FIFO. The must-analysis borrows basic ideas from LRU-analysis [3]. To predict cache hits, it infers upper bounds on cache misses to prove containedness of memory blocks. To predict cache misses, the may-analysis infers lower bounds on cache misses to prove eviction. By taking into account the order in which hits and misses happen, we improve the may-analysis, thereby increasing the number of predicted cache misses. Through the cooperation of the two analyses in the generic framework, this also improves the precision of the must-analysis.

After describing related work in Section 5, we report on our evaluation in Section 6. Using the generic framework, we compare three may-analyses with each other and to the collecting semantics of FIFO. We show that our analysis yields better results than the generic approach using relative competitiveness. Additionally, using the collecting semantics, we illustrate the limits for any static analysis. This supplements analytical bounds derived in [7] and reveals opportunities of how to improve abstract domains for FIFO.

2   Foundations

2.1   Caches

Caches are fast but small memories that store a subset of the main memory's contents to bridge the latency gap between CPU and main memory. To profit from spatial locality and to reduce management overhead, main memory is logically partitioned into a set of *memory blocks* B of size b bytes. Blocks are cached as a whole in cache lines of equal size. Usually, b is a power of two. This way, the block number is determined by the most significant bits of a memory address.

When accessing a memory block, the cache logic has to determine whether the block is stored in the cache ("cache hit") or not ("cache miss"). To enable an efficient look-up, each block can only be stored in a small number of cache lines. For this purpose, caches are partitioned into equally-sized *cache sets* S. The size of a cache set is called the *associativity* k of the cache. A cache with associativity k is often called k-*way* set-associative. It consists of k *ways*, each of which consists of one cache line in each cache set. In the context of a cache set, the term *way* thus refers to a single cache line. The number of such equally-sized cache sets s is usually a power of two such that the set number, also called *index*, is determined by the least significant bits of the block number. The remaining bits of an address are known as the *tag*. To finally decide whether and where a block is cached within a set, tags $t_i \in \mathcal{T}$ are stored along with the data.

Since the number of memory blocks that map to a set is usually far greater than the associativity of the cache, a so-called *replacement policy* must decide which memory block to replace upon a cache miss. Replacement policies try to exploit temporal locality and base their decisions on the history of memory accesses. Usually, cache sets are treated independently of each other such that accesses to one set do not influence replacement decisions in other sets.

Well-known policies for individual cache sets are least-recently used (LRU), a more cost-efficient variant of it (PLRU), and first-in first-out (FIFO). For details on the implementation of caches in hardware refer to Jacob [9].

2.2   Static Analysis

The goal of static analysis is to automatically determine properties of programs without actually executing the programs. Since the properties to determine are commonly incomputable, abstraction has to be employed. In general, there is a trade-off between analysis precision on the one hand and computability and analysis complexity on the other hand.

One formal method in static analysis, which our work is based on, is abstract interpretation. Instead of representing concrete semantic information in a concrete domain D, one represents more abstract information in an abstract domain $\widehat{D}$. The relation between concrete and abstract can be given by an abstraction function $\alpha : \mathcal{P}(D) \to \widehat{D}$ and a concretization function $\gamma : \widehat{D} \to \mathcal{P}(D)$.

To determine the properties, a data-flow analysis computes invariants for each program point, which are represented by values of $\widehat{D}$. A *transfer function* $\mathcal{U} : \widehat{D} \times I \to \widehat{D}$ models the effect of instructions I on abstract values. With the transfer function it is possible to set up a system of data-flow equations that correlates values before and after each instruction. If an instruction has multiple predecessors, a *join function* $\mathcal{J} : \widehat{D} \times \widehat{D} \to \widehat{D}$ combines all incoming values into a single one. If a data-flow framework meets certain conditions, the induced system of equations for a given program has a least solution, which can be obtained by a fixed-point computation. If the transfer- and the join-function satisfy certain conditions, the analysis is sound with respect to α and γ: True properties in the abstract map to true properties in the concrete. For an overview article with pointers to details on abstract interpretation refer to Cousot and Cousot [10].

2.3   Static Cache Analysis

Static cache analysis by abstract interpretation computes *may*- and *must*-cache information at program points: may- and must-cache information are used to derive upper and lower approximations, respectively, to the *contents* of all concrete cache states that will occur whenever program execution reaches a program point.

Must-cache information is used to derive safe information about cache hits. The more cache hits can be predicted, the better the upper bound on the execution times. May-cache information is used to safely predict cache misses.

Predicting more cache misses will result in a better lower bound on the execution times. Generally, the lower the number of unclassified accesses (neither hit nor miss can be predicted), the lower the runtime of a WCET analysis is because it has to consider fewer cases.

As most cache architectures manage their cache sets independently from each other, cache analyses can analyze them independently as well. Thus, we limit ourselves to the analysis of a single cache set. For details on (LRU-)cache analysis refer to Ferdinand et al. [11,3].

3 The FIFO Policy

The policy. Conceptually, a FIFO cache set maintains a fixed-size queue of tags T. A concrete k-way FIFO cache set s can therefore be modeled as a k-tuple of cache tags, which are ordered from last-in to first-in from left to right:

$$s = [t_0, \ldots, t_{k-1}] \in \mathcal{S} := T^k$$

A cache hit does not change the cache set. A cache miss inserts the new tag at position 0, shifting the others to the right and evicting the one at the rightmost position. The update function $\mathcal{U}_{\mathcal{S}} : \mathcal{S} \times T \to \mathcal{S}$ models the effect on a cache set when accessing a memory block with tag t:

$$\mathcal{U}_{\mathcal{S}}([t_0, \ldots, t_{k-1}], t) := \begin{cases} [t_0, \ldots, t_{k-1}] & : \exists i : t = t_i \quad \text{``cache hit''} \\ [t, t_0, \ldots, t_{k-2}] & : \text{otherwise} \quad \text{``cache miss''} \end{cases}$$

In hardware, the FIFO-update can be implemented more efficiently than the LRU-update and the resulting circuit has a lower latency.

Challenges for static analysis. For FIFO, it is difficult to obtain may-information. At the same time, may-information is necessary to obtain precise must-information. Consider a FIFO cache set with unknown contents. After observing a cache access to a block a, one knows that a must be cached—trivial must-information is available. If one cannot classify the access to a as a miss, another access to a different block b may immediately evict a. This is the case if the access to a is a hit on the first-in, i.e., right-most, position and the access to b is a miss. Thus, without (implicitly or explicitly) classifying some accesses as misses, it is not possible to infer that two or more blocks are cached.

Hence, may-information is important to obtain precise must-information, and thus to be able to classify a significant amount of accesses as hits. However, Reineke et al. [7] give the following bound for a k-way FIFO cache set. Assuming accesses to pairwise different blocks, it is impossible to classify an individual access as a miss before $2k - 1$ accesses have been observed.

One way to attenuate the lack of FIFO may-information is to invalidate the cache contents at the start of the program. This way, one can safely assume an empty cache, i.e., at program start one gets complete may- and must-information. However, cache information can be lost during the analysis, e.g., due to control-flow joins. Furthermore, an architecture might not support cache invalidation.

4 The FIFO Cache Analysis

Our analysis is an instance of a generic framework for cache analysis that allows *several* cache analyses to cooperate by exchanging classifications of memory accesses. Instead of first describing the framework itself, we immediately describe our instance for FIFO that composes *two* analyses. Then, we present our main contribution: a may- and a must-analysis for FIFO used in this instance of the framework. In our case, the framework is instantiated with one must- and one may-analysis; its abstract domain is:

$$Fifo := Must \times May$$

Cache accesses are classified as hit (H), miss (M), or unclassified ($\top$). See Figure 1 for the definition of the classification semi-lattice $Class := \{H, M\}^\top$. To classify an access to some block with tag $t \in \mathcal{T}$, the classification function of the framework combines the classifications of the may- and the must-analysis. Since these two classifications are sound, they cannot contradict each other. Thus, their meet ($\sqcap$) is always defined.

$$\mathcal{C}_{Fifo} : Fifo \times \mathcal{T} \to Class$$
$$\mathcal{C}_{Fifo}((mst, may), t) := \mathcal{C}_{Must}(mst, t) \sqcap \mathcal{C}_{May}(may, t)$$

The goal of our analysis is to gain better may-information and leverage it more than existing analyses. To enable these synergies, one has to introduce some information flow between the may- and the must-analysis. To this end, the update functions of may- and must-information are refined by an additional parameter that is used to pass the classification of the current access. This classification depends on both analyses, may and must. The main update function hence is defined as:

$$\mathcal{U}_{Fifo} : Fifo \times \mathcal{T} \to Fifo$$
$$\mathcal{U}_{Fifo}((mst, may), t) := (\mathcal{U}_{Must}(mst, t, cl), \mathcal{U}_{May}(may, t, cl)),$$

where $cl = \mathcal{C}_{Fifo}((mst, may), t)$, and $\mathcal{U}_{Must}$ and $\mathcal{U}_{May}$ are the update functions of the must- and the may-analysis. This is a form of domain cooperation as described in Cousot et al. [12]. In our case, the additional information allows to define more precise update functions for both analyses.

The main join function is simply defined component-wise:

$$\mathcal{J}_{Fifo} : Fifo \times Fifo \to Fifo$$
$$\mathcal{J}_{Fifo}((mst_1, may_1), (mst_2, may_2)) := (\mathcal{J}_{Must}(mst_1, mst_2), \mathcal{J}_{May}(may_1, may_2))$$

$\sqcup$	H	M	$\top$
H	H	$\top$	$\top$
M	$\top$	M	$\top$
$\top$	$\top$	$\top$	$\top$

$\sqcap$	H	M	$\top$
H	H		H
M		M	M
$\top$	H	M	$\top$

H : cache hit
M : cache miss
$\top$: unclassified

Fig. 1. Classification join semi-lattice *Class* and induced join ($\sqcup$) and meet ($\sqcap$)

The remainder of this section details the must- and the may-analysis and defines their classification-, update-, and join-functions, which we have used above.

4.1   Must Analysis

In a concrete k-way cache set, k misses must happen to evict a newly inserted memory block. To predict hits, our must-analysis approximates this number from above, it counts potential misses. We define the abstract domain as follows:

$$Must := Must_{Fifo_k} := [T_0, \dots, T_{k-1}],$$

where $T_i \subseteq T, \forall i \neq j : T_i \cap T_j = \emptyset$, and $\forall j \leq k : \sum_{i=0}^{j-1} |T_i| \leq j$. The position of a tag in the tuple is an upper bound on the number of misses that happened since the insertion of the block with that tag. If a tag $t \in T_i$, there have been at most i misses since the block with t was inserted into the cache set. It will not be evicted before at least $k - i$ further misses have happened. One must allow for sets of tags because multiple tags may have the same upper bound. However, at most j tags may have an upper bound $\leq j - 1$. Since it is senseless to specify multiple bounds for one tag, all k sets are defined to be disjoint. Otherwise, all but the least bound would be redundant.

The set of concrete cache sets represented by an abstract must cache set is given by the concretization function:

$$\gamma_{Must} : Must \rightarrow \mathcal{P}(\mathcal{S})$$
$$\gamma_{Must}([T_0, \dots, T_{k-1}]) := \{[t_0, \dots, t_{k-1}] \in \mathcal{S} \mid \forall i \, \forall t \in T_i \, \exists j \leq i : t_j = t\}$$

In other words: If a tag t is contained in some T_i in an abstract must cache set, the block with tag t must be located at one of the first i positions in the concrete cache set. Consider $mst_1 := [\{f\}, \{\}, \{a, c\}, \{b\}]$ and $mst_2 := [\{\}, \{d\}, \{b, c\}, \{a\}]$ as an example. Their concretizations are $\gamma_{Must}(mst_1) = \{[f, c, a, b], [f, a, c, b]\}$ and $\gamma_{Must}(mst_2) = \{[c, d, b, a], [b, d, c, a], [d, c, b, a], [d, b, c, a]\}$.

The classification function is straightforward. If the accessed tag is contained in any of the T_i-sets, the analysis can predict a hit. If k tags must be cached, no other tag may be cached; in this case, the analysis can predict a miss.

$$\mathcal{C}_{Must} : Must \times T \rightarrow Class$$
$$\mathcal{C}_{Must}([T_0, \dots, T_{k-1}], t) := \begin{cases} \text{H} : t \in \cup_i T_i \\ \text{M} : t \notin \cup_i T_i =: C, |C| = k \\ \top : \text{otherwise} \end{cases}$$

The update function has three cases. If the analysis can predict a hit, the must-information remains unchanged as FIFO does not change its state upon a hit. If, with the help of may-information, the analysis can predict a miss, one can update the must-information similarly to the concrete semantics. If neither hit nor miss can be predicted, the analysis has to account for both possibilities:

Since the access might be a miss, all sets are shifted to the right. Since it might be a hit on the first-in position, the tag can only be added to the rightmost position. This results in:

$$\mathcal{U}_{Must} : Must \times \mathcal{T} \times Class \rightarrow Must$$

$$\mathcal{U}_{Must}([T_0,\ldots,T_{k-1}],t,cl) := \begin{cases} [T_0,\ldots,T_{k-1}] & : cl = \text{H} \\ [\{t\},T_0,\ldots,T_{k-2}] & : cl = \text{M} \\ [\emptyset,T_0,\ldots,T_{k-2} \cup \{t\}] & : \text{otherwise} \end{cases}$$

If a cache access is not a hit, either the second or the third case of the update applies. They are identical, except for the position where t is inserted. Predicting a miss on the block with tag t allows to predict hits for t until k further misses might have happened. In contrast, the third case only allows to predict hits for t until the next miss might have happened.

The join function has to be sound w.r.t. the concretization function. Therefore, a tag may only be contained in the result if it is present in both operands. The position of such a tag must be the maximum of the two positions in the operands. The best possible join function for our domain is:

$$\mathcal{J}_{Must} : Must \times Must \rightarrow Must$$

$$\mathcal{J}_{Must}([X_0,\ldots,X_{k-1}],[Y_0,\ldots,Y_{k-1}]) := [Z_0,\ldots,Z_{k-1}],$$

with $Z_l := \{t \in \mathcal{T} \mid \exists i,j : t \in X_i \cap Y_j, l = \max\{i,j\}\}$. As an example consider the join of the two must cache sets from above. $mst_3 := \mathcal{J}_{Must}(mst_1, mst_2) = [\{\},\{\},\{c\},\{a,b\}]$. The concretization of mst_3 is "infinite", i.e., $|\gamma_{Must}(mst_3)| = 18 * (|\mathcal{T}| - 3)$: if less than k tags are contained in $\bigcup_i T_i$, any of the other $|\mathcal{T}| - |\bigcup_i T_i|$ tags may also be contained in the cache set.

4.2 May Analysis

The goal of the may-analysis is to infer information that allows for classifying accesses as misses. Our may-analysis associates information with each cache tag. This results in the abstract domain:

$$May := May_{Fifo_k} := \mathcal{T} \rightarrow TInfo_k$$

In the following paragraphs, we will motivate and describe all parts of $TInfo_k$. After describing $TInfo_k$, we define the classification-, update-, and join-functions.

Consider a k-way associative FIFO cache set s and a block with tag t that has just been inserted into s. If k misses happen, the block with t is evicted from s and the next access to that block can be predicted to be a miss. Hence, the may-analysis approximates the number of misses from below.[1] Thus, one constituent of $TInfo_k$ is the number of *definite misses*:

$$DM_k := \{0,\ldots,k-1\}$$

---

[1] This is analogous to must-information: May-information gives a lower bound on the number of misses (definite misses) while must-information gives an upper bound (potential misses). Must-information can also be represented as a mapping $\mathcal{T} \rightarrow PM$.

Before an analysis can predict a miss for a block, it must predict its eviction, i.e., it must prove that k misses have happened since the insertion of that block. Hence, there is a "bootstrapping problem" if the analysis starts with the worst may-information (i.e., any block could be cached). Similar problems arise if may-information is (partially) lost during the analysis, e.g., due to joins. To solve this problem, a may-analysis *must* infer and maintain additional information.

The only solution to this bootstrapping problem are amortizing observations like "k of $a \geq k$ accesses must have been misses". Consider the following lemma, which holds independently of the replacement policy.

Lemma 1. *Let s be a k-way cache set. Furthermore, let (t_n) be an access sequence (finite series of tags). If (t_n) contains $p \geq k$ pairwise different tags, at least $p - k$ misses must happen if (t_n) is carried out on s.*

Proof. Initially, s can contain at most k pairwise different blocks. Since only accessed blocks are inserted into the set, at most k of the p pairwise different accesses may therefore be hits.   □

With FIFO, a block is replaced after k misses.[2] Together with Lemma 1, this means that after at most $2k - 1$ accesses to pairwise different blocks, blocks that are not contained in this access sequence cannot be cached. Subsequent accesses to them can be predicted as misses.

To prove that k misses have happened, a FIFO may-analysis *must* be able to distinguish repeating accesses from pairwise different ones. For each tag t, our analysis maintains a set of tags that may have been accessed since the insertion of t. Hence, another constituent of $TInfo_k$ is the set of *possibly accessed tags*:

$$PAT := \mathcal{P}(T)$$

Note that the lower bound on the number of misses provided by Lemma 1 is implicitly based on an upper bound on the number of hits. If one could improve the upper bound on hits, one could predict misses earlier.

Example 1. Consider the FIFO cache set $s = [x, c, b, a]$ and the four access sequences $\langle a, b, c, e, f, g, h \rangle$, $\langle a, e, b, f, c, g, h \rangle$, $\langle e, f, g, h \rangle$, and $\langle a, e, f, c, g, h \rangle$. Although being of different length, carrying out any of the sequences results in the final cache set state $[h, g, f, e]$. In case of the first two sequences, it takes exactly $2k - 1 = 7$ accesses to pairwise different blocks to evict all blocks not contained in the sequence. This is because all of the original contents of s, except x, are accessed before their eviction. The third sequence evicts the original contents without accessing them. Sequence four lies in between the two extremes. Note that after accessing a, e, f, it is not possible to access more than three pairwise different blocks without evicting x because a hit on b is impossible.

As Example 1 shows and Figure 2(a) depicts, the order in which hits and misses happen matters. "Early misses", as in $\langle a, e, f, c, g, h \rangle$, preclude hits and reduce

---

[2] For other replacement policies, this does not necessarily hold, e.g., for PLRU.

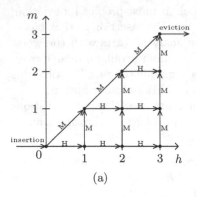
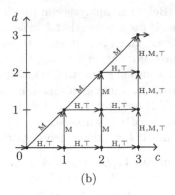

(a)   (b)

Fig. 2. (a) The paths illustrate all possible sequences of hits (H) and misses (M) between the insertion and eviction of a block in a 4-way associative FIFO cache set. Thereby, only accesses on pairwise different blocks trigger a transition. A block "enters" the cache set at $(0, 0)$. At (h, m), m misses and at most h hits have happened. At $(3, 3)$, the next accesses on a furthermore pairwise different block must be a miss; the block is evicted. (b) Evolution of the number of definite misses d and covered ways c depending on the classifications of accesses. $\top$ denotes the transition upon an unclassified access.

the overall number of accesses to pairwise different blocks until x's eviction. Our analysis exploits that by maintaining a lower bound on the number of *covered ways*, which is the last constituent of $TInfo_k$:

$$CW_k := \{0, \ldots, k-1\}$$

A way is covered if it is occupied by a block whose tag is also contained in the set of potentially accessed tags $A \in PAT$. For each tag t, covered ways $c \in CW_k$ is a lower bound on the number of covered ways, *assuming* that all unclassified accesses were hits. Eventually, c reaches $k - 1$, i.e., the cache set would have to be filled with blocks whose tags are in A. Then, there are two possibilities for further accesses to tags not contained in A. Either such an access is a miss. Or the access is a hit, which indicates that one of the previously unclassified accesses must have been a miss. In either case, the lower bound d on the number of definite misses can be incremented.

Figure 2(b) illustrates the evolution of the lower bounds $d \in DM_k$ and $c \in CW_k$. Accesses that are classified as hit (H) or as unclassified ($\top$) increase c (arrows from left to right). Although misses (M) insert a block into the cache set (cover a way), c is usually not incremented (upwards arrows). This is because the miss might evict a block whose tag is contained in A. Still, the number of definite misses is a lower bound on the number of covered ways. Thus, c can be incremented if $d = c$ (diagonal arrows). As explained above, the analysis can increase the number of definite misses if $c = k - 1$, even if the current access cannot be classified as a miss (the upwards arrows at $c = 3 = 4 - 1$).

In summary, the domain for the information maintained per cache tag $t \in \mathcal{T}$ is $CW_k \times DM_k \times PAT$. Adding $\perp$ to indicate that a tag is definitely not cached yields $TInfo_k := (CW_k \times DM_k \times PAT)_\perp$. Substituting this in the definition of our abstract may cache sets results in:

$$May = \mathcal{T} \to (CW_k \times DM_k \times PAT)_\perp$$

$t \mapsto \perp$ indicates that t cannot be cached. Otherwise, $t \mapsto (c, d, A)$, where:

- A, potentially accessed tags, is an upper approximation of the set of tags that have been accessed since the last insertion of t.
- d, definite misses, is a lower bound on the number of misses that happened since the insertion of t into s.
- c, covered ways, is a lower bound on the number of ways that are occupied by tags in A, assuming that all unclassified accesses were hits.

The concretization function for May is:

$$\gamma_{May} : May \to \mathcal{P}(\mathcal{S})$$

$$\gamma_{May}(may) := \bigcap_{t \in \mathcal{T}} \gamma_{TInfo_k}(t, may(t))$$

The $TInfo_k$ of each tag constrains the set of possible cache sets. γ_{TInfo_k} defines such a constraint for one tag. Hence, the concretization function of May is the conjunction (intersection) of all these constraints (sets). Let $C_n([t_0, \ldots, t_{k-1}]) := \bigcup_{0 \le i < n}\{t_i\}$, i.e., the cache contents of the n leftmost positions in a cache set. If $may(t) = \perp$, tag t is evicted and cannot be contained in a cache set represented by may. Hence,

$$\gamma^\perp_{TInfo_k}(t) := \{s \in \mathcal{S} \mid t \notin C_k(s)\}$$

Otherwise,

$$\gamma^{\not\perp}_{TInfo_k}(t, (c, d, A)) := \{s \in \mathcal{S} \mid o := |C_k(s) \cap A|, C_{\max\{d, d+c-o\}}(s) \subseteq A\}$$

Here, o is the number of ways *actually* covered by A in a particular concrete cache set state s. c was defined to be the number of ways covered by A, given that all unclassified accesses were hits. Hence, if $c > o$, $c - o$ unclassified accesses must have been misses. Together with the d definite misses, at least $\max\{d, d+c-o\}$ of the tags in A must occupy the leftmost positions of s ($C_{\max\{\ldots\}}(s) \subseteq A$).[3] As $t \notin A$ by construction, this also constrains t's position in s. The concretization function for $TInfo_k$ is:

$$\gamma_{TInfo_k}(t, \perp) \quad := \gamma^\perp_{TInfo_k}(t)$$

$$\gamma_{TInfo_k}(t, (c, d, A)) := \gamma^\perp_{TInfo_k}(t) \cup \gamma^{\not\perp}_{TInfo_k}(t, (c, d, A))$$

In the latter case, $\gamma^\perp_{TInfo_k}(t)$ reflects that t might not be cached, and the second part defines constraints for the case that t is cached.

---

[3] Recall that tags are inserted in the leftmost position upon a miss.

In the remaining part of this section, we will describe the classification-, update-, and join-functions for *May*. The classification function is straightforward:

$$\mathcal{C}_{May} : May \times \mathcal{T} \to Class$$

$$\mathcal{C}_{May}(may, t) := \begin{cases} \text{M} : may(t) = \bot \\ \top : \text{otherwise} \end{cases}$$

The update function is defined separately for each of the three possible cases (H, M, $\top$) of the classification parameter.

$$\mathcal{U}_{May} : May \times \mathcal{T} \times Class \to May$$

$$\mathcal{U}_{May}(may, t, \text{H}) := \lambda x.$$

$$\begin{cases} may(x) & : \begin{cases} x = t \\ x \neq t, may(x) = \bot \\ x \neq t, may(x) = (c, d, A), t \in A \end{cases} \\ (c + 1, d, A \cup \{t\}) : x \neq t, may(x) = (c, d, A), t \notin A, c < k - 1 \\ (c, d + 1, A \cup \{t\}) : x \neq t, may(x) = (c, d, A), t \notin A, c = k - 1, d < k - 1 \\ \bot & : x \neq t, may(x) = (c, d, A), t \notin A, c = k - 1, d = k - 1 \end{cases}$$

FIFO does not change its state upon a hit. Furthermore, the $TInfo_k$ of a tag is only updated if the accessed tag is not contained in A. This explains the first case where nothing is changed. The remaining three cases update the $TInfo_k$ of tags different from the accessed one ($x \neq t$), that may be cached ($may(x) = (c, d, A)$), and t has definitely not been accessed since the insertion of x ($t \notin A$). If $c < k-1$, the number of covered ways is incremented. If $c = k - 1$ and a hit happens, the number of definite misses is soundly incremented: Since no more than $k - 1$ hits on pairwise different elements can happen, a previous access, which also incremented c, must have been a miss though the analysis could not classify it as a miss. In the last case, the number of definite misses reaches k; the block with tag x is definitely evicted.

$$\mathcal{U}_{May}(may, t, \text{M}) := \lambda x.$$

$$\begin{cases} (0, 0, \emptyset) & : x = t \\ may(x) & : \begin{cases} x \neq t, may(x) = \bot \\ x \neq t, may(x) = (c, d, A), t \in A \end{cases} \\ (\max\{c, d + 1\}, d + 1, A \cup \{t\}) : x \neq t, may(x) = (c, d, A), t \notin A, d < k - 1 \\ \bot & : x \neq t, may(x) = (c, d, A), t \notin A, d = k - 1 \end{cases}$$

The first case resets the information associated with a tag to $(0, 0, \emptyset)$ if a miss on this tag happens. The $TInfo_k$ of a tag is not updated if it is already evicted or if the accessed tag is contained in A (second case). In the third case, the number of definite misses is incremented. Furthermore, as explained above ("the diagonal"), c can be incremented if $d = c$. This can be abbreviated by the max expression. In the last case, the analysis can prove eviction of the tag.

The update for an unclassified access is defined as the join of the hit- and miss-update.

$$\mathcal{U}_{May}(may, t, \top) := \mathcal{J}_{May}(\mathcal{U}_{May}(may, t, \text{H}), \mathcal{U}_{May}(may, t, \text{M}))$$

The most interesting cases when spelling this out are

$(c + 1, d, A \cup \{t\}) : x \neq t, may(x) = (c, d, A), t \notin A, c < k - 1$

$(c, d + 1, A \cup \{t\}) : x \neq t, may(x) = (c, d, A), t \notin A, c = k - 1, d < k - 1$

$\bot \qquad\qquad : x \neq t, may(x) = (c, d, A), t \notin A, c = k - 1, d = k - 1$

This shows that the analysis can "bootstrap"; i.e., it can prove eviction of memory blocks without relying on explicit miss-classifications.

Finally, the join of may-information is defined as the component-wise join of the $TInfo_k$ for each tag:

$$\mathcal{J}_{May} : May \times May \rightarrow May$$

$$\mathcal{J}_{May}(may_1, may_2) := \lambda x. \begin{cases} may_1(x) & : may_2(x) = \bot \\ may_2(x) & : may_1(x) = \bot \\ (c', d', A_1 \cup A_2) & : may_i(x) = (c_i, d_i, A_i) \end{cases}$$

where $d' := \min\{d_1, d_2\}$ and $c' := \min\{c_1 + d_1, c_2 + d_2\} - d'$. In the first two cases, one of the operands maps $x \mapsto \bot$. Since $\forall I \in TInfo_k : \gamma_{TInfo_k}(t, \bot) \subseteq \gamma_{TInfo_k}(t, I)$, the other operand must be the least upper bound of the two. In the last case, the $TInfo_k$ of x of both operands is $\neq \bot$. As the set of potentially accessed tags must be an overapproximation, the join of A_1 and A_2 is the set union $A_1 \cup A_2$. The number of definite misses is an underapproximation. Hence, the join is the minimum $\min\{d_1, d_2\}$. For c one would also expect $\min\{c_1, c_2\}$. However, note that $\gamma_{TInfo_k}(t, (c, d, A)) \subseteq \gamma_{TInfo_k}(t, (c+\delta, d-\delta, A))$, i.e., one can "trade misses for hits". The join may result in a loss of precision for the definite misses, i.e., the difference $d_i - d'$. Due to the relation above, one can add $d_i - d'$ to c_i before taking the minimum, i.e., $c' = \min\{c_1 + (d_1 - d'), c_2 + (d_2 - d')\}$.

Theorem 1 (Soundness). *The abstract interpretation $(Fifo, \mathcal{J}_{Fifo}, \mathcal{U}_{Fifo}, \gamma_{Fifo})$ is a sound abstraction of the concrete FIFO semantics.*

Theorem 2 (Termination). *The update function $\mathcal{U}_{Fifo}$ is monotone and the abstract domain Fifo satisfies the ascending-chain condition.*

5   Related Work

There are different types of static cache analysis. Cache analyses directed at compiler optimizations compute bounds on the number of misses for larger program fragments, e.g., loop nests, whereas analyses directed at WCET analyses classify individual cache accesses as hits or misses.

Representatives of the first class are Ghosh et al. [13] and Chatterjee et al. [6]. Ghosh et al. [13] introduce *Cache Miss Equations* that characterize the cache behavior of loop-nests in direct-mapped caches by Diophantine equations. In subsequent work [5,14], they generalize their approach to set-associative caches with LRU replacement. Chatterjee et al. [6] propose an exact model of cache behavior of loop nests. It can handle imperfect loop nests and modest levels of associativity with LRU replacement.

Representatives of the second class include Mueller et al. [15], White et al. [4], Li et al. [16], and Ferdinand et al. [11,3]. Mueller et al. [15] present a *static cache simulation* for direct-mapped instruction caches. It classifies instructions as *always-miss*, *always-hit*, *first-miss*, or *conflict*. White et al. [4] extend this work to data caches, where the main challenges lie in the analysis of accessed addresses. Furthermore, an instruction cache analysis for set-associative LRU caches is sketched. Li et al. [16] present a timing analysis based on integer linear programming (ILP) formulations. It can handle set-associative caches by encoding their concrete semantics using linear constraints. However, since this approach integrates pipeline, cache, and path analysis into one ILP, it suffers from complexity problems. In practice it is limited to direct-mapped caches and simple pipelines. Ferdinand et al. [11,3] introduce the concepts of may- and must-caches and present an LRU analysis that is based on abstract interpretation.

Almost all cache analyses assume LRU replacement. As explained in Section 3 statically analyzing FIFO is inherently more difficult than LRU. In contrast to FIFO, it is possible to obtain precise must-information for LRU replacement without any may-analysis.

The concept of relative competitiveness [8] bounds the performance of one replacement policy relative to the performance of another one. This allows to use cache analyses for one policy as cache analyses for other policies. This implies that all of the existing analyses for LRU can be used as either may- or must-analyses for FIFO and PLRU. For instance, an LRU may-analysis for a $2k - 1$-way associative cache can be reused as a may-analysis for a k-way FIFO. Due to the generic nature of this approach, however, the resulting analyses may be rather imprecise. In the case of FIFO, one would expect that a $2k - 1$-way LRU performs much better than a k-way FIFO, i.e., the number of misses is much lower. Hence, the gap between actual and predicted number of misses might be large. The analysis presented in this work is tailored precisely to FIFO behavior and can therefore deliver more precise results.

Finally, our work is different from the analysis of so-called FIFO channels [17,18,19]. Such channels mostly model communication and have different characteristics than caches with FIFO replacement.

6   Evaluation

In the following, we compare three FIFO analyses with each other and to the collecting semantics. The collecting semantics is computed using a powerset domain of concrete cache set states and is denoted by COLLSEM. The three analyses are different instantiations of our framework. All analyses use the canonical must-analysis CM presented in this paper and only differ in their may-analysis.

- No+CM: An analysis that uses no may-analysis at all, i.e., the classification returned by the may-analysis is always ⊤.
- RC+CM: An analysis that uses a may-analysis based on relative competitiveness, as explained in Section 5, and the canonical must-analysis given in Section 4.1.
- EMX+CM: "Early Miss eXploitation"; the analysis proposed in this paper.

The analyses can be partially ordered according to their precision. Let $A \preccurlyeq B$ denote that analysis A is at least as precise as B for all programs. More precisely, $A \preccurlyeq B$ if for each access to be classified, the classification by A is equal or better than the respective classification of B. $A \prec B$ if $A \preccurlyeq B$ and $B \not\preccurlyeq A$.

Theorem 3 (Relative Precision)

$$\text{COLLSEM} \begin{matrix} \overset{\prec}{} & \text{EMX+CM} & \overset{\curlyvee}{} \\ {\underset{\curlyvee}{}} & \curlyvee\!\!\!\!\curlyvee\ \curlyvee\!\!\!\!\curlyvee & \text{No+CM} \\ & \text{RC+CM} & \underset{\prec}{} \end{matrix}$$

To quantify the precision of the analyses, we analyzed random access sequences and program fragments. In a first experiment, for each $1 \le n \le 31$, we generated 100 random access sequences that contain 500 accesses to n pairwise different tags. The parameter n controls the locality in the sequences: the greater the n, the lower is the locality.

Figure 3 shows the results; i.e., hit- and miss-rates guaranteed by the four analyses. The shape of the plot marks identify the analysis, e.g., circles for No+CM. The number of different tags (n) in the generated access sequences is plotted against the x-axis. The percentage of classifications (H, T, M) is plotted against the y-axis. For each analysis there are two curves, which partition the 100%. The lower curve, with filled plot marks, shows the guaranteed hit-rate. The upper one, with empty plot marks, is plotted bottom-up (from 100% downwards) and shows the guaranteed miss-rate. The difference between the upper and the lower curve gives the percentage of unclassified accesses.

For example consider the squares at $n = 24$. For 100 access sequences, each 500 accesses long and containing $n = 24$ different tags, the average guaranteed hit-rate obtained by RC+CM was 20%. The average guaranteed miss-rate was 42%, and on average 38% could not be classified.

Discussion: No+CM cannot predict any misses, hence the upper curve is constantly at 100%. As explained in Section 3, without may-information, it is impossible to infer that more than one memory block must be cached. Thus, with increasing n, the lower curve decreases as it gets more unlikely to access the same tag twice in a row.

Both, RC+CM and EMX+CM cannot predict any misses until 15 pairwise different tags have been accessed. This is in line with the "evict" bound $2k - 1 = 15$ determined in [7]. Hence, the curves of RC+CM and EMX+CM coincide with the one of No+CM up to $n = 15$. For larger n, both analyses predict misses, which in turn allows to predict more hits.

EMX+CM predicts more misses than RC+CM. For $n = 16, 17$ the difference is relatively small. This is because the benefit of predicting "early misses" is self-energizing. The more misses are predicted, the more does the "diagonal" in Figure 2(b) help, the more misses are predicted. ... Due to the domain cooperation, the must-analysis also profits from the prediction of misses, i.e., more hits can be predicted. Put simply, RC+CM "takes the long way" and always takes the T-transitions in Figure 2(b).

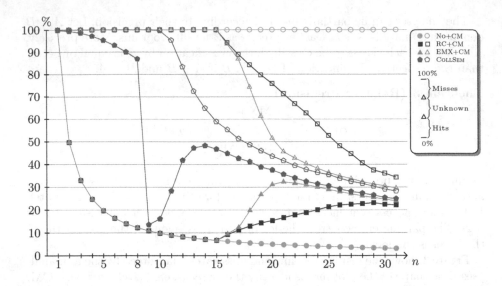

Fig. 3. Average guaranteed hit- and miss-rates for an 8-way cache set

Interestingly, COLLSEM shows that one could statically predict misses with accesses to less than $2k - 1$ pairwise different blocks. EMX+CM and RC+CM require at least $2k - 1$ pairwise different blocks because they do not gain information from repeating accesses. For $n \leq k$, COLLSEM shows that one could predict a large fraction of the accesses as hits. This is due to the fact that in any concrete cache set at most n misses might occur if $n \leq k$. However, one cannot predict all but those n misses as hits since one has to account for all initial cache set states. Depending on the initial position of a tag within a cache set, what is a hit in one concrete cache set is a miss in another. Hence, the lower curve decreases super-linearly. At $n = 9 = k + 1$, the percentage of predictable hits drops extremely. Since $n > k$, the cache cannot hold all accessed blocks. At the same time, almost no may-information is available in the collecting semantics.

Similarly to static analyses, which cannot gain precise must-information without may-information, there are not many guaranteed hits in the collecting semantics. For larger n, the number of predictable (and actually occurring) misses increases, causing initially different cache set states to converge more quickly. This allows to predict more accesses as hits.

In a second experiment, we generated program fragments with a large number of control-flow join points to evaluate the join functions of the analyses.

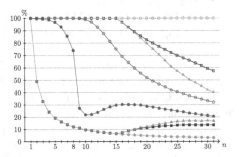

Fig. 4. Results of the join experiment

We generated recursively nested if-then-else patterns, i.e., $\circ \rightarrow \diamond$. All nodes of the flow-graph contain 10 random memory accesses. This way, we tested the ability of the analyses to recover from (partially) lost information before the next join point was reached. 4 shows the results. Generally, the relative evolution of the curves are the same as in Figure 3. The main difference is that all guarantees are worse since even in the collecting semantics the uncertainty is large.

7 Conclusions and Future Work

We presented the first abstract domain specifically tailored to the analysis of caches with FIFO replacement. With information about the order in which hits and misses have happened, our analysis can predict more misses than previous approaches. Due to an effective cooperation between our may- and must-analysis, this also improves the number of predicted hits.

Our evaluation clearly showed the characteristics of three different analyses, i.e., when and why an analysis is better than another one. Additionally, the illustration of the collecting semantics revealed characteristics of FIFO itself: While EMX+CM and RC+CM need to observe accesses to at least $2k - 1$ pairwise different blocks to obtain may-information, may-information may be available after accessing fewer pairwise different blocks. How to exploit this in an abstract domain? Furthermore, there is room for a better must-analysis for $n \leq k$, which, however, would have to rely on implicit miss-classifications.

Acknowledgements. We want to express our gratitude to Sebastian Hack for his helpful remarks on drafts of this paper. We also thank the anonymous reviewers for their fair and thorough reviews. The research leading to these results has received funding from the European Community's Seventh Framework Programme FP7/2007-2013 under grant agreement n° 216008 (Predator). This work was supported by the DFG as part of the Transregional Collaborative Research Center SFB/TR 14 (AVACS).

References

1. Wilhelm, R., Engblom, J., Ermedahl, A., Holsti, N., Thesing, S., Whalley, D., Bernat, G., Ferdinand, C., Heckmann, R., Mitra, T., Mueller, F., Puaut, I., Puschner, P., Staschulat, J., Stenström, P.: The worst-case execution-time problem—overview of methods and survey of tools. Transactions on Embedded Computing Systems 7(3), 1–53 (2008)
2. Alt, M., Ferdinand, C., Martin, F., Wilhelm, R.: Cache behavior prediction by abstract interpretation. In: Cousot, R., Schmidt, D.A. (eds.) SAS 1996. LNCS, vol. 1145, pp. 52–66. Springer, Heidelberg (1996)
3. Ferdinand, C., Wilhelm, R.: Efficient and precise cache behavior prediction for real-time systems. Real-Time Systems 17(2-3), 131–181 (1999)

4. White, R.T., Healy, C.A., Whalley, D.B., Mueller, F., Harmon, M.G.: Timing analysis for data caches and set-associative caches. In: RTAS 1997: Proceedings of the 3rd IEEE Real-Time Technology and Applications Symposium, Washington, DC, USA, p. 192. IEEE Computer Society, Los Alamitos (1997)
5. Ghosh, S., Martonosi, M., Malik, S.: Precise miss analysis for program transformations with caches of arbitrary associativity. In: ASPLOS-VIII: Proceedings of the Eighth International Conference on Architectural Support for Programming Languages and Operating Systems, pp. 228–239. ACM Press, New York (1998)
6. Chatterjee, S., Parker, E., Hanlon, P.J., Lebeck, A.R.: Exact analysis of the cache behavior of nested loops. In: PLDI 2001: Proceedings of the ACM SIGPLAN 2001 Conference on Programming Language Design and Implementation, pp. 286–297. ACM Press, New York (2001)
7. Reineke, J., Grund, D., Berg, C., Wilhelm, R.: Timing predictability of cache replacement policies. Real-Time Systems 37(2), 99–122 (2007)
8. Reineke, J., Grund, D.: Relative competitive analysis of cache replacement policies. In: LCTES 2008: Proceedings of the 2008 ACM SIGPLAN-SIGBED Conference on Languages, Compilers, and Tools for Embedded Systems, pp. 51–60. ACM Press, New York (2008)
9. Jacob, B., Ng, S.W., Wang, D.T.: Memory Systems: Cache, DRAM, Disk. Morgan Kaufmann Publishers, San Francisco (2008)
10. Cousot, P., Cousot, R.: Basic Concepts of Abstract Interpretation. In: Building the Information Society, pp. 359–366. Kluwer Academic Publishers, Dordrecht (2004)
11. Ferdinand, C.: Cache Behaviour Prediction for Real-Time Systems. PhD thesis, Saarland University (1997)
12. Cousot, P., Cousot, R., Feret, J., Mauborgne, L., Miné, A., Monniaux, D., Rival, X.: Combination of abstractions in the ASTRÉE static analyzer. In: Okada, M., Satoh, I. (eds.) ASIAN 2006. LNCS, vol. 4435, pp. 272–300. Springer, Heidelberg (2008)
13. Ghosh, S., Martonosi, M., Malik, S.: Cache miss equations: An analytical representation of cache misses. In: ICS 1997: Proceedings of the 11th International Conference on Supercomputing, pp. 317–324. ACM Press, New York (1997)
14. Ghosh, S., Martonosi, M., Malik, S.: Cache miss equations: A compiler framework for analyzing and tuning memory behavior. ACM Transactions on Programming Languages and Systems 21(4), 703–746 (1999)
15. Mueller, F., Whalley, D.B., Harmon, M.: Predicting instruction cache behavior. In: LCTRTS 1994: Proceedings of the ACM SIGPLAN Workshop on Language, Compiler, and Tool Support for Real-Time Systems (1994)
16. Li, Y.T.S., Malik, S., Wolfe, A.: Cache modeling for real-time software: Beyond direct mapped instruction caches. In: RTSS 1996: Proceedings of the 17th IEEE Real-Time Systems Symposium, Washington, DC, USA, p. 254. IEEE Computer Society, Los Alamitos (1996)
17. Brand, D., Zafiropulo, P.: On communicating finite-state machines. Journal of the ACM 30(2), 323–342 (1983)
18. Peng, W., Iyer, S.P.: Data flow analysis of communicating finite-state machines. ACM Transactions on Programming Languages and Systems 13(3), 399–442 (1991)
19. Bouajjani, A., Habermehl, P.: Symbolic reachability analysis of FIFO-channel systems with nonregular sets of configurations. Theoretical Computer Science 221(1-2), 211–250 (1999)

A Verifiable, Control Flow Aware Constraint Analyzer for Bounds Check Elimination*

David Niedzielski, Jeffery von Ronne, Andreas Gampe, and Kleanthis Psarris

The University of Texas, San Antonio
{dniedzie,vonronne,agampe,psarris}@cs.utsa.edu

Abstract. The Java platform requires that out-of-bounds array accesses produce runtime exceptions. In general, this requires a dynamic bounds check each time an array element is accessed. However, if it can be proven that the array index is within the bounds of the array, the check can be eliminated. We present a new algorithm based on extended Static Single Assignment (eSSA) form that builds a constraint system representing control flow qualified, linear constraints among program variables derived from program statements. Our system then derives relationships among variables, and provides a verifiable proof of its conclusions. This proof can be verified by a runtime system to minimize the analysis's performance impact. Our system simultaneously considers both control flow and data flow when analyzing the constraint system, handles general linear inequalities instead of simple difference constraints, and provides verifiable proofs for its claims. We present experimental results demonstrating that this method eliminates more bounds checks, and when combined with runtime verification, results in a lower runtime cost than prior work. Our algorithm improves benchmark performance by up to nearly 10% over the baseline SafeTSA system.

1 Introduction

The Java Virtual Machine specification requires all array accesses to be checked at run time and that each out-of-bounds reference cause an *ArrayIndexOutOfBoundsException* to be thrown. However, these run time checks (especially those occurring in nested loops) degrade performance, and so eliminating redundant checks can significantly increase the the performance of Java programs.

Redundant bounds check elimination for Java programs relies on the optimizer's ability to determine that the index used to access an array element is always both strictly less than the array's length and also non-negative. If the optimizer is able to make that determination, then the bounds check can be safely eliminated. If this analysis is performed at run-time, then it must be done as efficiently as possible so as not to degrade performance. However, techniques that sacrifice precision for efficiency detect fewer redundant checks with resulting

---

* Supported in part by AFRL grant F30602-02-1-001, and NSF grants EIA-0117255 and CCF-0702527.

J. Palsberg and Z. Su (Eds.): SAS 2009, LNCS 5673, pp. 137–153, 2009.

sub-optimal run time performance. Alternatively, if optimization is performed at compile time, then it is possible to devote more time to the analysis in an attempt to locate more redundant checks. However, any system that relies solely on compile time analysis is susceptible to a malicious optimizer that claims that an unsafe access is actually safe, thereby compromising system integrity. Therefore, the results of the compile time analysis must be encoded, communicated to the run time system, decoded, and verified at run time.

Optimization techniques generally sacrifice performance for precision, or vice versa. For example, in an attempt to reduce the cost of the analysis, some systems [4,14] restrict the relationship among the variables to simple difference constraints of the form $x - y + c \leq 0$, where x and y are program variables, and c is a constant. Other more precise techniques [9,3] are neither efficient enough to be used at run time, nor are capable of producing verifiable proofs.

We have previously described how proofs of the redundancy of a check can be efficiently represented and verified [16]. This paper describes the Constraint Analysis System (CAS), a symbolic program constraint analyzer that can be used to detect redundant checks and provides a proof of its redundancy claims that can be passed to and verified by a run time system. As described here, CAS is intraprocedural, but in Gampe et al. [11], we describe how many bounds-checks that would otherwise require inter-procedural analysis, can be eliminated by combining CAS with a technique similar to that of Würthinger et al. [17]. This technique removes expensive bounds checks (such as those inside loops) by inserting dynamic tests which guarantee sufficient conditions for the removed bounds check to be redundant at program locations which minimize the cost of the tests (such as the entry of methods).

CAS builds a *Constraint System (CS)* out of general linear relationships among program variables. These have the form:

$$\sum_{1 \leq i \leq n} a_i x_i + c \leq 0 \tag{1}$$

The CS is populated with linear constraints known as *program constraints* that are known to hold because they are derived directly from the statements in the program. CAS then determines if a *proposed inequality constraint* (a conjectured relationship among program variables) is consistent with those program constraints. That is, CAS attempts to determine if the proposed constraint is plausible in the context of a particular program. CAS does so using negative logic: it tries to find sequences of program constraint combinations that are consistent with valid program control flow and which produce an inconsistent result (i.e., $c \leq 0$, where c is a positive constant) when combined with the proposed constraint. Constraints are combined via elementary row operations to produce an equivalent constraint with fewer variables. If CAS can determine that, regardless of the control path taken to reach the variables in a constraint, there is a corresponding set of program constraint combinations that can be combined with the proposed constraint to produce an inconsistency, then the proposed constraint can be rejected. Specifically, in the case where the rejected constraint states that an index is out of bounds, the array access using that index will be safe and its runtime bounds check can be eliminated. CAS records the sequence of constraint combinations from which an inconsistency or consistency was derived, enabling its reasoning to be later checked by verification systems.

The contribution of CAS is two fold. First, CAS specializes Fourier-Motzkin Variable Elimination for use with eSSA program representations so that only those constraint pairs corresponding to valid control flow (CF) paths are combined to eliminate a variable. Additionally, ϕ-function variables are summarized to obtain constraints that apply to all relevent control flow paths in the program. Second, in CAS, the sequence of constraint combinations leading to a inconsistency can be recorded so as to be quickly validated as authentic by a properly-equipped run time system. Lastly, CAS is more general than runtime algorithm based on difference constraints such as ABCD [4], which also operates on eSSA but only considers a limited set of difference constraints.

1.1   eSSA Representation

Our system simultaneously considers program control and data flow to make meaningful conclusions about how program variables relate to one another because the CS used by our system is derived from the program's eSSA [4] representation. eSSA extends traditional SSA [10] representation with "π-assignments", which reflect constraints resulting from control flow paths taken subsequent to conditional statements. These π-assignments create new variables (aliases) along control flow paths that are dominated by the outcome of a conditional expression. The π-variables referenced in constraints implicitly identify a particular control flow path within the program, and are later combined via an SSA ϕ-assignment at a control flow merge point. The SSA code fragment in Figure 1 would be transformed into the equivalent eSSA fragment shown in Figure 2.

```
                      read(a)
                      read(b)
                      if (a < b) then
                          a_1 = pi(a)
                          b_1 = pi(b)    /* a_1 + 1 <= b_1 */
                          {Block A}      /* a,b replaced with a_1, b_1 */
read(a);              else
read(b);                 a_2 = pi(a)
if (a < b) then          b_2 = pi(b)    /* b_2 <= a_2 */
   {Block A}             {Block B}      /* a,b replaced with a_2, b_2 */
else                  end
   {Block B}          a_3 = phi(a_1, a_2)
end                   b_3 = phi(b_1, b_2)
{Rest of program}     {Rest of program} /* a,b replaced with a_3, b_3 */
```

Fig. 1. SSA Example   **Fig. 2.** eSSA Example

1.2   Elementary Row Operations

CAS reduces the problem of determining whether a proposed constraint holds in the context of a program to deciding whether a system of linear inequalities is consistent. Several of the techniques used to solve this and related problems (such as Gaussian, Gauss-Jordan, and Fourier-Motzkin elimination) operate on the principle of iteratively reducing the original system to simpler but equivalent forms until it is able to determine consistency (or solutions). One of the fundamental concepts underlying such techniques is that of *elementary row operations*, which are transformations to the set of linear inequalities which do not change the solution set of the system. Techniques such as Gaussian and Gauss-Jordan elimination reduce a matrix representing a system of linear equations into an equivalent but simpler form by performing only the following row operations:

Row Switching. A row within the matrix can be switched with another row
Row Multiplication. A row can be multiplied by a positive constant
Row Addition. A row can be replaced by the sum of that row and a multiple
   of another row

A related technique to determine the consistency of a system of linear inequalities via elementary row operations is Fourier-Motzkin Variable Elimination (FMVE) [15]. FMVE applies elementary row operations to eliminate variables from the system until its consistency is readily decidable. It eliminates a variable by combining all upper bounds on a variable x with all lower bounds on x. Whenever a lower bound on x is paired with an upper bound on x, a new inequality constraint is produced in which x does not appear. After all variables have been eliminated, the system contains constraints of the form $c \leq 0$. If all such constraints are valid (that is, c is negative or zero), then the original system is consistent. Otherwise, the original system is inconsistent.

2   The Constraint Analysis System (CAS)

CAS's approach is based on FMVE: it eliminates a variable from all constraints in a single step. CAS constructs a *Constraint System* (CS) and combines constraints within it to reason about relationships among program variables. We now describe these two facets of CAS: representation via the CS and reasoning via constraint combination.

2.1   The CAS Constraint System

CAS builds and manipulates a *Constraint System* ($\mathbf{CS} = (\mathbf{V},\mathbf{C})$) to represent relationships among program variables. $\mathbf{V}$ contains representations of the variables in the program, while $\mathbf{C}$ contains linear inequalities that represent constraints over those variables. These elements of $\mathbf{CS}$ are derived from the program's assignment and conditional statements. CAS continually reduces $\mathbf{CS}$ by eliminating variables in $\mathbf{V}$ until it is able to determine consistency. To eliminate a variable x_n in **V**, CAS combines each lower bound (LB) on x_n in **C** (i.e., constraint in which x_n's coefficient is negative) with every upper bound (UB) on x_n (i.e., constraints in which x_n's coefficient is positive) in **C** via elementary row operations that produce a zero coefficient for x_n in the result. At the conclusion of this step, x_n is removed from **V**, all new constraints formed by these combinations are added to **C**, and all former bounds on x_n are removed from **C**. Thus, as processing continues, the set **V** becomes progressively smaller, while **C** (potentially) becomes larger. Note that **C** does not increase if all constraints are difference constraints, whereas the elimination of variables involved in general linear constrains causes the number of edges to increase.

Vertices in CS and their Properties **CS** contains a vertex for each variable in the eSSA representation of the program (including π and ϕ variables). Each vertex $v \in$ **V** has several properties, including:

v.LB the set of constraints $e \in$ **C** representing lower bounds on x_n.
v.UB the set of constraints $e \in$ **C** representing upper bounds on x_n.
v.PHI a boolean indicating whether v is a ϕ variable

Constraints in CS and their Properties. The constraints in **C** represent linear constraints over the program's variables. CAS deals generally with two kinds of constraints: the constraints in **C** that are derived from program statements are called *program constraints*, and are known to be mutually consistent if they all lie on a non-cyclic feasible control flow path, whereas a *proposed constraint* represents a linear constraint over variables that CAS attempts to disprove. In our work, a proposed constraint represents an unsafe condition that would lead to an array-out-of-bounds exception (either upper or lower bound). Since the program constraints are self-consistent (arising directly from program logic), and since a proposed constraint states an access is unsafe (exceeds array bounds), an inconsistent system means that the array access is actually safe. Since all constraints represent less-than-or-equal relationships, assignments and equalities are represented by a pair of inverted edges. That is, if the assignment statement $x = y$ or equality statement $x == y$ occurs in the program, then two constraints are added to **C**: $x - y \leq 0$ and $y - x \leq 0$. In order to ensure combined constraints lie on consistent control-flow paths, constraints in **C** have a "direction" flag associated with them to distinguish whether the assigned variable has a negative coefficient ("forward" direction) or a positive coefficient ("reverse" direction). For example, the constraint $-x + y \leq 0$ resulting from the assignment statement $x = y$ is assigned a "forward" direction, since the variable being assigned to x has a negative coefficient. The other constraint resulting from this assignment $(x - y \leq 0)$ is assigned a "reverse" direction since the assigned variable carries a positive coefficient. Constraints arising from equality and inequality statements are assigned an "independent" direction, but as we shall see later, if an "independent" constraint is combined with a constraint from an assignment, the new constraint will carry the direction of the assignment. Additionally, proposed constraints are initially assigned an "independent" direction as well. Another flag associated with a constraint is the *proposed* flag, which is a binary indication of whether a constraint is a program or proposed constraint. If a proposed constraint is combined with a non-proposed constraint, the *proposed* attribute is set to true on the result.

Any constraint in which x_n's coefficient is negative is a lower bound on x_n, and is added to the collection $x_n.LB$, while those with positive coefficients for x_n are upper bounds and are added to $x_n.UB$. Since a single constraint can contain terms for multiple variables, the same constraint can simultaneously be in multiple UB or LB collections.

As an example, consider a simple program that allocates an integer array of y elements, and then assigns to each element in ascending order. The eSSA listing is shown in Figure 3, and the resulting **CS** is shown in Figure 4.

```
      int A[] = new int[y0];
      /* y0 == A.length */
      x0 = 0
  L:  x1 = phi(x0, x3)
      if (x1 >= y0) goto E:
      x2 = pi(x1)
      y1 = pi(y0)
      /* x2 < y2 */
      A[x2] = ...
      x3 = x2 + 1
      goto L:
  E:  x4 = pi(x1)
      y2 = pi(y0)
      /* y2 <= x4 */
      ...
```

Constraint	Direction
$x0 + 0 \leq 0$	Rev
$-x0 + 0 \leq 0$	Fwd
$A.length - y0 + 0 \leq 0$	Ind
$-A.length + y0 + 0 \leq 0$	Ind
$x0 - x1 + 0 \leq 0$	Fwd
$-x0 + x1 + 0 \leq 0$	Rev
$x2 - x1 + 0 \leq 0$	Rev
$-x2 + x1 + 0 \leq 0$	Fwd
$y1 - y0 + 0 \leq 0$	Rev
$-y1 + y + 0 \leq 0$	Fwd
$x2 - y1 + 1 \leq 0$	Ind
$x2 - x3 + 1 + 0 \leq 0$	Fwd
$-x2 + x3 - 1 - 0 \leq 0$	Rev
$x3 - x1 + 0 \leq 0$	Fwd
$-x3 + x1 + 0 \leq 0$	Rev
$x4 - x1 + 0 \leq 0$	Rev
$-x4 + x1 + 0 \leq 0$	Fwd
$y2 - y0 + 0 \leq 0$	Rev
$-y2 + y + 0 \leq 0$	Fwd
$y2 - x4 + 0 \leq 0$	Ind

Fig. 3. eSSA Version   **Fig. 4.** Constraint System (CS)

2.2 Constraint Combination in CAS

Once all program constraints and the proposed constraint are added to **CS**, CAS determines the plausibility of the proposed constraint by eliminating variables. Unlike conventional FMVE where each upper bound on a variable is indiscriminately combined with each lower bound on a variable to eliminate it from the system, CAS restricts which constraints can be combined in order to ensure the resulting constraint corresponds to a valid control flow path in the program.

Direction Compatibility. Some constraints, in particular, the 'coupling' of a ϕ result variable with each of its operand variables, are only valid when certain control flow graph edges are traversed. An example of this can be seen in the case of the coupling constraints derived from the instruction $x1 = \phi(x0, x3)$ in Figure 3: $x1 - x0 + 0 \leq 0$, $-x1 + x0 \leq 0$, $-x1 + x3 \leq 0$, and $x1 - x3 \leq 0$. If the lower and upper bounds on $x1$ in these constraints were allowed to be combined arbitrarily, it would yield $0 \leq 0$, $0 \leq 0$, $x0 - x3 \leq 0$ and $-x0 + x3 \leq 0$. The first two of these constraints are consistent but redundant, whereas the second two are together equivalent to $x0 == x3$. If this were true, then the value of $x4$ at the loop exit in Figure 3 would always be 0, but this relationship does not follow from the code, since the coupling between $x0$ and $x1$ and between $x1$ and $x3$ exist on different loop iterations.

CAS avoids this by flagging these 'ϕ-coupling' constraints (like $-x1 + x0 + 0 \leq 0$) where the ϕ-variable is negative as "forward" and those where the ϕ-variable is positive as "reverse." CAS then prohibits the combination of bounds with opposing directions. That is, CAS will generally never combine a forward constraint with a reverse constraint. If a forward or reverse constraint is combined with another constraint, then the resulting constraint will carry the forward or reverse direction, respectively. In this way, combined constraints derived from at least one non-independent constraint inherit the direction of the non-independent constraint, while a combined constraint is "independent" only if both "parent" constraints were "independent."

In the case of the ϕ-function in Figure 3, the constraint $-x1 + x0 \leq 0$ has forward direction and the constraint $x1 - x3 \leq 0$ has reverse direction. Combining them to eliminate $x1$ is therefore not allowed. This will always be true for ϕ-coupling constraints. Since the ϕ-variable ($x1$, in the example) is the variable being assigned, it will always have a coefficient of -1 in the forward ϕ-coupling constraints. Conversely, it will always have a coefficient of $+1$ in reverse ϕ-coupling constraints. For two constraints to be combined, they need to have opposite signs on the coefficient of the variable being eliminated, so because coupling constraints with opposite signs will also also have opposite directions, the direction compatibility test effectively prevents CAS from using the ϕ-coupling constraints to inappropriately combine the constraints on the different ϕ operands. (They can, however, still be combined in the case of loops as described in the section of Sub-Cycle Elimination below).

In addition, direction flags on "π-coupling" constraints (such as $x2 - x1 + 0 \leq 0$) play a role in ensuring that constraints derived from conditional branches are only applied on the control flow path dependent on that conditional branch. An example of this is the constraint $x2 - y1 + 1 \leq 0$ in Figure 4 which is derived from the conditional branch in Figure 3. In general, constraints are presumed to hold wherever all of the variables involved in the constraint are in scope; eSSA π-variables are introduced for variables involved in conditionals, so that constraints for control-conditions are implicitly scoped to the control-dependent region. The direction rules ensure that a constraint obtained by combining condition constraints with constraints that are neither ϕ-coupling constraints nor proposed constraints will always contain at least one variable that is control dependent on the condition. As a result, those variables can only be eliminated from the constraint if it is combined with a constraint derived from the coupling of a ϕ-function operand that is control-dependent on the condition or from an original proposed constraint that contained a variable that is control dependent on the condition; in either case, it is appropriate to include the condition-derived constraint. Otherwise, if it is inappropriate, the variable will be left unbounded at will not be able to be used to show an inconsistency.

Sub-Cycle Elimination. CAS detects (in)consistencies through the formation of inequalities in which all variables have been eliminated, leaving only the constant term (we refer to these as 'reduced' constraints). This can be viewed as a 'cycle' in which each term with a positive coefficient is paired with a term with an negative coefficient. In the example program (Figure 3 and 4), this would occur if the proposed constraint for the upper-bound being violated $-x2+A.length \leq 0$ is combined with $x2-y1+1 \leq 0$ by eliminating $x2$ to produce $A.length-y1+1 \leq 0$ which combines with $y1 - y + 0 \leq 0$ to produce $A.length - y + 1 \leq 0$, which combines with $-A.length + y + 0 \leq 0$ to produce the inconsistency $1 \leq 0$. (Note how the final constraint completed the cycle $A.length \leftarrow x2 \leftarrow y1 \leftarrow A.length$ eliminating all of the variables.)

Smaller sub-cycles can also be formed if there are constraints derived from equality relationships (i.e., $x - y \leq 0$ and $y - x \leq 0$) which are not qualified with direction flags or in the case of loops. To handle the former situation, CAS keeps track of variables that were eliminated to derive each constraint and does not allowing constraints to be combined if the same variable was eliminated from both sides of the inequality. The latter case is handled by eliminating phi-variables last and detecting cycles during phi-variable elimination. In such cases, CAS summarizes the loop under the assumption that the back edge is traversed either an infinite number of times, or else not taken at all, depending on which gives the most conservative (safest) summary for that constraint.

Phi nodes. CAS uses a map to compare multiple constraints with the same set of terms and propagates only the "best" one. The definition of "best" affects precision as well as safety decisions and depends upon whether the variable being eliminated is a ϕ node. As described in [4], ϕ nodes are "maximum" nodes, whereas other nodes are "minimum" nodes. We ensure that only the weakest constraints are propagated when a ϕ node is eliminated, and the strongest constraint otherwise. To achieve this, CAS maintains a map effectively keyed by a set of terms (excluding a constant), combined with a direction. The value of the entry is the "best" constraint with those terms and direction. This map initially is populated by program and proposed constraints as they are added to the system. Thereafter, when a new constraint is produced via LB-UB combinations, the map is consulted to see if a 'better' value (depending on the type of eliminated variable) has already been produced. This is done by comparing the constant in the new constraint with the constant in the map entry corresponding to the new constraints terms and direction. If the new constraint and mapped constraint are of equal strength, a constraint carrying the "proposed" indicator takes preference. If not, the map is updated and the old constraint is deleted.

Mapping a reduced result requires explanation. Consider the combination of $z - y \leq 0$ (Forward) and $y - z \leq 0$ (Forward) to eliminate y. The reduced result $(0 \leq 0)$ (Forward) has no terms, and the map key cannot directly be derived. In this case, CAS constructs a *key constraint* to be used as a map key. The key constraint is of the the form $(\alpha,\ direction)$, where α is the set of all terms in the LB, excluding the variable being eliminated, and *direction* is the direction of the reduced constraint. For example, suppose we wish to combine $3x + 4y - 2z <= 0$ (Forward) with $-3x - 4y + 2z \leq 0$ (Forward) to eliminate z. Since the result is reduced, our key constraint is $(3x + 4y,\ \text{Forward})$. Furthermore, if the constant in the reduced constraint is negative and composed from the combination of exclusively assignment statements, then the constant in the key constraint is set to $-\infty$ to reflect the fact that the loop is unsafe when taken in this direction and must be assumed to be taken an arbitrary number of times (since each iteration weakens the constraint). Alternatively, since taking a safe (incrementing) loop in a particular direction makes the constraint stronger (by incrementing the constant), we assume the loop is *never* executed by setting the constant in the the key constraint to the constant in the reduced constraint.

Unbound Variables. When a proposed LB is selected for pairing, a check is done to see if the variable being eliminated is unbound. If so, CAS conservatively reports that the proposed constraint holds. Equivalently, the unbound variable will remain after all other variables are eliminated, but this approach allows us to terminate the algorithm quickly. In future work, we plan to extend CAS with the ability to generate run-time checks that resolve unbound variables during program execution.

Initialization. CAS processing begins by initializing an empty **CS**, and program constraints are added as the program is being parsed. CAS creates the internal representations of the constraint and referenced variables, adds new variables to **V**, sets the direction vector in the new constraint, ands adds the new constraint to the appropriate variable's LB and UB sets, and adds the constraint to the map. Additionally, if the constraint arises from an assignment or equality, the constraint is copied, the coefficients and directions inverted in the copy, and the copy is added to UB and LB sets as well as the map. Once all the program constraints are added, a proposed constraint is formulated and passed to the `propose()` method. This routine creates and initializes a new constraint, sets it's proposed flag, and adds it to appropriate UB and LB collections and the map. Next, assignments in the program are examined. For each assignment constraint where none of the variables are ϕ or π variables, the direction of the constraint is changed to "independent." This enables CAS to infer relationships between x and y in cases such as $x = 5; y = 6$ where there is no intermediate variable to eliminate and direction incompatibility would otherwise prevent the necessary constraint combinations.

Processing. Next, `propose()` calls `eliminate()` to remove a variables from the constraint system. This method combines each LB on a variable with all compatible UBs on the variable, checks for unbound variables, and invokes the method `update_map()` to manage the map of "best" constraints. As part of the combination, a new direction is computed, and the parent UB, parent LB, and the eliminated variable are recorded in the result, so they can be used to generate a proof. Importantly, `update_map()` checks that the proposed constraint is not equal to or weaker than a program constraint that arises either through combinations or from the original set of constraints from the program. If that is the case, then `update_map()` immediately returns "true" to indicate the proposed constraint is consistent with the program constraints. If a cycle is detected, this is recorded by calling `update_map()` after first generating the appropriate key constraint as described previously.

CAS first eliminates all non-ϕ variables, leaving only the strongest constraints linking the ϕ variables. Thereafter, the ϕ variables are eliminated taking only the weakest results at each intermediate stage. After CAS eliminates a variable v, it checks the map with key $(v, \text{Independent})$, $(v, \text{Forward})$, and $(v, \text{Reverse})$ for a non-negative proposed cycle. If one is found, it immediately returns 'true' meaning that the unsafe proposed constraint may hold. Otherwise, if a negative proposed constraint is found, a counter is updated that reflects the number of proposed inconsistencies encountered.

Termination. Once all variables have been eliminated without discovering a proposed consistency, `propose()` returns 'false' if at least one proposed inconsistency was discovered. Otherwise, `propose()` conservatively returns 'true.'

2.3 Arithmetic Overflow

The algorithm described above finds symbolic solutions in the integer domain $\mathbb{Z}$. Java's integer type int, however, is restricted to integers representable in 2's complement 32-bit words and "wrap around" when operations underflow/overflow. Thus, the verification system requires supplementary proofs that the arithmetic operations from which constraints are drawn do not invalidate those constraints through arithmetic underflow or overflow. These are generated by examining the eliminations used by CAS, identifying the constraints derived from arithmetic operations, and invoking the CAS algorithm on a proposed constraint representing the underflow or overflow condition. Proving these constraints may, in turn, require further invocations to check for underflow or overflow in the arithmetic instructions providing constraints used in those proofs and so on.

3   Experimental Results

CAS was implemented in the SafeTSA compiler [1] and was used to identify redundant bound checks and produce verifiable proofs of its redundancy claims. These proofs were encoded in the form of annotations and were passed to a run-time system for verification. Additionally, we added an annotation verifier and

---

Procedure propose(*pc*)

```
/* Check if the proposed constraint pc is provably inconsistent with the program
   constraints in this CS                                                       */
proposed_inconsistencies = 0 ;
/* Add the proposed constraints to the UB and LB collections of the variables it
   references                                                                   */
foreach v in pc's terms do
    if v's coefficient is negative then
        Add pc to v.LB;
    else
        Add pc to v.UB;
    end
end
update_map(pc, null);
/* Convert assignments into inequalities where safe to do so                    */
foreach non-φ v in V do
    if v is assigned in constraint c, c has no φs, and c is not a Pi-Assignment then
        c.direction = Independent;
    end
end
/* Eliminate all variables in the system. We'll return early if we see a proposed
   consistency preventing us from disproving the proposed constraint            */
foreach non-φ v in CS do
    eliminate(v);
end
foreach φ v in CS do
    eliminate(v);
end
/* No proposed inconsistencies -- check if proposed inconsistencies detected    */
if proposed_inconsistencies > 0 then
    return FALSE;
else
    return TRUE;
end
```

---

annotation directed optimization into the SafeTSA class loader and JIT compiler of the SafeTSA virtual machine (which is based on Jikes RVM 2.2.0).

For comparison, we also took the implementation of ABCD [4] found in the Jikes RVM Optimizing compiler [6] and ported it to work with the SafeTSA data structures. Several features of SafeTSA required extensions to the original algorithm, most notably, SafeTSA's type infrastructure. SafeTSA includes several explicit type coercion instructions to simplify type-checking; these were accommodated in ABCD by extending ABCD's existing Global Value Numbering system. In addition, since the existing ABCD implementation analyzed only upper-bounds checks, we extended ABCD to support lower-bounds checks.

We evaluated our prototype system using the Java Grande Forum benchmarks [5]. The benchmarks were modified to express some of the array bounds limits as symbolic constants rather than passed in as parameters so that more array bounds could be eliminated with conservative, intraprocedural analysis. These benchmarks were compiled into SafeTSA and then optimized using common subexpression elimination, which eliminates duplicate bounds checks using SafeTSA's safe-element-reference type. This version of each class was used as the baseline to which CAS and ABCD were applied. All of the experiments were conducted on a 1.5GHz G4 PowerMac with 1GB of RAM running

---

Procedure eliminate(v)

```
foreach LB in v.LB do
    if LB.proposed AND v has no upper bounds then
        /* Unbound variable detected                                        */
        EXIT(TRUE);
    end
    foreach UB in v.UB do
        if LB and UB have compatible directions AND do not form a sub-cycle then
            /* Combine the constraints to eliminate v                       */
            new_con = combine(LB,v,UB);
            if new_con is reduced then
                /* All variables have been eliminated, leaving only a constant term.
                   If this is a proposed constraint or is not a harmless cycle, then
                   create a key constraint from the terms eliminated terms (excluding
                   v) so we can consult the map                             */
                if (new_con.constant ¡ 0 AND new_constant.isAssignmentCycle) OR
                new_con.proposed then
                    calculate key_constraint from LB and UB;
                    if new_con.proposed then
                        /* Assume a proposed constraint is not strengthened by safe
                           loop traversals                                  */
                        key_constraint.constant = new_con.constant;
                    else
                        /* Assume unsafe loops are taken indefinitely       */
                        key_constraint.constant = −∞;
                    end
                    key_constraint.direction = new_con.direction;
                    update_map(key_constraint, v);
                end
            else
                /* There are more variables to eliminate -- see if this new constraint
                   is ''better'' than one we've already seen               */
                if (update_map(new_con, v) == true then
                    Add new_con to the UB and LB sets of remaining variables;
                else
                    Discard new_con;
                end
            end
        end
    end
end
delete all bounds in v.UB and v.LB;
if map[v, *].constant ≤ 0 and is proposed then
    /* A consistency exists -- indicate we cannot disprove proposed constraint */
    EXIT(TRUE)
end
if map[v, *].constant ¿ 0 and is proposed then
    /* Inconsistent proposed cycle -- increment counter and keep checking  */
    proposed_constraints += 1
end
```

---

a Linux 2.6.15 kernel. All timing measurements were made by repeatedly running the benchmark program in a fresh virtual machine at least 200 times. The first fifty runs were discarded and the mean of the subsequent runs reported.

Figure 5 shows the number of bounds checks (beyond those eliminated by common subexpression elimination) that were eliminated by CAS and ABCD, respectively, in each of the benchmark classes. Since CAS can reason about a more general class of linear constraints while ABCD is limited to a subclass of difference constraints, one would expect CAS to eliminate more bounds

---

Procedure update_map(*con*, *v*)

```
/* Manage a map of the ''best'' constraints seen thus far. The definition of ''best''
   depends on whether the term just eliminated to create a new constraint is a φ node
   or not                                                                          */
if map[(con.terms,con.direction)] exists then
       /* A constraint with the same terms and direction as the new constraint has already
          been processed. See if the new constraint is ''better''                 */
       old_con = map[(con.terms,con.direction)];
       /* If old_con is proposed and con is a program constraint (or vice versa) verify
          that the proposed constraint is not the original proposed constraint and equal
          to or weaker than the program constraint. If so, return ''true''         */
       if v is non-φ then
              /* Test the constant in the old constraint to see if the new constraint is
                 stronger. Replace and delete the old constraint if it is weaker, or if it is
                 not proposed while the new constraint is proposed (to be conservative).
                 Return ''true'' if we updated the map, ''false'' otherwise         */
       else
              /* Test the constant in the old constraint to see if the new constraint is
                 weaker, or if the new constraint is proposed and is the same strength as the
                 old constraint. If so, replace and delete the old constraint. Return
                 ''true'' if we updated the map, ''false'' otherwise               */
       end
else
       /* This is a new map entry                                                  */
       map[(con.terms,con.direction)] = con;
       return "true";
end
```

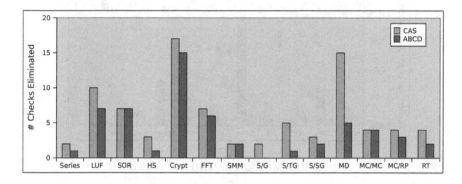

Fig. 5. Precision of CAS and ABCD

checks than ABCD. For our benchmarks, all of the bounds checks removed by ABCD were also eliminated by CAS, and in nearly three-quarters of the classes, CAS's extra precision enabled it to eliminate more bounds checks. Notably, for the the Moldyn benchmark, CAS was able to eliminate 15 bounds checks where ABCD could only remove 5. Manual inspection of several bounds checks revealed that these were bounds checks that the ABCD is unable to prove because ABCD can only reason about difference constraints constraining the variable being defined relative to the variables being used in that definition. This restriction speeds up ABCD significantly (since it allows ABCD to piggy back on the existing compiler data structures) but does so at the cost of precision. The following code fragment from MolDyn is typical:

```
particle[] one = new particle [mdsize];
for(i=0;i<mdsize;i++) {
    sp = sp + one[i].xvelocity;
}
```

ABCD cannot infer that the access is safe in this case because `particle` is defined in terms of `mdsize` instead of `mdsize` being defined in terms of `a.length`, but CAS can prove such accesses safe.

Figure 6 shows the cost of the runtime verification of CAS's proofs vs. the runtime use of ABCD as a percentage of baseline JIT compilation time. For CAS this is primarily the time required to verify annotations at run-time, whereas for ABCD this is the time required to carry out the analysis. With one exception (RayTracer), verification has a lower runtime cost than ABCD. For some of the benchmarks (notably Crypt, Search, and LUFact), verification is several times faster. For bounds checks both ABCD and CAS can eliminate (chains of difference constraints), CAS verification and ABCD take about the same time. The primary reason that verification outperforms ABCD is because verification only needs to verify those bounds checks that are actually unnecessary, whereas

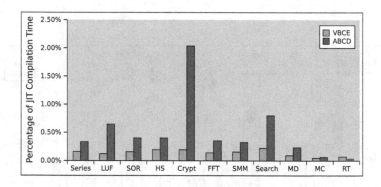

Fig. 6. Runtime Cost of CAS and ABCD

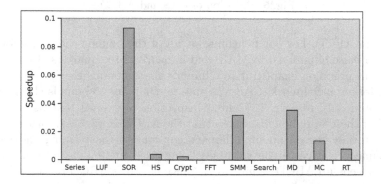

Fig. 7. Overall Execution Speedup with CAS

ABCD analyzes all bounds checks. Compared to the total JIT compilation time, both methods impose a very small runtime cost (up to about 0.2% for CAS verification and up to about 2.0% for ABCD).

Figure 7 shows the speedup in total benchmark execution time resulting from the use of verification compared to the baseline SafeTSA version of the benchmark. The bounds check elimination resulted in improvements of nearly 10% on the SOR benchmark and over 3% on the SparseMatMult and MolDyn benchmarks. On the other benchmarks the speedup was small or negligible; this is because most of the bounds checks that could be eliminated in those benchmarks were not in the benchmark's inner loop. Since time spent in verification was relatively small (a couple of milliseconds) compared to the total execution time (15s–200s), the effect of verification cost was negligible.

4 Related Work

There have been several works addressing the array bounds check problems in Java. Moreira et al. [13] used heavy-weight loop-based transformations and optimizations to optimize bounds checks in scientific applications; their goal was to provide a traditional static compiler for Java programs that provides performance approaching that of traditional optimizing compilers for Fortran, so their approach does not support just-in-time compilation and is not a general solution to the Java bounds check problem.

The ABCD algorithm [4] provides a runtime global bounds check elimination based on extended-SSA (eSSA) form and difference constraints, it is quite efficient but has some limitations since it can only obtain difference constraints that can be overlayed onto the eSSA graph. Menon et al. [12] extended the ABCD algorithm to produce optimized programs augmented with verifiable proof variables. Like ABCD, CAS represents programs using eSSA, but CAS's constraint system is more general allowing it to reason about linear inequalities. Linear programming techniques such as Fourier-Motzkin Variable Elimination [15] also handle such inequalities, but CAS is adapted to simultaneously consider restrictions arising from control flow.

Qian et al.[14] use an iterative dataflow analysis based on difference constraints to annotate bytecode with an indication of which bounds checks are unnecessary, but it does not provide verifiable proofs of its claims. Chen and Kandemir [7] describe a method for annotating the fixed point of a iterative dataflow analysis of integer variable ranges which can then be verified using a single iteration of the same algorithm, but their constraints are limited to a subset of difference constraints.

Zhao et al.'s [18] optimization is restricted to limited loop forms (and is, therefore, less comprehensive than our approach) but is quite efficient during JIT compilation. Würthinger et al. [17] have developed a bounds check elimination for use in the HotSpot JIT compiler, which similarly identifies simple patterns in the source code but adds speculation to reduce the overhead of some of the bounds checks that cannot be completely eliminated statically.

Besson et al.'s [2] proof-carrying code architecture is based on Cousot's abstract interpretation [8] and produces a certificate at analysis time that is passed to a consumer for certified verification. Their system checks if all accesses within a program are safe, rather than testing the safety of individual array accesses.

5 Conclusion

We present in this paper a static analysis for determining whether a proposed constraint over variables is consistent with the semantics of a particular code fragment. CAS uses eSSA representation to form a constraint system expressing relationships among variables with sufficient control flow information to ensure semantically meaningful conclusions. It then simplifies the system until it can determine whether the proposed constraint is consistent with the system. This information can be used to determine that array bounds checking is not necessary along particular control flow paths. We present experimental results that demonstrate that CAS finds more redundant checks than previous work, and improves the runtime of JAVA benchmarks up to 10%. Our results show how CAS is useful when used at compile time to identify fully redundant bounds checks and having its conclusions encoded in the form of annotations which are efficiently verified at run-time.

References

1. Amme, W., von Ronne, J., Franz, M.: Ssa-based mobile code: Implementation and empirical evaluation. ACM Trans. Archit. Code Optim. 4(2), Article 13 (2007)
2. Besson, F., Jensen, T., Pichardie, D.: Proof-carrying code from certified abstract interpretation and fixpoint compression. Theoretical Computer Science 364(3), 273–291 (2006); Applied Semantics
3. Blume, W., Eigenmann, R.: Demand-driven, symbolic range propagation. In: Huang, C.-H., Sadayappan, P., Banerjee, U., Gelernter, D., Nicolau, A., Padua, D.A. (eds.) LCPC 1995. LNCS, vol. 1033, pp. 141–160. Springer, Heidelberg (1996)
4. Bodík, R., Gupta, R., Sarkar, V.: Abcd: eliminating array bounds checks on demand. In: PLDI 2000: Proceedings of the ACM SIGPLAN 2000 conference on Programming language design and implementation, pp. 321–333. ACM Press, New York (2000)
5. Bull, J.M., Smith, L.A., Westhead, M.D., Henty, D.S., Davey, R.A.: A benchmark suite for high performance Java. Concurrency: Practice and Experience 12(6), 375–388 (2000)
6. Burke, M.G., Choi, J.-D., Fink, S., Grove, D., Hind, M., Sarkar, V., Serrano, M.J., Sreedhar, V.C., Srinivasan, H., Whaley, J.: The jalapeño dynamic optimizing compiler for java. In: JAVA 1999: Proceedings of the ACM 1999 conference on Java Grande, pp. 129–141. ACM, New York (1999)
7. Chen, G., Kandemir, M.: Verifiable annotations for embedded java environments. In: CASES 2005: Proceedings of the 2005 international conference on Compilers, architectures and synthesis for embedded systems, pp. 105–114. ACM Press, New York (2005)

8. Cousot, P., Cousot, R.: Abstract interpretation: a unified lattice model for static analysis of programs by construction or approximation of fixpoints. In: POPL 1977: Proceedings of the 4th ACM SIGACT-SIGPLAN symposium on Principles of programming languages, pp. 238–252. ACM, New York (1977)

9. Cousot, P., Halbwachs, N.: Automatic discovery of linear restraints among variables of a program. In: POPL 1978: Proceedings of the 5th ACM SIGACT-SIGPLAN symposium on Principles of programming languages, pp. 84–96. ACM Press, New York (1978)

10. Cytron, R., Ferrante, J., Rosen, B.K., Wegman, M.N., Zadeck, F.K.: Efficiently computing static single assignment form and the control dependence graph. ACM Transactions on Programming Languages and Systems (TOPLAS) 13(4), 451–490 (1991)

11. Gampe, A., von Ronne, J., Niedzielski, D., Psarris, K.: Speculative improvements to verifiable bounds check elimination. In: Proceedings of the International Conference on Principles and Practice of Programming In Java (PPPJ 2008). ACM Press, New York (2008)

12. Menon, V.S., Glew, N., Murphy, B.R., McCreight, A., Shpeisman, T., Adl-Tabatabai, A.-R., Petersen, L.: A verifiable ssa program representation for aggressive compiler optimization. In: POPL 2006: Conference record of the 33rd ACM SIGPLAN-SIGACT symposium on Principles of programming languages, pp. 397–408. ACM Press, New York (2006)

13. Moreira, J.E., Midkiff, S.P., Gupta, M.: From flop to megaflops: Java for technical computing. ACM Trans. Program. Lang. Syst. 22(2), 265–295 (2000)

14. Qian, F., Hendren, L.J., Verbrugge, C.: A comprehensive approach to array bounds check elimination for java. In: Horspool, R.N. (ed.) CC 2002. LNCS, vol. 2304, pp. 325–342. Springer, Heidelberg (2002)

15. Schrijver, A.: Theory of Linear and Integer Programming. Wiley and Sons, Chichester (1986)

16. von Ronne, J., Gampe, A., Niedzielski, D., Psarris, K.: Safe bounds check annotations. Concurrency and Computations: Practice and Experience (2008), doi:10.1002/cpe.1341

17. Würthinger, T., Wimmer, C., Mössenböck, H.: Array bounds check elimination for the java hotspot client compiler. In: PPPJ 2007: Proceedings of the 5th international symposium on Principles and practice of programming in Java, pp. 125–133. ACM, New York (2007)

18. Zhao, J., Rogers, I., Kirkham, C., Watson, I.: Loop parallelisation for the jikes rvm. In: Proceedings of the Sixth International Conference on Parallel and Distributed Computing (PDCAT 2005), pp. 35–39. IEEE Computer Society Press, Los Alamitos (2005)

Increasing the Scope and Resolution of Interprocedural Static Single Assignment

Silvian Calman and Jianwen Zhu

Department of Electrical and Computer Engineering
University of Toronto, Toronto, Ontario, Canada
{calman,jzhu}@eecg.toronto.edu

Abstract. While intraprocedural Static Single Assignment (SSA) is ubiquitous in modern compilers, the use of interprocedural SSA, although seemingly a natural extension, is limited. We find that part of the impediment is due to the narrow scope of variables handled by previously reported approaches, leading to limited benefits in optimization.

In this study, we increase the scope of Interprocedural SSA (ISSA) to record elements and singleton heap variables. We show that ISSA scales reasonably well (to all MediaBench and most of the SPEC2K), while resolving on average 1.72 times more loads to their definition. We propose and evaluate an interprocedural copy propagation and an interprocedural liveness analysis and demonstrate their effectiveness on reducing input and output instructions by 44.5% and 23.3%, respectively. ISSA is then leveraged for constant propagation and dead code removal, where 11.8% additional expressions are folded.

Keywords: SSA, interprocedural, dataflow, constant propagation.

1   Introduction

When the *Intermediate Representation* (IR) is in *Static Single Assignment* (SSA) form, each use of a variable is associated with the point where it is defined. To convert the IR into SSA form an algorithm based on Cytron [1] can be used to replace loads and stores for a set of program variables, which we refer to as *SSA variables* and insert ϕ instructions at control flow merge points.

Not all program variables are SSA variables. Usually, they are limited to scalar stack variables, whose address is never taken. This scope can be extended to other stack variables, global variables, and variables allocated on the heap. This extension is usually referred to as *Interprocedural SSA* (ISSA) as it is required to trace the dataflow for SSA variables across procedure boundaries.

SSA form can simplify analysis and optimization algorithms. Due to ϕ instructions, we can distinguish values associated with incoming edges, a property utilized to apply constant propagation, dead code removal [2], and other transformations [3, 4]. Moreover, ϕ instructions can also be used to analyze cyclical dataflow, such as in induction variable analysis [5]. Beyond this, SSA is also used to simplify other client applications [6, 7, 8] by decoupling the dataflow

J. Palsberg and Z. Su (Eds.): SAS 2009, LNCS 5673, pp. 154–170, 2009.
© Springer-Verlag Berlin Heidelberg 2009

analysis from the implementation. Naturally, it can be expected that ISSA form can help extend these intraprocedural analysis and optimization algorithms to their interprocedural counterparts.

We review two recent ISSA construction algorithms. Liao [9] applied a unification based pointer analysis (Steensgaard's [10]), and renamed memory accesses to the corresponding alias set. Staiger et al. [11] used symbolic variables, called locators, to represent program variables at each procedure. In this work, values are passed interprocedurally by mapping locators to one another and SSA is generated in a traditional way [1], after a pointer analysis step maps all loads and stores to the corresponding locator. Staiger showed that an inclusion-based pointer analysis (Andersen's [12]) reduces memory consumption and considerably speeds up the formation of ISSA, compared to the unification-based pointer analysis (Steensgaard).

The ISSA construction described by Liao [9] and Staiger [11] has a number of shortfalls. First, their ISSA has limited resolution, as some SSA variables represent more than one program variable, creating *may def-use* relations. More specifically, full resolution was only available for scalar globals and as such, copy propagation (and strong updates, etc.) could only be applied to scalar globals. Furthermore, in contrast to traditional SSA form, client applications would have to distinguish between must def-use and may def-use relations. Second, neither Liao [9], nor Staiger [11] applied interprocedural copy propagation, which can fold false merge points or liveness analysis to reduce unnecessary dataflow propagation. The lack of a mechanism to remove redundant ϕ instructions and unused expressions during ISSA construction results in a much greater code size and less precise dataflow.

We propose and evaluate an ISSA form without may def-use relations, implemented in the compiler IR by extending the instruction set. Our implementation considers both scalars as well as scalar elements of records. We handle global and stack variables, as well as variables corresponding to a single dynamic memory location. Using this implementation, we contrast ourselves with previous work and make the following contributions:

- We quantify why the previous approach, in which a flow-insensitive pointer analysis is used and only strong updates to scalars globals are handled (similar to Staiger [11]), is less effective. By handling record elements and singleton heap locations, we replace 1.72 times (on average) more load instructions with their definition. In addition, we observed that the field-insensitive pointer analysis increases the input into procedures by a factor of 12.2, on average.
- We define the value of an instruction in terms of its parent's last invocation and we propose an interprocedural copy propagation algorithm, which reduces input and output instructions by 44.5%, on average. To the best of our knowledge, this is the first paper describing the challenges involved as well as proposing a solution.

- We incorporate a revised interprocedural liveness analysis to limit the variables propagated into and out of procedures, which reduces the input and output instructions by 23.3%, on average.
- We evaluate the benefit of ISSA by applying constant-folding and dead code elimination on the IR (ISSA form) and fold on average 11.8% more instructions than what was provided by the LLVM infrastructure.

In Section 2, we describe the IR extensions for ISSA and the challenges involved in copy propagation. In Section 3, we provide details regarding the implementation and present the algorithms used to identify heap allocated SSA variables, compute liveness analysis, and apply copy propagation. In Section 4, we provide experimental data for the performance and precision of our ISSA form and the improvement observed in constant propagation. Section 5 discusses related work and Section 6 summarizes the major conclusions.

2   Interprocedural SSA

In this section, we present the IR extensions used to handle dereferences and interprocedural value propagation and demonstrate ISSA form construction using an example. In Section 2.1, we describe the difference between intraprocedural and interprocedural copy propagation and outline our algorithm.

In ISSA, dereferences might correspond to multiple locations, including SSA variables. Similar to previous work [13, 6, 14, 15], we extend the IR with the conditional load and store instructions (ϕ^L and ϕ^S, respectively). Another issue is value passing at call instructions; we introduce two new instructions, ϕ^V and ϕ^C, to pass the value of a variable across procedure boundaries. These new instructions are discussed in more detail below:

ϕ^S: $pExpr.\phi^S(var, curr, val)$ is used to handle store instructions, where $pExpr$ is the pointer expression. If $pExpr$ is equal to var, then the value of this instruction becomes val, otherwise, the value is $curr$.

ϕ^L: $pExpr.\phi^L(\langle var_1, val_1\rangle, \ldots, \langle var_n, val_n\rangle)$ is used to handle load instructions, where $pExpr$ is the pointer expression. If $pExpr$ is equal to var_i, then the value of this instruction will be val_i.

ϕ^V: $\phi^V_{\langle var, p\rangle}(\langle ci_1, val_1\rangle, \langle ci_2, val_2\rangle, \ldots)$ is used to pass the value of variable var to the entry of procedure p, from a call instruction ci. When entering p from ci_i, the value of this instruction is val_i.

ϕ^C: $pExpr.\phi^C_{\langle var, ci\rangle}(\langle func_1, val_1\rangle, \langle func_2, val_2\rangle, \ldots)$ is used to pass the value of variable var, at the exit from a call instruction ci, where $pExpr$ is the pointer expression for ci, if ci is an indirect call. If $pExpr$ is equal to $func_i$, then the value of this instruction will be val_i. For direct calls, we omit the pointer expression.

In Example 1(d), we show the ISSA form of Example 1(a). The ISSA form is derived by leveraging the pointer analysis result along with the new instructions

Example 1. Interprocedural SSA Example

```
int   y = 5, z = 10, *x, **g;     1
C( ) { print( **g ); }            2
B( ) { *g = &z; }                 3
main( ) {                         4
  g = &x;                         5
  x = &y;                         6
S1:  B( );                        7
  **g = 20;                       8
S2:  C( );                        9

}
```

(a) Code before SSA is applied.
Point-to graph is shown in
Example 1(b).

(b) Point-to
graph for
Example 1(a)

```
int   y = 5, z = 10,     1
  *x, **g;               2
C( ) {                   3
  print( 20 );           4
}                        5
main( ) {                6
  C( );                  7

}
```

(c) Code after copy propagation

```
int   y = 5, z = 10, *x, **g;                           1
C( ) {                                                  2
  x2 = φ^V_{⟨x,C⟩}(CI_2, x1);                            3
  y2 = φ^V_{⟨y,C⟩}(CI_2, y1);                            4
  z2 = φ^V_{⟨z,C⟩}(CI_2, z1);                            5
  print( x2.φ^L(⟨&y, y2⟩, ⟨&z, z2⟩) );                   6
}                                                       7
B( ) { }                                                8
main( ) {                                               9
CI_1:  B( );                                            10
  x1 = φ^C_{⟨x,CI_1⟩}(B, &z)                             11
  y1 = x1.φ^S(&y, 5, 20);                                12
  z1 = x1.φ^S(&z, 10, 20);                               13
CI_2:  C( );                                            14

}
```

(d) Code after ϕ^S, ϕ^L, ϕ^V, and ϕ^C instructions are inserted

(ϕ^L, ϕ^S, ϕ^V, ϕ^C). In Example 1(a), all four global variables g, x, y, and z are SSA variables. A flow-insensitive pointer analysis indicates that x points to either y or z, and g points to x. Since the dereference in Example 1(a) on Line 8 corresponds to either y or z, we need to insert two ϕ^S instructions to handle the store, as illustrated in Example 1(d) on Lines 12–13. Similarly, due to the dereference in Example 1(a) on Line 2, we need to insert a ϕ^L instruction in Example 1(d) on Line 6. Note that procedure B produces the variable x, whereas procedure C uses the variable x and possibly the variables y or z. Hence, we generate the appropriate input and output mappings for procedure B on Line 11 and procedure C on Lines 3–5.

2.1   Copy Propagation

Copy propagation simplifies the IR, as we remove and fold ϕ, ϕ^S, ϕ^L, ϕ^V, and ϕ^C instructions. For instance, by applying copy propagation, we determine the value of $x1$ (Line 11 in Example 1(d)) to be $&z$ and by folding the ϕ^S and ϕ^L instructions, we produce the code in Example 1(c).

The scope of a value in our framework is the whole program, enabling us to fold ϕ^V and ϕ^C instructions. The benefit of this approach is IR size reduction and the simplification of the def-use relation, as values passed in and out of procedures are masked by ϕ^V and ϕ^C instructions. To this end, we define the value of instruction I in procedure P as the value of I in the last call frame of

P, or otherwise (P is not on the stack) as the value of I in the last invocation of P. Under this definition, the value of I varies with its usage points, but at any program point in P, it is identical in both SSA and ISSA, and as such, ISSA can be constructed on IR in SSA form. Copy propagation is straight forward with the exception of ϕ^V and ϕ^C instructions, which we discuss in the rest of this section.

Let us consider a ϕ^V instruction I^V used in procedure P, merging a single value V. Under our definition, replacing I^V with V is legal as long as V is not located in P. However, V cannot be located in P since V must dominate I^V, and I^V dominates all instructions inside procedure P. Hence, under our definition, ϕ^V instructions merging a single value V, can always be substituted with V.

Example 2. Examples for invalid ϕ^C copy propagation

```
int Sum(                              1
    int a, int b, int c ) {           2
S1: return a + b + c; }               3
void main( ) {                        4
    int    e, f;                      5
                                      6
    e=Sum( 1,2,3 );                   7
    f=Sum( 20,21,315 );               8
    printf("%d,%d\n", f, e );         9
}
```

```
StructPtr recursiveProc(              1
    StructPtr a, StructPtr b ) {      2
    resA = recursiveProc(             3
        a->right, b->right );         4
    resB = recursiveProc(             5
        a->left, b->left );           6
    ...                               7
    if( resA == resB )                8
    ... ;                             9
}
```

(a) Interprocedural copy propaga-   (b) Recursive procedure dataflow
tion

Let us consider a ϕ^C instruction I^C merging a single value V located in procedure P_V. Replacing I^C with V is not always legal, as the invocation of P_V which V corresponds to depends on the usage point of I^C. This is illustrated in Example 2, where we present two cases in which the same value can correspond to different instances of an instruction. In Example 2(a), both the first and second return values from procedure *Sum* would correspond to $S1$. If we propagate $S1$ through both ϕ^C instructions corresponding to it, then we would lose the reference to $S1$ returned from the first call. To further emphasize this, in Example 2(b), the values produced in two previous invocation of a recursive procedure are compared. Without distinguishing between such instances, we will erroneously conclude that the branch is always taken.

To discuss a solution for the substitution of ϕ^C instructions, let us assume I^C is in procedure P_{I^C} and defined at call instruction ci. First, if the value I^C merged was a constant (i.e. not V), then it could be substituted at all usage points of I^C. Otherwise, to prevent the propagation of values whose parent might still be on the stack, we make sure that **P_{I^C} and P_V do not belong to the same maximal Strongly Connected Component**. Then, we can substitute I^C with V if no other call to P_V is reachable between ci and the usage program point (V not redefined – thus it corresponds to value at ci). Note that our copy propagation algorithm must be flow-sensitive, since we need to determine the last instance of values substituted for ϕ^C instructions.

3 Interprocedural SSA Generation

ISSA is generated in a stepwise procedure, as is illustrated in Figure 1. First, in Section 3.1, we discuss the field-sensitive pointer analysis. In Section 3.2, we describe the SSA variables handled and present the algorithm used to identify singleton heap variables. Similar to Staiger [11], we convert load and store instructions as described in Section 3.3 and map input and output values at call instructions, as detailed in Section 3.4. In Section 3.4, we also describe the interprocedural liveness analysis used to constrain the variables propagated across procedures. Next, we place ϕ instructions to merge values, both interprocedurally and intraprocedurally. We treat the newly inserted ϕ^S, ϕ^V, and ϕ^C as storage instructions; ϕ^L as a load instruction; and we use Cytron's [1] algorithm, unmodified. Lastly, we apply interprocedural copy propagation, as described in Section 3.5.

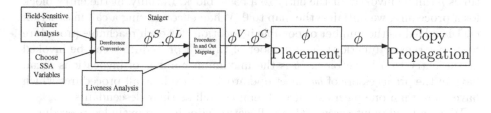

Fig. 1. Overall procedure for ISSA generation

3.1 Pointer Analysis

Pointer analysis is used to update the call graph and to resolve pointer dereferences into loads, stores, ϕ^S, and ϕ^L instructions (Section 3.3). From practical experimentation on a large number of C benchmarks, we observed that field-insensitivity results in a large number of spurious point-to edges and an increase in the number of variables passed across procedures.

We observed that distinguishing between heap objects reduced the number of spurious point-to edges and therefore, false loads and assignments. Moreover, many benchmarks use memory managers, and distinguishing between heap locations, allocated using interface functions, reduced both the runtime of the pointer analysis and spurious point-to edges (and hence, spurious memory accesses).

3.2 Choosing SSA Variables

Currently, we consider scalar variables and fields of aggregates as potential SSA variables. We handle local variables in non-recursive procedures and in addition to previous work on ISSA, we also handle SSA variables residing in allocation sites, executed at most once in a program, which we refer to as *singular*. If an allocation site A_i is executed at most once, then each dereference resolved to A_i corresponds to the same memory location. Furthermore, since only a single instance of this instruction exists, each variable v, allocated at A_i, can be an SSA variable.

Singular allocation sites are identified by using the *maximal Strongly Connected Component* (SCC) partitioned call graph and control flow graph. Singular allocations can occur on mutually exclusive paths in the program. As such, we propose an algorithm called *Exclusive Path Singular Allocation Site Identifier* (**EPSASI**). Initially, EPSASI excludes from consideration all procedures in a SCC, or procedures called from a control flow graph SCC, as well as their descendants. In EPSASI, the procedures reached from every call instruction in non-excluded procedures are summed up (using bottom-up traversal). The rest of the algorithm is formulated as an intraprocedural dataflow analysis, identifying procedures invoked more than once on a given path. In the analysis, the domain is a mapping between every procedure p and the maximum number of times p can be invoked, at the entry to a basic block. Initially, at the entry block for a procedure, we initialize the map to 0. When encountering a call instruction ci, 1 is added to the number of possible invocations for each reachable procedure from ci (transfer function). The number of times a procedure p can be invoked at the entry to a basic block bb is the maximum number of invocations p can have in the predecessors of bb (meet operator). We exclude all procedures which have more than one path executing them, as well as their descendants.

When a fixed point is reached, all allocation sites in non-excluded procedures, not located in control flow graph SCCs, are singular.

3.3   Dereference Conversion

We convert dereferences to load and store instructions, which can reference SSA variables. If $pExpr$ is the pointer expression for a load or store instruction and it references a single memory location (according to pointer analysis) for SSA variable var, then we replace $pExpr$ with var.

Let us consider a store instruction, assigning value val, that references more than one memory location, including at least one SSA variable. We will replace this instruction with a series of ϕ^S instructions, with the form $pExpr.\phi^S(var, curr, val)$, for each SSA variable var, with current value $curr$. If $pExpr$ can also reference a non-SSA variable, we also insert a default ϕ^S instruction, which is executed if none of the other ϕ^S instructions have $pExpr == var$.

In the case of a load instruction that can reference SSA variables $var_0 \ldots var_n$, and non-SSA variables $var_{n+1} \ldots var_{n+1+m}$, where $n + m > 1$, we insert a ϕ^L instruction. If $m == 0$, then the load is replaced with $pExpr.\phi^L(\langle var_0, val_0 \rangle, \ldots \langle var_n, val_n \rangle)$. If $m \neq 0$, then we also add a default value to the ϕ^L instruction, which is taken if none of the other addresses match.

The effect of external call instructions is captured by replacing the call using the load, store, ϕ^L, and ϕ^S instructions. In cases where this can't be done, we commit the value of the variable prior to the call and assign it afterwards.

Note that during copy propagation and constant folding, the pointer expression, $pExpr$, for various ϕ^L or ϕ^S instructions, is resolved. We can then fold these instructions to their corresponding value.

3.4 Procedure Input and Output Mapping

In the rest of this section (and in Section 3.5), we use the following terms:

- $\mathcal{PR} \subset [0, \infty)$ is the set of procedures in the program.
- $\mathcal{BB} \subset [0, \infty)$ is the set of basic blocks in the program.
- $\mathcal{INS} \subset [0, \infty)$ is the set of instructions in the program.
- $\mathcal{VR} \subset [0, \infty)$ is the set of SSA variables in the program.
- $\mathcal{RV} : \mathcal{PR} \mapsto 2^{\mathcal{VR}}$ is a mapping between a given procedure $p \in \mathcal{PR}$ and the set of variables $V \subseteq \mathcal{VR}$ possibly read in p or its descendants.
- $\mathcal{WV} : \mathcal{PR} \mapsto 2^{\mathcal{VR}}$ is a mapping between a given procedure $p \in \mathcal{PR}$ and the set of variables $V \subseteq \mathcal{VR}$ possibly written in p or its descendants.

We use the load, store, ϕ^S, and ϕ^L instructions to determine the initial values of $\mathcal{RV}$ and $\mathcal{WV}$, for each procedure. We then partition the call graph into SCCs and traverse the partitioned call graph using a postorder traversal (bottom-up pass), adding up the read and write sets in the program. The computation of $\mathcal{RV}$ and $\mathcal{WV}$ using this approach is very coarse and we refine it by using a revised liveness analysis. For every procedure $p \in \mathcal{PR}$, we compute $\mathcal{ARV}(p)$, which is the set of variables read after p exits. In addition, we compute the set of variables written before p is first invoked, $\mathcal{BWV}(p)$. Then, we constrain the set of variables passed in and out of procedure p using $\mathcal{BWV}(p)$ and $\mathcal{ARV}(p)$, respectively.

We compute these two sets by using the SCC partitioned call graph to derive a topological visitation order, $TopCG : \mathcal{Z} \mapsto 2^{\mathcal{PR}}$. Likewise, for each procedure $p \in \mathcal{PR}$, we derive a topological control flow graph visitation order $TopCFG : \mathcal{Z} \mapsto 2^{\mathcal{BB}}$. Next, we apply procedure $deriveLimitSets$, presented in Algorithm 1, which visits the call graph in topological order. When $TopCG(i)$ is a SCC, then $\mathcal{RV}$ and $\mathcal{WV}$ are added to $\mathcal{ARV}$ and $\mathcal{BWV}$, respectively, since each procedure in $TopCG(i)$ might be executed multiple times (Lines 9–15). Otherwise, a topological traversal over the SCC partitioned control flow graph of $TopCG(i)$ is applied, using $TopCFG$. During the pass, the set of variables written so far, $WritesSoFar$ (Line 28), and the set of procedures invoked so far, $ProcsSoFar$ (Line 29), are maintained. Conceptually, when visiting a call instruction where the callee is $cp \in \mathcal{PR}$, $WritesSoFar$ are added to $\mathcal{BWV}(cp)$, and when encountering a read to variable var, then var is added to $\mathcal{ARV}$ for each procedure in $ProcsSoFar$. In Algorithm 1, on Line 30, the routine $Summarize$ is used to retrieve the set of procedures called in $TopCFG(i)$, along with the set of variables read and written. If $TopCFG(i)$ is not a SCC, then $Summarize$ excludes variables written in procedures called from $TopCFG(i)$ and their descendants. In our algorithm $\mathcal{BWV}$ is updated for each called procedure $cp \in Callees$ with $WritesSoFar$, and $\mathcal{ARV}$ is updated for each procedure $psf \in ProcsSoFar$ with the current reads $(currR)$. Lastly, if $TopCFG(i)$ is a SCC, then we also update $\mathcal{ARV}$ for psf (Line 35).

Algorithm 1. Top-down computation of $BW\mathcal{V}$ and $AR\mathcal{V}$

```
updateComp = func(                              1
  Uset : PR ↦ 2^VR,                             2
  update : 2^VR, callee : PR ) {                3
  if( ∃i, callee ∈ TopCG(i) )                   4
    forall( p ∈ TopCG(i) )                      5
      Uset(p) = Uset(p) ∪ update;               6
}                                               7
deriveLimitSetsSCC = func( i : Z ) {            8
  forall( p ∈ TopCG(i) ) {                      9
    forall( q ∈ TopCG(i) ) {                   10
      BWV(p) = BWV(q) ∪ WV(q);                 11
      ARV(p) = ARV(q) ∪ RV(q);}                12
    forall( callee of p, cp ) {               13
      updateComp(BWV, BWV(p), cp);             14
      updateComp(ARV, ARV(p), cp); } }         15
                                               16
}                                              17
deriveLimitSets = func( ) {                    18
  for( i = 0; i < |TopCG|; i + + ) {           19
    if( |TopCG(i)| > 1 ∨                        
      TopCG(i) recursive )                     20
      deriveLimitSetsSCC(i);                   21
    else                                       22
      deriveLimitSetsNormal(i);                23
  } }
```

```
deriveLimitSetsNormal = func(i : Z ) {          24
  ProcsSoFar : 2^PR = ∅                         25
  WritesSoFar : 2^VR = BWV(TopCG(i))            26
  for(j = 0; j < |TopCFG|; j + +) {             27
    CurrW, CurrR : 2^VR;                        28
    Callees : 2^PR;                             29
    ⟨CurrW, CurrR, Callees⟩ =
               Summarize(TopCFG(j));            30
    WritesSoFar =
               WritesSoFar ∪ CurrW;             31
    forall( cp ∈ Callees ) {                    32
      updateComp(BWV, WritesSoFar, cp);         33
      if( TopCFG(i) recursive )                 34
        updateComp(ARV, CurrR, psf);            35
    }                                           36
    forall( psf ∈ ProcsSoFar )                  37
      updateComp(ARV, CurrR, psf);              38
    ProcsSoFar ⋃ = Callees;                     39
    WritesSoFar ⋃ = ⋃_{cp∈Callees} WV(cp);      40
  }                                             41
  forall( psf ∈ ProcsSoFar )                    42
    updateComp(
      ARV, ARV(TopCG(i)), psf);                 43
}                                               44
```

After $W\mathcal{V}$ and $R\mathcal{V}$ are computed, we insert ϕ^V and ϕ^C instructions. Let us assume that $ci \in \mathcal{INS}$ is the call instruction, $p \in \mathcal{PR}$ is the caller, and $ProcCallees \in 2^{\mathcal{PR}}$ is the set of callees. First, we compute the set of variables propagated to $cle \in ProcCallees$, which we refer to as $PropTo = R\mathcal{V}(cle) \cup W\mathcal{V}(cle)$. Then, for each variable $var \in PropTo$, we add the tuple $\langle ci, val \rangle$ to $\phi^V_{\langle var, cle \rangle}$, where val is the value of var prior to ci. Next, we compute the set of variables written in $ProcCallees$, which we refer to as $PropFrom = \bigsqcup_{cle \in ProcCallees} W\mathcal{V}(cle)$. Afterwards, for each variable $var \in PropFrom$, and each $cle \in ProcCallees$, we add the tuple $\langle cle, val \rangle$ to $\phi^C_{\langle var, ci \rangle}$, where val is the value of var at the exit from cle.

3.5 Interprocedural Copy Propagation

During ϕ-placement, the ϕ^V instructions merging a single value are substituted and we follow up by applying copy propagation to ϕ^C instructions. As described in Section 2.1, we substitute a $\phi^C_{\langle var, ci \rangle}(cle, val)$ instruction merging a single value $val \in \mathcal{INS}$ defined in procedure $pval \in \mathcal{PR}$, as long as $pval$ cannot be called on any path from the ϕ^C instruction, up to the respective use. In basic cases, where val is either a constant or if $pval$ is equal to cle and is called from only one call instruction (not in a SCC), we replace ϕ^C with val.

Otherwise, in order to determine where a ϕ^C can be replaced by val, we identify the call instruction corresponding to the last instance of $pval$, for each procedure at every basic block. To this end, in our implementation, described in 2 (and illustrated, using an example in Appendix A), we construct a virtual SSA form, using a quasi variable p_v for each procedure $p \in \mathcal{PR}$, in the program. The value of p_v will be the call instruction corresponding to the last invocation of p, or $\oslash$ otherwise. Prior to calling procedure $interCopyProp$, we use a bottom-up pass over the SCC partitioned call graph to summarize the set of procedures reached (in $ReachedProcedures$) from every call instruction, $ci \in \mathcal{INS}$. When visiting a procedure, we compute the iterated dominance frontier, $IDF \subset \mathcal{BB}$, for each call instruction, ci. We then add to the $\mathcal{VID}$ relation a mapping from each basic block $bb \in IDF$, to each procedure reached from ci ($ReachedProcedures(ci)$).

Algorithm 2. Interprocedural Copy Propagation

```
SCC : PR ↦ Z;                                        1
ReachedProcedures : INS ↦ 2^PR;                       2
VID : BB ↦ 2^PR;                                      3
Vals : Z ↦ BB × (PR ↦ INS);                           4
SP : Z;                                               5
replOuts = func(                                      6
    p : PR, ci : INS,                                 7
    currV : PR ↦ INS) {                               8
  forall( φ^C_(var,ci)((pval, val)) ) {               9
    if( IsAConstant(val) )                           10
      replWithVal(φ^C_(var,ci), val);                11
    else if( SCC(pval) ≠ SCC(p) ) {                  12
      if( IsCalledOnce(pval) )                       13
        replWithVal(φ^C_(var,ci), val);              14
      else if( currV(pval) == ci )                   15
        replWithVal(φ^C_(var,ci), val);              16
  } }                                                17
  forall( rp ∈ ReachedProcedures(ci) )              18
    currV(rp) = ci;                                  19
}

depthFirstVisit = func (                            20
    p : PR, bb : BB,                                 21
    currV : PR ↦ INS) {                              22
  forall( pdef ∈ VID(bb) )                          23
    currV(pdef) = ⊘;                                 24
  forall( ins ∈ bb.INS )                            25
    replOuts(p, ci, currV);                          26
  forall( succ ∈ getSuccs(bb) )                     27
    Vals(SP + +) = (succ, currV);                   28
}                                                   29
interCopyProp = func ( ) {                          30
  forall( p ∈ PR ) {                                31
    SP = 0;                                         32
    deriveVID( );                                   33
    Vals(SP + +) = (p.entry, ⊘)                     34
    while( SP! = 0 ) {                              35
      (bb, currV) = Vals(- - SP);                   36
      depthFirstVisit(p, bb, currV);                37
    }                                               38
  }                                                 39
}
```

After $\mathcal{VID}$ is computed, we begin a depth-first traversal of the control flow graph for p, to perform copy propagation for the quasi variables. We treat a call instruction ci as an assignment to each reachable procedure's ($pv \in ReachedProcedures(ci)$) quasi variable, indicating ci was the last call instruction to reach pv. We use $\mathcal{VID}$ to identify basic blocks where a procedure pv might be reached through more than one call instruction and we invalidate the value stored in the quasi variable for pv (on Line 24). Through the copy propagation of the quasi variables, we identify the call instruction associated with the last invocation of each reachable procedure. We can substitute a reference to $\phi^C_{(...,ci)}$ (passed out at call instruction ci), with its value val (derived in procedure p), if $Vals(p) == ci$, at the site of the use (see procedure $replOuts$ in Algorithm 2).

4   Experiment

In this study, we report on the performance of the interprocedural SSA construction algorithm and we contrast the design choices to previous work. Aside from the runtime, we present and discuss the impact of increasing the scope and resolution of ISSA, applying copy propagation and liveness analysis, pointer analysis, and lastly, the impact on constant propagation.

4.1 Setup, Benchmarks, and Runtime

We implemented the interprocedural SSA in the LLVM [16] compiler infrastructure. The experiments were performed on an Intel CORE 2 Duo 1.66 GHz processor, with 4 GB memory, and running 64-bit ubuntu. These results were collected on IR in intraprocedural SSA form, with constant propagation and dead code removal already applied.

We evaluated our work on a set of MediaBench [17] and SPEC2K [18] benchmarks. In Table 1, we list the various benchmarks used and their lines of code, along with the number of call sites present in the benchmarks.

Table 1. Benchmark characteristics and the runtime (column labeled T(s)), in seconds

MediaBench				SPEC2K				SPEC2K			
Name	Lines	Call Sites	T(s)	Name	Lines	Call Sites	T(s)	Name	Lines	Call Sites	T(s)
GSM	4626	258	1.4	164.gzip	8218	306	0.95	197.parser	10932	1691	21.52
JPEG	26173	942	10.8	175.vpr	16984	1902	5.88	254.gap	59493	9773	91.17
MPEG2[1]	7283	654	2.3	181.mcf	1913	81	1.02	256.bzip2	4665	299	0.74
G721	1476	53	0.3	186.crafty	19478	2252	8.32	300.twolf	19756	1883	38.63

In Table 1, we also present the runtime for ISSA generation (does not include pointer analysis runtime). All the MediaBench [17] benchmarks complete within a few seconds and we handle a very large number of variables in them. In comparison, the runtime takes longer for the SPEC2K [18] benchmarks, which is understandable as the benchmarks have more lines of code and more call sites. Furthermore, SPEC2K benchmarks use a greater set of the C language features, including recursion, indirect calls, and cast accesses, which increase the number of inputs and output across call sites.

4.2 Impact of Increasing Scope and Resolution

We evaluate the impact of increasing the scope and resolution of ISSA using the number of SSA variables and the number of load instructions resolved to the corresponding definition. A greater number can provide a higher benefit to clients of ISSA.

In Table 2 we compare our ISSA construction algorithm (columns labeled *All*) to an algorithm which is similar to Staiger [11] as it only considers scalar globals (columns labeled *Globals*), and provide the ratio between them (columns labeled *X*).

---

[1] Decoder.

Table 2. Number of variables handled, load instructions replaced, and singular allocation sites identified

Benchmark	SSA Variables			Loads Replaced			Allocation Sites	
	All	Globals	X	All	Globals	X	Singular	%
GSM	73	20	3.65	191	164	1.16	0	0.0
JPEG	249	7	35.57	1564	588	2.66	33	55.0
MPEG2	186	133	1.4	814	650	1.25	1	7.1
G721	14	5	2.8	43	15	2.87	0	0.0
164.gzip	151	100	1.51	575	530	1.08	1	20.0
175.vpr	280	96	2.92	2471	2008	1.23	31	30.4
181.mcf	39	6	6.5	140	15	9.33	3	100.0
186.crafty	403	266	1.52	3406	1501	2.27	5	41.7
197.parser	229	82	2.79	570	520	1.10	2	1.8
254.gap	222	207	1.07	1412	1409	1.00	1	50.0
256.bzip2	41	41	1	478	478	1.00	5	50.0
300.twolf	378	293	1.29	6808	6669	1.02	0	0.0
Average			5.17			1.72		

We first present the number of SSA variables (heading) for the two algorithm in Table 2. As indicated, we are handling on average *5.17* times more variables than an ISSA formation similar to Staiger [11]. Second, this shows a precise field-sensitive analysis is useful in increasing the scope of ISSA, making it more useful for structure intensive benchmarks.

Furthermore, in Table 2, we also illustrate the impact of increasing the scope and resolution of ISSA construction on the number of load instructions substituted with their definition (columns underneath *Loads Replaced*). On average, we substituted *1.72* times more load instructions with their definition, than Staiger [11], increasing the scope of the dataflow analysis and its potential benefit.

Lastly, we present the number of singular allocation sites and their percentage (of total allocation sites), in the last two columns (*Allocation Sites* heading). While a large percentage of singular allocation sites were identified in a number of benchmarks, only in *JPEG* this translated to a substantial increase in SSA variables. In other benchmarks, such memory was primarily used for arrays, which we currently do not handle.

4.3   Impact of Copy Propagation and Liveness Analysis

To evaluate the impact of copy propagation and liveness analysis we compute the the sum of ϕ^V and ϕ^C instructions. A lower number indicates both performance (less instructions) and precision improvement, as a lower number results from folding various instructions (i.e. propagation through ϕ^V or ϕ^C instructions), associating additional uses with the corresponding definition.

Table 3. Impact of liveness analysis and copy propagation measured by the reduction of the read and write sets, along with the effectiveness of constant propagation

Benchmark	Liveness Analysis			Copy Propagation			Constant Propagation		
	Total ϕ^V,ϕ^C		Δ	Total ϕ^V,ϕ^C		Δ	Extra Folded	Δ	Extra Dead Blocks
	Before	After		Before	After				
GSM	494	319	35.4 %	319	136	57.4%	9	2.23 %	1
JPEG	10261	9115	11.2 %	9115	4600	49.5%	35	13.01 %	15
MPEG2	6279	5408	13.9 %	5408	3418	36.8%	9	3.59 %	11
G721	133	100	24.8 %	100	66	34.0%	0	0 %	1
164.gzip	2606	2074	20.4 %	2074	1037	50.0%	105	23.6 %	4
175.vpr	5702	4457	21.8 %	4457	2412	45.9%	15	1.81 %	10
181.mcf	262	181	30.9 %	181	12	93.4%	3	7.32 %	2
186.crafty	20935	16373	21.8 %	16373	13276	18.9%	119	2.13 %	3
197.parser	23037	22015	4.4 %	22015	17109	22.3%	133	19.97 %	0
254.gap	100678	61684	38.7 %	61684	48332	21.6%	29	0.55 %	5
256.bzip2	942	614	34.8 %	614	269	56.2%	115	59.28 %	7
300.twolf	5211	4106	21.2 %	4106	2130	48.1%	113	8.67 %	10
Average			23.3 %			44.5%		11.8 %	

We apply copy propagation as described in Section 3.5, and fold ϕ^V and ϕ^C instructions. As shown in Table 3, copy propagation reduced the number of ϕ^V and ϕ^C instructions at call sites, and procedure entries, by 44.5% on average. In addition, during copy propagation we folded 30% of the ϕ^V instructions merging values from multiple call sites, as well as a number of ϕ^L and ϕ^S instructions. This demonstrates a significant improvement over previous work, as copy propagation reduced both the size of the IR as well as the number of spurious merge points.

In Table 3, we detail the impact of the liveness analysis, presented in Section 3.4, on reducing the read and write sets into various procedures. The second and third columns contain the sum of ϕ^V and ϕ^C instructions before and after liveness analysis, respectively. The average number of ϕ^V and ϕ^C instructions removed was 23.3%, demonstrating the benefit of liveness analysis in reducing the size of the IR, thus making ISSA construction more efficient.

4.4   Impact of Pointer Analysis

In Table 4, we illustrate the difference between the input sets derived using the field-insensitive pointer analysis available in LLVM and our field-sensitive pointer analysis. The size of the input sets is on average *12.2* times higher in the field-insensitive version, mainly because of the greater point-to set size. Furthermore, since the pointer analysis is used to resolve indirect calls, the field-insensitive version usually contains spurious paths in the call graph. This increases the size of the input sets, as data must be propagated to various unreachable destinations.

Table 4. Size of input and output sets for a field-insensitive and field-sensitive pointer analysis

Benchmark	Field-Sensitive	Field-Insensitive	X
GSM	214	818	3.82
JPEG	330	2480	7.52
MPEG2	1256	12185	9.7
G721	10	83	8.3
164.gzip	1024	4348	4.25
175.vpr	2265	18341	8.1
181.mcf	49	136	2.78
186.crafty	2660	11236	4.22
197.vpr	8239	21398	2.6
300.twolf	581	40806	70.23
Average			12.15

Larger sets result in increased code size and runtime and hence, by using the field-sensitive pointer analysis, we are able to reduce code size and runtime, in addition to handling more variables.

4.5 Impact on Constant Propagation

We implemented a pass that performs constant propagation and dead code removal using ISSA, based on the Wegman and Zadeck algorithm [19]. In Table 3 we show the effectiveness of ISSA based constant propagation in comparison to the LLVM [16] constant propagation and dead code removal passes (*-instcombine, -adce, -ipconstprop*). In the last three columns, we present the number of additional constant folded expressions (and their percentage in relation to LLVM), along with the number of dead basic blocks in the benchmarks. On average, excluding all expressions folded during dereference conversion and copy propagation, we fold an additional 11.8% of instructions, on top of the LLVM passes.

5 Related Work

The challenge in handling pointers in SSA form is that pointer dereferences are not always resolved to a singular memory location and as such, merge points have to sometimes be inserted for pointer dereferences. One way to handle this challenge is to use an aliasing query, as was done by Cytron [13] and others [14, 15].

For interprocedural SSA, dereferences must be handled. In Liao's [20] ISSA form, SSA variables are alias sets (equivalence classes) computed by applying Steensgaard's unification-based pointer analysis [10]. Such derivation creates more merge points than an inclusion-based pointer analysis [11], due to the relatively lower precision which impacts the construction in two ways. First, more spurious assignments are inserted due to a greater point-to set size, and second, the call graph which is used to propagate definitions and uses is less precise as well (in programs with indirect calls). Staiger [11] considered each variable individually, in a manner similar to Horwitz [21]. When encountering unresolvable dereferences, Staiger merged dataflow by assigning a common allocator to aliased objects. Staiger showed that using more precise pointer analysis would result in a drastically lower number of ϕ instructions; Andersen's pointer analysis had 20× less ϕ instructions than Steensgaard's in some benchmarks. However, Staiger does not apply copy propagation and the analysis outputs its results in graph form – making it harder to directly apply traditional clients of SSA. Along the same lines, the representation is may def-use (e.g. locators correspond to recursive data structures), where only accesses to scalar globals are marked with must use edges. Lastly, Staiger did not evaluate ISSA using a target application.

As shown in Section 4, our approach reduces input and output instructions, while we handle more SSA Variables and replace more load instructions than Staiger [11]. In addition, we demonstrate the benefit of ISSA to constant propagation.

6   Conclusion

SSA can be used for various analysis and optimization algorithms and this paper presents an extension of SSA to the scope of a whole program. We have shown that while handling a large number of variables, we are still able to construct ISSA in seconds. ISSA improves precision by handling a large percentage of load instructions, and by resolving a few pointer dereferences. We have also demonstrated the benefit of liveness analysis and interprocedural copy propagation on ISSA, as well as an improvement in constant propagation and dead code removal, due to ISSA.

From our experiment, ISSA usually performed better in the MediaBench [17] benchmarks, in terms of runtime and precision improvement. This occurred because there was little use of recursive data structures, recursive procedures, and hashtables in MediaBench. Such features make it difficult to resolve dereferences to singular objects and propagate values interprocedurally.

Acknowledgments

We would like to thank the anonymous reviewers for their helpful comments.

References

[1] Cytron, R., Ferrante, J., Rosen, B.K., Wegman, M.N., Zadeck, F.K.: Efficiently computing static single assignment form and the control dependence graph. ACM Transactions on Programming Languages and Systems 13(4), 451–490 (1991)

[2] Wegman, M.N., Zadeck, F.K.: Constant propagation with conditional branches. ACM Transactions on Programming Languages and Systems 13(2), 181–210 (1991)

[3] Gal, A., Probst, C.W., Franz, M.: HotpathVM: an effective JIT compiler for resource-constrained devices. In: VEE 2006: Proceedings of the 2nd international conference on Virtual execution environments, pp. 144–153. ACM, New York (2006)

[4] Stoutchinin, A., Gao, G.: If-conversion in SSA form. In: Danelutto, M., Vanneschi, M., Laforenza, D. (eds.) Euro-Par 2004. LNCS, vol. 3149, pp. 336–345. Springer, Heidelberg (2004)

[5] Wolfe, M.: Beyond induction variables. In: Proceedings of the Conference on Programming Language Design and Implementation (PLDI), vol. 7(27), pp. 162–174. ACM Press, New York (1992)

[6] Hasti, R., Horwitz, S.: Using static single assignment form to improve flow-insensitive pointer analysis. In: Proceedings of SIGPLAN Conference on Programming Language Design and Implementation, pp. 97–105 (1998)

[7] Kennedy, R., Chan, S., Liu, S.M., Lo, R., Tu, P., Chow, F.: Partial redundancy elimination in SSA form. ACM Trans. Program. Lang. Syst. 21(3), 627–676 (1999)

[8] Brisk, P., Verma, A.K., Ienne, P.: Optimal polynomial-time interprocedural register allocation for high-level synthesis and asip design. In: ICCAD 2007: Proceedings of the 2007 IEEE/ACM international conference on Computer-aided design, Piscataway, NJ, USA, pp. 172–179. IEEE Press, Los Alamitos (2007)

[9] Liao, S.W.: SUIF Explorer: An interactive and interprocedural parallelizer. PhD thesis, Stanford University, CA, USA, Adviser-Monica S. Lam (2000)

[10] Steensgaard, B.: Efficient context-sensitive pointer analysis for C programs. In: Proceedings of the 1996 International Conference on Compiler Construction, April 1996, pp. 136–150 (1996)

[11] Staiger, S., Vogel, G., Keul, S., Wiebe, E.: Interprocedural Static Single Assignment Form. In: Proceedings of the 14th Working Conference on Reverse Engineering, pp. 1–10 (2007)

[12] Andersen, O.: Program Analysis and Specialization for the C Programming Language. PhD thesis, Computer Science Department, University of Copenhagen (1994)

[13] Cytron, R., Gershbein, R.: Efficient accommodation of alias information in SSA form. In: Proceedings of the ACM SIGPLAN 1993 Conference on Programming Language Design and Implementation, pp. 36–45 (1993)

[14] Chow, F.C., Chan, S., Liu, S.M., Lo, R., Streich, M.: Effective representation of aliases and indirect memory operations in SSA form. In: Gyimóthy, T. (ed.) CC 1996. LNCS, vol. 1060, pp. 253–267. Springer, Heidelberg (1996)

[15] Choi, J.D., Cytron, R., Ferrante, J.: On the efficient engineering of ambitious program analysis. IEEE Trans. Softw. Eng. 20(2), 105–114 (1994)

[16] Lattner, C.: LLVM: An infrastructure for multi-stage optimization. Master's thesis, Computer Science Dept., University of Illinois at Urbana-Champaign (December 2002)

[17] Lee, C., Potkonjak, M., Mangione-Smith, W.H.: Mediabench: A tool for evaluating and synthesizing multimedia and communications systems. In: Micro 30 (1997)

[18] Standard Performance Evaluation Corporation: SPEC CPU2000 benchmarks, http://www.specbench.org/cpu2000/

[19] Wegman, M.N., Zadeck, F.K.: Constant propagation with conditional branches. ACM Trans. Program. Lang. Syst. 13(2), 181–210 (1991)

[20] Liao, S.W., Diwan, A., Bosch Jr., R.P., Ghuloum, A., Lam, M.S.: SUIF Explorer: An interactive and interprocedural parallelizer. In: Proceedings of the 7th ACM SIGPLAN Symposium on Principles and Practice of Parallel Programming, pp. 37–48 (1999)

[21] Horwitz, S., Reps, T., Binkley, D.: Interprocedural slicing using dependence graphs. In: PLDI 1988: Proceedings of the ACM SIGPLAN 1988 conference on Programming Language design and Implementation, pp. 35–46. ACM, New York (1988)

A   Example for Copy Propagation Algorithm

In this section, we illustrate the solution process for Algorithm 2, shown in Section 3.5. Let us consider the example shown in Figure 2 (a). First, we assign identifiers for functions starting at 0 and call sites, starting at 1. For each call site CI, we compute its reachable functions, shown in Figure 2 (b), in the fifth column and add it to $\mathcal{VID}(bb)$, where bb is a basic block in CI's iterated dominance frontier (eighth column).

The reference solution for Figure 2 (a) is shown in the sixth and ninth columns of Figure 2 (b), where the vector index corresponds to the function. After CI_1 the latest call to X and Z is CI_1 and to Y is undefined (similar reasoning applies to CI_2,CI_3 with different functions). Since functions Y and Z are in $\mathcal{VID}(BB_2)$, their value gets invalidated when entering BB_2. The actual replacement of ϕ^C instructions occurs during the traversal, as we query the table to determine whether substitution is possible at various program points.

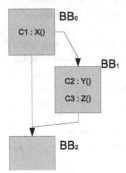

Function	ID	Call Site	ID	Reachable Functions	Values	Basic Block	$\mathcal{VID}$	Values
X	0	$C1$	1	X,Z	[1,0,1]	BB_0	$\oslash$	[0,0,0]
Y	1	$C2$	2	Y,Z	[1,2,2]	BB_1	$\oslash$	[1,0,1]
Z	2	$C3$	3	Z	[1,2,3]	BB_2	Y,Z	[1,0,0]

(a) Structure for currently analyzed procedure.

(b) Table with data computed prior and during the algorithm. It shows the identifiers for call sites and procedures, as well as the values of quasi variables.

Fig. 2. Example illustrating Algorithm 2, from Section 3.5

Region Analysis for Race Detection

Helmut Seidl and Vesal Vojdani

Lehrstuhl für Informatik II, Technische Universität München
Boltzmannstraße 3, D-85748 Garching b. München, Germany
{seidl,vojdanig}@in.tum.de

Abstract. Automatic race detection of C programs requires fast, yet sufficiently precise analysis of dynamic memory. Therefore, we present a region-based pointer analysis which seeks to identify disjoint *regions* of dynamically allocated objects to ensure that write accesses to the same region are always protected by the same mutexes. Our approach has been implemented within the interprocedural analyzer of concurrent C programs GobLint and we have successfully applied it on code from the Linux kernel, such as the access vector cache. This code relies on a synchronized hash table where an array of doubly linked lists is protected by an array of locks.

1 Introduction

Writing multi-threaded code which both is correct and manipulates complicated data-structures can be cumbersome. Programmers of low-level software therefore mostly adhere to simple and conservative programming styles. Accordingly, dynamic shared data-structures are avoided whenever possible, and when dynamic allocation of memory is inevitable, one common idiom is to rely on *non-overlapping* data-structures and protect each of these *memory regions* by a dedicated lock. This occurs naturally when resources are main-

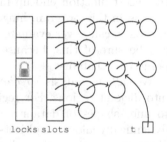

Fig. 1. Memory regions

tained in hash-table-like data-structures, i.e., arrays of linked lists where each list is protected by its own lock as illustrated in Figure 1.

There are different levels of granularity at which locking schemes for shared data-structures operate: at one extreme, an individual mutex is maintained for each data element separately, known as *per-element locking* [20]; at the other extreme, coarse-grained locking schemes use a single mutex to protect all data nodes allocated at a given point in the program. In between, there are subtler cases of medium-grained locking where certain dynamically allocated elements protect a bunch of other elements (not quite per-element), or elements allocated at a given point are not all protected by the same mutex (not quite coarse-grained). Here, we are concerned with the latter case. In many applications, we found that the dynamic data-structures protected by one mutex are disjoint from

J. Palsberg and Z. Su (Eds.): SAS 2009, LNCS 5673, pp. 171–187, 2009.

```
typedef struct node { int data; struct node *next; } node;
node *even_list, *odd_list;

void insert(int data) {
    node *t = new(data);
    if (even(data)) { t→next = even_list; even_list = t; }
    else { t→next = odd_list; odd_list = t; } }
```

```
void even_worker() {          void odd_worker() {
    node *t1 = even_list;          node *t2 = odd_list;
    while (t1 != NULL) {           while (t2 != NULL) {
        lock(even_mutex);             lock(odd_mutex);
        t1 = even_list;               t2 = odd_list;
        access(t1→data);              access(t2→data);
        t1 = t1→next;                 t2 = t2→next;
        unlock(even_mutex); } }        unlock(odd_mutex); } }
```

Fig. 2. Elements placed into linked lists

the data-structures protected by other mutexes. The *number* of protected disjoint data-structures, however, can be large. This is the case, e.g., for synchronized hash-tables where each bucket is protected by an individual mutex.

Consider the two-bucket hash-table in Figure 2 where elements allocated by the insert function end up in two distinct lists. The correctness of the locking scheme in this program hinges on the fact that the expressions t1→data and t2→data can never evaluate to the same address, i.e., they can never *alias*. We can be sure of this, because the two lists are disjoint and thus closed under pointer reachability.

We call an analysis a *region analysis* if it infers a safe partitioning of the heap into disjoint regions. For region analysis, one could use sophisticated analyses to infer shapes of data-structures. Another approach would be to summarize dynamically allocated objects as *blobs* of memory associated with finitely many abstract locations such as allocation sites. While the first approach has difficulties scaling to larger programs, the second approach fails when elements allocated at the same program point end up in distinct data-structures protected by distinct mutexes, as in the above example.

We present a region analysis which is reasonably fast, yet sufficiently precise to deal with programs that manipulate disjoint heap regions. It identifies the set of static globals within the region accessed by local pointers. It also deals with arrays of regions by allowing regions to be indexed with symbolic index expressions. For the example above, the analysis would maintain that the two lists are disjoint, t1 is pointing into the region of even_list, and t2 is pointing into the region of odd_list.

Our region analysis can be extended to a race detection method by adding two components. First, a must alias analysis which provides information on which global address are definitely pointed to by a pointer variable, e.g., provided by [17]. Second, a symbolic lock set analysis which determines for every program point a *representation*, which may involve symbolic address expressions, of the set of definitely held locks when reaching this program point.

2   Region Inference

For the purpose of this paper, we spell out our approach for a minimalistic programming model which is just rich enough to exhibit the key ideas of our analysis of multi-threaded programs using dynamic data-structures and arrays. At first, we restrict ourselves to programs which consist of only a single procedure represented by a finite control-flow graph where each edge is labeled with a basic operation s; in Section 3, we will extend to an interprocedural setting. We only track the values of local variables pointing into the global memory. The global memory is shared between different processes and consists of blocks, which either may be statically allocated at program start or dynamically allocated during program execution through some operator new τ (for some type τ). For the moment, we rule out pointers into the stack as well as pointer arithmetic and assume that pointers always point to the beginning of blocks. In Section 5, we will add global arrays, and in Section 6, we indicate how the basic approach can be extended to work also in presence of (well-behaved) pointer-arithmetic as required for the analysis of, e.g., the Linux kernel API for doubly linked lists.

We assume that the frontend provides us with a normalized representation of assignments. For the beginning, we consider the following forms of expressions and assignments:

adr	$::= \mathbf{y}$	local pointer variable
	$\mid \&a$	static global address
$pexp$	$::= \mathbf{y} \rightarrow b$	dereferencing of pointers
val	$::= adr \mid \mathsf{null}$	pointer value
	$\mid \mathsf{new}(\tau)$	memory allocation
$pass$	$::= pexp = val;$	memory write
	$\mid \mathbf{y} = val; \mid \mathbf{y} = pexp;$	variable assignment

Let L and G denote the set of local pointer variables and the set of addresses of static global memory cells, respectively. Region analysis aims at inferring *potential reachability* between elements from $G \cup L$. Our analyzer therefore maintains for every program point an equivalence relation π on globals. Two elements $x_1, x_2 \in G$ are put into the same equivalence class when some memory cell is jointly reachable from both x_1 and x_2 through iterated field selection and dereferencing. Additionally, we maintain for every program point a function $\rho : L \rightarrow 2^{G \cup \{\bullet\}}$ mapping each local $\mathbf{y}$ to a set of globals identifying the region into which $\mathbf{y}$ may possibly point. The bullet $\bullet$ identifies the region of all thread-local dynamically allocated memory cells. When a thread allocates an object and initializes its fields, the object is seen as residing within this thread-local region until it is reachable from, or can itself reach, one of the global regions.

Equivalence relations have also been used for *may-alias* analysis [12]. There, two expressions are considered equivalent if they may denote the same address. May-alias equivalence classes do not collapse when one is reachable from the other. On the other hand, while non-reachability *implies* non-equality, we cannot extract definite non-reachability information from non-equality. Thus, ensuring that pointers which traverse complicated structures may not alias is extremely difficult without the explicit notion of disjointness: one must precisely express the aliasing relationship, or all information about non-reachability is lost.

Here, an equivalence relation π is represented by the set of two-element subsets $\{x, y\}$ with $(x, y) \in \pi$ — implying that the *trivial* equivalence relation is represented by the empty set. Let $\mathbf{P}$ and $\mathbf{R}$ denote the set of all equivalence relations on G and the set of all maps from L to $2^{G \cup \{\bullet\}}$, respectively. Both sets form complete lattices for the orderings induced by the subset orderings on the set of two-element subsets of G and $G \cup \{\bullet\}$, respectively. In particular, for equivalence relations $\pi_1, \pi_2 \in \mathbf{P}$, the greatest lower bound $\pi_1 \sqcap \pi_2$ is given by the intersection of the sets of unordered pairs corresponding to π_1 and π_2, respectively; whereas the least upper bound $\pi_1 \sqcup \pi_2$ is the least equivalence relation containing all pairs from π_1 and π_2.

Using a suitable data-structure for partitions, the operations "$\sqcap$", "$\sqcup$" in $\mathbf{P}$ can be executed in polynomial time. Consider a pair $T = \langle \pi, \rho \rangle$ describing the current program state. We assume that all sets $\rho(\mathbf{y})$ are *closed* under π. We call a set X *closed* under the equivalence relation π, if $x \in X$ and $\{x, x'\} \in \pi$ implies that also $x' \in X$. For an arbitrary pair $\langle \pi, \rho \rangle$, let $\mathsf{cl}_\pi X$ denote the least set X' with $X \subseteq X'$ which is closed under π.

We now specify how a pair $T = \langle \pi, \rho \rangle$ describing the program state before an assignment s is transformed into a pair $\langle \pi', \rho' \rangle$ describing the program state after the assignment, i.e., we define the *abstract* meaning $[\![s]\!]^\sharp$ of the statement s. First, consider statements where local pointers are set:

$$[\![\mathbf{y} = \&a]\!]^\sharp \, T = \langle \pi, \rho \oplus \{\mathbf{y} \mapsto \mathsf{cl}_\pi\{\&a\}\} \rangle$$

$$[\![\mathbf{y} = \mathbf{y}']\!]^\sharp \, T = [\![\mathbf{y} = \mathbf{y}' \to b]\!]^\sharp \, T = \langle \pi, \rho \oplus \{\mathbf{y} \mapsto \rho(\mathbf{y}')\} \rangle$$

$$[\![\mathbf{y} = \mathsf{null}]\!]^\sharp \, T = \langle \pi, \rho \oplus \{\mathbf{y} \mapsto \emptyset\} \rangle$$

$$[\![\mathbf{y} = \mathsf{new}(\tau)]\!]^\sharp \, T = \langle \pi, \rho \oplus \{\mathbf{y} \mapsto \{\bullet\}\} \rangle$$

where $\rho \oplus \{\mathbf{y}_i \mapsto X_i \mid i \in I\}$ is the function obtained from ρ by updating the image of $\mathbf{y}_i$ to X_i for all $i \in I$. Now, consider a write to memory through local pointers. In case either null or a pointer to a fresh memory block is written, the abstract state does not change:

$$[\![\mathbf{y} \to b = \mathsf{null}]\!]^\sharp \, T = [\![\mathbf{y} \to b = \mathsf{new}(\tau)]\!]^\sharp \, T = T$$

Finally, consider a write to memory of the form $\mathbf{y} \to b = \mathbf{y}'$. If neither $\rho(\mathbf{y})$ nor $\rho(\mathbf{y}')$ contain $\bullet$, then we join the equivalence classes of $\mathbf{y}$ and $\mathbf{y}'$:

$$[\![\mathbf{y} \to b = \mathbf{y}']\!]^\sharp \, T = \langle \pi', \{\mathbf{y} \mapsto \mathsf{cl}_{\pi'}(\rho(\mathbf{y})) \mid \mathbf{y} \in L\} \rangle \qquad \text{where}$$

$$\pi' = \pi \sqcup \{\{x, x'\} \mid x \neq x', x, x' \in \rho(\mathbf{y}) \cup \rho(\mathbf{y}')\}$$

If the bullet is involved, but $\rho(\mathbf{y}), \rho(\mathbf{y}') \subseteq \{\bullet\}$, then simply $[\![\mathbf{y} \to b = \mathbf{y}']\!]^{\sharp} T = T$; however, when $\bullet \in \rho(\mathbf{y}) \cup \rho(\mathbf{y}') \not\subseteq \{\bullet\}$, we additionally consider all pointers that may point into the thread-local region denoted by $\bullet$. Let $Y = \{\mathbf{y}, \mathbf{y}'\} \cup \{\mathbf{y}'' \in L \mid \bullet \in \rho(\mathbf{y}'')\}$ and $X = \bigcup\{\rho(\mathbf{y}'') \mid \mathbf{y}'' \in Y\}\setminus\{\bullet\}$. We join all globals from X into one equivalence class to which all variables from Y may now point:

$$[\![\mathbf{y} \to b = \mathbf{y}']\!]^{\sharp} T = \langle \pi', \rho' \rangle \qquad \text{where}$$
$$\pi' = \pi \sqcup \{\{x, x'\} \mid x \neq x', x, x' \in X\}$$
$$\rho' = \{\mathbf{y} \mapsto \mathsf{cl}_{\pi'}(\rho(\mathbf{y})) \mid \mathbf{y} \notin Y\} \cup \{\mathbf{y}'' \mapsto \mathsf{cl}_{\pi'} X \mid \mathbf{y}'' \in Y\}$$

For proving the soundness of the analysis, we rely on a small-step operational semantics of heap-manipulating programs. Since we have currently ruled out procedures, the concrete program state when reaching a program point u consists of a pair $\sigma = \langle \mu, \lambda \rangle$ where λ maps the local pointers to the start addresses of blocks and μ describes the current global memory. We represent the memory μ by a map which assigns a value to every address-field pair (l, b). Type-safety requires that l is the address of a block in the global memory of struct type τ which has a field b. For convenience, we assume that every field of pointer type which has not yet been initialized, holds the value null.

In μ, the address l_1 is *reachable* from the address l_2 iff l_2 can be obtained from l_1 by repeated field selection and dereferencing. A *region* in μ is a set R of addresses in μ such that every $l_1 \in R$ satisfies the condition: $l_2 \in R$ whenever $\mu(l_1, b) = l_2$ for some field name b of the struct at address l_1. This definition implies that the set of regions of μ form a *partition* of the addresses in μ. In particular, no address in the region R is reachable from any address outside the region R.

Assume that the concrete program state $\sigma = \langle \mu, \lambda \rangle$ induces a partition $\Pi = \{R_1, \ldots, R_m\}$ of the addresses in μ. Then σ is in the *concretization* of the abstract state $T = \langle \pi, \rho \rangle$, i.e., $\sigma \in \gamma(T)$, iff the following holds:

1. Whenever $\{x, x'\} \notin \pi$ for global static addresses $x \neq x'$, then x and x' are not in the same region of μ.
2. Whenever $x \notin \rho(\mathbf{y})$, then x and $\lambda(\mathbf{y})$ are not in the same region of μ.
3. Whenever $\rho(\mathbf{y}) = \emptyset$, then $\lambda(\mathbf{y})$ equals null.

This implies that if $\rho(\mathbf{y}) = \{\bullet\}$, then all memory cells reachable from $\lambda(\mathbf{y})$ are definitely not reachable from globals and thus not accessible from other threads. Accordingly, write accesses through $\mathbf{y}$ need not be protected. If on the other hand, $\rho(\mathbf{y})$ contains a global static address, the address of $\mathbf{y}$ must be considered as *published*, i.e., possibly accessible for other threads. The set of static global addresses occurring in ρ (and π) can be considered as the set of *possible owners* of a region for which locks should be provided. The following theorem states that our definitions of the abstract transformers for basic program statements are sound.

Theorem 1 (Soundness of Transfer Functions). *Let s denote a program statement and T denote an abstract state. If $\sigma \in \gamma(T)$ and σ' denotes the concrete program state obtained from σ by the execution of s, then $\sigma' \in \gamma([\![s]\!]^{\sharp} T)$.* □

3   Interprocedural Analysis

In this section we present an interprocedural formulation of the region analysis. We model communication between procedures by assuming that every function has the same set L of local variables and that all locals of the caller are passed by value to the callee; however, in our simplified setting, we only pass locals into procedures but do not return them back. Thus, the effect of a procedure call is limited to possible collapses within the partition of globals and the possible joining of thread-local data structures with some global regions. In order to deal with the latter, we extend the points-into map ρ for local pointer variables with an extra variable $\diamond$ representing the thread-local data structures before the call. The abstract transformer $\mathsf{enter}^\sharp$ initializes the abstract state at procedure entry based on the abstract state before the call:

$$\mathsf{enter}^\sharp(\langle \pi, \rho \rangle) = \langle \pi, \rho \oplus \{\diamond \mapsto \{\bullet\}\} \rangle$$

While analyzing a procedure q, updates through pointers into thread-local memory may result in globals being added to the region tracked by $\diamond$ (just as for any other variable with $\bullet$ in its points-into set). At procedure exit, the local variables of the called procedure q are removed, while the points-into information accumulated by $\diamond$ are added to every local $\mathbf{y}$ of the caller which before the call may have pointed into the thread-local region. Assume that $T_1 = \langle \pi_1, \rho_1 \rangle, T_2 = \langle \pi_2, \rho_2 \rangle$ are the abstract states before the call and at procedure exit, respectively. Then this combination is achieved by the function $\mathsf{combine}^\sharp$:

$$\mathsf{combine}^\sharp(T_1, T_2) = \langle \pi_2, \rho \rangle \qquad \text{where}$$
$$\rho = \{z \mapsto \mathsf{cl}_{\pi_2}(\rho_1(z)) \mid z \in L \cup \{\diamond\}, \bullet \notin \rho_1(z)\} \cup$$
$$\{z \mapsto \mathsf{cl}_{\pi_2}(\rho_1(z) \cup \rho_2(\diamond)) \mid z \in L \cup \{\diamond\}, \bullet \in \rho_1(z)\}$$

The abstract functions $\mathsf{enter}^\sharp$ and $\mathsf{combine}^\sharp$ allow us to apply general frameworks for interprocedural analysis [26]. Here, we follow the approach advocated, e.g., by Cousot [5], which relies on *partially tabulating* the abstract value tables of called procedures. A multi-threaded variant of this approach [25] has been implemented by the analyzer Goblint [28]. The analyzer solves a constraint system for the abstract values returned by the summary function for f when called on abstract values a. Given a complete lattice $\mathcal{L}$ of abstract values, abstract transformers $[\![s]\!]^\sharp$ for basic statements, and abstract transformers $\mathsf{enter}^\sharp$ and $\mathsf{combine}^\sharp$ for parameter passing and function return, the constraint system is set up as follows:

$$\langle v, a \rangle \sqsupseteq a \qquad\qquad\qquad\qquad \text{for a function entry point } v$$
$$\langle v, a \rangle \sqsupseteq [\![s]\!]^\sharp(\langle u, a \rangle) \qquad\qquad\quad \text{for edge } (u, v) \text{ with statement } s$$
$$\langle v, a \rangle \sqsupseteq \mathsf{combine}^\sharp(\langle u, a \rangle, \langle \mathsf{ret}_f, \mathsf{enter}^\sharp(\langle u, a \rangle) \rangle) \text{ for edge } (u, v) \text{ calling } f()$$

where $a \in \mathcal{L}$, f denotes functions with return point ret_f, and u, v are program points. For a program point v of a function g, the variable $\langle v, a \rangle$ of the constraint system represents the abstract value attained at v in a call to g where evaluation of the body of g starts with the abstract value a. The soundness of the least solution of this constraint system instantiated to our region analysis follows from Theorem 1 and [5, 14]:

Theorem 2 (Soundness of Region Analysis). *Assume that $\varphi\langle v, a\rangle$, for program point v of a procedure f and abstract state a, is the least solution of the constraint system over the complete lattice $\mathcal{L}$. Let $\varphi\langle v, a_e\rangle = \langle \pi, \rho\rangle$, and assume that the pair $\sigma_e = \langle \mu_e, \lambda_e\rangle$ of a heap μ_e and assignment λ_e of locals is in the concretization of a_e, i.e., $\sigma_e \in \gamma(a_e)$. Moreover, assume that R_e is the set of thread-local memory cells at procedure entry, i.e., the set of addresses which can only be reached from the locals in σ_e.*

Then every same-level execution starting in σ_e at the entry point of f and reaching program point v in state $\sigma = \langle \mu, \lambda\rangle$ satisfies the following properties:

- $\sigma \in \gamma(\langle \pi, \rho\rangle)$;
- *For every global x, if x is reachable from an address in R_e (w.r.t. μ), or an address in R_e is reachable from x (w.r.t. μ), then $\&x \in \rho(\diamond)$.*   □

The given constraint system may be huge depending on the complete lattice of the analysis. *Local fixpoint iteration* is a general technique to partially explore large (or possibly infinite) systems of constraints [7]. Starting from a subset Y of *interesting* unknowns, local fixpoint iteration explores only those other unknowns which may *contribute* to the values of unknowns from Y. This technique is well-suited if the interesting values can be computed by consulting only a small (though possibly unknown) fraction of the constraint variables. This is the case in our application. Here, fixpoint iteration starts with the set $Y = \{\langle \mathsf{ret_{main}}, \mathsf{enter}^\sharp a\rangle\}$ if main is the start function of the thread currently under consideration, and the abstract value a describes the program state before program execution [7]. Local fixpoint iteration then will trigger the evaluation of all pairs $\langle v, \mathsf{enter}^\sharp a'\rangle$ where v is the program point of a procedure which (during fixpoint iteration) is called for the abstract program state a'. In our experiments with the analyzer Goblint, we found that the number of different calls of the same procedure is mostly quite small.

4   Relating Locks and Regions

In order to relate accessed regions of the global memory with acquired locks, we can rely on any analysis providing *must-alias* information for static global addresses. For clarity of presentation, we just consider the simplest instance of such an analysis, which tracks conjunctions of equalities of the form $\mathbf{y} \doteq x$ where $\mathbf{y} \in L$ is a local pointer variable and $x \in L \cup G$ is either a local pointer variable or a global static address. Such a domain has been suggested in [17] where efficient algorithms for the basic operations have been presented.

Let $\mathbf{E}$ denote the lattice of equalities. Technically, each element $\phi \in \mathbf{E}$ either is equivalent to false or is equivalent to a satisfiable finite conjunction of equalities. We write $\phi \models (x \doteq x')$ if the equality $x \doteq x'$ is logically implied by ϕ. The ordering on $\mathbf{E}$ is given by logical implication, i.e., $\phi \sqsubseteq \phi'$ iff either $\phi = \mathsf{false}$ or both ϕ and ϕ' are different from false, and $\phi \models (x \doteq x')$ for every equality $x \doteq x'$ in ϕ'. Thus, the greatest lower bound of ϕ_1, ϕ_2 is given by their conjunction $\phi_1 \wedge \phi_2$, whereas the least upper bound of two satisfiable conjunctions ϕ_1, ϕ_2 is equivalent to the conjunction of all equalities $x \doteq x'$ which are both implied by ϕ_1 and ϕ_2. Here, we consider the abstract functions for procedure calls. According to our assumption, all locals are passed as actual parameters to called procedures. The locals of the caller, on the other hand, are not affected by the changes to locals of the callee. This means that the abstract functions $\mathsf{enter}_E^\sharp, \mathsf{combine}_E^\sharp$ for procedure calls are defined by:

$$\mathsf{enter}_E^\sharp \, \phi = \phi \qquad \mathsf{combine}_E^\sharp(\phi_1, \_) = \phi_1$$

As a third component, our analysis requires information about the set of locks which are definitely held when reaching a program point. For the moment, every lock is identified by static addresses or addresses pointed at by local pointers. For every reachable program point u (in every analyzed invocation of a procedure), our analysis therefore identifies a finite subset S of descriptions of locks which are definitely held when reaching u (in the given invocation). Let $\mathbf{S}$ denote the set of finite subsets of global static addresses of locks. Since we are interested in *definite* information, finite sets of lock address expressions are ordered by the *superset* relation.

While region and must-alias analysis are independent, the analysis of sets of definitely held locks may profit from the results of both. The must-alias analysis is applied to identify all address expressions which denote the acquired lock, the may-alias information which we infer from the region information, helps to narrow down the set of locks which may no longer be held after releasing a lock. More precisely, assume that $T = \langle \pi, \rho \rangle$ is an abstract description of memory regions. We infer non-equality information as follows. If $\{x, x'\} \notin \pi$ for two pointer expressions x, x', then $x \neq x'$ for every program state $\langle \mu, \lambda \rangle$ in the concretization of π. Likewise, if $x \notin \rho(\mathbf{y})$, then also $\lambda(\mathbf{y}) \neq x$. Finally, if $\rho(\mathbf{y}) \cap \rho(\mathbf{y}') = \emptyset$ while $\rho(\mathbf{y}) \cup \rho(\mathbf{y}') \neq \emptyset$, then also $\lambda(\mathbf{y}) \neq \lambda(\mathbf{y}')$. We denote these facts by $T \models (x \neq x')$, $T \models (\mathbf{y} \neq x)$ and $T \models (\mathbf{y} \neq \mathbf{y}')$, respectively.

Assume that the current program state $T = \langle \pi, \rho, \phi, S \rangle$ consists of the partition of globals π, the points-into information ρ, the conjunction of must-equalities ϕ, and the lock set S. Then the sets of definitely held locks after operations lock and unlock for locks inside static structs are defined by:

$$[\![\mathsf{lock}(\&(z \to b)]\!]_S^\sharp T \quad = S \cup \{\&(x \to b) \mid x \in G, \phi \models z \doteq x\}$$
$$[\![\mathsf{unlock}(\&(z \to b))]\!]_S^\sharp T = S \setminus \{\&(x \to b) \mid \neg(\pi \models z \neq x)\}$$

for $z \in L \cup G$, respectively. When entering or leaving a procedure, the set of definitely held locks does not change. Therefore, we have:

$$\mathsf{enter}_L^\sharp \, S = S \qquad \mathsf{combine}_L^\sharp(\_, S_2) = S_2$$

```
struct list { int key; int data; struct list *next; };
struct list *slots[512];
spinlock_t    locks[512];

struct list *insert(int key, int data) {
    struct list *t; int hv = hash(key);
    spin_lock(&locks[hv]);
    t = slots[hv];
    if (t == NULL) {
        slots[hv] = new_list(key, data); goto fd; }
    while(1) {
        if (t→key == key) {
            t→data = data; goto fd; }
        if (t→next == NULL) {
            t→next = new_list(key, data); goto fd; }
        t = t→next; }
fd: spin_unlock(&locks[hv]);
    return t; }
```

Fig. 3. Simplified insert-function

5 Extension with Arrays

So far, our analysis is able to deal with dynamic data structures and a fixed finite set of mutexes. In the next step, we extend this base approach to global data structures which may contain arrays and thus also arrays of mutexes.

Example 1. Figure 3 shows a simplified version of the insert-function from the access vector cache of Security Enhanced Linux.[1] At every program point, at most one lock is held which is taken from a possibly large set of locks contained in the array locks. For a sound data-race analysis of the function insert, it does not suffice to verify that *some* lock from this array is held when the hash map is modified. Instead, it also must check the (statically unknown) *index* of the lock coincides with the index of the list in slots.   □

We now extend our core language by additionally allowing arrays within global shared data structures. Here, we consider non-nested arrays only. The address of a memory cell from a *static* global data structure with arrays is identified by $\&a[i]$ where i is an index. Accordingly, we consider address expressions of the form $\&a[e]$ where e is a side-effect free index expression depending on int-variables only. Furthermore, we extend our notion of abstract heap partitions π and points-into maps ρ. Besides sets of two-element sets, we now also allow *singleton* sets $\{\&a\}$ in partitions. Such a singleton indicates that different entries

---

[1] The most notable simplification is the use of singly linked lists instead of the doubly linked lists from the Linux kernel; however, since our technique is based on a conservative partitioning of the heap into disjoint regions, dealing with doubly linked lists and even structured use of pointer arithmetic posed no significant further challenge.

of the array $\&a$ may belong to the same memory region. We thus consider the set $\mathbf{P}$ of abstract heap partitions π with the following properties:

1. If $\{x,y\}, \{y,z\} \in \pi$ for $x \neq z$, then $\{x,z\} \in \pi$.
2. If $\{\&a, x\} \in \pi$, then also $\{\&a\} \in \pi$.
3. If $\{\&a\} \in \pi$, then $\&a[e]$ does not occur in π.
4. For the same array $\&a$, π may have at most one address expression e with $\&a[e]$ occurring in π.

We could have allowed multiple index expressions e_i referring to the same array $\&a$ as long as all e_i definitely evaluate to distinct values. In our experiments, the restriction to a single expression, however, has always been sufficient. The partial ordering on $\mathbf{P}$ is given by $\pi_1 \sqsubseteq \pi_2$ iff the following holds:

1. If $\{\&a[e], x\} \in \pi_1$ then $\{\&a[e], x\} \in \pi_2$ or $\{\&a\}, \{\&a, x\} \in \pi_2$.
2. If $\{x, y\} \in \pi_1$ where neither x nor y contains an index expression, then also $\{x, y\} \in \pi_2$.

Thus, e.g., for $\pi_1 = \emptyset$, $\pi_2 = \{\{\mathbf{p}, \&a[i]\}\}$, $\pi_3 = \{\{\&a\}, \{\mathbf{p}, \&a\}\}$, $\pi_1 \sqsubseteq \pi_2 \sqsubseteq \pi_3$.

Accordingly, we now consider points-into maps ρ where a set X occurring as the image of a local (or $\diamond$) satisfies the following additional restrictions:

1. If $\&a[e], \&a[e'] \in X$, then $e \equiv e'$;
2. If $\&a \in X$ then for every e, $\&a[e] \notin X$

where the ordering on two such sets is the natural extension of $\emptyset \sqsubseteq \{x\}$ for all x, and $\{\&a[e]\} \sqsubseteq \{\&a\}$.

Also, we extend the closure operation cl_π such that $\mathsf{cl}_\pi X$ for a set X of global static address expressions or $\bullet$, now additionally replaces an indexed expression $\&a[e]$ with $\&a$ whenever $\{\&a\} \in \pi$. Likewise, we extend the domain of must equalities and finite lock sets to address expressions containing indexing. The occurring index expressions may depend on **int**-variables; however, we here ignore definite equalities between **int**-variables. Thus, we consider two index expressions e_1, e_2 as *definitely* equal only if they are *syntactically* equal. Technically, this allows us to use a similar domain for must equalities and lock sets as in section 4 — only that we now additionally consider indexed static addresses $\&a[e]$ instead of static addresses $\&a$ alone.

This simplistic setting is still able to deal with increments or decrements of **int**-variables. Accordingly, our analysis will track assignments to **int**-variables i of the form $i = i + c$ for $c \in \mathbf{Z}$ whereas all other assignments to i are approximated by the *non-deterministic* assignment $i = ?$ which is meant to assign to i an *unknown* value. The effect of the assignment $i = i + c$ on a triple $T = \langle \pi, \phi, S \rangle$ consists in substituting i in all index expressions occurring in T with $i - c$. The effect of the assignment $i = ?$ on the other hand, assigns an unknown value to i and thus must remove all occurrences of $\mathbf{x}_i$ from T. For a partition π, $\mathsf{delete}(\pi, i)$ replaces all expressions $\&a[e]$ where i occurs in e with $\&a$ (if there are any) and adds the set $\{\&a\}$ (given that there are any). For a points-into map ρ, $\mathsf{delete}(\pi, i)$ replaces in every image $\rho(z)$ elements $\&a[e]$ where i occurs in e with $\&a$. For component ϕ, delete(ϕ, **i**) removes all equalities involving **i**. Likewise for S, delete(S, **i**) removes all lock expressions $\&a[e].b$ where **i** occurs in e.

$$\llbracket \mathbf{i} = \mathbf{i} + c \rrbracket^\sharp T = T[\mathbf{i} - c/\mathbf{i}]$$
$$\llbracket \mathbf{i} = ? \rrbracket^\sharp T = \langle \text{delete}(\pi, \mathbf{i}), \text{delete}(\rho, \mathbf{i}), \text{delete}(\phi, \mathbf{i}), \text{delete}(S, \mathbf{i}) \rangle$$

The effects of assignments involving local pointers and global memory, are defined componentwise on the first three components, while the set of definitely held locks remains unchanged. We omit the details but instead apply the technique to a typical example.

Example 2. Assume we start the execution of the insert-function from Figure 3 with the abstract value $T_0 = \langle \emptyset, \{\diamond \mapsto \{\bullet\}, \mathbf{t} \mapsto \emptyset\}, \text{true}, \emptyset \rangle$. After having called spin_lock() and reaching the *while*-loop, we have:

$$T_1 = \langle \emptyset, \rho_1, \phi_1, S_1 \rangle \quad \text{where}$$
$$\rho_1 = \{\diamond \mapsto \{\bullet\}, \mathbf{t} \mapsto \{\&\text{slots}[\mathbf{hv}]\}\}$$
$$\phi_1 = \mathbf{t} \doteq \&\text{slots}[\mathbf{hv}]$$
$$S_1 = \{\&\text{locks}[\mathbf{hv}]\}$$

although the precise value of **hv** is unknown. Inside the loop the must-equality $\mathbf{t} \doteq \&\text{slots}[\mathbf{hv}]$ is lost, while the region information as well as the lock set are preserved. Unlocking resets the set of held locks to $\emptyset$.   □

Our analysis can be enhanced by jointly performing constant propagation or, more generally, any analysis of **int** variables which provides us with more precise information about how index expressions are related. Such information could be provided, e.g., by Karr's analysis of affine equalities [13, 16].

While the complete lattice for the combined analysis of regions, must equalities and abstract lock sets in presence of arrays is no longer finite, it still satisfies the ascending chain condition. In order to apply the interprocedural framework from Section 3, we generalize the functions enter$^\sharp$ and combine$^\sharp$ for abstract parameter passing and procedure return from the last sections. Additionally, we now must track the values of local **int** variables. We could do so by additionally maintaining, e.g., affine must equalities between these. Here, we prefer a simpler analysis which just tracks the set of local **int** variables which may have changed their values since procedure entry. Assume that before the call, we have the abstract state $T = \langle \pi, \rho, I, \phi, S \rangle$ where π, ρ, ϕ, and S are as before and I now denotes a set of **int** variables whose value possibly has changed since procedure entry. When entering a newly called procedure, we initialize this set to $\emptyset$. We define:

$$\text{enter}^\sharp \langle \pi, \rho, I, \phi, S \rangle = \langle \pi, \rho_1, \emptyset, \phi, S \rangle \quad \text{where}$$
$$\rho_1 = \rho \oplus \{\diamond \mapsto \{\bullet\}\}$$

Likewise, at procedure exit, the local variables of the called procedure q must be removed. Also all equivalences $\{x, \&a[e]\}$ in the returned must be collapsed to

$\{x, \&a\}$ for index expressions e depending on **int**-variables which have changed their values. This is achieved by:

$$\text{combine}^\sharp(\langle\pi_1, \rho_1, I_1, \phi_1, S_1\rangle, \langle\pi_2, \rho_2, I_2, \_, S_2\rangle) \quad = \quad \langle\pi, \rho, I_1, \phi_1, S\rangle \quad \text{where}$$
$$\pi = \text{delete}(\pi_2, I_2)$$
$$\rho = \{z \mapsto \text{cl}_\pi(\rho_1(z)) \mid z \in L \cup \{\diamond\}, \bullet \notin \rho_1(z)\} \cup$$
$$\{z \mapsto \text{cl}_\pi(\rho_1(z) \cup \rho_2(\diamond)) \mid z \in L \cup \{\diamond\}, \bullet \in \rho_1(z)\}$$
$$S = \text{delete}(S_2, I_2)$$

Here, the calls to delete() for a set I of **int** variables abbreviate repeated application of delete() for each element $i \in I$.

Example 3. Consider the insert-function from Figure 3. Assume that at the program point before the call to this function we have the abstract state: $T_0 = \langle\emptyset, \{\diamond, t \mapsto \{\bullet\}\}, \emptyset, \text{true}, \emptyset\rangle$. Then $\text{enter}^\sharp(T_0) = T_1$ is the abstract value for the start point of the corresponding abstract call to the function `insert()` where:

$$T_1 = \langle\emptyset, \rho_1, \emptyset, \phi_1, \emptyset\rangle \quad \text{where}$$
$$\rho_1 = \{\diamond \mapsto \{\bullet\}, t \mapsto \{\&\text{slots}[\text{hv}]\}\}$$
$$\phi_1 = t \doteq \&\text{slots}[\text{hv}]$$

At the program point before the lock operation, we have $T_2 = \langle\emptyset, \rho_1, \{\text{hv}\}, \phi_1, \emptyset\rangle$. After locking, we thus have $T_3 = \langle\emptyset, \rho_1, \{\text{hv}\}, \phi_1, \{\&\text{locks}[\text{hv}]\}\rangle$ — implying that the elements accessed through the pointer t belong to the region $\text{slots}[\text{hv}]$ and that these accesses are protected by the corresponding lock $\text{locks}[\text{hv}]$. At function exit, we finally arrive at $T_4 = \langle\emptyset, \rho_1, \{\text{hv}\}, \phi_1, \emptyset\rangle$. Combining this state with the state T_0 before the call will recover the set of possibly modified **int** variables as well as the must equalities before the call. In the example, we just recover the abstract state T_0. □

6 Analyzing the Linux Kernel

We have implemented our analysis in the Goblint analyser and applied it to Linux kernel modules such as device drivers. One challenge in analyzing device drivers is how to model the rest of the kernel. Goblint uses a driver *harness* that assumes the worst possible interleavings of the device's file operations and interrupt handlers. Starting from the module initialization code, we track function pointers that are held in structs. Pointers passed to library functions are assumed to be potential call-backs and are analyzed as separate threads. These may interleave with each other as well as with the rest of the initialization code.

In the implementation, we also extended the basic approach to deal with nested static global data-structures such as structs containing arrays as well as well-behaved pointer arithmetic within structs. This is necessary for the analysis of the Linux API for doubly linked lists. This API provides macros which, e.g., calculate the start address of a struct from the address of a component. While these macros have a clean semantics, their implementation makes extensive use

Table 1. Result of analysing kernel modules

File	Size (merged)	Time	Verified	Warnings
atmel_tclib	1317 lines	0,07 s	1	0
hwmon	1434 lines	0,23 s	1	0
enclosure	1510 lines	0,19 s	1	1
scsi_dh	4370 lines	0,57 s	2	0
dmaengine	4449 lines	0,83 s	3	0
scsi_rdac	4744 lines	0,81 s	1	0
usb_hcd	7340 lines	3,32 s	3	2
avc	7466 lines	1,68 s	2	1
ppp_generic	10818 lines	4,70 s	4	1

of type casts, and addition and subtraction of pointers. Therefore, our implementation allows application of the address operator to arbitrary expressions evaluating to global addresses. Thus, pointers may no longer point to the beginnings of blocks. Moreover, a pointer variable whose value is obtained from the value of the pointer variable q by means of such kind of pointer arithmetic is put into the same region as q.

The results of running our analyzer on a number of different modules from the kernel is summarized in Table 1. We use the CIL analysis framework [19] as a front-end to parse and process these files. The sizes of the files in the table are the sizes of CIL's outputs after merging the modules with included headers and removing unused definitions. We ran these experiments on an Athlon 64 X2 3800+ machine under Kubuntu.[2]

For all these benchmarks, we are successful in automatically inferring the correlations between elements of lists and their corresponding locks and to verify that all accesses are protected. The numbers of shared variables for which we could verify a consistent locking scheme as well those for which conflicting accesses were found are listed in the table. The analyzer registers accesses to each element in a region separately; thus, if k linked lists have collapsed into a single region and there is a conflicting access through a pointer into this region, the number of warnings would be k and not one. The false alarms for these benchmakrs are mostly due to our imprecise harness. We will comment here only on two interesting benchmarks. The file avc is the access vector cache code of Security Enhanced Linux which served as the inspiration for the examples in this paper. The analyzer's output is the following:

```
Found correlation: avc_cache.latest_notif is guarded by
    lockset {notif_lock}
Found correlation: avc_cache.slots is guarded by
    lockset {avc_cache.slots_lock[*]}
Datarace over avc_callbacks:
    write in some thread with lockset: {} (avc.c:6953)
```

---

[2] The goblint website, http://goblint.at.mt.ut.ee, has detailed instructions on reproducing these benchmarks.

The asterisk in the second lockset is the analyzer's modest way of indicating that it has verified the correlation between the index expressions used when accessing list elements in the array of slots and the index expressions used to acquire a mutex from the array of locks. The analyzer warns about a "race" for avc_callbacks. While this is indeed a race in the context of this module alone, the function for registering callbacks are only used in the initialization code by the files using this module.

The file dmaengine is part of the hardware-neutral interface to the DMA subsystem. The programmers have commented in the source file: "The subsystem keeps two global lists, dma_device_list and dma_client_list. Both of these are protected by a mutex, dma_list_mutex." Our analyzer succeeds in verifying this.

7   Related Work

Regions and ownership types have been used for compile-time garbage collection [27] or to ensure encapsulation in object-oriented languages [4]. More recently, analyzers have been developed for checking correct usage of region-based memory management APIs [1, 29]. Note, however, that the regions there need not be closed under reachability. For analyzing pointers, Gulwani and Tiwari [10] present a domain of quantified may- and must-equality pairs which can express similar invariants to ours. This analysis, while being extremely precise, has problems with dealing with doubly linked lists. Reachability in the presence of pointer arithmetic has been studied by Chatterjee et al. [3] who provide an annotation language for reasoning about the linked list API of Windows device drivers.

Precise abstractions of the heap have been provided by separation logic [22] and shape analysis [24]. Gopan et al. [8] present a shape analysis which allows reasoning about dynamic memory and the values of array elements, Gulwani et al. [9] present a *set cardinality analysis* which combines shape and numeric abstractions to reason about sizes of data-structures. Hackett and Rugina [11] present a shape analysis which is built on top of a partitioning of the heap into disjoint regions. These regions are derived from a standard points-to analysis and again not necessarily closed under reachability. Recent work has also provided methods for making shape analysis scale better [31, 2, 15] — at a certain loss in precision, e.g., by no longer tracking arrays.

Our main interest has been to provide efficient methods which are precise enough for analyzing data races in presence of dynamic data-structures and arrays. Rugina and Rinard [23] present techniques to avoid races by analyzing disjointness of accessed memory blocks. Naik and Aiken [18] propose *conditional must-not aliasing* to deal with locking schemes of various levels of granularity in Java. They introduce *disjoint reachability* analysis for dealing with medium-grained locking; however, their notion of disjointness is based on allocation sites, which is not helpful in cases such as Figure 2. We have experimented with some analyzers that perform race detection for C. We compared the following analyzers: Locksmith, a sound race detection tool based on type-based

Table 2. Summary of comparison. For each idiom, "+" indicates success, while "−" indicates the existence of a False Negative / False Positive

Test	Goblint	Locksmith	Coverity	DDVerify
static	+/+	+/+	+/+	−/+
single list	+/+	+/−	−/+	
shared lists	+/+	+/−	−/+	
simple array	+/+	+/−	−/+	
shared array	+/+	+/−	−/+	

label-flow [21]; Coverity Prevent, a commercial bug-detection tool based on meta-compilation techniques [6]; and DDVerify, a device driver model-checker that checks for proper use of the kernel API [30].

We compared the tools on small test programs. For each test, there is a version with a race and one without races. The test *static* is the simplest possible race example, has a static global variable that should be protected by a static lock; *single list* contains a linked list where access to its nodes are protected by a single lock; *shared lists* has two lists that are protected by their own locks; still, there might be races due to sharing between elements in the lists; *simple array* contains an array of locks and an array of linked lists where the accesses should be properly correlated as in the examples of this paper; *shared array* is like the previous test, except there might be sharing between the linked lists of different array elements, hence there may a race although the correct lock is acquired. The summary of this comparison is shown in Table 2.

It seems that DDVerify checks other properties related to mutexes, e.g., double-acquisition of locks, but not whether accesses to globals are protected by the same locks. Locksmith and Coverity Prevent pass the first test, but already the simple linked list example is beyond their current capabilities. Locksmith complains on all tests, even when the program is perfectly safe; Coverity remains completely silent, even in the presence of races. Naturally, these analyzers have their advantages: Coverity checks a host of other properties, Locksmith deals with per-element locking, and DDVerify has an extremely precise automatic device driver harness mechanism; nevertheless, for medium-grained locking, Goblint is the clear winner.

8 Conclusion

We have presented a general approach to certify absence of data-races in C. In order to deal with dynamic data-structures, we provided a simple region analysis which allows to analyze reachability through field selection and dereferencing. We also indicated how this method can be extended to deal with arrays of regions and (well-behaved) pointer arithmetic. Our methods have been implemented in the efficient interprocedural data-race analyzer Goblint allowing us to verify locking schemes for dynamic data structures and arrays in the Linux kernel.

While we have analyzed benchmarks without modifying the original kernel code, in four of the benchmarks we only considered conflicts between write accesses. Read accesses are often protected by reader/writer locks, or more recently, the Read-Copy-Update mechanism. This poses a problem when the read accesses are protected at a coarser level of granularity than that of the write accesses. Thus, our failure to distinguish these would generate false alarms. Another challenge is to combine our technique here with methods dealing with per-element locking [20] in order to verify programs where some dynamically allocated structures, such as the per-device structure, contain linked lists and associated mutexes.

Acknowledgments. We thank Kalmer Apinis for assistance with the programming. Development of the analyzer is partially supported by the Estonian Science Foundation under grant no. 6713.

References

1. Boyapati, C., Salcianu, A., Beebee, W., Rinard, M.: Ownership types for safe region-based memory management in real-time java. In: PLDI 2003, pp. 324–337. ACM Press, New York (2003)
2. Calcagno, C., Distefano, D., O'Hearn, P., Yang, H.: Compositional shape analysis by means of bi-abduction. In: POPL 2009, pp. 289–300. ACM Press, New York (2009)
3. Chatterjee, S., Lahiri, S., Qadeer, S., Rakamarić, Z.: A reachability predicate for analyzing Low-Level software. In: Grumberg, O., Huth, M. (eds.) TACAS 2007. LNCS, vol. 4424, pp. 19–33. Springer, Heidelberg (2007)
4. Clarke, D.G., Potter, J.M., Noble, J.: Ownership types for flexible alias protection. In: OOPSLA 1998, pp. 48–64. ACM Press, New York (1998)
5. Cousot, P., Cousot, R.: Static Determination of Dynamic Properties of Recursive Programs. In: Neuhold, E. (ed.) Formal Descriptions of Programming Concepts, pp. 237–277. North-Holland Publishing Company, Amsterdam (1977)
6. Engler, D., Chelf, B., Chou, A., Hallem, S.: Checking system rules using system-specific, programmer-written compiler extensions. In: OSDI 2000, pp. 1–16. USENIX Association (2000)
7. Fecht, C., Seidl, H.: A Faster Solver for General Systems of Equations. Sci. Comput. Programming 35(2), 137–161 (1999)
8. Gopan, D., Reps, T., Sagiv, M.: A framework for numeric analysis of array operations. In: POPL 2005, pp. 338–350. ACM Press, New York (2005)
9. Gulwani, S., Lev-Ami, T., Sagiv, M.: A combination framework for tracking partition sizes. In: POPL 2009, pp. 239–251. ACM Press, New York (2009)
10. Gulwani, S., Tiwari, A.: An abstract domain for analyzing heap-manipulating low-level software. In: Damm, W., Hermanns, H. (eds.) CAV 2007. LNCS, vol. 4590, pp. 379–392. Springer, Heidelberg (2007)
11. Hackett, B., Rugina, R.: Region-based shape analysis with tracked locations. In: POPL 2005, pp. 310–323. ACM Press, New York (2005)
12. Hind, M., Burke, M., Carini, P., Choi, J.-D.: Interprocedural pointer alias analysis. ACM Trans. Prog. Lang. Syst. 21(4), 848–894 (1999)
13. Karr, M.: Affine relationships among variables of a program. Acta Inf. 6(2), 133–151 (1976)

14. Knoop, J., Steffen, B.: The Interprocedural Coincidence Theorem. In: Pfahler, P., Kastens, U. (eds.) CC 1992. LNCS, vol. 641, pp. 125–140. Springer, Heidelberg (1992)
15. Manevich, R., Lev-Ami, T., Sagiv, M., Ramalingam, G., Berdine, J.: Heap decomposition for concurrent shape analysis. In: Alpuente, M., Vidal, G. (eds.) SAS 2008. LNCS, vol. 5079, pp. 363–377. Springer, Heidelberg (2008)
16. Müller-Olm, M., Seidl, H.: A note on Karr's algorithm. In: Díaz, J., Karhumäki, J., Lepistö, A., Sannella, D. (eds.) ICALP 2004. LNCS, vol. 3142, pp. 1016–1028. Springer, Heidelberg (2004)
17. Müller-Olm, M., Seidl, H.: Upper adjoints for fast inter-procedural variable equalities. In: Drossopoulou, S. (ed.) ESOP 2008. LNCS, vol. 4960, pp. 178–192. Springer, Heidelberg (2008)
18. Naik, M., Aiken, A.: Conditional must not aliasing for static race detection. In: POPL 2007, pp. 327–338. ACM Press, New York (2007)
19. Necula, G.C., McPeak, S., Rahul, S.P., Weimer, W.: Cil: An infrastructure for C program analysis and transformation. In: Horspool, R.N. (ed.) CC 2002. LNCS, vol. 2304, pp. 213–228. Springer, Heidelberg (2002)
20. Pratikakis, P., Foster, J.S., Hicks, M.: Existential label flow inference via CFL reachability. In: Yi, K. (ed.) SAS 2006. LNCS, vol. 4134, pp. 88–106. Springer, Heidelberg (2006)
21. Pratikakis, P., Foster, J.S., Hicks, M.: Locksmith: Context-sensitive correlation analysis for detecting races. In: PLDI 2006, pp. 320–331. ACM Press, New York (2006)
22. Reynolds, J.C.: Separation logic: A logic for shared mutable data structures. In: LICS 2002, pp. 55–74. IEEE Computer Society Press, Los Alamitos (2002)
23. Rugina, R., Rinard, M.C.: Symbolic bounds analysis of pointers, array indices, and accessed memory regions. ACM Trans. Prog. Lang. Syst. 27(2), 185–235 (2005)
24. Sagiv, M., Reps, T., Wilhelm, R.: Parametric shape analysis via 3-valued logic. ACM Trans. Prog. Lang. Syst. 24(3), 217–298 (2002)
25. Seidl, H., Vene, V., Müller-Olm, M.: Global invariants for analyzing multithreaded applications. Proc. of the Estonian Academy of Sciences: Phys., Math. 52(4), 413–436 (2003)
26. Sharir, M., Pnueli, A.: Two approaches to interprocedural data flow analysis. In: Program Flow Analysis: Theory and Applications, pp. 189–234 (1981)
27. Tofte, M., Birkedal, L.: A region inference algorithm. ACM Trans. Prog. Lang. Syst. 20(4), 724–767 (1998)
28. Vojdani, V., Vene, V.: Goblint: Path-sensitive data race analysis. Annales Univ. Sci. Budapest., Sect. Comp. 30, 141–155 (2009)
29. Wang, X., Xu, Z., Liu, X., Guo, Z., Wang, X., Zhang, Z.: Conditional correlation analysis for safe region-based memory management. In: PLDI 2008, pp. 45–55. ACM Press, New York (2008)
30. Witkowski, T., Blanc, N., Kroening, D., Weissenbacher, G.: Model checking concurrent linux device drivers. In: ASE 2007, pp. 501–504. ACM Press, New York (2007)
31. Yang, H., Lee, O., Berdine, J., Calcagno, C., Cook, B., Distefano, D., O'Hearn, P.: Scalable shape analysis for systems code. In: Gupta, A., Malik, S. (eds.) CAV 2008. LNCS, vol. 5123, pp. 385–398. Springer, Heidelberg (2008)

Bottom-Up Shape Analysis

Bhargav S. Gulavani[1], Supratik Chakraborty[1], Ganesan Ramalingam[2],
and Aditya V. Nori[2]

[1] IIT Bombay
[2] Microsoft Research Bangalore

Abstract. In this paper we present a new shape analysis algorithm.
The key distinguishing aspect of our algorithm is that it is completely
compositional, bottom-up and non-iterative. We present our algorithm
as an inference system for computing Hoare triples summarizing heap
manipulating programs. Our inference rules are compositional: Hoare
triples for a compound statement are computed from the Hoare triples
of its component statements. These inference rules are used as the basis
for a bottom-up shape analysis of programs.

Specifically, we present a logic of iterated separation formula (LISF)
which uses the iterated separating conjunct of Reynolds [17] to represent
program states. A key ingredient of our inference rules is a strong bi-
abduction operation between two logical formulas. We describe sound
strong bi-abduction and satisfiability decision procedures for LISF.

We have built a prototype tool that implements these inference rules
and have evaluated it on standard shape analysis benchmark programs.
Preliminary results show that our tool can generate expressive summaries, which are complete functional specifications in many cases.

1 Introduction

In this paper we present a new shape analysis algorithm: an algorithm for analyzing programs that manipulate dynamic data structures such as lists. The
key distinguishing aspect of our algorithm is that it is *completely bottom-up
and non-iterative*. It computes summaries describing the effect of a statement
or procedure in a modular, compositional, non-iterative way: the summary for a
compound statement is computed from the summaries of the simpler statements
that make up the compound statement.

Shape analysis is intrinsically challenging. Bottom-up shape analysis is particularly challenging because it requires analyzing complex pointer manipulations
when nothing is known about the initial state. Hence, traditional shape analyses are based on an iterative top-down (forward) analysis, where the statements
are analyzed in the context of a particular (abstract) state. Though challenging,
a bottom-up shape analysis appears worth pursuing because the compositional
nature of the analysis promises much better scalability, as illustrated by the
recent work of Calcagno *et al.* [8]. The algorithm we present is based on ideas
introduced by Calcagno *et al.* [8].

J. Palsberg and Z. Su (Eds.): SAS 2009, LNCS 5673, pp. 188–204, 2009.

Motivating Example. Consider the procedure shown in Figure 1. Given a list, pointed to by parameter h, this procedure deletes the fragment of the list demarcated by parameters a and b. Our goal is an analysis that, given a procedure S such as this, computes a set of Hoare triples $[\varphi]$ S $[\widehat{\varphi}]$ that summarize the procedure. We use the above notation to indicate that the Hoare triples inferred are *total*: the triple $[\varphi]$ S $[\widehat{\varphi}]$ indicates that, given an initial state satisfying φ, the execution of S will terminate safely (with no memory errors) in a state satisfying $\widehat{\varphi}$.

```
delete(struct node *h, *a, *b)
1.    y=h;
2.    while (y!=a && y!=0) {
3.        y=y->next;
      }
4.    x=y;
5.    if (y!=0) {y=y->next;}
6.    while (y!=b && y!=0) {
7.        t=y;
8.        y=y->next;
9.        delete(t);
      }
10.   if (x !=0) {
11.       x->next=y;
12.       if (y!=0) y->prev=x;
      }
```

Fig. 1. Motivating example – deletion of the list segment

Inferring Preconditions. There are several challenges in meeting our goal. First, note that there are a number of interesting cases to consider: the list pointed to by h may be an acyclic list, or a complete cyclic list, or a lasso (an acyclic fragment followed by a cycle). The behavior of the code also depends on whether the pointers a and b point to an element in the list or not. Furthermore, the behavior of the procedure also depends on the order in which the elements pointed to by a and b occur in the list.

With traditional shape analyses, a user would have to supply a precondition describing the input to enable the analysis of the procedure delete. Alternatively, an analysis of the calling procedure would identify the abstract state σ in which the procedure delete is called, and delete would be analyzed in an initial state σ. In contrast, a bottom-up shape analysis automatically infers relevant preconditions and computes a *set* of Hoare triples, each triple describing the procedure's behavior for a particular case (such as the cases described in the previous paragraph).

Inferring Postconditions. However, even for a given φ, many different correct Hoare triples can be produced, differing in the information captured by the postcondition $\widehat{\varphi}$. As an example consider the case where h points to an acyclic list, and a and b point to elements in the list, with a pointing to an element that occurs before the element that b points to. In this case, the following are all valid properties that can be expressed as suitable Hoare triples: (a) The procedure is *memory-safe*: it causes no pointer error such as dereferencing a null pointer. (b) Finally, h points to an acyclic list. (c) Finally, h points to an acyclic list, which is the same as the list h pointed to at procedure entry, with the fragment from a to b deleted. Clearly, these triples provide increasingly more information.

A distinguishing feature of our inference algorithm is that it seeks to infer triples describing properties similar to (c) above, which yield a *functional specification* for the analyzed procedure. One of the key challenges in shape analysis is relating the value of the final data-structure to the value of the initial data-structure. We utilize an extension of separation logic, described later, to achieve this.

Composition via Strong Bi-Abduction. We now informally describe how summaries $[\varphi_1]$ S1 $[\widehat{\varphi}_1]$ and $[\varphi_2]$ S2 $[\widehat{\varphi}_2]$, in separation logic, can be composed to obtain summaries for S1;S2. The intuition behind the composition rule, which is similar to the composition rule in [8], is as follows. Suppose we can identify φ_{pre} and φ_{post} such that $\widehat{\varphi}_1 * \varphi_{pre}$ and $\varphi_{post} * \varphi_2$ are equivalent. We can then infer summaries $[\varphi_1 * \varphi_{pre}]$ S1 $[\widehat{\varphi}_1 * \varphi_{pre}]$ and $[\varphi_{post} * \varphi_2]$ S2 $[\varphi_{post} * \widehat{\varphi}_2]$ by application of Frame rule [15], where $*$ is the separating conjunction of Separation Logic [17] (subject to the usual Frame rule conditions: φ_{pre} and φ_{post} should not involve variables modified by S1 and S2 respectively). We can then compose these summaries trivially and get $[\varphi_1 * \varphi_{pre}]$ S1; S2 $[\varphi_{post} * \widehat{\varphi}_2]$. Given $\widehat{\varphi}_1$ and φ_2, we refer to the identification of φ_{pre}, φ_{post} such that $\widehat{\varphi}_1 * \varphi_{pre} \Leftrightarrow \varphi_{post} * \varphi_2$ as *strong bi-abduction*. Strong bi-abduction also allows for existentially quantifying some auxiliary variables from the right hand side of the equivalence. Refer Section 2 for details.

Iterative Composition. A primary contribution of this paper is to extend the above intuition to obtain loop summaries. Suppose we have a summary $[\varphi]$ S $[\widehat{\varphi}]$, where S is the body of a loop (including the loop condition). We can apply strong bi-abduction to compose this summary with itself: for simplicity, suppose we identify φ_{post} and φ_{pre} such that $\widehat{\varphi} * \varphi_{pre} \Leftrightarrow \varphi_{post} * \varphi$. If we now inductively apply the composition rule, we can then infer a summary of the form $[\varphi * \varphi_{pre}^k]$ S^k $[\varphi_{post}^k * \widehat{\varphi}]$ that summarizes k executions of the loop. Here, we have abused notation to convey the intuition behind the idea. If our logic permits a representation of the repetition of a structure φ_{pre} an unspecified number of times k, we can then directly compute a Hoare triple summarizing the loop from a Hoare triple summarizing the loop body.

Logic Of Iterated Separation Formulas. In this paper, we introduce LISF, an extension of separation logic that enables us to meet our goal, and present sound procedures for strong bi-abduction and satisfiability in LISF. LISF has two key aspects: (i) It contains a variant of Reynolds' iterated separating conjunct construct that allows the computation of a loop summary from a loop body summary. (ii) It uses an indexed symbolic notation that allows us to give names to values occurring in a recursive (or iterative) data-structure. This is key to meeting the goal described earlier of computing functional specifications that can relate the value of the final data-structure to the value of the initial data-structure. LISF gives us a generic ability to define recursive predicates useful for describing recursive data-structures. The use of LISF, instead of specific recursive predicates, such as those describing singly-linked lists or doubly-linked lists, allows us to compute more precise descriptions of recursive data-structures in preconditions. Though we use LISF for a bottom-up analysis, it can also be used to represent program states in top down interprocedural analysis.

Empirical Evaluation. We have implemented our inference rules in a prototype bottom-up analyzer and evaluated it on several shape analysis benchmarks. On most of the examples we could generate 'complete' functional specifications. On the example program in Figure 1, we could generate several summaries with cyclic and lasso structures, although a complete specification was not obtained. This is due to the incompleteness of our strong bi-abduction algorithm.

Related Work. Our work is most closely related to the recent compositional shape analysis algorithm presented by Calcagno *et al.* [8], which derives from the earlier work in [9]. The algorithm described by Calcagno *et al.* is a hybrid algorithm that combines compositional analysis with an iterative forward analysis. The first phase of this algorithm computes candidate preconditions for a procedure, and the second phase utilizes a forward analysis to either discard the precondition, if the precondition is found to potentially lead to a memory error, or find a corresponding sound postcondition. The key idea in the Calcagno *et al.* approach, which we borrow and extend, is the use of *bi-abduction* to handle procedure calls compositionally. Given $\widehat{\varphi}_1$, the state at a callsite, and φ_2, a precondition of a Hoare triple for the called procedure, Calcagno *et al.* compute φ_{pre} and φ_{post} such that $\widehat{\varphi}_1 * \varphi_{pre} \Rightarrow \varphi_{post} * \varphi_2$. Our approach differs from the Calcagno *et al.* work in the following ways. We present a *completely* bottom-up analysis which does not use any iterative analysis whatsoever. Instead, it relies on a "stronger" form of bi-abduction (where we seek equivalence instead of implication but allow some auxiliary variables to be quantified) to compute the post-condition simultaneously. Furthermore, our approach extends the composition rule to treat loops in a similar fashion. Our approach also computes preconditions that guarantee termination. We present LISF, which serves as the basis for our algorithm, while their work uses a set of abstract recursive predicates. We also focus on computing more informative triples that can relate the final value of a data-structure to the initial data-structure.

Several recent papers [16,2,13] describe techniques to obtain preconditions by going backwards starting from some bad states. Unlike our approach, these techniques are not compositional or bottom-up. The work on regular model-checking [1,6,5,7] represents input-output relations by a transducer, which can be looked upon as a functional specification. But these works do not provide compositional techniques to compute the transducer for a loop.

Extrapolation techniques proposed in [18,4] compute sound overapproximations by identifying the growth in successive applications of transducers and iterating that growth. Similarly, [12] proposes a technique to guess the recursive predicates characterizing a data structure by identifying the growth in successive iterations of the loop and repeating that growth. In contrast, we identify the growth in both the pre and postconditions by strong bi-abduction and iterate it to compute Hoare triples that are guaranteed to be sound. Furthermore, our analysis is bottom-up and compositional in contrast to these top-down (forward) analyses.

Program Syntax
e ::= v | null
C ::= v = e | v != e
S ::= v.f := e | v := u.f | v := new | dispose v | S; S
    | assert(C) | v := e | if(C, S, S) | while(C) S

Assertion Logic Syntax   ($\sim$ $\in \{=, \neq\}$)
e ::= null | v | ...
P ::= $e \sim e$ | **false** | **true** | $P \wedge P$ | ...
S ::= **emp** | $e \mapsto (f : e)$ | **true** | $S * S$ | ...
SH ::= $P \wedge S$ | $\exists v. \, SH$

Fig. 2. Program syntax and assertion logic syntax

Contributions. (i) We present the logic of iterated separation formulas LISF (Section 3) and give sound algorithms for satisfiability checking and strong bi-abduction in this logic (Section 5). (ii) We present inference rules to compute Hoare triples in a compositional bottom-up manner (Section 4). (iii) We have a prototype implementation of our technique. We discuss its performance on several challenging programs (Section 6).

2   Composition via Strong Bi-abduction

In this section we introduce the idea of composing Hoare triples using strong bi-abduction.

2.1   Preliminaries

Programming language. We address a simple language whose syntax appears in Figure 2. The primitives assert(v = e) and assert(v != e) are used primarily to present inference rules for conditionals and loops (as will be seen later). Here v, u are program variables, and e is an expression which could either be a variable or a constant **null**. This language does not support address arithmetic.

Semantically, we use a value domain Locs (which represents an unbounded set of locations). Each location in the heap represents a cell with n fields, where n is statically fixed. A computational state contains two components: a stack, mapping program variables to their values (Locs $\cup$ {**null**}), and a heap, mapping a finite set of non-null locations to their values, which is a n-tuple of (primitive) values.

Assertion Logic. We illustrate some of the key ideas using standard Separation Logic, using the syntax shown in Figure 2. The '...' in Figure 2 refer to constructs and extensions we will introduce in Section 3. We assume the reader is familiar with the basic ideas in Separation Logic. An expressions e evaluates to a location. Given a stack s, a variable v evaluates to a location. A symbolic heap representation consists of a pure part P and a spatial part S. The pure part P consists of equalities and disequalities of expressions. The spatial part S describes the shape of the graph in the heap. **emp** denotes that the heap has no allocated cells. $x \mapsto (f : l)$ denotes a heap consisting of a single allocated cell pointed to by x, and the f field of this cell has value l. The $*$ operator is called the separating conjunct; $s_1 * s_2$ denotes that s_1 and s_2 refer to disjoint portions of the heap and the current heap is the disjoint union of these sub-heaps. The meaning of pure assertions depends only on the stack, and the meaning of spatial assertions depends on both the stack and the heap.

Table 1. Local reasoning rules for primitive statements

Mutation	$[v \mapsto (f : \_w; \ldots)]$ v.f := e $[v \mapsto (f : e; \ldots)]$
Deallocation	$[v \mapsto (f^1 : \_w^1, \ldots, f^n : \_w^n)]$ dispose v $[v \neq \mathbf{null} \wedge \mathbf{emp}]$
Allocation (modifies v)	$[v = \_x]$ v := new $[\exists \_w^1 \ldots \_w^n. \; v \mapsto (f^1 : \_w^1, \ldots, f^n : \_w^n)]$
Lookup (modifies v)	$[v = \_x \wedge u \mapsto (f : \_w; \ldots)]$ v := u.f $[v = \_w \wedge u \mapsto (f : \_w; \ldots)]$
	$[v = \_x \wedge v \mapsto (f : \_w; \ldots)]$ v := v.f $[v = \_w \wedge \_x \mapsto (f : \_w; \ldots)]$
Copy (modifies v)	$[v = \_x]$ v := e $[v = e\langle v \to \_x\rangle]$
Guard	$[v = e]$ assert(v = e) $[v = e]$
	$[v \neq e]$ assert(v! = e) $[v \neq e]$

Hoare triples. The specification $[\varphi]$ S $[\widehat{\varphi}]$ means that when S is run in a state satisfying φ it terminates without any memory error (such as null dereference) in a state satisfying $\widehat{\varphi}$. Thus, we use *total correctness specifications*. Additionally, we call the specification $[\varphi]$ S $[\widehat{\varphi}]$ *strong* if $\widehat{\varphi}$ is the strongest postcondition of φ with respect to S. We use the logical variable v to refer to the value of program variable v in the pre and postcondition of a statement S. The specification may refer to auxiliary logical variables, called Aux, that do not correspond to the value of any program variable. For the present discussion, we prefix all auxiliary variable names with '$\_$'. A Hoare triple with auxiliary variables is said to be valid iff it is valid for any value binding for the auxiliary variables occurring in both the pre and postcondition. The local Hoare triples for reasoning about primitive program statements are given in Table 1. These are similar to the small axioms of [15].

We use the following short-hand notations for the remainder of the paper. Formulae $\mathbf{true} \wedge S$ and $P \wedge \mathbf{emp}$ in pre or post conditions are represented simply as S and P respectively. The notation $\theta : \langle v \to x \rangle$ refers to a renaming θ that replaces variable v with x, and $e\theta$ refers to the expression obtained by applying renaming θ to e. For sets A and B of variables, we write $\theta : \langle A \hookrightarrow B \rangle$ to denote renaming of a subset of variables in A by variables in B. We use $free(\varphi)$ to refer to the set of free variables in φ. Similarly, $mod(\mathsf{S})$ denotes the set of logical variables corresponding to program variables modified by S. We denote sets of variables by upper-case letters like $V, W, X, Y, Z, \ldots$. For every such set V, V_i denotes the set of i subscripted versions of variables in V. We use φ^s and φ^p to refer to the pure and spatial parts, respectively, of φ. The notation $\exists X.\varphi * \exists Y.\psi$ is used to denote $\exists X, Y. \; \varphi^p \wedge \psi^p \wedge \varphi^s * \psi^s$, when φ and ψ are quantifier free and do not have free Y and X variables, respectively.

2.2 Composing Hoare Triples

Given two summaries $[\varphi_1]$ S1 $[\widehat{\varphi}_1]$ and $[\varphi_2]$ S2 $[\widehat{\varphi}_2]$, we wish to compute a summary for the composite statement S1; S2. If we can compute formulas φ_{pre} and φ_{post} that are independent of $mod(\mathsf{S1})$ and $mod(\mathsf{S2})$, respectively, such that $\widehat{\varphi}_1 * \varphi_{pre} \Leftrightarrow \varphi_{post} * \varphi_2$, then by application of Frame rule we can infer the summary $[\varphi_1 * \varphi_{pre}]$ S1; S2 $[\varphi_{post} * \widehat{\varphi}_2]$. We can compose the two given summaries even under the slightly modified condition $\widehat{\varphi}_1 * \varphi_{pre} \Leftrightarrow \exists Z. \; (\varphi_{post} * \varphi_2)$, if $Z \subseteq$ Aux. The summary inferred in this case is $[\varphi_1 * \varphi_{pre}]$ S1; S2 $[\exists Z. \; (\varphi_{post} * \widehat{\varphi}_2)]$.

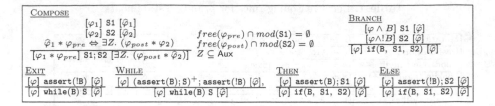

Fig. 3. Inference rules for sequential composition, loops, and branch statements

Given $\widehat{\varphi}_1$ and φ_2, we refer to the determination of φ_{pre}, φ_{post} and a set Z of variables such that $\widehat{\varphi}_1 * \varphi_{pre} \Leftrightarrow \exists Z. (\varphi_{post} * \varphi_2)$ as *strong bi-abduction*. The concept of strong bi-abduction is similar to that of bi-abduction presented in [8] (in the context of using a Hoare triple computed for a procedure at a particular callsite to the procedure). Key differences are that bi-abduction requires the condition $\widehat{\varphi}_2 * \varphi_{pre} \Rightarrow \varphi_{post} * \varphi_2$, whereas we seek equivalence instead of implication while allowing some auxiliary variables to be existentially quantified in the right hand side of the equivalence. While the above composition rule is sound even if we use bi-abduction, bi-abduction may not yield good post-conditions. Specifically, 'total' and 'strong' properties of specifications are preserved under composition using strong bi-abduction. The 'strong' property is not preserved under composition using bi-abduction, although composition is sound. A drawback of using strong bi-abduction, though, is that there exist Hoare triples which cannot be composed using strong bi-abduction but can be composed using bi-abduction. However, even with this drawback our tool could generate complete functional specification for most of the benchmark programs using strong bi-abduction in a bottom-up analysis.

Example 1. In this and subsequent examples, we use $v \mapsto w$ as a short-hand for $v \mapsto (next : w)$. Let us compose two summaries, $[v = \_a]$ v := new $[\exists\_b.\ v \mapsto \_b]$ and $[v = \_c \wedge \_c \mapsto \_d]$ v := v.next $[v = \_d \wedge \_c \mapsto \_d]$. Note that all variables other than v are distinct in the two summaries, as they represent implicitly existentially quantified auxiliary variables in each of the two summaries. Since $(\exists\_b.\ v \mapsto \_b) *$ **emp** $\Leftrightarrow \exists\_c\_d.$ **emp** $* (v = \_c \wedge \_c \mapsto \_d)$ we can compose the two summaries and deduce $[v = \_a]$ v := new; v := v.next $[\exists\_c\_d.\ v = \_d \wedge \_c \mapsto \_d]$.

We now present a set of Hoare inference rules in Separation Logic for our programming language. The rules are formally presented in Figure 3. The COM-POSE rule captures the above idea of using strong bi-abduction for the sequential composition of statements. The rules WHILE, THEN and ELSE use the COMPOSE rule to derive the fact in their antecedent.

The rules EXIT and WHILE are straightforward rules that decompose analysis of loops into two cases. Rule EXIT handles the case where the loop executes zero times, while rule WHILE applies when the loop executes one or more times. Rule WHILE leaves the bulk of the work to the computation of triples of the form $[\varphi]$ S$^+$ $[\widehat{\varphi}]$. The triple $[\varphi]$ S$^+$ $[\widehat{\varphi}]$ means that for every initial state satisfying φ, there exists a $k \geq 1$ such that the state resulting after k executions of S satisfies $\widehat{\varphi}$. In next two sections we present a technique for computing triples of this form.

3   Logic of Iterated Separation Formulae: LISF

Let S be the loop: while (v!=null) v := v.next. Let us use $\odot_{i=0}^{k} \psi^i$ informally to represent the iterated separating conjunction $\psi^0 * \cdots * \psi^k$ [17]. We would like to infer the following summary for S: $[v = \_x_0 \wedge \_x_k = \text{null} \wedge \odot_{i=0}^{k-1} \_x_i \mapsto \_x_{i+1}]$ S $[v = \_x_k \wedge \_x_k = \text{null} \wedge \odot_{i=0}^{k-1} \_x_i \mapsto \_x_{i+1}]$. In this section, we present a formal extension of Separation Logic that lets us express such triples involving iterated separating conjunction, in a restricted form. We first motivate this restricted form of iteration by informally explaining how we plan to infer summaries such as the one above.

Assume that we have a Hoare triple $[\varphi]$ S $[\widehat{\varphi}]$ where φ and $\widehat{\varphi}$ are quantifier free formulas. We can compute a Hoare triple for k executions of S by repeated applications of the COMPOSE rule as follows. Let φ^i (resp. $\widehat{\varphi}^i$) denote φ (resp. $\widehat{\varphi}$) with every variable $x \in \text{Aux}$ replaced by an indexed variable x_i. Consider the following valid Hoare triples with variables renamed, $[\varphi^i]$ S $[\widehat{\varphi}^i]$ and $[\varphi^{i+1}]$ S $[\widehat{\varphi}^{i+1}]$. Let φ_{pre}^i and φ_{post}^i be such that, $free(\varphi_{pre}^i) \cap mod(\text{S}) = free(\varphi_{post}^i) \cap mod(\text{S}) = \emptyset$, and $\widehat{\varphi}^i * \varphi_{pre}^i \Leftrightarrow \varphi_{post}^i * \varphi^{i+1}$. Note that unlike φ^i or $\widehat{\varphi}^i$, φ_{pre}^i and φ_{post}^i may have free variables with index i as well as $i+1$. We can now inductively apply the compose rule and conclude the following Hoare triple.

$$[\varphi^0 * (\odot_{i=0}^{k-1} \varphi_{pre}^i)]\text{S}^{k+1}[(\odot_{i=0}^{k-1} \varphi_{post}^i) * \widehat{\varphi}^k] \tag{3.1}$$

Example 2. Let S be the statement: $\text{assert}(v! = \text{null}); v := v.\text{next}$. Let us compose the two summaries $[v = \_x_0 \wedge \_x_0 \mapsto \_y_0]$ S $[v = \_y_0 \wedge \_x_0 \mapsto \_y_0]$ and $[v = \_x_1 \wedge \_x_1 \mapsto \_y_1]$ S $[v = \_y_1 \wedge \_x_1 \mapsto \_y_1]$, which are identical, except for renaming of auxiliary variables. Let $\varphi_{pre} \equiv \_x_1 = \_y_0 \wedge \_x_1 \mapsto \_y_1$ and $\varphi_{post} \equiv \_x_1 = \_y_0 \wedge \_x_0 \mapsto \_y_0$. Application of the COMPOSE rule results in the following summary. $[(v = \_x_0 \wedge \_x_0 \mapsto \_y_0) * (\_x_1 = \_y_0 \wedge \_x_1 \mapsto \_y_1)]$ S; S $[(\_x_1 = \_y_0 \wedge \_x_0 \mapsto \_y_0) * (v = \_y_1 \wedge \_x_1 \mapsto \_y_1)]$. Iterative application of compose gives the summary: $[v = \_x_0 \wedge \_x_0 \mapsto \_y_0 * \odot_{i=0}^{k-1}(\_x_{i+1} = \_y_i \wedge \_x_{i+1} \mapsto \_y_{i+1})]$ S^+ $[\odot_{i=0}^{k-1}(\_x_{i+1} = \_y_i \wedge \_x_i \mapsto \_y_i) * (v = \_y_k \wedge \_x_k \mapsto \_y_k)]$.

$ae ::= arr \mid ae[\cdot] \mid ae[\cdot + 1] \mid ae[c] \mid ae[\$c]$

$e ::= \ldots \mid ae[\cdot] \mid ae[\cdot + 1] \mid ae[c] \mid ae[\$c]$

$P ::= \ldots \mid \text{RP}(P, l, u)$

$S ::= \ldots \mid \text{RS}(S, l, u)$

$SH ::= P \wedge S \mid \exists v. \, SH \mid \exists arr. \, SH$

Fig. 4. LISF assertion syntax

LISF *Syntax and Informal Semantics:* We now formally introduce a restricted form of the iterated separating conjunct illustrated above. Fig. 4 presents the syntax of LISF, where "…" represents standard constructs of Separation Logic from Figure 2. We first illustrate the syntax with an example relating the informal notation introduced earlier to the formal syntax. The informal notation $v = \_x_0 \wedge \_x_k = \text{null} \wedge \odot_{i=0}^{k-1} \_x_i \mapsto \_x_{i+1}$ is represented in LISF as $v = \text{A}[0] \wedge \text{A}[\$0] = \text{null} \wedge \text{RS}(\text{A}[\cdot] \mapsto \text{A}[\cdot + 1], 0, 0)$. This represents an acyclic singly linked list pointed to by v.

$$m \models e_1 \sim e_2 \qquad \text{iff } \mathcal{E}(e_1, L, s, \mathcal{V}) \sim \mathcal{E}(e_2, L, s, \mathcal{V})$$

$$m \models \mathsf{RP}(P, l, u) \qquad \text{iff } \exists k.\ k + 1 = len(\mathcal{V}, L, P) \wedge \forall l \leq i \leq k - 1 - u.\ (s, h, \mathcal{V}, i :: L) \models P$$

$$m \models e_1 \mapsto (f : e_2) \text{ iff } h(\mathcal{E}(e_1, L, s, \mathcal{V})) = (f : \mathcal{E}(e_2, L, s, \mathcal{V})) \wedge dom(h) = \{\mathcal{E}(e_1, L, s, \mathcal{V})\}$$

$$m \models \mathsf{RS}(S, l, u) \qquad \text{iff } \exists k, u', h_l, \ldots, h_{u'}.\ k + 1 = len(\mathcal{V}, L, S) \wedge u' = k - 1 - u \wedge h = \bigsqcup_{i=l}^{u'} h_i \wedge$$
$$\forall l \leq i, j \leq u'.\ i \neq j \Rightarrow h_i \# h_j \wedge \forall l \leq i \leq u'.\ (s, h_i, \mathcal{V}, i :: L) \models S$$

Fig. 5. Subset of semantics of LISF. m is $(s, h, \mathcal{V}, L)$, len is as explained in text.

A LISF formula may reference a new type of logical variable such as $\mathbf{A}$, which we call an *array variable*. We will denote array variable names with bold-faced upper case letters, as a convention. As we will see later, the semantics of LISF will utilize a mapping from such array variables to a *sequence* of values $(v_0, \cdots, v_k)$. LISF also utilizes multi-dimensional arrays to handle nested recursive data-structures. In such cases, the values v_i may themselves be sequences.

Expressions are extended in LISF to permit indexed variable references, which consist of an array variable name followed by a sequence of one or more indices. An index can take one of the following four forms: (i) $arr[c]$, (ii) $arr[\$c]$, (iii) $arr[\cdot]$, or (iv) $arr[\cdot + 1]$. *Fixed indices* $arr[c]$ and $arr[\$c]$ refer to the element at an offset c from the beginning or end of the sequence that arr denotes, respectively. E.g., if $\mathbf{A}$ is bound to $(v_0, \cdots, v_k)$, then $\mathbf{A}[0]$ and $\mathbf{A}[\$0]$ evaluate to v_0 and v_k respectively. *Iterated indices* $arr[\cdot]$ and $arr[\cdot + 1]$ will be explained soon.

We extend the pure and spatial formulas with predicates $\mathsf{RP}(P, l, u)$ and $\mathsf{RS}(S, l, u)$, respectively, to capture repeated structures. Loosely speaking, $\mathsf{RS}(S, l, u)$ corresponds to our informal notation $\odot_{i=l}^{k-1-u} S$, except that there is no explicit representation of the index variable i or the bound k. The values of i and k are actually provided by the evaluation context in the semantics. The dot in the *iterated indices* $arr[\cdot]$ and $arr[\cdot + 1]$ is used to refer to the implicit index variable i. Thus, $arr[\cdot]$ refers to the element at offset i, and $arr[\cdot + 1]$ refers to the element at offset $i + 1$. Expressions with iterated indices are used within RP or RS predicates. For example, consider the predicate $\mathsf{RS}(\mathbf{A}[\cdot] \mapsto \mathbf{A}[\cdot + 1], 0, 0)$, where $\mathbf{A}$ is bound to a sequence of length $k + 1$. This predicate asserts that for all $i \in [0, k - 1]$, the ith element of $\mathbf{A}$ is the location of a cell in the heap whose next field has the same value as the $i + 1^{th}$ element of $\mathbf{A}$. Further, the predicate also asserts that the elements $\mathbf{A}[0]$ to $\mathbf{A}[k - 1]$ are distinct. For notational convenience we denote the formulas $\mathsf{RP}(P, l, u)$ and $\mathsf{RS}(S, l, u)$ by $\mathsf{RP}(P)$ and $\mathsf{RS}(S)$, respectively, when both l and u are 0.

LISF *Semantics* Expression evaluation semantics is extended in a straightforward fashion to evaluate indexed variable references. Expressions involving array variable with multiple indices require the value of that array and a list of indices, one for every iterated index, for their evaluation. The semantics of an expression e, which evaluates to a location, is given by the function $\mathcal{E}(e, L, s, \mathcal{V})$ where L is the index list (provided by the evaluation context), s is the stack, and $\mathcal{V}$ is the mapping of array names to their values (uni or multi-dimensional sequences of locations). Definition of $\mathcal{E}$ and detailed semantics are provided in the extended version [11].

The structures modeling LISF formulas are $(s, h, \mathcal{V})$ where s is the stack, h is the heap, and $\mathcal{V}$ is the mapping of array names to their values. The semantics of assertions is given by the satisfaction relation ($\models$) between a structure extended with a list of indices L, and an assertion φ. The list of indices L facilitates evaluation of expressions by the function $\mathcal{E}$. The structure $(s, h, \mathcal{V})$ models φ iff $(s, h, \mathcal{V}, []) \models \varphi$. Semantics of constructs novel to LISF are given in Figure 5. We assume that φ is a well formed formula (wff) and $(s, h, \mathcal{V})$ is a well formed structure for φ (wfs_φ). Intuitively, wff and wfs_φ avoid indexing error in the evaluation of φ. We write $h_1 \# h_2$ to indicate that h_1 and h_2 have disjoint domains, and $h_1 \sqcup h_2$ to indicate the disjoint union of such heaps.

Consider a RP(P, l, u) (or RS(S, l, u)) predicate nested inside $n - 1$ other RP (or RS) predicates. The length of the array accessed by the nth iterated index of every expression in P (or S) is guaranteed to be identical by the requirement of well formed structures of a formula. Given a list L of $n - 1$ index values corresponding to the evaluation context arising from the outer RP (or RS) predicates, function $len(\mathcal{V}, L, P)$ (or $len(\mathcal{V}, L, S)$) determines the length, say $k + 1$, of the array accessed by the nth iterated index of any expression in P (or S). The semantics of RP(P, l, u) requires that P holds for each array index i ranging from l to $k - 1 - u$. Similarly, the semantics of RS(S, l, u) requires that S holds over a sub-heap h_i of h for each array index i ranging from l to $k - 1 - u$, with the additional constraint that the h_is are pair-wise disjoint.

4   Inductive Composition

INDUCT

Given

1. $[\varphi]$ S $[\exists X.\ \widehat{\varphi}]$
2. $\widehat{\varphi}^0$: $\widehat{\varphi}$ with every $w \in W$ replaced by w_0
3. φ^1 : φ with every $w \in W$ replaced by w_1
4. $free(\varphi_{pre}^0) \cap mod(\text{S}) = \emptyset$
5. $free(\varphi_{post}^0) \cap mod(\text{S}) = \emptyset$
6. $(\exists X.\ \widehat{\varphi}^0) * \varphi_{pre}^0 \Leftrightarrow \varphi_{post}^0 * \varphi^1$
7. α : $\langle x \to \mathbf{X}[0] \rangle$, for each x in W
8. β : $\langle x \to \mathbf{X}[\$0] \rangle$, for each x in W
9. Function Iter as explained in following text

Infer

$[\varphi\alpha * \text{Iter}(\varphi_{pre}^0)]$ S$^+$ $[\exists X.\ \text{Iter}(\varphi_{post}^0) * \widehat{\varphi}\beta]$

Fig. 6. Inference rule for acceleration

The rules introduced in Figure 3 are valid even with LISF extension of Separation Logic. The set of auxiliary variables, Aux, includes the array variables in this extension. For clarity, we adopt the following convention in the remainder of the paper: (i) unless explicitly stated, all formulas in LISF are quantifier free, (ii) Hoare triples are always expressed as $[\varphi]$ S $[\exists X.\ \widehat{\varphi}]$, (iii) $free(\varphi) = V \cup W$ and $free(\widehat{\varphi}) = V \cup W \cup X$, where V denotes the set of logical variables representing values of program variables, and W, X are sets of auxiliary variables, including array variables[1]. Thus W is the set of free auxiliary variables occurring in φ and in $\exists X.\ \widehat{\varphi}$.

Let $[\varphi]$ S $[\exists X.\ \widehat{\varphi}]$ be a Hoare triple. We wish to compute a strong summary for S$^+$. Figure 6 presents the rule INDUCT to compute such a summary. As in the previous Section, we use φ^i (resp. $\widehat{\varphi}^i$) to denote φ (resp. $\widehat{\varphi}$) with every free auxiliary variable $w \in W$ replaced by an indexed variable w_i. Let $\varphi_{pre}^0, \varphi_{post}^0$ be formulas such

---

[1] By restricting preconditions to quantifier free formulas we do not sacrifice expressiveness. Indeed, the Hoare triple $[\exists Y.\ \psi(V, W, Y)]$ S $[\exists X.\ \widehat{\psi}(V, W, X)]$ is valid iff $[\psi(V, W, Y)]$ S $[\exists X.\ \widehat{\psi}(V, W, X)]$ is valid, where W, X, Y are disjoint sets of auxiliary variables (see defn. 124 in [10]).

that $free(\varphi^0_{pre})$ and $free(\varphi^0_{post})$ are disjoint from $mod(\mathbf{S})$ and $(\exists X.\ \widehat{\varphi}^0) * \varphi^0_{pre} \Leftrightarrow \varphi^0_{post} * \varphi^1$. Note that the premises 4, 5, and 6 of INDUCT imply that $free(\varphi^i_{pre})$ and $free(\varphi^i_{post})$ are disjoint from $mod(\mathbf{S})$, and that $(\exists X.\ \widehat{\varphi}^i) * \varphi^i_{pre} \Leftrightarrow \varphi^i_{post} * \varphi^{i+1}$ for any i. Given these conditions, the COMPOSE rule can be iteratively applied to obtain an accelerated summary similar to that in (3.1).

We use α, β, and Iter to express φ^0, $\widehat{\varphi}^k$ and the iterated separating conjunct of accelerated summary (3.1) in LISF. The renaming α replaces every variable $x \in W$ in φ by $\mathbf{x}[0]$. Similarly β replaces every $x \in W$ in $\widehat{\varphi}$ by $\mathbf{x}[\$0]$.

The function Iter in premise 9 takes an LISF formula ψ, computes an intermediate formula ψ_{ren}, and returns $\mathsf{RP}(\psi^p_{ren}) \wedge \mathsf{RS}(\psi^s_{ren})$. The formula ψ_{ren} is computed by applying a function called warp to ψ. warp makes at most two passes over the syntax tree of ψ in a bottom-up manner. In the first pass it renames every indexed auxiliary variable w_0 (resp. w_1) by a fresh array with iterated index $\mathbf{w}[\cdot]$ (resp. $\mathbf{w}[\cdot + 1]$). If ψ^p_{ren} and ψ^s_{ren} do not have any common array variable, it performs a second pass in which every sub-formula $e_1 \mapsto e_2$ in ψ^s_{ren} is replaced by $e_1 \neq \mathbf{null} \wedge e_1 \mapsto e_2$. All resulting sub-formulas of the form $\mathsf{RS}(P \wedge S, l, u)$ are finally replaced by $\mathsf{RP}(P, l, u) \wedge \mathsf{RS}(S, l, u)$. This ensures that

---

INDUCTQ

Given

1. $[\varphi]\ \mathbf{S}\ [\exists X.\ \widehat{\varphi}]$
2. $\widehat{\varphi}^0$: $\widehat{\varphi}$ with every $w \in W$ and $x \in X$ replaced by w_0 and x_1, resp.
3. φ^1 : φ with every $w \in W$ replaced by w_1
4. $free(\varphi^0_{pre}) \cap mod(\mathbf{S}) = \emptyset$
5. $free(\varphi^0_{post}) \cap mod(\mathbf{S}) = \emptyset$
6. $(\exists X.\ \widehat{\varphi}^0) * \varphi^0_{pre} \Leftrightarrow \exists Z_1.\ (\varphi^0_{post} * \varphi^1)$
7. $Z_1 \subseteq W_1 \cup X_1 \subseteq \text{Aux}$ and $|Z_1| = r$
8. $free(\varphi^0_{pre}) \cap Z_0 = \emptyset$
9. $\alpha, \beta,$ Iter, same as described in INDUCT

Infer

$$\frac{[\varphi\alpha * \mathsf{Iter}(\varphi^0_{pre})]}{\mathbf{s}^+}$$
$$[\exists X, \mathbf{Z}^1, \ldots, \mathbf{Z}^r.\ \mathsf{Iter}(\varphi^0_{post}) * \widehat{\varphi}\beta]$$

Fig. 7. Inference rule INDUCTQ

ψ^p_{ren} and ψ^s_{ren} always have at least one common array variable, unless ψ^s is **emp**. The length of these common arrays determines the implicit upper bound in the universal quantifier of RP and RS predicates in $\mathsf{Iter}(\psi)$.

In general, the strong bi-abduction of $\exists X.\ \widehat{\varphi}^0$ and φ^1 in premise 6 may require variables to be existentially quantified on the right hand side. The INDUCT rule needs to be slightly modified in this case. The modified rule INDUCTQ is presented in Figure 7. We use a refined notation in INDUCTQ where φ^i (resp. $\widehat{\varphi}^i$) denotes φ (resp. $\widehat{\varphi}$) with every variable $w \in W$ replaced by an indexed variable w_i and every variable $x \in X$ replaced by x_{i+1}. Let the bi-abduction between $\widehat{\varphi}^0$ and φ^1 be $(\exists X_1.\ \widehat{\varphi}^0) * \varphi^0_{pre} \Leftrightarrow \exists Z_1.\ (\varphi^0_{post} * \varphi^1)$, where $Z_1 \subseteq W_1 \cup X_1$ is the set of auxiliary variables. If the additional side-condition $free(\varphi^0_{pre}) \cap Z_0 = \emptyset$ holds, we can infer the accelerated summary in the conclusion of INDUCTQ.

Let Z_i be the set of variables $\{z^1_i, \ldots, z^r_i\}$. The values of variables in $Z_0 = \{z^1_0, \ldots z^r_0\}, \ldots, Z_k = \{z^1_k, \ldots z^r_k\}$ are represented as elements of r arrays $\mathbf{z}^1 = \{z^1_0, \ldots, z^1_k\}, \ldots, \mathbf{z}^r = \{z^r_0, \ldots, z^r_k\}$ in the postcondition of conclusion of INDUCTQ. These two representations are analogous to representing elements of the same matrix row-wise and column-wise. The variables representing the values of variables in $Z_1 \cup \ldots \cup Z_k$ need to be existentially quantified in the postcondition of the conclusion of INDUCTQ because of the existential quantification of Z_1 in strong bi-abduction. Hence we existentially quantify the array variables $\mathbf{z}^1, \ldots, \mathbf{z}^r$ in the conclusion of INDUCTQ. As a technical subtlety, the variables in Z_0 need not be quantified. This is taken care of by adding extra equalities in $\mathsf{Iter}(\varphi_{post}^0)$ (see [11] for details).

Soundness of INDUCT and INDUCTQ can be proved by appealing to the soundness of the COMPOSE rule, and by using structural induction. Note that if any Hoare triple in the premise of an inference rule in Figure 3, 6, or 7 is partial (i.e., termination is not guaranteed starting from a state satisfying precondition), then the Hoare triple in the conclusion will also be partial.

Lemma 1. *Inference rules* INDUCT *and* INDUCTQ *are sound.*

Example 3. Recall Example 2 where two instances of the summary $[v = \_x \wedge \_x \mapsto \_y]$ s $[v = \_y \wedge \_x \mapsto \_y]$ are composed using $\varphi_{pre}^0 : (\_x_1 = \_y_0 \wedge \_x_1 \mapsto \_y_1)$ and $\varphi_{post}^0 : (\_x_1 = \_y_0 \wedge \_x_0 \mapsto \_y_0)$. For this example, $\mathsf{Iter}(\varphi_{pre}^0)$ generates the LISF formula $\mathsf{RP}(\mathbf{X}[\cdot + 1] = \mathbf{Y}[\cdot]) \wedge \mathsf{RS}(\mathbf{X}[\cdot + 1] \mapsto \mathbf{Y}[\cdot + 1])$, and $\mathsf{Iter}(\varphi_{post}^0)$ generates the formula $\mathsf{RP}(\mathbf{X}[\cdot + 1] = \mathbf{Y}[\cdot]) \wedge \mathsf{RS}(\mathbf{X}[\cdot] \mapsto \mathbf{Y}[\cdot])$. In this representation, the arrays $\mathbf{X}$ and $\mathbf{Y}$ represent the sequences $\_x_0, \ldots, \_x_k$ and $\_y_0, \ldots, \_y_k$, respectively. The renamed formulas $\varphi\alpha$ and $\widehat{\varphi}\beta$ correspond to the formulas $v = \mathbf{X}[0] \wedge \mathbf{X}[0] \mapsto \mathbf{Y}[0]$ and $v = \mathbf{Y}[\$0] \wedge \mathbf{X}[\$0] \mapsto \mathbf{Y}[\$0]$ respectively. The application of INDUCT thus generates the summary: $[v = \mathbf{X}[0] \wedge \mathsf{RP}(\mathbf{X}[\cdot + 1] = \mathbf{Y}[\cdot]) \wedge \mathbf{X}[0] \mapsto \mathbf{Y}[0] * \mathsf{RS}(\mathbf{X}[\cdot + 1] \mapsto \mathbf{Y}[\cdot + 1])]$ s$^+$ $[v = \mathbf{Y}[\$0] \wedge \mathsf{RP}(\mathbf{X}[\cdot + 1] = \mathbf{Y}[\cdot]) \wedge \mathsf{RS}(\mathbf{X}[\cdot] \mapsto \mathbf{Y}[\cdot]) * \mathbf{X}[\$0] \mapsto \mathbf{Y}[\$0]]$.

Discussion. In the above example, the equality $\_x_1 = \_y_0$ in φ_{pre}^0 and φ_{post}^0 identifies *folding points* of the repeated sub-heaps. Hence we can rewrite the pre and postcondition as $v = \_x_0 \wedge \odot_{i=0}^{k-1} \_x_i \mapsto \_x_{i+1}$ and $v = \_x_k \wedge \odot_{i=0}^{k-1} \_x_i \mapsto \_x_{i+1}$, respectively, using the equality $\_y_0 = \_x_1$ to eliminate $\_y_0$ in both the formulas. The corresponding summary in LISF is: $[v = \mathbf{X}[0] \wedge \mathsf{RS}(\mathbf{X}[\cdot] \mapsto \mathbf{X}[\cdot + 1])]$ s$^+$ $[v = \mathbf{X}[\$0] \wedge \mathsf{RS}(\mathbf{X}[\cdot] \mapsto \mathbf{X}[\cdot + 1])]$.

Instead of translating a recurrence into a LISF formula, one could also translate it into a recursive predicate. For example, the recurrence $\odot_{i=0}^{k-1} \_x_i \mapsto \_x_{i+1}$ obtained above can be translated into a recursive predicate $\mathsf{Rec}(\_x_0, \_x_k)$, where $\mathsf{Rec}(\_x_0, \_x_k) \equiv \_x_0 \mapsto \_x_k \vee \exists \_x_1 . \_x_0 \mapsto \_x_1 * \mathsf{Rec}(\_x_1, \_x_k)$. We choose to represent the values of variables in successive instances of a repeated formula by an array rather than hiding them under an existential quantifier of a recursive predicate. This enables us to relate the data-structures before and after the execution of a loop. For example, this enables our analysis to establish the fact that traversing a list using **next** field does not modify contents of the cells or the relative links between them.

The COMPOSE and EXIT rules can be used to obtain summaries of loop free code fragments and trivial summaries of loops, respectively. Given a loop body summary, the INDUCT and INDUCTQ rules generate an accelerated summary for use in the WHILE rule. Any pair of accelerated summaries can also be composed to obtain new accelerated summaries. In general, determining the sequence of application of the rules COMPOSE, INDUCTQ, EXIT and WHILE to obtain useful loop summaries is an important but orthogonal issue and needs to be guided by heuristics. Heuristics used for acceleration in [3] can be adapted to guide the application of these rules for synthesizing useful loop summaries. Given procedure summaries, non-recursive procedure calls can be analyzed by the COMPOSE rule, as in [8]. The INDUCTQ rule can also be used to compute accelerated summaries of tail recursive procedures having at most one self-recursive call.

5   A Strong Bi-abduction Algorithm for LISF

BiAbduct(φ, ψ, mod_1, mod_2)
1: $res \leftarrow \{\}$
2: **for all** $(M, C, L_1, L_2) \in \mathsf{Match}(\varphi^s, \psi^s)$ **do**
3:      $\Delta \leftarrow (\varphi^p \wedge L_1) * (M \wedge C) * (\psi^p \wedge L_2)$
4:      **if** $\mathsf{sat}(\Delta)$ **then**
5:          $\delta_1 \leftarrow \mathsf{RemoveVar}(M \wedge \psi^p \wedge L_2, \varphi, mod_1, V \cup W)$

6:          $\delta_2 \leftarrow \mathsf{RemoveVar}(M \wedge \varphi^p \wedge L_1, \psi, mod_2, V \cup Y)$

7:          $\gamma \leftarrow \mathsf{ComputeRenaming}(\delta_1, mod_1, Y)$
8:          $\kappa_1 \leftarrow \delta_1 \gamma$
9:          $\hat{Z} \leftarrow \mathsf{Range}(\gamma)$
10:         **if** $\mathsf{IsIndep}(\kappa_1, mod_1)$ **and** $\mathsf{IsIndep}(\delta_2, mod_2)$
            then
11:             $\theta \leftarrow \mathsf{ComputeRenaming}(\kappa_1, X \cup Y, X)$
12:             $\tilde{Z} \leftarrow \mathsf{Domain}(\theta)$
13:             **if** $\mathsf{IsIndep}(\kappa_1\theta, X)$ **then**
14:                 $res \leftarrow res \cup (\kappa_1\theta, \delta_2\bar{\theta}, \hat{Z} \cup \tilde{Z})$
15: **return** res

Fig. 8. Algorithm BiAbduct

We now present a sound algorithm for computing $\varphi_{pre}, \varphi_{post}$ and Z in the equivalence $(\exists X.\ \widehat{\varphi}) * \varphi_{pre} \Leftrightarrow \exists Z.\ (\varphi_{post} * \varphi)$ in the premise of the COMPOSE and INDUCTQ rules. Simplifying notation, the problem can be stated as follows: given variable sets mod_1 and mod_2, and two LISF formulas $\exists X.\ \varphi(V, W, X)$ and $\psi(V, Y)$ where V, W, X, Y are disjoint sets of variables, we wish to compute $\varphi_{pre}, \varphi_{post}$, and a set $Z \subseteq X \cup Y$ such that (i) $(\exists X.\ \varphi) * \varphi_{pre} \Leftrightarrow \exists Z.\ (\varphi_{post} * \psi)$, (ii) $free(\varphi_{pre}) \cap mod_1 = \emptyset$, and (iii) $free(\varphi_{post}) \cap mod_2 = \emptyset$.

Our strong bi-abduction algorithm, BiAbduct, is presented in Figure 8. We illustrate the algorithm through the following example: $\varphi \equiv v \mapsto \_x_0$, $\psi \equiv v = \_y_0 \wedge \_y_0 \mapsto \_y_1$, $V = \{v\}, W = \{\}, X = \{\_x_0\}, Y = \{\_y_0, \_y_1\}$ and $mod_1 = mod_2 = \{v\}$.

The key step in bi-abduction is the Match procedure used in line 2. Match takes as input two spatial formulas φ^s and ψ^s and returns a set of four tuples (M, C, L_1, L_2) where M is a pure formula and C, L_1, L_2 are spatial formulas. For each such tuple, M describes a constraint under which the heaps defined by φ^s and ψ^s can be decomposed into an overlapping part defined by C and non-overlapping parts defined by L_1 and L_2 respectively.

We present procedure Match as a set of inference rules in Figure 9. In these inference rules we use a set of spatial facts and a star conjunction of spatial facts interchangeably. The function $\mathsf{unroll_f}\ \mathsf{RS}(S, l, u)$ required by rule MIII *unrolls* RS once from the beginning. This is done by instantiating that iterated index $[\cdot]$ (resp. $[\cdot + 1]$) of every array expression in S corresponding to the nesting depth of S with fixed index $[l]$ (resp. $[l + 1]$). Similarly $\mathsf{unroll_b}\ \mathsf{RS}(S, l, u)$ unrolls RS once from the end. These rules can be easily implemented as a recursive algorithm. Note that in rules MIII and MIV, the size of the formula $L_1 * \mathsf{RS}(\_, \_, \_)$ in the conclusion may be larger than the size of formula k_1 in the premise. This may lead to non-termination of the recursion. In practice we circumvent this problem by limiting the number of applications of these rules.

Lemma 2. *Every* (M, C, L_1, L_2) *computed in line 2 of* BiAbduct *satisfies* (i) $M \wedge \varphi^s \Leftrightarrow (M \wedge C) * L_1$, *and* (ii) $M \wedge \psi^s \Leftrightarrow (M \wedge C) * L_2$.

$$\text{M0} \quad \overline{(\mathbf{true}, \mathbf{emp}, S_1, S_2) \in \mathsf{Match}(S_1, S_2)}$$

$$\text{MI} \quad \frac{k_1 \in S_1, \; k_2 \in S_2, \; S_1' = S_1 \setminus k_1, \; S_2' = S_2 \setminus k_2}{(M, C, L_1, L_2) \in \mathsf{Match}(k_1, k_2)} \\ \frac{(N, C', L_1', L_2') \in \mathsf{Match}(S_1' \cup L_1, S_2' \cup L_2)}{(M \wedge N, C * C', L_1', L_2') \in \mathsf{Match}(S_1, S_2)}$$

$$\text{MII} \quad \frac{k_1 \equiv x \mapsto (f^i : x^i), \; k_2 \equiv y \mapsto (f^i : y^i)}{M \equiv x = y \wedge \bigwedge \{x^i = y^i\}}{(M, x \mapsto (f^i : y^i), \{\}, \{\}) \in \mathsf{Match}(k_1, k_2)}$$

$$\text{MIII} \quad \frac{\begin{array}{c} k_1 : \; \mathsf{RS}(S, l, u), \; k_2 : \; x \mapsto (f : y), \\ S_1 : \; \mathsf{unroll_f} \; \mathsf{RS}(S, l, u) \\ (M, C, L_1, L_2) \in \mathsf{Match}(S_1, k_2) \end{array}}{(M, C, L_1 * \mathsf{RS}(S, l+1, u), L_2) \in \mathsf{Match}(k_1, k_2)}$$

$$\text{MIV} \quad \frac{\begin{array}{c} k_1 : \; \mathsf{RS}(S, l, u), \; k_2 : \; x \mapsto (f : y), \\ S_1 : \; \mathsf{unroll_b} \; \mathsf{RS}(S, l, u) \\ (M, C, L_1, L_2) \in \mathsf{Match}(S_1, k_2) \end{array}}{(M, C, L_1 * \mathsf{RS}(S, l, u+1), L_2) \in \mathsf{Match}(k_1, k_2)}$$

$$\text{MV} \quad \frac{k_1 : \; \mathsf{RS}(S_1, l, u), \; k_2 : \; \mathsf{RS}(S_2, l, u),}{(M, C, \{\}, \{\}) \in \mathsf{Match}(S_1, S_2)}{(\mathsf{RP}(M, l, u), \mathsf{RS}(C, l, u), \{\}, \{\}) \in \mathsf{Match}(k_1, k_2)}$$

Fig. 9. Rules for procedure Match

Given a possible decomposition (M, C, L_1, L_2) of φ^s and ψ^s, line 4 checks whether this decomposition is consistent with φ^p and ψ^p. This is done by checking the satisfiability of $(\varphi^p \wedge L_1) * (M \wedge C) * (\psi^p \wedge L_2)$. If this formula is found to be satisfiable, δ_1 and δ_2 are computed from $M \wedge \psi^p \wedge L_2$ and $M \wedge \varphi^p \wedge L_1$, respectively, using function RemoveVar (lines 5, 6). The function RemoveVar(ϕ_1, ϕ_2, A, B) replaces every free variable $v \in A$ in ϕ_1 by e if ϕ_2 implies $v = e$ and $free(e) \in B \setminus A$. For our running example $\delta_1 \equiv v = {}_{-}y_0 \wedge {}_{-}x_0 = {}_{-}y_1$ and $\delta_2 \equiv {}_{-}x_0 = {}_{-}y_1$ is one such pair.

Lemma 3. *Every* (δ_1, δ_2) *pair computed in lines 5 and 6 of* BiAbduct *satisfies* $\varphi * \delta_1 \Leftrightarrow \delta_2 * \psi$.

Next, we process the formula δ_1 so as to make it independent of mod_1. In line 7, we compute a renaming $\gamma : \langle mod_1 \hookrightarrow Y \rangle$ such that if κ_1 represents $\delta_1 \gamma$ and $\hat{Z}$ equals the range of γ, then $\varphi * \kappa_1 \Leftrightarrow \exists \hat{Z}. (\delta_2 * \psi)$. This is done by invoking function ComputeRenaming. The function ComputeRenaming(ϕ, A, B) renames a variable $a \in A$ by $b \in B$ if ϕ^p implies the equality $a = b$. If $\delta_1 \gamma$ is not independent of mod_1 or δ_2 is not independent of mod_2, we discard the pair (δ_1, δ_2) (line 10). Note the asymmetry in dealing with δ_1 and δ_2, which stems from the asymmetric structure ($\exists Z$ only on right side) of the required solution $(\exists X. \varphi) * \varphi_{pre} \Leftrightarrow \exists Z. (\varphi_{post} * \psi)$. For our running example, $\hat{Z} = \{{}_{-}y_0\}$ and $\gamma : \langle {}_{-}y_0 \to v \rangle$ gives a valid renaming, since $\delta_1 \gamma \equiv {}_{-}x_0 = {}_{-}y_1$ is independent of v.

Lemma 4. *Every* κ_1 *and* $\hat{Z}$ *computed in lines 8 and 9 of* BiAbduct *satisfy* $\varphi * \kappa_1 \Leftrightarrow \exists \hat{Z}. (\delta_2 * \psi)$.

For every κ_1 at line 11 we compute a renaming $\theta : \langle \tilde{Z} \hookrightarrow X \rangle$, where $\tilde{Z} \subseteq X \cup Y$, so as to render $\kappa_1 \theta$ independent of X (lines 11, 12, 13). The function ComputeRenaming$(\kappa_1, X \cup Y, X)$ computes the renaming θ. Let $\bar{\theta} : \langle X \hookrightarrow \tilde{Z} \rangle$ be a renaming such that $\bar{\theta}(x) = z$ only if $\theta(z) = x$. If $\kappa_1 \theta$ is independent of X, then algorithm BiAbduct returns $(\kappa_1 \theta, \delta_2 \bar{\theta}, \tilde{Z} \cup \hat{Z})$ as one of the solutions of strong bi-abduction.

The invocations of ComputeRenaming in lines 7 and 11 have one important difference: in line 7 only non-array variables in mod_1 are renamed, whereas in line 11 array variables in $X \cup Y$ may be renamed. The function ComputeRenaming(ϕ, A, B) renames array variables as follows. An array variable

Table 2. Experimental results on (a) list manipulating example, (b) functions from Firewire Windows Device Drivers, and (c) examples from [2,14]. Experiments performed on Pentium 4 CPU, 2.66GHz, 1 GB RAM. All programs are available at [11].

Progs	LOC	Time (s)	# triples discovered	Complete?
init	16	0.010	2	Yes
del-all	21	0.009	2	Yes
del-circ	23	0.013	2	Yes
delete	42	0.090	* 19	No
append	23	0.013	3	Yes
ap-disp	52	0.047	6	Yes
copy	33	0.532	3	Yes
find	28	0.023	4	Yes
insert	53	1.270	6	Yes
merge	60	0.880	12	No
reverse	20	0.015	* 3	No

(a)

Progs	LOC	Time (s)	# triples discovered	Complete?
BusReset	145	0.080	* 3	Yes
CancelIrp	87	1.060	* 32	Yes
SetAddress	96	0.185	* 6	Yes
GetAddress	94	0.185	* 6	Yes
PnpRemove	460	75.321	34	No

(b)

Progs	LOC	Time (s)	# triples discovered	Complete?
dll-reverse	23	0.130	3	No
fumble	20	0.017	2	Yes
zip	37	0.650	4	No
nested	20	0.130	10	Yes

(c)

$a \in A$ is renamed to another array variable $b \in B$ if ϕ^p implies one of the following facts: (i) $\mathsf{RP}(a[\cdot] = b[\cdot]) \wedge a[\$0] = b[\$0]$, or (ii) $\mathsf{RP}(a[\cdot + 1] = b[\cdot + 1]) \wedge a[0] = b[0]$, or (iii) $\mathsf{RP}(a[\cdot] = b[\cdot] \wedge a[\cdot + 1] = b[\cdot + 1])$. Higher dimensional arrays can be renamed by performing similar checks for each dimension. For our running example, we have $X = \{\_x_0\}, \widetilde{Z} = \{\_y_1\}$ and $\theta : \langle \_y_1 \rightarrow \_x_0 \rangle$. It is evident that $(\exists \_x_0.\ v \mapsto \_x_0) * (\mathbf{true}) \Leftrightarrow \exists \_y_0, \_y_1.\ (\mathbf{true}) * (v = \_y_0 \wedge \_y_0 \mapsto \_y_1)$. Thus $\varphi_{pre} \equiv \kappa_1 \theta \equiv \mathbf{true}$, $\varphi_{post} \equiv \cdot \delta_2 \bar{\theta} \equiv \mathbf{true}$, and and $Z = \{\_y_0, \_y_1\}$ is a solution of strong bi-abduction between $\exists \_x_0.\ \varphi \equiv \exists \_x_0.\ v \mapsto \_x_0$ and $\psi \equiv v = \_y_0 \wedge \_y_0 \mapsto \_y_1$.

Lemma 5. *Every θ and $\widetilde{Z}$ at line 14 of* BiAbduct *satisfy* $(\exists X.\ \varphi) * \kappa_1 \theta \Leftrightarrow \exists \widehat{Z}, \widetilde{Z}.\ (\delta_2 \bar{\theta} * \psi).$

Satisfiability checking. We provide a sound algorithm for checking satisfiability of LISF formulas. The basic idea is to convert a LISF formula to a formula in separation logic without iterated predicates. This is achieved by instantiating the lengths of all dimensions of all arrays to fixed constants, and by soundly unrolling the RP and RS predicates. The array lengths are so chosen that the offsets specified in the fixed indices of all expressions in the formula are within the respective array bounds. See [11] for details.

6   Experimental Evaluation

We have implemented our inference rules to generate specifications of programs in a bottom-up and compositional manner. Our implementation takes as input a C program and outputs summaries for each procedure in the program. We currently do not handle pointer arithmetic.

The results of running our tool on a set of challenging programs are tabulated in Table 2. Programs in Table 2(a) are adopted from [9]. Program delete is the same as the motivating example in Section 1. All programs in Table 2 (c) except nested are adopted from [2,14]. These programs manipulate singly or doubly linked lists. Program nested traverses nested linked lists. In each of these tables, the fourth column indicates the number of summaries inferred by our tool. The last column indicates whether the inferred summaries provide a complete specification for the corresponding program. Our tool inferred richer summaries than those inferred by the tool in [9]. For example, for the programs delete and reverse, our tool infers preconditions with cyclic lists (indicated by * in fourth column). For the program delete some of the inferred preconditions even have a lasso structure.

The examples in Table 2(b) are program fragments modifying linked structures in the Firewire Windows Device Driver. We report only the summaries discovered for the main procedures in these programs. A complete set of summaries is discovered for all the other procedures in these programs. The original programs and data structures have been modified slightly so as to remove pointer arithmetic. These programs perform selective deletion or search through doubly linked lists. The program PnpRemove iterates over five different cyclic lists and deletes all of them; it has significant branching structure. All programs except CancelIrp refer to only the next field of list nodes. The program CancelIrp also refers the prev field of list nodes. The increased number of inferred summaries for CancelIrp is due to the exploration of different combinations of prev and next fields in the the pre and postconditions. The summaries inferred for all programs except for PnpRemove have been manually checked and found to be complete. These summaries capture the transformations on an unbounded number of heap cells, although they constrain only the next fields of list nodes. Hence these summaries can be plugged in contexts where richer structural invariants involving both next and prev fields are desired.

7   Conclusion

We have presented inference rules for bottom-up and compositional shape analysis. Strong bi-abduction forms the basis of our inference rules. We have introduced a new logic, LISF, along with sound procedures for strong bi-abduction and satisfiability checking in LISF.

In future we would like to (i) enrich the Match procedure by additional lemmas so that our tool can generate more expressive summaries, (ii) extend strong bi-abduction procedure to operate over disjunctions of LISF formulas, and (iii) extend our technique to analyze programs manipulating tree-like structures.

Acknowledgment. We thank Hongseok Yang and Dino Distefano for introducing us to the idea of abduction and for providing us with benchmark programs. The first author was supported by Microsoft Corporation and Microsoft Research India under the Microsoft Research India PhD Fellowship Award.

References

1. Abdulla, P.A., Jonsson, B., Nilsson, M., Saksena, M.: A survey of regular model checking. In: Gardner, P., Yoshida, N. (eds.) CONCUR 2004. LNCS, vol. 3170, pp. 35–48. Springer, Heidelberg (2004)
2. Abdulla, P.A., Bouajjani, A., Cederberg, J., Haziza, F., Rezine, A.: Monotonic abstraction for programs with dynamic memory heaps. In: Gupta, A., Malik, S. (eds.) CAV 2008. LNCS, vol. 5123, pp. 341–354. Springer, Heidelberg (2008)
3. Bardin, S., Finkel, A., Leroux, J., Schnoebelen, P.: Flat acceleration in symbolic model checking. In: Peled, D.A., Tsay, Y.-K. (eds.) ATVA 2005. LNCS, vol. 3707, pp. 474–488. Springer, Heidelberg (2005)
4. Boigelot, B., Legay, A., Wolper, P.: Iterating transducers in the large. In: Hunt Jr., W.A., Somenzi, F. (eds.) CAV 2003. LNCS, vol. 2725, pp. 223–235. Springer, Heidelberg (2003)
5. Bouajjani, A., Habermehl, P., Moro, P., Vojnar, T.: Verifying programs with dynamic 1-selector-linked structures in reg ular model checking. In: Halbwachs, N., Zuck, L.D. (eds.) TACAS 2005. LNCS, vol. 3440, pp. 13–29. Springer, Heidelberg (2005)
6. Bouajjani, A., Habermehl, P., Rogalewicz, A.: Abstract regular tree model checking of complex dynamic data structures. In: Yi, K. (ed.) SAS 2006. LNCS, vol. 4134, pp. 52–70. Springer, Heidelberg (2006)
7. Bouajjani, A., Habermehl, P., Tomas, V.: Abstract regular model checking. In: Alur, R., Peled, D.A. (eds.) CAV 2004. LNCS, vol. 3114, pp. 372–386. Springer, Heidelberg (2004)
8. Calcagno, C., Distefano, D., O'Hearn, P., Yang, H.: Compositional shape analysis by means of bi-abduction. In: Proc. of POPL (2009)
9. Calcagno, C., Distefano, D., O'Hearn, P.W., Yang, H.: Footprint analysis: A shape analysis that discovers preconditions. In: Riis Nielson, H., Filé, G. (eds.) SAS 2007. LNCS, vol. 4634, pp. 402–418. Springer, Heidelberg (2007)
10. Cousot, P.: Methods and logics for proving programs. In: van Leeuwen, J. (ed.) Formal Models and Semantics. Handbook of Theoretical Computer Science, vol. B, Ch. 15., pp. 843–993. Elsevier Science Publishers B.V., Amsterdam (1990)
11. Gulavani, B.S., Chakraborty, S., Ramalingam, G., Nori, A.V.: Bottom-up shape analysis. Technical Report TR-09-27, CFDVS, IIT Bombay (2009), www.cfdvs.iitb.ac.in/~bhargav/shape-analysis.html
12. Guo, B., Vachharajani, N., August, D.I.: Shape analysis with inductive recursion synthesis. In: Proc. of PLDI, pp. 256–265 (2007)
13. Lev-Ami, T., Sagiv, M., Reps, T., Gulwani, S.: Backward analysis for inferring quantified preconditions. Technical Report TR-2007-12-01, Tel Aviv University (2007)
14. Møller, A., Schwartzbach, M.I.: The pointer assertion logic engine. In: Proc. of PLDI (June 2001); also in SIGPLAN Notices 36(5) (May 2001)
15. O'Hearn, P.W., Reynolds, J.C., Yang, H.: Local reasoning about programs that alter data structures. In: Fribourg, L. (ed.) CSL 2001 and EACSL 2001. LNCS, vol. 2142, pp. 1–19. Springer, Heidelberg (2001)
16. Podelski, A., Rybalchenko, A., Wies, T.: Heap assumptions on demand. In: Gupta, A., Malik, S. (eds.) CAV 2008. LNCS, vol. 5123, pp. 314–327. Springer, Heidelberg (2008)
17. Reynolds, J.C.: Separation logic: A logic for shared mutable data structures. In: Proc. of LICS, pp. 55–74 (2002)
18. Touili, T.: Regular model checking using widening techniques. In: Proc. of VEPAS 2001 (2001)

The Complexity of Andersen's Analysis in Practice

Manu Sridharan and Stephen J. Fink

IBM T.J. Watson Research Center
{msridhar,sjfink}@us.ibm.com

Abstract. While the tightest proven worst-case complexity for Andersen's points-to analysis is nearly cubic, the analysis seems to scale better on real-world codes. We examine algorithmic factors that help account for this gap. In particular, we show that a simple algorithm can compute Andersen's analysis in worst-case quadratic time as long as the input program is k-sparse, i.e., it has at most k statements dereferencing each variable and a sparse flow graph. We then argue that for strongly-typed languages like Java, typical structure makes programs likely to be k-sparse, and we give empirical measurements across a suite of Java programs that confirm this hypothesis. We also discuss how various standard implementation techniques yield further constant-factor speedups.

1 Introduction

The scalability of Andersen's points-to analysis [1] has received much attention, as scalable points-to analysis lies on the critical path for many static analyses. Andersen's analysis implementations [6, 9, 13, 16, 20, 22, 27, 29] have scaled to increasingly large programs through clever algorithms and careful engineering. Despite this progress, the best known worst-case complexity bound for Andersen's analysis remains (nearly) cubic.[1]

If Andersen's analysis required time cubic in program size for *typical* inputs, implementations would not scale as well as the literature reports. On the contrary, experiences from real implementations suggest that the worst-case bound rarely governs performance in practice. For example, Heintze and McAllester suggested that a standard algorithm for 0-CFA [23], similar to Andersen's analysis, "rarely exhibit[s] cubic behavior" [10]. Similarly, Goldsmith et al. [8] observed no worse than quadratic scaling for an implementation of Andersen's analysis for C [14].

In this paper, we show that (1) Andersen's analysis can be computed in worst-case quadratic time for a restricted class of inputs and that (2) realistic Java programs usually belong to this class.

Andersen's analysis can be formulated as a *dynamic transitive closure* problem over a *flow graph* representing the flow of pointers in the program, where the

---

[1] One can reduce Andersen's analysis to CFL-reachability [21, 25], for which Chaudhuri's algorithm is slightly sub-cubic [5].

J. Palsberg and Z. Su (Eds.): SAS 2009, LNCS 5673, pp. 205–221, 2009.

flow graph grows dynamically to capture value flow through pointer dereferences (details in §3). We show that when the input program is *k-sparse*, Andersen's analysis can be computed in quadratic time. A *k*-sparse program must have (1) at most *k* statements dereferencing each variable and (2) a sparse flow graph *at analysis termination*, i.e., including all dynamically inserted edges. The key insight behind the bound is that *difference propagation* [7, 20] limits both the closure work and edge insertion work to quadratic time for *k*-sparse programs (details in §4).

For strongly-typed languages like Java, program structure typically constrains programs to be *k*-sparse and hence analyzable in quadratic time. In particular, types associated with heap allocated data in Java limit flow analysis to a small number of named instance fields per object. Furthermore, modularity of typical Java programs—in particular, the common use of "getter" and "setter" methods to encapsulate field accesses—limits the number of statements accessing any particular field. We show that programs with no arrays or dynamic dispatch that use fields in this manner must be *k*-sparse, and we argue that dispatch and arrays usually do not materially compromise *k*-sparseness in practice. Furthermore, we present empirical evidence of *k*-sparseness across a suite of large Java programs.

Perhaps surprisingly, our quadratic complexity bound does not rely on many engineering details that have been shown to have a significant impact on the real-world performance of Andersen's analysis. We include a discussion of many of these issues (set implementation, worklist ordering, cycle elimination, etc.), describing potential constant-factor speedups, space consumption, and the relative importance of the techniques for strongly-typed languages like Java vs. weakly-typed languages like C.

Contributions. This paper makes the following contributions:

- We show that a simple algorithm for Andersen's analysis runs in worst-case quadratic time for *k*-sparse programs.
- We show that Java's type system and typical program structure suggest that realistic programs will be *k*-sparse.
- We present measurements across a suite of large Java programs that show they are *k*-sparse, with the number of flow graph edges being at most 4.5X the number of nodes. We also show that the implementation we tested [28] scales roughly quadratically.

2   Andersen's Analysis for Java

Here, we briefly review Andersen's points-to analysis [1] for Java, as treated in detail in previous work [16, 22, 25, 29]. A points-to analysis computes an overapproximation of the heap locations that program variables may point to, where a finite heap abstraction represents configurations of the runtime heap. The analysis result is typically represented as a *points-to set* $pt(x)$ for each variable x. Andersen's points-to analysis has the following properties:

Table 1. Canonical statements for Java points-to analysis and the corresponding points-to set constraints

Statement	Constraint
i: x = new T()	$\{o_i\} \subseteq pt(x)$ [New]
x = y	$pt(y) \subseteq pt(x)$ [Assign]
x = y.f	$\dfrac{o_i \in pt(y)}{pt(o_i.f) \subseteq pt(x)}$ [Load]
x.f = y	$\dfrac{o_i \in pt(x)}{pt(y) \subseteq pt(o_i.f)}$ [Store]

- *Abstract location per allocation*: The heap abstraction represents all objects potentially allocated by a statement with a single abstract location.
- *Flow insensitive*: The analysis assumes statements in a procedure can execute in any order and any number of times.
- *Subset based*: The analysis models directionality of assignments; *i.e.*, a statement x = y implies $pt(y) \subseteq pt(x)$. In contrast, an equality-based analysis (*e.g.*, [26]) would require $pt(y) = pt(x)$ for the same statement, a coarser approximation.

As is typical for Java points-to analyses, we also desire *field sensitivity*, which requires separate reasoning about each abstract location instance field. Finally, we restrict our attention to *context-insensitive* analysis, which computes a single result for each procedure, merging the behaviors from all call sites.

Table 1 presents the canonical statements for Java points-to analysis and the corresponding points-to set constraints, as seen previously (*e.g.*, in [16]). More complex statements (*e.g.*, x.f = y.g.h) are handled through suitable introduction of temporary variables. We assume that all accesses to global variables (static fields in Java) occur via a copy assignment to a local, implying that load and store statements do not directly dereference globals; this model matches Java putstatic and getstatic bytecodes. Since we focus on context-insensitive analysis, we elide method calls and assume copy statements for parameter passing and return values via some precomputed call graph. (§5.2 discusses on-the-fly call graph construction.) Arrays are modeled with a single field representing the contents of all array indices. For simplicity, we ignore the effects of reflection and native code in this exposition.

3   Algorithm

Here we present an algorithm for Andersen's analysis for Java, as specified in §2. The algorithm is most similar to Pearce et al.'s algorithm for C [20] and also resembles existing algorithms for Java (*e.g.*, [16]).

The algorithm constructs a flow graph G representing the pointer flow for a program and computes its (partial) transitive closure, a standard points-to analysis technique (*e.g.*, see [6, 10, 13]). G has nodes for variables, abstract locations, and fields of abstract locations. At algorithm termination, G has an edge $n \to n'$ iff one of the following two conditions holds:

1. n is an abstract location o_i representing a statement x = new T(), and n' is x.
2. $pt(n) \subseteq pt(n')$ according to some rule in Table 1.

Given a graph G satisfying these conditions, it is clear that $o_i \in pt(x)$ iff x is reachable from o_i in G. Hence, the transitive closure of G—where only abstract location nodes are considered sources—yields the desired points-to analysis result.

Since flow relationships for abstract location fields depend on the points-to sets of base pointers for field accesses (see [Load] and [Store] rules referencing $pt(o_i.f)$ in Table 1), certain edges in G can only be inserted after some reachability has been determined, yielding a *dynamic transitive closure* (DTC) problem. Note that Andersen's analysis differs from a general DTC problem in two key ways. First, unlike general DTC, edge deletions from G need not be handled. Second, as observed in [10], adding new edges to G is part of the points-to analysis work— edge insertion work is typically not considered in discussions of DTC algorithms. The second point is important, as we must consider edge insertion work when reasoning about analysis complexity.

Pseudocode for the analysis algorithm appears in Figure 1. The DoAnalysis routine takes a set of program statements of the forms shown in Table 1 as input. (We assume suitable data structures that, given a variable x, yield all load statements y = x.f and store statements x.f = y in constant time per statement.) The algorithm maintains a flow graph G as just described and computes a points-to set $pt(x)$ for each variable x, representing the transitive closure in G from abstract locations. Note that abstract location nodes are eschewed, and instead the relevant points-to sets are initialized appropriately (line 2).

The algorithm employs *difference propagation* [7, 16, 20] to reduce the work of propagating reachability facts. For each node n in G, $pt_\Delta(n)$ holds those abstract locations o_i such that (1) the algorithm has discovered that n is reachable from o_i and (2) this reachability information has not yet propagated to n's successors in G. $pt(n)$ holds those abstract locations for which (1) holds and propagation to successors of n is complete. The DiffProp routine updates a difference set $pt_\Delta(n)$ with those values from *srcSet* not already contained in $pt(n)$. After a node n has been removed from the worklist and processed, all current reachability information has been propagated to n's successors, so $pt_\Delta(n)$ is added to $pt(n)$ and emptied (lines 21 and 22).

Theorem 1. DoAnalysis *terminates and computes the points-to analysis result specified in Table 1.*

Proof. (*Sketch*) DoAnalysis terminates since (1) the constructed graph is finite and (2) a node n is only added to the worklist when $pt_\Delta(n)$ changes (line 2 of

DoAnalysis()

```
1   for each statement i: x = new T() do
2           pt_Δ(x) ← pt_Δ(x) ∪ {o_i}, o_i fresh
3           add x to worklist
4   for each statement x = y do
5           add edge y → x to G
6   while worklist ≠ ∅ do
7           remove n from worklist
8           for each edge n → n' ∈ G do
9                   DiffProp(pt_Δ(n), n')
10          if n represents a local x
11          then for each statement x.f = y do
12                   for each o_i ∈ pt_Δ(n) do
13                       if y → o_i.f ∉ G
14                       then add edge y → o_i.f to G
15                           DiffProp(pt(y), o_i.f)
16               for each statement y = x.f do
17                   for each o_i ∈ pt_Δ(n) do
18                       if o_i.f → y ∉ G
19                       then add edge o_i.f → y to G
20                           DiffProp(pt(o_i.f), y)
21          pt(n) ← pt(n) ∪ pt_Δ(n)
22          pt_Δ(n) ← ∅
```

DiffProp(srcSet, n)

```
1   pt_Δ(n) ← pt_Δ(n) ∪ (srcSet − pt(n))
2   if pt_Δ(n) changed then add n to worklist
```

Fig. 1. Pseudocode for the points-to analysis algorithm

DiffProp), which can only occur a finite number of times. For the most part, the correspondence of the computed result to the rules of Table 1 is straightforward. One subtlety is the handling of the addition of new graph edges due to field accesses. When an edge $y \rightarrow o_i.f$ is added to G to handle a putfield statement (line 14), only $pt(y)$ is propagated across the edge, not $pt_\Delta(y)$ (line 15). This operation is correct because if $pt_\Delta(y) \neq \emptyset$, then y must be on the worklist, and hence $pt_\Delta(y)$ will be propagated across the edge when y is removed from the worklist. A similar argument holds for the propagation of $pt(o_i.f)$ at line 20.   □

4   Complexity for k-Sparse Programs

Here, we show that the algorithm of Figure 1 has quadratic worst-case time complexity for k-sparse input programs (§4.1). We then argue that, due to strong types and typical program structure, realistic Java programs are likely to be k-sparse (§4.2).

4.1   Quadratic Bound

Let N be the number of variables in an input program plus the number of **new** statements in the program (*i.e.*, the number of abstract locations in the heap abstraction).[2] Also, let $D(x)$ be the number of statements dereferencing variable x, and let E be the number of edges in G at analysis termination. We show that DoAnalysis from Figure 1 runs in worst-case $O(N^2 \max_x D(x) + NE)$ time.

Definition 1. *A program is k-sparse if (1) $\max_x D(x) \leq k$ and (2) $E \leq kN$.*

For k-sparse programs with k being constant, DoAnalysis runs in worst-case $O(N^2)$ time.

Note that our definition of k-sparsity depends on both the input program *and* the analysis computing its flow graph. In particular, variants of Andersen's analysis with different levels of context sensitivity may compute different flow graphs for the same input program, yielding different values of k. When discussing k-sparsity in this paper, we assume flow graphs are constructed with the context-insensitive analysis described in §2.[3]

We begin with a key lemma characterizing the effect of difference propagation.

Lemma 1. *For each abstract location o_i and node p in G, there is at most one execution of the loop at lines 6-22 of DoAnalysis for which $n = p \wedge o_i \in pt_\Delta(p)$.*

Proof. If there exists a loop execution where $n = p \wedge o_i \in pt_\Delta(p)$, line 21 of DoAnalysis adds o_i to $pt(p)$ and line 22 removes o_i from $pt_\Delta(p)$. Subsequently, $pt_\Delta(p)$ may only be modified by line 1 of DiffProp, which ensures that elements of $pt(p)$ cannot be re-added to $pt_\Delta(p)$.   □

DoAnalysis does four kinds of work:

1. *Initialization*: Lines 1 through 5, which handle **new** statements and add the initial edges to G.
2. *Edge Adding*: Lines 13, 14, 18, and 19, which add new edges to or from abstract location field nodes in G as needed.
3. *Propagation*: All calls to the DiffProp routine.
4. *Flushing Difference Sets*: Lines 21 and 22.

The cost of the algorithm is the sum of the costs of these four types of work, which we analyze in turn. In this sub-section, we assume a points-to set data structure which allows for (1) constant time membership checks, (2) constant time addition of a single element, and (3) iteration in constant time per set element, *e.g.*, an array of bits (for (1) and (2)) combined with a linked list (for (3)). (Note that this is not a space-efficient data structure; we discuss space / time

---

[2] Note that N must be no greater than the number of statements in a program, since each statement can introduce at most one variable.

[3] Alternately, k-sparsity could be defined in terms of the possible value flow in the input program with a dynamic semantics that matches the pointer analysis model; we include the flow graph in the definition for clarity.

tradeoffs in §5.1 and §5.4.) We also assume a worklist data structure that prevents duplicate worklist entries and allows for constant-time removal of a node.

Initialization. The loop from lines 1 to 3 clearly takes $O(N)$ time. The loop on lines 4 and 5 takes time proportional to the number of copy assignments in the program, which could be $O(N^2)$ in the worst case. Hence, we have an $O(N^2)$ bound for initialization.[4]

Edge Adding. We assume a suitable graph data structure so that lines 13, 14, 18, and 19 each execute in constant time. For each statement dereferencing a given variable x, the algorithm performs at most $|pt(x)|$ edge adding work, since by Lemma 1 the loops headed at lines 12 and 17 can execute at most $|pt(x)|$ times per such statement. Since $|pt(x)|$ is $O(N)$ and we have $O(N)$ variables, the edge adding work is bounded by $O(N^2 \max_x D(x))$.

Propagation. To reason about propagation work, we first prove the following lemmas.

Lemma 2. *For each graph node p, at any time during execution of* DOANALYSIS *except between lines 21 and 22, $pt_\Delta(p) \cap pt(p) = \emptyset$.*

Proof. The condition clearly holds before the first iteration of the loop starting at line 6. Afterward, for any node p, $pt_\Delta(p)$ can only be changed by line 22 or by a call to DIFFPROP. The condition clearly holds after line 22 since $pt_\Delta(n)$ is emptied. DIFFPROP also preserves the condition, since it only adds abstract locations to $pt_\Delta(n)$ that are not contained in $pt(n)$. □

Lemma 3. *For each abstract location o_i and each edge $e = n \rightarrow n'$ in G, o_i is propagated across e at most once during execution of* DOANALYSIS.

Proof. Propagation across edges occurs via the DIFFPROP calls at lines 9, 15, and 20. By Lemma 1, line 9 can propagate o_i across e at most once. By Lemma 2, we know that $pt_\Delta(y) \cap pt(y) = \emptyset$ at line 15 and that elements from $pt(y)$ cannot later be re-added to $pt_\Delta(y)$. Hence, if an abstract location is propagated across $y \rightarrow o_i.f$ at line 15, it cannot again be propagated across the same edge by line 9 in a later loop iteration. Similar reasoning holds for the propagation at line 20. □

By Lemma 3, propagation work is bounded by $O(NE)$, where E is the final number of edges in G.

Flushing Difference Sets. By Lemma 1, each abstract location can be flushed from a difference set at most once per variable, immediately yielding an $O(N^2)$ bound for this work.

---

[4] A tighter bound would be the number of statements, which we expect to be $O(N)$ in practice. This is irrelevant to our proof since initialization costs are dominated by edge adding.

In the worst case, the work of initialization and flushing difference sets will be dominated by edge adding and propagation. So, we have a worst-case bound of $O(N^2 \max_x D(x) + NE)$ for the algorithm, or $O(N^2)$ for k-sparse programs (see Definition 1), as desired.

We note that if the average points-to set size is $O(N)$, the $O(N^2)$ bound for k-sparse programs is tight, as the result itself would be quadratic in the size of the program. In §6, we give evidence that average points-to set size grows with the size of the program (see Figure 3(a)). Sub-quadratic bounds may be possible in practice for clients that do not require all points-to sets [10].

4.2   Realistic Java Programs

Here, we argue that the Java type system and typical program structure imply that realistic Java programs are likely to be k-sparse. In particular, we show that method size limits imply that $\max_x D(x)$ is bounded and that the type system and modular programming imply that G will most likely be sparse.

The structure of Java methods ensures that $\max_x D(x)$ does not grow with program size. For $\max_x D(x)$ to grow with program size, methods would have to become larger in bigger programs.[5] In practice, Java programs tend to have many small methods, and in fact the Java virtual machine enforces a fixed bound on method size.

Java programs must have $E = O(N)$ if they exclusively use "getters" and "setters" to access fields and do not use arrays or dynamic dispatch. Edges in G correspond to either (1) copy assignments or (2) flow through abstract location fields. For (1), the number of intraprocedural copy assignments in a program can only grow linearly (due to limited method size), and without dynamic dispatch, the number of interprocedural copies must grow linearly as well. For (2), we can bound the number of inserted edges for abstract location fields as follows. Let K be the maximum number of accesses of any field, and let F be the maximum number of instance fields in any class. The maximum number of field edges is $O(NFK)$: there are at most NF abstract location field nodes, and each such node can have at most K incident edges. Java enforces a bound on class size, which yields a constant limit for F. Furthermore, if all fields are only accessed via "getter" and "setter" methods, then $K = 2$ for all fields.[6] Hence, the number of edge insertions for abstract location fields must be $O(N)$ for this class of programs.

In practice, the number of statements accessing any given field tends to be small due to encapsulation. However, the synthetic field arr used to model array contents is an exception: the number of array access statements (i.e., accesses of arr) increases with the size of the program, potentially leading to a quadratic number of flow graph edges. If the base pointers of array accesses have points-to sets of bounded size, then only a linear number of inserted edges will be required

---

[5] This assumes that static fields cannot be directly dereferenced, which holds for Java bytecode.

[6] Note that this bound relies on the context-*insensitive* analysis of the these methods, i.e., it is independent of the number of calls to the methods.

for these accesses, maintaining flow graph sparseness. While array base pointers usually have small points-to sets (again due to encapsulation), exceptions can occur due to context-insensitive analysis of frequently used library methods; we discuss this issue further in §6.

Hypothetically, dynamic dispatch could also cause a quadratic number of flow graph edges, in the case where there were $O(N)$ call sites of a method, each of which could dispatch to $O(N)$ possible targets. In practice, this phenomenon could only occur for methods defined in the root `java.lang.Object` class like `toString()`, and its likelihood is mitigated by on-the-fly call graph construction (see §5.2); we have not observed such a blowup in practice.

5   Other Factors

The literature presents myriad other implementation techniques that, at the least, yield significant constant-factor time improvements. Furthermore, when performing points-to analysis on large programs, space concerns often dominate, necessitating space-saving techniques that complicate analysis of running time. In this section, we briefly discuss several other factors relevant to Andersen's analysis performance and relate them to our complexity result.

5.1   Bit-Vector Parallelism and Worklist Ordering

The use of bit-wise operations for propagation can yield significant constant-factor speedups in practice. The complexity proof of §4 assumes that abstract locations are propagated across edges one at a time. With an appropriate set representation, bit-wise operators can effectively propagate up to k abstract locations across an edge in constant time, where k is the machine word size (*e.g.*, 64). When using such operations, our proof of a quadratic bound no longer applies, since propagation across an edge becomes proportional to the total number of abstract locations instead of the size of the source set. Nevertheless, using bit-wise operations usually improves performance in practice, since the cost model on real machines usually depends more on cache locality than the number of register-level arithmetic instructions.

The speedup due to bit-wise operations depends on an effective worklist ordering [19]. For a node n, the analysis would ideally complete all propagation to n before removing n from the worklist, since this maximizes the benefits of using bit-wise operations when propagating to n's successors. If the analysis only required computing standard transitive closure over a DAG, the best worklist ordering would be topological, in which case the algorithm would propagate across each edge at most once.

With dynamic transitive closure, even if the final flow graph G is a DAG, it may not be possible to do propagation in topological order due to cyclic data dependences. Consider the following example program:

```
x = new Obj(); // o1
z = new Obj(); // o2
y = x; y.f = z; x = y.f;
```

Note that $y = x$ and $x = y.f$ are cyclically data dependent on each other. Initially, G only contains the edge $e = x \rightarrow y$. After o_1 is propagated across e, the analysis can add incident edges for $o_1.f$, yielding the graph $z \rightarrow o_1.f \rightarrow x \rightarrow y$. After these edge insertions, the analysis must repeat propagation across e to add o_2 to $pt(y)$. Hence, repeated work across edges may be required even when G is a DAG. It would be interesting to characterize how much cyclic data dependences affect performance in practice.

In real programs, cycles in the flow graph G further complicate matters. On-line cycle elimination can lessen the impact of flow graph cycles, as we shall discuss further in §5.5. In WALA [28], the analysis implementation used for our measurements, worklist order is determined by a pseudo-topological ordering of the flow graph, periodically updated as edges are added. Further discussion of worklist ordering heuristics appears in [19].

5.2   Function Calls

Direct handling of higher-order functions, *i.e.*, on-the-fly call graph construction, does not affect the $O(N^2)$ bound for k-sparse programs. For Java, on-the-fly call graph construction requires (1) reasoning about possible virtual call targets using receiver points-to sets and (2) incorporating constraints for discovered call targets, as described previously [16, 22, 29]. Both of these operations can be performed for all relevant call sites in quadratic time, and the core propagation and edge adding operations of the analysis are unaffected.

Though it does not affect our worst-case bound, on-the-fly call graph building has a significant impact on real-world performance. If constraint generation costs are ignored, on-the-fly call graph reasoning can slow down analysis, as more iterations are required to reach a fixed point [29]. However, if the costs of constraint generation are considered (which we believe is a more realistic model), on-the-fly call graph building improves performance, since constraints need not be generated for unreachable library code. Also, as suggested in §4.2, on-the-fly call graph reasoning can make the flow graph for a program more sparse, improving performance.

Much recent work on Java points-to analysis employs some context-sensitive handling of method calls [17, 18, 29]. Cloning-based context sensitivity causes a blowup in input size; an m-limited call-string or m-object-sensitive analysis may require $O(N^m)$ clones. Our bound implies that Andersen's analysis can run in time quadratic in the size of the program after cloning, assuming the program with clones is still k-sparse. In some cases selective cloning can yield a significantly sparser flow graph, thereby improving both precision and running time (further discussion in §6). BDDs have been employed to make the space explosion from cloning more manageable, as we shall discuss in §5.4.

5.3   Exploiting Types

Type filters [3, 16], which ensure that points-to sets for variables are consistent with their declared types, are critical to good performance for Java points-to analysis. Type filters do not affect our worst-case bound for sparse programs: a quadratic pre-processing step can create an appropriate mask for each type to use during propagation. The filters improve performance by dramatically reducing the size of points-to sets and hence the amount of propagation work [16].

We remark that only applying type filters at propagation for downcasting operations, whether explicit (a JVM `checkcast` bytecode) or implicit (passing the receiver parameter at a virtual call site), yields the same precision benefit as applying them for all propagation operations (as was formulated in some previous work [3, 29]). Reducing the use of type filters without affecting precision can be a significant performance win, since they make propagation more expensive.

5.4   Space

Space usage often presents a bigger bottleneck for points-to analysis than running time, especially for context-sensitive analyses. Here, we discuss some space optimizations performed by points-to analyses and their effects on running time.

Employing difference propagation exhaustively as in Figure 1 may double space requirements and hence represent an unattractive space-time tradeoff. Our complexity proof relies on exhaustive use of difference propagation since it assumes that propagating a single abstract location requires one unit of work. A set implementation that enables propagation of abstract locations in parallel (see §5.1) lessens the need for exhaustive difference propagation in practice. In our experience, the key benefit of difference propagation lies in operations performed for each abstract location in a points-to set, *e.g.*, edge adding (see lines 12 and 17 in Figure 1). To save space, WALA [28] only uses difference propagation for edge adding and for handling virtual call receivers (since with on-the-fly call graph construction, each receiver abstract location may yield a new call target). Also note that the best data structure for the $pt_\Delta(x)$ sets may differ from the $pt(x)$ sets to support smaller sets and iteration efficiently; see [16, 19] for further discussion.

Many points-to analyses use set data structures that exploit redundancy between points-to sets, like shared bit sets [13] or BDDs [3, 29, 30], to dramatically reduce space requirements. Their effects on running time are difficult to analyze, since the propagation cost model is very different: running times for BDD operations are highly dependent on variable orderings, and shared bit set operations depend on the current bit set cache state. Further understanding of the use of these data structures for analyzing k-sparse programs is a topic for future work.

5.5   Other Languages

Our main result of quadratic time complexity for points-to analysis of k-sparse programs can be adapted to other languages fairly easily. We believe the algorithm of Pearce et al. for C points-to analysis with difference propagation [20, Figure 7], very similar to the algorithm of Figure 1, would run in quadratic time for k-sparse C programs. The Figure 1 algorithm could also be adapted to perform control-flow analysis for functional languages [23] (formulated as dynamic transitive closure in [10]). For this case the notion of k-sparseness (see Definition 1) would be slightly transformed: rather than counting the number of dereferences of a variable $D(x)$, one would count the number of function applications of a variable / expression.

It is an open question as to whether typical programs in other languages are k-sparse. Pearce et al. [20] present some evidence that for C, the number of flow graph edges increases much more quickly with program size than for Java. They present a benchmark gawk with less than 20,000 LOC where the number of flow graph edges added during analysis is over 40X the number of variables; in contrast, our measurements in the next section never saw a factor more than 4.5X. This increased edge density in C may be due to the use of the * operator rather than named fields and the weaker type system. It may also explain the greater importance of projection merging [27] and online cycle elimination [6, 9, 13] for C.[7] In our experience, when respecting declared types in Java, relatively few cycles are discovered (also observed in [16]).

6   Measurements

We used the Watson Libraries for Analysis (WALA) [28] for our measurements. The WALA implementation of Andersen's analysis differs from the algorithm of Figure 1 in a few ways. WALA employs on-the-fly call graph construction (§5.2) and type filters (§5.3), both of which reduce the size of the constraint graph without increasing worst-case complexity. WALA also models some Java reflective methods (*e.g.*, Class.newInstance()) and native methods with synthetic code generated during analysis.[8] Program sizes for the presented programs may differ from other published numbers due to variations in library versions and handling of reflection; we analyzed the IBM Java 1.6.0 libraries.

Table 2 lists the programs used in this study. They include all of the DaCapo 2006-10-MR2 benchmarks [4] and Apache Ant 1.7.1 [2], another large Java program. The table reports program sizes as determined by the methods discovered during on-the-fly call graph construction.

Density of Flow Graphs. The second-to-last column of Table 2 reports the density of the final flow graph constructed during pointer analysis. The Table shows that for all programs, the number of edges (E) per node (N) is less than 4.5. The fop program seems to be an outlier; all other programs have less than 2.2 edges per node in the flow graph.

Figure 2(a) displays the edges in flow graphs as a function of the number of nodes. The figure shows the best linear fit, which would have E grow as $3.46N$. Figure 2(b) shows the same data on a log-log scale. The best linear fit on a

---

[7] Note that conceptually, cycle elimination is orthogonal to difference propagation; the former eliminates redundancy across variables with provably equivalent points-to sets, while the latter prevents redundant propagation of abstract locations.

[8] Reflection and native code may still cause the analysis to be unsound.

Table 2. Characteristics of programs analyzed

Benchmark	Methods	Bytecodes (KB)	Flow Graph Nodes (K)	Flow Graph Edges (K)	Edges / Nodes	Runtime (s)
antlr	3381	238	54	101	1.87	20
bloat	6438	456	99	218	2.20	43
chart	19089	1359	310	617	1.99	414
eclipse	17021	1169	275	563	2.05	359
fop	25542	2225	459	2039	4.44	2920
hsqldb	4600	330	79	138	1.75	25
jython	5291	386	85	157	1.85	35
luindex	4114	296	64	113	1.77	15
lusearch	16826	1160	268	530	1.98	312
pmd	18125	1248	286	569	1.99	361
xalan	2691	176	43	79	1.84	9
apache-ant	18404	1449	294	577	1.96	378

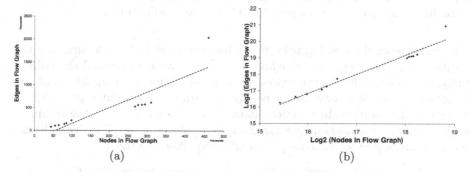

(a)   (b)

Fig. 2. Sparsity measure for flow graphs. Each data point represents one benchmark analyzed. We show a standard scale in (a) and a log scale in (b). The lines show the best fit via linear regression, with a slope of 3.46 in (a) and 1.17 in (b).

log-log scale has slope 1.17, indicating that the best polynomial fit to the data has E growing as $N^{1.17}$. If we exclude fop as an outlier, the best polynomial fit indicates E grows as $N^{1.05}$. We conclude the flow graphs are mostly sparse. As discussed in §4.2, we expect $E = O(N)$, with exceptions arising from arrays and dispatch, and the data support this conclusion.

We examined fop in detail. Most of the edges in the fop flow graph result from the failure of the pointer analysis to adequately disambiguate the contents of object arrays passed to library routines, due to context insensitivity. In a practical pointer analysis client, we would recommend a context-sensitivity policy designed to clone common library routines that manipulate arrays, such as the java.util.Arrays utilities. As suggested in §5.2, though such cloning increases the size of the program, it can make the flow graph significantly sparser (since many infeasible flows are ruled out), improving both performance and precision. Further study of increased sparsity via context sensitivity would be an interesting topic for future work.

Size of pointer analysis result. Figure 3(a) shows the total size of the computed points-to sets, as a function of the node count in the flow graph on a log scale.

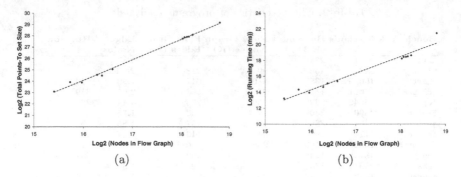

Fig. 3. Total size of computed points-to sets in (a) and pointer analysis running time in (b) on log scales, both as functions of nodes in flow graph. The lines show the best fit via linear regression, with a slope of 1.79 in (a) and 2.10 in (b).

The figure shows the best linear fit, which has a slope of 1.79, indicating that the points-to solution size grows roughly as $N^{1.79}$. As we have defined the pointer analysis problem, this factor represents a lower bound on complexity of the Andersen's analysis in practice, since any algorithm will take at least $O(N^{1.79})$ to output the solution. In practice, many clients do not demand the complete analysis result, instead issuing a targeted set of alias queries. For these clients, demand-driven pointer analysis [12, 24, 25] may offer a better fit.

Observed analysis performance. Figure 3(b) shows the running time of the pointer analysis as a function of the node count in the flow graph on a log scale.[9] The figure shows the best linear fit, which has a slope of 2.10, indicating that running time grows roughly as $N^{2.10}$. If we exclude **fop** from the regression, running time grows as $N^{1.92}$. The running of time of a real implementation depends on many factors, including those discussed in §4.2 and §5. The results here show that on this benchmark suite, our implementation scales roughly quadratically with program size. It remains for future studies to determine whether quadratic scaling holds for other implementations and benchmarks.

7   Related Work

Our work is most closely related to the studies of points-to analysis complexity of Pearce et al. [19, 20]. Our algorithm is very similar to that of [20, Figure 7], but adapted to Java. Pearce was the first to show difference propagation can affect worst-case complexity, in his case improving a worklist-based algorithm from quartic to cubic time [19, §4.1.3]. We further improve the bound to quadratic time for k-sparse programs, which requires additionally reasoning about the cost of edge-adding work. Difference propagation was first presented by Fecht and Seidl in [7].

---

[9] We ran the analysis on a Linux machine with an Intel Xeon 3.8GHz CPU and 5GB RAM, using the Sun 1.5.0_06 virtual machine with a 1.8GB heap.

Lhoták and Hendren present a Java points-to analysis algorithm with difference propagation (there termed an "incremental worklist" algorithm) and showed its performance benefits [16]. Their algorithm does not fully employ difference propagation for abstract location fields, as it periodically does full propagation for field access statements [15, §4.4.3]. Hence, it is not clear if the quadratic bound for k-sparse programs holds for their algorithm.

Heintze and McAllester present a sub-cubic control-flow analysis algorithm for bounded-typed programs [10]. They formulate the analysis problem as dynamic transitive closure and distinguish edge addition work from closure work (in fact, they occur in separate phases in their algorithm). As their algorithm does not allow for recursive types, it is not immediately applicable to Java.

Various other work studies points-to analysis complexity. Heintze and McAllester relate the difficulty of flow analysis to the 2NPDA complexity class [11]. Melski and Reps formulate Andersen's analysis for C as a CFL-reachability problem, immediately yielding a cubic algorithm [21]. Fändrich et al. use a probability-based analytic model over random graphs to study online cycle elimination for set constraints in inductive form [6]. Chaudhuri presents a slightly sub-cubic algorithm for CFL-reachability, thereby breaking the "cubic bottleneck" for Andersen's analysis [5].

8   Conclusions

We have proven a quadratic worst-case time bound for computing Andersen's analysis for k-sparse input programs, and we have given empirical evidence that Java programs are usually k-sparse. These results help account for the gap between the nearly cubic worst-case complexity of Andersen's analysis and its scalability in practice. The notion of k-sparsity may also be useful in understanding the real-world performance of other program analyses.

Acknowledgments. We thank the anonymous reviewers for their helpful comments and Ras Bodík for input on earlier versions of this work.

References

[1] Andersen, L.O.: Program Analysis and Specialization for the C Programming Language. PhD thesis, University of Copenhagen, DIKU (1994)
[2] Apache Ant, http://ant.apache.org
[3] Berndl, M., Lhoták, O., Qian, F., Hendren, L., Umanee, N.: Points-to analysis using BDDs. In: Conference on Programming Language Design and Implementation (PLDI) (June 2003)
[4] Blackburn, S.M., Garner, R., Hoffman, C., Khan, A.M., McKinley, K.S., Bentzur, R., Diwan, A., Feinberg, D., Frampton, D., Guyer, S.Z., Hirzel, M., Hosking, A., Jump, M., Lee, H., Moss, J.E.B., Phansalkar, A., Stefanović, D., VanDrunen, T., von Dincklage, D., Wiedermann, B.: The DaCapo benchmarks: Java benchmarking development and analysis. In: Conference on Object-Oriented Programming, Systems, Languages, and Applications (OOPSLA) (2006)

[5] Chaudhuri, S.: Subcubic algorithms for recursive state machines. In: POPL 2008: Proceedings of the 35th annual ACM SIGPLAN-SIGACT symposium on Principles of programming languages, pp. 159–169. ACM, New York (2008)

[6] Fändrich, M., Foster, J.S., Su, Z., Aiken, A.: Partial online cycle elimination in inclusion constraint graphs. In: Conference on Programming Language Design and Implementation (PLDI), Montreal, Canada (June 1998)

[7] Fecht, C., Seidl, H.: Propagating differences: an efficient new fixpoint algorithm for distributive constraint systems. Nordic J. of Computing 5(4), 304–329 (1998)

[8] Goldsmith, S.F., Aiken, A.S., Wilkerson, D.S.: Measuring empirical computational complexity. In: ESEC-FSE 2007: Proceedings of the the 6th joint meeting of the European software engineering conference and the ACM SIGSOFT symposium on The foundations of software engineering, pp. 395–404. ACM Press, New York (2007)

[9] Hardekopf, B., Lin, C.: The ant and the grasshopper: fast and accurate pointer analysis for millions of lines of code. In: PLDI, pp. 290–299 (2007)

[10] Heintze, N., McAllester, D.: Linear-time subtransitive control flow analysis. SIGPLAN Not. 32(5), 261–272 (1997)

[11] Heintze, N., McAllester, D.: On the cubic bottleneck in subtyping and flow analysis. In: LICS 1997: Proceedings of the 12th Annual IEEE Symposium on Logic in Computer Science, Washington, DC, USA, 1997, p. 342. IEEE Computer Society, Los Alamitos (1997)

[12] Heintze, N., Tardieu, O.: Demand-driven pointer analysis. In: Conference on Programming Language Design and Implementation (PLDI), Snowbird, Utah (June 2001)

[13] Heintze, N., Tardieu, O.: Ultra-fast aliasing analysis using CLA: A million lines of C code in a second. In: Conference on Programming Language Design and Implementation (PLDI), Snowbird, Utah (June 2001)

[14] Kodumal, J., Aiken, A.: Banshee: A scalable constraint-based analysis toolkit. In: Hankin, C., Siveroni, I. (eds.) SAS 2005. LNCS, vol. 3672, pp. 218–234. Springer, Heidelberg (2005)

[15] Lhoták, O.: Spark: A flexible points-to analysis framework for Java. Master's thesis, McGill University (December 2002)

[16] Lhoták, O., Hendren, L.: Scaling Java points-to analysis using Spark. In: Hedin, G. (ed.) CC 2003. LNCS, vol. 2622, pp. 153–169. Springer, Heidelberg (2003)

[17] Lhoták, O., Hendren, L.: Context-sensitive points-to analysis: Is it worth it? In: Mycroft, A., Zeller, A. (eds.) CC 2006. LNCS, vol. 3923, pp. 47–64. Springer, Heidelberg (2006)

[18] Milanova, A., Rountev, A., Ryder, B.G.: Parameterized object sensitivity for points-to analysis for java. ACM Trans. Softw. Eng. Methodol. 14(1), 1–41 (2005)

[19] Pearce, D.J.: Some directed graph algorithms and their application to pointer analysis. PhD thesis, Imperial College of Science, Technology and Medicine, University of London (2005)

[20] Pearce, D.J., Kelly, P.H.J., Hankin, C.: Online cycle detection and difference propagation for pointer analysis. In: Proceedings of the third international IEEE Workshop on Source Code Analysis and Manipulation (2003)

[21] Reps, T.: Program analysis via graph reachability. Information and Software Technology 40(11-12), 701–726 (1998)

[22] Rountev, A., Milanova, A., Ryder, B.G.: Points-to analysis for Java using annotated constraints. In: Conference on Object-Oriented Programming, Systems, Languages, and Applications (OOPSLA), Tampa Bay, Florida (October 2001)

[23] Shivers, O.: Control flow analysis in scheme. In: Conference on Programming Language Design and Implementation (PLDI) (1988)
[24] Sridharan, M., Bodík, R.: Refinement-based context-sensitive points-to analysis for Java. In: Conference on Programming Language Design and Implementation (PLDI) (2006)
[25] Sridharan, M., Gopan, D., Shan, L., Bodík, R.: Demand-driven points-to analysis for Java. In: Conference on Object-Oriented Programming, Systems, Languages, and Applications (OOPSLA) (2005)
[26] Steensgaard, B.: Points-to analysis in almost linear time. In: ACM Symposium on Principles of Programming Languages (POPL) (1996)
[27] Su, Z., Fähndrich, M., Aiken, A.: Projection merging: Reducing redundancies in inclusion constraint graphs. In: ACM Symposium on Principles of Programming Languages (POPL), Boston, Massachusetts, January 2000, pp. 81–95 (2000)
[28] T.J. Watson Libraries for Analysis (WALA), http://wala.sf.net
[29] Whaley, J., Lam, M.S.: Cloning-based context-sensitive pointer alias analysis using binary decision diagrams. In: Conference on Programming Language Design and Implementation (PLDI) (2004)
[30] Zhu, J., Calman, S.: Symbolic pointer analysis revisited. In: Conference on Programming Language Design and Implementation (PLDI) (2004)

Optimizing Pointer Analysis Using Bisimilarity

Luke Simon

Metallect Corp.
660 North Central Expressway, Suite 235
Plano, TX 75074, USA
luke.simon@gmail.com

Abstract. We introduce a new technique for dramatically improving
the performance of inclusion-based points-to analysis, by using bisimilarity in order to detect pointer equivalences before constraint resolution.
We present the design and correctness proof of this technique, along with
an implementation prototype, and a series of benchmarks. The benchmarks indicate that our technique dramatically improves the scalability
of inclusion-based points-to analysis, beating the current leading offline
optimizations for inclusion-based points-to analysis.

1 Introduction

Points-to analysis is a static program analysis that computes a conservative
abstraction of the values of pointers. More precise points-to analyses perform
a whole-program inter-procedural data-flow analysis, which causes scalability
issues when analyzing real world programs. Andersen's points-to analysis [2],
also known as inclusion-based points-to analysis, is a class of the most precise
flow and context-insensitive points-to analyses that have been demonstrated to
scale to programs consisting of millions of lines of code [9].

Inclusion-based points-to analysis can be treated as a constraint resolution
problem. A set of inclusion constraints is extracted from the analyzed program's
code, and a subsequent resolution of the constraints yields the results of the
analysis. A typical approach for a constraint resolution algorithm is to represent
the extracted set of constraints as a graph. The nodes of this constraint graph
correspond to variables and addresses, and the edges represent the inclusion
constraints on the set of abstract values of each variable. A solution to the
constraint graph is then calculated by determining the set of address nodes
that can reach each variable node, with constraints corresponding to pointer
dereferencing causing new edges to be added to the graph based on the address
nodes that can reach the dereferenced variables. In the worst case, this takes
$O(n^3)$ time and $O(n^2)$ space.[1,2] Hence a small reduction in the size of the input
can dramatically improve the performance of the analysis.

---

[1] In this paper, when discussing worst-case complexity, n denotes the number of variables in the given points-to analysis constraint graph.

[2] Note that it is possible for the initial constraint graph to contain $O(n^2)$ edges. For this
reason, discussing worst-case complexity solely in terms of the number of variables
may simplify the discussion, but it does so without hiding nonlinear factors.

J. Palsberg and Z. Su (Eds.): SAS 2009, LNCS 5673, pp. 222–237, 2009.
© Springer-Verlag Berlin Heidelberg 2009

The most prominent technique for reducing the input size of points-to analysis constraint resolution involves detecting and contracting equivalence classes of variables. Online cycle detection is such a technique. Every variable in the same strongly connected component will have the same points-to set. Since new cycles can be introduced as constraint resolution approaches equilibrium, it is worthwhile to perform cycle detection periodically during the progression to equilibrium.

When and where online cycle detection is performed greatly influences the overall performance of inclusion-based points-to analysis. The algorithm of Fahndrich et al. [7] searches for cycles when a new edge is added to the constraint graph, while the algorithm of Heintze et al. [11] searches for cycles during reachability queries. The former approach can unnecessarily prevent certain cycles from being detected, while the latter approach may perform excessive redundant work. A more straightforward approach is used by the algorithm described in Pearce et al. [15], which periodically searches the entire constraint graph for cycles.

In contrast, Hardekopf et al. [9] present an algorithm that uses a heuristic to efficiently determine when and where a periodic search for cycles should be performed. While this heuristic may prevent some cycles from being detected, empirical evidence shows that: (i) the heuristic reduces the overhead of online cycle detection by preventing some unnecessary searches and (ii) the heuristic detects cycles more quickly after their introduction than the simple periodic sweep used by Pearce et al. [15]. Hardekopf et al. further improve upon these two points by introducing a technique called Hybrid Cycle Detection (HCD). HCD is an extremely fast pre-processing pass on the input that creates metadata for performing a restricted form of online cycle detection with minimal overhead.

A completely different approach for reducing the size of the constraint graph was presented by Berndl et al. [3]. They show how reduced, ordered binary decision diagrams (BDDs) can be used to efficiently perform inclusion-based points-to analysis. BDDs effectively reduce the size of the constraint graph by hash-consing binary trie representations of the constraint graph. This results in the partial contraction of the representations of variables that have similar points-to sets.

In addition to contracting equivalence classes online, another practical means of reducing the size of the input is to use a fast pre-processing phase before running the constraint solver. The pre-processing phase is called an "offline optimization" because it reduces the size of the input before performing constraint resolution.

The first prominent offline optimization for inclusion-based points-to analysis was presented by Rountev et al. [17]. Their technique, known as *Offline Variable Substitution* (OVS), uses offline cycle detection and value numbering in order to detect and contract pointer equivalent variables. Variables are pointer equivalent when they have the same points-to set.

Hardekopf et al. [10] introduced HRU+LE, an offline optimization that improves upon OVS by iterating more sophisticated value numbering techniques in order to detect more equivalences. HRU+LE also introduced the notion of location equivalence as a means of optimizing the input passed to a constraint solver. Location equivalence equates variables whose addresses appear in the same points-to sets, which means that location equivalent variables can share the same symbol when stored in a points-to set of a constraint solver.

In this paper, we identify bisimilarity as a practical basis for developing an effective offline optimization for points-to analysis, and we make the following additional contributions:

- In section 4, we present the design and correctness proof of BSM (**BiSiM**ilarity-based pointer equivalence detection), a new offline optimization that improves upon previous offline optimizations by efficiently identifying a coarser partitioning of variables into equivalence classes.
- In section 5, we describe techniques for efficiently implementing BSM, so that it has a better asymptotic complexity than HRU+LE and lower overhead for real world benchmarks.
- In section 6, we present empirical results by benchmarking, on several prominent open-source applications, a BSM prototype along with the leading offline optimizations. The results show BSM outperforming the other leading offline optimizations.

The next two sections cover background material. Section 2 briefly compares and contrasts the contributions of this paper with related work, and section 3 covers the salient concepts necessary to understand the remaining sections, which detail this paper's contributions.

2   Related Work

Offline Variable Substitution (OVS), introduced by Rountev et al. [17], is an offline optimization that attempts to collapse pointer equivalent variables by using a $O(n^2)$ time and space algorithm based on cycle detection and value numbering. OVS is actually linear in the size of initial constraint graph, but since the constraint graph can have $O(n^2)$ edges, OVS's complexity is quadratic in the number of constraint variables in the given constraint graph. Even when taking OVS's overhead into consideration, the empirical results presented in section 6 show that OVS significantly improves the total analysis time and the peak memory usage of points-to analysis.

Before the development of BSM, Hardekopf et al. [10] introduced HRU+LE, which has a higher worst-case complexity than OVS, using $O(n^4)$ time and $O(n^2)$ space, but as demonstrated by Hardekopf et al. [10] and reiterated in section 6 of this paper, HRU+LE improves the total analysis time and peak memory usage, when compared to OVS. The fact that HRU+LE's worst-case time complexity is greater than the worst-case time complexity of constraint resolution seems to be a theoretical disadvantage that does not manifest itself in empirical results. In addition, HRU+LE and BSM use both pointer equivalence and location equivalence, while OVS only uses pointer equivalence.

BSM improves upon both OVS and HRU+LE by detecting more pointer equivalent variables, which allows for a greater reduction in the size of the input fed into the inclusion constraint solver. The empirical evidence presented in section 6 demonstrates how this dramatically improves the scalability of whole-program points-to analysis.

In addition to improving upon OVS and HRU+LE in terms of scalability, BSM also improves upon OVS and HRU+LE in terms of precision. OVS and HRU+LE assume that a dereference expression *d corresponds to a load or store of a variable that is pointed to by the variable d. However, it is possible that d does not point to anything, and so this assumption can reduce the precision of the points-to analysis.

Example 1. For the following fragment of C source code, OVS and HRU+LE detect a cycle containing a and c. This false cycle causes them to place variables a and c in the same pointer equivalence class, even though they are not pointer equivalent.

```
// types and ordering of statements are irrelevant
// for Andersen's points-to analysis of C
a = &c;    a = &d;    b = &c;    b = &d;    c = &b;
x = &a;    y = &a;    x = *x;    y = *y;
c = *d;    *d = a;    a = c;
```

Contracting a small number of *pointer inequivalent* variables in the input can have a cascading effect on the precision of individual points-to sets because the abstract values of these collapsed variables can be propagated throughout the constraint graph.

Since BSM completely ignores store constraints, it does not suffer from this problem, and as theoretically demonstrated in section 4, BSM does not decrease the precision of inclusion-based points-to analysis.

BSM is not the first application of bisimilarity to static program analysis, and the range of applications from compilers [1] to concurrency analysis [5] to computer security [8] to model checking [4] is so vast that we will not attempt to provide an overview of such works. Instead we limit ourselves to works directly related to BSM's implementation.

The first algorithm capable of efficiently computing a coarsest partitioning of a graph into bisimilar equivalence classes was presented by Paige et al. [14]. Their algorithm was presented in terms of the relational coarsest partition problem, which is effectively synonymous to the problem of determining the coarsest partitioning of a graph into bisimilar equivalence classes.

The worst-case complexity of Paige et al.'s algorithm hasn't been improved upon, but progress has been made on improving the performance of bisimulation equivalence detection algorithms that are based upon Paige et al.'s algorithm, when used on real world input. Dovier et al. [6] present several techniques for improving the performance of coarsest partitioning of a graph into bisimilar equivalence classes. The most effective technique is to stratify the graph into a sequence of ranks, so that Paige et al. [14]'s algorithm only needs to be applied to individual subsets of the entire graph. In section 5, we apply a similar technique in order to efficiently stratify the bisimulation graph into a topologically sorted sequence of ranks.

3   Inclusion-Based Points-to Analysis

Inclusion-based points-to analysis involves extracting a collection of inclusion constraints from the analyzed program, and then by iteratively applying inference rules, the constraints are solved. The solution of these constraints induces the results of the points-to analysis, which are the points-to sets of each pointer. Informally, a pointer's points-to set contains the variables that the pointer may point to. The specifics of how constraints are extracted from an analyzed program's code is an implementation detail that is not covered in this paper.

Definition 1. *We write* offset(x, k), *where x is a variable and k is a natural number, to denote the variable at offset k from variable x. It is required that for every variable $x =$ offset$(x, 0)$, and for some constant $c > 0$, offset(x, k) is undefined for every value of $k > c$.*

Variable offsets are used to model fields of structs as well as the formal parameters and returns of functions called indirectly through a function pointer.

Definition 2. *Inclusion constraints are of the following four forms:*

1. A *points-to* constraint $x \supseteq \{y\}$ asserts that the points-to set of variable x contains the variable y.
2. A *copy* constraint $x \supseteq y$ asserts that the points-to set of variable x is a superset of the points-to set of y.
3. A *load* constraint $x \supseteq *(y + k)$ asserts that the points-to set of variable x is a superset of the points-to sets of every variable $z = $ *offset*(w, k), where w is in y's points-to set.
4. A *store* constraint $*(y+k) \supseteq x$ asserts that the points-to set of every variable $z = $ *offset*(w, k) is a superset of the points-to set of x, where w is in y's points-to set.

If the offset $k = 0$, then a load constraint $x \supseteq *(y + k)$ can be abbreviated as $x \supseteq *y$ and a store constraint $*(y + k) \supseteq x$ can be abbreviated as $*y \supseteq x$.

Note 1. It is a common practice to abuse notation by using the same variable when referring to a program variable and its corresponding constraint variable [9, 11, 16].

Example 2. The constraints extracted from the code presented in example 1 are:

$$a \supseteq \{c\} \; a \supseteq \{d\} \; b \supseteq \{c\} \; b \supseteq \{d\} \; c \supseteq \{b\}$$
$$x \supseteq \{a\} \; y \supseteq \{a\} \; x \supseteq *x \; y \supseteq *y$$
$$c \supseteq *d \;\; *d \supseteq a \;\; a \supseteq c$$

Definition 3. *The* solution *to a given set of constraints is the set of points-to constraints of the form* $x \supseteq \{y\}$, *which are either in the given set of constraints or can be inferred from the given set of constraints by repeated application of the following inference rules:*

$$\frac{x \supseteq y \quad y \supseteq \{a\}}{x \supseteq \{a\}}[copy] \qquad \frac{x \supseteq *(y+k) \quad y \supseteq \{a\} \quad z = \text{offset}(a,k)}{x \supseteq z}[load]$$

$$\frac{*(y+k) \supseteq x \quad y \supseteq \{a\} \quad z = \text{offset}(a,k)}{z \supseteq x}[store]$$

Definition 4. *The* points-to set *of a variable* x *is the set of variables* y *such that* $x \supseteq \{y\}$ *is in the solution of the given set of constraints. We write* $P(x)$ *to denote the points-to set of variable* x.

Example 3. The points-to sets of the variables from example 2 are: $P(a) = \{b, c, d\}$, $P(b) = \{c, d\}$, $P(c) = \{b\}$, $P(d) = \{\}$, and $P(x) = P(y) = \{a, b, c, d\}$.

3.1 Offline Optimization

As previously mentioned, solving inclusion constraints takes $O(n^3)$ time and uses $O(n^2)$ space in the worst case, and so decreasing the size of the constraint graph can substantially improve performance. The main technique for accomplishing this is to merge equivalent variables.

Since there are two distinct representations of a variable in a constraint graph, two kinds of variable equivalence are used to merge the corresponding representations of equivalent variables. The two mergeable representations of a variable are: (i) the representation of a variable as a node and (ii) the representation of a variable as an element of points-to sets.

Definition 5. *Two variables are* pointer equivalent *if they have the same points-to set.*

Example 4. According to example 3, the only two pointer equivalent variables are x and y.

Constraint graph nodes corresponding to pointer equivalent variables can be collapsed into a single node. Determining the coarsest partitioning of a constraint graph's variables into pointer equivalence classes can be performed by calculating the solution to the given constraints, but since the objective is to optimize the performance of pointer analysis, such a naive approach provides no benefit. Instead, more efficient partitioning algorithms are used, which are conservative in that they never group inequivalent variables into the same class, yet they may assign equivalent variables to distinct classes.

Definition 6. *Two variables are* location equivalent *if the inclusion of one variable in a points-to set means the other variable is also included in the points-to set.*

Example 5. According to example 3, the only two location equivalent variables are c and d.

Location equivalent variables can be represented as a single symbol in a points-to set that contains the location equivalent variables. This helps decrease the size of the representations used to store intermediate points-to sets. Some care has to be taken when adding new edges to the constraint graph due to load and store constraints. Exploiting location equivalence requires a pointer analysis algorithm to translate each element of a points-to set into a set of constraint graph nodes, when adding edges inferred from load and store constraints.

4   Bisimilarity-Based Pointer Equivalence Detection

Compared to other offline optimizations for inclusion-based points-to analysis, the novel aspect of BSM is its technique for detecting pointer equivalences. This section introduces the theory behind this technique, while section 5 describes its implementation.

4.1   Superset Graphs

Instead of using the kind of constraint graphs used by constraint solvers, BSM uses two alternative kinds of graphs: superset graphs and simulation graphs.

Definition 7. *The* superset graph *is generated from the input constraint set. It represents points-to sets as nodes and containment relationships as edges. For variables x and y, we write $x \to y$ to denote that there is an edge in the superset graph from node x to node y. The superset graph is the smallest graph such that $x \to y$ if and only if $x \supseteq y$.*

Note 2. We further overload our notation such that the same variable is used to refer to a program variable, a corresponding constraint variable, and a corresponding graph node. This helps simplify our notation by making an implicit correspondence between a program variable, constraint variable, and simulation graph node.

Note 3. The variables in a strongly connected component (SCC) of the superset graph are pointer equivalent.

In order to serve as an offline optimization for points-to analysis, BSM must not attempt to solve the constraints because doing so would be too costly. This is why BSM does not interpret load and store constraints by adding new edges to the superset graph. In addition, the points-to sets calculated by BSM are more abstract than those computed by an actual constraint solver. In a constraint solver, points-to sets are modeled as sets of constraint variables, while in BSM they are modeled as unions of abstract points-to subsets.

Definition 8. *Constraint variable x is said to be* addressed, *if there exists variables y and z such that $x = \text{offset}(y, k)$ and $z \supseteq \{y\}$.*

The contents of addressed variables can be changed indirectly, and so their contents are modeled more abstractly by BSM than they are by a constraint solver.

Definition 9. *The abstract points-to subsets of a superset graph have the following forms:*

- x, such that x is addressed. This form of abstract points-to subset denotes the set of locations that can be copied from x.
- $\&x$, which denotes the singleton set containing the location of variable x.
- $*(x + k)$, which denotes the set of locations that can be loaded from offset k of the variables that x points to.

A variable's union of abstract points-to subsets is defined in terms of reachability in the superset graph.

Definition 10. *Let $A(x)$ denote the set of abstract points-to subsets whose union defines the points-to set of variable x. Formally, $A(x)$ is the smallest set such that:*

- $x \in A(x)$ whenever x is addressed.
- $\&y \in A(x)$ whenever $x \supseteq \{y\}$.
- $*(y + k) \in A(x)$ whenever $x \supseteq *(y + k)$.
- $A(x)$ contains every element of $A(y)$ whenever x can reach y in the superset graph.

Location Equivalence. Note that for any two variables x and y, x is location equivalent to y if and only if for every z such that $\&x \in A(z)$, it is also true that $\&y \in A(z)$.

Note 4. When it comes to detecting location equivalence, the difference between BSM and HRU+LE is that HRU+LE treats dereference expressions of the form $*x$ as nodes in the superset graph . Since HRU+LE also treats load and store constraints as edges in the superset graph, more variables may be determined to be location equivalent by HRU+LE. However, HRU+LE may incorrectly determine that two variables are location equivalent for the same reasons that HRU+LE may incorrectly determine that two variables are pointer equivalent (see example 1). So the additional location equivalences discovered by HRU+LE may or may not be valid equivalences, which means that precision may be adversely affected by HRU+LE. However, a thorough investigation of the magnitude of the loss of precision caused by HRU+LE is out of the scope of this paper.

4.2 Simulation Graphs

As previously stated, the novel aspect of BSM is that it uses bisimilarity in order to detect more pointer equivalences than previous offline optimizations for inclusion-based points-to analysis. The bisimilarity equivalence relation used by BSM is defined in terms of the simulation graph corresponding to the given constraints. This is typical for the definition of a bisimilarity relation, but the following definition of BSM's simulation graphs is the most conceptually complicated aspect of BSM.

Definition 11. *For nodes n and m and label l, we write $n \xrightarrow{l} m$ to denote that there is an l-labeled edge in the simulation graph from node n to node m. For each variable x, the simulation graph contains two kinds of nodes. A node x represents the points-to set of the variable x, while a node $N(x)$ represents the subset of x's points-to set that can be inferred without using the load or store inference rules. The simulation graph for a given set of constraints is the smallest graph such that:*

- $x \xrightarrow{sup} N(x)$ for every variable x. This kind of edge is called a *superset edge*, and it denotes the fact that $N(x)$ is a subset of x.
- $N(x) \xrightarrow{\&y} y$ whenever $\&y \in A(x)$. This kind of edge is called an *address edge*, and it denotes that x points to the location of variable y.
- $x \xrightarrow{load(k)} y$ whenever $*(y + k) \in A(x)$. This kind of edge is called a *load edge*, and it denotes the fact that x's points-to set may contain values that are loaded from the dereferencing of y offset by k.
- $x \xrightarrow{ref} N(y)$ whenever $z \in A(x)$ and $\&z \in A(y)$. This kind of edge is called a *reference edge*, and it denotes the fact that x's points-to set may contain values copied from a variable which is indirectly modified via the pointer y.
- $x \xrightarrow{off(k)} y$ whenever $k > 0$, $z \in A(x)$, and $z = offset(y, k)$. This kind of edge is called an *offset edge*, and it denotes the fact that x's points-to set may contain values copied from a variable which is indirectly modified by stores involving pointers to y offset by k.

If the offset $k = 0$, then a load edge $x \xrightarrow{load(k)} y$ can be abbreviated as $x \xrightarrow{load} y$. In addition, note that $N(x) \xrightarrow{\&y} z$ if and only if y and z are the same variable, and also note that $N(x) \xrightarrow{\&y} y$ if and only if $y \xrightarrow{ref} N(x)$.

Example 6. Figure 1 shows the simulation graph corresponding to the constraints in example 2.

4.3 Bisimilarity

Intuitively, the bisimilarity relation used by BSM equates two variables x and y, whenever their corresponding inclusion constraints have a similar structure. This can be seen as a generalization of the value numbering techniques used by OVS and HRU+LE.

Definition 12. *The bisimilarity relation $\sim$ is the largest binary relation between nodes of the simulation graph, such that whenever $x \sim y$, both of the following are true:*

- For every label l, if $x \xrightarrow{l} x'$ then there exists y' such that $y \xrightarrow{l} y'$ and $x' \sim y'$.
- For every label l, if $y \xrightarrow{l} y'$ then there exists x' such that $x \xrightarrow{l} x'$ and $y' \sim x'$.

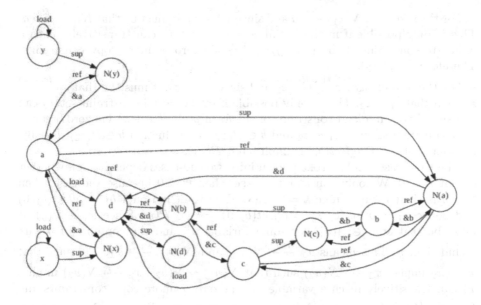

Fig. 1. The simulation graph described in example 6

Example 7. In the simulation graph described in example 6, the only two pairs of bisimilar nodes are $x \sim y$ and $N(x) \sim N(y)$. Therefore, the set of equivalence classes is:

$$\{\{a\},\ \{b\},\ \{c\},\ \{d\},\ \{x, y\},\ \{N(a)\},\ \{N(b)\},\ \{N(c)\},\ \{N(d)\},\ \{N(x), N(y)\}\}$$

Note that this corresponds to the coarsest partitioning of the variables into pointer equivalence classes, and also note that both OVS and HRU+LE are unable to detect the pointer equivalence between variables x and y, while BSM does detect the equivalence. Theorem 1 states the correctness of using bisimilarity as a means of detecting pointer equivalence.

Theorem 1. *If two variables are bisimilar, then they are pointer equivalent.*

Proof. Since the bisimilarity relation is symmetric, it is sufficient to prove that $x_1 \sim x_2$ and $a \in P(x_1)$ implies $a \in P(x_2)$. So in the following, assume $x_1 \sim x_2$ and $a \in P(x_1)$. The proof proceeds by induction on the size of the derivation of the inferred points-to constraints.

According to the inference rules specified in definition 3, there are three ways in which $a \in P(x_1)$: (i) in the initial constraint set x_1 can transitively reach a points-to constraint of the form $y_1 \supseteq \{a\}$ via zero or more copy constraints, (ii) in the initial constraint set x_1 can transitively reach a load constraint of the form $y_1 \supseteq *(z_1 + k)$ via zero or more copy constraints and there is a variable $b \in P(z_1)$ such that $a \in P(offset(b, k))$, or (iii) there is a constraint of the form $*(y + k) \supseteq z$ in the initial constraint set and x_1 can transitively reach a variable w_1 via zero or more copy constraints such that $a \in P(z)$, $b_1 \in P(y)$, and $w_1 = offset(b_1, k)$.

For the first case, $N(x_1) \xrightarrow{\&a} a$ and since $x_1 \sim x_2$, it must be that $N(x_2) \xrightarrow{\&a} a$. This is only possible if in the initial constraint set x_2 can transitively reach a points-to constraint of the form $y_2 \supseteq \{a\}$ via zero or more copy constraints. Therefore $a \in P(x_2)$.

For the second case, $x_1 \xrightarrow{load(k)} z_1$ and since $x_1 \sim x_2$, it must be that $x_2 \xrightarrow{load(k)} z_2$ such that $z_1 \sim z_2$. This is only possible if in the initial constraint set x_2 can transitively reach a load constraint of the form $y_2 \supseteq *(z_2 + k)$ via zero or more copy constraints. Since $z_1 \sim z_2$ and $b \in P(z_1)$, by induction $b \in P(z_2)$. Finally, the fact that $a \in P(offset(b, k))$ implies $a \in P(x_2)$.

The third case can be broken down into two sub-cases depending on whether or not $k > 0$. We only consider the case when $k = 0$ because the case when $k > 0$ is similar. So assume $k = 0$. According to definition 1 $b_1 = offset(b_1, 0)$ and hence $w_1 = offset(b_1, k) = offset(b_1, 0) = b_1 \in P(y)$. Since $w_1 \in P(y)$, it must be that $\&w_1 \in A(u_1)$ for some variable u_1, and the contents of u_1 are included in y. This means $x_1 \xrightarrow{ref} N(u_1)$ and $N(u_1) \xrightarrow{\&w_1} w_1$. The fact that $x_1 \sim x_2$ implies $x_2 \xrightarrow{ref} N(u_2)$ such that $N(u_1) \sim N(u_2)$. $x_2 \xrightarrow{ref} N(u_2)$ implies x_2 can transitively reach a variable w_2 via zero or more copy constraints and $\&w_2 \in A(u_2)$. This means $N(u_2) \xrightarrow{\&w_2} w_2$, and since $N(u_1) \sim N(u_2)$ we can conclude that $N(u_1) \xrightarrow{\&w_2} w_2$, which implies $w_2 \in P(u_1) \subseteq P(y)$. Therefore the store constraint $*(y + k) \supseteq z$ also includes a in the points-to set of w_2, and hence $a \in P(x_2)$.

In addition to discussing the partitioning of variables into location equivalence classes, the next section describes how to efficiently calculate the coarsest partitioning of variables into bisimilar equivalence classes. According to theorem 1, such a partitioning is a valid grouping of variables into pointer equivalence classes.

5   Implementation

The BSM offline optimization uses the bisimilarity relation presented in the previous section to detect and collapse pointer equivalence classes, and like HRU+LE, BSM also uses hashing of reference sets in order to detect and collapse location equivalences. This section outlines the implementation of BSM.

5.1   Preprocess Constraints

The first stage of BSM consists of two preprocessing passes on the input constraints. This is done in order to reduce the size of the input that is passed to the more costly, core part of BSM.

Filter Empty Pointers. BSM first preprocesses the input constraints in order to filter out pointers that can be efficiently determined to be empty. This is accomplished by collapsing the SCCs of the superset graph using the algorithm presented by Nuutila et al. [13], and augmenting the superset graph with additional edges of the form $x \to y$ whenever $x \supseteq \{y\}$ or $x \supseteq *(y + k)$.

Finally, a depth-first search is performed in order to determine the variables that can reach addressed variables (see definition 8) in the residual augmented superset graph. The variables that cannot reach addressed variables are removed from the constraint set, as their points-to set is empty.

Simplify Constraints. Like HRU+LE, BSM uses hash-based value numbering (HVN), introduced in by Hardekopf et al. [10], in order to reduce the size of the input that is fed into the more costly core part of the offline optimization.

5.2 Build Simulation Graph

After BSM has simplified the input constraints using the preprocessing passes described in section 5.1, a new superset graph is constructed from the preprocessed constraint set. The SCCs of this new superset graph are collapsed, and then the $A(x)$ sets are calculated by propagating the elements of the sets in reverse topological order. These sets are needed for assigning variables to location equivalence classes and for constructing the simulation graph.

Calculating these sets has a worst-case complexity of $O(n^3)$ time and $O(n^2)$ space. Since this is the most costly part of BSM, this establishes BSM's worst-case complexity: $O(n^3)$ time and $O(n^2)$ space, where n is the number of constraint variables.

Assign Location Equivalence Classes. The set of variables y such that $x \in A(y)$ is used to identify the location equivalence class to which variable x should be assigned. This technique was introduced by Hardekopf et al. [10], but since BSM doesn't make the precision sacrificing assumptions about dereference expressions that HRU+LE makes (see note 4 in section 4.1), BSM discovers slightly fewer location equivalence classes. However, empirical evidence indicates that very few additional location equivalences are detected by HRU+LE, so this difference has little impact on scalability.

Create Simulation Graph Nodes. For performance reasons, BSM explicitly creates a simulation graph that does not contain the $N(x)$ nodes, superset edges, address edges, reference edges, or offset edges. This is accomplished by assigning simulation graph nodes to initial partitions, which are potentially split during a later phase of BSM. A node's initial partition is identified by a tuple of three IDs: (i) an address set ID, (ii) a reference set ID, and (iii) an offset set ID.

Address set IDs are assigned by mapping each address set $\{y \mid y \in A(x)\}$ to a unique number, and then each node of the form x is mapped to the ID for its address set $\{y \mid y \in A(x)\}$. The reference set ID of a node x is determined in a similar manner, but this time by using the set of address set IDs of variables y such that $x \xrightarrow{ref} N(y)$. Finally, the offset set ID of a node x is also determined in a similar manner, using the set of pairs $(k,$ reference set ID of $y)$ such that $x \xrightarrow{load(k)} N(y)$.

Add Simulation Graph Edges. Because nodes are initially partitioned based on the superset, address, reference, and offset edges, the simulation graph created by BSM only contains nodes of the form x (as opposed to nodes of the form $N(x)$), and it only needs to have load edges added to it.

5.3 Partition Nodes

BSM uses a technique similar to the one introduced by Dovier et al. [6], in order to split the initially partitioned simulation graph into a set of subgraphs called ranks, and then BSM uses the relational coarsest partitioning algorithm introduced by Paige et al. [14] in order to partition each rank into bisimilar equivalence classes.

6   Benchmarks

This section presents empirical results obtained from running an implementation of the BSM algorithm introduced in this paper against a points-to analysis benchmark suite introduced by Hardekopf et al. [9, 10]. The benchmark suite contains implementations of the leading inclusion-based points-to analysis algorithms for analyzing C programs (Heintze et al.'s algorithm "HT" [11], Pearce et al.'s algorithm "PKH" [15], and Hardekopf et al.'s algorithm "LCD+HCD" [9]). The benchmark suite also contains implementations of the offline optimizations OVS and HRU+LE, in addition to sample sets of constraints extracted from six prominent open-source C programs.

As mentioned in [10], the benchmark constraint sets were generated using the CIL front-end for the C programming language [12]. Assignments involving types that are too small to hold a pointer are ignored and standard library calls are modeled using manually created stubs. The details of the benchmark constraint sets are listed in the following table:

Application	KLOCs	Constraints	Variables
Emacs-21.4a	169	83,213	43,236
GhostScript-8.15	242	168,312	103,876
Gimp-2.2.8	554	411,783	245,677
Insight-6.5	603	243,404	143,677
Linux-2.4.26	2,172	574,788	414,489
Wine-0.9.21	1,338	713,065	501,214

Originally, the benchmark suite did not implement any means of translating the results of the analysis back in terms of the original input variables, and so we augmented the suite with this functionality. This led to the discovery of a bug in the implementation of HRU+LE, which caused a significant number of variables to be incorrectly removed from the constraints. Since the implementation was the source of this bug, as opposed to the design of the HRU+LE algorithm itself, we used the corrected HRU+LE implementation in our benchmarks.

Our main addition to the benchmark suite is an implementation of BSM, written in C++. The details of the implementation's design and implementation are discussed in the previous sections. Our experiments were run using the Fedora 9 (i686) Linux distribution on a Dell XPS M1710 with 4GB of RAM and a "Core 2 Duo T7200" CPU running at 2Ghz, and the prototypes were compiled with GCC 4.3 using the "-O3" optimization level.

The source code for the BSM prototype and the benchmark suite can be obtained from the authors upon request.

6.1 Empirical Results

We used all possible pairings of each offline optimization with each of the leading inclusion-based points-to analysis algorithms, in order to obtain the empirical results presented in this section.

Figure 2 presents the combined execution time and peak memory usage for points-to analysis for the LCD+HCD constraint solver paired with each offline optimization. For every benchmark except the smallest (Emacs), compared to the other two leading offline optimizations BSM improves the scalability of the analysis. In the Emacs benchmark, BSM is only marginally one-upped in terms of speed by HRU+LE.

BSM significantly outperforms the competition in the two largest benchmarks: Linux and Wine. In the case of Wine, when using BSM, the performance of points-to analysis is improved by approximately a factor of 3× over the previously leading offline optimization: HRU+LE. This improvement is due to the

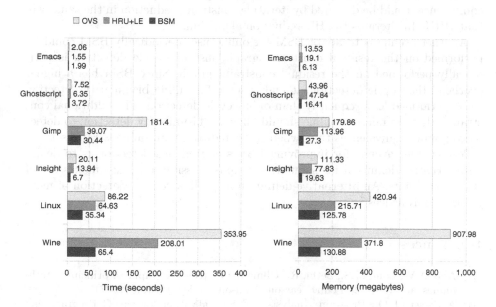

Fig. 2. Total time and peak memory used by points-to analysis for each offline optimization paired with the LCD+HCD algorithm

fact that BSM's bisimilarity relation generalizes HRU+LE's value numbering technique for detecting and collapsing pointer equivalent variables.

With or without offline optimizations, LCD+HCD is currently the fastest, sound, inclusion-based points-to analysis algorithm for analyzing C programs [9]. Due to space limitations, this section only presents the results obtained when using LCD+HCD. The results for the other two algorithms HT and PKH are similar. In fact, BSM outperforms the other leading offline optimizations by an even greater margin in the cases of HT and PKH.

7   Conclusions and Future Work

We have demonstrated that coarsest partitioning of pointers into bisimilar equivalence classes is an efficient technique for offline optimization of inclusion-based points-to analysis, without decreasing the precision of the calculated points-to sets. Our empirical results indicate that BSM, the offline optimization introduced in this paper, outperforms the other leading offline optimizations. However, greater performance improvements could be obtained by improving BSM's equivalence detection.

If the input constraints could be efficiently preprocessed so as to remove every variable with an empty points-to set, BSM could be augmented to interpret store constraints in a manner similar to the interpretation used by OVS and HRU+LE, without adversely affecting precision. This would allow for paths in the superset graph to traverse dereference expressions, which would result in detecting more location equivalences and more pointer equivalences. Even more equivalences could be detected by iterating constraint reduction in the same way that HRU+LE iterates the HU reduction algorithm.

Another avenue is to adapt BSM for online use. Periodically BSM could be performed on the residual constraint graph, just like cycle detection is periodically performed on the residual constraint graph. Since BSM has a higher overhead than cycle detection, it makes sense for online bisimilarity detection to be performed less frequently than online cycle detection. The additional constraints that are inferred online should allow for bisimilarity detection to detect more pointer equivalences than when restricted to the initial constraint set.

Yet another avenue for improving BSM's equivalence detection is to devise an alternative definition for simulation graphs, possibly one that makes use of store constraints. An alternative definition may allow for the detection of more pointer equivalences.

References

[1] Aho, A.V., Lam, M.S., Sethi, R., Ullman, J.D. (eds.): Compilers: principles, techniques, and tools, 2nd edn. Pearson/Addison Wesley, Boston (2007)
[2] Andersen, L.O.: Program Analysis and Specialization for the C Programming Language. PhD thesis, DIKU, University of Copenhagen (DIKU report 94/19) (May 1994)

[3] Berndl, M., Lhoták, O., Qian, F., Hendren, L., Umanee, N.: Points-to analysis using BDDs. ACM SIGPLAN Notices 38(5), 103–114 (2003)

[4] Clarke, E.M., Grumberg, O., Peled, D.A.: Model Checking. MIT Press, Cambridge (1999)

[5] Cleaveland, R.: The concurrency workbench: A semantics-based verification tool for the verification of concurrent systems. ACM Transactions on Programming Languages and Systems 15(1), 36–72 (1993)

[6] Dovier, A., Piazza, C., Policriti, A.: An efficient algorithm for computing bisimulation equivalence. Theor. Comput. Sci. 311(1-3), 221–256 (2004)

[7] Fähndrich, M., Foster, J.S., Su, Z., Aiken, A.: Partial online cycle elimination in inclusion constraint graphs. ACM SIGPLAN Notices 33(5), 85–96 (1998)

[8] Focardi, R., Gorrieri, R.: The compositional security checker: A tool for the verification of information flow security properties. IEEE Trans. Software Eng. 23(9), 550–571 (1997)

[9] Hardekopf, B., Lin, C.: The ant and the grasshopper: fast and accurate pointer analysis for millions of lines of code. In: Ferrante, J., McKinley, K.S. (eds.) PLDI, pp. 290–299. ACM Press, New York (2007)

[10] Hardekopf, B., Lin, C.: Exploiting pointer and location equivalence to optimize pointer analysis. In: Riis Nielson, H., Filé, G. (eds.) SAS 2007. LNCS, vol. 4634, pp. 265–280. Springer, Heidelberg (2007)

[11] Heintze, N., Tardieu, O.: Ultra-fast aliasing analysis using CLA: A million lines of C code in a second. ACM SIGPLAN Notices 36(5), 254–263 (2001)

[12] Necula, G.C., McPeak, S., Rahul, S.P., Weimer, W.: CIL: Intermediate language and tools for analysis and transformation of C programs. In: Horspool, R.N. (ed.) CC 2002. LNCS, vol. 2304, pp. 213–228. Springer, Heidelberg (2002)

[13] Nuutila, E., Soisalon-Soininen, E.: On finding the strongly connected components in a directed graph. Information Processing Letters 49, 9–14 (1993)

[14] Paige, R., Tarjan, R.E.: Three partition refinement algorithms. SIAM J. Comput. 16(6), 973–989 (1987)

[15] Pearce, D.J., Kelly, P.H.J., Hankin, C.: Efficient field-sensitive pointer analysis for C. In: Flanagan, C., Zeller, A. (eds.) PASTE, pp. 37–42. ACM Press, New York (2004)

[16] Pearce, D.J., Kelly, P.H.J., Hankin, C.: Efficient field-sensitive pointer analysis of C. ACM Transactions on Programming Languages and Systems 30(1), 4:1–4:42 (2007)

[17] Rountev, A., Chandra, S.: Off-line variable substitution for scaling points-to analysis. ACM SIGPLAN Notices 35(5), 47–56 (2000)

Type Analysis for JavaScript

Simon Holm Jensen[1,*], Anders Møller[1,**], and Peter Thiemann[2]

[1] Aarhus University, Denmark
{simonhj,amoeller}@cs.au.dk
[2] Universität Freiburg, Germany
thiemann@informatik.uni-freiburg.de

Abstract. JavaScript is the main scripting language for Web browsers, and it is essential to modern Web applications. Programmers have started using it for writing complex applications, but there is still little tool support available during development.

We present a static program analysis infrastructure that can infer detailed and sound type information for JavaScript programs using abstract interpretation. The analysis is designed to support the full language as defined in the ECMAScript standard, including its peculiar object model and all built-in functions. The analysis results can be used to detect common programming errors – or rather, prove their absence, and for producing type information for program comprehension.

Preliminary experiments conducted on real-life JavaScript code indicate that the approach is promising regarding analysis precision on small and medium size programs, which constitute the majority of JavaScript applications. With potential for further improvement, we propose the analysis as a foundation for building tools that can aid JavaScript programmers.

1   Introduction

In 1995, Netscape announced JavaScript as an "easy-to-use object scripting language designed for creating live online applications that link together objects and resources on both clients and servers" [25]. Since then, it has become the de facto standard for client-side scripting in Web browsers but many other applications also include a JavaScript engine. This prevalence has lead developers to write large programs in a language which has been conceived for scripting, but not for programming in the large. Hence, tool support is badly needed to help debug and maintain these programs.

The development of sound programming tools that go beyond checking mere syntactic properties requires some sort of program analysis. In particular, type analysis is crucial to catch representation errors, which e.g. confuse numbers with strings or booleans with functions, early in the development process. Type

---

* Supported by The Danish Research Council for Technology and Production, grant no. 274-07-0488.
** Corresponding author.

J. Palsberg and Z. Su (Eds.): SAS 2009, LNCS 5673, pp. 238–255, 2009.

analysis is a valuable tool to a programmer because it rules out this class of programming errors entirely.

Applying type analysis to JavaScript is a subtle business because, like most other scripting languages, JavaScript has a weak, dynamic typing discipline which resolves many representation mismatches by silent type conversions. As JavaScript supports objects, first-class functions, and exceptions, tracking the flow of data and control is nontrivial. Moreover, JavaScript's peculiarities present a number of challenges that set it apart from most other programming languages:

- JavaScript is an object-based language that uses prototype objects to model inheritance. As virtually all predefined operations are accessed via prototype objects, it is imperative that the analysis models these objects precisely.
- Objects are mappings from strings (property names) to values. In general, properties can be added and removed during execution and property names may be dynamically computed.
- Undefined results, such as accessing a non-existing property of an object, are represented by a particular value **undefined**, but there is a subtle distinction between an object that lacks a property and an object that has the property set to **undefined**.
- Values are freely converted from one type to another type with few exceptions. In fact, there are only a few cases where no automatic conversion applies: the values **null** and **undefined** cannot be converted to objects and only function values can be invoked as functions. Some of the automatic conversions are non-intuitive and programmers should be aware of them.
- The language distinguishes primitive values and wrapped primitive values, which behave subtly different in certain circumstances.
- Variables can be created by simple assignments without explicit declarations, but an attempt to read an absent variable results in a runtime error. JavaScript's **with** statement breaks ordinary lexical scoping rules, so even resolving variable names is a nontrivial task.
- Object properties can have attributes, like ReadOnly. These attributes cannot be changed by programs but they must be taken into account by the analysis to maintain soundness and precision.
- Functions can be created and called with variable numbers of parameters.
- Function objects serve as first-class functions, methods, and constructors with subtly different behavior. An analysis must keep these uses apart and detect initialization patterns.
- With the **eval** function, a dynamically constructed string can be interpreted as a program fragment and executed in the current scope.
- The language includes features that prescribe certain structures (the global object, activation objects, argument objects) in the implementation of the runtime system. These structures must be modeled in an analysis to obtain sufficient precision.

This paper reports on the design and implementation of a program analyzer for the full JavaScript language. In principle, the design is an application of abstract interpretation using the monotone framework [9,21]. However, the challenges explained above result in a complicated lattice structure that forms the basis of our analysis. Starting from a simple type lattice, the lattice has evolved in a number of steps driven by an observed lack of precision on small test cases. As the lattice includes precise singleton values, the analyzer duplicates a large amount of the functionality of a JavaScript interpreter including the implementation of predefined functions. Operating efficiently on the elements of the lattice is another non-trivial challenge.

The analyzer is targeted at hand-written programs consisting of a few thousand lines of code. We conjecture that most existing JavaScript programs fit into this category.

One key requirement of the analysis is *soundness*. Although several recent bug finding tools for other languages sacrifice soundness to obtain fewer false positives [5,12], soundness enables our analysis to guarantee the absence of certain errors. Moreover, the analysis is *fully automatic*. It neither requires program annotations nor formal specifications.

While some programming errors result in exceptions being thrown, other errors are masked by dynamic type conversion and **undefined** values. Some of these conversions appear unintuitive in isolation but make sense in certain circumstances and some programmers may deliberately exploit such behavior, so there is no clear-cut definition of what constitutes an "error". Nevertheless, we choose to draw the programmer's attention to such potential errors. These situations include

1. invoking a non-function value (e.g. **undefined**) as a function,
2. reading an absent variable,
3. accessing a property of **null** or **undefined**,
4. reading an absent property of an object,
5. writing to variables or object properties that are never read,
6. implicitly converting a primitive value to an object (as an example, the primitive value **false** may be converted into a **Boolean** object, and later converting that back to a primitive value results in **true**, which surprises many JavaScript programmers),
7. implicitly converting **undefined** to a number (which yields **NaN** that often triggers undesired behavior in arithmetic operations),
8. calling a function object both as a function and as a constructor (i.e. perhaps forgetting **new**) or passing function parameters with varying types (e.g. at one place passing a number and another place passing a string or no value),
9. calling a built-in function with an invalid number of parameters (which may result in runtime errors, unlike the situation for user defined functions) or with a parameter of an unexpected type (e.g. the second parameter to the **apply** function must be an array).

The first three on this list cause runtime errors (exceptions) if the operation in concern is ever executed, so these warnings have a higher priority than the others. In many situations, the analysis can report a warning as a definite error rather than a potential error. For example, the analysis may detect that a property read operation will always result in undefined because the given property is never present, in which case that specific warning gets high priority. As the analysis is sound, the absence of errors and warnings guarantees that the operations concerned will not fail. The analysis can also detect dead code.

The following tiny but convoluted program shows one way of using JavaScript's prototype mechanism to model inheritance:

```
function Person(n) {
  this.setName(n);
  Person.prototype.count++;
}
Person.prototype.count = 0;
Person.prototype.setName = function(n) { this.name = n; }
function Student(n,s) {
  this.b = Person;
  this.b(n);
  delete this.b;
  this.studentid = s.toString();
}
Student.prototype = new Person;
```

The code defines two "classes" with constructors Person and Student. Person has a static field count and a method setName. Student inherits count and setName and defines an additional studentid field. The definition and deletion of b in Student invokes the super class constructor Person. A small test case illustrates its behavior:

```
var t = 100026.0;
var x = new Student("Joe Average", t++);
var y = new Student("John Doe", t);
y.setName("John Q. Doe");
assert(x.name === "Joe Average");
assert(y.name === "John Q. Doe");
assert(y.studentid === "100027");
assert(x.count == 3);
```

Even for a tiny program like this, many things could go wrong – keeping the different errors discussed above in mind – but our analysis is able to prove that none of the errors can occur here. Due to the forgiving nature of JavaScript, errors may surface only as mysterious undefined values. Simple errors, like misspelling prototype or name in just a single place or writing toString instead of toString(), are detected by the static type analysis instead of causing failure at runtime. The warning messages being produced by the analysis can help the programmer not only to detect errors early but also to pinpoint their cause.

Contributions

This work is the first step towards a full-blown JavaScript program analyzer, which can be incorporated into an IDE to supply on-the-fly error detection as well as support for auto-completion and documentation hints. It focuses on JavaScript version 1.5, corresponding to ECMAScript 3rd edition [11], which is currently the most widely used variant of the language and which is a subset of the upcoming revision of the JavaScript language.

In summary, the contributions of this paper are the following:

- We define a type analysis for JavaScript based on abstract interpretation [9]. Its main contribution is the design of an intricate lattice structure that fits with the peculiarities of the language. We design the analysis building on existing techniques, in particular recency abstraction [3].
- We describe our prototype implementation of the analysis, which covers the full JavaScript language as specified in the ECMAScript standard [11], and we report on preliminary experiments on real-life benchmark programs and measure the effectiveness of the various analysis techniques being used.
- We identify opportunities for further improvements of precision and speed of the analysis, and we discuss the potential for additional applications of the analysis technique.

Additional information about the project is available online at

$$http://www.brics.dk/TAJS$$

2   Related Work

The present work builds on a large body of work and experience in abstract interpretation and draws inspiration from work on soft typing and dynamic typing. The main novelty consists of the way it combines known techniques, leading to the construction of the first full-scale implementation of a high precision program analyzer for JavaScript. It thus forms the basis to further investigate the applicability of techniques in this new domain.

Dolby [10] explains the need for program analysis for scripting languages to support the interactive completion and error spotting facilities of an IDE. He sketches the design of the WALA framework [13], which is an adaptable program analysis framework suitable for a range of languages, including Java, JavaScript, Python, and PHP. While our first prototype was built on parts of the WALA framework, we found that the idiosyncrasies of the JavaScript language required more radical changes than were anticipated in WALA's design.

Eclipse includes JSDT [7], which mainly focuses on providing instantaneous documentation and provides many shortcuts for common programming and documentation patterns as well as some refactoring operations. It also features some unspecified kind of prototype-aware flow analysis to predict object types and thus enable primitive completion of property names. JSEclipse [1] is another Eclipse plugin, which includes built-in knowledge about some popular JavaScript frameworks and uses the Rhino JavaScript engine to run parts of the code to improve support for code completion. Neither of these plugins can generate warnings for unintended conversions or other errors discussed above.

Program analysis for scripting languages has evolved from earlier work on type analysis for dynamically typed languages like Scheme and Smalltalk [6,31,16]. These works have clarified the need for a type structure involving union types and recursive types. They issue warnings and insert dynamic tests in programs that cannot be type checked. MrSpidey [14] is a flow-based implementation of these ideas with visual feedback about the location of the checks in a programming environment. In contrast, our analysis only reports warnings because the usefulness of checks is not clear in a weakly typed setting.

Thiemann's typing framework for JavaScript programs [30] has inspired the design of the abstract domain for the present work. That work concentrates on the design and soundness proof, but does not present a typing algorithm. In later work, Heidegger and Thiemann [17] propose a recency-based type system for a core language of JavaScript, present its soundness proof, sketch an inference algorithm, and argue the usefulness of this concept.

Anderson and others [2] present a type system with an inference algorithm for a primitive subset of JavaScript based on a notion of definite presence and potential absence of properties in objects. Their system does not model type change and the transition between presence and absence of a property is harder to predict than in a recency-based system.

Furr and others [15] have developed a typed dialect of Ruby, a scripting language with features very similar to JavaScript. Their approach requires the programmer to supply type annotations to library functions. Then they employ standard constraint solving techniques to infer types of user-defined functions. There is support for universal types and intersection types (to model overloading), but these types can only be declared, not inferred. They aim for simplicity in favor of precision also to keep the type language manageable, whereas our design aims for precision. Their paper contains a good overview of further, more pragmatic approaches to typing for scripting languages like Ruby and Python.

Similar techniques have been applied to the Erlang language by Marlow and Wadler [24] as well as by Nyström [27]. These ideas have been extended and implemented in a practical tool by Lindahl and Sagonas [23]. Their work builds on success typings, a notion which seems closely related to abstract interpretation.

One program analysis that has been developed particularly for JavaScript is points-to analysis [20]. The goal of that analysis is not program understanding, but enabling program optimization. The paper demonstrates that the results from the analysis enable partial redundancy elimination. The analysis is flow and context insensitive and it is limited to a small first-order core language. In contrast, our analysis framework deals with the entire language and performs points-to analysis as part of the type analysis. As our analysis is flow and context sensitive, it yields more precise results than the dedicated points-to analysis.

Balakrishnan and Reps [3] were first to propose the notion of recency in abstract interpretation. They use it to create a sound points-to analysis with sufficient precision to resolve the majority of virtual method calls in compiled C++ code. Like ourselves, they note that context sensitivity is indispensable in the presence of recency abstraction. However, the rest of their framework is substantially different as it is targeted to analyzing binary code. Its value representation is based on a stride domain and the interprocedural part uses a standard k-limited call-chain abstraction.

Shape analysis [28] is yet more powerful than recency abstraction. For example, it can recover strongly updatable abstractions for list elements from a summary description of a list data structure. This capability is beyond recency abstraction. However, the superior precision of shape analysis requires a much more resource-intensive implementation.

Finally, our analysis uses abstract garbage collection. This notion has been investigated in depth in a polyvariant setting by Might and Shivers [26], who attribute its origin to Jagannathan and others [19]. They, as well as Balakrishnan and Reps [3], also propose abstract counting which is not integrated in our work as the pay-off is not yet clear.

3   Flow Graphs for JavaScript

The analysis represents a JavaScript program as a flow graph, in which each node contains an instruction and each edge represents potential control flow between instructions in the program. The graph has a designated program entry node corresponding to the first instruction of the global code in the program. Instructions refer to *temporary variables*, which have no counterpart in JavaScript, but which are introduced by the analyzer when breaking down composite expressions and statements to instructions. The nodes can have different kinds:

declare-variable[x]: declares a program variable named x with value undefined.

read-variable[x, v]: reads the value of a program variable named x into a temporary variable v.

write-variable[v, x]: writes the value of a temporary variable v into a program variable named x.

constant[c, v]: assigns a constant value c to the temporary variable v.

read-property[v_1, v_2, v_3]: performs an object property lookup, where v_1 holds the base object, v_2 holds the property name, and v_3 gets the resulting value.

write-property[v_1, v_2, v_3]: performs an object property write, where v_1 holds the base object, v_2 holds the property name, and v_3 holds the value to be written.

delete-property[v_1, v_2, v_3]: deletes an object property, where v_1 holds the base object, v_2 holds the property name, and v_3 gets the resulting value.

if[v]: represents conditional flow for e.g. if and while statements.

entry[$f, x_1, \ldots, x_n$], exit, and exit-exc: used for marking the unique entry and exit (normal/exceptional) of a function body. Here, f is the (optional) function name, and $x_1, \ldots, x_n$ are formal parameters.

call[$w, v_0, \ldots, v_n$], construct[$w, v_0, \ldots, v_n$], and after-call[v]: A function call is represented by a pair of a call node and an after-call node. For a call node, w holds the function value and $v_0, \ldots, v_n$ hold the values of this and the parameters. An after-call node is returned to after the call and contains a single variable for the returned value. The construct nodes are similar to call nodes and are used for new expressions.

return[v]: a function return.

throw[v] and catch[x]: represent **throw** statements and entries of **catch** blocks.

$<op>[v_1, v_2]$ and $<op>[v_1, v_2, v_3]$: represent unary and binary operators, where the result is stored in v_2 or v_3, respectively.

This instruction set is reminiscent of the bytecode language used in some interpreters [18] but tailored to program analysis. Due to the limited space, we here omit the instructions related to **for-in** and **with** blocks and settle for this informal description of the central instructions. They closely correspond to the ECMAScript specification – for example, read-property is essentially the [[Get]] operation from the specification.

We distinguish between different kinds of edges. *Ordinary* edges correspond to intra-procedural control flow. These edges may be labeled to distinguish branches at if nodes. Each node that may raise an exception has an *exception* edge to a catch node or an exit-exc node. Finally, *call* and *return* edges describe flow from call or construct nodes to entry nodes and from exit nodes to after-call nodes.

All nodes as well as ordinary edges and exception edges are created before the fixpoint iteration starts, whereas the call and return edges are added on the fly when data flow is discovered, as explained in Section 4.

4   The Analysis Lattice and Transfer Functions

The classical approach of abstract interpretation [9] and the monotone framework [21] requires a lattice of abstract states. Our lattice structure is similar to a lattice used for constant propagation with JavaScript's type structure on top. Numbers and strings are further refined to recognize array indices. For objects, the analysis performs a context-sensitive flow analysis that discovers points-to information.

For a given flow graph, we let N denote the set of nodes, T is the set of temporary variables, and L is the set of *object labels* corresponding to the possible allocation sites (including construct nodes, constant nodes for function declarations, and objects defined in the standard library).

Abstract values are described by the lattice Value:

$$\mathsf{Value} = \mathsf{Undef} \times \mathsf{Null} \times \mathsf{Bool} \times \mathsf{Num} \times \mathsf{String} \times \mathcal{P}(L)$$

The components of Value describe the different types of values.

For example, the abstract value $(\bot, \mathsf{null}, \bot, \bot, \mathsf{baz}, \emptyset)$ describes a concrete value that is either null or the string "baz", and $(\mathsf{undef}, \bot, \bot, \bot, \bot, \{\ell_{42}, \ell_{87}\})$ describes a value that is $\mathsf{undefined}$ or an object originating from ℓ_{42} or ℓ_{87}.

Objects are modeled as follows:

$$\mathsf{Obj} = (P \hookrightarrow \mathsf{Value} \times \mathsf{Absent} \times \mathsf{Attributes} \times \mathsf{Modified}) \times \mathcal{P}(\mathsf{ScopeChain})$$

Here, P is the infinite set of property names (i.e. all strings). The partial map provides an abstract value for every possible property name. There are four special property names: [[Prototype]], [[Value]], *default_index*, and *default_other*. The former two correspond to the internal properties used by ECMAScript; *default_index* and *default_other* are always in the domain of the map and provide an abstract value for all property names that are not in the domain of the map (hence the map is effectively total): *default_index* covers property names that match $\mathsf{UIntString}$ (array indices), and *default_other* covers all other strings. This distinction is crucial when analyzing programs involving array operations. Section 4.3 explains the $\mathsf{ScopeChain}$ component, which models the special internal property [[Scope]].

Each value stored in an object has additional components. Absent models potentially absent properties, $\mathsf{Modified}$ is related to interprocedural analysis as explained in Section 4.3, and $\mathsf{Attributes}$ models the property attributes Read-Only, DontDelete, and DontEnum.

$$\mathsf{Absent} = \begin{array}{c} \mathsf{absent} \\ | \\ \bot \end{array} \qquad \mathsf{Modified} = \begin{array}{c} \mathsf{modified} \\ | \\ \bot \end{array}$$

$$\mathsf{Attributes} = \mathsf{ReadOnly} \times \mathsf{DontDelete} \times \mathsf{DontEnum}$$

$$\mathsf{ReadOnly} = \begin{array}{c} \top \\ \diagup \diagdown \\ \mathsf{RO} \quad \mathsf{notRO} \\ \diagdown \diagup \\ \bot \end{array} \qquad \mathsf{DontDelete} = \begin{array}{c} \top \\ \diagup \diagdown \\ \mathsf{DD} \quad \mathsf{notDD} \\ \diagdown \diagup \\ \bot \end{array} \qquad \mathsf{DontEnum} = \begin{array}{c} \top \\ \diagup \diagdown \\ \mathsf{DE} \quad \mathsf{notDE} \\ \diagdown \diagup \\ \bot \end{array}$$

An abstract state consists of an abstract store, which is a partial map from object labels to abstract objects, together with an abstract stack:

$$\mathsf{State} = (L \hookrightarrow \mathsf{Obj}) \times \mathsf{Stack} \times \mathcal{P}(L) \times \mathcal{P}(L)$$

The last two object label sets in State are explained in Section 4.3.

The stack is modeled as follows:

$$\mathsf{Stack} = (T \to \mathsf{Value}) \times \mathcal{P}(\mathsf{ExecutionContext}) \times \mathcal{P}(L)$$
$$\mathsf{ExecutionContext} = \mathsf{ScopeChain} \times L \times L$$
$$\mathsf{ScopeChain} = L^*$$

The first component of Stack provides values for the temporary variables. The $\mathcal{P}(\mathsf{ExecutionContext})$ component models the top-most execution context[1] and the $\mathcal{P}(L)$ component contains object labels of all references in the stack. An

---

[1] The ECMAScript standard [11] calls a stack frame an *execution context* and also defines the terms *scope chain* and *variable object*.

execution context contains a scope chain, which is here a sequence of object labels, together with two additional object labels that identify the variable object and the `this` object.

Finally, we define the analysis lattice, which assigns a set of abstract states to each node (corresponding to the program points *before* the nodes):

$$\mathsf{AnalysisLattice} = V \times N \;\rightarrow\; \mathsf{State}$$

V is the set of version names of abstract states for implementing context sensitivity. As a simple heuristic, we currently keep two abstract states separate if they have different values for `this`, which we model by $V = \mathcal{P}(L)$.

The lattice order is defined as follows: For the components of Value, the Hasse diagrams define the lattice order for each component. All maps and products are ordered pointwise, and power sets are ordered by subset inclusion – except the last $\mathcal{P}(L)$ component of State, which uses $\supseteq$ instead of $\subseteq$ (see Section 4.3).

These definitions are the culmination of tedious twiddling and experimentation. Note, for example, that for two abstract stores σ_1 and σ_2 where $\sigma_1(\ell)$ is undefined and $\sigma_2(\ell)$ is defined (i.e. the object ℓ is absent in the former and present in the latter), the join simply takes the content of ℓ from σ_2, i.e. $(\sigma_1 \sqcup \sigma_2)(\ell) = \sigma_2(\ell)$, as desired. Also, for every abstract store σ and every ℓ where $\sigma(\ell) = (\omega, s)$ is defined, we have absent set in $\omega(default\_index)$ and in $\omega(default\_other)$ to reflect the fact that in every object, *some* properties are absent. Thereby, joining two stores where an object ℓ is present in both but some property p is only present in one (and mapped to the bottom Value in the other) results in a store where ℓ is present and p is marked as absent (meaning that it is *maybe* absent).

The analysis proceeds by fixpoint iteration, as in the classical monotone framework, using the transfer functions described in Section 4.1. The initial abstract state for the program entry node consists of 161 abstract objects (mostly function objects) defined in the standard library.

We omit a formal description of the abstraction/concretization relation between the ECMAScript specification and this abstract interpretation lattice. However, we note that during fixpoint iteration, an abstract state never has dangling references (i.e. in every abstract state σ, every object label ℓ that appears anywhere within σ is always in the domain of the store component of σ). With this invariant in place, it should be clear how every abstract state describes a set of concrete states.

The detailed models of object structures represented in an abstract state allows us to perform *abstract garbage collection* [26]. An object ℓ can safely be removed from the store unless ℓ is reachable from the abstract call stack. This technique may improve both performance and precision (see Section 5).

Section 5 contains an illustration of the single abstract state appearing at the final node of the example program after the fixpoint is reached.

4.1 Transfer Functions

For each kind of node n in the flow graph, a monotone transfer function maps an abstract state before n to a abstract state after n. In addition, we provide a transfer function for each predefined function in the ECMAScript standard library. Some edges (in particular, call and return edges) also carry transfer functions. As usual, the before state of node n is the join of the after states of all predecessors of n.

The transfer function for read-property$[v_{obj}, v_{prop}, v_{target}]$ serves as an illustrative example. If v_{obj} is not an object, it gets converted into one. If v_{obj} abstracts many objects, then the result is the join of reading all of them. The read operation for a single abstract object descends the prototype chain and joins the results of looking up the property until the property was definitely present in a prototype. If v_{prop} is not a specific string, then the *default_index* and *default_other* fields of the object and its prototypes are also considered. Finally, the temporary variable v_{target} is overwritten with the result; all temporaries can be strongly updated. As this example indicates, it is essential that the analysis models all aspects of the JavaScript execution model, including prototype chains and type coercions.

A special case is the transfer function for the built-in functions eval and Function that dynamically construct new program code. The analyzer cannot model such a dynamic extension of the program because the fixpoint solver requires N and L to be fixed. Hence, the analyzer issues a warning if these functions are used. This approach is likely satisfactory as these functions are mostly used in stylized ways, e.g. for JSON data, according to a study of existing JavaScript code [22].

4.2 Recency Abstraction

A common pattern in JavaScript code is creating an object with a constructor function that adds properties to the object using write-property operations. In general, an abstract object may describe multiple concrete objects, so such operations must be modeled with weak updates of the relevant abstract objects. Subsequent read-property operations then read potentially absent properties, which quickly leads to a proliferation of undefined values, resulting in poor analysis precision. Fortunately, a solution exists which fits perfectly with our analysis framework: *recency abstraction* [3].

In essence, each allocation site ℓ (in particular, those identified by the construct instructions) is described by *two* object labels: $\ell^@$ (called the *singleton*) always describes exactly one concrete object (if present in the domain of the store), and ℓ^* (the *summary*) describes an unknown number of concrete objects. Typically, $\ell^@$ refers to the *most recently allocated* object from ℓ (hence the name of the technique), and ℓ^* refers to older objects – however the addition of interprocedural analysis (Section 4.3) changes this slightly.

In an intra-procedural setting, this mechanism is straightforward to incorporate. Informally, the transfer function for a node n of type construct$[v]$ joins the $n^@$ object into the n^* object, redirects all pointers from $n^@$ to n^*, sets $n^@$ to an empty object, and assigns $n^@$ to v. Henceforth, v refers to a singleton abstract object, which permits strong updates.

The effect of incorporating recency abstraction on the analysis precision is substantial, as shown in Section 5.

4.3   Interprocedural Analysis

Function calls have a remarkably complicated semantics in JavaScript, but each step can be modeled precisely with our lattice definition. The transfer function for a call node n, $\mathsf{call}[w, v_0, \ldots]$, extracts all function objects from w and then, as a side-effect, adds call edges to the entry nodes of these functions and return edges from their exit nodes back to the after-call node n' of n. To handle exception flow, return edges are also added from the exit-exc nodes to n'_{exc}, where n' has an exception edge to n'_{exc}. The call edge transfer function models parameter passing. It also models the new execution context being pushed onto the call stack. The base object, v_0, is used for setting this and the scope chain of the new execution context (which is why we need $\mathcal{P}(\mathsf{ScopeChain})$ in Obj).

A classical challenge in interprocedural analysis is to avoid flow through infeasible paths when a function is called from several sites [29]. Ignoring this effect may lead to a considerable loss of precision. We use the Modified component of Obj to keep track of object properties that may have been modified since the current function was entered. For an abstract state σ_m at an exit node m with a return edge to an after-call node n', which belongs to a call node n, the edge transfer function checks whether the definitely non-modified parts of σ_m are inconsistent with σ_n, in which case it can safely discard the flow. (A given object property that is non-modified in σ_m is *consistent* with σ_n if its abstract value according to σ_n is less than or equal to its value according to σ_m.) If consistent, the transfer function replaces all non-modified parts of σ_m by the corresponding potentially more precise information from σ_n, together with the abstract stack. When propagating this flow along return edges, we must take into account the use of recency abstraction to "undo" the shuffling of singleton and summary objects. To this end, two sets of object labels are part of State to keep track of those object labels that are definitely/maybe summarized since entering the current function.

4.4   Termination of the Analysis

The usual termination requirement that the lattice should have finite height does not apply here, now even for a fixed program. We informally argue that the analysis nevertheless always terminates by the following observations: (1) The length of the ScopeChain object label sequences is always bounded by the lexical nesting depth of the program being analyzed. (2) The number of abstract states maintained for each node is solely determined by the choice of context sensitivity criteria. The simple heuristic proposed in Section 4 ensure the sizes of these sets to be bounded for any program. (3) The partial map in Obj has a potentially unbounded domain. However, at any point during fixpoint iteration a property name p can only occur in the domain if it was put in by a write-variable or write-property instruction. The property name for such an instruction comes from a temporary variable whose value is drawn from Value and coerced to String. In case that value is not a constant string, the use of *default_index* and *default_other* ensures that the domain is unmodified, and there are clearly only finitely many nodes that contain such an instruction. Together, these observations ensure that a fixpoint will be reached for any input program. The theoretical worst case complexity is obviously high, because of the complex analysis lattice. Nevertheless, our tool analyzes sizable programs within minutes, as shown in the next section.

5 Experiments

Our prototype is implemented on top of the JavaScript parser from Rhino [4] with around 17,000 lines of Java code. For testing that the prototype behaves as expected on the full JavaScript language, we have collected a corpus of more than 150 programs. These test programs are mostly in the range 5–50 lines of code and include 28 example programs[2] from Anderson et al. [2].

For the Anderson programs, our analysis detects all errors without spurious warnings and provides type information consistent with that of Anderson [2]. Our own programs were written to exercise various parts of the system and to provoke certain error messages, so it is not surprising that the analysis handles these well.

Running the analysis on the example program from Section 1 results in two warnings. First, the analysis correctly detects that the expression s.toString() involves a coercion from a primitive type to an object (which was deliberate by the programmer, in this case). Second, the analysis is able to prove that y.studentid is a string after the call to y.setName, but not that the string is a particular string, which results in a warning at the second assert statement. The reason is that setName is called twice on the same object with different strings (once through the constructor and once directly). A stronger heuristic for context sensitivity might resolve this issue.

Figure 1 shows the abstract state for the final program point of the example program, as obtained by running the prototype implementation. Each box describes an abstract object. For this simple program, each of them is a singleton (see Section 4.2). Edges correspond to references. For obvious reasons, only the used parts of the standard library are included in the illustration. The activation objects that are used during execution of the function calls have been removed by the abstract garbage collection. GLOBAL describes the global object, which also acts as execution context for the top-level code. OBJECT_PROTOTYPE and FUNCTION_PROTO model the prototype objects of the central built-in objects Object and Function, respectively. F_Person, F_Student, and F_0 correspond to the three functions defined in the program, and F_Person_PROTO, F_Student_PROTO, and F_0_PROTO are their prototype objects. Finally, L0 and L1 describe the two Student objects being created. The special property names [[Prototype]], [[Scope]], and [[Value]] are the so-called internal properties. For an example prototype chain, consider the object referred to by the variable x using

---

[2] http://www.doc.ic.ac.uk/~cla97/js0impl/

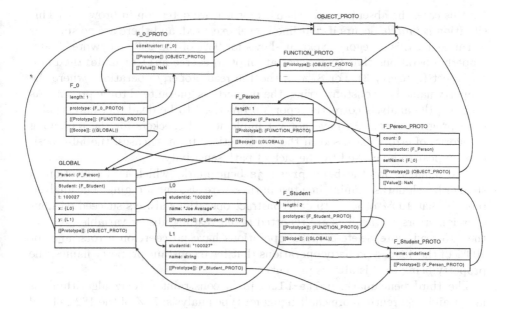

Fig. 1. Abstract state for the final program point of the example program

the global object as variable object. Its prototype chain consists of L0, followed by F_Student_PROTO and F_Person_PROTO, which reflects the sequence of objects relevant for resolving the expression x.count. As the illustration shows, even small JavaScript programs give rise to complex object structures, which our analysis lattice captures in sufficient detail.

The tool also outputs a call graph for the program in form of the call edges that are produced during fixpoint iteration, which can be useful for program comprehension.

The Google V8 benchmark suite[3] is our main testbed to evaluate the precision of the analysis on real code. It consists of four complex, standalone JavaScript programs. Although developed for testing performance of JavaScript interpreters, they are also highly demanding subjects for a static type analysis. In addition, we use the four most complex SunSpider benchmarks[4].

Clearly we do not expect to find bugs in such thoroughly tested programs, so instead we measure precision by counting the number of operations where the analysis does *not* produce a warning (for different categories), i.e. is capable of proving that the error cannot occur at that point.

For the richards.js benchmark (which simulates the task dispatcher of an operating system), the analysis shows for 95% of the 58 call/construct nodes that the value being invoked is always a function (i.e. category 1 from Section 1). Moreover, it detects one location where an absent variable is read (category 2).

---

[3] http://v8.googlecode.com/svn/data/benchmarks/v1/
[4] http://www2.webkit.org/perf/sunspider-0.9/sunspider.html

(In this case, the absent variable is used for feature detection in browsers.) This situation *definitely* occurs if that line is ever executed, and there are no spurious warnings for this category. Next, it shows for 93% of the 259 read/write/delete-property operations that they never attempt to coerce null or undefined into an object (category 3). For 87% of the 156 read-property operations where the property name is a constant string, the property is guaranteed to be present. As a bonus, the analysis correctly reports 6 functions to be dead, i.e. unreachable from program entry. We have not yet implemented checkers for the remaining categories of errors discussed in the introduction. In most cases, the false positives appear to be caused by the lack of path sensitivity.

The numbers for the benchpress.js benchmark (which is a collection of smaller benchmarks running in a test harness) are also encouraging: The analysis reports that 100% of the 119 call/construct operations always succeed without coercion errors, 0 warnings are reported about reading absent variables, 89% of the 113 read/write/delete-property operations have no coercion errors, and for 100% of the 48 read-property operations that have constant property names, the property being read is always present.

The third benchmark, delta-blue.js (a constraint solving algorithm), is larger and apparently more challenging for type analysis: 78% of the 182 call and construct instructions are guaranteed to succeed, 8 absent variables are correctly detected (all of them are functions that are defined in browser APIs, which we do not model), 82% of 492 read/write/delete-property instructions are proved safe, and 61% of 365 read-property with constant names are shown to be safe. For this benchmark, many of the false positives would likely be eliminated by better context sensitivity heuristics.

The results for the first three V8 benchmarks and the four SunSpider benchmarks are summarized in Figure 2. For each of the categories discussed above, the table shows the ratio between precise answers obtained and the number of nodes of the relevant kind.

The fourth (and largest) V8 benchmark, cryptobench.js, presently causes our prototype to run out of memory (with a limit of 512MB). For the other benchmarks, analysis time is less than 10 seconds, except 3d-raytrace.js and delta-blue.js which require 30 seconds and 6 minutes, respectively. Although

	lines	call / construct	variable read	property access	fixed-property read
richards.js	529	95%	100%	93%	87%
benchpress.js	463	100%	100%	89%	100%
delta-blue.js	853	78%	100%	82%	61%
3d-cube.js	342	100%	100%	92%	100%
3d-raytrace.js	446	99%	100%	94%	94%
crypto-md5.js	291	100%	100%	100%	100%
access-nbody.js	174	100%	100%	93%	100%

Fig. 2. Analysis precision

analysis speed and memory consumption have not been key objectives for this prototype, we naturally pursue this matter further. Most likely, the work list ordering used by the fixpoint solver can be improved.

We can disable various features in the analysis to obtain a rough measure of their effect. Disabling abstract garbage collection has little consequence on the precision of the analysis on these programs, however it is cheap to apply and it generally reduces memory consumption. Using recency abstraction is crucial: With this technique disabled, the analysis of `richards.js` can only guarantee that a constant property is present in 2 of the 156 read-property nodes (i.e. less than 2%, compared to 87% before) and the number of warnings about potential dereferences of null or undefined rises from 19 to 90. These numbers confirm our hypothesis that recency abstraction is essential to the precision of the analysis. The Modified component of State is important for some benchmarks; for example, the number of warnings about dereferences of null or undefined in `3d-raytrace.js` rises from 21 to 61 if disabling this component. Finally, we observe that context sensitivity has a significant effect on e.g. `delta-blue.js`.

6 Conclusion

Scripting languages are a sweet-spot for applying static analysis techniques: There is yet little tool support for catching errors before code deployment and the programs are often relatively small. Our type analyzer is the first sound and detailed tool of this kind for real JavaScript code. The use of the monotone framework with an elaborate lattice structure, combined with recency abstraction, results in an analysis with good precision on demanding benchmarks.

We envision an IDE for JavaScript programming with features known from strongly typed languages, such as highlighting of type-related errors and support for precise content assists and safe refactorings. This goal requires further work, especially to improve the analysis speed. Our primary objectives for the prototype have been soundness and precision, so there are plenty of opportunities for improving performance. For example, we currently use a naive work list heuristic and the representation of abstract states employs little sharing.

In further experiments, we want to investigate if there is a need for even higher precision. For example, the String component could be replaced by regular languages obtained using a variant of string analysis [8]. It may also be fruitful to tune the context sensitivity heuristic or incorporate simple path sensitivity.

Another area is the consideration of the DOM, which is heavily used by most JavaScript programs. Our work provides a basis for modeling the different DOM implementations provided by the main browsers and hence for catching browser specific programming errors. Additionally, it paves the way for analyzing code that uses libraries (Dojo, Prototype, Yahoo! UI, FBJS, jQuery, etc.). With these further challenges ahead, the work presented here constitutes a starting point for developing precise and efficient program analysis techniques and tools that can detect errors (recall the list from Section 1) and provide type information for JavaScript programs used in modern Web applications.

Acknowledgments. We thank Julian Dolby and Stephen Fink for contributing the WALA framework to the research community, which helped us in the early phases of the project. Our work also benefited from inspiring discussions about JavaScript with Lars Bak and the Google Aarhus team.

References

1. Adobe. JSEclipse, http://labs.adobe.com/technologies/jseclipse/
2. Anderson, C., Giannini, P., Drossopoulou, S.: Towards type inference for JavaScript. In: Black, A.P. (ed.) ECOOP 2005. LNCS, vol. 3586, pp. 428–452. Springer, Heidelberg (2005)
3. Balakrishnan, G., Reps, T.W.: Recency-abstraction for heap-allocated storage. In: Yi, K. (ed.) SAS 2006. LNCS, vol. 4134, pp. 221–239. Springer, Heidelberg (2006)
4. Boyd, N., et al.: Rhino: JavaScript for Java, http://www.mozilla.org/rhino/
5. Bush, W.R., Pincus, J.D., Sielaff, D.J.: A static analyzer for finding dynamic programming errors. Software: Practice and Experience 30(7), 775–802 (2000)
6. Cartwright, R., Fagan, M.: Soft typing. In: Proc. ACM SIGPLAN Conference on Programming Language Design and Implementation, PLDI 1991 (June 1991)
7. Childs, B.: JavaScript development toolkit (JSDT) features (July 2008), http://live.eclipse.org/node/569
8. Christensen, A.S., Møller, A., Schwartzbach, M.I.: Precise analysis of string expressions. In: Cousot, R. (ed.) SAS 2003. LNCS, vol. 2694, pp. 1–18. Springer, Heidelberg (2003)
9. Cousot, P., Cousot, R.: Abstract interpretation: a unified lattice model for static analysis of programs by construction or approximation of fixpoints. In: Proc. 4th ACM SIGPLAN-SIGACT Symposium on Principles of Programming Languages, POPL 1977, pp. 238–252 (1977)
10. Dolby, J.: Using static analysis for IDE's for dynamic languages, 2005. In: The Eclipse Languages Symposium (2005)
11. ECMA. ECMAScript Language Specification, 3rd edn. ECMA-262
12. Engler, D.R., Chelf, B., Chou, A., Hallem, S.: Checking system rules using system-specific, programmer-written compiler extensions. In: 4th Symposium on Operating System Design and Implementation, OSDI 2000, USENIX (October 2000)
13. Fink, S., Dolby, J.: WALA – The T.J. Watson Libraries for Analysis, http://wala.sourceforge.net/
14. Flanagan, C., Flatt, M., Krishnamurthi, S., Weirich, S., Felleisen, M.: Catching bugs in the web of program invariants. In: Proc. ACM SIGPLAN Conference on Programming Language Design and Implementation, PLDI 1996, pp. 23–32 (1996)
15. Furr, M., (David) An, J-h., Foster, J.S., Hicks, M.: Static type inference for Ruby. In: Proc. 24th Annual ACM Symposium on Applied Computing, SAC 2009, Object Oriented Programming Languages and Systems Track (March 2009)
16. Graver, J.O., Johnson, R.E.: A type system for Smalltalk. In: Proc. 17th ACM SIGPLAN-SIGACT Symposium on Principles of Programming Languages, POPL 1990, pp. 136–150 (1990)
17. Heidegger, P., Thiemann, P.: Recency types for dynamically-typed object-based languages. In: Proc. International Workshops on Foundations of Object-Oriented Languages, FOOL 2009 (January 2009)
18. Apple Inc. Squirrelfish bytecodes, http://webkit.org/specs/squirrelfish-3bytecode.html

19. Jagannathan, S., Thiemann, P., Weeks, S., Wright, A.: Single and loving it: Must-alias analysis for higher-order languages. In: Proc. 25th ACM SIGPLAN-SIGACT Symposium on Principles of Programming Languages, POPL 1998, pp. 329–341 (1998)
20. Jang, D., Choe, K.-M.: Points-to analysis for JavaScript. In: Proc. 24th Annual ACM Symposium on Applied Computing, SAC 2009, Programming Language Track (March 2009)
21. Kam, J.B., Ullman, J.D.: Monotone data flow analysis frameworks. Acta Informatica 7, 305–317 (1977)
22. Kromann-Larsen, R., Simonsen, R.: Statisk analyse af JavaScript: Indledende arbejde. Master's thesis, Department of Computer Science, University of Aarhus (2007) (in Danish)
23. Lindahl, T., Sagonas, K.: Practical type inference based on success typings. In: Proc. 8th ACM SIGPLAN International Conference on Principles and Practice of Declarative Programming, PPDP 2006, pp. 167–178 (2006)
24. Marlow, S., Wadler, P.: A practical subtyping system for Erlang. In: Proc. 2nd ACM SIGPLAN International Conference on Functional Programming, ICFP 1997, pp. 136–149 (1997)
25. Sun Microsystems and Netscape Inc. Netscape and Sun announce Javascript(TM), the open, cross-platform object scripting language for enterprise networks and the internet (1995), http://sunsite.nus.sg/hotjava/pr951204-03.html
26. Might, M., Shivers, O.: Improving flow analyses via ΓCFA: abstract garbage collection and counting. In: Proc. 11th ACM SIGPLAN International Conference on Functional Programming, ICFP 2006 (2006)
27. Nyström, S.-O.: A soft-typing system for Erlang. In: Proc. 2nd ACM SIGPLAN Erlang Workshop, ERLANG 2003, pp. 56–71 (2003)
28. Sagiv, S., Reps, T.W., Wilhelm, R.: Parametric shape analysis via 3-valued logic. ACM Transactions on Programming Languages and Systems 24(3), 217–298 (2002)
29. Sharir, M., Pnueli, A.: Two approaches to interprocedural dataflow analysis. In: Program Flow Analysis: Theory and Applications, pp. 189–233. Prentice-Hall, Englewood Cliffs (1981)
30. Thiemann, P.: Towards a type system for analyzing JavaScript programs. In: Sagiv, M. (ed.) ESOP 2005. LNCS, vol. 3444, pp. 408–422. Springer, Heidelberg (2005)
31. Wright, A.K., Cartwright, R.: A practical soft type system for Scheme. ACM Transactions on Programming Languages and Systems 19(1), 87–152 (1997)

Abstract Parsing:
Static Analysis of Dynamically Generated String Output Using LR-Parsing Technology

Kyung-Goo Doh[1,*], Hyunha Kim[1,*], and David A. Schmidt[2,**]

[1] Hanyang University, Ansan, South Korea
[2] Kansas State University, Manhattan, Kansas, USA

Abstract. We combine LR(k)-parsing technology and data-flow analysis to analyze, in advance of execution, the documents generated dynamically by a program. Based on the document language's context-free reference grammar and the program's control structure, the analysis *predicts* how the documents will be generated and *parses* the predicted documents. Our strategy remembers context-free structure by computing *abstract LR-parse stacks*. The technique is implemented in Objective Caml and has statically validated a suite of PHP programs that dynamically generate HTML documents.

1 Introduction

Scripting languages like PHP, Perl, Ruby, and Python use strings as a "universal data structure" to communicate values, commands, and programs. For example, one might write a PHP script that assembles within a string variable an SQL query or an HTML page or an XML document. Typically, the well-formedness of the assembled string is verified when the string is supplied as input to its intended processor (database, web browser, or interpreter), and an incorrectly assembled string might cause processor failure. Worse still, a malicious user might deliberately supply misleading input that generates a document that attempts a cross-site-scripting or injection attack.

As a first step towards preventing failures and attacks, the well-formedness of a dynamically generated, "grammatically structured" string (document) should be checked with respect to the document's context-free *reference grammar* (for SQL or HTML or XML) before the document is supplied to its processor. Better still, the document generator program *itself* should be analyzed to validate that all its generated documents are well formed with respect to the reference grammar, like an application program is type checked in advance of execution. Such an

---

* Supported in part by grant R01-2006-000-10926-0 from the Basic Research Program of the Korea Science and Engineering Foundation and in part by the Engineering Research Center of Excellence Program of Korea Ministry of Education, Science and Technology(MEST) / Korea Science and Engineering Foundation(KOSEF), R11-2008-007-01003-0.
** Supported by NSF ITR-0326577.

J. Palsberg and Z. Su (Eds.): SAS 2009, LNCS 5673, pp. 256–272, 2009.

analysis should indicate the grammatical structure of the generated documents so that there is clear indication of those positions within the document where unsanitized data or potential attacks might appear. This level of precision goes further than what is provided by regular-expression-based analysis techniques.

In this paper, we employ LR(k)-parsing technology and data-flow analysis to *analyze* statically a program that dynamically generates documents as strings, and at the same time, *parse* the dynamically generated strings with the context-free reference grammar for the document language. We compute *abstract parse stacks* that remember the context-free structure of the strings.

Our approach requires that the reference grammar is LR(k) and that the program analyzed is annotated with "hot spots" (those program points where critically important strings are generated). Starting from each hot spot, the static analysis conducts demand-driven *abstract parsing* of the string assembled at the hot-spot. We have implemented an abstract-parsing analyzer and applied it to PHP programs that dynamically generate strings of HTML documents.

The paper is organized as follows: The next section reviews research on string analysis, and Section 3 summarizes our contributions. Sections 4 and 5 present a motivating example and the key concepts behind abstract parsing. Section 6 surveys the worklist algorithm that implements the flow analysis, and Sections 7 and 8 discuss technical issues regarding input variables and string-update operations. Section 9 sketches our implementation, and Section 10 concludes.

2   Previous Efforts

Because of the popularity of document generators and the dangers that they introduce, there exist a variety of approaches for validating document generators and their generated documents:

Parsing the generated strings: From the perspective of the document processor, it is important to protect oneself from malicious incoming queries. Wassermann and Su [20] studied the format of command-injection attacks on SQL servers and devised an SQL reference grammar with annotations that identify in the grammar the positions where injection attacks might be inserted. A parser based on the grammar is inserted as a front-end filter to the SQL database — every incoming query must be parsed before it proceeds to the database.

Document-generation languages: One might limit malformed document generation by restricting the language used to write document-generator programs. XDuce [9,10] is an ML-like language for building XML documents that are struct-like values statically typed with regular-expressions. The typing ensures that dynamically generated documents conform to "templates" defined by the document types. In a similar vein, <bigwig> [3] and JWIG [6] are domain-specific languages for XHTML-document generation. JWIG, an extension of Java, provides Java-encoded templates, and an accompanying static analyzer validates regular-expression well-formedness of the assembled documents.

Thiemann [18] studied the problem of inferring string-data types that are exactly the reference grammar's nonterminals: His extension of ML's type checker generates a set of typing constraints, expressed as grammar rules, for the strings generated by a program and checks containment of the constraint-set language in the reference-grammar language with Early's parsing algorithm, searching for grammar nonterminals that are solutions to the constraint set.

Regular-expression-based static analysis: Checking context-free grammar inclusion is costly, so analyses based on regular expressions are typically employed. One example is Christensen, et al.'s string analyzer [5], which extracts from a Java program a set of data-flow equations for the generated strings, treating the equations as a context-free grammar. Rather than check for context-free language inclusion, the flow equations are overapproximated into a regular grammar, using a conversion due to Mohri and Nederhof. Queries about grammatical well-formedness are posed as regular expressions, and finite-state machinery decides the answers.

Using Christensen, et al.'s string analyzer and a context-free-language reachability algorithm, Wasserman, et al.[19] devised a static analysis that type checks dynamically generated SQL queries in Java database applications. Kirkegaard and Møller [13] adapted Christensen, et al.'s work and Knuth's balanced grammars to check whether the approximated regular grammar conforms to a balanced XML grammar, statically predicting generated XML documents to be well-formed.

Minamide's analysis [14] also uses Christensen, et al.'s string analyzer and extracts a flow-equation set for a string expression, treating the equation set as if it were a context-free grammar. The novelty is the application of finite-state-automata transducers to revise the flow equations due to string-update operations embedded in the program. The transducers are also used to sanitize suspect user input before it is injected into a dynamically generated document. Subsequently, Minamide's group developed exponential-time algorithms that validate a context-free grammar against a subclass of balanced context-free grammars, which can be used to validate dynamically generated XML and HTML documents [15,17].

Choi, et al. [4] used abstract-interpretation with heuristic widening to devise a string analyzer that handles heap variables and context sensitivity. Its regular-expression-based machinery shares the same limitations with earlier efforts.

Flow-analysis techniques: When a user supplies malicious input data for inclusion into a dynamically generated document, a flow analyzer might track the input's flow and determine whether unsanitized input is injected into a dynamically generated document. Xie and Aiken [22] devised and applied an interprocedural flow analyzer that detects potential SQL injection errors in PHP programs. Jovanovich, et al., [12] implemented a tool with similar aims.

Combining the regular-expression and flow-analysis approaches are Wassermann and Su [21], who use Minamide's approach to extract data-flow equations from a program. They then annotate the flow equations as to which strings are untrustworthy so that solving the equations implements a data-flow analysis that tracks potential injection errors.

```
x = 'a'                      X0 = a
r = ']'                      R = ]
while ...                    X1 = X0 ⊔ X2
   x = '[' . x . r           X2 = [ · X1 · R
print x                      X3 = X1
```

(Read . as an infix string-append operation.)

Fig. 1. Sample program and its data-flow equations

3   Our Contribution

Our work means to complement these approaches by improving their precision:

1. We use the data-flow equations extracted from a program as a higher-order schema from which we generate first-order flow equations that *calculate the parse stacks generated when the dynamically generated strings are parsed (by the context-free reference grammar)*. The solved equations convey context information more precise than that given by regular-expression techniques.
2. We cannot retain *all* parse information and ensure termination, so we "fold" "repeating" parse stacks into single-entry, single-exit graphs (with cycles).
3. Rather than implement string-update operations as f.s.a.-transductions on the original flow equation set (cf. [14]), we use an *invariance property* for string updates, which means a string can be updated only if the outcome of the string's LR-parse is left unaltered.

It is easy to envision how our abstract parsing technique can be augmented by semantic-processing functions [2] so that a Xie-and-Aiken or Wassermann-and-Su tainting analysis can be conducted along with the abstract parse.

4   Motivating Example

We can compare the approaches just surveyed with a small example. Say that a script must generate an output string that conforms to this grammar,

$$S \rightarrow a \,|\, [S]$$

where S is the only nonterminal. (HTML, XML, and SQL are such bracket languages.) The grammar is LR(0), but it can be difficult to enforce even for simple programs, like the one in Figure 1, left column. Perhaps we require this program to print only well-formed S-phrases — the occurrence of x at "`print x`" is a "hot spot" and we must analyze x's possible values.

An analysis based on type checking assigns types (reference-grammar nonterminals) to the program's variables. The occurrences of x can indeed be data-typed as S, but r has no data type that corresponds to a nonterminal.

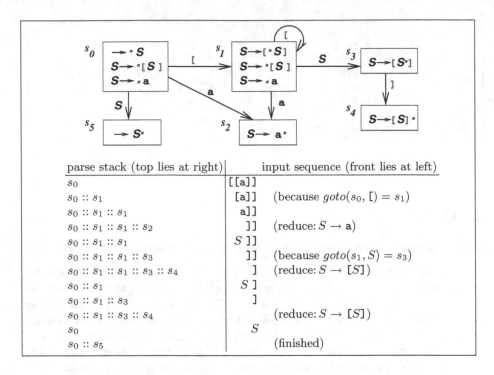

parse stack (top lies at right)	input sequence (front lies at left)
s_0	$[[a]]$
$s_0 :: s_1$	$[a]]$ (because $goto(s_0, [) = s_1$)
$s_0 :: s_1 :: s_1$	$a]]$
$s_0 :: s_1 :: s_1 :: s_2$	$]]$ (reduce: $S \to a$)
$s_0 :: s_1 :: s_1$	$S\,]]$
$s_0 :: s_1 :: s_1 :: s_3$	$]]$ (because $goto(s_1, S) = s_3$)
$s_0 :: s_1 :: s_1 :: s_3 :: s_4$	$]$ (reduce: $S \to [S]$)
$s_0 :: s_1$	$S\,]$
$s_0 :: s_1 :: s_3$	$]$
$s_0 :: s_1 :: s_3 :: s_4$	(reduce: $S \to [S]$)
s_0	S
$s_0 :: s_5$	(finished)

Fig. 2. *goto* controller for $S \to [S] \mid a$ and an example parse of $[[a]]$

An analysis based on regular expressions solves flow equations shown in Figure 1's right column in the domain of regular expressions, determining that the hot spot's ($X3$'s) values conform to the regular expression, $[^* \cdot a \cdot]^*$, but this does not validate the assertion. A grammar-based analysis does not solve the flow equations, but treats them instead as a set of grammar rules. The "type" of x at the hot spot is $X3$. Next, a language-inclusion check tries to prove that all $X3$-generated strings are S-generable.

Our approach solves the flow equations in the domain of *parse stacks* — $X3$'s meaning is the *set of LR-parses* of the strings that might be denoted by x. Assume that the reference grammar is LR(k); we first calculate its LR-items and build its parse ("*goto*") controller; see Figure 2. (This example, and the others in this paper, are LR(0) for simplicity.) The Figure displays an example parse.

We interpret the flow equations in Figure 1 as *functions* that map an input parse state to (a set of) output parse stacks. Figure 3 defines the collecting interpretation, but the informal explanation of Figure 1 conveys the intuitions:

The demand in Figure 1 to analyze the hot spot at $X3$ generates the function call, $X3(s_0)$, where s_0 is the start state for parsing an S-phrase. The flow equation, $X3 = X1$, generates the function,

$$X3(s_0) = X1(s_0)$$

Concrete semantics: A source program computes a store that maps variables to strings. The *concrete collecting semantics* computes a set of stores for each program point; the collecting semantics is then abstracted so that it computes, for each program point, a single store that maps each variable to a set of strings.

The collecting semantics is overapproximated by the *data-flow semantics*, which uses flow equations to compute the set of strings denoted by each variable at each program point. In Figure 1, the data-flow semantics computes these values of variable x at the program points:

$$X0 = \{a\} \quad X2 = \{[s_1] \mid s_1 \in X1\} \quad R = \{]\} \quad X1 = X0 \cup X2 = X3$$

Let Σ name the states in the parser's *goto*-controller. A parse stack, $st \in \Sigma^+$, models those strings that parse to st. Function $\gamma : \mathcal{P}(\Sigma^+) \to \mathcal{P}(String)$ concretizes a set of parse stacks into a set of strings:

$$\gamma(S) = \{t \in String \mid s_0 :: s_1 :: \cdots :: s_k \in S \text{ and } parse(s_0, t) = s_0 :: s_1 :: \cdots :: s_k\}$$

The *abstract collecting interpretation*, $\mathcal{X}$, computes the set of parse stacks denoted by a program variable. For flow equation, $Xi = E_i$, the function, $\mathcal{X}_i : \Sigma \to \mathcal{P}(\Sigma^*)$, is defined as $\mathcal{X}_i(s) = [\![E_i]\!](s)$, where $s \in \Sigma$ and

$[\![t]\!]s = \{reduce(s, goto(s, t))\}$, where t is a terminal symbol

$[\![E_1 \sqcup E_2]\!]s = [\![E_1]\!]s \cup [\![E_2]\!]s$

$[\![Xj]\!]s = [\![E_j]\!]s$, where $Xj = E_j$ is the flow equation for Xj

$[\![E_1 \cdot E_2]\!]s = \{reduce(s, p') \mid p' \in ([\![E_1]\!]s) \oplus [\![E_2]\!]\}$,

　　where $S \oplus g = \{p :: g(top(p)) \mid p \in S\}$

where $reduce(s, p)$ reduces the final states within parse stack, $s :: p$.
　$reduce(s, p) =$
　　$t := top(p)$
　　if $t = s_m$, the final state for item, $T \to U_1 U_2 \cdots U_m\cdot$,
　　then $p' := pop(m, p)$　// pop m states, corresponding to $U_1 U_2 \cdots U_m$
　　　　$p'' := p' :: goto(top(s :: p'), T)$
　　　　return $reduce(s, p'')$　// repeat till finished
　　else return p　// t was not a final state, so nothing to reduce

Fig. 3. Abstract collecting interpretation: $\mathcal{X}_i(s) = [\![E_i]\!]s$ denotes the set of parse stacks generated by parsing the strings denoted by E_i, starting from parse state s

which itself demands a parse of the string generated at point $X1$ from state s_0:

$$X1(s_0) = X0(s_0) \cup X2(s_0)$$

The union of the parses from $X0$ and $X2$ must be computed.[1] Consider $X0(s_0)$:

---

[1] As Figure 3 indicates, the functions compute sets of parse stacks; in this motivating example, all the sets are singletons.

$$X0(s_0) = goto(s_0, \mathtt{a}) = s_2 \quad (\text{reduce: } S \to \mathtt{a})$$
$$\Rightarrow goto(s_0, S) = s_5$$

showing that a parse of string 'a' from state s_0 generates state s_2, a final state, that reduces to nonterminal S, which generates state s_5 — an S-phrase has been parsed. (The $\Rightarrow$ signifies when the parser makes a *reduce* step to a nonterminal.) The completed stack is therefore $s_0 :: s_5$. The remaining call, $X2(s_0)$, commences like this ($\oplus$ is explained two lines below):

$$X2(s_0) = (\mathtt{[} \cdot X1 \cdot R)(s_0) = goto(s_0, \mathtt{[}) \oplus (X1 \cdot R)$$
$$= s_1 \oplus (X1 \cdot R) = s_1 :: (X1(s_1) \oplus R)$$

The $\oplus$ operator sequences the parse steps: for parse stack, st, and function, E, $st \oplus E = st :: E(top(st))$, that is, the stack made by *appending* st to the stack returned by $E(top(st))$. Then, $X1(s_1) = X0(s_1) \cup X2(s_1)$ computes to s_3, and

$$X2(s_0) = s_1 :: (X1(s_1) \oplus R) = s_1 :: (s_3 \oplus R) = s_1 :: s_3 :: R(s_3)$$
$$= s_1 :: s_3 :: s_4 \quad (\text{reduce: } S \to \mathtt{[}S\mathtt{]})$$
$$\Rightarrow goto(s_0, S) = s_5$$

That is, $X2(s_0)$ built the stack, $s_1 :: s_3 :: s_4$, denoting a parse of $\mathtt{[}S\mathtt{]}$, which reduced to S, giving s_5. Here is the complete list of solved function calls:

$$X3(s_0) = X1(s_0)$$
$$X1(s_0) = X0(s_0) \cup X2(s_0) = \cdots = s_5 \cup s_5 = s_5$$
$$X0(s_0) = goto(s_0, \mathtt{a}) = s_2 \Rightarrow goto(s_0, S) = s_5$$
$$X2(s_0) = goto(s_0, \mathtt{[}) \oplus (X1 \cdot R) = s_1 :: X1(s_1) \oplus R$$
$$\qquad = \cdots = s_1 :: s_3 :: R(s_3) = s_1 :: s_3 :: s_4 \Rightarrow goto(s_0, S) = s_5$$
$$R(s_3) \;\; = goto(s_3, \mathtt{]}) = s_4$$
$$X1(s_1) = X0(s_1) \cup X2(s_1) = \cdots = s_3 \cup s_3 = s_3 \;\; (\text{see comment below})$$
$$X0(s_1) = goto(s_1, \mathtt{a}) = s_2 \Rightarrow goto(s_1, S) = s_3$$
$$X2(s_1) = goto(s_1, \mathtt{[}) \oplus (X1 \cdot R)$$
$$\qquad = s_1 :: (X1(s_1) \oplus R) = \cdots = s_1 :: s_3 :: R(s_3) \;\; (\text{see comment below})$$
$$\qquad = s_1 :: s_3 :: s_4 \Rightarrow goto(s_1, S) = s_3$$

The solution is $X3(s_0) = s_5$, validating that the strings printed at the hot spot must be S-phrases.

Each equation instance, $X_i(s_j) = E_{ij}$, is *a first-order data-flow equation*. In the example, $X1(s_1)$ and $X2(s_1)$ are mutually recursively defined, and their solutions are obtained by iteration-until-convergence. The flow-equation set is *generated dynamically while the equations are being solved*. This is a demand-driven analysis [1,7,8], called *minimal function-graph semantics* [11], computed by a worklist algorithm, described later.

5   Abstract Parse Stacks

In the previous example, the result for each $X_i(s_j)$ was a single stack. In general, a set of parse stacks can result, e.g., for

<table>
<tr><td>x = '['</td><td>$X0 = $ [</td></tr>
<tr><td>while ...</td><td>$X1 = X0 \sqcup X2$</td></tr>
<tr><td> x = x . '['</td><td>$X2 = X1 \cdot$ [</td></tr>
<tr><td> x = x . 'a' . ']'</td><td>$X3 = X1 \cdot a \cdot$]</td></tr>
</table>

at conclusion, x holds zero or more left brackets and an S-phrase; $X3(s_0)$ is the infinite set, $\{s_5,\ s_1 :: s_3,\ s_1 :: s_1 :: s_3,\ s_1 :: s_1 :: s_1 :: s_3,\ \cdots\}$.

To bound the set, we abstract it by "folding" its stacks so that no parse state repeats in a stack. Since Σ, the set of parse-state names, is finite, folding produces a finite set of finite-sized stacks (that contain cycles).

The abstract interpretation based on abstract, folded stacks is defined in Figure 4. Here is the intuition: A stack segment like $p = s_1 :: s_1$ is a linked list, a graph, $\overset{\leftarrow}{s_1} \leftarrow \overset{\leftarrow}{s_1}$, where the stack's top and bottom are marked by pointers; when we push a state, e.g., $p :: s_2$, we get $\overset{\leftarrow}{s_1} \leftarrow \overset{\leftarrow}{s_1} \leftarrow \overset{\leftarrow}{s_2}$. The folded stack is formed by merging same-state objects and retaining all links: $\overset{\curvearrowright}{\leftarrow s_1} \leftarrow \overset{\leftarrow}{s_2}$. (This can be written as the regular expression, $s_1^+ :: s_2$.) Folding can apply to multiple states, e.g., $\leftarrow \overset{}{s_6} \leftarrow \overset{}{s_7} \leftarrow \overset{}{s_6} \leftarrow \overset{}{s_7} \leftarrow \overset{}{s_6} \leftarrow \overset{}{s_8} \leftarrow$ folds to $\leftarrow \overset{}{s_6} \overset{\curvearrowright}{\leftarrow s_7} \overset{}{s_8} \leftarrow$.

The abstract interpretation of the loop program that began this section is defined with abstract stacks in Figure 5. The result, $X3(s_0) = \{s_1^+ :: s_3,\ s_5\}$, asserts that the string at $X3$ might be a well-formed S phrase, or it might contain a surplus of unmatched left brackets.

At the end of the calculation in Figure 5, the reduction of $S \rightarrow [S]$ is done on the folded stack segment, $s_1^+ :: s_3 :: s_4$, that is, the complete stack is $\overset{}{s_0} \overset{\curvearrowright}{\leftarrow s_1} \leftarrow \overset{}{s_3} \leftarrow \overset{}{s_4} \leftarrow$, meaning that three states must be popped: we traverse s_4, s_3, and s_1, and follow the links from the last state, s_1, to see what the remaining stack might be. There are two possibilities: $\overset{}{s_0} \overset{\curvearrowright}{\leftarrow s_1} \leftarrow$ and $\overset{}{s_0} \leftarrow$. We compute the result for each case, as shown in the Figure.

6   Worklist Algorithm

The algorithm that computes the solution to a hot-spot is a variation of the conventional worklist algorithm.

In the conventional worklist algorithm, there is a fixed flowgraph that indicates flows to nodes and a flow equation for each node. The initialization step builds the entire flowgraph and places demands on the worklist to calculate the value at every node in the graph. The algorithm then iterates, extracting a demand from the worklist, computing the value of that demand, and placing into the

A set of parse stacks can be soundly approximated by a single, abstract stack: For label set Σ, a Σ-*labelled graph*, g, is a tuple, $\langle nodes_g, edges_g, label_g \rangle$, where

- $nodes_g$ is a set of nodes,
- $edges_g \subseteq nodes_g \times nodes_g$ is a set of directed edges (at most one per source, target node pair),
- and $label_g : nodes_g \rightarrow \Sigma$ assigns a label to each node.

Let $Graph_\Sigma$ be the set of Σ-labelled graphs.

An *abstract stack* is a triple, (g, bot, top), such that $g \in Graph_\Sigma$ and $bot, top \in nodes_g$ mark the bottom and top nodes of the stack. Let $AbsStack_\Sigma$ be the set of abstract stacks labelled with Σ-values.

Example: the stack, $s_1 :: s_1 :: s_3$, is modeled as $(\langle \{a, b, c\}, \{(c, b), (b, a)\}, [a \mapsto s_1, b \mapsto s_1, c \mapsto s_3] \rangle, a, c)$.

An abstract stack, $(g, bot, top) \in AbsStack_\Sigma$, concretizes to a set of parse stacks:

$$\gamma(g, bot, top) = \{st \in \mathcal{P}(\Sigma^+) \mid st \text{ is a finite path through } g \text{ from } top \text{ to } bot\}$$

Two abstract stacks, $G_1 = (g_1, bot_1, top_1)$ and $G_2 = (g_2, bot_2, top_2)$, are composed by :: into the disjoint union of g_1 and g_2 plus one new edge from bot_2 to top_1:

$$G_1 :: G_2 = (\langle nodes_{g_1} \uplus nodes_{g_2},$$
$$edges_{g_1} \cup edges_{g_2} \cup \{(bot_2, top_1)\},$$
$$label_{g_1} + label_{g_2}\rangle, \ bot_1, \ top_2)$$

An abstract stack is folded (widened) by merging all nodes that share the same label, in effect, equating the nodes with the labels:

$$fold(g, bot, top) = (\langle \{s \in \Sigma \mid \exists n \in nodes_g, label_g(n) = s\},$$
$$\{(s, s') \mid \exists (n, n') \in edges_g, label_g(n) = s, label_g(n') = s'\},$$
$$\lambda s.s\rangle, \ label_g(bot), \ label_g(top))$$

The abstract interpretation of flow equation, $Xi = E_i$, is the function, $\mathcal{X}_i : \Sigma \rightarrow \mathcal{P}_{fin}(AbsStack_\Sigma)$, defined as

$$\mathcal{X}_i(s) = \{fold(p) \mid p \in [\![E_i]\!](s)\}.$$

This interpretation is sound for the abstract collecting semantics in Figure 3.

A set of abstract stacks can be further abstracted into a *single* stack of form, $Graph_\Sigma \times \mathcal{P}(\Sigma) \times \mathcal{P}(\Sigma)$, by unioning the stacks' node sets, edge sets, *bot*-values and *top*-values. The resulting "stack" is a *subgraph* of the parser's *goto*-controller.

Fig. 4. Abstract interpretation defined in terms of abstract, folded, parse stacks

---

Flow equation set generated from demand, $X3(s_0)$:

$$X0(s_0) = [(s_0) \qquad\qquad X2(s_0) = X1(s_0) \oplus [$$
$$X1(s_0) = X0(s_0) \cup X2(s_0) \qquad X3(s_0) = X1(s_0) \oplus (\mathbf{a}.])$$

Least fixed-point solution expressed with abstract parse stacks:

$X0(s_0) \;=\; [(s_0) \;=\; \{s_1\}$

Because $X1$ and $X2$ are mutually defined, we iterate to a solution, where Xi's value at iteration j is denoted Xi_j:

$X1_1(s_0) = \{s_1\} \cup \emptyset = \{s_1\}$

$X2_1(s_0) = X1_1(s_0) \oplus [= \mathit{fold}\{s_1 :: s_1\} = \{s_1^+\}$

$X1_2(s_0) = \{s_1\} \cup \{s_1^+\} = \{s_1, s_1^+\}$
$\qquad\quad\;\; = \{s_1^+\}$. (We can merge the two stack segments since the first is a prefix of the second and has the same bottom and top states.)

$X2_2(s_0) = X1_2(s_0) \oplus [= \{s_1^+ :: [(s_1)\} = \mathit{fold}\{s_1^+ :: s_1\} = \{s_1^+\}$

$X1_3(s_0) = \{s_1\} \cup \{s_1^+\} = \{s_1, s_1^+\} = \{s_1^+\} = X1_2(s_0)$

$X2_3(s_0) = \{s_1^+\} = X2_2(s_0)$

$X3(s_0) \;=\; \{s_1^+ :: \mathbf{a}(s_1) \oplus]\}$

First, $s_1^+ :: \mathbf{a}(s_1) = s_1^+ :: s_2 \Rightarrow s_1^+ :: \mathit{goto}(s_1, S) = s_1^+ :: s_3$.
$= \{s_1^+ :: s_3 ::](s_3)\} = \{s_1^+ :: s_3 :: s_4\}$
The reduction, $S \to [S]$, splits the stack into two cases:
(i) there are multiple s_1s within s_1^+; (ii) there is only one s_1:
$= (i)\{s_1^+ :: \mathit{goto}(s_1, S)\} \cup (ii)\{\mathit{goto}(s_0, S)\}$
$= \{s_1^+ :: s_3, \;\; s_5\}$

Fig. 5. Iterative solution with folded parse stacks, depicted as regular expressions

worklist new demands to evaluate those nodes whose values are affected by the one just updated. Iteration terminates when the worklist is empty [16].

In our worklist algorithm, the flowgraph is constructed while iteration is undertaken. The algorithm uses three data structures: the worklist of unresolved calls, $Xi(s_j)$; a *Cache* that maps each call to its current (partial) solution (a set of abstract parse stacks); and the flowgraph of call dependencies, which is dynamically constructed.

The algorithm is defined in the Appendix, but here is an overview: The initialization step places the initial call, $X0(s_0)$, into the worklist and into the call graph and then assigns to the cache the partial solution, $Cache[X0(s_0)] := \emptyset$. The iteration step repeats the following until the worklist is empty:

1. Extract a call, $X(s)$, from the worklist, and for the corresponding flow equation, $X = E$, compute $E(s)$, folding abstract stacks as necessary. (In the Appendix, this is done by $compute_{X(s)}(s, E)$).
2. While computing $E(s)$, if a call, $X'(s')$ is encountered, *(i)* add the dependency, $X'(s') \to X(s)$, to the call graph (if it is not already present); *(ii)* if

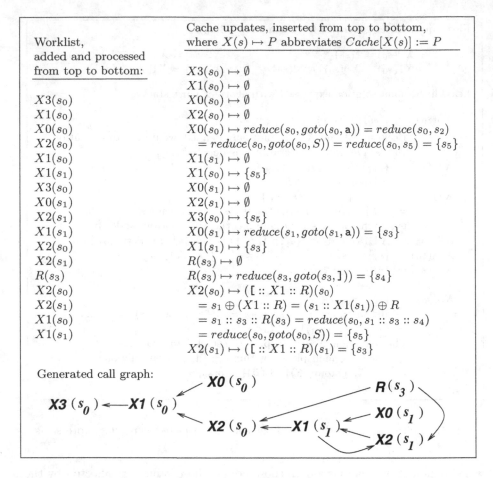

Worklist, added and processed from top to bottom:	Cache updates, inserted from top to bottom, where $X(s) \mapsto P$ abbreviates $Cache[X(s)] := P$
	$X3(s_0) \mapsto \emptyset$
	$X1(s_0) \mapsto \emptyset$
$X3(s_0)$	$X0(s_0) \mapsto \emptyset$
$X1(s_0)$	$X2(s_0) \mapsto \emptyset$
$X0(s_0)$	$X0(s_0) \mapsto reduce(s_0, goto(s_0, \mathtt{a})) = reduce(s_0, s_2)$
$X2(s_0)$	$\quad = reduce(s_0, goto(s_0, S)) = reduce(s_0, s_5) = \{s_5\}$
$X1(s_0)$	$X1(s_1) \mapsto \emptyset$
$X1(s_1)$	$X1(s_0) \mapsto \{s_5\}$
$X3(s_0)$	$X0(s_1) \mapsto \emptyset$
$X0(s_1)$	$X2(s_1) \mapsto \emptyset$
$X2(s_1)$	$X3(s_0) \mapsto \{s_5\}$
$X1(s_1)$	$X0(s_1) \mapsto reduce(s_1, goto(s_1, \mathtt{a})) = \{s_3\}$
$X2(s_0)$	$X1(s_1) \mapsto \{s_3\}$
$X2(s_1)$	$R(s_3) \mapsto \emptyset$
$R(s_3)$	$R(s_3) \mapsto reduce(s_3, goto(s_3, \mathtt{]})) = \{s_4\}$
$X2(s_0)$	$X2(s_0) \mapsto ([\ ::\ X1\ ::\ R)(s_0)$
$X2(s_1)$	$\quad = s_1 \oplus (X1\ ::\ R) = (s_1\ ::\ X1(s_1)) \oplus R$
$X1(s_0)$	$\quad = s_1\ ::\ s_3\ ::\ R(s_3) = reduce(s_0, s_1\ ::\ s_3\ ::\ s_4)$
$X1(s_1)$	$\quad = reduce(s_0, goto(s_0, S)) = \{s_5\}$
	$X2(s_1) \mapsto ([\ ::\ X1\ ::\ R)(s_1) = \{s_3\}$

Generated call graph:

Fig. 6. Worklist-algorithm calculation of call, $X3(s_0)$, in Figure 1

there is no entry for $X'(s')$ in the cache, then assign $Cache[X'(s')] := \emptyset$ and place $X'(s')$ on the worklist.

3. When $E(s)$ computes to an answer set, P, and P contains an abstract parse stack not already listed in $Cache[X(s)]$, then assign $Cache[X(s)] := (Cache[X(s)] \cup P)$ and add to the worklist all $X''(s'')$ such that the dependency, $X(s) \rightarrow X''(s'')$, appears in the flowgraph.

Figure 6 shows the worklist calculation for $X3(s_0)$ in Figure 1.

7   Input Variables

Input and nonlocal variables present the usual difficulties for a static analysis. If we require that such variables hold grammatically well-structured strings as their values, then we can use the nonterminal symbols of the reference grammar as "data types." For example, we might set the type of input variable, x, to be nonterminal S and use Figure 2 to analyze

$$\text{read}_S \text{ x} \qquad\qquad X = S$$
$$\text{y = '[' . x . ']'} \qquad Y = [\cdot X \cdot]$$

We solve the flow equations,

$$Y(s_0) = ([\cdot X \cdot])(s_0) = goto(s_0, [) \oplus (X \cdot]) = s_1 :: (X(s_1) \oplus])$$
$$X(s_1) = goto(s_1, S) = \{s_3\}$$

and compute that $Y(s_0) = s_1 :: s_3 :: goto(s_3,]) = s_1 :: s_3 :: s_4 \Rightarrow goto(s_0, S)$ $= \{s_5\}$, because we assumed that input variable x denotes a parsed S-phrase.

8 String-Update Operations

String-manipulating languages use operations like `replace` and `substring`, which can be employed foolishly or sensibly on strings that represent well-structured values. An example of the former is x = '[[a]]'; replace('a', '[', x), which replaces occurrences of 'a' in x by '[', changing x's value to the grammatically ill-formed phrase, '[[[]]'. A more sensible replacement would be replace('[a]', 'a', x), which preserves x's grammatical structure.

To validate an operation, replace(U,V,x), we require that U and V "parse the same" in every possible context where they might appear (within x): Say that replace(U,V,x) is *update-invariant for* x iff for all (nonfinal) parse states, $s \in \Sigma$, $U(s) = V(s)$. This means replacing U by V preserves x's parse.

When we analyze a program, we may first *ignore* the replace operations, treating them as "no-ops." Once the flow equations are solved, we validate the invariance of each replace(U,V,x) by generating hot-spot requests for strings U and V for all possible parse states, building on the cached results of the worklist algorithm. Finally, we compare the results to see if replace(U,V,x) is update-invariant for x. Here is an example:

$$\begin{aligned}
&\text{y = '[[[a]]]'} &&Y0 = [\cdot[\cdot[\cdot a\cdot]\cdot]\cdot] \\
&\text{x = 'a'} &&X0 = a \\
&\text{while ...} &&X1 = X0 \cup X2 \\
&\quad\text{x = '['. x .']'} &&X2 = [\cdot X1\cdot] \\
&\text{replace(x, 'a', y)} &&Y1 = replace(X1, a, Y0)
\end{aligned}$$

Say that the program must be analyzed for y's final value: $Y1(s_0)$. We initially ignore the replacement operation at $Y1$ and solve the simpler equation, $Y1(s_0) = Y0(s_0)$, instead, which quickly computes to $\{s_5\}$. Next, we analyze the replace operation by generating these hot-spot requests for all the nonfinal parse states:

$$a(s_0), X1(s_0), a(s_1), X1(s_1), a(s_3), X1(s_3)$$

For example, the first request computes to

$$a(s_0) = goto(s_0, a) = s_2 \Rightarrow goto(s_0, S) = s_5$$

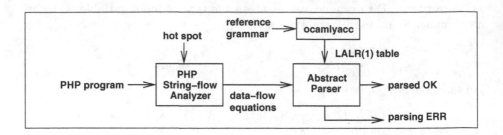

Fig. 7. Implementation

and the second repeats an earlier example,

$$X1(s_0) = X0(s_0) \cup X2(s_0)$$
$$X2(s_0) = \cdots = s_1 :: s_3 :: s_4 \Rightarrow goto(s_0, S)) = s_5$$

showing that both strings compute to the same parse-stack segments in starting context s_0. The other hot spots compute this same way. Once all the hot spots are solved, we confirm that $X1$ and a have identical outcomes for all possible parse contexts. This validates the invariance of `replace(x,'a',y)` at $Y1$, preserving the original solution.

It is important that we validate update-invariance for *all* possible contexts. Consider the reference grammar,

$$N \rightarrow a \,|\, b \,|\, [a]$$

Although both a and b are N-phrases, `replace('a','b','[a]')` violates [a]'s grammatical structure.

9   Implementation and Experiments

The abstract parser, essentially the worklist algorithm, is implemented in Objective Caml, structured as in Figure 7. The front end of Minamide's analyzer for PHP [14] was modified to accept a PHP program with a hot-spot location and to return data-flow equations with string operations for the hot spot. A parser generator, `ocamlyacc`, produces an LALR(1) parsing table for the reference grammar, and the abstract parser uses the data-flow equations and the parsing table to parse statically the strings generated by the PHP program. Since abstract parsing works directly on characters (and not tokens), the reference grammar is given at the same level, like a grammar for scannerless parsing. (Our experiment showed that the performance of character-based parsing was good enough for practical use.) The algorithm in the Appendix is defined for LR(0) grammars, but its extension to LR(1) required only minor modification.

We applied our abstract parser to publicly available PHP programs that dynamically generate HTML documents, the same suite of programs Minamide

used in his paper [14]. Experiments were done on a MacOSX with an Intel Core
2 Duo Processor (2.56GHz) and 4 GByte memory. The table below summarizes
our experiments:

	webchess	faqforge	phpwims	timeclock	schoolmate
files	21	11	30	6	54
lines	2918	1115	6606	1006	6822
no. of hot spots	6	14	30	7	1
no. of parsings	6	16	36	7	19
parsed OK	5	1	19	0	1
parsed ERR	1	15	17	7	18
no. of alarms	1	31	16	14	20
true positives	1	31	13	14	17
false positives	0	0	3	0	3
time(sec)	0.224	0.155	1.979	0.228	2.077

We manually identified the hot spots and ran our abstract parser for each hot
spot. There were multiple parsings in some hot spots, as expected. Since we do
not yet have parse-error recovery, each time a parse error was identified by our
analyzer, we located the source of the error in the program, fixed it, and tried
again until no parse errors were detected. In the case of phpwims, the number
of alarms is smaller than that of parsing errors because two parsings share the
same parsing error in control flows of this form:

> parsed ERR
> if ... then parsed OK else parsed OK;

All the false-positive alarms that appeared were caused by ignoring the tests
within conditional commands. The parsing time shown in the table is the sum
of all execution times needed to find all parsing errors for all hot spots. The
reference grammar's parse table took 1.323 seconds to construct; this is not
included in the analysis times. The alarms are classified below:

classification	occurrences
open/close tag syntax error	11
open/close tag missing	45
superfluous tag	5
improperly nested	14
misplaced tag	5
escaped character syntax error	2

All in all, our abstract parser works without limiting the nesting depth of tags,
validates the syntax reasonably fast, and is guaranteed to find all parsing errors
reducing inevitable false alarms to a minimum.

Minamide excluded one PHP application, named tagit, from his experiments
[14], since tagit generates an arbitrary nesting depth of tags. In principle, our
abstract parser should be able to validate tagit, but we also excluded tagit
from our studies because the current version of our abstract parser checks that

string-update operations satisfy the update-invariance property (cf. Section 8). Unexpectedly (to us!), so many string updates in `tagit` violated update invariance that our abstract parser generated too many false-positives to be helpful.

We can reduce false positives due to violation of update invariance by selectively employing Minamide's f.s.a.-transducer technique [14], where a string update is analyzed separately from the flow analysis with its own f.s.a. transducer. For example, the last flow equation in this program,

$$
\begin{array}{ll}
\texttt{x = 'a'} & X0 = \texttt{a} \\
\texttt{while ...} & X1 = X0 \cup X2 \\
\quad \texttt{x = '[['. x .']'} & X2 = \texttt{[} \cdot \texttt{[} \cdot X1 \cdot \texttt{]} \\
\texttt{replace('[[', '[', x)} & X3 = replace(\texttt{[[}, \texttt{[}, X1)
\end{array}
$$

could be replaced by just $X3 = X1$, and we would use a separate transducer to analyze $replace(\texttt{[[}, \texttt{[}, X1)$. We leave this as a future work.

On the other hand, one might argue that *any* string-update operator that violates update invariance is dubiously employed and deserves closer scrutiny. In this regard, the abstract parser's "false positives" are healthy warnings.

10   Conclusion

Injection and cross-site-scripting attacks can be reduced by analyzing the programs that dynamically generate documents [21]. In this paper, we have improved the precision of such analyses by employing LR-parsing technology to validate the context-free grammatical structure of generated documents.

A parse tree is but the first stage in calculating a string's meaning. The parsed string has a semantics (as enforced by its interpreter), and one can encode this semantics with semantics-processing functions, like those written for use with a parser-generator. (Tainting analysis — tracking unsanitized data — is an example semantic property that can be encoded this way.) The semantics can then be approximated by the static analysis so that abstract parsing and abstract semantic processing proceed simultaneously. This is future work.

Acknowledgements. We thank GTOne's CEO Soo-Yong Lee for inspiration and support and the anonymous referees for valuable suggestions and comments.

References

1. Agrawal, G.: Simultaneous demand-driven data-flow and call graph analysis. In: Proc. Int'l. Conf. Software Maintenance, Oxford (1999)
2. Aho, A., Ullman, J.: Principles of Compiler Design. Addison-Wesley, Reading (1977)
3. Brabrand, C., Møller, A., Schwartzbach, M.I.: The <bigwig> project. ACM Trans. Internet Technology 2 (2002)
4. Choi, T.-H., Lee, O., Kim, H., Doh, K.-G.: A practical string analyzer by the widening approach. In: Kobayashi, N. (ed.) APLAS 2006. LNCS, vol. 4279, pp. 374–388. Springer, Heidelberg (2006)

5. Christensen, A.S., Møller, A., Schwartzbach, M.I.: Static analysis for dynamic XML. In: Proc. PLAN-X 2002 (2002)
6. Christensen, A.S., Møller, A., Schwartzbach, M.I.: Extending Java for high-level web service construction. ACM TOPLAS 25 (2003)
7. Duesterwald, E., Gupta, R., Soffa, M.L.: A practical framework for demand-driven interprocedural data flow analysis. ACM TOPLAS 19, 992–1030 (1997)
8. Horwitz, S., Reps, T., Sagiv, M.: Demand interprocedural dataflow analysis. In: Proc. 3rd ACM SIGSOFT Symp. Foundations of Software Engg. (1995)
9. Hosoya, H.: XDuce: A typed XML processing language. Technical Report (2008), http://xduce.sourceforge.net/
10. Hosoya, H., Vouillon, J., Pierce, B.C.: Regular expression types for XML. ACM TOPLAS 27, 46–90 (2005)
11. Jones, N.D., Mycroft, A.: Data flow analysis of applicative programs using minimal function graphs. In: Proc. 13th Symp. POPL, pp. 296–306. ACM Press, New York (1986)
12. Jovanovich, N., Kruegel, C., Kirda, E.: Pixy: A static analysis tool for detecting web application vulnerabilities. In: Proc. IEEE Symp. on Security and Privacy, pp. 258–263 (2006)
13. Kirkegaard, C., Møller, A.: Static analysis for Java Servlets and JSP. In: Yi, K. (ed.) SAS 2006. LNCS, vol. 4134, pp. 336–352. Springer, Heidelberg (2006)
14. Minamide, Y.: Static approximation of dynamically generated web pages. In: Proc. 14th ACM Int'l Conf. on the World Wide Web, pp. 432–441 (2005)
15. Minimide, Y., Tozawa, A.: XML validation for context-free grammars. In: Kobayashi, N. (ed.) APLAS 2006. LNCS, vol. 4279, pp. 357–373. Springer, Heidelberg (2006)
16. Nielson, F., Nielson, H.R., Hankin, C.: Principles of Program Analysis. Springer, Heidelberg (1999)
17. Nishiyama, T., Minimide, Y.: A translation from the HTML DTD into a regular hedge grammar. In: Ibarra, O.H., Ravikumar, B. (eds.) CIAA 2008. LNCS, vol. 5148, pp. 122–131. Springer, Heidelberg (2008)
18. Thiemann, P.: Grammar-based analysis of string expressions. In: Proc. ACM workshop Types in languages design and implementation, pp. 59–70 (2005)
19. Wassermann, G., Gould, C., Su, Z., Devanbu, P.: Static checking of dymanically generated queries in database applications. ACM Trans. Software Engineering and Methodology 16(4), 1–27 (2007)
20. Wassermann, G., Su, Z.: The essence of command injection attacks in web applications. In: Proc. 33d ACM POPL, pp. 372–382 (2006)
21. Wassermann, G., Su, Z.: Sound and precise analysis of web applications for injection vulnerabilities. In: Proc. ACM PLDI, pp. 32–41 (2007)
22. Xie, Y., Aiken, A.: Static detection of security vulnerabilities in scripting languages. In: Proc. 15th USENIX Security Symp. (2006)

Appendix: Worklist Algorithm

Input:
- controller (*goto* function) for parser;
- flow-equation schemes, $\{X_i = E_i\}_{0 < i \leq n}$;
- initial demand, $X_0(s_0)$.

Data structures:

- $W \in Call^* =$ worklist of demands (calls) of form, $X_j(s)$, $s \in ParseState$;
- F: dynamically generated call graph, consisting of arcs of form, $X(s) \to X'(s')$, read as, "$X(s)$'s value flows to $X'(s')$";
- $Cache : Call \to \mathcal{P}(AbsStack)$: dynamic array mapping calls to sets of abstract stacks, where
  $AbsStack =$ graphs whose nodes are $ParseStates$, such that one node is marked the stack bottom and another the stack top.
  There is a unique entry, $Cache[X(s)] := P$, in the cache array iff the node, $X(s)$, appears in F.

Algorithm:
1. *Initialize:* $W := [X_0(s_0)]$; $F := \{X_0(s_0)\}$; $Cache[X_0(s_0)] := \emptyset$

2. *Iterate:*   while $W \neq []$ do :
$\qquad X(s) := head(W)$; $W := tail(W)$;
$\qquad$ let $X = E$ be the flow equation that matches $X(s)$;
$\qquad P := compute_{X(s)}(s, E)$;   (see below)
$\qquad$ if $P \not\subseteq Cache[X(s)]$
$\qquad$ then $Cache[X(s)] := Cache[X(s)] \cup P$;
$\qquad\qquad$ forall $X'(s')$ such that $X(s) \to X'(s') \in F$,
$\qquad\qquad\qquad W := W + [X'(s')]$;

where $compute_{Call} : ParseState \times FlowExpression \to \mathcal{P}(AbsStack)$ is
$compute_c\ (s, a) = return\ reduce(s, goto(s, a))$
$compute_c(s, E_1 \sqcup E_2) = return\ compute_c(s, E_1) \cup compute_c(s, E_2)$
$compute_c\ (s, X) =$
$\qquad$ if $Cache[X(s)]$ is undefined (has no entry),
$\qquad$ then $Cache[X(s)] := \emptyset$;
$\qquad\qquad$ add the edge, $X(s) \to c$, to F;
$\qquad\qquad W := W + [X(s)]$;
$\qquad$ if $c < X$ (that is, $c \to X(s)$ is a program back-arc),
$\qquad$ then return $fold(Cache[X(s)])$
$\qquad$ else return $Cache[X(s)]$
$compute_c\ (s, E_1 \cdot E_2) =$
$\qquad P := \bigcup\{p \oplus E_2 \mid p \in compute_c(s, E_1)\}$
$\qquad$ where $p \oplus E_2 = \{p :: p' \mid p' \in compute_c(top(p), E_2)\}$
$\qquad$ return $\bigcup\{reduce(s, p'') \mid p'' \in P\}$

Auxiliary function $reduce(s, p)$ reduces parse stack, $s :: p$, as needed, never popping stack bottom, s. If the stack needs no reduction, $reduce(s, p) = \{p\}$:
$reduce : ParseState \times AbsStack \to \mathcal{P}(AbsStack)$
$reduce(s, p) = \quad t := top(p)$;
$\qquad$ if $t = s_m$, a final state for item, $T \to U_1 U_2 \cdots U_m$,
$\qquad\qquad$ and the path, $s_1 \leftarrow s_2 \leftarrow \cdots \leftarrow s_m = top(p)$ in p matches the item,
$\qquad$ then
$\qquad\qquad newTops := \{s' \mid s' \leftarrow s_1 \in p\}$ // the predecessor states to s_1 in p
$\qquad\qquad$ if $newTops = \emptyset$, // popped stack empty?
$\qquad\qquad$ then $R := \{goto(s, T)\}$
$\qquad\qquad$ else $poppedStacks := \{p$ with s' marked as top $\mid s' \in newTops\}$
$\qquad\qquad\qquad R := \{p' :: goto(top(p'), T) \mid p' \in poppedStacks\}$ // "split" the stacks
$\qquad\qquad$ return $\bigcup\{reduce(s, p'') \mid p'' \in R\}$ // repeat till finished
$\qquad$ else return $\{p\}$ // t not a final state, nothing to reduce

Creating Transformations for Matrix Obfuscation

Stephen Drape and Irina Voiculescu

Oxford University Computing Laboratory,
Wolfosn Building, Parks Road,
Oxford, UK, OX1 3QD
{sjd,irina}@comlab.ox.ac.uk

Abstract. There are many programming situations where it would be convenient to conceal the meaning of code, or the meaning of certain variables. This can be achieved through program transformations which are grouped under the term *obfuscation*. Obfuscation is one of a number of techniques that can be employed to protect sensitive areas of code. This paper presents obfuscation methods for the purpose of concealing the meaning of matrices by changing the pattern of the elements.

We give two separate methods: one which, through splitting a matrix, changes its size and shape, and one which, through a change of basis in a ring of polynomials, changes the values of the matrix and any patterns formed by these. Furthermore, the paper illustrates how matrices can be used in order to obfuscate a scalar value. This is an improvement on previous methods for matrix obfuscation because we will provide a range of techniques which can be used in concert.

This paper considers obfuscations as data refinements. Thus we consider obfuscations at a more abstract level without worrying about implementation issues. For our obfuscations, we can construct proofs of correctness easily. We show how the refinement approach enables us to generalise and combine existing obfuscations. We then evaluate our methods by considering how our obfuscations perform under certain relevant program analysis-based attacks.

Keywords: Obfuscation, Matrix Operations, Information Hiding, Program Transformations.

1 Introduction

An *obfuscation* is a behaviour-preserving program transformation whose aim is to make an input program "harder to understand". The landmark paper by Collberg et al. [6] gives a range of transformations which can be used as obfuscating transformations. The purpose of such transformations is to decrease the opportunities for a user to reverse engineer a commercially supplied program [1,6]. In this paper, we interpret "harder to understand" as keeping some information secret for as long as possible from some set of adversaries.

After the proof of Barak et al. [1], there seems little hope of designing a perfectly-secure software black-box, for any broad class of programs. To date,

J. Palsberg and Z. Su (Eds.): SAS 2009, LNCS 5673, pp. 273–292, 2009.

no one has devised an alternative to Barak's model, in which we would be able to derive proofs of security for systems of practical interest. These theoretical difficulties do not lessen practical interest in obfuscation, nor should they prevent us from placing appropriate levels of reliance on obfuscated systems in cases where the alternative of a hardware black-box is infeasible or uneconomic [10].

The view of obfuscation from Collberg *et al.* [6] concentrates on concrete data structures such as variables and arrays. However, the thesis of Drape [8] viewed obfuscations at a more abstract level by considering an abstract data-type and defining operations for this data-type — thus we should obfuscate the data-type according to these operations. This work had lead to the development of the specification of obfuscations for imperative programs [10] and for creating obfuscations which impede the effectiveness of program slicing [18].

The focus of this paper consists of a data-type for finite matrices having four operations: scalar multiplication, addition, transposition and multiplication, specified mathematically. We use data refinement [7] to provide a way of proving the correctness of our obfuscated operations. Thus we are guaranteed that our obfuscations are behaviour-preserving. We will review a previous matrix obfuscation, called matrix splitting [8], and we will discuss problems with this obfuscation. We will then describe a new technique for matrix obfuscation and we also show how matrices can be used to obfuscate another data-type. Since we consider our operations at a more abstract level than program code, we will be able to discuss how we can generalise our obfuscations.

The notion of "harder to understand" can be a little vague as it is not easy to measure — the creation of a suitable measure of the quality of an obfuscation is an open problem. When creating obfuscations we will make reference to an attack model including what analysis techniques we expect to perform. In the work of Majumdar *et al.* [18], the obfuscations were created with the intention of trying to protect against an attacker armed with a program slicer. In this paper, we adopt the attack model of Drape [8] in which, when defining data-types, we also specify a set of assertions which are true for the operations of that data-type. According to [8], the comparison between the assertions proofs for unobfuscated and obfuscated operations gives a measure of the effectiveness of the obfuscation. In this paper, we do not show such proofs but example proofs for various data-types can be found in [8].

2 Preliminaries

In this section we will discuss how we can prove the correctness of our obfuscations and we will define a data-type for matrices.

2.1 Obfuscation as Data Refinement

In Drape's thesis [8], data obfuscation was considered as a data refinement [7]. Suppose that a data-type D is obfuscated using an obfuscation $\mathcal{O}$ to produce a data-type E. Under the refinement approach, an abstraction function

$$af :: E \to D$$

and a data-type invariant *dti* are needed such that, for $x :: D$ and $y :: E$:

$$x \rightsquigarrow y \iff (x = af(y)) \wedge dti(y) \tag{1}$$

The term $x \rightsquigarrow y$ is read as "*x is obfuscated by y*".

For a function $f :: D \to D$, an obfuscated function $f^{\mathcal{O}}$ is correct with respect to f if it satisfies:

$$(\forall x :: D; y :: E) \; x \rightsquigarrow y \Rightarrow f(x) \rightsquigarrow f^{\mathcal{O}}(y)$$

Using Equation (1) we can rewrite this as

$$f \cdot af = af \cdot f^{\mathcal{O}} \tag{2}$$

The abstraction function *af* is surjective and so we have a function $cf :: D \to E$, called the conversion function, which satisfies $af \cdot cf = id$. Thus we can rewrite Equation (2) to obtain:

$$f = af \cdot f^{\mathcal{O}} \cdot cf \tag{3}$$

and we can use this equation to prove the correctness of $f^{\mathcal{O}}$.

If we also have that $cf \cdot af = id$ then we can rewrite Equation (2) to obtain:

$$f^{\mathcal{O}} = cf \cdot f \cdot af \tag{4}$$

Thus when *af* is bijective then we can use Equation (4) to give us a way of deriving an obfuscated operation $f^{\mathcal{O}}$ from the original operation f.

2.2 Matrices

A matrix is an array of numbers which are arranged in a meaningful tabular form. It is usually two-dimensional and can have any width and height. It is also possible to use multi-dimensional matrices and, even though these are harder to write down, it is fairly easy to manipulate them in a computer program.

The matrix **M** which has r rows and c columns (for natural numbers r and c) will be denoted by $\mathbf{M}^{r \times c}$. The element of **M** that is located at row i and column j will be written as $\mathbf{M}(i, j)$, and, for simplicity, assumed to be rational. The operation $dim(\mathbf{M})$ returns the dimensions of **M**.

In Figure 1 we define a data-type for matrices — for the rest of the paper we will suppose that *Matrix* α is $\mathbb{Q}^{r \times c}$ which denotes matrices with r rows and c columns with rational number elements. From our data-type, we would like to obfuscate matrices with the following matrix operations: *scalar multiplication, addition, transposition* and *multiplication*. In the lower part of Figure 1 we have a possible (but not complete) set of assertions. As we stated in Section 1, we should aim to obfuscate our operations with the intention that they make the proofs of correctness for assertions harder.

Note that for addition the matrices must have the same size and for multiplication we need the matrices to be *conformable*, i.e. the number of columns of the first is equal to the number of rows in the second. We can define the operations

---

Matrix (α)

---

scale :: $\alpha \rightarrow Matrix\ \alpha \rightarrow Matrix\ \alpha$
add :: $Matrix\ \alpha \times Matrix\ \alpha \rightarrow Matrix\ \alpha$
transpose :: $Matrix\ \alpha \rightarrow Matrix\ \alpha$
mult :: $Matrix\ \alpha \times Matrix\ \alpha \rightarrow Matrix\ \alpha$

---

transpose $\cdot$ transpose $= id$
transpose $\cdot$ (scale s) $=$ (scale s) $\cdot$ transpose
transpose (mult($\mathbf{M}, \mathbf{N}$)) $=$ mult (transpose $\mathbf{N}$, transpose $\mathbf{M}$)
add($\mathbf{M}, \mathbf{N}$) $=$ add($\mathbf{N}, \mathbf{M}$)

Fig. 1. A data-type for Matrices

element-wise in the usual way. We assume that basic arithmetic operations take constant time and so the computational complexities of add($\mathbf{M}, \mathbf{N}$), scale s $\mathbf{M}$ and transpose $\mathbf{M}$ are all $r \times c$ and the complexity of mult($\mathbf{M}, \mathbf{P}$) is $r \times c \times d$ where $(r, c) = dim(\mathbf{M}) = dim(\mathbf{N})$ and $(c, d) = dim(\mathbf{P})$.

Matrices are used for a wide variety of applications such as solving systems of equations, wavelets, graph theory and graphics. There are applications when it is desirable to hide the meaning of a matrix. One such case is when, in expressing a rigid body transformation by way of a matrix, the matrix has a particular structure. For example, the two-dimensional translation of an object by displacements (d_x, d_y) is usually written in the form

$$\begin{pmatrix} 1 & 0 & d_x \\ 0 & 1 & d_y \\ 0 & 0 & 1 \end{pmatrix}$$

Should somebody wish to hide the fact that a particular matrix is a translation matrix, they should aim to design an obfuscation method which changes not only the values, but also the visible pattern of these values.

3 Splitting Method

Now that we have defined our data-type for matrices and given equations for proving the correctness of matrix obfuscations we are ready to discuss our first obfuscation technique. Collberg *et al.* [6] discuss an obfuscation called an *array split*. This obfuscation was generalised in Drape [9] and so we can apply the concept of splitting to other data-types such as matrices.

3.1   Defining a Matrix Split

Suppose that we want to split a matrix $\mathbf{M}^{r \times c}$ into n matrices, called the *split components*,

$$\mathbf{M} \rightsquigarrow \langle \mathbf{M}_0, \ldots, \mathbf{M}_{n-1} \rangle_{sp}$$

where $\mathbf{M}_i$ has size $r_i \times c_i$ for $i : [0..n)$.

For this characterisation, $\mathbf{M}$ is represented by n matrices using a split, called sp, which consists of a *choice function*:

$$ch :: [0..r) \times [0..c) \rightarrow [0..n)$$

and a family $\mathcal{F}$ of injective functions where $\mathcal{F} = \{f_t\}_{t:[0..n)}$ such that for each t:

$$f_t :: ch^{-1}\{t\} \rightarrowtail [0..r_t) \times [0..c_t)$$

We define the relationship between $\mathbf{M}$ and the split components element-wise by using the choice function and the appropriate function from $\mathcal{F}$ to decide where an element is mapped to:

$$\mathbf{M}_t(f_t(i, j)) = \mathbf{M}(i, j) \text{ where } t = ch(i, j) \tag{5}$$

The requirement that we have a family of injective functions ensures that we can recover a matrix (and thus its properties) from the split components.

Equation (5) can be considered to be the definition of a conversion function and so for a matrix split

$$cf(\mathbf{M}(i, j)) = \mathbf{M}_t(f_t(i, j)) \qquad \text{where } t = ch(i, j) \tag{6}$$

The corresponding abstraction function for some split component $\mathbf{M}_t$ is

$$af(\mathbf{M}_t(i, j)) = \mathbf{M}(f_t^{-1}(i, j)) \tag{7}$$

where $f_t^{-1} \cdot f_t = id$ (which is valid as f_t is injective). Using these definitions we can check that $af \cdot cf = id$.

As an example, consider how we could define a split in which a matrix $\mathbf{M}^{r \times 2c}$ is split vertically into two matrices $\mathbf{M}_0^{r \times c}$ and $\mathbf{M}_1^{r \times c}$. The choice function is defined to be

$$ch(i, j) = j \text{ div } c$$

and the family of functions is:

$$\mathcal{F} = \{f_t = (\lambda\,(i, j)\,.\,(i, j \bmod c)) \,|\, t = 0 \lor t = 1\}$$

The process of splitting a matrix is analogous to the concept of a *partitioned* (or *block*) matrix discussed by Horn and Johnson [15] in which a matrix can be represented by a sequence of smaller submatrices.

3.2   Splitting in Squares

We now describe a simple matrix split that splits a square matrix into four matrices — two of which are square. Suppose that we have a square matrix $\mathbf{M}^{r \times r}$ and choose a positive integer k such that $k < r$. The choice function $ch(i, j)$ is defined as

$$ch(i, j) = 2\,sgn\,(i\ \text{div}\ k) + sgn\,(j\ \text{div}\ k)$$

where sgn is the signum function. The family of functions $\mathcal{F}$ is defined to be

$$\mathcal{F} = \{f_p = (\lambda\,(i, j)\,.\,(i - k\,(p\ \text{div}\ 2),\ j - k\,(p\ \text{mod}\ 2))) \mid p \in [0..3]\}$$

We call this split the $(k \times k)$-*square split* since the first component of the split is a $k \times k$ square matrix.

So if

$$\mathbf{M}(i, j) = \mathbf{M}_t(f_t(i, j)) \text{ where } t = ch(i, j)$$

then we can write

$$\mathbf{M}^{n \times n} \rightsquigarrow \langle \mathbf{M}_0^{k \times k}, \mathbf{M}_1^{k \times (n-k)}, \mathbf{M}_2^{(n-k) \times k}, \mathbf{M}_3^{(n-k) \times (n-k)} \rangle_{s_k}$$

where the subscript s_k denotes the $(k \times k)$-square split. Using this split, how can we define our matrix operations given in Figure 1?

The operations for scale and add are fairly straightforward. If

$$\mathbf{M} \rightsquigarrow \langle \mathbf{M}_0, \ldots, \mathbf{M}_3 \rangle_{s_k} \quad \text{and} \quad \mathbf{N} \rightsquigarrow \langle \mathbf{N}_0, \ldots, \mathbf{N}_3 \rangle_{s_k}$$

then

$$\text{scale } s\ \mathbf{M} \rightsquigarrow \langle \text{scale } s\ \mathbf{M}_0, \ldots, \text{scale } s\ \mathbf{M}_3 \rangle_{s_k}$$
$$\text{add}(\mathbf{M}, \mathbf{N}) \rightsquigarrow \langle \text{add}(\mathbf{M}_0, \mathbf{N}_0), \ldots, \text{add}(\mathbf{M}_3, \mathbf{N}_3) \rangle_{s_k}$$

The proofs for these definitions can be found in [8]. Also in [8] it was shown that

$$\mathbf{M}^T \rightsquigarrow \langle \mathbf{M}_0^T, \mathbf{M}_2^T, \mathbf{M}_1^T, \mathbf{M}_3^T \rangle_{s_k}$$

which corresponds to the following property for partitioned matrices:

$$\begin{pmatrix} \mathbf{M}_0\ \mathbf{M}_1 \\ \mathbf{M}_2\ \mathbf{M}_3 \end{pmatrix}^T = \begin{pmatrix} \mathbf{M}_0^T\ \mathbf{M}_2^T \\ \mathbf{M}_1^T\ \mathbf{M}_3^T \end{pmatrix}$$

The obfuscated operation has complexity $n \times n$.

Finally let us consider how we can multiply split matrices. Let

$$\mathbf{M}^{n \times n} \rightsquigarrow \langle \mathbf{M}_0,\ \mathbf{M}_1,\ \mathbf{M}_2,\ \mathbf{M}_2 \rangle_{s_k}$$
$$\mathbf{N}^{n \times n} \rightsquigarrow \langle \mathbf{N}_0,\ \mathbf{N}_1,\ \mathbf{N}_2,\ \mathbf{N}_3 \rangle_{s_k}$$

By considering the partitioned matrix product

$$\begin{pmatrix} \mathbf{M}_0\ \mathbf{M}_1 \\ \mathbf{M}_2\ \mathbf{M}_3 \end{pmatrix} \times \begin{pmatrix} \mathbf{N}_0\ \mathbf{N}_1 \\ \mathbf{N}_2\ \mathbf{N}_3 \end{pmatrix}$$

we obtain the following result:

$$\mathbf{M} \times \mathbf{N} \rightsquigarrow \langle (\mathbf{M}_0 \times \mathbf{N}_0) + (\mathbf{M}_1 \times \mathbf{N}_2), \ (\mathbf{M}_0 \times \mathbf{N}_1) + (\mathbf{M}_1 \times \mathbf{N}_3),$$
$$(\mathbf{M}_2 \times \mathbf{N}_0) + (\mathbf{M}_3 \times \mathbf{N}_2), \ (\mathbf{M}_2 \times \mathbf{N}_1) + (\mathbf{M}_3 \times \mathbf{N}_3) \rangle_{s_k}$$

The computation of $\mathbf{M} \times \mathbf{N}$ using normal matrix multiplication requires n^3 element multiplications. If we multiply the split matrices, does this calculation require more multiplications? If we use the definition of split matrices to add up the number of multiplications required by each component then we find that the total number of multiplications is still n^3.

3.3   Review of Matrix Splitting

Using our matrix split, we have seen that we can easily define obfuscated operations for our matrix data-type. All of the obfuscated operations have a similar complexity to the original versions. Since the matrix split is a generalisation of an array split then we could use matrix splits as obfuscation for arrays. We could do this by folding an array into a matrix, splitting the matrix and then flattening the components back into arrays.

For our matrix data-type (defined in Figure 1) we considered four matrix operations. Could we define obfuscations for other matrix operations? Computing inverses and determinants for dense matrices which have been split can prove to be difficult. We can, however, define obfuscations of these operations using results for partitioned matrices — we omit the details here.

4   Using the Bernstein Basis

We have seen that we can obfuscate a matrix by splitting it into many matrices. We can easily define obfuscations for simple operations but it is harder to define obfuscations for calculating inverses and determinants. We will now define an obfuscation that is based on the fact that the elements of a two-dimensional matrix can be used to define the coefficients of a bivariate polynomial.

We denote by $\mathcal{P}[x, y]$ the set of polynomials of variables x and y, with rational coefficients. For a given $n \in \mathbb{N}$, there are several ways to define bases for the ring of degree-n polynomials (see, for example, Lorentz [17]). One is the power basis $\left(1 \ x \ \ldots \ x^n\right)$ and another is the Bernstein basis $\left(B_0^n(x) \ B_1^n(x) \ \ldots \ B_n^n(x)\right)$ where $B_k^n(x) = \binom{n}{k} x^k (1 - x)^{n-k}$, $\forall x \in [0, 1]$, $k = 0, \ldots, n$ are the corresponding Bernstein Polynomials [3].

4.1   Power-Form and Bernstein-Form Polynomials

A power-form polynomial $p \in \mathcal{P}[x, y]$ of degree $m \in \mathbb{N}$ in x and $n \in \mathbb{N}$ in y is given by:

$$p(x, y) = \sum_{i=0}^{m} \sum_{j=0}^{n} a_{ij} x^i y^j, \tag{8}$$

where $a_{ij} \in \mathbb{Q}$. For given $m, n \in \mathbb{N}$ there are $m+1$ univariate degree-m Bernstein polynomials in x, and $n+1$ univariate degree-n Bernstein polynomials in y. Any bivariate power-form polynomial can be represented on the interval $[0, 1]$ using its equivalent Bernstein form as

$$p_\mathcal{B}(x, y) = \sum_{i=0}^{m} \sum_{j=0}^{n} c_{ij} B_i^m(x) B_j^n(y) \qquad (9)$$

where c_{ij} are the Bernstein coefficients corresponding to the degree-n base. The two representations $p(x, y)$ and $p_\mathcal{B}(x, y)$ are equivalent and it is possible to convert one into the other. In the case of bivariate polynomials this conversion requires some care and is based on the univariate case shown by Farouki and Rajan [11].

The polynomials in Equations (8) and (9) can also be written as matrix multiplications:

$$p(x, y) = \begin{pmatrix} 1 & x & \dots & x^m \end{pmatrix} \begin{pmatrix} a_{00} & \dots & a_{0n} \\ \vdots & \ddots & \vdots \\ a_{m0} & \dots & a_{mn} \end{pmatrix} \begin{pmatrix} 1 \\ y \\ \vdots \\ y^n \end{pmatrix} = \mathbf{X} \mathbf{A} \mathbf{Y}$$

$$p_\mathcal{B}(x, y) = \begin{pmatrix} B_0^m(x) & B_1^m(x) & \dots & B_m^m(x) \end{pmatrix} \begin{pmatrix} c_{00} & \dots & c_{0n} \\ \vdots & \ddots & \vdots \\ c_{m0} & \dots & c_{mn} \end{pmatrix} \begin{pmatrix} B_0^n(y) \\ B_1^n(y) \\ \vdots \\ B_n^n(y) \end{pmatrix} = \mathbf{B}_m^X \mathbf{C} \mathbf{B}_n^Y$$

Rewriting the vector $\mathbf{B}_m^X$ of Bernstein polynomials in terms of matrix multiplication gives:

$$\begin{aligned} \mathbf{B}_m^X &= \begin{pmatrix} B_0^m(x) & B_1^m(x) & \dots & B_m^m(x) \end{pmatrix} \\ &= \begin{pmatrix} \binom{m}{0}(1-x)^m & \dots & \binom{m}{m}x^m \end{pmatrix} \\ &= \begin{pmatrix} \binom{m}{0}\left(1 + \binom{m}{1}(-x) + \dots + \binom{m}{m}(-x)^m\right) & \dots & \binom{m}{m}x^m \end{pmatrix} \end{aligned}$$

$$= \underbrace{\begin{pmatrix} 1 & x & \dots & x^m \end{pmatrix}}_{X} \underbrace{\begin{pmatrix} 1 & & & \mathbf{O} \\ \binom{m}{0}\binom{m}{1}(-1)^1 & \binom{m}{1}\binom{m-1}{0}(-1)^0 & & \\ \vdots & & \ddots & \\ \binom{m}{0}\binom{m}{m}(-1)^m & \binom{m}{1}\binom{m-1}{m-1}(-1)^{m-1} & \dots & \binom{m}{m}\binom{m-m}{0}(-1)^0 \end{pmatrix}}_{U_m}$$

$$= \mathbf{X} \mathbf{U}_m, \qquad \forall x \in [0, 1].$$

So $$\mathbf{B}_m^X = \mathbf{X} \mathbf{U}_m$$

Similarly $$\mathbf{B}_n^Y = \mathbf{V}_n \mathbf{Y}$$

and $$p_\mathcal{B}(x, y) = \mathbf{B}_m^X \mathbf{C} \mathbf{B}_n^Y = \mathbf{X} \mathbf{U}_m \mathbf{C} \mathbf{V}_n \mathbf{Y}$$

Now we can compute the Bernstein coefficients matrix $\mathbf{C}$:

$$\mathbf{X}\,\mathbf{A}\,\mathbf{Y} = \mathbf{X}\,\mathbf{U}_m\,\mathbf{C}\,\mathbf{V}_n\,\mathbf{Y}$$
$$\mathbf{C} = (\mathbf{U}_m)^{-1}\,\mathbf{A}\,(\mathbf{V}_n)^{-1} \qquad \forall x, y \in [0, 1]$$

4.2   Bernstein Coefficients and Obfuscation of Matrices

The correspondence shown in Section 4.1 between the matrix of a polynomial's power-form coefficients and that of the Bernstein-form coefficients of the same polynomial is unique, because they represent the same element in the ring of polynomials. We have also shown that the transformation between the matrix representations is well-defined.

$(\forall \mathbf{A} \in \mathbb{Q}^{\alpha \times \beta})\ (\exists!\ p \in \mathcal{P}[x, y]$ of degree $\alpha - 1$ in x and $\beta - 1$ in $y)\quad p = \mathbf{X}\,\mathbf{A}\,\mathbf{Y}$
Furthermore $(\exists!\ \mathbf{C} \in \mathbb{Q}^{\alpha \times \beta})\quad p = p_\mathcal{B} = \mathbf{X}\,\mathbf{U}_{\alpha-1}\,\mathbf{C}\,\mathbf{V}_{\beta-1}\,\mathbf{Y}$

Thus $\mathbf{C}$ is the matrix of coefficients of the Bernstein-form polynomial $p_\mathcal{B}$. We will call the operation that transforms $\mathbf{A}$ into $\mathbf{C}$ the *Bernstein Obfuscation* of $\mathbf{A}$, thus $\mathbf{A} \rightsquigarrow \mathbf{C}$. For matrix $\mathbf{S}$ the abstraction function af for this obfuscation is:

$$af(\mathbf{S}) = \mathbf{U}_a\,\mathbf{S}\,\mathbf{V}_b \qquad \text{where } (a + 1, b + 1) = dim(\mathbf{S}) \qquad (10)$$

We can also define a conversion function cf as follows:

$$cf(\mathbf{S}) = \mathbf{U}_a^{-1}\,\mathbf{S}\,\mathbf{V}_b^{-1} \qquad \text{where } (a + 1, b + 1) = dim(\mathbf{S}) \qquad (11)$$

It is straightforward to show that these functions are bijections.

4.3   Bernstein Example

Using the formulae in Section 4.1, it is possible to work out the Bernstein form of a polynomial given in power form. Let us take the two-dimensional translation matrix defined in Section 2.2

$$\mathbf{A} = \begin{pmatrix} 1 & 0 & d_x \\ 0 & 1 & d_y \\ 0 & 0 & 1 \end{pmatrix}$$

The corresponding Bernstein-form matrix is

$$\mathbf{C} = \mathbf{U}_2^{-1}\mathbf{A}\mathbf{V}_2^{-1} = \begin{pmatrix} 1 & 1 & 1 + d_x \\ 1 & \frac{5}{4} & \frac{3}{2} + d_x + \frac{1}{2}d_y \\ 1 & \frac{3}{2} & 3 + d_x + d_y \end{pmatrix}$$

It is easy to verify that the polynomials corresponding to $\mathbf{A}$ and $\mathbf{C}$ are the same, that is $\mathbf{X}\,\mathbf{A}\,\mathbf{Y} = \mathbf{X}\,\mathbf{U}_2\,\mathbf{C}\,\mathbf{V}_2\,\mathbf{Y}$. We can see that this obfuscation conceals the fact that $\mathbf{C}$ represents a translation.

4.4   Operations for the Bernstein Obfuscation

Now that we have an obfuscation for matrices we can define obfuscations for our matrix operations (given in Figure 1). If op denotes a matrix operation then $\text{op}_\mathcal{B}$ will denote the Bernstein obfuscated operation. In the following definitions, for matrix $\mathbf{S}$ we assume $dim(\mathbf{S}) = (a + 1, b + 1)$.

We can use Equation (4) to derive the Bernstein obfuscated scalar multiplication (we omit the details). We find that $\text{scale}_\mathcal{B} \, \mathbf{S} = \text{scale} \, \mathbf{S}$ and so the operation is unchanged by the obfuscation.

In Appendix A.2 we prove that for a matrix $\mathbf{S}$

$$\text{transpose}_\mathcal{B}(\mathbf{S}) = \mathbf{U}_b^{-1} \, \mathbf{V}_b^{T} \, \mathbf{S}^{T} \, \mathbf{U}_a^{T} \, \mathbf{V}_a^{-1}$$

When performing matrix splits, it was hard to write an obfuscation for matrix inversion. However using the Bernstein obfuscation we are able to write such an obfuscation. For some square obfuscated matrix $\mathbf{S}$:

$$\text{inverse}_\mathcal{B}(\mathbf{S}) = \mathbf{U}_a^{-1} \, \mathbf{V}_a^{-1} \, \mathbf{S}^{-1} \, \mathbf{U}_a^{-1} \, \mathbf{V}_a^{-1}$$

We omit the details of the proof.

We also found it difficult, for split matrices, to define a determinant operation. However, in Appendix A.2, we derive the following obfuscation of the determinant operation under the Bernstein operation:

$$\text{det}_\mathcal{B}(\mathbf{S}) = \det(\mathbf{U}_a) \times \det(\mathbf{S}) \times \det(\mathbf{V}_b)$$

As with scalar multiplication, matrix addition is unchanged under the Bernstein obfuscation:

$$\text{add}_\mathcal{B}(\mathbf{S}, \mathbf{T}) = \mathbf{S} + \mathbf{T}$$

We omit the details of the proof.

Finally, we can derive an obfuscation for matrix multiplication

$$\text{mult}_\mathcal{B}(\mathbf{S}, \mathbf{T}) = \mathbf{S} \, \mathbf{V}_b \, \mathbf{U}_b \, \mathbf{T}$$

This derivation can be found in Appendix A.3.

4.5   Review of the Bernstein Obfuscation

In Section 4.4 we stated that determinants and inverses of matrices can be computed easily when matrices have been obfuscated using the Bernstein method — this is an immediate advantage of this method over the matrix splitting method.

One drawback of obfuscating matrices with the Bernstein method is, as shown in Section 4.4, that when scaling and adding matrices, the operations themselves are not obfuscated. This slight disadvantage is clearly outweighed by the method's major advantage, namely that the obfuscated matrices have an entirely different structure from the original entities. Any symmetry or other patterns are shuffled in the transformation, thus making it difficult for an attacker to guess their original meaning. This obfuscation technique would work with any change of basis transformation, which would help to strengthen this technique by allowing us to create a set of different obfuscations.

We have explained how the bivariate case works because most programs use two-dimensional matrices. However, conversion between the power form and the Bernstein representation is possible regardless of the number of variables (see Geisow [13] and Garloff [12,19]). Berchtold's thesis [2] and the book [14] give formulae and algorithms for the computation of the Bernstein form of bivariate and trivariate polynomials. Thus we could adapt the method to more (or, indeed, fewer) variables for use in programs with matrices of higher dimensions (or with arrays).

The important advantages of this method are obtained at the cost of its complexity. For each obfuscated matrix there are several matrices to compute, invert and multiply together. One way in which these computations can be kept low is by way of storing (rather than calculating) a table of the $\binom{n}{k}$ combinations (such as in the form of Pascal's triangle). If the matrices to be obfuscated are of similar sizes, then it should be possible to store, for significant values of a, the matrices U_a and U_a^{-1}.

5   Using Matrices to Obfuscate a Number

Up to now we have discussed creating obfuscation for a matrix data-type but we can use matrices to obfuscate other data-types. As an example, let us see how we could use matrices to obfuscate rational numbers with three rational operations: $+$, $\times$ and $\_^{-1}$. So, for a number n we want a matrix $\mathbf{S}$ such that $n \rightsquigarrow \mathbf{S}$ for some abstraction function af. We need matrix operations plus, times and recip such that, if $n \rightsquigarrow \mathbf{S}$ and $p \rightsquigarrow \mathbf{T}$ then

$$n + p \rightsquigarrow \mathsf{plus}(\mathbf{S}, \mathbf{T}) \qquad n \times p \rightsquigarrow \mathsf{times}(\mathbf{S}, \mathbf{T}) \qquad n^{-1} \rightsquigarrow \mathsf{recip}(\mathbf{S})$$

5.1   Using Determinants

We can define the abstraction function to be the determinant of the matrix. So, for example,

$$af \begin{pmatrix} a & b \\ c & d \end{pmatrix} = \det \begin{pmatrix} a & b \\ c & d \end{pmatrix} = a \times d - b \times c$$

We now need to define a suitable conversion function — remember that we are free to choose any conversion function cf such that $af \cdot cf = id$. We could choose the conversion function to be:

$$cf(n) = \begin{pmatrix} n & 0 \\ 0 & 1 \end{pmatrix}$$

We can immediately see that $af(cf(n)) = n$ (but $cf \cdot af = id$ does not hold). We can define plus to be

$$\mathsf{plus}(\begin{pmatrix} m & 0 \\ 0 & 1 \end{pmatrix}, \begin{pmatrix} n & 0 \\ 0 & 1 \end{pmatrix}) = \begin{pmatrix} m+n & 0 \\ 0 & 1 \end{pmatrix}$$

However we can only use this definition of plus for matrices that are in a very specific form — it is fairly easy to understand what the function is doing and so it is not a good obfuscation. (Referring back to the assertion definition of obfuscation, any assertions about plus, such as commutativity, can be proved easily for this matrix version.) Instead we would like a function that can be applied to more general matrices and so we need a different conversion function.

Let us suppose that to obfuscate a number n we pick a matrix $\mathbf{S}$ that has n as an eigenvalue. If $\mathbf{S}$ is a 2×2 matrix then $\mathbf{S}$ has two eigenvalues (which may be the same). So that we can recover n from $\mathbf{S}$ then we could fix the other eigenvalue of $\mathbf{S}$ and we will suppose that $\mathbf{S}$ had the eigenvalues 1 and n. With these eigenvalues, the trace of the matrix must be $n + 1$. Thus, we can define

$$cf(n) = \begin{pmatrix} a & b \\ c & d \end{pmatrix} \text{ where } ad - bc = n \wedge a + d = n + 1$$

This conversion function allows some freedom in choosing the elements of the matrix that represents n. Suppose that we choose values of a and non-zero b. We propose the following conversion function:

$$cf(n) = \begin{pmatrix} a & b \\ \frac{(a-1)(n-a)}{b} & n+1-a \end{pmatrix} \text{ where } b \neq 0 \qquad (12)$$

We can check that $\mathsf{trace}(cf(n)) = n + 1$ and $\mathsf{det}(cf(n)) = af(cf(n)) = n$. Thus, we can define

$$n \rightsquigarrow \begin{pmatrix} a & b \\ c & d \end{pmatrix} \iff n = af(\begin{pmatrix} a & b \\ c & d \end{pmatrix}) \wedge a + d = n + 1$$

5.2 Arithmetic Operations

Now let us define arithmetic operations using our obfuscation. We suppose that $n \rightsquigarrow \begin{pmatrix} a & b \\ c & d \end{pmatrix}$ and $p \rightsquigarrow \begin{pmatrix} e & f \\ g & h \end{pmatrix}$ using the conversion function. We need to find definitions for plus, times and recip.

First we want an operation that adds together n and p. We propose

$$\mathsf{plus}(\begin{pmatrix} a & b \\ c & d \end{pmatrix}, \begin{pmatrix} e & f \\ g & h \end{pmatrix}) = \begin{pmatrix} a+e-1 & bf \\ \frac{(a+e-2)(d+h-1)}{bf} & d+h \end{pmatrix}$$

We can check that the trace of the resulting matrix is

$$a + e - 1 + d + h = (a + d - 1) + (e + h - 1) + 1 = n + p + 1$$

as required. We can also check that the determinant is $n + p$.

For a multiplication operation, we propose

$$\mathsf{times}(\begin{pmatrix} a & b \\ c & d \end{pmatrix}, \begin{pmatrix} e & f \\ g & h \end{pmatrix}) = \begin{pmatrix} (a+d)(e+h)+1 & bf \\ \frac{-(a+d)(e+h)(a+d+e+h)}{bf} & 1-a-d-e-h \end{pmatrix}$$

Finally, for a reciprocal operation, we propose:

$$\text{recip}\left(\begin{pmatrix} a \; b \\ c \; d \end{pmatrix}\right) = \begin{pmatrix} \frac{d}{a+d-1} & b \\ \frac{(a-1)(d-1)}{b(a+d-1)^2} & \frac{a}{a+d-1} \end{pmatrix}$$

Note that this operation is undefined if $a + d - 1 = 0$ *i.e.* if $n = 0$.

More details of the development of the definitions for these operations can be found in Appendix A.4. Note that we are free to create many different definitions for each of these operations since we have some degree of flexibility in our conversion function.

5.3   Review of Number Obfuscation

Under this obfuscation, several arithmetic operations (on four numbers) are required, hence the complexity of each operation is increased. Thus this obfuscation should not be used where an increase of complexity is a concern.

We could use this obfuscation to obfuscate certain constants in a program or to obfuscate a variable (in a similar way to a variable split that was discussed in Collberg *et al.* [6]). If we choose this matrix transformation to obfuscate a rational variable then we risk adversely affecting the efficiency of a program. If the variable that we choose is used extensively then the obfuscation will add many arithmetic operations whenever the variable is used.

6   Evaluation of Techniques

As stated in the Introduction, when creating obfuscations we should make reference to an attack model and any analyses we expect to run. For a human reader, our obfuscated operations are harder to understand because the obfuscated operations are not the expected matrix operations. To understand the Bernstein obfuscated operations, an attacker needs to have familiarity with change of basis transformations and, more importantly, needs to realise the connection between matrices and polynomial bases.

Following the assertion attack model of Drape [8], when defining the matrix data-type (as seen in Figure 1) we stated a number of assertions that we expect our operations to satisfy. In most cases (except for the Bernstein obfuscations of add and scale), the proofs of the assertions (which we omit) are more complicated — example assertion proofs can be found in Drape [8]. One way of at least checking whether the assertions of the obfuscated operations hold is to generate a large set of random examples. In the case of functional languages (e.g. Haskell), such a checking exists in the form of QuickCheck [5], which is based precisely on sets of otherwise difficult to prove assertions.

Majumdar *et al.* [18] describe another attack model for obfuscation in which obfuscations were created with the aim of protecting against an adversary armed with a static program slicer. Majumdar *et al.* found that adding arrays to code fragments reduces the effectiveness of program slicing. Thus a particularly effective obfuscation against a slicing attack should be the determinant obfuscation described in Section 5.1 as it replaces numbers by array-like objects.

The data refinement approach means that we create obfuscations for a set of defined operations. If we want to obfuscate other operations or data-types then we may have to use different obfuscations. For instance, the determinant operation (discussed in Section 5.1) would not be suitable to obfuscate the individual elements of a matrix as the complexity of the matrix operations would drastically increase. Future work would be to see whether these obfuscations would be suitable if we allowed an update operation so that we could change individual elements of a matrix (rather than by using algebraic matrix operations).

One advantage of specifying obfuscations as data refinements is that we can easily produce equations which help us to prove the correctness of our obfuscations. In the Appendix we give some examples of correctness proofs using equations given in Section 2.1. Another advantage of using data refinement is we can compose our obfuscation functions to help us create more complicated obfuscations. For example, we can create an inverse operation for split matrices by using the Bernstein obfuscation:

$$\mathsf{inverse}_{sp} = cf_{sp} \cdot af_{\mathcal{B}} \cdot \mathsf{inverse}_{\mathcal{B}} \cdot cf_{\mathcal{B}} \cdot af_{sp}$$

In a similar way we can combine our number obfuscation (from Section 5.1) with our other matrix obfuscations so that we can build a more complicated obfuscation for numbers and we could also combine different change of basis transformations.

7   Conclusions

An obfuscation should make a program (or a method within a program) harder to understand. When obfuscating matrices one ideally aims to change the structure or the elements within the matrix. Our splitting obfuscation (Section 3.2) changes the size and shape of the matrix (but not the individual elements), whereas the Bernstein obfuscation (Section 4.2) does not alter the size and shape of the matrix, but changes its elements (thus changing their pattern). An advantage of considering obfuscations as data refinements is that obfuscations can then be written as functions, which gives us the ability to compose different obfuscations together. Thus, we can create an obfuscation that changes both the structure and the elements. Obviously, if efficiency is a concern then we have to restrict how complicated we make our obfuscations — there is usually a trade-off between how complicated the obfuscations are and efficiency. One way to alleviate the slow-down of a program is, as discussed in Section 4.5, is to pre-compute and store some of the data used frequently. The trade-off between space and time complexity will depend on the individual applications for which the obfuscation method is used.

Evidently, these operations rely on exact arithmetic being available for rational numbers. This is not a major inconvenience, though, since multi-precision rational operations nowadays are either supported by programming languages (e.g. Java) or through integrated packages (see, for example, MP [4] or LiDIA [16]).

In this paper we have used a variety of methods, both from number theory and from previous work in obfuscation. Our methods bring improvements on previous methods for matrix (and array) obfuscation because, as discussed in Section 6, we have provided a range of techniques that can be used to create transformations which provide greater obscurity. We do not give concrete programming details of our matrix operations, since we considered obfuscation at an appropriate level of abstraction, such that implementing these operations (and their obfuscations) is a straightforward exercise.

References

1. Barak, B., Goldreich, O., Impagliazzo, R., Rudich, S., Sahai, A., Vadhan, S.P., Yang, K.: On the (im)possibility of obfuscating programs. In: Kilian, J. (ed.) CRYPTO 2001. LNCS, vol. 2139, pp. 1–18. Springer, Heidelberg (2001)
2. Berchtold, J.: The Bernstein basis in set-theoretic geometric modelling. PhD thesis, University of Bath (2000)
3. Bernstein, S.: Démonstration du théorème de Weierstrass fondée sur le calcul des probabilités. Comm. Kharkov Math. Soc. 13(1-2), 49–194 (1912)
4. Brent, R.P.: A FORTRAN multiple–precision arithmetic package. ACM Transactions on Mathematical Software 4(1), 57–70 (1978)
5. Claessen, K., Hughes, J.: QuickCheck: a lightweight tool for random testing of Haskell programs. ACM SIGPLAN Notices (2000)
6. Collberg, C., Thomborson, C., Low, D.: A taxonomy of obfuscating transformations. Technical Report 148, Department of Computer Science, University of Auckland (July 1997)
7. de Roever, W.-P., Engelhardt, K.: Data Refinement: Model-Oriented Proof Methods and their Comparison. Cambridge Tracts in Theoretical Computer Science. Cambridge University Press, Cambridge (1998)
8. Drape, S.: Obfuscation of Abstract Data-Types. DPhil thesis, Oxford University Computing Laboratory (2004)
9. Drape, S.: Generalising the array split obfuscation. Information Sciences 177(1), 202–219 (2007)
10. Drape, S., Thomborson, C., Majumdar, A.: Specifying imperative data obfuscations. In: Garay, J.A., et al. (eds.) ISC 2007. LNCS, vol. 4779, pp. 299–314. Springer, Heidelberg (2007)
11. Farouki, R.T., Rajan, V.T.: Algorithms for polynomials in Bernstein form. Computer Aided Geometric Design 5, 1–26 (1988)
12. Garloff, J.: Convergent bounds for the range of multivariate polynomials. In: Nickel, K. (ed.) Interval Mathematics 1985. LNCS, vol. 212, pp. 37–56. Springer, Heidelberg (1986)
13. Geisow, A.: Surface Interrogations. PhD thesis, University of East Anglia (1983)
14. Gomes, A., Voiculescu, I., Jorge, J., Wyvill, B., Galbraith, C.: Implicit Curves and Surfaces: Mathematics, Data Structures and Algorithms. Springer, Heidelberg (2009)

15. Horn, R.A., Johnson, C.R.: Matrix Analysis. Cambridge University Press, Cambridge (1985)
16. LiDIA Group, Darmstadt University of Technology,
    `www.cdc.informatik.tu-darmstadt.de/TI/LiDIA`
17. Lorentz, G.G.: Bernstein Polynomials. Chelsea Publishing Company, New York (1986)
18. Majumdar, A., Drape, S.J., Thomborson, C.D.: Slicing obfuscations: design, correctness, and evaluation. In: DRM 2007: Proceedings of the 2007 ACM workshop on Digital Rights Management, pp. 70–81. ACM, New York (2007)
19. Zettler, M., Garloff, J.: Robustness analysis of polynomials with polynomial parameter dependency using Bernstein expansion. IEEE Transactions on Automatic Control 43(3), 425–431 (1998)

A   Correctness Proofs

In this appendix we outline some proofs of correctness for the various obfuscations given in the main body of the paper. For our proofs we will use the results of Section 2.1 along with the results of the following section.

A.1   Non-homogeneous Operations

Suppose that we have a operation

$$f :: B \to C$$

where B and C are the state spaces of two data-types. Let af_B and af_C be abstraction functions for some obfuscations of B and C. How do we define a correct obfuscation f^O of f? Suppose $x :: B$ and $x \rightsquigarrow y$ and consider:

$$f(x) \rightsquigarrow f^O(y)$$
$$\equiv \quad \{\text{Equation (1) using } af_C\}$$
$$f(x) = af_C(f^O(y))$$
$$\equiv \quad \{\text{Equation (1) using } af_B\}$$
$$f(af_B(y)) = af_C(f^O(y))$$

Thus

$$f \cdot af_B = af_C \cdot f^O \tag{13}$$

Some operations, have type:

$$f :: D \times D \to D$$

for some data-type D. If af is an abstraction function for D then the corresponding abstraction for $D \times D$ is

$$cross(af, af)$$

where *cross* is an operation with type

$$cross :: (\alpha \rightarrow \gamma, \beta \rightarrow \delta) \rightarrow (\alpha, \beta) \rightarrow (\gamma, \delta)$$

which satisfies

$$cross\ (f, g)\ (a, b) = (f\ a, g\ b) \tag{14}$$

Thus if $f^{\mathcal{O}}$ is an obfuscation of f then using Equation (13) we have that

$$f \cdot cross(af, af) = af \cdot f^{\mathcal{O}} \tag{15}$$

We will be able to use this equation to prove the correctness of binary matrix operations such as addition and multiplication.

A.2   Unary Operations under the Bernstein Obfuscation

Let us consider the operation transpose. As a shorthand, we will use the usual ^{T} notation. For a matrix $\mathbf{S}$ we propose that if $f = {}^T$ then

$$f_\mathcal{B}(\mathbf{S}) = \mathbf{U}_b^{-1} \mathbf{V}_b^T \mathbf{S}^T \mathbf{U}_a^T \mathbf{V}_a^{-1} \text{ where } (a+1, b+1) = dim(\mathbf{S})$$

We prove this using Equation (3) for some unobfuscated matrix $\mathbf{M}$:

$af(f_\mathcal{B}(cf(\mathbf{M})))$
= {definition of cf}
$af(f_\mathcal{B}(\mathbf{U}_a^{-1} \mathbf{M} \mathbf{V}_b^{-1}))$
= {definition of $f_\mathcal{B}$ with $(a+1, b+1) = dim(\mathbf{U}_a^{-1} \mathbf{M} \mathbf{V}_b^{-1})$}
$af(\mathbf{U}_b^{-1} \mathbf{V}_b^T (\mathbf{U}_a^{-1} \mathbf{M} \mathbf{V}_b^{-1})^T \mathbf{U}_a^T \mathbf{V}_a^{-1})$
= {$(\mathbf{B}\,\mathbf{C})^T = \mathbf{C}^T \mathbf{B}^T$}
$af(\mathbf{U}_b^{-1} \mathbf{V}_b^T \mathbf{V}_b^{-1^T} \mathbf{M}^T \mathbf{U}_a^{-1^T} \mathbf{U}_a^T \mathbf{V}_a^{-1})$
= {$\mathbf{C}^T (\mathbf{C}^{-1})^T = (\mathbf{C}^{-1} \mathbf{C})^T = \mathbf{I}^T = \mathbf{I}$}
$af(\mathbf{U}_b^{-1} \mathbf{M}^T \mathbf{V}_a^{-1})$
= {definition of af with $(b+1, a+1) = dim(\mathbf{U}_b^{-1} \mathbf{M}^T \mathbf{V}_a^{-1})$}
$\mathbf{U}_b(\mathbf{U}_b^{-1} \mathbf{M}^T \mathbf{V}_a^{-1}) \mathbf{V}_a$
= {associativity of matrix multiplication and inverses}
$\mathbf{M}^T$
= {definition of f}
$f(\mathbf{M})$

The determinant operation det is different to the other matrix operations we have considered as the output from this operation is a number rather than another matrix. Thus to derive a determinant operation for Bernstein obfuscated matrices we consider det $\cdot$ af (since numbers are not obfuscated, the conversion function is id) as follows:

$$\det_{\mathcal{B}}(\mathbf{S})$$
$$= \quad \{\text{deriving equation}\}$$
$$\det(af(\mathbf{S}))$$
$$= \quad \{\text{definition of } af \text{ with } (a+1, b+1) = dim(\mathbf{S})\}$$
$$\det(\mathbf{U}_a\,\mathbf{S}\,\mathbf{V}_b)$$
$$= \quad \{\det(\mathbf{B\,C}) = \det(\mathbf{B}) \times \det\mathbf{C}\}$$
$$\det(\mathbf{U}_a) \times \det(\mathbf{S}) \times \det(\mathbf{V}_b)$$

A.3   Binary Operations under the Bernstein Obfuscation

For a binary matrix operation $\otimes$, we use the non-homogeneous equations defined in Section A.1. If $cross(af, af)$ is the abstraction function for $Matrix\ \alpha \times Matrix\ \alpha$ then the corresponding conversion function is $cross(cf, cf)$ (this follows from the definition of $cross$). So, for example, to obfuscate an operation $\otimes$ we use Equation (15) and multiply by cf to get $cf \cdot (\otimes) \cdot cross(af, af)$.

Now we will use this equation to derive a definition for multiplication. Suppose that we have two matrices $\mathbf{S}$ and $\mathbf{T}$ with $(a+1, b+1) = dim(\mathbf{S})$ and $(b+1, c+1) = dim(\mathbf{T})$ (thus the matrices are conformable). Then, writing mult as the prefix matrix multiplication operator in the place of $\otimes$ in the equation above (but using normal matrix multiplication elsewhere), we can use this equation to derive an obfuscation:

$$cf(\text{mult}(cross(af, af)\,(\mathbf{S}, \mathbf{T})))$$
$$= \quad \{\text{definition of } cross\}$$
$$cf(\text{mult}(af(\mathbf{S}), af(\mathbf{T})))$$
$$= \quad \{\text{definition of } af \text{ with appropriate dimensions}\}$$
$$cf(\text{mult}(\mathbf{U}_a\,\mathbf{S}\,\mathbf{V}_b, \mathbf{U}_b\,\mathbf{T}\,\mathbf{V}_c))$$
$$= \quad \{\text{definition of mult}\}$$
$$cf(\mathbf{U}_a\,\mathbf{S}\,\mathbf{V}_b\,\mathbf{U}_b\,\mathbf{T}\,\mathbf{V}_c)$$
$$= \quad \{\text{definition of } cf \text{ with } (a+1, c+1) = dim(\mathbf{U}_a\,\mathbf{S}\,\mathbf{V}_b\,\mathbf{U}_b\,\mathbf{T}\,\mathbf{V}_c)\}$$
$$\mathbf{U}_a^{-1}\,(\mathbf{U}_a\,\mathbf{S}\,\mathbf{V}_b\,\mathbf{U}_b\,\mathbf{T}\,\mathbf{V}_c)\,\mathbf{V}_c^{-1}$$
$$= \quad \{\text{associativity of matrix multiplication and inverses}\}$$
$$\mathbf{S}\,\mathbf{V}_b\,\mathbf{U}_b\,\mathbf{T}$$

Thus, $\text{mult}_{\mathcal{B}}(\mathbf{S}, \mathbf{T}) = \mathbf{S}\,\mathbf{V}_b\,\mathbf{U}_b\,\mathbf{T}$ where $(a+1, b+1) = dim(\mathbf{S})$.

A.4   Arithmetic Operations for the Number Obfuscation

In Section 5.1 we define an obfuscation for numbers by representing a number as the determinant of a matrix. In this section, we discuss the definitions of the arithmetic operations in more details. We suppose that $n \rightsquigarrow \begin{pmatrix} a & b \\ c & d \end{pmatrix}$ and $p \rightsquigarrow \begin{pmatrix} e & f \\ g & h \end{pmatrix}$ using the conversion function defined in Section 5.1. We need to find definitions for plus, times and recip.

First we want an operation that adds together n and p. We need to find a matrix that satisfies

$$\begin{pmatrix} j & k \\ l & m \end{pmatrix} = \mathsf{plus}(\begin{pmatrix} a & b \\ c & d \end{pmatrix}, \begin{pmatrix} e & f \\ g & h \end{pmatrix})$$

Under our obfuscation we know that $a + d = n + 1$ and $e + h = p + 1$ and so the resulting matrix must obfuscate $n + p = a + d + e + h - 2$. Thus we need $j + m = a + d + e + h - 1$ so let us take $j = a + e - 1$ and $m = d + h$. We are free to choose any non-zero value for k so we take $k = b \times f$. Finally, from the definition of cf we need

$$l = \frac{(j-1)(n+p-j)}{k}$$
$$= \frac{((a+e-1)-1)((a+d+e+h-2)-(a+e-1))}{bf}$$
$$= \frac{(a+e-2)(d+h-1)}{bf}$$

Thus,

$$\mathsf{plus}(\begin{pmatrix} a & b \\ c & d \end{pmatrix}, \begin{pmatrix} e & f \\ g & h \end{pmatrix}) = \begin{pmatrix} a+e-1 & bf \\ \frac{(a+e-2)(d+h-1)}{bf} & d+h \end{pmatrix}$$

Note that this operation is commutative (as with $+$) but, as we free to choose any non-zero value of k, we could easily make this operation non-commutative.

Next, we need to a find a matrix that satisfies

$$\begin{pmatrix} j & k \\ l & m \end{pmatrix} = \mathsf{times}(\begin{pmatrix} a & b \\ c & d \end{pmatrix}, \begin{pmatrix} e & f \\ g & h \end{pmatrix})$$

We know that $n = a + d - 1$ and $p = e + h - 1$ and so we need our resulting matrix to obfuscate $n \times p = (a + d - 1)(e + h - 1)$. Expanding this expression we obtain:

$$n \times p = (a + d)(e + h) - (e + h) - (a + d) + 1$$

So we take $j = (a + d)(e + h) + 1$ and $m = 1 - (a + d) - (e + h)$. We can choose any non-zero value for k so (as before) let us take $k = b \times f$. Using the definition of cf, we have that

$$l = \frac{(j-1)(n \times p - j)}{k}$$
$$= \frac{(((a+d)(e+h)+1)-1)((a+d-1)(e+h-1)-((a+d)(e+h)+1))}{bf}$$
$$= \frac{-(a+d)(e+h)(a+d+e+h)}{bf}$$

Thus

$$\text{times}\left(\begin{pmatrix} a & b \\ c & d \end{pmatrix}, \begin{pmatrix} e & f \\ g & h \end{pmatrix}\right) = \begin{pmatrix} (a+d)(e+h)+1 & bf \\ \frac{-(a+d)(e+h)(a+d+e+h)}{bf} & 1-a-d-e-h \end{pmatrix}$$

Finally, we would like to find a matrix that satisfies

$$\begin{pmatrix} j & k \\ l & m \end{pmatrix} = \text{recip}\left(\begin{pmatrix} a & b \\ c & d \end{pmatrix}\right)$$

Under our obfuscation, we know that $n = a+d-1$ and so we need the result of the operation to obfuscate $\frac{1}{n} = \frac{1}{a+d-1}$. We need the trace of the result matrix to be $1 + \frac{1}{n}$ and so:

$$j + m = 1 + \frac{1}{n} = 1 + \frac{1}{a+d-1} = \frac{a+d}{a+d-1}$$

So let us take $j = \frac{d}{a+d-1}$ and $m = \frac{a}{a+d-1}$. Again, we have a free choice for non-zero k so let's take $k = b$. From the definition of cf we need

$$l = \frac{(j-1)(\frac{1}{n} - j)}{k}$$

$$= \left(\frac{1}{b}\right)\left(\frac{d}{a+d-1} - 1\right)\left(\frac{1}{a+d-1} - \frac{d}{a+d-1}\right)$$

$$= \left(\frac{1}{b}\right)\left(\frac{1-a}{a+d-1}\right)\left(\frac{1-d}{a+d-1}\right)$$

$$= \frac{(1-a)(1-d)}{b(a+d-1)^2}$$

Hence,

$$\text{recip}\left(\begin{pmatrix} a & b \\ c & d \end{pmatrix}\right) = \begin{pmatrix} \frac{d}{a+d-1} & b \\ \frac{(a-1)(d-1)}{b(a+d-1)^2} & \frac{a}{a+d-1} \end{pmatrix}$$

Note that this operation is undefined if $a+d-1 = 0$ *i.e.* if $n = 0$.

We can easily prove that these operations are correct by using Equations (2) or (15) as appropriate. The proofs of correctness are fairly straightforward (as we used our conversion function to define our matrices); they essentially check that the determinants of the matrices are correct.

Abstract Interpretation
from a Topological Perspective

David A. Schmidt*

Kansas State University, Manhattan, Kansas, USA
schmidt@cis.ksu.edu

Abstract. We develop abstract interpretation from topological principles by relaxing the definitions of open set and continuity; key results
still hold. We study families of closed and open sets and show they generate post- and pre-condition analyses, respectively. Giacobazzi's forwards-
and backwards-complete functions are characterized by the topologically
closed and continuous maps, respectively. Finally, we show that Smyth's
upper and lower topologies for powersets induce the overapproximating and underapproximating transition functions used for abstract-model
checking.

1 Introduction

Topology is a major force in mathematics — it is the study of properties (*open
sets*) and functions that behave well (are *continuous*) regarding the properties.
For example, the real line, $\mathbb{R}$, has as open sets the open intervals, (a, b). A
number $r \in \mathbb{R}$ has property (a, b) when $r \in (a, b)$, e.g., $\pi \in (3, 4)$. A function
$f : \mathbb{R} \to \mathbb{R}$ is topologically continuous when it maps arguments "close together"
(sharing many open sets) to answers "close together" (sharing equally many open
sets), e.g., $area(r) = \pi r^2$ is continuous with respect to intervals. The continuous
functions on the real line are exactly the topologically continuous functions.[1]

One application of topology to computing is Scott-domain theory [19]: To
solve the domain equation, $D = D \to D$, Scott needed to limit the cardinality of
functions on D. Continuity was the appropriate criterion: For complete lattice
L, Scott defined L's open sets to be those subsets of L that are *(i)* upwards
closed and *(ii)* closed under tails of chains.[2] Scott proved that the functions that
are topologically continuous for his *Scott topology* of L are exactly the chain-
continuous functions on L. By restricting $D \to D$ to the continuous functions,
Scott limited its cardinality so that the recursive domain equation had a solution.

Smyth [24] suggested that a domain's Scott topology defines all the *computable
properties* of the domain, and he established correspondences between "upper,"

---

* Supported by NSF ITR-0326577.

[1] In contrast, $g(r) = $ *if* $r \neq 9$ *then* r^2 *else* 0 is discontinuous — the "closeness" of
answers is destroyed at argument 9.

[2] That is, for every chain, $C = \{c_0, c_1, \cdots c_i, \cdots\} \subseteq L$, when $\sqcup C \in U$, for open set
$U \subseteq L$, then there exists some $c_k \in C$ such that $c_k \in U$ also. This means C's tail,
from c_k onwards, is in U.

J. Palsberg and Z. Su (Eds.): SAS 2009, LNCS 5673, pp. 293–308, 2009.

"lower," and "convex" topologies to the three main variants of powerdomains [15]. Smyth's observations generated intensive research on the Stone duality within domain theory, leading to "domain theory in logical form" [1].

Given that topology is the study of computing on properties, one would believe that it would be central to the theory of abstract interpretation [7], which studies exactly this topic. There are indeed some precedents.

In [8], Cousot and Cousot employed topology to establish soundness of convergence: They proposed a T0-topology, the $\sqcup$-topology, for complete lattices, where the basic open sets are up-closed and closed under finite meets. As with the Scott topology, a function is chain continuous iff it is $\sqcup$-topologically continuous. (The two topologies coincide for algebraic lattices.) The $\sqcup$-topology explains how computation on an abstract interpretation preserves properties: When lattice L's abstract interpretation is defined by an upper closure operation, $\rho : L \to L$, the $\sqcup$-topology on $\rho[L]$ is exactly the relative topology on L: every open $U' \subseteq \rho[L]$ equals $U \cap \rho[L]$, for some open $U \subseteq L$.

One application where topology has been employed is backwards strictness analysis. A characterization of a strictness-analysis domain as open-set properties was made by Hunt [16], who observed that Clack and Peyton Jones's backwards strictness analysis employed abstract values called *frontiers*, which were finite subsets of a finite lattice, D, that represented up-closed subsets of D. Since up-closed subsets of a finite lattice are Scott-open, all monotone functions $f : D \to D$ are Scott-continuous, implying f^{-1} maps frontiers to frontiers, ensuring that the analysis preserved strictness properties "on the nose." (In the present paper, we will show that such functions f are therefore backwards complete [14].)

Dybjer formalized this property for denotational semantics definitions and domain equations, axiomatizing the Scott topology of the latter as well as the law that the inverse of a Scott-continuous function maps open sets to open sets. He then showed strictness analysis is an instance of his axiomatization [12].

The most striking application of topology to abstract domains came from Jensen [17], who utilized Abramsky's domain theory in logical form [1]. Recall that Abramsky applied Stone duality [18] to domain theory, generating a Scott domain from a set of atomic elements that act as primitive propositions in a domain logic, closing them under a set of frame axioms. Jensen observed that one can use a finite subset of the atomic elements with the frame axioms to generate an abstract domain that approximates the domain generated from all the atomic elements. Jensen called his methodology *abstract interpretation in logical form* and applied it to strictness analysis, as did Benton, who proposed his own "strictness logic" [2].

The present paper steps back from strictness analysis and frame structures and poses a general question: "Starting from naive set theory, in what sense does an abstract domain define a "topology" on the concrete domain that it approximates?" Based on this "topology," what does it mean for a function to preserve and reflect the "open" and "closed" sets? How do these notions define both forwards and backwards static analyses and how do they ensure soundness and completeness of the analyses?

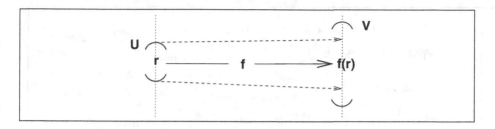

Fig. 1. Continuous function, f: When $f(r)$ falls within property (open set) V, then f maps some property, U, of r within V also

To answer these questions, we develop abstract interpretation from topological principles by relaxing the definitions of open set and continuity so that they apply to arbitrary families of property sets. Surprisingly, key results still hold. When we study families of closed sets and open sets (induced from closure and interior operations), we discover that closed families generate postcondition analyses and open families generate precondition analyses (e.g., backwards strictness analyses). Even more striking, Giacobazzi's forwards- and backwards-complete functions [13,14] are characterized as the topologically closed and continuous maps, respectively. Finally, we show that Smyth's upper and lower topologies for powersets [25] induce the overapproximating and underapproximating transition functions proposed by Cleaveland, et al. [5], and Dams, et al. [11], for abstract-model checking.

2   Basics of Topology and Abstract Interpretation

We provide here the bare essentials of topology; details appear later as needed. (Willard [26] is a good reference.) For a set, Σ, a *topology*, $\mathcal{O}_\Sigma \subseteq \mathcal{P}(\Sigma)$, is a family of property sets, called the *open sets*, that are closed under union (for all $S \subseteq \mathcal{O}_\Sigma, \bigcup S \in \mathcal{O}_\Sigma$) and binary intersection ($U_1 \cap U_2 \in \mathcal{O}_\Sigma$ when $U_1, U_2 \in \mathcal{O}_\Sigma$) and include Σ ($\bigcup \mathcal{O}_\Sigma = \Sigma$). The complement, $\sim U = \Sigma - U$, of an open set U is a *closed set*; define $\mathcal{C}_\Sigma = \{\sim U \mid U \in \mathcal{O}_\Sigma\}$. For topology $\mathcal{O}_\Sigma$, a *base* is a subset, $\mathcal{B}_\Sigma \subseteq \mathcal{O}_\Sigma$, such that every $U \in \mathcal{O}_\Sigma$ is the union of some members of the base (for all $U \in \mathcal{O}_\Sigma$, there exists $S \subseteq \mathcal{B}_\Sigma$ such that $\cup S = U$). The members of the base are called *basic-open sets*. The topology on the real line uses open intervals, (a, b), for $a, b \in \mathbb{R}$, as its base.

For $S \subseteq \Sigma$, its *interior*, $\iota(S)$, is the largest open set within S. Indeed, $\iota(S) = \bigcup\{U \in \mathcal{O}_\Sigma \mid U \subseteq S\}$. The smallest closed set enclosing S is its *closure*, $\rho(S) = \bigcap\{K \mid S \subseteq K, K \in \mathcal{C}_\Sigma\}$.

Given topologies for sets Σ and Δ, there are standard definitions for the coarsest topologies for $\Sigma \times \Delta$, $\Sigma \to \Delta$, etc. [26].

A function, $f : \Sigma \to \Sigma$, is *(topologically) continuous* iff for all $s \in \Sigma$ and $V \in \mathcal{O}_\Sigma$, if $f(s) \in V$, then there exists some $U \in \mathcal{O}_\Sigma$ such that $s \in U$ and $f[U] \subseteq V$ (where lift f to $\mathcal{P}(\Sigma) \to \mathcal{P}(\Sigma)$: $f[U] = \{f(x) \mid x \in U\}$). See Figure 1.

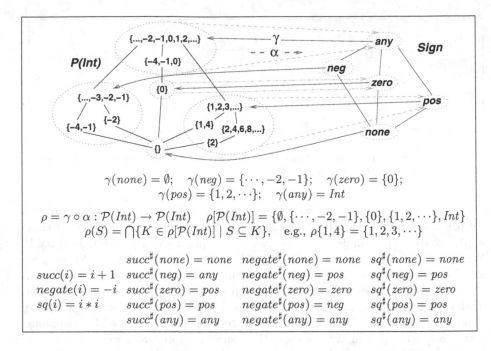

$$\gamma(none) = \emptyset; \quad \gamma(neg) = \{\cdots, -2, -1\}; \quad \gamma(zero) = \{0\};$$
$$\gamma(pos) = \{1, 2, \cdots\}; \quad \gamma(any) = Int$$

$$\rho = \gamma \circ \alpha : \mathcal{P}(Int) \to \mathcal{P}(Int) \quad \rho[\mathcal{P}(Int)] = \{\emptyset, \{\cdots, -2, -1\}, \{0\}, \{1, 2, \cdots\}, Int\}$$
$$\rho(S) = \bigcap\{K \in \rho[\mathcal{P}(Int)] \mid S \subseteq K\}, \quad \text{e.g., } \rho\{1, 4\} = \{1, 2, 3, \cdots\}$$

	$succ^\sharp(none) = none$	$negate^\sharp(none) = none$	$sq^\sharp(none) = none$
$succ(i) = i + 1$	$succ^\sharp(neg) = any$	$negate^\sharp(neg) = pos$	$sq^\sharp(neg) = pos$
$negate(i) = -i$	$succ^\sharp(zero) = pos$	$negate^\sharp(zero) = zero$	$sq^\sharp(zero) = zero$
$sq(i) = i * i$	$succ^\sharp(pos) = pos$	$negate^\sharp(pos) = neg$	$sq^\sharp(pos) = pos$
	$succ^\sharp(any) = any$	$negate^\sharp(any) = any$	$sq^\sharp(any) = any$

Fig. 2. Abstract domain, *Sign*, and the properties, $\rho[\mathcal{P}(Int)]$, it represents

A crucial result is that f is continuous iff for all $U \in \mathcal{O}_\Sigma$, $f^{-1}(U) \in \mathcal{O}_\Sigma$ also, where $f^{-1}(U) = \{x \in \Sigma \mid f(x) \in U\}$. Function f is an *open map* iff for all $U \in \mathcal{O}_\Sigma$, $f[U] \in \mathcal{O}_\Sigma$ and it is a *closed map* iff for all $K \in \mathcal{C}_\Sigma$, $f[K] \in \mathcal{C}_\Sigma$.

Abstract interpretation is computational approximation by computation on properties: For concrete data domain, Σ, select a set of property names, A, such that each $a \in A$ names the set $\gamma(a) \subseteq \Sigma$, for $\gamma : A \to \mathcal{P}(\Sigma)$. γ identifies the family of properties modelled by A. Order A s.t. $a \sqsubseteq a'$ iff $\gamma(a) \subseteq \gamma(a')$ — it should be a partial ordering.

Figure 2 displays an approximation of the integers, *Int*, by sign properties, *Sign*. (Notice *how few* properties are identified — just $\{none, neg, zero, pos, any\}$.)

When γ possesses an adjoint, $\alpha : \mathcal{P}(\Sigma) \to Sign$, then there is a Galois connection[3] and $\rho = \gamma \circ \alpha$ is an *upper closure operator* — $\rho : \mathcal{P}(\Sigma) \to \mathcal{P}(\Sigma)$ is monotone, extensive ($S \subseteq \rho(S)$), and idempotent ($\rho \circ \rho = \rho$). ρ's range, $\rho[\mathcal{P}(\Sigma)]$, identifies a family of property sets, but the family is typically *not* a topology, although it *is* closed under intersection (for all $S \subseteq \rho[\mathcal{P}(\Sigma)], \bigcap S \in \rho[\mathcal{P}(\Sigma)]$).

Computation functions, $f : \Sigma \to \Sigma$, are *soundly approximated* by $f^\sharp : A \to A$ iff $\alpha(f[S]) \sqsubseteq f^\sharp(\alpha(S))$, for all $S \in \mathcal{P}(\Sigma)$ (equivalently, iff $f[\gamma(a)] \subseteq \gamma(f^\sharp(a))$, for all $a \in A$) where we "lift" f to $f[S] = \{f(s) \mid s \in S\}$. See Figure 2.

The most precise such $f^\sharp$ is defined $f_0^\sharp = \alpha \circ f \circ \gamma$, where again, f is "lifted." When f is approximated exactly by $f_0^\sharp$ such that $f \circ \gamma = \gamma \circ f_0^\sharp$, we say f is *forwards*

---

[3] That is, $S \subseteq \gamma(a)$ iff $\alpha(S) \sqsubseteq a$, for all $S \in \mathcal{P}(\Sigma)$ and $a \in A$.

For $f : \mathcal{P}(\Sigma) \to \mathcal{P}(\Sigma)$, $f^\sharp : A \to A$ is *sound* iff

$$\alpha \circ f \sqsubseteq f^\sharp \circ \alpha \quad \text{or, equivalently,} \quad f \circ \gamma \sqsubseteq \gamma \circ f^\sharp$$

$$
\begin{array}{ccc}
S & \xrightarrow{\ f\ } & f(S) \\
\alpha \downarrow & & \downarrow \alpha \\
\alpha(S) & \xrightarrow[f^\#]{\ \ \ \sqcap\sqcap\ } & f^\#(\alpha(S))
\end{array}
\qquad
\begin{array}{ccc}
\gamma(a) & \xrightarrow{\ f\ } & f(\gamma(a)) \\
\gamma \uparrow & & \uparrow \gamma \\
a & \xrightarrow[f^\#]{\ \ \ \ } & f^\#(a)
\end{array}
$$

α and γ act as *semi-homomorphisms*; $f^\sharp$ is a *postcondition transformer*. The strongest transformer is $f_0^\sharp = \alpha \circ f \circ \gamma$. Next, define $\rho = \gamma \circ \alpha : \mathcal{P}(\Sigma) \to \mathcal{P}(\Sigma)$:

Forwards completeness [13]:

$$f \circ \gamma = \gamma \circ f^\sharp$$

$$
\begin{array}{ccc}
\gamma(a) & \xrightarrow{\ f\ } & f(\gamma(a)) \\
\gamma \uparrow & & \uparrow \gamma \\
a & \xrightarrow[f^\#]{\ \ \ \ } & f^\#(a)
\end{array}
$$

γ is a homomorphism from A to $\mathcal{P}(\Sigma)$. f is forwards complete (with respect to $f_0^\sharp$) iff for all $K \in \rho[\mathcal{P}(\Sigma)]$, $f[K] \in \rho[\mathcal{P}(\Sigma)]$.

Backwards completeness [9,14]:

$$\alpha \circ f = f^\sharp \circ \alpha$$

$$
\begin{array}{ccc}
S & \xrightarrow{\ f\ } & f(S) \\
\alpha \downarrow & & \downarrow \alpha \\
\alpha(S) & \xrightarrow[f^\#]{\ \ \ \ } & f^\#(\alpha(S))
\end{array}
$$

α is a homomorphism from $\mathcal{P}(\Sigma)$ to A. f is backwards complete (w.r.t. $f_0^\natural$) iff for all $S, S' \in \mathcal{P}(\Sigma)$, $\rho(S) = \rho(S')$ implies $\rho(f[S]) = \rho(f[S'])$.

Fig. 3. Sound and complete forms of abstract functions

complete; f is forwards complete iff for all $K \in \rho[\mathcal{P}(\Sigma)]$, $f[K] \in \rho[\mathcal{P}(\Sigma)]$, that is, iff $f \circ \rho = \rho \circ f \circ \rho$ [13]. That is, f maps properties to properties "on the nose." When f is approximated exactly such that $\alpha \circ f = f_0^\sharp \circ \alpha$, we say f is *backwards complete*; f is backwards complete iff for all $S, S' \in \mathcal{P}(\Sigma)$, $\rho(S) = \rho(S')$ implies $\rho(f[S]) = \rho(f[S'])$, that is, iff $\rho \circ f = \rho \circ f \circ \rho$. [14,21]. That is, f maps ρ-equivalent arguments to ρ-equivalent answers. See Figure 3. In Figure 2, sq is backwards but not forwards complete; *negate* is both backwards and forwards complete, and *succ* is neither.

Giacobazzi and his colleagues defined iterative refinement methods, called *shell constructions*, that add new elements to an abstract domain so that a incomplete function f becomes forwards or backwards complete, as desired [13,14]. They showed that the shell constructions formalize the CEGAR refinement method of abstract model checking [3].

This paper's main result is the equivalence of backwards and forwards completeness to topological continuity and topologically closed maps, respectively.

3   Property Families, Function Preservation and Reflection

We now develop abstract interpretation with topological concepts.

For a concrete state set, Σ, choose some $\mathcal{F}_\Sigma \subseteq \mathcal{P}(\Sigma)$ as a family of properties. (In Figure 2, the family $Sign_{Int}$ is $\{\emptyset, \{i \mid i < 0\}, \{0\}, \{i \mid i > 0\}, Int\}$.)

For each $U \in \mathcal{F}_\Sigma$, its complement is $\sim U = \Sigma - U$; for $\mathcal{F}_\Sigma$, its *complement family*, $\sim \mathcal{F}_\Sigma$, is $\{\sim U \mid U \in \mathcal{F}_\Sigma\}$. (E.g., $\sim Sign_{Int}$ is $\{Int, \{i \mid i \geq 0\}, \{i \mid i \neq 0\}, \{i \mid i \leq 0\}, \emptyset\}$.)

When property family $\mathcal{O}_\Sigma \subseteq \mathcal{P}(\Sigma)$ is closed under unions, then $\mathcal{O}_\Sigma$ is an *open family*. Every open family has an *interior* operation, ι, which computes the largest property contained within a set: $\iota : \mathcal{P}(\Sigma) \to \mathcal{O}_\Sigma$ is defined $\iota(S) = \cup\{U \in \mathcal{O}_\Sigma \mid U \subseteq S\}$.

Dually, if a property family $\mathcal{C}_\Sigma$ is closed under intersections, it is a *closed family* (*Moore family* [9]). Every closed family has a *closure* operation, ρ, which computes the smallest property covering a set: $\rho : \Sigma \to \mathcal{C}_\Sigma$ is defined $\rho(S) = \cap\{K \in \mathcal{C}_\Sigma \mid S \subseteq K\}$. ($Sign_{Int}$ in Figure 2 is a closed (but not open) family, whose closure operation is the ρ stated in the Figure.)

If $\mathcal{O}_\Sigma$ is an open family, then its complement is a closed family (and vice versa), where $\bigcap_{i \in I} K_i = \sim \bigcup_{i \in I} \sim K_i$ (where $\bigcup_{i \in I} U_i = \sim \bigcap_{i \in I} \sim U_i$).

Let $f : \Sigma \to \Delta$ be a function; define $f : \mathcal{P}(\Sigma) \to \mathcal{P}(\Delta)$ as $f[S] = \{f(s) \mid s \in S\}$. Next, define function inverse, $f^{-1} : \mathcal{P}(\Delta) \to \mathcal{P}(\Sigma)$, as $f^{-1}(T) = \{s \in \Sigma \mid f(s) \in T\}$.

For property families, $\mathcal{F}_\Sigma$ and $\mathcal{F}_\Delta$, $f : \Sigma \to \Delta$ is $\mathcal{F}_\Sigma\mathcal{F}_\Delta$-*preserving* iff for all $U \in \mathcal{F}_\Sigma$, $f[U] \in \mathcal{F}_\Delta$. In such a case, $f : \mathcal{F}_\Sigma \to \mathcal{F}_\Delta$ is well defined. To reduce notation, we use functions, $f : \Sigma \to \Sigma$, with the same domain and codomain (and we say, "f is $\mathcal{F}_\Sigma$-preserving"), but all results that follow hold for functions with distinct codomains and domains, too. (In Figure 2, *negate* is $Sign_{Int}$-preserving.)

Definition 1. *For $s \in \Sigma$ and $S \subseteq \Sigma$, let U_s (respectively, U_S) denote a member of $\mathcal{F}_\Sigma$ such that $s \in U_s$ (respectively, $S \subseteq U_S$).*

(i) *For $s \in \Sigma$, $f : \Sigma \to \Sigma$ is continuous at s iff for all $V_{f(s)} \in \mathcal{F}_\Sigma$, there exists some $U_s \in \mathcal{F}_\Sigma$ such that $f[U_s] \subseteq V_{f(s)}$.*

(ii) *For $S \subseteq \Sigma$, f is continuous at S iff for all $V_{f[S]} \in \mathcal{F}_\Sigma$, there exists some $U_S \in \mathcal{F}_\Sigma$ such that $f[U_S] \subseteq V_{f[S]}$.*

(iii) *f is $\mathcal{F}_\Sigma$-reflecting iff for all $V \in \mathcal{F}_\Sigma$, $f^{-1}(V) \in \mathcal{F}_\Sigma$, that is, f^{-1} is $\mathcal{F}_\Sigma$-preserving.*

Proposition 2. *(i) f is $\mathcal{F}_\Sigma$-reflecting iff f is continuous at S, for all $S \subseteq \Sigma$. (ii) If $\mathcal{F}_\Sigma$ is an open family, then f is $\mathcal{F}_\Sigma$-reflecting iff f is continuous at s, for all $s \in \Sigma$.*

Proof. We prove (i); (ii) is a standard result [26]. Only if: for $V \in \mathcal{F}_\Sigma$, consider $f^{-1}(V)$. Because f is continuous at all $S \subseteq \Sigma$, there is some $U_{f^{-1}(V)} \in \mathcal{F}_\Sigma$ such that $f[U_{f^{-1}(V)}] \subseteq V$. But $U_{f^{-1}(V)}$ must equal $f^{-1}(V)$ for this to hold.

If: for $S \subseteq \Sigma$, say that $V_S \in \mathcal{F}_\Sigma$. Since f is reflecting, $f^{-1}(V_S) \in \mathcal{F}_\Sigma$. Thus, $f[f^{-1}(V_S)] \subseteq V_S$. □

The proofs in this paper rely on naive-set reasoning (cf. Willard [26]) and will often be omitted. We retain these critical dualities for all f and $\mathcal{F}_\Sigma$:

Proposition 3. $f : \Sigma \to \Sigma$ is $\sim\!\mathcal{F}_\Sigma$-reflecting iff f is $\mathcal{F}_\Sigma$-reflecting.
f is $\mathcal{F}_\Sigma$-preserving iff $\tilde{f} = \sim \circ f \circ \sim$ is $\sim\!\mathcal{F}_\Sigma$-preserving.

In Figure 2, *negate* and *square* are $Sign_{Int}$-reflecting (but *succ* is not). This makes the two functions $\sim Sign_{Int}$ reflecting, where $\sim Sign_{Int} = \{Int, \{i \mid i \geq 0\}, \{i \mid i \neq 0\}, \{i \mid i \leq 0\}, \emptyset\}$. Since *negate* is $Sign_{Int}$-preserving, *negate* is $\sim Sign_{Int}$-preserving, e.g., $\underline{negate\{i \mid i \geq 0\}} = \{i \mid i \leq 0\}$. We exploit such dualities in the next section.

4   Applications: Logics, Postconditions, Preconditions

A property family lists the properties that can be computed by an abstract interpretation. To implement it, we name each of the sets in the family, e.g., Figure 2 shows that $Sign = \{none, neg, zero, pos, any\}$ are the names for $Sign_{Int}$ and $\gamma : Sign \to Sign_{Int}$ concretizes each name to its property set. Within $Sign$, $a \sqsubseteq a'$ iff $\gamma(a) \subseteq \gamma(a')$. To reduce notation, the abstract interpretations in this paper are defined directly upon the property sets rather upon than the names of the sets [6,14]. For example, we write $succ^\sharp\{0\} = \{i \mid i > 0\}$ rather than $succ^\sharp(zero) = pos$.

There is a weakened form of Stone duality here [1,18]: a property family $\mathcal{F}_\Sigma$ has a frame-like "logic" whose "primitive propositions" are the $U \in \mathcal{F}_\Sigma$ and "connectives" are the functions that are $\mathcal{F}_\Sigma$-preserving. Based on Figure 2, we know that $Sign_{Int}$'s logic includes

$$\phi ::= U \mid \phi_1 \cap \phi_2 \mid negate\,\phi$$

where $U \in Sign_{Int}$. $\cap$ appears because the family is closed; *negate* appears because it is $Sign_{Int}$-preserving. A set S *has property* ϕ iff $S \subseteq \phi$, e.g., $\{1,3\}$ has property $negate\{i \mid i < 0\}$. (When $\mathcal{F}_\Sigma$ is a topology, its logic is a frame [18] and includes *false* (empty set), *true* (Σ), disjunction (union), and conjunction (intersection).)

Ideally, for conducting an abstract interpretation, a program's transition functions, $f : \Sigma \to \Sigma$, are A-preserving — fall within the logic (cf. [16]). This rarely happens, e.g., a program that counts by ones uses the transition function, $succ : Int \to Int$, $succ(i) = i + 1$, which is not $Sign_{Int}$-preserving. In this case, we must define a $succ^\sharp : Sign_{Int} \to Sign_{Int}$ to soundly approximate *succ*.

If property family $\mathcal{C}_\Sigma$ is closed, we use its closure operator, ρ, to define from $f : \Sigma \to \Sigma$ its *overapproximation* $f^\sharp : \mathcal{C}_\Sigma \to \mathcal{C}_\Sigma$ as $f^\sharp = \rho \circ f$. Function $f^\sharp$ generates sound postconditions, because this relational assertion ("Hoare triple"),

$$\{\phi\}f\{f^\sharp(\phi)\}$$

holds true (where $\{\phi\}f\{\psi\}$ asserts $f[\phi] \subseteq \psi$, for $\phi, \psi \in \mathcal{C}_\Sigma$). Because $f^\sharp(\phi) = \rho(f[\phi])$ is the *smallest* set in $\mathcal{C}_\Sigma$ that contains $f[\phi]$, it is the *strongest postcondition of f and ϕ expressible in $\mathcal{C}_\Sigma$*: $\{\phi\}f\{\psi\}$ implies $\{\phi\}f\{f^\sharp(\phi)\}$ and $f^\sharp(\phi) \subseteq \psi$.[4]

---

[4] If $\mathcal{F}_\Sigma$ is not closed, then the $f : \Sigma \to \Sigma$ must be approximated by some $f^\sharp : \mathcal{F}_\Sigma \to \mathcal{F}_\Sigma$ such that $\{U\}f\{f^\sharp(U)\}$ holds for all $U \in \mathcal{F}_\Sigma$.

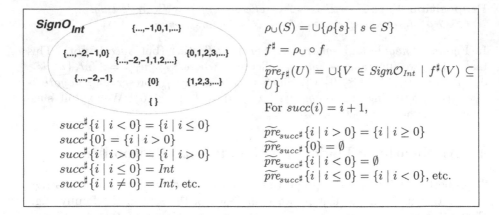

$$succ^\sharp\{i \mid i < 0\} = \{i \mid i \le 0\}$$
$$succ^\sharp\{0\} = \{i \mid i > 0\}$$
$$succ^\sharp\{i \mid i > 0\} = \{i \mid i > 0\}$$
$$succ^\sharp\{i \mid i \le 0\} = Int$$
$$succ^\sharp\{i \mid i \ne 0\} = Int, \text{ etc.}$$

$$\rho_\cup(S) = \cup\{\rho\{s\} \mid s \in S\}$$
$$f^\sharp = \rho_\cup \circ f$$
$$\widetilde{pre}_{f^\sharp}(U) = \cup\{V \in SignO_{Int} \mid f^\sharp(V) \subseteq U\}$$

For $succ(i) = i + 1$,

$$\widetilde{pre}_{succ^\sharp}\{i \mid i > 0\} = \{i \mid i \ge 0\}$$
$$\widetilde{pre}_{succ^\sharp}\{0\} = \emptyset$$
$$\widetilde{pre}_{succ^\sharp}\{i \mid i < 0\} = \emptyset$$
$$\widetilde{pre}_{succ^\sharp}\{i \mid i \le 0\} = \{i \mid i < 0\}, \text{ etc.}$$

Fig. 4. Using $Sign_{Int} = \{\emptyset, \{i \mid i < 0\}, \{0\}, \{i \mid i > 0\}, Int\}$ as a base for a topology

(For example, for $Sign_{Int}$, $succ^\sharp = \rho \circ succ$, so that $succ^\sharp\{0\} = \rho(succ\{0\}) = \rho\{1\} = \{i \mid i \ge 0\}$, etc.)

When f is forwards complete (cf. Figure 3), we have completeness in the entire codomain: for *every* $S \subseteq \mathcal{P}(\Sigma)$, $\{\phi\}f\{S\}$ implies $\{\phi\}f\{f^\sharp(\phi)\}$ and $f^\sharp(\phi) \subseteq S$. When f is backwards complete, completeness extends to the entire domain: for every $S \subseteq \mathcal{P}(\Sigma)$, $\{S\}f\{\psi\}$ implies $\{S\}f\{f^\sharp(\rho(S))\}$ and $f^\sharp(\rho(S)) \subseteq \psi$. But each completeness notion yields nothing more in the logic than the strongest postcondition — what deeper property is hiding here? (See the next section.)

In summary, a forwards static analysis calculates postconditions [6,7], and the development suggests this moral:

Use a closed family of properties to generate a postcondition analysis.

What if we desire preconditions from a forwards analysis? We must first define $f^\sharp$'s inverse, $f^{\sharp-}_{\mathcal{C}_\Sigma} : \mathcal{C}_\Sigma \to \mathcal{P}(\mathcal{C}_\Sigma)$, as

$$(\star) \qquad\qquad f^{\sharp-}_{\mathcal{C}_\Sigma}(U) = \{V \in \mathcal{C}_\Sigma \mid f^\sharp(V) \subseteq U\}$$

We have, for all $V \in f^{\sharp-}_{\mathcal{C}_\Sigma}(\phi)$, that $\{V\}f\{\phi\}$ holds true, but $\cup f^{\sharp-}_{\mathcal{C}_\Sigma}(U)$ *itself* is not necessarily expressible in the closed family, $\mathcal{C}_\Sigma$.

To repair the flaw, we close $\mathcal{C}_\Sigma$ under unions, that is, *we use it as a base for a topology* on Σ, namely, $\mathcal{CO}_\Sigma = \{\cup T \mid T \subseteq \mathcal{C}_\Sigma\}$, which is both an open *and* a closed family. (The closure map $\rho_\cup : \mathcal{CO}_\Sigma \to \mathcal{CO}_\Sigma$ equals $\rho_\cup(S) = \cup\{\rho\{s\} \mid s \in S\}$.) Now, we approximate with $\mathcal{CO}_\Sigma$: for $f : \Sigma \to \Sigma$, we define $f^\sharp : \mathcal{CO}_\Sigma \to \mathcal{CO}_\Sigma$ as $f^\sharp = \rho_\cup \circ f$; we define $f^{\sharp-}_{\mathcal{CO}_\Sigma} : \mathcal{CO}_\Sigma \to \mathcal{P}(\mathcal{CO}_\Sigma)$ as $f^{\sharp-}_{\mathcal{CO}_\Sigma}(U) = \{V \in \mathcal{CO}_\Sigma \mid f^\sharp(V) \subseteq U\}$, like before; and this makes $f^\sharp$'s weakest precondition, $\widetilde{pre}_{f^\sharp} : \mathcal{CO}_\Sigma \to \mathcal{CO}_\Sigma$, well defined: $\widetilde{pre}_{f^\sharp}(U) = \cup f^{\sharp-}_{\mathcal{CO}_\Sigma}(U)$.[5]

---

[5] Since $\mathcal{CO}_\Sigma$ possesses an interior operation, ι, we can define the precondition as merely $\iota \circ f^{-1}$, and one can prove that $\widetilde{pre}_{f^\sharp} = \iota \circ f^{-1}$ [22].

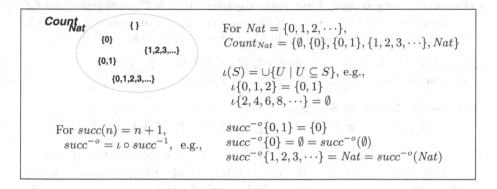

$$Count_{Nat}$$

For $Nat = \{0, 1, 2, \cdots\}$,
$Count_{Nat} = \{\emptyset, \{0\}, \{0, 1\}, \{1, 2, 3, \cdots\}, Nat\}$

$\iota(S) = \cup\{U \mid U \subseteq S\}$, e.g.,
$\iota\{0, 1, 2\} = \{0, 1\}$
$\iota\{2, 4, 6, 8, \cdots\} = \emptyset$

For $succ(n) = n + 1$,
$succ^{-o} = \iota \circ succ^{-1}$, e.g.,

$succ^{-o}\{0, 1\} = \{0\}$
$succ^{-o}\{0\} = \emptyset = succ^{-o}(\emptyset)$
$succ^{-o}\{1, 2, 3, \cdots\} = Nat = succ^{-o}(Nat)$

Fig. 5. Open family for counting analysis

In lattice theory, closure under unions is called *disjunctive completion* [10]. Figure 4 shows the disjunctive completion of $Sign_{Int}$ to $Sign\mathcal{O}_{Int}$ and the precondition function for $succ^{\sharp}$. Now, we have preconditions, but the extra sets generated by the disjunctive completion may make the abstract domain *too large* for a practical static analysis.

If we are primarily interested in preconditions, we should start with an *open family* of properties (one closed under unions), $\mathcal{O}_\Sigma \subseteq \mathcal{P}(\Sigma)$, so that we have straightaway an interior operation, $\iota : \Sigma \to \mathcal{O}_\Sigma$. An open family's logic includes disjunction as well as the inverses of those functions that are $\mathcal{O}_\Sigma$-reflecting.

We *underapproximate* the inverses of transition functions: For $f : \Sigma \to \Sigma$, define $f^{-o} : \mathcal{O}_\Sigma \to \mathcal{O}_\Sigma$ as $f^{-o} = \iota \circ f^{-1}$. This implies

$$\{f^{-o}(\psi)\}f\{\psi\}$$

holds true and $f^{-o}(\psi)$ is the *weakest precondition of f and ψ expressible in $\mathcal{O}_\Sigma$*: $\{\phi\}f\{\psi\}$ implies $\{f^{-o}(\psi)\}f\{\psi\}$ and $\phi \subseteq f^{-o}(\psi)$. Further, we can formalize the two forms of completeness with respect to ι, but we see in the next section a topological characterization.

Figure 5 defines an open (but not closed) family, $Count_{Nat}$, for a backwards counting analysis. The successor operation, $succ : Nat \to Nat$, is $Count_{Nat}$-reflecting, so $succ^{-1}$ lives in the family's logic and $succ^{-o} = succ^{-1}$. (See the Figure.) Predecessor $(pred(n) = n - 1)$ is not reflecting, and $pred^{-o} = \iota \circ pred^{-1}$ yields $pred^{-o}\{0, 1\} = \iota\{0, 1, 2\} = \{1\}$, etc. Abstract domain $Count_{Nat}$ is imperfect, e.g., it cannot prove the assertion, $\{\{0\}\}succ; pred\{\{0\}\}$. As indicated by research on backwards strictness analysis [2,12,16,17], the moral is:

> Use an open family of properties to generate a precondition analysis.

There is no need to work from a closed property family.[6]

Because the complement of a closed family is open (and vice versa), we can move from a postcondition analysis to a precondition one: Say that $\mathcal{C}_\Sigma$ is closed

---

[6] But there is an adjoint here, $\mathcal{P}(\Sigma)^{op}\langle\iota, id\rangle\mathcal{O}_\Sigma^{op}$ — $\subseteq$ becomes $\supseteq$.

so that $\mathcal{O}_\Sigma = \sim\!\mathcal{C}_\Sigma$ is open. First, every $\mathcal{C}_\Sigma$-reflecting f is $\mathcal{O}_\Sigma$-reflecting, and for every $\mathcal{C}_\Sigma$-preserving $f : \Sigma \to \Sigma$, $\hat{f}$ is $\mathcal{O}_\Sigma$-preserving, by Proposition 3. (So, $\mathcal{C}_\Sigma$'s conjunction operation is preserved in $\mathcal{O}_\Sigma$'s logic as disjunction.) We have

Lemma 4. *For all $f : \Sigma \to \Sigma$ and $S \subseteq \Sigma$, $\sim\!f^{-1}(S) = f^{-1}(\sim\!S)$.*
For closed family $\mathcal{C}_\Sigma$ and $\mathcal{O}_\Sigma = \sim\!\mathcal{C}_\Sigma$, $\sim \circ \rho = \iota \circ \sim$.

Proposition 5. *For all $S \subseteq \Sigma$, $\widetilde{f^{-1}}(S) = f^{-1}(S)$.*
   $(\widetilde{f^{-1}})^\sharp(U) = f^{-\circ}(U)$, *for all $U \in \mathcal{O}_\Sigma$.   (Note: $(\widetilde{f^{-1}})^\sharp = \sim \circ (f^{-1})^\sharp \circ \sim$.)*

Proof. We prove the second claim, $(\widetilde{f^{-1}})^\sharp(U) = \sim \circ \rho \circ f^{-1} \circ \sim (\sim\!K)$, where $U = \sim\!K$. This equals $\sim\!\rho(f^{-1}(K)) = \iota(\sim f^{-1}(K))$, by the previous lemma, which equals $\iota(f^{-1}(\sim\!K))$, by the lemma, which equals $f^{-\circ}(U)$.   □

The last result says that, by using $\mathcal{C}_\Sigma$'s closure operator to define the overapproximating $(f^{-1})^\sharp$, we can compute an *underapproximating*, weakest-precondition analysis on $\mathcal{O}_\Sigma = \sim\!\mathcal{C}_\Sigma$ defined as $(\widetilde{f^{-1}})^\sharp$.

As an example, consider $\sim Sign_{Int} = \{Int, \{i \mid i \geq 0\}, \{i \mid i \neq 0\}, \{i \mid i \leq 0\}, \emptyset\}$, based on Figure 2. This open family's logic includes

$$\psi ::= \sim\!U \mid \psi_1 \cup \psi_2 \mid negate^{-1}\psi \mid sq^{-1}\psi, \quad \text{for } U \in Sign_{Int}$$

Because $succ$ is not $Sign_{Int}$-reflecting, we underapproximate it by $succ^{-\circ} = (\widetilde{succ^{-1}})^\sharp$. We have $succ^{-\circ}\{i \mid i \neq 0\} = \{i \mid i \geq 0\}$; $succ^{-\circ}Int = Int$; and $succ^{-\circ}(U) = \emptyset$, otherwise. In this fashion, a postcondition analysis based on $\mathcal{C}_\Sigma$ defines a precondition analysis on $\sim\!\mathcal{C}_\Sigma$.

Finally, every $\mathcal{F}_\Sigma$ possesses both a logic for validation (viz., $\mathcal{F}_\Sigma$'s sets and its preserving operators) as well as a dual, *refutation logic*: $\sim \mathcal{F}_\Sigma$'s logic. We say that S *has property* $\neg\phi$ if $S \subseteq \sim\!\phi$, for $\sim\!\phi \in \sim \mathcal{F}_\Sigma$. This is the foundation for three-valued static analyses [20], where one uses a single abstract domain to compute validation, refutation, and "don't know" judgements.

5   From Continuity to Completeness

As stated earlier, there is a correspondence between functions that preserve and reflect property sets and abstract-interpretation-complete functions:

   Recall that $f : \Sigma \to \Sigma$ is $\mathcal{F}_\Sigma$-preserving iff for all $S \in \mathcal{F}_\Sigma$, $f[S] \in \mathcal{F}_\Sigma$. But this is *exactly the definition of abstract-interpretation forwards completeness* when $\mathcal{F}_\Sigma$ is a closed family. In topological terms, f is a closed map.

   We now prove that $\mathcal{F}_\Sigma$-reflection is exactly backwards completeness when $\mathcal{F}_\Sigma$ is a closed family. For $S, S' \subseteq \Sigma$, write $S \leq_{\mathcal{F}_\Sigma} S'$ iff for all $K \in \mathcal{F}_\Sigma, S \subseteq K$ implies $S' \subseteq K$. This is called the *specialization ordering* in topology. Write $S \equiv_{\mathcal{F}_\Sigma} S'$ iff $S \leq_{\mathcal{F}_\Sigma} S'$ and $S' \leq_{\mathcal{F}_\Sigma} S$. The following definition is the usual one for abstract-interpretation backwards completeness:

Definition 6. *For property family, $\mathcal{F}_\Sigma$, $f : \Sigma \to \Sigma$ is $B_{\mathcal{F}_\Sigma}$-complete iff for all $S, S' \subseteq \Sigma$, $S \equiv_{\mathcal{F}_\Sigma} S'$ implies $f[S] \equiv_{\mathcal{F}_\Sigma} f[S']$.*

Proposition 7. *If f is $\mathcal{F}_\Sigma$-reflecting, then it is $B_{\mathcal{F}_\Sigma}$-complete.*

Proof. Assume $S \leq_\Sigma S'$ and show $f[S] \leq_\Sigma f[S']$: Say that $f[S] \subseteq K \in \mathcal{F}_\Sigma$; since f is reflecting, $f^{-1}(K) \in \mathcal{F}_\Sigma$, too, and $S \subseteq f^{-1}(K)$. Because $S \leq_\Sigma S'$, $S' \subseteq f^{-1}(K)$, implying $f[S'] \subseteq K$. □

The converse of the above might not hold, but say that $\mathcal{C}_\Sigma$ is a closed family so that $\rho(S) = \cap\{K \in \mathcal{C}_\Sigma \mid S \subseteq K\}$; we can prove the converse:

Lemma 8. *For all $S \subseteq \Sigma$, $S \equiv_{\mathcal{C}_\Sigma} \rho(S)$.*
For all $S, S' \subseteq \Sigma$, $S \equiv_{\mathcal{C}_\Sigma} S'$ iff $\rho(S) = \rho(S')$.

Lemma 9. *The following are equivalent for closed family, $\mathcal{C}_\Sigma$:*
(i) f is $B_{\mathcal{C}_\Sigma}$-complete;
(ii) for all $S \subseteq \Sigma$, $f[S] \equiv_{\mathcal{C}_\Sigma} f[\rho(S)]$;
(iii) $\rho \circ f = \rho \circ f \circ \rho$.

For a closed family, reflection (topological continuity) is backwards completeness:

Theorem 10. *For $\mathcal{C}_\Sigma$, $f : \Sigma \to \Sigma$ is $B_{\mathcal{C}_\Sigma}$-complete iff f is $\mathcal{C}_\Sigma$-reflecting.*

Proof. The if-part is already proved. For the only-if part, assume $f[S] \subseteq K \in \mathcal{C}_\Sigma$ and show there is some $L_S \in \mathcal{C}_\Sigma$ such that $f[L_S] \subseteq K$. Let $\rho(S)$ be the L_S: we have $f[\rho(S)] \equiv_{\mathcal{C}_\Sigma} f[S]$ which implies $f[\rho(S)] \subseteq K$. Use the Lemma above. □

Corollary 11. *(i) if f is backwards complete for $\mathcal{C}_\Sigma$, then f^{-1} is forwards complete for both $\mathcal{C}_\Sigma$ and $\sim\mathcal{C}_\Sigma$.*
(ii) f is forwards complete for $\mathcal{C}_\Sigma$ iff $\tilde{f}$ is forwards complete for $\sim\mathcal{C}_\Sigma$.

Proof. By Proposition 3 and the previous Theorem.

The characterizations of forwards completeness as property preservation and backwards completeness as property reflection (continuity) apply to open families as well. They also link the shell constructions of Giacobazzi, et al. [13,14], to refinements of topologies and the characterization of function continuity to convergence of nets [26].

6   Relation to Partial-Order Backwards Completeness

The crucial characterization of backwards completeness by Giacobazzi, et al. [14] is made in a "frame-theory" presentation [18], where $(\mathcal{P}(\Sigma), \subseteq)$ is abstracted to a complete lattice, $(D, \sqsubseteq)$, and $\mathcal{C}_\Sigma$ is abstracted to $\rho[D] \subseteq D$, namely, the fixed points of upper closure map, $\rho : D \to D$. We can rephrase their work in terms of our development:

First, define $f^- : D \to \mathcal{P}(D)$ as $f^-(d) = \{e \in D \mid f(e) \sqsubseteq d\}$. When f^- is chain-continuous, then $f^-(d)$ has a set of maximal points, denoted by $max(f^-(d))$. When f is an *additive* function, that is, $f(\sqcup S) = \sqcup_{d \in S} f(d)$, for all

$S \subseteq D$, then $max(f^-(d))$ is a singleton set. *This is the case for the point-set topology used in the previous section.*

Let $\rho[D]$ define D's closed family of "properties" and let $f : D \to D$ be chain-continuous. First, (i) f is *continuous at* $d \in D$ iff for all $e \in \rho[D]$, if $f(d) \sqsubseteq e$, then there exists $d' \in \rho[D]$ such that $d \sqsubseteq d'$ and $f(d') \sqsubseteq e$. Next, (ii) f is *ρ-reflecting* iff for all $e \in \rho[D]$, $max((f^-(d)) \subseteq \rho[D]$ (that is, the maximum elements of $f^-(d)$ are in $\rho[D]$). It is easy to prove that (i) and (ii) are equivalent.

We define $d \equiv_{\rho[D]} d'$ iff for all $e \in \rho[D]$, $d \sqsubseteq e$ iff $d' \sqsubseteq e$, that is, iff $\rho(d) = \rho(d')$. This yields the definition of backwards completeness: f is backwards-ρ-complete if $d \equiv_{\rho[D]} d'$ implies $f(d) \equiv_{\rho[D]} f(d')$ for all $d, d' \in D$, that is, $\rho \circ f = \rho \circ f \circ \rho$. We have immediately the main result of Giacobazzi, et al. [14] in the "frame theory": $f : D \to D$ is backwards-ρ-complete iff it is ρ-reflecting.

7   Nondeterminism and semicontinuity

Model-checking applications of abstract interpretation commence with transition *relations* on $\Sigma \times \Sigma$, which we will treat as functions of arity, $f : \Sigma \to \mathcal{P}(\Sigma)$. The property family for $\mathcal{P}(\Sigma)$ is different from Σ's and depends on how we define f's preimage, a map, $\mathcal{P}(\Sigma) \to \mathcal{P}(\Sigma)$. We have two choices: for $S \subseteq \Sigma$,

$$pre_f(S) = \{c \in \Sigma \mid f(c) \cap S \neq \emptyset\}$$
$$\widetilde{pre}_f(S) = \{c \in \Sigma \mid f(c) \subseteq S\}$$

The following definitions come from Vietoris [25]:

Definition 12. *For property family,* $\mathcal{F}_\Sigma \subseteq \Sigma$,
   $f : \Sigma \to \mathcal{P}(\Sigma)$ *is* lower semicontinuous *for* $\mathcal{F}_\Sigma$ *iff* pre_f *is* $\mathcal{F}_\Sigma$-*preserving.*
   $f : \Sigma \to \mathcal{P}(\Sigma)$ *is* upper semicontinuous *for* $\mathcal{F}_\Sigma$ *iff* $\widetilde{pre}_f$ *is* $\mathcal{F}_\Sigma$-*preserving.*

Say we want pre_f in the logic for $\mathcal{F}_\Sigma$; what property family for $\mathcal{P}(\Sigma)$ is appropriate? The answer was found by Smyth [25]: define $\mathcal{O}_{\mathcal{F}_\Sigma}^L \subseteq \mathcal{P}(\mathcal{P}(\Sigma))$ to be the open family generated by taking all unions of the base, $\mathcal{B}_{\mathcal{F}_\Sigma}^L = \{\exists U \mid U \in \mathcal{F}_\Sigma\}$, where $\exists U = \{S \subseteq \Sigma \mid S \cap U \neq \emptyset\}$. (Read $\exists U$ as "all the sets that meet property U"). Indeed, for all $U \in \mathcal{F}_\Sigma$, $f^{-1}(\exists U) = pre_f(U)$. $\mathcal{O}_{\mathcal{F}_\Sigma}^L$ is called the *lower topology based on* $\mathcal{F}_\Sigma$. This result is due to Smyth [25]:

Proposition 13. *If* $\mathcal{O}_\Sigma \subseteq \Sigma$ *is an open family for* Σ, *then* $f : \Sigma \to \mathcal{P}(\Sigma)$ *is lower semicontinuous for* $\mathcal{O}_\Sigma$ *iff* f *is* $\mathcal{O}_\Sigma \mathcal{O}_{\mathcal{O}_\Sigma}^L$-*reflecting.*

That is, pre_f lies in the logic for $\mathcal{O}_\Sigma$ iff f is $\mathcal{O}_\Sigma \mathcal{O}_{\mathcal{O}_\Sigma}^L$-reflecting. When $f : \Sigma \to \mathcal{P}(\Sigma)$ is not lower semicontinuous, we simply use $\mathcal{O}_\Sigma$'s interior operator, ι, to approximate pre_f by $\iota \circ pre_f : \mathcal{O}_\Sigma \to \mathcal{O}_\Sigma$, like in Section 4.

We can rephrase the previous Proposition in terms of its dual, closed family and discover a well-travelled path: For open family, $\mathcal{O}_\Sigma$, and $\mathcal{C}_\Sigma = \sim \mathcal{O}_\Sigma$, we have that $\sim \mathcal{O}_{\mathcal{O}_\Sigma}^L$ is a closed family whose members are all the intersections of sets taken from the (co)base, $\mathcal{B}_{\mathcal{C}_\Sigma}^U = \{\forall K \mid K \in \mathcal{C}_\Sigma\}$, where $\forall K = \{S \subseteq \Sigma \mid S \subseteq K\}$. (Read $\forall K$ as "all the sets covered by property K.") Indeed, for all $K \in \mathcal{C}_\Sigma$, $f^{-1}(\forall K) = \widetilde{pre}_f(K)$. We name the closed family: $\mathcal{C}_{\mathcal{C}_\Sigma}^U = \sim \mathcal{O}_{\mathcal{O}_\Sigma}^L$.

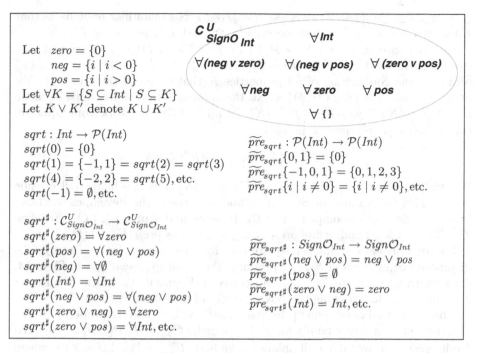

Fig. 6. *sqrt*, upper topology on $SignO_{Int}$, and $sqrt^{\sharp}$

Corollary 14. *Let $\mathcal{C}_\Sigma$ be a closed family and define $\mathcal{O}_\Sigma = \sim\mathcal{C}_\Sigma$.*

pre_f is $\mathcal{O}_\Sigma$-preserving iff $\widetilde{pre}_f$ is $\mathcal{C}_\Sigma$-preserving.

f is $\mathcal{O}_\Sigma\mathcal{O}_{\mathcal{O}_\Sigma}^L$-reflecting iff it is $\mathcal{C}_\Sigma\mathcal{C}_{\mathcal{C}_\Sigma}^U$-reflecting.

Hence, $\widetilde{pre}_f$ is $\mathcal{C}_\Sigma$-preserving iff f is $\mathcal{C}_\Sigma\mathcal{C}_{\mathcal{C}_\Sigma}^U$-reflecting iff f is upper semicontinuous for $\mathcal{C}_\Sigma$.

Proof. By Propositions 3 and 13. □

The corollary tells us $\widetilde{pre}_f$ lies in $\mathcal{C}_\Sigma$'s logic when $f : \Sigma \to \mathcal{P}(\Sigma)$ is upper semicontinuous. But what if f is not? Then we must approximate it by some $f^{\sharp} : \mathcal{C}_\Sigma \to \mathcal{C}_{\mathcal{C}_\Sigma}^U$ from which we induce a $\mathcal{C}_\Sigma$-preserving $\widetilde{pre}_{f^{\sharp}}$. (Alas, we have no interior map to aid us, only a closure map.)

To do this, we need some insight: First, each $M \in \mathcal{C}_{\mathcal{C}_\Sigma}^U$ is a set of sets formed as $M = \bigcap_{i \in I}\{\forall K_i \mid K_i \in \mathcal{C}_\Sigma\}$. Read property M as "$\forall K_1 \wedge \forall K_2 \wedge \cdots \wedge \forall K_i \wedge \cdots$" — M's members are sets covered by property K_1 and covered by property K_2 and ... covered by property K_i and so on. For $f : \Sigma \to \mathcal{P}(\Sigma)$, we express its relational assertions in the form,

$$\{\phi\}f\{\forall\psi_1 \wedge \forall\psi_2 \wedge \cdots \wedge \forall\psi_i \wedge \cdots\}$$

By pointwise reasoning, the M defined above equals $\forall\bigcap\{K_i \mid K_i \in \mathcal{C}_\Sigma\}$, read as "$\forall(K_1 \wedge K_2 \wedge \cdots \wedge K_i \wedge \cdots)$." But $\bigcap\{K_i \mid K_i \in \mathcal{C}_\Sigma\} \in \mathcal{C}_\Sigma$, meaning that the relational assertion reverts to this benign format:

$$\{\phi\}f\{\forall\psi\}$$

for $\phi, \psi \in \mathcal{C}_\Sigma$. (You can write it as "$\phi \models [f]\psi$.") The quantifier reminds us that f's answer is a *set* of Σ-values, covered by ψ. And, $\phi \subseteq \widetilde{pre}_f(\psi) = f^{-1}(\forall\psi)$.

Say we approximate $f : \Sigma \to \mathcal{P}(\Sigma)$ by $f^\sharp(K) = \rho_U(f[K])$, where ρ_U is the closure operation for $\mathcal{C}^U_{\mathcal{C}_\Sigma}$: $\rho_U(T) = \bigcap\{\forall K \mid T \subseteq \forall K, K \in \mathcal{C}_\Sigma\}$. That is, $\rho_U(T)$ computes the conjunction of all properties K that cover all the sets in T. We have, as usual, that $\{\phi\}f\{f^\sharp(\phi)\}$. Next, the approximation of $\widetilde{pre}_f$ must be made sound: $\widetilde{pre}_{f^\sharp}(K) \subseteq \widetilde{pre}_f(K) = f^{-1}(\forall K)$, for all $K \in \mathcal{C}_\Sigma$. We work from Equation $(\star)$ in Section 4; $f^\sharp$'s inverse image is

$$f^{\sharp-}_{\mathcal{C}_\Sigma}(K) = \{K' \in \mathcal{C}_\Sigma \mid f^\sharp(K') \subseteq \forall K\}$$

We wish to define $\widetilde{pre}_{f^\sharp}(K) = \cup f^{\sharp-}(K)$, but $\widetilde{pre}_{f^\sharp}$'s image might fall outside of $\mathcal{C}_\Sigma$. This issue arose in Section 4, and we repeat the development there: build the disjunctive completion of $\mathcal{C}_\Sigma$ (closure under unions), $\mathcal{CO}_\Sigma$; redefine $f^\sharp : \mathcal{CO}_\Sigma \to \mathcal{C}^U_{\mathcal{CO}_\Sigma}$; and define $\widetilde{pre}_{f^\sharp} : \mathcal{CO}_\Sigma \to \mathcal{CO}_\Sigma$ as $\widetilde{pre}_{f^\sharp}(K) = \cup f^{\sharp-}_{\mathcal{CO}_\Sigma}(K)$.

Figure 6 displays an integer square-root function, $sqrt : Int \to \mathcal{P}(Int)$. The disjunctive completion of $Sign_{Int}$ produces the topology, $SignO_{Int}$, in Figure 4, from which we generate $\mathcal{C}^U_{SignO_{Int}}$, illustrated in Figure 6. This form of abstract domain is used for checking the box-modality of modal-mu calculus.

There is a dual development. Starting again with Σ and its property family, $\mathcal{F}_\Sigma$, define the property family for $\mathcal{P}(\Sigma)$, namely, $\mathcal{O}^U_{\mathcal{F}_\Sigma} \subseteq \mathcal{P}(\mathcal{P}(\Sigma))$, as the open family generated by taking all unions of the base, $\mathcal{B}^U_{\mathcal{F}_\Sigma} = \{\forall U \mid U \in \mathcal{F}_\Sigma\}$, where $\forall U = \{S \subseteq \Sigma \mid S \subseteq U\}$. This is the *upper topology based on* $\mathcal{F}_\Sigma$. (Recall, for all $U \in \mathcal{F}_\Sigma$, that $f^{-1}(\forall U) = \widetilde{pre}_f(U)$.)

Proposition 15. *[25] Let $\mathcal{O}_\Sigma \subseteq \Sigma$ be an open family. $f : \Sigma \to \mathcal{P}(\Sigma)$ is upper semicontinuous for $\mathcal{O}_\Sigma$ iff f is $\mathcal{O}_\Sigma \mathcal{O}^U_{\mathcal{O}_\Sigma}$-reflecting.*

When f is not upper semicontinuous, we may use $\iota \circ \widetilde{pre}_f : \mathcal{O}_\Sigma \to \mathcal{O}_\Sigma$, where ι is $\mathcal{O}_\Sigma$'s interior operator. The dual goes as follows: $\mathcal{C}^L_{\mathcal{C}_\Sigma} = {\sim}\mathcal{O}^U_{\mathcal{O}_\Sigma}$, whose members are all intersections of sets from the (co)base, $\mathcal{B}^L_{\mathcal{C}_\Sigma} = \{\exists K \mid K \in \mathcal{C}_\Sigma\}$, where $\exists K = \{S \subseteq \Sigma \mid S \cap K \neq \emptyset\}$. For all $K \in \mathcal{C}_\Sigma$, $f^{-1}(\exists K) = pre_f(K)$.

Corollary 16. $\widetilde{pre}_f$ *is $\mathcal{O}_\Sigma$-preserving iff pre_f is $\mathcal{C}_\Sigma$-preserving.*

f is $\mathcal{O}_\Sigma \mathcal{O}^U_{\mathcal{O}_\Sigma}$-reflecting iff it is $\mathcal{C}_\Sigma \mathcal{C}^L_{\mathcal{C}_\Sigma}$-reflecting.

Hence, pre_f is $\mathcal{C}_\Sigma$-preserving iff f is $\mathcal{C}_\Sigma \mathcal{C}^L_{\mathcal{C}_\Sigma}$-reflecting iff f is lower semicontinuous for $\mathcal{C}_\Sigma$.

Say that $f : \Sigma \to \mathcal{P}(\Sigma)$ is not lower semicontinuous. When we approximate it by $f^\flat : \mathcal{C}_\Sigma \to \mathcal{C}^L_{\mathcal{C}_\Sigma}$, what is the result? What is $pre_{f^\flat}$? The answer summarizes significant research on underapproximation [5,11,23].

Each $M \in \mathcal{C}^L_{\mathcal{C}_\Sigma}$ is a set of sets of form $M = \bigcap_{i \in I}\{\exists K_i \mid K_i \in \mathcal{C}_\Sigma\}$. Read M as "$\exists K_1 \wedge \exists K_2 \wedge \cdots \wedge \exists K_i \wedge \cdots$" — each of M's members is a set that meets (*witnesses*) K_1 and K_2 and ... K_i and so on. For $f : \Sigma \to \mathcal{P}(\Sigma)$, we express its relational assertions in the form,

$$\{\phi\}f\{\exists\psi_1 \wedge \exists\psi_2 \wedge \cdots \wedge \exists\psi_i \wedge \cdots\}$$

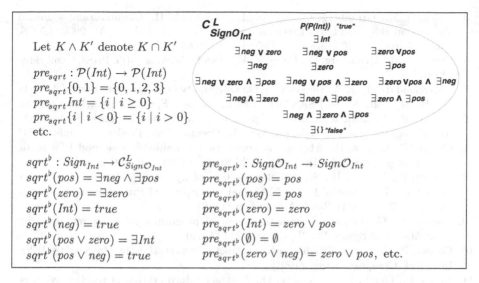

Let $K \wedge K'$ denote $K \cap K'$

$pre_{sqrt} : \mathcal{P}(Int) \to \mathcal{P}(Int)$
$pre_{sqrt}\{0,1\} = \{0,1,2,3\}$
$pre_{sqrt}Int = \{i \mid i \geq 0\}$
$pre_{sqrt}\{i \mid i < 0\} = \{i \mid i > 0\}$
etc.

$sqrt^{\flat} : Sign_{Int} \to \mathcal{C}^L_{SignO_{Int}}$
$sqrt^{\flat}(pos) = \exists neg \wedge \exists pos$
$sqrt^{\flat}(zero) = \exists zero$
$sqrt^{\flat}(Int) = true$
$sqrt^{\flat}(neg) = true$
$sqrt^{\flat}(pos \vee zero) = \exists Int$
$sqrt^{\flat}(pos \vee neg) = true$

$pre_{sqrt^{\flat}} : SignO_{Int} \to SignO_{Int}$
$pre_{sqrt^{\flat}}(pos) = pos$
$pre_{sqrt^{\flat}}(neg) = pos$
$pre_{sqrt^{\flat}}(zero) = zero$
$pre_{sqrt^{\flat}}(Int) = zero \vee pos$
$pre_{sqrt^{\flat}}(\emptyset) = \emptyset$
$pre_{sqrt^{\flat}}(zero \vee neg) = zero \vee pos$, etc.

Fig. 7. Lower topology on $SignO_{Int}$ and $sqrt^{\flat}$

for $\psi_i \in \mathcal{C}_{\Sigma}$. (In the case of $\{\phi\}f\{\exists\psi\}$ you can write "$\phi \models \langle f \rangle \psi$." And, $\phi \subseteq pre_f(\psi) = f^{-1}(\exists\psi)$.)

We approximate $f : \Sigma \to \mathcal{P}(\Sigma)$ by $f^{\flat}(K) = \rho_L(f[K])$, where ρ_L is the closure operation for $\mathcal{C}^L_{\mathcal{C}_{\Sigma}}$: $\rho_L(T) = \bigcap\{\exists K \mid T \subseteq \exists K, K \in \mathcal{C}_{\Sigma}\}$. That is, $\rho_L(T)$ collects all the properties, K, that are witnessed (met) by each of the sets in T. We have $\{\phi\}f\{f^{\flat}(\phi)\}$, and $f^{\flat}(\phi)$ is the strongest postcondition in the logic associated with $\mathcal{C}^L_{\mathcal{C}_{\Sigma}}$, the "language of witnesses." Once again, we define $f^{\flat -}_{\mathcal{C}_{\Sigma}}(K) = \{K' \in \mathcal{C}_{\Sigma} \mid f^{\flat}(K') \subseteq \exists K\}$ and $pre_{f^{\flat}}(K) = \cup f^{\flat -}_{\mathcal{C}_{\Sigma}}(K)$. This is the definition used by Cleaveland [5], Dams [11], and Schmidt [23] to prove that $pre_{f^{\flat}}$ computes weakest preconditions for f within the logics for $\mathcal{C}_{\Sigma}$ and $\mathcal{C}^L_{\mathcal{C}_{\Sigma}}$. When $pre_{f^{\flat}}$'s image does not fall within $\mathcal{C}_{\Sigma}$ — see $pre_{sqrt^{\flat}}(Int)$ in Figure 7, for example — disjunctive completion of $\mathcal{C}_{\Sigma}$ to a topology again saves the day. The final moral, contained in Cousot and Cousot's use of topology in 1977 [8], is:

Every abstract domain defines a base for a topology on the corresponding concrete domain.

Acknowledgements. This paper was inspired by a presentation Mike Smyth gave in Edinburgh in December 1982; I thank Mike for his clear, intuitive papers and explanations. The trailblazing works of Radhia and Patrick Cousot and Roberto Giacobazzi and his colleagues are also greatly appreciated. I also thank the referees for their detailed comments and many helpful suggestions.

References

1. Abramsky, S.: Domain theory in logical form. Ann. Pure Appl. Logic 51, 1–77 (1991)
2. Benton, N.: Strictness logic and polymorphic invariance. In: Proc. Logical Found. Comp. Sci, pp. 33–44 (1992)

3. Clarke, E.M., Grumberg, O., Jha, S., Lu, Y., Veith, H.: Counterexample-guided abstraction refinement. In: Emerson, E.A., Sistla, A.P. (eds.) CAV 2000. LNCS, vol. 1855, pp. 154–169. Springer, Heidelberg (2000)
4. Clarke, E.M., Grumberg, O., Peled, D.A.: Model Checking. MIT Press, Cambridge (2000)
5. Cleaveland, R., Iyer, P., Yankelevich, D.: Optimality in abstractions of model checking. In: Mycroft, A. (ed.) SAS 1995. LNCS, vol. 983. Springer, Heidelberg (1995)
6. Cousot, P.: Semantic foundations of program analysis. In: Muchnick, S., Jones, N. (eds.) Program Flow Analysis, pp. 303–342. Prentice-Hall, Englewood Cliffs (1981)
7. Cousot, P., Cousot, R.: Abstract interpretation: a unified lattice model for static analysis of programs. In: Proc. 4th ACM Symp. POPL, pp. 238–252 (1977)
8. Cousot, P., Cousot, R.: Static determination of dynamic properties of recursive procedures. In: Neuhold, E.J. (ed.) Formal Description of Programming Concepts, pp. 238–277. North-Holland, Amsterdam (1978)
9. Cousot, P., Cousot, R.: Systematic design of program analysis frameworks. In: Proc. 6th ACM Symp. POPL, pp. 269–282 (1979)
10. Cousot, P., Cousot, R.: Higher-order abstract interpretation. In: Proceedings IEEE Int. Conf. Computer Lang. (1994)
11. Dams, D., Gerth, R., Grumberg, O.: Abstract interpretation of reactive systems. ACM Trans. Prog. Lang. Systems 19, 253–291 (1997)
12. Dybjer, P.: Inverse image analysis generalises strictness analysis. Information and Computation 90, 194–216 (1991)
13. Giacobazzi, R., Quintarelli, E.: Incompleteness, counterexamples, and refinements in abstract model checking. In: Cousot, P. (ed.) SAS 2001. LNCS, vol. 2126, pp. 356–373. Springer, Heidelberg (2001)
14. Giacobazzi, R., Ranzato, F., Scozzari, F.: Making abstract interpretations complete. J. ACM 47, 361–416 (2000)
15. Gunter, C., Scott, D.S.: Semantic domains. In: Handbook of Theoretical Computer Science, vol. B, pp. 633–674. MIT Press, Cambridge (1991)
16. Hunt, S.: Frontiers and open sets in abstract intepretation. In: Proc. ACM Symp. Functional Prog. and Comp. Architecture, pp. 194–216 (1989)
17. Jensen, T.: Abstract Interpretation in Logical Form. PhD thesis, Imperial College, London (1992)
18. Johnstone, P.: Stone Spaces. Cambridge University Press, Cambridge (1986)
19. Reynolds, J.C.: Notes on a lattice-theoretic approach to the theory of computation. Technical report, Computer Science, Syracuse University (1972)
20. Sagiv, M., Reps, T., Wilhelm, R.: Parametric shape analysis via 3-valued logic. ACM TOPLAS 24, 217–298 (2002)
21. Schmidt, D.A.: Comparing completeness properties of static analyses and their logics. In: Kobayashi, N. (ed.) APLAS 2006. LNCS, vol. 4279, pp. 183–199. Springer, Heidelberg (2006)
22. Schmidt, D.A.: Underapproximating predicate transformers. In: Yi, K. (ed.) SAS 2006. LNCS, vol. 4134, pp. 127–143. Springer, Heidelberg (2006)
23. Schmidt, D.A.: A calculus of logical relations for over- and underapproximating static analyses. Science of Computer Programming 64, 29–53 (2007)
24. Smyth, M.B.: Effectively given domains. Theoretical Comp. Sci. 5, 257–274 (1977)
25. Smyth, M.B.: Powerdomains and predicate transformers: a topological view. In: Díaz, J. (ed.) ICALP 1983. LNCS, vol. 154, pp. 662–675. Springer, Heidelberg (1983)
26. Willard, S.: General Topology. Dover Publications (2004)

Interval Polyhedra: An Abstract Domain to Infer Interval Linear Relationships[*]

Liqian Chen[1,2], Antoine Miné[2,3], Ji Wang[1], and Patrick Cousot[2,4]

[1] National Laboratory for Parallel and Distributed Processing, Changsha, P.R.China
wj@nudt.edu.cn
[2] École Normale Supérieure, Paris, France
{chen,mine,cousot}@di.ens.fr
[3] CNRS, France
[4] CIMS, New York University, New York, NY, USA

Abstract. We introduce a new numerical abstract domain, so-called *interval polyhedra (itvPol)*, to infer and propagate interval linear constraints over program variables. *itvPol*, which allows to represent constraints of the form $\sum_k [a_k, b_k] x_k \leq c$, is more expressive than the classic convex polyhedra domain and allows to express certain non-convex (even unconnected) properties. The implementation of *itvPol* can be constructed based on interval linear programming and an interval variant of Fourier-Motzkin elimination. The preliminary experimental results of our prototype are encouraging, especially for programs affected by interval uncertainty, e.g., due to uncertain input data or interval-based abstractions of disjunctive, non-linear, or floating-point expressions. To our knowledge, this is the first application of interval linear algebra to static analysis.

1 Introduction

Abstract interpretation [7] is a theory of semantics approximation. One application is to design computable abstractions and achieve a trade-off between efficiency and precision. Abstract interpretation provides a generic framework for devising static analyses to automatically infer dynamic properties of programs. The notion of an *abstract domain* is a core concept in this framework, and is used to denote a specific kind of computer-representable properties (such as a family of constraints) together with efficient manipulation algorithms to perform abstract operations (such as join, meet, widening, etc.). In particular, *numerical* abstract domains focus on numerical relationships among program variables. There exists a wide variety of numerical abstract domains with different expressiveness and complexity, such as intervals ($a \leq x \leq b$) [6], octagons ($\pm x \pm y \leq c$) [20], convex polyhedra ($\Sigma_k a_k x_k \leq b$) [10].

In the analysis and verification of hardware and software systems, after modeling or abstraction, the given application data may be inexact or affected by uncertainty, that is, they are only known to lie in certain intervals. Particularly, to analyze programs involving non-linear operations (e.g., multiplication or division of two expressions) or

---

[*] This work is supported by the INRIA project "Abstraction" common to CNRS and ENS in France, and by the National Natural Science Foundation of China under Grant No.60725206.

floating-point arithmetic, one may resort to a so-called *linearization* technique to abstract non-linear or floating-point expressions into linear expressions with interval coefficients ($\sum_k[a_k, b_k]x_k+[c, d]$) [19,21]. Furthermore, when analyzing numerical programs using a floating-point implementation (e.g., [4]) of a numerical abstract domain, a real number in the analyzed program might be abstracted as an interval of two neighboring floating-point numbers for soundness. Moreover, many floating-point algorithms can only output safe bounds, even when the input is an exact singleton value (e.g., adding two floating-point numbers in the floating-point interval domain). In other words, intervals appear naturally in practice. Hence, it is useful to have a numerical abstract domain that allows interval linear relationships among numerical program quantities to be maintained during the analysis.

This paper presents a new abstract domain, *interval polyhedra (itvPol)*, to infer relationships of the form $\sum_k[a_k, b_k] \times x_k \le b$ over program variables x_k ($k = 1, \ldots, n$), where constants $a_k, b_k, c \in \mathbb{R}$ are automatically inferred by the analysis. Intuitively, *itvPol* is an interval version of the classic convex polyhedra domain. In general, an interval polyhedron is non-convex (even unconnected); it is the union of a family of convex polyhedra. Thus, *itvPol* can naturally encode certain disjunctive information. In this paper, we propose a method to abstract disjunctions using interval linear constraints. The *itvPol* domain is implemented based on interval linear programming and an interval variant of Fourier-Motzkin variable elimination. The preliminary experimental results of the prototype implementation are promising on benchmark programs; *itvPol* can find more precise invariants than the convex polyhedra domain without too much overhead.

The rest of the paper is organized as follows. Section 2 discusses some related work. Section 3 reviews the basic theory of interval linear systems and interval linear programming. Section 4 defines our numerical abstract domain *itvPol*. Section 5 describes the domain operations of *itvPol*. In Section 6, possible applications of the *itvPol* domain are discussed. Section 7 presents our prototype implementation together with preliminary experimental results before Section 8 concludes.

2 Related Work

Numerical Abstract Domains. Most of the current numerical abstract domains can only represent *convex* properties using a subset of standard linear constraints, which makes the analysis tractable. Examples include intervals [6], octagons [20], convex polyhedra [10], SubPolyhedra [17], etc. Few abstract domains natively allow representing non-convex sets (i.e., that are not disjunctive completion of known convex domains), e.g., congruences [12], max-plus polyhedra [2], domain lifting by max expressions [13]. To deal with disjunctions, a well-known solution is to use *disjunctive completion* [8,9,11] or *reduced cardinal power* [8]. Unfortunately, it can be very costly and also the widening operators for such domains are difficult to design (e.g., as discussed in [3]).

The *itvPol* domain that we introduce in this article is closest to the classic domain of convex polyhedra [10] but is strictly more expressive, since the coefficients of variables are generalized to intervals. Our domain is orthogonal to max-plus polyhedra [2] in that *itvPol* generalizes convex polyhedra [10] while max-plus polyhedra generalize octagons [20][1]. Moreover, *itvPol* can describe even some unconnected sets.

Interval Linear Systems. Solving interval linear systems is a challenging problem in the community of interval analysis and interval linear algebra. This problem was first considered by Oettli and Prager [22] in the middle of the 1960s. And since then, this problem has received much attention [23,24]. A deep insight of the topological and graph theoretical properties of the solution set was given in [14]. However, both checking the solvability and finding the solution set of an interval linear system are NP-hard [24]. Some algorithms have also been proposed for interval linear programming [5,15].

   In contrast to the above community, we are interested in designing an abstract domain, and thus, need to design new operators tailored to the semantics of programs.

3   Preliminaries

In this section we briefly recall the basic theory and results on interval linear systems, most of which can be found in [23,24]. We use the following notations. Let $A \in \mathbb{R}^{m \times n}$ be a matrix. Intervals are denoted using boldface letters, such as $\mathbf{x}$, and their bounds are denoted as $\underline{x}$ and $\overline{x}$ so that $\mathbf{x} = [\underline{x}, \overline{x}]$. This notation is extended to linear algebra over intervals. Let $\mathbb{IR}$ be the set of all intervals on $\mathbb{R}$. Throughout the paper, intervals and other interval objects in interval algebra are typeset in boldface letters.

3.1   Interval Linear System

Let $\underline{A}, \overline{A} \in \mathbb{R}^{m \times n}$ be two matrices with $\underline{A} \le \overline{A}$, where comparison operators are defined element-wise, then the set of matrices

$$\mathbf{A} = [\underline{A}, \overline{A}] = \{A \in \mathbb{R}^{m \times n} : \underline{A} \le A \le \overline{A}\}$$

is called an *interval matrix*, and the matrices $\underline{A}, \overline{A}$ are called its bounds. Let us define the *center matrix* of $\mathbf{A}$ as $A_c = \frac{1}{2}(\underline{A} + \overline{A})$ and the *radius matrix* as $\triangle_A = \frac{1}{2}(\overline{A} - \underline{A})$. Then, $\mathbf{A} = [\underline{A}, \overline{A}] = [A_c - \triangle_A, A_c + \triangle_A]$. An *interval vector* is a one-column interval matrix $\mathbf{d} = [\underline{d}, \overline{d}] = \{d \in \mathbb{R}^m : \underline{d} \le d \le \overline{d}\}$, where $\underline{d}, \overline{d} \in \mathbb{R}^m$ and $\underline{d} \le \overline{d}$.

   Let $\mathbf{A}$ be an $m \times n$ interval matrix and b be a vector of size m. The following system of interval linear inequalities

$$\mathbf{A}x \le b$$

denotes an *interval linear system*, that is, the *family* of all systems of linear inequalities $Ax \le b$ such that $A \in \mathbf{A}$.

Definition 1 (Weak solution). *A vector $x \in \mathbb{R}^n$ is called a* weak solution *of the interval linear system* $\mathbf{A}x \le b$, *if it satisfies* $Ax \le b$ *for some* $A \in \mathbf{A}$. *Furthermore, the set*

$$\Sigma_{\exists}(\mathbf{A}, b) = \{x \in \mathbb{R}^n : \exists A \in \mathbf{A}. Ax \le b\}$$

is said to be the weak solution set *of the system* $\mathbf{A}x \le b$.

---

[1] As an example, Fig. 1(1.a) depicts an *itvPol* element which cannot be represented by max-plus polyhedra while Fig. 1(2.b) shows a max-plus polyhedron that is not in *itvPol*.

The weak solution set of an interval linear system is characterized by the following theorem [24].

Theorem 1. *A vector $x \in \mathbb{R}^n$ is a weak solution of $\mathbf{A}x \leq b$ iff it satisfies $A_c x - \Delta_A |x| \leq b$.*

In general, the weak solution set can be *non-convex*, and even unconnected (Fig. 1(1)). The non-convexity can be derived from the non-linear factor $|x|$ in Theorem 1. A (closed) *orthant* is one of the 2^n subsets of an n-dimensional Euclidean space defined by constraining each Cartesian coordinate axis to be either nonnegative or nonpositive. Note that, in a given orthant, each component of x keeps a constant sign, so the intersection of the weak solution set with each orthant can be described as a (possibly empty) convex polyhedron. However, not all unions of convex polyhedra with at most one in each orthant can be exactly encoded as interval linear systems (e.g., Fig. 1(2.c)).

The narrowest interval vector $\mathbf{x}^H$ containing the weak solution set $\Sigma_\exists(\mathbf{A}, b)$, is called the *interval hull* of $\Sigma_\exists(\mathbf{A}, b)$, i.e., $\mathbf{x}_k^H = [\underline{x}_k^H, \overline{x}_k^H]$, where $\underline{x}_k^H = \min\{x_k : x \in \Sigma_\exists(\mathbf{A}, b)\}$, $\overline{x}_k^H = \max\{x_k : x \in \Sigma_\exists(\mathbf{A}, b)\}$, for $k = 1, \dots, n$. Computing the interval hull of the solution set $\Sigma_\exists(\mathbf{A}, b)$ is an NP-hard problem [23].

3.2 Interval Linear Programming

Let $\mathbf{A} \in \mathbb{IR}^{m \times n}$ be an $m \times n$ interval matrix, $b \in \mathbb{R}^m$ be an m-dimensional vector, and $\mathbf{c} \in \mathbb{IR}^n$ be an n-dimensional interval vector. The *family* of linear programming (LP) problems

$$f(A, b, c) = \min\{c^T x : Ax \leq b\}$$

with data satisfying

$$A \in \mathbf{A}, c \in \mathbf{c}$$

is called an *interval linear programming (ILP)* problem.

The interval $[\underline{f}(\mathbf{A}, b, \mathbf{c}), \overline{f}(\mathbf{A}, b, \mathbf{c})]$, where $\underline{f}(\mathbf{A}, b, \mathbf{c}) = \inf\{f(A, b, c) : A \in \mathbf{A}, c \in \mathbf{c}\}$, and $\overline{f}(\mathbf{A}, b, \mathbf{c}) = \sup\{f(A, b, c) : A \in \mathbf{A}, c \in \mathbf{c}\}$, is called the *range of the optimal value* of the above ILP problem.

In this paper, we are only interested in computing the lower bound $\underline{f}(\mathbf{A}, b, \mathbf{c})$. However, in general, to compute the exact $\underline{f}(\mathbf{A}, b, \mathbf{c})$, in the worst case up to 2^n LP problems have to be solved, one for each orthant. In practice, [5] proposed an enumerative approach which can considerably reduce the number of LPs in many cases. Recently, Jansson [15] proposed an iterative method to compute a safe lower bound for $\underline{f}(\mathbf{A}, b, \mathbf{c})$ by solving a sequence of midpoint problems, and in many cases, only a small computational effort is required. In the following sections, we use ILP as a black box.

4   The Interval Polyhedra Domain

We now introduce the *interval polyhedra* abstract domain (*itvPol*). The main idea is to use interval linear inequality constraints in the representation of the new domain. An important similarity between the *itvPol* domain and most existing numerical abstract domains is that their elements can be defined as the solutions of systems of finitely many constraints from a certain family. To some extent, one may consider the *itvPol* domain as an interval version of the classic convex polyhedra domain which only supports standard (non-interval) linear constraints.

4.1 Representation

An *interval polyhedron* **P** is described as an interval linear system $\mathbf{A}x \le b$, where $\mathbf{A} \in \mathbb{IR}^{m \times n}$ is an interval matrix and $b \in \mathbb{R}^m$ is a plain vector of real numbers. It represents the set $\gamma(\mathbf{P}) = \Sigma_\exists(\mathbf{A}, b)$, and each point $x \in \gamma(\mathbf{P})$ is a possible program environment (or state), i.e., an assignment of numerical/real values to program variables. Note that with respect to the weak solution set, an interval linear equation $\varphi: \Sigma_k [\underline{a}_k, \overline{a}_k] \times x_k = [\underline{b}, \overline{b}]$ can be represented as a pair of interval linear inequalities $\varphi': \Sigma_k [\underline{a}_k, \overline{a}_k] \times x_k \le \overline{b}$ and $\varphi'': \Sigma_k [-\overline{a}_k, -\underline{a}_k] \times x_k \le -\underline{b}$. The set of interval polyhedra has the following properties:

- Non-convexity: an interval polyhedron is *non-convex* in general, but its intersection with each orthant in $\mathbb{R}^n$ gives a (possibly empty) convex polyhedron.
- Closed for intersection: the intersection of two interval polyhedra is also an interval polyhedron.
- Non-closed for union: the union of two interval polyhedra may not be an interval polyhedron.

In general, an interval polyhedron has a complicated shape. Fig. 1 shows some examples of interval polyhedra (1) as well as examples that are not interval polyhedra (2). Specifically, (2.a), (2.b), (2.d) are not interval polyhedra because their intersection with some orthant (e.g., the (+,+)-orthant) is not convex. (2.c) and (2.e) are not interval polyhedra as they do not satisfy the topological properties described in [14].

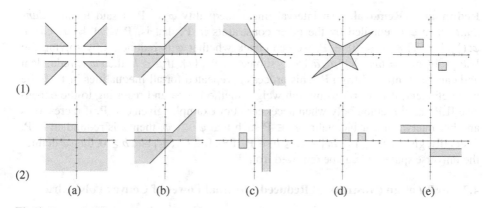

Fig. 1. Examples that are (1) or are not (2) interval polyhedra in two dimensions. The examples (1) correspond to the following interval linear systems: (1.a) $\{[-1,1]x + y = 0, [-1,1]y = 1\}$, (1.b) $\{[-1,0]x + y = [0,1]\}$, (1.c) $\{[1,2]x + [1,2]y = [1,2]\}$, (1.d) $\{[-1,1]x + 2y = [-2,2], 2x + [-2,1]y = [-2,2]\}$, (1.e) $\{[-1,1]x = 1, [-1,1]y = 1, x = [-2,2], y = [-2,2], x + y = [-1,1]\}$.

An interval linear inequality φ is entailed by an interval polyhedron **P**, denoted as $\mathbf{P} \models \varphi$, iff $\gamma(\mathbf{P}) \subseteq \gamma(\varphi)$. The order relation $\sqsubseteq$ on interval polyhedra is defined as $\mathbf{P}_1 \sqsubseteq \mathbf{P}_2$ iff $\gamma(\mathbf{P}_1) \subseteq \gamma(\mathbf{P}_2)$, i.e., $\forall \varphi \in \mathbf{P}_2 . \mathbf{P}_1 \models \varphi$, which can be implemented using ILP. The inclusion $\mathbf{P}_1 \sqsubseteq \mathbf{P}_2$ holds iff for all $(\Sigma_k [\underline{a}_k, \overline{a}_k] \times x_k \le b) \in \mathbf{P}_2$, $\mu \le b$ holds where $\mu = \max \Sigma_k [\underline{a}_k, \overline{a}_k] \times x_k$ subject to $\mathbf{P}_1$. However, $\sqsubseteq$ may be too expensive to compute. We define an approximate order relation $\sqsubseteq_s$ on interval polyhedra based on syntactic representations. Given $\varphi: \Sigma_k [\underline{a}_k, \overline{a}_k] \times x_k \le b$ and $\varphi': \Sigma_k [\underline{a}'_k, \overline{a}'_k] \times x_k \le b'$, $\varphi \sqsubseteq_s \varphi'$ iff $b \le b'$ and

$\forall k.[\underline{a}_k, \overline{a}_k] \subseteq [\underline{a}'_k, \overline{a}'_k]$. And $\mathbf{P}_1 \sqsubseteq_s \mathbf{P}_2$ iff for all $\varphi_2 \in \mathbf{P}_2$ there exists some $\varphi_1 \in \mathbf{P}_1$ such that $\varphi_1 \sqsubseteq_s \varphi_2$. Then, $\mathbf{P}_1 \sqsubseteq_s \mathbf{P}_2$ implies $\mathbf{P}_1 \sqsubseteq \mathbf{P}_2$, while the converse does not hold. The intersection of $\mathbf{P}_1$ and $\mathbf{P}_2$, denoted as $\mathbf{P}_1 \sqcap \mathbf{P}_2$, is an interval polyhedron whose constraint system is the conjunction of those of $\mathbf{P}_1$ and $\mathbf{P}_2$, thus $\gamma(\mathbf{P}_1 \sqcap \mathbf{P}_2) = \gamma(\mathbf{P}_1) \cap \gamma(\mathbf{P}_2)$. Also, we use the term *bounding box* of an interval polyhedron $\mathbf{P}$, denoted as $BB(\mathbf{P})$, to refer to the interval hull $\mathbf{x}^H$ of $\Sigma_\exists(\mathbf{A}, b)$. $BB(\mathbf{P})$ can be computed by ILP, namely by calculating $\max(\min) x_k$ subject to $\mathbf{P}$, which is NP-hard (Sect. 3.1). In practice, $BB(\mathbf{P})$ is updated on-the-fly, and an over-approximated bounding box which is sound can be obtained by cheaper methods, as in [4].

As in the classic convex polyhedra abstract domain, the constraint representation of an interval polyhedron is not unique. E.g., the interval linear equation $[-1, 1]x = 1$ and the inequality $[-1, 1]x \le -1$ have the same weak solution set $\{x \in [-\infty, -1] \cup [1, +\infty]\}$. For efficiency reasons, it is desirable to have as few and simple constraints as possible.

Reduction. According to Theorem 1, an interval linear inequality $\varphi: \sum_k [\underline{a}_k, \overline{a}_k] \times x_k \le b$ can be reduced to $\varphi': \sum_k [\underline{a}'_k, \overline{a}'_k] \times x_k \le b$, where $x_k \in [\underline{x}^H_k, \overline{x}^H_k]$ and

$$[\underline{a}'_k, \overline{a}'_k] = \begin{cases} [\underline{a}_k, \underline{a}_k] & \text{if } \underline{x}^H_k \ge 0, \\ [\overline{a}_k, \overline{a}_k] & \text{if } \overline{x}^H_k \le 0, \\ [\underline{a}_k, \overline{a}_k] & \text{otherwise.} \end{cases}$$

The reduction is useful in practice, since φ' will cause less precision loss in the subsequent computations, e.g., in the interval combination operation (see Sect. 5.2.1).

Redundancy Removal. An interval linear inequality $\varphi \in \mathbf{P}$ is said to be *redundant* when φ is entailed by the other constraints in $\mathbf{P}$, that is, $\mathbf{P} \setminus \{\varphi\} \models \varphi$. Given $\varphi: (\sum_k [\underline{a}_k, \overline{a}_k] \times x_k \le b) \in \mathbf{P}$, we can check whether φ is redundant by solving the ILP problem: $\mu = \max \sum_k [\underline{a}_k, \overline{a}_k] \times x_k$ subject to $\mathbf{P} \setminus \{\varphi\}$. If $\mu \le b$, then φ is redundant and can be eliminated from $\mathbf{P}$. This process is repeated for all inequalities in $\mathbf{P}$. To be more efficient, it is worth using lightweight methods first and resorting to the expensive ILP-based method only when necessary. For example, given $\varphi \in \mathbf{P}$, if there exists another interval linear inequality $\varphi' \in \mathbf{P}$ such that $\varphi' \sqsubseteq_s \varphi$, then φ is redundant in $\mathbf{P}$. Secondly, given $\varphi: (\sum_k [\underline{a}_k, \overline{a}_k] \times x_k \le b) \in \mathbf{P}$, if $\forall k.0 \in [\underline{a}_k, \overline{a}_k]$ and $b \ge 0$, then φ defines the universe space and can be removed from $\mathbf{P}$.

4.2 *itvPol* as an (Abstracted) Reduced Cardinal Power of Convex Polyhedra

In this section we consider *itvPol* as a reduced cardinal power (see Sect. 10.2 of [8]) that maps each orthant to a convex polyhedron, by exploiting the fact that the intersection of an interval polyhedron with an orthant is a (possibly empty) convex polyhedron. An n-dimensional interval polyhedron is at worst a set of 2^n convex polyhedra. More precisely, let p be the number of variables in an interval polyhedron that are unrestricted in sign and are associated with at least one (non-singleton) interval coefficient, then the interval polyhedron is partitioned into a set of at most 2^p convex polyhedra.

In the general case, we maintain one (possibly empty) convex polyhedron in each orthant. Each operation on the *itvPol* domain is obtained by "lifting" the corresponding operation from the convex polyhedra domain. E.g., to join two interval polyhedra, one would compute pair-wisely the convex hull of the convex polyhedra in each orthant. The assignment transfer function needs more care, since applying an assignment transfer function on a convex polyhedron in one orthant may cause it to "enter" other orthants. In such a case, the result in each orthant is then updated to be the polyhedral convex hull of the regions which belong to that orthant after the transfer operation. Thus, this domain is not simply equivalent to a finite disjunctive completion of convex polyhedra. In our case, it is perhaps better called an orthant partitioning domain of convex polyhedra.

In order to enjoy the benefits of the compact representation of interval polyhedra, one may abstract further a set of convex polyhedra with at most one in each orthant back to an interval polyhedron after each operation. However, there may not exist an interval polyhedron that exactly defines the union of those convex polyhedra, e.g., by referring to Fig. 1(2.c). And, to our knowledge, up to now there exists no method to compute the smallest interval polyhedron that encloses those convex polyhedra.

We propose an algorithm to calculate a (not necessarily smallest) interval polyhedron that soundly encloses those convex polyhedra. Given a variable ordering, an n-dimensional space is described by a binary tree with variables at internal nodes and convex polyhedra at leaves. Each node represents a variable x, and its left (right) branch specifies the subspace in which $x \leq 0$ ($x \geq 0$). Thus the path from the root to a leaf (involving all variables with respect to the given ordering) defines an orthant, and the convex polyhedron attached at the leaf corresponds to the convex polyhedron in that orthant. At each internal node $Node_x$, an interval polyhedron is constructed in a bottom-up manner, to enclose all the convex polyhedra within the subtree rooted at $Node_x$, using the weak join operation $\sqcup_w$ defined in Sect. 5.2.2. When a variable has a fixed sign, one of its subtrees is empty, which speeds up the computation. Finally, the interval polyhedron at the root of the whole binary tree is an interval polyhedron that encloses all the convex polyhedra in each orthant.

Example 1. Given the interval polyhedron $\mathbf{P} = \{[-1,0]x + y = [0,1]\}$ shown in Fig. 1(1.b), after performing the assignment transfer function $[[x := x + 1]]^\#$ on $\mathbf{P}$ in the powerset domain of convex polyhedra, we obtain the region shown in Fig. 1(2.b), which cannot be exactly encoded by any interval polyhedron. Then, by computing the polyhedral convex hull in each orthant, we get the convex polyhedra $\{x \geq 0, y \geq 0, -x + y \leq 1\}$ in the $(+, +)$-orthant and $\{x \geq 0, -1 \leq y \leq 0\}$ in the $(+, -)$-orthant. Finally, we obtain the interval polyhedron $\{[-1,0]x + y = [-1,1]\}$ using the above algorithm.

As an abstracted reduced cardinal power of convex polyhedra, *itvPol* is at worst exponentially more complex than the convex polyhedra domain. However, in some real-life applications, many of the variables do not change their signs, that is, the weak solution set intersects only a few orthants. In such situations, *itvPol* as an abstracted reduced cardinal power of convex polyhedra has a reasonable complexity.

5   *itvPol* as a New Abstract Domain

In general, *itvPol* as an abstracted reduced cardinal power of convex polyhedra may be too complex to be applied to program analysis. To solve this problem, we present an alternative construction based on faster approximate algorithms. Similarly to the constraint-based convex polyhedra abstract domain [4], this construction is based on two main operations: projection and (interval) linear programming. We will now briefly describe the implementation of the most common domain operations.

5.1 Projection

The projection operation is used to remove all information pertaining to a variable x_i while preserving the relational information between other variables. It can be computed by eliminating all occurrences of x_i in the constraints defining **P**, using an Interval Fourier-Motzkin Elimination (IFME) algorithm defined below, which is an adaptation of the classic Fourier-Motzkin elimination algorithm to interval arithmetic.

Let $\mathbf{P} = \{Ax \leq b\}$ be an interval polyhedron and x_i be a variable to be eliminated. If all non-zero interval coefficients of x_i in **P** do not contain zero, the classic Fourier-Motzkin elimination algorithm can be easily adapted to interval arithmetic. However, in general, the constraint $\varphi: (\sum_k [\underline{a}_k, \overline{a}_k] x_k \leq b) \in P$ in which $[\underline{a}_i, \overline{a}_i] \neq [0, 0]$ but $0 \in [\underline{a}_i, \overline{a}_i]$, will break the algorithm due to division by an interval containing zero. To avoid this, we apply the following linearization operator $\zeta(\varphi, x_i)$ beforehand.

Definition 2 (Linearization operator). *Let* $\varphi: \sum_k [\underline{a}_k, \overline{a}_k] \times x_k \leq b$ *be an interval linear inequality and* $x_i \in [\underline{x}_i^H, \overline{x}_i^H]$.

$$
\zeta(\varphi, x_i) \stackrel{\text{def}}{=}
\begin{cases}
\underline{a}_i \times x_i + \sum_{k \neq i} [\underline{a}_k, \overline{a}_k] \times x_k \leq b & \text{if } \underline{x}_i^H \geq 0 \\
\overline{a}_i \times x_i + \sum_{k \neq i} [\underline{a}_k, \overline{a}_k] \times x_k \leq b & \text{if } \overline{x}_i^H \leq 0 \\
c \times x_i + \sum_{k \neq i} [\underline{a}_k, \overline{a}_k] \times x_k \leq \sup(b - [\underline{a}_i - c, \overline{a}_i - c] \times [\underline{x}_i^H, \overline{x}_i^H]) & \text{otherwise}
\end{cases}
$$

where c *can be any real number.*

In practice, we often choose $c = (\underline{a}_i + \overline{a}_i)/2$ that is the midpoint of the interval $[\underline{a}_i, \overline{a}_i]$, which causes the least loss of precision (minimizing $\sup(b - [\underline{a}_i - c, \overline{a}_i - c] \times [\underline{x}_i^H, \overline{x}_i^H])$).

Example 2. Consider the interval linear inequality $[0, 2]x + y \leq 2$ with respect to the bounds $x, y \in [-2, 4]$. If we choose the midpoint of $[0, 2]$ as c, $\zeta(\varphi, x)$ will give $x+y \leq 6$. Note that some loss of precision happens here, e.g., the point $(0,4)$ satisfies the result inequality $x + y \leq 6$ but does not satisfy the original interval inequality $[0, 2]x + y \leq 2$.

Theorem 2 (Soundness of the linearization operator). *Given an interval linear inequality* φ *and a variable* $x_i \in [\underline{x}_i^H, \overline{x}_i^H]$, $\zeta(\varphi, x_i)$ *soundly over-approximates* φ, *that is,* $\forall x.(x_i \in [\underline{x}_i^H, \overline{x}_i^H] \wedge x \in \gamma(\varphi)) \Rightarrow x \in \gamma(\zeta(\varphi, x_i))$.

By falling back to the above linearization technique, IFME can be applied to general interval polyhedra. Given an inequality $\varphi: \sum_k [\underline{a}_k, \overline{a}_k] x_k \leq b$, we define $\iota(\varphi, x_i)$ as

$$
\iota(\varphi, x_i) \stackrel{\text{def}}{=}
\begin{cases}
\zeta(\varphi, x_i) & \text{if } 0 \in [\underline{a}_i, \overline{a}_i] \wedge [\underline{a}_i, \overline{a}_i] \neq [0, 0], \\
\varphi & \text{otherwise.}
\end{cases}
$$

Then, the Interval Fourier-Motzkin Elimination algorithm can be defined as

$$
\text{IFME}(\mathbf{P}, x_i) \stackrel{\text{def}}{=} \{ (\sum_k [\underline{a}_k, \overline{a}_k] x_k \leq b) \in \mathbf{P}' \mid [\underline{a}_i, \overline{a}_i] = [0, 0] \}
$$
$$
\cup \left\{ \sum_{k \neq i} \left(\frac{[\underline{a}_k^+, \overline{a}_k^+]}{[\underline{a}_i^+, \overline{a}_i^+]} + \frac{[\underline{a}_k^-, \overline{a}_k^-]}{[-\overline{a}_i^-, -\underline{a}_i^-]} \right) x_k \leq b' \; \middle| \; \begin{matrix} (\sum_k [\underline{a}_k^+, \overline{a}_k^+] x_k \leq b^+) \in \mathbf{P}', \underline{a}_i^+ > 0 \\ (\sum_k [\underline{a}_k^-, \overline{a}_k^-] x_k \leq b^-) \in \mathbf{P}', \overline{a}_i^- < 0 \end{matrix} \right\}
$$

where $\mathbf{P}' = \{\iota(\varphi, x_i) \mid \varphi \in \mathbf{P}\}$ and $b' = \sup\left(\frac{b^+}{[\underline{a}_i^+, \overline{a}_i^+]} + \frac{b^-}{[-\overline{a}_i^-, -\underline{a}_i^-]} \right)$.

Theorem 3 (Soundness of the Interval Fourier-Motzkin Elimination). *Given an interval polyhedron* **P** *and a variable* x_i, *any point satisfying* **P** *also satisfies* IFME$(\mathbf{P}, x_i)$, *that is,* $\forall x \in \gamma(\mathbf{P}) \Rightarrow x \in \gamma(\text{IFME}(\mathbf{P}, x_i))$.

5.2 Join

In order to abstract the control-flow join, we need to compute the union of environments of program variables. However, to our knowledge, no existing method is available to compute the smallest interval polyhedron enclosing this union. We propose to compute an overapproximation of this union cheaply using an operation that we call *weak join*.

The main idea is as follows. We first define an operation $\uplus$ on constraints that over-approximates the set union $\cup$ such that $\gamma(\varphi') \cup \gamma(\varphi'') \subseteq \gamma(\varphi' \uplus \varphi'')$. Given two interval polyhedra $\mathbf{P}'$ and $\mathbf{P}''$, by distributivity

$$\gamma(\mathbf{P}') \cup \gamma(\mathbf{P}'') = (\bigcap_{\varphi' \in \mathbf{P}'} \gamma(\varphi')) \cup (\bigcap_{\varphi'' \in \mathbf{P}''} \gamma(\varphi'')) = \bigcap_{\substack{\varphi' \in \mathbf{P}' \\ \varphi'' \in \mathbf{P}''}} (\gamma(\varphi') \cup \gamma(\varphi'')) \subseteq \bigcap_{\substack{\varphi' \in \mathbf{P}' \\ \varphi'' \in \mathbf{P}''}} (\gamma(\varphi' \uplus \varphi'')).$$

Our weak join can be constructed basically by pairwise combinations of inequalities from $\mathbf{P}_1$ with those from $\mathbf{P}_2$ using the $\uplus$ operation.

5.2.1 Interval Combination

Definition 3 (Interval Combination). *Given two interval linear inequalities φ':* $\sum_k [\underline{a}'_k, \overline{a}'_k] \times x_k \leq b'$ *and φ'':* $\sum_k [\underline{a}''_k, \overline{a}''_k] \times x_k \leq b''$, *the interval combination of φ' and φ'' is defined as*

$$\varphi' \uplus \varphi'' \overset{\text{def}}{=} \left(\sum_k [\underline{a}_k, \overline{a}_k] \times x_k \leq b \right),$$

where $b = \max(b', b'')$ and $[\underline{a}_k, \overline{a}_k] = [\min(\underline{a}'_k, \underline{a}''_k), \max(\overline{a}'_k, \overline{a}''_k)]$.

This definition straightforwardly lifts to interval polyhedra. Given two interval polyhedra $\mathbf{P}'$ and $\mathbf{P}''$, $\mathbf{P}' \uplus \mathbf{P}'' \overset{\text{def}}{=} \{\varphi' \uplus \varphi'' \mid \varphi' \in \mathbf{P}' \wedge \varphi'' \in \mathbf{P}''\}$.

Example 3. Consider two interval polyhedra $\mathbf{P}' = \{y \leq 1, -y \leq -1\}$ and $\mathbf{P}'' = \{-x + y \leq 0, x - y \leq 0\}$. By interval combination, we obtain $\mathbf{P} = \mathbf{P}' \uplus \mathbf{P}'' = \{[-1, 0]x + y = [0, 1]\}$, whose weak solution set is depicted in Fig. 1(1.b). Note that some loss of precision happens here, e.g., the point $(1,0)$ satisfies the result $\mathbf{P}$ but satisfies neither $\mathbf{P}'$ nor $\mathbf{P}''$.

Theorem 4 (Soundness of the interval combination). *Given two interval linear inequalities φ' and φ'', their interval combination $\varphi' \uplus \varphi''$ soundly over-approximates the union of φ' and φ'', that is, $\forall x.(x \in \gamma(\varphi') \vee x \in \gamma(\varphi'')) \Rightarrow x \in \gamma(\varphi' \uplus \varphi'')$.*

The above theorem implies the soundness of $\uplus$ on interval polyhedra, i.e., $\forall x.(x \in \gamma(\mathbf{P}') \vee x \in \gamma(\mathbf{P}'')) \Rightarrow x \in \gamma(\mathbf{P}' \uplus \mathbf{P}'')$. However, the result of $\varphi' \uplus \varphi''$ may not be the tightest interval linear inequality whose weak solution set encloses the union of the weak solution sets of φ' and φ''. Moreover, the precision of the interval combination depends on the representation of the input. The tighter the input coefficient intervals are, the more precise the result will be. Hence, the reduction operation (in Sect. 4.1) is often used before performing interval combinations.

In some cases, the interval combination can be improved. Given φ': $\sum_k [\underline{a}'_k, \overline{a}'_k] \times x_k \leq b'$ and φ'': $\sum_k [\underline{a}''_k, \overline{a}''_k] \times x_k \leq b''$, if there exists a positive *multiplier* λ such that $\lambda \times [\underline{a}'_i, \overline{a}'_i] = [\underline{a}''_i, \overline{a}''_i]$ (i.e., $\lambda \underline{a}'_i = \underline{a}''_i$ and $\lambda \overline{a}'_i = \overline{a}''_i$) for some i, then the interval combination of φ' and φ'' can be computed as $\varphi' \uplus \varphi'' = (\sum_k [\underline{a}_k, \overline{a}_k] \times x_k \leq b)$, where $b = \max(\lambda b', b'')$ and $[\underline{a}_k, \overline{a}_k] = [\min(\lambda \underline{a}'_k, \underline{a}''_k), \max(\lambda \overline{a}'_k, \overline{a}''_k)]$. In most cases, the interval combination with multiplier is more precise than the general one. E.g., given $\varphi_1 : x + y \leq 2$ and $\varphi_2 : -x + 2y \leq 2$, $\varphi_1 \uplus \varphi_2$ gives $\varphi : [-1, 1]x + [1, 2]y \leq 2$. However, if we use a version with multiplier (i.e., rewrite $\varphi_1 : x + y \leq 2$ as $\varphi'_1 : 2x + 2y \leq 4$), $\varphi'_1 \uplus \varphi_2$ will give $\varphi' : [-1, 2]x + 2y \leq 4$, and the result φ' is more precise than the previous one φ.

5.2.2 Weak Join

Definition 4 (Envelope). *Given two interval polyhedra* $\mathbf{P}_1$ *and* $\mathbf{P}_2$, *the envelope of* $\mathbf{P}_1$ *and* $\mathbf{P}_2$ *is defined as*

$$env(\mathbf{P}_1, \mathbf{P}_2) \overset{\text{def}}{=} S_1 \cup S_2$$

where $S_1 = \{ \varphi_1 \in \mathbf{P}_1 \mid \mathbf{P}_2 \models \varphi_1 \}, S_2 = \{ \varphi_2 \in \mathbf{P}_2 \mid \mathbf{P}_1 \models \varphi_2 \}$.

Let $i \in \{1, 2\}$, for any $\varphi \in \mathbf{P}_i$, if $\varphi \in env(\mathbf{P}_1, \mathbf{P}_2)$, we say that φ is an *envelope constraint* in $\mathbf{P}_i$, otherwise φ is a *nonenvelope constraint* in $\mathbf{P}_i$. We denote the set of nonenvelope constraints in $\mathbf{P}_i$ as $\overline{env}(\mathbf{P}_i)$. Given two boxes $\mathbf{B}' = [\underline{b}', \overline{b}']$ and $\mathbf{B}'' = [\underline{b}'', \overline{b}'']$, their join in the interval abstract domain is defined as $\mathbf{B}' \sqcup_I \mathbf{B}'' = [\min(\underline{b}', \underline{b}''), \max(\overline{b}', \overline{b}'')]$. Note that $BB(\gamma(\mathbf{P}_1) \cup \gamma(\mathbf{P}_2)) = BB(\mathbf{P}_1) \sqcup_I BB(\mathbf{P}_2)$.

Definition 5 (Weak Join). *Given two interval polyhedra* $\mathbf{P}_1$ *and* $\mathbf{P}_2$, *we define a* weak join *operation for the itvPol domain as*

$$\mathbf{P}_1 \sqcup_w \mathbf{P}_2 \overset{\text{def}}{=} env(\mathbf{P}_1, \mathbf{P}_2) \sqcap (\overline{env}(\mathbf{P}_1) \uplus \overline{env}(\mathbf{P}_2)) \sqcap (BB(\mathbf{P}_1) \sqcup_I BB(\mathbf{P}_2)).$$

Note that the weak join operation may introduce redundant constraints in the result, but most of them can be eliminated by syntactic means (see Sect. 4.1).

Example 4. Consider two interval polyhedra $\mathbf{P}_1 = \{[-1, 1]x + 2y \leq 2, -2x - y \leq 2, x - y \leq 1, -y \leq 0\}$ (i.e., the region above the x-axis in Fig. 1(1.d)) and $\mathbf{P}_2 = \{[-1, 1]x - 2y \leq 2, 2x + y \leq 2, -x + y \leq 1, y \leq 0\}$ (i.e., the region below the x-axis in Fig. 1(1.d)). $env(\mathbf{P}_1, \mathbf{P}_2) = \{[-1, 1]x + 2y \leq 2, [-1, 1]x - 2y \leq 2\} = \{[-1, 1]x + 2y = [-2, 2]\}$. $\overline{env}(\mathbf{P}_1) \uplus \overline{env}(\mathbf{P}_2) = \{-2x - y \leq 2, x - y \leq 1, -y \leq 0\} \uplus \{2x + y \leq 2, -x + y \leq 1, y \leq 0\} = \{2x + [-2, 1]y = [-2, 2]\}$. Thus, $\mathbf{P}_1 \sqcup_w \mathbf{P}_2 = \{[-1, 1]x + 2y = [-2, 2], 2x + [-2, 1]y = [-2, 2]\}$, whose weak solution set is depicted in Fig. 1(1.d).

Theorem 5 (Soundness of the Weak Join). *Given two interval polyhedra* $\mathbf{P}_1$ *and* $\mathbf{P}_2$, *the weak join* $\mathbf{P}_1 \sqcup_w \mathbf{P}_2$ *is an overapproximation of both* $\mathbf{P}_1$ *and* $\mathbf{P}_2$, *that is,* $\forall x.(x \in \gamma(\mathbf{P}_1) \vee x \in \gamma(\mathbf{P}_2)) \Rightarrow x \in \gamma(\mathbf{P}_1 \sqcup_w \mathbf{P}_2)$.

The above weak join can construct constraints that are satisfied by the set-union of the input interval polyhedra but not satisfied by their convex hull (e.g., $\gamma(\mathbf{P}_1 \sqcup_w \mathbf{P}_2) = \gamma(\mathbf{P}_1) \cup \gamma(\mathbf{P}_2)$ holds in Example 4). However, when both interval polyhedra $\mathbf{P}_1$ and $\mathbf{P}_2$ are convex polyhedra and in the same orthant, $\mathbf{P}_1 \sqcup_w \mathbf{P}_2$ is less precise than their polyhedral convex hull. In such a case, one may use the polyhedral convex hull instead. E.g., given two points $(0, 0)$ and $(1, 1)$ in the $(+, +)$-orthant of the x-y plane, $\sqcup_w$ can only give $\{0 \leq x \leq 1, 0 \leq y \leq 1\}$, which is less precise than the result of their polyhedral convex hull (i.e., $\{0 \leq x \leq 1, y = x\}$).

5.3 Emptiness Test

An interval polyhedron $\mathbf{P}$ is *empty* iff its constraint set is not weakly solvable, that is, $\gamma(\mathbf{P}) = \emptyset$. Theorem 1 shows that checking weak solvability of interval linear systems can be in principle performed by checking solvability of one linear system per orthant, by some finite procedure (e.g., linear programming). During program analysis, constraints are often added one by one. Thus, the emptiness test can be done incrementally. When adding a new constraint $\sum_k [a_k, b_k] \times x_k \leq b$ to a nonempty interval polyhedron $\mathbf{P}$, we solve the ILP problem: $\mu = \min \sum_k [a_k, b_k] \times x_k$ subject to $\mathbf{P}$. If $\mu > b$, the new interval polyhedron is indeed empty.

5.4 Transfer Functions

Test Transfer Function. The result of a test $[\![\sum_k [\underline{a_k}, \overline{a}_k] \times x_k \leq b]\!]^{\#}(\mathbf{P})$ is simply the interval polyhedron $\mathbf{P}$ with the constraint $\sum_k [\underline{a_k}, \overline{a}_k] \times x_k \leq b$ added, where $[\![\cdot]\!]^{\#}(\mathbf{P})$ denotes the effect of a program statement on the interval polyhedron $\mathbf{P}$. More complicated cases, such as tests involving disjunctive, non-linear or floating-point expressions can be soundly abstracted to the form $\sum_k [\underline{a_k}, \overline{a}_k] \times x_k \leq b$, as discussed in Sect. 6.

Assignment Transfer Function. The assignment of a certain expression e to the variable x_j can be modeled using test, projection and variable renaming as follows:

$$[\![x_j := e]\!]^{\#}(\mathbf{P}) \stackrel{\text{def}}{=} (IFME([\![x'_j - e = 0]\!]^{\#}(\mathbf{P}), x_j))[x'_j / x_j]. \tag{1}$$

The fresh variable x'_j, introduced to hold the value of the expression e, is necessary when x_j also appears on the right hand of the assignment, e.g., $x := [-1, 2]x + [2, 3]$.

Alternatively, the assignment transfer function can be implemented by substitution, when the coefficient of x_j in e does not contain zero. Let $e = \sum_k [\underline{d_k}, \overline{d}_k]x_k + [\underline{c}, \overline{c}]$, where $0 \notin [\underline{d_j}, \overline{d}_j]$. Then the assignment transfer function by substitution is defined as

$$[\![x_j := e]\!]^{\#}(\mathbf{P}) \stackrel{\text{def}}{=} \left\{ [\underline{a'_j}, \overline{a'_j}]x_j + \sum_{k \neq j} [\underline{a'_k}, \overline{a'_k}]x_k \leq b' \mid (\sum_k [\underline{a_k}, \overline{a}_k]x_k \leq b) \in \mathbf{P} \right\} \tag{2}$$

where $[\underline{a'_j}, \overline{a'_j}] = \dfrac{[\underline{a_j}, \overline{a}_j]}{[\underline{d_j}, \overline{d}_j]}$, $[\underline{a'_k}, \overline{a'_k}] = \left([\underline{a_k}, \overline{a}_k] - \dfrac{[\underline{d_k}, \overline{d}_k]}{[\underline{d_j}, \overline{d}_j]} \right)$ and $b' = sup\left(b + \dfrac{[\underline{c}, \overline{c}]}{[\underline{d_j}, \overline{d}_j]} \right)$.

Note that unlike the case of convex polyhedra, neither (1) nor (2) is an exact or best abstraction for interval polyhedra. In most cases, (2) gives more precise results than (1). E.g., given an interval polyhedron $\mathbf{P} = \{[-1, 1]x \leq -1\}$, for the assignment $x := -x$, (1) will give the whole space as the result while (2) will result in $\mathbf{P}' = \{[-1, 1]x \leq -1\}$ which is exact.

5.5 Widening

itvPol does not satisfy the ascending chain condition. Thus, a widening [7] operator is needed to ensure convergence of fixpoint computations (used to analyze loops). We define the widening in the *itvPol* domain as follows:

Definition 6 (Widening). *Given a threshold k and two interval polyhedra* $\mathbf{P}_1 \sqsubseteq \mathbf{P}_2$ *in the i-th iteration, we define the* widening *in the i-th iteration as*

$$\mathbf{P}_1 \, \triangledown_i^{[k]} \, \mathbf{P}_2 \stackrel{\text{def}}{=} \begin{cases} S_1 \cup S_2 & \text{if } i \leq k \\ S_1 & \text{otherwise} \end{cases}$$

where $S_1 = \{\varphi_1 \in \mathbf{P}_1 \,|\, \mathbf{P}_2 \models \varphi_1\}, S_2 = \{\varphi_2 \in \mathbf{P}_2 \,|\, \exists \varphi_1 \in \mathbf{P}_1, \gamma(\mathbf{P}_1) = \gamma((\mathbf{P}_1 \setminus \{\varphi_1\}) \cup \{\varphi_2\})\}.$

S_1 keeps stable inequalities from $\mathbf{P}_1$. S_2 recovers precision by adding those inequalities from $\mathbf{P}_2$ that are mutually redundant with an inequality of $\mathbf{P}_1$ with respect to $\mathbf{P}_1$. Unlike the classic convex polyhedra domain where the widening is defined as $S_1 \cup S_2$ in all cases, *itvPol* needs a threshold k to guarantee convergence of the above widening by disabling S_2 after the k-th iteration. Given a chain $(X_i)_{i \in \mathbb{N}}$, the increasing chain $(Y_i)_{i \in \mathbb{N}}$ defined by $Y_0 = X_0$ and $Y_{i+1} = Y_i \, \triangledown_i^{[k]} X_{i+1}$, is stable after a finite time, since after the k-th iteration, the set of constraints in Y_{j+1} is a subset of the constraints in Y_j $(j > k)$.

6 Applications of the Interval Polyhedra Domain

6.1 Handling Disjunctions

We propose to apply the technique of *interval combination* to abstract disjunctions of linear constraints by interval linear inequalities. In general, given a DNF (Disjunctive Normal Form) formula, each DNF-term can be considered as a convex polyhedron. The disjunction of those convex polyhedra can be abstracted as an interval polyhedron using the join operation of *itvPol* (Sect. 5.2). On the other hand, given a CNF (Conjunctive Normal Form) formula, each CNF-term can be abstracted as one interval linear inequality by interval combination (Sect. 5.2.1), thus the whole CNF formula can be abstracted as an interval polyhedron.

For example, consider the program in Fig. 2. At ②, the negation of $-1 \leq x \leq 1$ on integers gives $x \leq -2 \lor -x \leq -2$, which can be exactly encoded as an interval linear inequality $[-1, 1]x \leq -2$. And, using *itvPol*, we can obtain the exact information at ⑤, i.e., $y = -1$, which implies $y \neq 0$. However, the convex polyhedra domain can only obtain $-1 \leq y \leq 0$ at ⑤ which fails to prove the assertion $y \neq 0$.

```
int x, y;
if ( x ≥ −1 and x ≤ 1 ) then
    y := x − 1; ①
else ②
    y := x; ③
endif; ④
if( x == 0 ) then
⑤   assert(y ≠ 0);
endif;
```

Loc	Convex Polyhedra	Interval Polyhedra
①	$x - y = 1 \land -1 \leq x \leq 1$	$x - y = 1 \land -1 \leq x \leq 1$
②	⊤ (no information)	$[-1, 1]x \leq -2$
③	$y = x$	$y = x \land [-1, 1]x \leq -2$
④	$0 \leq x - y \leq 1$	$0 \leq x - y \leq 1$
		$\land [-1, 1]x + [0, 1]y \leq -1$
		$\land x + [-1, 0]y \leq 1$
⑤	$x = 0 \land -1 \leq y \leq 0$	$x = 0 \land y = -1$

Fig. 2. Example program1 (left) and the generated invariants (right)

6.2 Handling Non-linear Expressions

Miné has proposed a so-called *linearization* algorithm able to abstract arbitrary expressions into interval linear form $\Sigma_k[\underline{a_k}, \overline{a_k}] \times x_k + [\underline{c}, \overline{c}]$ [21]. However, most current numerical abstract domains, such as the convex polyhedra domain, cannot deal with interval linear forms directly. Thus, one has to employ a so-called *quasi-linearization* technique to convert the interval linear form $\Sigma_k[\underline{a_k}, \overline{a_k}] \times x_k + [\underline{c}, \overline{c}]$ into quasi-linear form $\Sigma_k a_k' \times x_k + [\underline{c}', \overline{c}']$ [19]. The quasi-linearization process may cause precision loss. However, using *itvPol*, one can avoid (at least delay) such precision loss, since *itvPol* directly supports the representation of interval linear forms.

Given the program in Fig. 3, after the linearization of the non-linear expression $z \times x + 1$, we obtain $[-5, 5]x + y = 1$ at ①. When using the convex polyhedra domain, we have to apply quasi-linearization to $[-5, 5]x + y = 1$. And the best quasi-linearization will be $-5x + y \leq 21 \wedge -5x - y \leq 19$. Note that some precision loss happens here, e.g., the point $(0, 0)$ satisfies $-5x + y \leq 21 \wedge -5x - y \leq 19$ but does not satisfy $[-5, 5]x + y = 1$. Finally, the convex polyhedra domain can only obtain $x \geq -1$ at ② while using *itvPol* we can prove $x \geq 3$ at ②.

int x, y, z;	Loc	Convex Polyhedra	Interval Polyhedra
assume $-5 \leq z \leq 5$;	①	$-5 \leq z \leq 5 \wedge x \geq -2$	$-5 \leq z \leq 5 \wedge x \geq -2$
assume $x \geq -2$;		$\wedge -5x + y \leq 21 \wedge -5x - y \leq 19$	$\wedge [-5, 5]x + y = 1$
$y := z \times x + 1$; ①	②	$y = -14 \wedge -5 \leq z \leq 5$	$y = -14 \wedge -5 \leq z \leq 5$
assume $y == -14$; ②		$\wedge x \geq -1$	$\wedge x \geq 3$

Fig. 3. Example program2 (left) and the generated invariants (right)

6.3 Handling Floating-Point Arithmetic

Real-life programming languages do not manipulate rationals or reals, but floating-point numbers, which are much more difficult to abstract. One solution is to approximate floating-point expressions as linear expressions in the real field with interval coefficients by making rounding explicit [19]. Rounding is highly non-linear but can be abstracted using intervals. For instance, $X + Y$ in the floating-point world can be abstracted into $[1 - p, 1 + p] \times X + [1 - p, 1 + p] \times Y + [-mf, mf]$ with the relative error p and the absolute error mf (the smallest non-zero positive value in the floating-point format), e.g., $p = 2^{-23}$ and $mf = 2^{-149}$ in the single precision floating-point format. This fits the linearization framework which can be extended to treat floating-point arithmetic soundly. Thus, floating-point programs can be directly analyzed using *itvPol* after applying floating-point abstractions.

Let us consider the program in Fig. 4. The quasi-linearization of both floating-point assignments $y := -2 \otimes_r x \oplus_r 1$ and $y := -x \oplus_r 1$ will give $y \leftarrow [-\infty, +\infty]$, since x is unbounded. Thus, the convex polyhedra domain will obtain no useful information, while *itvPol* can prove $0.4999998 \leq x \leq 1.0000002$ at ②, which indicates that x is bounded and thus there is no overflow exception in the last statement (i.e., $x := x \oplus_r 1$).

```
real x, y;
if random() then
    y := -2 ⊗ᵣ x ⊕ᵣ 1;
else
    y := -x ⊕ᵣ 1;
endif; ①
assume y == 0; ②
x := x ⊕ᵣ 1;
```

Loc	Convex Polyhedra	Interval Polyhedra
①	⊤(no information)	$[0.9999999, 2.0000005]x + y \leq 1.0000001$ $\wedge [0.9999999, 2.0000005]x + y \geq 0.9999999$
②	$y = 0$	$y = 0 \wedge 0.4999998 \leq x \leq 1.0000002$

Fig. 4. Example program3 (left) and the generated invariants (right). $\odot_r$ denotes single precision floating-point semantics with arbitrary rounding mode ($\odot \in \{\otimes, \oplus\}, r \in \{+\infty, -\infty\}$).

7 Implementation and Experimental Results

Our prototype domain, *itvPol*, is developed based on Sect. 5 using double precision floating-point numbers. It makes use of GLPK (GNU Linear Programming Kit) [18] which implements the simplex algorithm for linear programming. We implemented an interval linear programming solver based on GLPK following the methods from [5,15]. The soundness of the floating-point LP/ILP solver is guaranteed by rigorous linear programming [4,15]. The whole *itvPol* domain is implemented based on interval arithmetic with outward rounding (i.e., rounding upper bounds upward and lower bounds downward), which guarantees the soundness of the floating-point implementation.

itvPol is interfaced to the APRON [1] numerical abstract domain library. Our experiments were conducted using the Interproc [16] static analyzer. We extended Interproc to support input data with intervals (such as expressions and constraints with interval coefficients). In order to assess the precision and efficiency of *itvPol*, we compare the obtained invariants as well as the performance of *itvPol* with our previous work FPPol [4] which is a sound floating-point implementation of the convex polyhedra domain.

To demonstrate the expressiveness of *itvPol*, two simple typical loops are shown in Fig. 5 and Fig. 6, together with the invariants generated by the analyzer. *program4* is a loop that reverses the sign of variable x at each iteration, and *program5* consists of two stages, increasing y in the inner loop first and then increasing x in the outer loop. For *program4* in Fig. 5, *itvPol* can prove that $x = -1 \vee x = 1$ at ①, which is exact and more precise than the invariant $-1 \leq x \leq 1$ given by FPPol. For *program5* in Fig. 6, *itvPol* can prove that $-20 \leq y \leq -10 \vee y \geq 10$ at ②, while FPPol can only prove $y \geq -20$.

Fig. 7 shows the comparison of performance and result invariants for a selection of benchmark examples[2]. The first set of benchmark programs, program1-5, corresponds to examples shown in Fig. 2-6. The second set of examples is reused from our previous work [4], most of which come from Interproc. For each program, "#vars" indicates the total number of program variables, and "#±" indicates the number of variables which have unrestricted sign. The column "#∇delay" specifies the value of the widening delay parameter for Interproc (i.e., the number of loop iterations performed before applying

---

[2] We also analyzed the benchmark programs using NewPolka which is implemented in exact arithmetic, and the result invariants are almost the same as those by FPPol. *itvPol* performs 2 times faster than NewPolka on ratelimiter_f and at worst 4 times slower on other programs.

```
real x, y;
x := -1;
while ( true ) do
①  x := -x;
done;
```

Loc	Convex Polyhedra	Interval Polyhedra
①	$-1 \leq x \leq 1$	$-1 \leq x \leq 1 \wedge [-1, 1]x \leq -1$

Fig. 5. program4 (left) and the generated invariants (right)

```
int x, y;
x := 1;
y := -20;
while (x ≤ 9) do
①    x := x + 1;
    while (y ≤ 9) do
        y := y + 1;
    done;
done; ②
```

Loc	Convex Polyhedra	Interval Polyhedra
①	$y \geq -20$	$y \geq -20$
	$\wedge 1 \leq x \leq 9$	$\wedge 1 \leq x \leq 9$
		$\wedge - x + [0, 1]y \leq -2$
		$\wedge [-1, 1]y \leq -10$
②	$y \geq -20 \wedge x \geq 10$	$y \geq -20 \wedge x \geq 10$
		$\wedge [-1, 1]y \leq -10$

Fig. 6. program5 (left) and the generated invariants (right)

Program		Analyzer		itvPol			FPPol			Result
name	#vars(#±)	#∇delay	#iterat.	#lp	time(ms)	#iterat.	#lp	time(ms)	Invar.
program1	2(2)	1	1	256	31	1	138	24	>
program2	3(3)	1	1	78	12	1	54	11	>
program3	2(2)	1	1	68	13	1	0	6	>
program4	1(1)	3	4	19	10	4	8	7	>
program5	2(1)	1	5	270	49	6	187	35	>
sequencewhiles	3(1)	1	9	368	61	9	237	46	>
ratelimiter_f	5(4)	4	4	5846	792	5	2966	1425	>
bubblesort	4(4)	1	8	845	123	8	646	101	>
maccarthy91	3(2)	1	4	609	83	4	442	63	>
heapsort	7(7)	1	4	1534	273	4	1929	374	<
symmetricalstairs	2(1)	1	5	245	45	6	469	78	<
ackerman	4(2)	1	4	883	127	6	1477	298	<

Fig. 7. Experimental results for benchmark examples

the widening operator with the fixed threshold $k = 10$ in Def. 6). "#iterat." gives the number of increasing iterations during the analysis.

Invariants. The column "Result Invar." compares the invariants obtained. A ">" ("<") indicates that *itvPol* outputs stronger (weaker) invariants than FPPol. For programs involving variables unrestricted in sign, *itvPol* can often find some interesting non-convex invariants. When all variables in the program are restricted in sign, in most cases *itvPol* generates no better invariants than FPPol, since *itvPol* uses the weak join $\sqcup_w$ which is weaker than the polyhedral convex hull of FPPol in such a case.

Performance. "time(ms)" presents the analysis times in milliseconds when the analyzer is run on a 1.6GHz PC with 768MB of RAM running Fedora 9. Fig. 7 shows that the overall computation cost of *itvPol* is not so high compared with FPPol. The reason can be derived mainly from the fact that *itvPol* uses the weak join $\sqcup_w$. In some cases, e.g., ratelimiter_f and heapsort, *itvPol* even outperforms FPPol. "#lp" shows the number of LP queries issued to GLPK. During our experiments, we found that the time spent in the LP solver frequently takes at least half of the total analysis time when using *itvPol*.

8   Conclusion

In this paper, a new numerical abstract domain called *interval polyhedra (itvPol)* was presented, which introduces interval linear algebra to static analysis. This domain can represent and manipulate linear constraints with interval coefficients. *itvPol* has some attractive features in that it natively allows expressing certain non-convex (even unconnected) properties without any explicit disjunctive representations. The domain operations can be constructed by interval linear programming and interval Fourier-Motzkin elimination. Possible applications of *itvPol* are described, e.g., to handle programs involving disjunctive, non-linear, or floating-point expressions. *itvPol* can discover interesting non-convex properties for programs involving variables unrestricted in sign.

It remains for future work to design more precise or even optimal abstractions for the join of the *itvPol* domain, and to test *itvPol* on large realistic programs. We also plan to improve the efficiency of *itvPol*, e.g., by reducing the number of LP queries.

Acknowledgements. We would like to thank Axel Simon and Jiri Rohn for useful discussions, and the anonymous reviewers for their helpful comments and suggestions.

References

1. APRON numerical abstract domain library, http://apron.cri.ensmp.fr/library/
2. Allamigeon, X., Gaubert, S., Goubault, E.: Inferring min and max invariants using max-plus polyhedra. In: Alpuente, M., Vidal, G. (eds.) SAS 2008. LNCS, vol. 5079, pp. 189–204. Springer, Heidelberg (2008)
3. Bagnara, R., Hill, P.M., Zaffanella, E.: Widening operators for powerset domains. In: Steffen, B., Levi, G. (eds.) VMCAI 2004. LNCS, vol. 2937, pp. 135–148. Springer, Heidelberg (2004)
4. Chen, L., Miné, A., Cousot, P.: A sound floating-point polyhedra abstract domain. In: Ramalingam, G. (ed.) APLAS 2008. LNCS, vol. 5356, pp. 3–18. Springer, Heidelberg (2008)
5. Chineck, J.W., Ramadan, K.: Linear programming with interval coefficients. Journal of the Operational Research Society 51(2), 209–220 (2000)
6. Cousot, P., Cousot, R.: Static determination of dynamic properties of programs. In: Proc. of the 2nd International Symposium on Programming, Dunod, Paris, pp. 106–130 (1976)
7. Cousot, P., Cousot, R.: Abstract interpretation: a unified lattice model for static analysis of programs by construction or approximation of fixpoints. In: ACM POPL 1977, pp. 238–252. ACM Press, New York (1977)
8. Cousot, P., Cousot, R.: Systematic design of program analysis frameworks. In: ACM POPL 1979, pp. 269–282. ACM Press, New York (1979)

9. Cousot, P., Cousot, R.: Higher-order abstract interpretation (and application to comportment analysis generalizing strictness, termination, projection and PER analysis of functional languages). In: ICCL 1994, pp. 95–112. IEEE Computer Society Press, Los Alamitos (1994)
10. Cousot, P., Halbwachs, N.: Automatic discovery of linear restraints among variables of a program. In: ACM POPL 1978, pp. 84–96. ACM Press, New York (1978)
11. Giacobazzi, R., Ranzato, F.: Optimal domains for disjunctive abstract interpretation. Sci. Comput. Program 32(1-3), 177–210 (1998)
12. Granger, P.: Static analysis of arithmetical congruences. International Journal of Computer Mathematics 30, 165–199 (1989)
13. Gulavani, B.S., Gulwani, S.: A numerical abstract domain based on expression abstraction and max operator with application in timing analysis. In: Gupta, A., Malik, S. (eds.) CAV 2008. LNCS, vol. 5123, pp. 370–384. Springer, Heidelberg (2008)
14. Jansson, C.: Calculation of exact bounds for the solution set of linear interval systems. Linear Algebra and Its Applications 251, 321–340 (1997)
15. Jansson, C.: Rigorous lower and upper bounds in linear programming. SIAM Journal on Optimization 14(3), 914–935 (2004)
16. Lalire, G., Argoud, M., Jeannet, B.: Interproc,
    http://pop-art.inrialpes.fr/people/bjeannet/bjeannet-forge/interproc/
17. Laviron, V., Logozzo, F.: Subpolyhedra: A (more) scalable approach to infer linear inequalities. In: Jones, N.D., Müller-Olm, M. (eds.) VMCAI 2009. LNCS, vol. 5403, pp. 229–244. Springer, Heidelberg (2009)
18. Makhorin, A.: The GNU Linear Programming Kit (2000),
    http://www.gnu.org/software/glpk/
19. Miné, A.: Relational abstract domains for the detection of floating-point run-time errors. In: Schmidt, D. (ed.) ESOP 2004. LNCS, vol. 2986, pp. 3–17. Springer, Heidelberg (2004)
20. Miné, A.: The octagon abstract domain. Higher-Order and Symbolic Computation 19(1), 31–100 (2006)
21. Miné, A.: Symbolic methods to enhance the precision of numerical abstract domains. In: Emerson, E.A., Namjoshi, K.S. (eds.) VMCAI 2006. LNCS, vol. 3855, pp. 348–363. Springer, Heidelberg (2005)
22. Oettli, W., Prager, W.: Compatibility of approximate solution of linear equations with given error bounds for coefficients and right-hand sides. Numer. Math. 6, 405–409 (1964)
23. Rohn, J.: A handbook of results on interval linear problems. Technical report, Czech Academy of Sciences, Prague, Czech Republic (April 2005)
24. Rohn, J.: Solvability of systems of interval linear equations and inequalities. In: Linear Optimization Problems with Inexact Data, pp. 35–77. Springer, US (2006)

Invariant Checking for Programs with Procedure Calls*

Guillem Godoy[1] and Ashish Tiwari[2]

[1] LSI Department, Technical University of Catalonia
Jordi Girona, 1-3 08034 Barcelona, Spain
ggodoy@lsi.upc.edu
[2] SRI International, 333 Ravenswood Ave, Menlo Park, CA, U.S.A
Tel.: +1.650.859.4774, Fax: +1.650.859.2844
tiwari@csl.sri.com

Abstract. Invariants are a crucial component of the overall correctness
of programs. We explore the theoretical limits for doing automatic invariant checking and show that invariant checking is decidable for a large
class of programs that includes some recursive programs. The proof uses
known results like the decidability of Presburger arithmetic and the semi-
linearity of the Parikh image of a regular language. Removing some of the
restrictions on the program model leads to undecidability of the invariant
checking problem.

1   Introduction

The ability to generate reliable and correct software depends crucially on the
development of tools for automatically verifying the correctness of programs.
Modern software development tools support automatic program analysis, but
only to a limited extent. Extending these analyses to richer and deeper properties
of programs is an active area of research.

Invariants are a crucial component of the overall correctness of programs.
An invariant is simply an expression that evaluates to "true" on all executions
(paths) of the program. The problem of checking whether a given expression is an
invariant is undecidable in general. However, there are simplified program models
for which invariant checking is decidable, even efficiently. These decidability
results are important in two respects: they help in developing efficient analysis
engines and understanding the causes of undecidability, which in turn is useful
for identifying places where any analysis engine will necessarily be incomplete.

There are several results on the decidability of invariant checking for restricted
program models. These decidability results are parameterized by three choices:
(a) the program model, (b) the theory of the expression language used in the

---

* The first author was supported by Spanish Ministry of Education and Science
through the FORMALISM project (TIN2007-66523) and the LOGICTOOLS-2
project (TIN2007-68093-C02-01). The second author was supported in part by NSF
grants CNS-0720721 and CNS-0834810 and NASA grant NNX08AB95A.

J. Palsberg and Z. Su (Eds.): SAS 2009, LNCS 5673, pp. 326–342, 2009.

program model, and (c) the form of the assertion. A common assumption on
the program model is that there are no procedure call nodes [6,11,12,7,8]. When
procedure call nodes are allowed, it is commonly assumed that variables can take
only *finitely* many values [4,3,1]. When (restricted) procedure call nodes are allowed, and also infinite domains for data values are allowed [16,13,14,10,9], then,
it is assumed that assertions are always equality of two program expressions. In
other words, there are no results for the case when procedure call nodes, infinite data values, and disequality assertions are all allowed. However, note that
checking invariance of *disequalities* is equally important; for example, for alias
analysis.

In this paper, we show that invariant checking is decidable in a setting which
allows (a) recursive procedure call nodes in the program model, (b) infinite
domains for values of variables, and (c) any Boolean combination of equality
and disequality of program expressions as the assertion. Specifically, we define
a programming model in which a program contains a *finite* number of program
variables, but each variable takes values over the *infinite* domain of (uninterpreted first-order) terms. The program variables are updated by assignments
and the control flow structure consists of non-deterministic conditionals, loops,
and (possibly recursive) procedure calls. We identify a subclass of programs in
this programming model for which the problem of checking if an equality or
disequality (or any Boolean combination thereof) is an invariant is decidable.

In the process of obtaining the main result, we also show that the following
problem is solvable: given $N + M$ substitutions, $\sigma_1, \ldots, \sigma_N, \beta_1, \ldots, \beta_M$, $N + M$
integer variables, $n_1, \ldots, n_N, m_1, \ldots, m_M$, and terms x, y, determine if there is
a value for the $N + M$ integer variables in a given semilinear set such that

$$\sigma_N^{n_N} \ldots \sigma_1^{n_1}(x) = \beta_M^{m_M} \ldots \beta_1^{m_1}(y).$$

This result can be of independent interest.

2   Preliminaries

Let $\mathcal{T}(\Sigma, \{X\})$ be the set of all the terms constructed over a fixed finite signature Σ and a set of variables X. The root symbol of a term t is denoted by
$\mathrm{root}(t)$. The *positions* $\mathrm{Pos}(t)$ in a term t are sequences of positive integers (ϵ,
the empty sequence, is the root position). A subterm of t at position p is written
$t|_p$. The concatenation of the positions p and q is denoted as $p.q$. A substitution
is a mapping from a set of variables X to $\mathcal{T}(\Sigma, \{X\})$. We denote substitutions by σ, θ and $\sigma(t)$ denotes the term obtained by replacing every variable in
t by its image by σ. Given substitutions σ and θ, their composition is denoted
by juxtaposition $\sigma\theta$, and is defined by $\sigma\theta(x) := \sigma(\theta(x))$.

A *linear* set is any subset of $\mathbb{N}^k$ that can be written in the form $\{c_0 +$
$\sum_{i=1}^{n} \alpha_i c_i \mid \alpha_i \in \mathbb{N}\}$ for some fixed $n + 1$ vectors $c_0, \ldots, c_n$ in $\mathbb{N}^k$. A *semilinear* set is a finite union of *linear* sets.

The *Parikh image* of a word $w \in \Sigma^*$ is a vector in $\mathbb{N}^{|\Sigma|}$ that contains the
number of occurrences in w of each symbol in Σ. For example, if $\Sigma = \{a_1, a_2\}$

and $w = a_1 a_2 a_1 a_1$, then the Parikh image of w is $\langle 3, 1 \rangle$. It is well known that Parikh image of a regular (even context-free) language is semilinear [15].

A Presburger arithmetic formula is a (possibly quantified) first-order formula over predicate symbols $=$ and $>$, and with terms constructed using the binary symbol $+$ and constant symbols $\mathbb{N}$ (that is, linear arithmetic expressions are allowed). Presburger arithmetic formulas are interpreted over the natural numbers in the standard way. If ϕ is a sentence in Presburger arithmetic, then $\models_{\mathbb{N}} \phi$ denotes validity of ϕ. We will use $\models$ to denote validity in the pure theory of equality over uninterpreted symbols (occasionally, this theory combined with Presburger arithmetic).

Every semilinear set can be represented using a Presburger formula. Hence, it follows that for every regular language L, there exists a Presburger formula ϕ_L whose solutions coincide with the Parikh image of L. In fact, the size of the formula ϕ_L can be bounded using the following result from Seidl et. al. [17].

Theorem 1 (Seidl et. al. [17], Theorem 1). *For any nondeterministic finite automaton A, an existential Presburger formula ϕ_A for the Parikh image of the language $\mathsf{L}(A)$ of A can be constructed in time $O(|A|)$, where $|A|$ is the number of states plus the number of transitions in A.*

3   Invariant Checking and Related Work

We illustrate the main ideas related to invariant checking via a simple example. Consider the program in Figure 1 (left). Given an assertion, say $x = 2y$, at the end of the program, the problem of invariant checking seeks to find out if the assertion is an invariant of the program, that is, if it evaluates to true for all executions of the program.

Since invariant checking is undecidable for general programs, often the program is abstracted and invariants are checked on the abstracted program. The program in Figure 1 (left) has already abstracted away the actual conditions (that were present in some original program) and replaced them with nondeterministic choices (*). This new program has more behaviors, and hence if an

```
if (*) then                         if (*) then
    ⟨x, y⟩ := ⟨x + x, x⟩;                ⟨x, y⟩ := ⟨f(x, x), x⟩;
else                                else
    while (*) do                        while (*) do
        ⟨x, y⟩ := ⟨sin(y) + sin(y), sin(y)⟩;    ⟨x, y⟩ := ⟨f(g(y), g(y)), g(y)⟩;
    endwhile                            endwhile
endif                               endif
assert (x = 2y)                     assert (x = f(y, y))
```

Fig. 1. A simple program (left) and its abstracted version (right). The abstract version is obtained by replacing the interpreted symbols $+, \sin$ by uninterpreted symbols f, g respectively.

expression is an invariant for this new program, it will be an invariant of the original. For the above example, it is easy to see that the assertion at the end of the program holds under all possible executions of this nondeterministic program.

The left program can be abstracted further by replacing the interpreted functions, + and sin, by uninterpreted functions, say f and g. Again, this is a sound abstraction – the new abstracted program, shown on the right-hand side of Figure 1, has more behaviors. The process of abstraction is attractive since it can give a program that lies in a class of programs for which invariant checking is decidable.

The decidability of the assertion checking problem is parameterized by three choices: (a) the program model, (b) the theory of the expression language used in the program model, and (c) the form of the assertion. We briefly describe the common choices made for obtaining decidability and point to related work.

(a) The program model: First note that including conditional branches in programs quickly leads to undecidability of invariant checking [12,11]. Hence, a commonly studied program model is one that contains only assignments, *nondeterministic* conditionals and *non-deterministic* loops. The two programs in Figure 1 fall into this category. Since interprocedural analysis is more difficult, procedure call nodes are often disallowed in the program model [6,11,12,7,8]. For this program model, invariant checking is decidable when the expressions are terms over uninterpreted symbols and assertions are term equalities [6,8]. For example, the invariant checking problem for the program in Figure 1 (right) falls into this class. However, the invariant checking problem becomes undecidable if we consider disequality assertions, such as $x \neq y$, rather than equality assertions [18]. It remains decidable when the assertion is a disjunction of conjunctions of equalities [8]. For the same program model, the above results also generalize to several other expression languages; the reader is referred to [8] for details.

A useful extension of the program model is obtained by including procedure calls. If the procedure calls are not recursive, the problem can be reduced to the original one by just inlining the procedures. When recursive procedure calls are allowed, the problem becomes more complex, and there are very few results on the decidability of invariant checking [9].

(b) The expression language: It is commonly assumed that infinite data types have been abstracted into finite types and this assumption forms the starting point for several investigations, especially when the program model allows recursive procedure calls [4,3,1]. Our work, however, takes a complementary path. We focus on *restricted and simpler control flow paths, but keep the data type domains infinite.*

(c) The form of assertion: There are some results for the case when procedure calls and infinite data types are both allowed [16,13,14,10,9], but in all these cases, as well as in most of the other works, assertions are restricted to equality between program expressions.

```
main () {                          P() {
    ⟨x,y⟩ := ⟨f(x,x),x⟩;               if (*) then // do nothing
    call P ;                           else
    y := f(y,y);                           x := g(x); call P ; y := g(y);
    assert(x = y);                     endif
}                                  }
```

Fig. 2. A simple program containing a main procedure (left) and a subprocedure (right)

In contrast to all the above mentioned works, we consider equality and disequality assertions in the presence of recursive procedure calls and infinite data types. Since the Post Correspondence Problem (PCP) can be reduced to checking a disequality assertion in a non-deterministic loop containing non-deterministic conditionals (see Figure 3 and [18]), we have to restrict the program model – by disallowing conditionals within loops – to achieve decidability.

Summary of the Main Ideas and Results

Consider the recursive program in Figure 2. We will view an assignment block $\langle x_1, \ldots, x_n \rangle := \langle s_1, \ldots, s_n \rangle$ as the substitution $\sigma_s = \{x_1 \mapsto s_1, \ldots x_n \mapsto s_n\}$. In the program in Figure 2, the five assignment blocks correspond to the following five substitutions:

$$\sigma_1 = \{x \mapsto f(x,x), y \mapsto x\} \quad \sigma_2 = \{x \mapsto x, y \mapsto f(y,y)\} \quad \sigma_3 = \{x \mapsto x, y \mapsto y\}$$
$$\sigma_4 = \{x \mapsto g(x), y \mapsto y\} \qquad \sigma_5 = \{x \mapsto x, y \mapsto g(y)\}$$

The assertion $x = y$ holds at the end of procedure main iff x and y have equal values at that point on all program paths. This is equivalent to deciding whether

$$\sigma_1 \underline{\sigma_4^N \sigma_3 \sigma_5^N} \sigma_2(x) = \sigma_1 \underline{\sigma_4^N \sigma_3 \sigma_5^N} \sigma_2(y), \qquad \text{for every } N \geq 0 \qquad (1)$$

Note that the underlined composition of substitutions capture the effect of the recursive procedure P, and N represents the total number of recursive calls to P in a certain execution.

Consider the negation of Condition 1:

$$\sigma_1 \sigma_4^N \sigma_3 \sigma_5^N \sigma_2(x) \neq \sigma_1 \sigma_4^N \sigma_3 \sigma_5^N \sigma_2(y), \qquad \text{for some } N \geq 0 \qquad (2)$$

We view the above literal as an instance of the general dis-unification problem: find all numerical values for the variables $i_1, \ldots, i_n, j_1, \ldots, j_m$ such that

$$\sigma_1^{i_1} \ldots \sigma_n^{i_n}(x) \neq \beta_1^{j_1} \ldots \beta_m^{j_m}(y). \qquad (3)$$

where σ_i, β_j's are given substitutions. We prove that the solutions for this dis-unification problem can be expressed with a Presburger arithmetic formula with free variables $i_1, \ldots, i_n, j_1, \ldots, j_m$. As a consequence, we prove decidability of any Boolean formula whose atoms are of Form 3, and in particular, we prove decidability of our original invariant checking problem.

In our example, we construct the Presburger sentence equivalent to Equation 1 by constructing a Presburger formula ϕ for the following "more general" set:

$$\{\langle i_1, \ldots, i_5, j_1, \ldots, j_5 \rangle \in \mathbb{N}^{10} \mid \sigma_1^{i_1} \sigma_4^{i_4} \sigma_3^{i_3} \sigma_5^{i_5} \sigma_2^{i_2}(x) \neq \sigma_1^{j_1} \sigma_4^{j_4} \sigma_3^{j_3} \sigma_5^{j_5} \sigma_2^{j_2}(y)\}$$

The Presburger formula ϕ is obtained in two steps. In the first step, we construct a non-deterministic finite automaton A on an alphabet with 10 symbols such that the Parikh image of the language accepted by A is equal to the above set. This construction is given in Section 5. In the second step, we construct a Presburger formula representing the Parikh image of A.

We characterize the class of programs for which the invariant checking problem can be decided using our approach. A program is in this class if the effect of all its execution paths can be described as a finite union of expressions of the form $\sigma_1^{i_1} \ldots \sigma_n^{i_n}$, with linear conditions relating the i_j's. We also define a general program model and a syntactic subclass, called *Sloopy Programs*, that falls in the decidable class. An important restriction is that Sloopy Programs disallow conditionals within loops.

The outline for the rest of the paper is as follows. In Section 4 we define the notion of *parameterized substitutions*, present our program model and the subset of Sloopy Programs. We show that parameterized substitutions are sufficient to finitely represent the semantics of Sloopy Programs. Thus, the invariant checking problem is reduced to deciding conditions of the form of Equation 1. In Section 5 we show that these conditions are decidable. Finally, we put forward our conclusions in Section 7 and discuss avenues for future research.

4   Program Model, Semantics, and Parameterized Substitutions

The programs considered in this paper do not have input and are non-deterministic. The semantics of a concrete execution of a program is the final value of its variables, which can be viewed as a substitution σ. The semantics of a program can then be defined as the set of substitutions corresponding to all its possible executions. We are interested in programs whose semantics is finitely representable in some formalism. In this setting, the following definition will be useful.

Definition 1. *A* parameterized substitution, $\theta(n_1, \ldots, n_N)$, *or* $\theta(\boldsymbol{n})$ *in short, is an expression of the form*

$$\sigma_N^{n_N} \cdots \sigma_3^{n_3} \sigma_2^{n_2} \sigma_1^{n_1}$$

where each n_i is a variable (ranging over the natural numbers) and each σ_i is a substitution. A parameterized substitution is succinctly written as $\boldsymbol{\sigma^n}$.

An instance *of $\theta(\boldsymbol{n})$ is a substitution obtained by fixing the valuation for the variables $\boldsymbol{n}$. If Θ is a set of parameterized substitutions, then the set* Instances(Θ) *is defined as*

$$\text{Instances}(\Theta) := \{\sigma \mid \sigma := \theta(\boldsymbol{c}), \ \boldsymbol{c} \in \mathbb{N}^N, \ \theta(\boldsymbol{n}) \in \Theta\}$$

An extended parameterized substitution *is a pair* $(\theta(\boldsymbol{n}); \chi(\boldsymbol{n}))$ *where* $\theta(\boldsymbol{n})$ *is a parameterized substitution and* $\chi(\boldsymbol{n})$ *is a Presburger formula with free variables* $\boldsymbol{n}$. *If* Θ *is a set of extended parameterized substitutions, then the set* Instances(Θ) *is defined as*

$$\text{Instances}(\Theta) := \{\sigma \mid \sigma := \theta(\boldsymbol{c}), \quad \boldsymbol{c} \in \mathbb{N}^N, \quad \models_{\mathbb{N}} \chi(\boldsymbol{c}), \quad (\theta(\boldsymbol{n}); \chi(\boldsymbol{n})) \in \Theta\}$$

For a given class of programs, we say that its semantics is effectively representable with extended parameterized substitutions *if, for every program* P *in the class, a finite set* Θ *of extended parameterized substitutions can be computed such that the semantics,* $\|P\|$, *of* P *is equal to* Instances(Θ).

Note that a parameterized substitution θ can be written as an extended parameterized substitution $(\theta; \text{true})$.

Program Model. We define a general class of programs syntactically and then identify its subclass that is effectively representable with extended parameterized substitutions. Let X be a finite set of variables, called program variables. A *program* is a finite ordered list of *procedures*, $\langle P_0, P_1, \ldots, P_k \rangle$, where a *procedure* is a string defined by the following grammar:

$$P ::= \boldsymbol{X} := \boldsymbol{t} \mid P ; P \mid$$
$$\quad \text{if } (*) \, P \text{ else } P \text{ endif} \mid \text{while } (*) \, P \text{ endwhile} \mid \text{call } n$$

where $n \in \{0, \ldots, k\}$ is an index (referring to the procedure at the n-th position in the ordered list above) and $\boldsymbol{t}$ is a vector of terms (of size exactly equal to $|\boldsymbol{X}|$).

We next define a subclass of programs called Sloopy Programs that only contain simple *loop*s. A Sloopy Procedure is defined as follows:

$$\text{Intr}_n ::= \boldsymbol{X} := \boldsymbol{t} \mid \text{while } (*) \, \boldsymbol{X} := \boldsymbol{t} \text{ endwhile} \mid \text{Intr}_n ; \text{Intr}_n \mid$$
$$\quad \text{if } (*) \, \text{Intr}_n \text{ else } \text{Intr}_n \text{ endif} \mid \text{call } m \text{ where } m > n$$
$$\text{SProc}_n ::= \text{Intr}_n \mid \text{if } (*) \, \text{Intr}_n \text{ else } \boldsymbol{X} := \boldsymbol{t}; \text{call } n; \, \boldsymbol{X} := \boldsymbol{t}' \text{ endif}$$

A Sloopy Program is an ordered list of procedures, $\langle P_0, P_1, \ldots, P_k \rangle$, where each P_i is generated by SProc_i. We assume that P_0 is the main procedure.

The class of Sloopy Programs has two main restrictions compared to the class of general programs defined above. First, it restricts what can occur inside a nondeterministic while loop. Specifically, it disallows conditionals inside while. If this is allowed, then invariant checking (of disequality assertions) becomes undecidable as shown by the program in Figure 3. The second restriction in Sloopy Programs concerns mutual recursion. Recursive calls are not allowed inside code generated by Intr_n, but Procedure P_n (generated by SProc_n) can recursively call itself.

Semantics. The semantics of the program constructs if else endif and while endwhile are standard, with the condition $(*)$ meaning that the control can flow in either direction in a nondeterministic way. The construct call n

SolvePCP$((u_1, v_1), \ldots, (u_k, v_k))$:
  $x := u_1(\epsilon)$; $y := v_1(\epsilon)$;
  while (*) {
     if (*) { $x := u_1(x)$; $y := v_1(y)$; }
     if (*) { $x := u_2(x)$; $y := v_2(y)$; }
     $\vdots$
     if (*) { $x := u_k(x)$; $y := v_k(y)$; }
  } **assert**$(x \neq y)$

The assertion $x \neq y$ is not an invariant of program SolvePCP iff $u_1 u_{i_1} \ldots u_{i_m} = v_1 v_{i_1} \ldots v_{i_m}$ for some $i_1, \ldots, i_m \in \{1, \ldots, k\}$. Thus, we can solve PCP by checking if certain disequalities are invariants.

Fig. 3. Undecidability of invariant checking for general programs

denotes a procedure call where control flows to the procedure with index n — with the understanding that all variables X are global variables. Thus, a program essentially represents a (possibly infinite) collection of paths, where a path is a sequence of assignments.

Definition 2 (Semantics of a program). *The semantics of a path $X :=$ $e_1; X := e_2; \cdots ; X := e_k;$ is the substitution obtained by composing the k substitutions as follows: $\langle X \mapsto e_1 \rangle \langle X \mapsto e_2 \rangle \cdots \langle X \mapsto e_k \rangle$. The semantics of a program $\|P\|$ is the collection of the semantics of all its paths.*

The following lemma says that the semantics of the class of Sloopy Programs is effectively representable with extended parameterized substitutions.

Lemma 1. *For any Sloopy Program P, a finite set Θ of extended parameterized substitutions can be computed such that $\|P\| = $ Instances(Θ).*

Since the semantics of a Sloopy Program P is, by definition, the semantics of the main procedure P_0, the proof of Lemma 1 follows immediately from the same claim for Sloopy Procedures generated by SProc$_n$ stated and proved in Appendix A. The intuition behind the proof is that each basic block corresponds to a substitution and the parameters in the parameterized substitution represent the number of times a basic block (which is part of a loop or procedure) is executed. The relationship between these numbers is encoded in the constraint in the extended parameterized substitution. The restrictions on Sloopy Programs ensure that its semantics are representable by extended parameterized substitutions in this way (Lemma 1).

5   Invariant Checking

We define the invariant checking problem for programs as follows. Given a program P and a postcondition ψ, we are interested in testing whether

$$\models \sigma(\psi), \qquad \text{for all } \sigma \in \|P\|,$$

where $\sigma(\psi)$ denotes the formula obtained by applying σ to all the terms in ψ, and $\models$ denotes validity in the pure theory of equality. The postcondition formula ψ is a (quantifier-free) formula built using equalities $t_1 = t_2$ as the atomic formulas, where t_1, t_2 are terms over $\mathcal{T}(\Sigma, \{X\})$. Without loss of generality, we can assume that t_1 and t_2 are variables, since the program P can always introduce two new variables, say x, y, and assignments, $x := t_1$; $y := t_2$, and instead check for $x = y$.

For programs whose semantics is effectively representable with extended parameterized substitutions, the invariant checking problem reduces to the following problem. Given a formula ψ and *one* extended parameterized substitution $(\theta(u); \chi(u))$, determine whether

$$\models \theta(c)(\psi), \qquad \text{for all } c \in \mathbb{N}^N \text{ s.t. } \models_\mathbb{N} \chi(c),$$

that is, determine whether all solutions c of χ are also solutions of $\theta(u)(\psi)$.

We solve this problem by mapping the formula $\theta(u)(\psi)$ to a formula in Presburger arithmetic $\phi(u)$ such that the two formulas have the same set of solutions; that is, for all $c \in \mathbb{N}^N$, $\models_\mathbb{N} \phi(c)$ iff $\models \theta(c)(\psi)$. We further simplify the proof by first considering only a disequality, $x \neq y$, in place of ψ. We will show that

Lemma 2. *Given a parameterized substitution $\theta(u)$ and variables x and y, there is a Presburger arithmetic formula $\phi_{x,y,\theta}(u)$ such that for all $c \in \mathbb{N}^N$, it is the case that $\models \theta(c)(x) \neq \theta(c)(y)$ iff $\models_\mathbb{N} \phi_{x,y,\theta}(c)$.*

Parameterized Disequation to Automaton. We prove Lemma 2 by solving a more general problem. Given substitutions $\sigma_1, \ldots, \sigma_N$ and $\beta_1, \ldots, \beta_M$, all with domain $\{x_1, \ldots, x_k\}$ and range $\mathcal{T}(\Sigma, \{x_1, \ldots, x_k\})$, we consider the problem of characterizing the solutions of the disequation

$$\sigma_N^{n_N} \ldots \sigma_1^{n_1}(x) \neq \beta_M^{m_M} \ldots \beta_1^{m_1}(y),$$

where $n_1, \ldots, n_N, m_1, \ldots, m_M$ are variables ranging over the natural numbers, and x, y are variables in $\{x_1, \ldots, x_k\}$. Our goal is to represent all the solutions of this disequation, written in short as $\sigma^n(x) \neq \beta^m(y)$, as a Presburger arithmetic formula with $N + M$ free variables n, m. To this end, we first construct an automaton A that accepts words over an alphabet of vectors $\{0, 1\}^{N+M}$ such that the following property holds: $\sigma^n(x)$ will be different from $\beta^m(y)$ iff there exists a word $w := v_1 \ldots v_l$ in the language accepted by A such that $Sum(w) := v_1 + \ldots + v_l$ is equal to the vector $\langle n, m \rangle \in \mathbb{N}^{N+M}$. In fact, only the vector $\mathbf{0}$ and the unit vectors of the canonical basis $e_1, \ldots, e_{N+M}$ will appear in the definition of A. (Here, $e_j \in \{0, 1\}^{N+M}$ is a vector that has 1 in the j-th position and 0's elsewhere.)

Intuitively, the automaton non-deterministically searches for the position in the terms $\sigma^n(x)$ and $\beta^m(y)$ where the two terms are different. Informally, call this position the *point of difference*. We use the notation N to denote the set $\{1, \ldots, N\}$. The non-deterministic automaton $A = (Q, \Sigma_A, q_{\text{init}}, Q_F, T)$ is defined as follows:

(1) The alphabet Σ_A is $\{\mathbf{0}, e_1, \ldots, e_{N+M}\}$. Informally, when the automaton A makes a transition on symbol e_i, for $i \in N$, then it means that the automaton

A decided to use one more application of σ_i in its search for the "point of difference". Analogously, when it makes a transition on symbol e_{N+j}, for $j \in M$, it decided to use one more application of β_j.

(2) The set of states Q of the automaton A is

$$Q = Q_1 \cup Q_F$$
$$Q_1 = \{\langle i, s, j, t\rangle \mid i \in N, s \text{ is a subterm of } \{x_1, \ldots, x_k\} \cup \{\sigma_i(x_1), \ldots, \sigma_i(x_k)\},$$
$$j \in M, t \text{ is a subterm of } \{x_1, \ldots, x_k\} \cup \{\beta_j(x_1), \ldots, \beta_j(x_k)\}\}$$
$$Q_F = \{q_{ij} \mid i \in N+1, j \in M+1\}$$

Here Q_F is the set of accepting states, and $q_{\text{init}} = \langle 1, x, 1, y\rangle$ is the initial state. Intuitively, when A is in the state $\langle i, s, j, t\rangle$, then it means that A is currently applying σ_i and β_j, respectively, and currently matching s and t, in its search for the "point of difference".

(3) The transitions T of A are given in Table 1. Informally speaking, in its search for the "point of difference" from state $\langle i, s, j, t\rangle$, the non-deterministic automaton A does the following: (a) if the top function symbols are different, then it moves into an accept state (T_1'), (b) if the top function symbols are identical, then it *guesses* under which subterms the "point of difference" may lie, and moves into the state with these subterms (T_1), (c) if the search reaches a variable, then it non-deterministically chooses to either apply the current substitution (T_2, T_2') and continue the search, or it moves to the next substitution (T_3, T_3'), (d) if the search reaches the last substitutions, then it moves into an accepting state if it finds the "point of difference" (T_4, T_4', T_5), and (e) if A is in an accepting state (that is, it has found the "point of difference"), but it has not used up all the available substitutions, then it accepts all possible choices for the remaining substitutions (T_6, T_6').

Table 1. Transitions of the automaton encoding solutions of a parameterized disequation

$$T = T_1 \cup T_1' \cup T_2 \cup T_2' \cup T_3 \cup T_3' \cup T_4 \cup T_4' \cup T_5 \cup T_6 \cup T_6'$$
$$T_1 = \{(\langle i, fs_1 \ldots s_n, j, ft_1 \ldots t_n\rangle, \mathbf{0}, \langle i, s_l, j, t_l\rangle) \mid i \in N, j \in M, l \in n\}$$
$$T_1' = \{(\langle i, fs_1 \ldots s_n, j, gt_1 \ldots t_m\rangle, \mathbf{0}, q_{ij}) \mid i \in N, j \in M, f \not\equiv g\}$$
$$T_2 = \{(\langle i, x, j, t\rangle, e_i, \langle i, \sigma_i(x), j, t\rangle) \mid i \in N, j \in M\}$$
$$T_2' = \{(\langle i, t, j, x\rangle, e_{N+j}, \langle i, t, j, \sigma_j(x)\rangle) \mid i \in N, j \in M\}$$
$$T_3 = \{(\langle i, x, j, t\rangle, \mathbf{0}, \langle i+1, x, j, t\rangle) \mid i \in N-1, j \in M\}$$
$$T_3' = \{(\langle i, t, j, x\rangle, \mathbf{0}, \langle i, t, j+1, x\rangle) \mid i \in N, j \in M-1\}$$
$$T_4 = \{(\langle N, x, j, t\rangle, \mathbf{0}, q_{N+1,j}) \mid j \in M, t \notin X\}$$
$$T_4' = \{(\langle i, t, M, x\rangle, \mathbf{0}, q_{i,M+1}) \mid i \in N, t \notin X\}$$
$$T_5 = \{(\langle N, s, M, t\rangle, \mathbf{0}, q_{N+1,M+1}) \mid s, t \in X, s \not\equiv t\}$$
$$T_6 = \{(q_{ij}, e_l, q_{ij}) \mid i \in N, j \in M+1, i \le l \le N\}$$
$$T_6' = \{(q_{ij}, e_{N+l}, q_{ij}) \mid i \in N+1, j \in M, j \le l \le M\}$$

The next two lemmas will capture the intuition behind the construction of A. The first lemma states that every run of A corresponds to some instance of x and y and some path on those instances.

Lemma 3. *Let A be an automaton constructed from x, y, σ and β as before. Let w be a word in Σ_A^*. Let $\langle 1, x, 1, y \rangle \xrightarrow{w} \langle i, s, j, t \rangle$ be a run of the automaton A. Let $Sum(w) = \langle n, m \rangle$, $u = \sigma^n(x)$ and $v = \beta^m(y)$. Then, there is a position p such that $s = u|_p$, $t = v|_p$, and $\mathrm{root}(u|_{p'}) = \mathrm{root}(v|_{p'})$ for all positions $p' < p$.*

Proof. We generate the required position p by annotating each state in the given run with a position. The initial state is annotated with position ϵ. If p is the annotation on the current state, then (a) if the next state is obtained using a transition from the set T_1, then the next state is annotated with $p.l$, and (b) if the next state is obtained using any other transition, then the next state is annotated with p.

Now, the lemma follows by induction on the length of the run. In the base case, the claim is clearly true for the initial state. It is easily verified that the claim is preserved on every transition that does not lead to some q_{ij} state. □

Conversely, we can show that given an instance of x and y and a position p on these instances, we can find a corresponding run of A.

Lemma 4. *Let A be an automaton constructed from x, y, σ and β as before. Let n, m be $N + M$ natural numbers and let u be $\sigma^n(x)$ and v be $\beta^m(y)$. If p is a position in u and v such that $\mathrm{root}(u|_{p'}) = \mathrm{root}(v|_{p'})$ for all $p' < p$, then there is a run of A, $\langle 1, x, 1, y \rangle \xrightarrow{w} \langle i, s, j, t \rangle$ such that $Sum(w) = \langle n_1, \dots, n_{i-1}, n', 0, \dots, 0, m_1, \dots, m_{j-1}, m', 0, \dots, 0 \rangle$, $n' \leq n_i$, $m' \leq m_j$, $s := (\sigma_i^{n'} \sigma_{i-1}^{n_{i-1}} \dots \sigma_1^{n_1}(x))|_p$, and $t := (\beta_j^{m'} \beta_{j-1}^{m_{j-1}} \dots \beta_1^{m_1}(y))|_p$.*

Proof. We construct the required run of automaton A by following the path p on terms u and v. We need to keep three auxiliary variables – two indices n', m', and a position p' – to guide this run of A. We just append the 3 auxiliary variables to the state to simplify presentation. The starting state is $\langle \langle 1, x, 1, y \rangle, 0, 0, \epsilon \rangle$.

Suppose that the current (extended) state of A is $\langle \langle i, s, j, t \rangle, n', m', p' \rangle$. The auxiliary variables will satisfy the invariant that $0 \leq n' \leq n_i$, $0 \leq m' \leq m_j$, $\epsilon \leq p' \leq p$, $s = (\sigma_i^{n'} \sigma_{i-1}^{n_{i-1}} \dots \sigma_1^{n_1}(x))|_p$, and $t = (\beta_j^{m'} \beta_{j-1}^{m_{j-1}} \dots \beta_1^{m_1}(y))|_p$. Now, the next state in the required run will be:

(1) $\langle \langle i, s|_l, j, t|_l \rangle, n', m', p'.l \rangle$ (using a transition from T_1), if neither s nor t is a variable and $p'.l \leq p$. Note that, by assumption, in this case, $\mathrm{root}(s) = \mathrm{root}(t)$ and hence a transition from T_1 will be enabled.

(2) $\langle \langle i, \sigma_i(s), j, t \rangle, n' + 1, m', p' \rangle$ (using a transition from T_2), if s is a variable and $n' < n_i$.

(2') $\langle \langle i, s, j, \beta_j(t) \rangle, n', m' + 1, p' \rangle$ (using a transition from T_2'), if t is a variable and $m' < m_j$.

(3) $\langle \langle i+1, s, j, t \rangle, 0, m', p' \rangle$ (using a transition from T_3), if s is a variable, $i < N$, and $n' = n_i$.

(3') $\langle\langle i, s, j+1, t\rangle, n', 0, p'\rangle$ (using a transition from T_3'), if t is a variable, $j < M$, and $m' = m_j$.

Using induction on the length of position p, it is easy to prove that the above run has all the desired properties (stated in the lemma). $\qquad\square$

We can now state the correctness of the construction of A, but leave the proof to Appendix A.

Lemma 5. *Let A be an automaton constructed from x, y, σ and β as before. Let n, m be $N + M$ natural numbers.*

Then $\sigma^n(x)$ is different from $\beta^m(y)$ iff there exists a word w accepted by A such that $Sum(w) = \langle n, m\rangle$.

For an automaton A, let $L(A)$ denote the language accepted by A and let $Sum(L(A))$ denote the set $\{Sum(w) \mid w \in L(A)\}$. Lemma 5 gives us the following result on representing solutions of parameterized disequations.

Theorem 2. *Let X be a finite set of variables and σ, β be $N + M$ substitutions mapping X to the set of terms $T(\Sigma, X)$. Given $x, y \in X$, there is a finite automaton A such that*

$$Sum(L(A)) = \{\langle c, d\rangle \in \mathbb{N}^{N+M} \mid \sigma^c(x) \neq \beta^d(y)\}$$

The number of states in A is bounded by $O(InputSize^4)$ and the number of transitions is bounded by $O(InputSize^8)$, where $InputSize$ is the size of the input σ, β.

Automaton to Presburger Formula. Let A be a finite automaton over the alphabet $\{0, e_1, \ldots, e_{N+M}\}$. If we treat 0 as the ϵ-symbol, then it is obvious that $Sum(L(A))$ is simply the Parikh image of $L(A)$. It follows from Theorem 1 that we can represent $Sum(L(A))$ by a Presburger formula ϕ_A.

Disequation to Arbitrary Formula. We can put together Theorems 2 and 1 to immediately get a proof of Lemma 2. In fact, Lemma 2 can now be easily generalized to arbitrary formulas ψ whose atomic formulas are equations between variables.

Theorem 3. *Given an extended parameterized substitution $(\theta(u); \chi(u))$ and a quantifier-free equality formula ψ, there is a Presburger formula $\phi_{\psi,(\theta;\chi)}(u)$ such that for all $c \in \mathbb{N}^N$, it is the case that $\models \chi(c) \Rightarrow \theta(c)(\psi)$ iff $\models_{\mathbb{N}} \phi_{\psi,(\theta;\chi)}(c)$.*

Proof. We proceed by structural induction on ψ. The base case is when ψ is $x = y$. By Lemma 2, we know there is a formula $\phi_{x \neq y, \theta}$ corresponding to $x \neq y$. Thus, for all $c \in \mathbb{N}^N$, we have the following inference:

$$\models \theta(c)(x) \neq \theta(c)(y) \text{ iff } \phi_{x\neq y,\theta}(c) \qquad \text{Lemma 2}$$
$$\therefore, \quad \models \theta(c)(x) = \theta(c)(y) \text{ iff } \neg\phi_{x\neq y,\theta}(c)$$
$$\therefore, \quad \models \chi(c) \Rightarrow \theta(c)(x) = \theta(c)(y) \text{ iff } \chi(c) \Rightarrow \neg\phi_{x\neq y,\theta}(c)$$
$$\therefore, \quad \phi_{\psi,(\theta;\chi)} := \phi_{x=y,(\theta;\chi)} := \chi(u) \Rightarrow \neg\phi_{x\neq y,\theta}(u)$$

For the inductive step, if ψ is $\psi_1 \vee \psi_2$, then it is easy to see that $\phi_{\psi,\theta}$ is $\phi_{\psi_1,\theta} \vee \phi_{\psi_2,\theta}$, and similarly for the cases when ψ is $\neg\psi_1$ and when ψ is $\psi_1 \wedge \psi_2$.   □

Note that $\phi_{\psi,\theta}$ is always an existentially quantified Presburger formula (with free variables). We can test the validity of the (universal closure) of $\phi_{\psi,\theta}$ and thus decide the invariant checking problem for Sloopy Programs.

Theorem 4. *Let P be a Sloopy Program and ψ be an assertion. The problem of checking if ψ is an invariant for P is decidable.*

Proof. Using Lemma 1, we first get a finite set Θ of extended parameterized substitutions that represent $\|P\|$, that is, $\|P\| = \texttt{Instances}(\Theta)$. For each parameterized substitution $(\theta; \chi) \in \Theta$, we use Theorem 3 to construct a Presburger formula $\phi_{\psi,(\theta;\chi)}$ and test the validity of (the universal closure of) $\phi_{\psi,(\theta;\chi)}$. If all such Presburger formulas are valid, then ψ is an invariant of P; otherwise, it is not. The correctness follows from the following reasoning:

ψ is an invariant of P

iff	$\models \sigma(\psi)$ for each $\sigma \in \|P\|$	By definition of invariant
iff	$\models \sigma(\psi)$ for each $\sigma \in \texttt{Instances}(\Theta)$	Lemma 1
iff	$\models \chi(\boldsymbol{c}) \Rightarrow \theta(\boldsymbol{c})(\psi)$ for each $(\theta;\chi) \in \Theta, \boldsymbol{c} \in \mathbb{N}^l$	Definition of $\texttt{Instances}$
iff	$\forall \boldsymbol{u}(\phi_{\psi,(\theta;\chi)}(\boldsymbol{u}))$ is valid	Theorem 3

This completes the proof.   □

6   Discussion

The class of Sloopy Programs has some severe restrictions compared to the class of general programs defined in Section 4. It disallows procedure calls and loops inside a loop and it supports only a limited form of recursion. If we allow arbitrary loops and recursive procedure calls (that is, use the general program model P from Section 4), but restrict to (positive) equations as assertions, then the decidability is not known, although it is known for some subcases [9,5]. If linear arithmetic is the expression language, then disequality checking remains undecidable (similar proof as Figure 3), but equality checking is known to be decidable [13,9].

The decidability result for the class of Sloopy Programs actually works more generally. It works for any program in which the mapping that maps a run of that program to the vector of the number of times a basic block is executed in that run is injective. In other words, given the number of times a basic block has executed in a run, it should be possible to extract the exact run of the program. For any such program, the decidability arguments given in this paper are applicable.

The proof of decidability given here performs two steps. The first step computes the semantics of the program using extended parameterized substitutions. Fixing the parameters fixes a program path. The second step constructs an automaton that characterizes all solutions for the parameters that make an assertion true. We can get a direct proof by merging these two steps. Note that applying a substitution (corresponding to a basic block) to an assertion is the same as computing the weakest precondition of the assertion with respect to the basic block.

Techniques used for deciding equality assertions do not directly apply for deciding disequality assertions. Decidability for equality assertions often relies on the fact that there can be only *finitely* many *non-redundant equations*. This is mostly not true for disequalities.

7   Conclusions

We presented two decidability results in this paper. First, we showed decidability of the following problem: given substitutions $\sigma_1, \ldots, \sigma_N, \beta_1, \ldots, \beta_M$ and terms x, y, is there a vector $(c_1, \ldots, c_N, d_1, \ldots, d_N)$ of natural numbers in a given semilinear set such that $\sigma_N^{c_N} \ldots \sigma_1^{c_1}(x) \neq \beta_M^{d_M} \ldots \beta_1^{d_1}(y)$? We also showed decidability of the above problem when the disequality is replaced by an equality or any Boolean combination of equalities and disequalities. Using the above result, we established decidability of invariant checking for a large class of programs with recursion. Our decidability result is valid for any class of programs whose semantics is effectively representable with extended parameterized substitutions, and Sloopy Programs are just a particular case. It would be interesting to study alternative classes of programs satisfying this property. Moreover, note that our assertions are just quantifier-free boolean formulas. Adding quantification to the assertions will be interesting, since the first order theory of term algebras is known to be decidable [2]. Other variants of the problem can also be considered for future research, such as allowing local variables or parameters in the procedures, and incorporating interpreted symbols in the signature.

Acknowledgments. We thank the reviewers for their helpful comments.

References

1. Bouajjani, A., Esparza, J., Touili, T.: A generic approach to the static analysis of concurrent programs with procedures. In: POPL, pp. 62–73 (2003)
2. Comon, H., Delor, C.: Equational formulae with membership constraints. Inf. Comput. 112, 167–216 (1994)
3. Esparza, J., Hansel, D., Rossmanith, P., Schwoon, S.: Efficient algorithm for model checking pushdown systems. In: Emerson, E.A., Sistla, A.P. (eds.) CAV 2000. LNCS, vol. 1855. Springer, Heidelberg (2000)
4. Esparza, J., Knoop, J.: An automata-theoretic approach to interprocedural dataflow analysis. In: Thomas, W. (ed.) FOSSACS 1999. LNCS, vol. 1578, pp. 14–30. Springer, Heidelberg (1999)

5. Gascon, A., Godoy, G., Schmidt-Schauß, M., Tiwari, A.: Context unification with one context variable. J. of symbolic computation (submitted, 2009)
6. Gulwani, S., Necula, G.C.: A polynomial-time algorithm for global value numbering. In: Giacobazzi, R. (ed.) SAS 2004. LNCS, vol. 3148, pp. 212–227. Springer, Heidelberg (2004)
7. Gulwani, S., Tiwari, A.: Assertion checking over combined abstraction of linear arithmetic & uninterpreted functions. In: Sestoft, P. (ed.) ESOP 2006. LNCS, vol. 3924, pp. 279–293. Springer, Heidelberg (2006)
8. Gulwani, S., Tiwari, A.: Assertion checking unified. In: Cook, B., Podelski, A. (eds.) VMCAI 2007. LNCS, vol. 4349, pp. 363–377. Springer, Heidelberg (2007)
9. Gulwani, S., Tiwari, A.: Computing procedure summaries for interprocedural analysis. In: De Nicola, R. (ed.) ESOP 2007. LNCS, vol. 4421, pp. 253–267. Springer, Heidelberg (2007)
10. Müller-Olm, M., Petter, M., Seidl, H.: Interprocedurally analyzing polynomial identities. In: Durand, B., Thomas, W. (eds.) STACS 2006. LNCS, vol. 3884, pp. 50–67. Springer, Heidelberg (2006)
11. Müller-Olm, M., Rüthing, O., Seidl, H.: Checking Herbrand equalities and beyond. In: Cousot, R. (ed.) VMCAI 2005. LNCS, vol. 3385, pp. 79–96. Springer, Heidelberg (2005)
12. Müller-Olm, M., Seidl, H.: A note on Karr's algorithm. In: 31st ICALP, pp. 1016–1028 (2004)
13. Müller-Olm, M., Seidl, H.: Precise interprocedural analysis through linear algebra. In: 31st ACM Symposium on POPL, January 2004, pp. 330–341 (2004)
14. Müller-Olm, M., Seidl, H., Steffen, B.: Interprocedural Herbrand equalities. In: Sagiv, M. (ed.) ESOP 2005. LNCS, vol. 3444, pp. 31–45. Springer, Heidelberg (2005)
15. Parikh, R.J.: On context-free languages. J. of the ACM 13(4), 570–581 (1966)
16. Reps, T., Horwitz, S., Sagiv, M.: Precise interprocedural dataflow analysis via graph reachability. In: 22nd ACM Symposium on POPL, pp. 49–61 (1995)
17. Seidl, H., Schwentick, T., Muscholl, A., Habermehl, P.: Counting in trees for free. In: Díaz, J., Karhumäki, J., Lepistö, A., Sannella, D. (eds.) ICALP 2004. LNCS, vol. 3142, pp. 1136–1149. Springer, Heidelberg (2004)
18. Tiwari, A., Gulwani, S.: Logical interpretation: Static program analysis using theorem proving. In: Pfenning, F. (ed.) CADE 2007. LNCS, vol. 4603, pp. 147–166. Springer, Heidelberg (2007)

A   Supplementary Lemmas and Proofs

Lemma 6. *For any Sloopy Procedure SP_n, there is a finite set Θ of extended parameterized substitutions such that $\|SP_n\| = \texttt{Instances}(\Theta)$.*

Proof. We prove this by structural induction on the structure of the Sloopy Procedure SP_n. By assumption programs are finite, and hence the structural induction process is well defined. The following equations define the set of extended parameterized substitutions that capture the semantics of Sloopy Procedure SP_n in terms of the the the semantics of its components.

$$\|X := t\| = \{(\langle X \mapsto t\rangle^n; n = 1)\}$$
$$\|\text{while } (*) \ X := t \ \text{endwhile}\| = \{(\langle X \mapsto t\rangle^n; \text{true})\}$$
$$\|\text{Intr}_n \ ; \ \text{Intr}_n'\| = \{(\theta\theta'; \chi \wedge \chi') \mid (\theta; \chi) \in \|\text{Intr}_n\|,$$
$$(\theta'; \chi') \in \|\text{Intr}_n'\|\}$$
$$\|\text{if } (*) \ \text{Intr}_n' \ \text{else} \ \text{Intr}_n' \ \text{endif}\| = \|\text{Intr}_n\| \cup \|\text{Intr}_n'\|$$
$$\|\text{call } m\| = \|P_m\|$$
$$\|\text{if } (*) \ \text{Intr}_n; \ \text{else} \ X := t; \ \text{call } n; \ \ X := t' \ \text{endif}\|$$
$$= \{(\langle X \mapsto t\rangle^{n_1}\theta\langle X \mapsto t'\rangle^{n_2}; \chi \wedge n_1 = n_2) \mid$$
$$(\theta; \chi) \in \|\text{Intr}_n\|\}$$

where n, n_1 and n_2 are always new variables ranging over the natural numbers. Recall that the side condition, $m > n$, guarantees that the above inductive way of obtaining parameterized representation of semantics is well defined. The correctness of the above definition is obvious. □

Proof (Lemma 5). $\Rightarrow$: Assume that $u = \sigma_N^{n_N} \ldots \sigma_1^{n_1}(x)$ is different from $v = \beta_M^{m_M} \ldots \beta_1^{m_1}(y)$. Then, there exists a position $p \in \text{Pos}(u) \cap \text{Pos}(v)$ such that $\text{root}(u|_p) \neq \text{root}(v|_p)$. Among all choices for such a p, we choose one with the minimal size/length. Hence, $\text{root}(u|_{p'}) = \text{root}(v|_{p'})$ for all $p' < p$.

Using Lemma 4 on this choice of position p, we infer that there is a run of automaton A, $\langle 1, x, 1, y\rangle \xrightarrow{w} \langle i, s, j, t\rangle$, such that

$$Sum(w) = \langle n_1, \ldots, n_{i-1}, n', 0, \ldots, 0, m_1, \ldots, m_{j-1}, m', 0, \ldots, 0\rangle,$$

with $n' \leq n_i$, $m' \leq m_j$, $s = (\sigma_i^{n'} \sigma_{i-1}^{n_{i-1}} \ldots \sigma_1^{n_1}(x))|_p$, and $t = (\beta_j^{m'} \beta_{j-1}^{m_{j-1}} \ldots \beta_1^{m_1}(y))|_p$. Among all the runs satisfying these conditions, we choose a run r maximum in length. Because of the choice of p, one of the following conditions is satisfied:

(a) *Neither s nor t is a variable*: In this case, a transition from set T_1' is applicable and we can complete the current run to get the following accepting run:

$$\langle 1, x, 1, y\rangle \xrightarrow{w} \langle i, s, j, t\rangle \xrightarrow[T_1']{0} q_{ij} \xrightarrow[T_6, T_6']{w'} q_{ij}$$

where w' is the word $e_i^{n_i - n'} e_{i+1}^{n_{i+1}} \ldots e_N^{n_N} e_{N+j}^{m_j - m'} e_{N+j+1}^{m_{j+1}} \ldots e_{N+M}^{m_M}$. By construction, we have $Sum(w0w') = \langle n_1, \ldots, n_N, m_1, \ldots, m_M\rangle$ in this accepting run.
(b) *Either s or t is a variable*: Suppose s is a variable, say x', and t is not a variable. If $i \neq N$ or $n' < n_i$, then we can apply a transition of T_2 or T_3 to obtain a larger run than r and with the same conditions, contradicting then the election of r. Hence, $i = N$ and $n' = n_N$. Thus, we can complete the current run as follows:

$$\langle 1, x, 1, y\rangle \xrightarrow{w} \langle i, x', j, t\rangle = \langle N, x', j, t\rangle \xrightarrow[T_4]{0} q_{N+1,j} \xrightarrow[T_6']{w'} q_{N+1,j}$$

where w' is the word $e_{N+j}^{m_j - m'} e_{N+j+1}^{m_{j+1}} \ldots e_{N+M}^{m_M}$. Again, by construction, we have $Sum(w0w') = \langle n_1, \ldots, n_N, m_1, \ldots, m_M\rangle$ in this accepting run. Finally, the other cases, when either t or both s and t are variables can be handled similarly and we get the desired accepting run in each case.

$\Leftarrow$: Suppose that A accepts w and $Sum(w) = \langle n_1, \ldots, n_N, m_1, \ldots, m_M \rangle$. Thus, we have an accepting run of A that can be written in the following form:

$$\langle 1, x, 1, y \rangle \xrightarrow{w'} \langle i, s, j, t \rangle \xrightarrow[T_1, T_4, T_4', T_5]{\mathbf{0}} q_{IJ} \xrightarrow[T_6, T_6']{w''} q_{IJ}$$

It holds that $Sum(w') = \langle n_1, \ldots, n_{i-1}, n', 0, \ldots, 0, m_1, \ldots, m_{j-1}, m', 0, \ldots, 0 \rangle$ for some $n' \leq n_i$ and $m' \leq m_j$. Let $u := \sigma_i^{n'} \sigma_{i-1}^{n_{i-1}} \ldots \sigma_1^{n_1}(x)$ and $v := \sigma_i^{n'} \sigma_{i-1}^{n_{i-1}} \ldots \sigma_1^{n_1}(x)$. Using Lemma 3 on the run $\langle 1, x, 1, y \rangle \xrightarrow{w'} \langle i, s, j, t \rangle$, we conclude that there is a position p such that s is $u|_p$, t is $v|_p$, and $\mathbf{root}(u|_{p'}) = \mathbf{root}(v|_{p'})$ for all $p' < p$.

We can now complete the proof depending on whether we used T_1, T_4, T_4', or T_5 in the accepting run above:

T_1 : In this case, u and v are different at a non-leaf position p. Hence, $\sigma_N^{n_N} \ldots \sigma_1^{n_1}(x)$ and $\beta_M^{m_M} \ldots \beta_1^{m_1}(y)$, which are just instances of u and v, will also differ at position p.

T_4 : In this case, s is a variable and t is not a variable. Furthermore, I is necessarily $N+1$ in this case. Consequently, the only transitions applicable on $q_{I,J}$ are those in T_6', and hence w'' cannot contain e_i for $i \leq N$. Hence, at position p, the term $\sigma_N^{n_N} \ldots \sigma_1^{n_1}(x)$ contains the variable s, whereas the term $\beta_M^{m_M} \ldots \beta_1^{m_1}(y)|_p$ will not be a variable.

T_4' : This case is similar to the previous case.

T_5 : In this case, $I = N+1$, $J = M+1$, and hence, at position p, the two terms $-\sigma_N^{n_N} \ldots \sigma_1^{n_1}(x)$ and $\beta_M^{m_M} \ldots \beta_1^{m_1}(y)$ – have *distinct* variables.

Thus, in all cases, the terms $\sigma_N^{n_N} \ldots \sigma_1^{n_1}(x)$ and $\beta_M^{m_M} \ldots \beta_1^{m_1}(y)$ are different. $\square$

Inter-program Properties

Andrei Voronkov[1] and Iman Narasamdya[2,*]

[1] The University of Manchester
voronkov@cs.man.ac.uk
[2] FBK-Irst
narasamdya@fbk.eu

Abstract. We develop foundations for proving properties relating two programs. Our formalization is based on a suitably adapted notion of program invariant for a single program. First, we give an abstract formulation of the theory of program invariants based on the notion of assertion function: a function that assigns assertions to program points. Then, we develop this abstract notion further so that it can be used to prove properties between two programs. We describe an application of the theory to proving program properties in translation validation.

Keywords: assertion function, invariant, translation validation.

1 Introduction

Recent work on the translation validation approach [15] to compiler correctness has shown the prominence of techniques for proving properties that relate two programs. In translation validation, especially for optimizing compilers, one proves that, for a *single* source program, the program and the result of optimization are *semantically equivalent*. Translation validation frameworks, such as [18,14,23,2,19,12], present program analysis and proof rules specialized for equivalence checking between programs and their optimized versions. However, one of the most bothersome and challenging problems in the work on translation validation or program logic for relating two programs is still present: *how to relate two programs whose control structures are loosely related?*

For instance, consider the programs P and P' in Figure 1. A compiler optimized the program P by unrolling the body of the loop L of P; the resulting program is P'. Variables in P correspond to their primed counterparts in P'. In this case, the loop L corresponds to the loops L'_1 and L'_2. However, two iterations of the loop L correspond to one iteration of the optimized loop L'_1. Note that the control flow of P is related to that of the optimized version P', but they are not identical. Now the problem is *how can we prove the equivalence between these two programs?* The existing solutions to this problem were not satisfactory. For example, Benton [2] included common program optimizations as part of his logic, and so those optimizations are provable just by axioms.

Suppose that one proves the equivalence of two programs using some translation validation method. All existing methods exploit, to a certain extent, that the two programs have much in common: for example, some variables in one of the programs may directly correspond (whatever it means) to variables of the other program. One of the important

---

* Supported in part by COCONUT project.

J. Palsberg and Z. Su (Eds.): SAS 2009, LNCS 5673, pp. 343–359, 2009.

P :

l_1 :

  do $_L\{$

    i := i + 4;

  l_2 :

  $\}$ **while** (i < n);

  return i;

l_3 :

P' :

l_1':

if (i' < n' − 8) {

  do $_{L_1'}$ {

    i' := i' + 8;

  l_2'' :

  $\}$ **while** (i' < n' − 8);

$\}$

do $_{L_2'}\{$

  i' := i' + 4;

l_2' :

$\}$ **while** (i' < n');

return i';

l_3' :

Fig. 1. Example of loop unrolling

questions in translation validation is how to present the results of equivalence-checking so that they can be checked by other systems, such as theorem provers or proof checkers. This problem is not trivial since translation validation methods do not have a common notion of verification conditions, proofs or certificates. This contrasts to program verification where there is a commonly accepted way of proving program properties based on Hoare's logic and invariants. One cannot use Hoare's logic for proving equivalence since we do not even have any specification of the programs.

This paper presents a new elegant way to address this problem. We develop foundations for relating two programs with very different control structures and for proving properties between these programs. Such properties in this paper are called *inter-program properties*. Our proof technique is not specialized for proving specific properties, such as program equivalence, nor for specific program transformations. We propose an abstract theory for expressing and proving inter-program properties; the theory also establishes a notion of certificate or proof about such properties.

Similar to the Floyd-Hoare proof technique [3,4], the main ingredients of our technique are assertions associated with program points. Our theory is based on the notion of *assertion function*: a function that assigns assertions to program points. For instance, one can define an assertion function I_1 that maps l_1 to (n − i)%8 = 0 ∧ n > i, l_2 to (n − i)%8 = 0 ∧ n ≥ i, and l_3 to n = i. Note that the assertions assigned to program points in a loop are not necessarily loop invariants, for example, the assertion assigned to l_2.

The formalization of our theory is based on a suitably adapted notion of program invariant for a single program. We propose the notion of *extendible assertion function* as a constructive characterization for expressing and proving program properties, including program invariants. An assertion function I of a program is extendible if for every run of the program reaching a point p_1 on which I is defined and the assertion $I(p_1)$ holds, we can always *extend* the run so that it reaches a point p_2 on which I is defined and the assertion $I(p_2)$ holds. Note that, on extending the run, the run can reach a point p_3 on which I is defined but the assertion $I(p_3)$ does not hold.

Consider again the assertion function I_1 defined above. This function is extendible with the following arguments. First, for every run of P starting from an initial state that satisfies $I_1(l_1)$, the run reaches l_2 with two iterations of the loop L such that $I_1(l_2)$ holds. Second, let now the run be at l_2 such that $I_1(l_2)$ holds. Then the run can be extended either by following the same path as in the first argument, or by following the path that exits the loop without going through the loop body again. For the latter path, the run reaches l_3 such that $I_1(l_3)$ holds. Note that, in this example, we prove a partial correctness property. That is, for every run of P starting from an initial state that satisfies $I_1(l_1)$, the final state of the run will satisfy $I_1(l_3)$ whenever the run terminates (or reaches l_3). Note in particular that we prove a partial correctness property *without* using loop invariants.

We develop further the notion of extendible assertion function so that it can be used to prove inter-program properties. To this end, we consider two programs P and P' as a *pair* (P, P') *of programs* whose runs are defined by the transitions in P and P', without any synchronization. We will show that meta properties that hold for the case of a single program also hold for the case of pairs of programs. Similar to the case of a single program, we prove inter-program properties using assertions between two specific points of P and P'. These assertions describe data abstractions and control mapping between P and P'. We call such assertions *inter-program assertions*. We extend the notion of assertion function so that it maps pairs of program points to inter-program assertions.

Consider again the programs P and P' of Figure 1. Suppose that two programs are equivalent if for every pair of runs of the two programs on the same input, one run is terminating if and only if the other is, and when the runs terminate, they return the same value. To prove that P and P' are equivalent, we first define an assertion function I_2 as follows: let ϕ be the assertion $\mathsf{i} = \mathsf{i}' \wedge \mathsf{n} = \mathsf{n}'$, we have $I_2(l_1, l_1') \Leftrightarrow I_2(l_2, l_2') \Leftrightarrow I_2(l_2, l_2'') \Leftrightarrow \phi$, and $I_2(l_3, l_3') \Leftrightarrow \mathsf{i} = \mathsf{i}'$.

We prove the equivalence between P and P' by showing that I_2 is extendible. First, for every run of (P, P') from the entries of both programs, that is (l_1, l_1'), such that $\mathsf{n} = \mathsf{n}' = v_1$ and $\mathsf{i} = \mathsf{i}' = v_2$ for some input values v_1 and v_2, the run can be extended either to (l_2, l_2') or to (l_2, l_2''). For the latter extension, the run of P iterates the loop L twice. For the former extension, the assertions $I_2(l_2, l_2')$ holds and for the latter one, the assertion $I_2(l_2, l_2'')$ holds. From (l_2, l_2''), the run can be extended either to (l_2, l_2'') by following the same path as before, or to (l_2, l_2'). Again, either the assertion $I_2(l_2, l_2'')$ or $I_2(l_2, l_2')$ holds, depending on the path of extension. From (l_2, l_2'), the run can be extended either to (l_2, l_2') again by iterating each loop L and L_2' once or to (l_3, l_3') by exiting the loops. For the former extension, the assertions $I_2(l_2, l_2')$ holds and for the latter one, the assertion $I_2(l_3, l_3')$ holds. Our reasoning on the extendibility of I_2 shows that for every pair runs of P and P' on the same input, one run is terminating if and only if so is the other, and since the assertion $I_2(l_3, l_3')$ holds at the program exits, then when the runs terminate, they return the same return value.

One of our main motivations is to give a notion of *certificate* that certifies inter-program properties. We define *verification conditions* that can be used as such a certificate. A verification condition itself is a *finite* set of assertions. A certificate can be turned into a proof by proving that every assertion in the verification condition is valid.

Note that we do not focus on how to find certificates (or verification conditions). Our main motivation is to establish a *unifying notion of certificate* so that program and inter-program properties obtained by various techniques could all become part of a certificate and eventually contribute to proving a required inter-program property, such as program equivalence.

In summary, the main contributions of this paper are the following: (1) new foundations for expressing and proving inter-program properties through the notion of extendibility, (2) a unifying notion of certificate about inter-program properties, and (3) an application of the theory to proving properties in translation validation for optimizing compilers. As briefly shown above, the notion of extendible assertion function is very flexible so that it allows one to formally relate two programs with loosely related control structures and to prove properties of those programs.

The outline of this paper is as follows. We first describe the formal model of programs and their semantics. We then develop a theory of properties of a single program based on the notion of extendible assertion function. Afterward we develop the theory further so that it can be used to describe and prove inter-program properties. We then describe the application of the theory to proving inter-program properties in translation validation for optimizing compilers. Finally, we discuss related and future work.

2   Main Assumptions

Our formalization will be based on standard assumptions about programs and their semantics. We assume that a program consists of a finite set of *program points*. We denote by $\mathbf{Point}_P$ the set of program points of P. A *program-point flow graph of P* is a finite directed graph whose nodes are the program points of P. In the sequel, we assume that every program P we are dealing with is associated with a program-point flow graph, denoted by $\mathbf{G}_P$. We assume that every program has a unique *entry point* and a unique *exit point*. Denote by $entry(P)$ and $exit(P)$, respectively, the entry and the exit point of program P.

We describe the run-time behavior of a program as sequences of configurations. A *configuration* of a program run is a pair (p, σ), where p is a program point and σ is a *state* mapping variables to values. The variables used in a state do not necessarily coincide with variables of the program. For example, we may consider *memory* to be a variable. A configuration (p, σ) is called an *entry configuration for P* if $p = entry(P)$, and an *exit configuration for P* if $p = exit(P)$. For a configuration γ, we denote by $pp(\gamma)$ the program point of γ.

We assume that the semantics of a program P is defined as a transition relation $\mapsto_P$ with transitions of the form $(p_1, \sigma_1) \mapsto_P (p_2, \sigma_2)$, where p_1, p_2 are program points, σ_1, σ_2 are states, and (p_1, p_2) is an edge in the program-point flow graph of P.

Definition 2.1 (Computation Sequence, Run). A *computation sequence of a program P* is either a finite or an infinite sequence of configurations

$$(p_0, \sigma_0), (p_1, \sigma_1), \dots, \tag{1}$$

where $(p_i, \sigma_i) \mapsto_P (p_{i+1}, \sigma_{i+1})$ for all i. A *run R of a program P from an initial state σ_0* is a computation sequence (1) such that $p_0 = entry(P)$. A run is *complete* if it cannot be extended, that is, it is either infinite or terminates at an exit configuration.   □

We introduce two restrictions on the semantics of programs. First, we assume that programs are deterministic. That is, for every program P, given a configuration γ_1, there exists at most one configuration γ_2 such that $\gamma_1 \mapsto_P \gamma_2$. Second, we assume that, for every program P and for every non-exit configuration γ_1 of P's run, there exists a configuration γ_2 such that $\gamma_1 \mapsto_P \gamma_2$, that is, a complete run may only terminate in an exit configuration. Our results can easily be generalized by relieving these restrictions. Indeed, for non-deterministic programs where the non-deterministic choices are visible, one can view such programs as deterministic programs having an additional input variable x whose value is an infinite sequence of numbers, these numbers are used to decide which of non-deterministic choices should be made. Further, if a program computation can terminate in a state different from the exit state, we can add an artificial transition from this state to the exit state.

Further, we assume some *assertion language* in which one can write *assertions* involving variables and express properties of states. The set of all assertions is denoted by **Assertion**. We write $\sigma \models \alpha$ to mean an assertion α is true in a state σ, and also say that σ *satisfies* α, or that α *holds at* σ. We say that an assertion α is valid if $\sigma \models \alpha$ for every state σ. We will also use a similar notation for configurations: for a configuration (p, σ) and assertion α we write $(p, \sigma) \models \alpha$ if $\sigma \models \alpha$. We assume that the assertion language is closed under the standard propositional connectives and respects their semantics.

3 Intra-program Properties

In this section we introduce the notion of program invariant for a single program and some related notions that make it more suitable to present inter-program properties later.

Program Invariants. We introduce the notion of assertion function that associates program points with assertions. An *assertion function* for a program P is a partial function

$$I : \textbf{Point}_P \to \textbf{Assertion}$$

mapping program points of P to assertions such that $I(entry(P))$ and $I(exit(P))$ are defined. The requirement that I is defined on the entry and exit points is purely technical and not restrictive, for one can always define $I(entry(P))$ and $I(exit(P))$ as $\top$, that is, an assertion that holds at every state.

Given an assertion function I, we call a program point p I-*observable* if $I(p)$ is defined. A configuration (p, σ) is called I-observable if so is its program point p. We say that a configuration $\gamma = (p, \sigma)$ *satisfies* I, denoted by $\gamma \models I$, if $I(p)$ is defined and $\sigma \models I(p)$. We will also say that I is defined on γ if it is defined on p and write $I(\gamma)$ to denote $I(p)$.

Definition 3.1 (Program Invariant). Let I be an assertion function of a program P. The function I is said to be a *program invariant* of P if for every run $\gamma_0, \gamma_1, \ldots$ of the program such that $\gamma_0 \models I$ and for all $i \geq 0$, we have $\gamma_i \models I$ whenever I is defined on γ_i. □

This notion of invariant is useful for asserting that a program satisfies some properties, including partial correctness of a problem. Recall that a program P is *partially correct* with respect to a precondition φ and a postcondition ψ, denoted by $\{\varphi\}P\{\psi\}$, if for every run of P from a configuration satisfying φ and reaching an exit configuration, this exit configuration satisfies ψ.

P:

```
i := 0;
j := 0;
while (j < 100) {
    if (i > j) j := j + 1;
    else i := i + 1;
q :
}
```

P':

```
i' := 0;
j' := 0;
while (j' < 100) {
    i' := i' + 1;
    j' := j' + 1;
q' :
}
```

Fig. 2. Example Programs

Theorem 3.2. *Let P be a program and φ, ψ be assertions. Let I be an assertion function for P such that $I(entry(P)) = \varphi$ and $I(exit(P)) = \psi$. If I is an invariant, then $\{\varphi\}P\{\psi\}$. If, in addition, I is only defined on the entry and the exit points, then I is an invariant if and only if $\{\varphi\}P\{\psi\}$.*   □

One can provide a similar characterization of loop invariants using our notion of invariant.

Extendible Assertion Functions. Our notion of invariant is not immediately useful for *proving* that a program satisfies some properties. For proving, we need a more constructive characterization of relations between I and P than just those expressed by program runs. We introduce the notion of extendible assertion function that provides such a characterization.

Definition 3.3. Let I be an assertion function of a program P. I is *strongly extendible* if for every run $\gamma_0, \ldots, \gamma_i$ of the program such that $i \geq 0$, $\gamma_0 \models I$, $\gamma_i \models I$, and γ_i is not an exit configuration, there exists a finite computation sequence $\gamma_i, \ldots, \gamma_{i+n}$ such that

1. $n > 0$,
2. $\gamma_{i+n} \models I$, and
3. for all j such that $i < j < i + n$, the configuration γ_j is not I-observable.

The definition of *weakly-extendible* assertion function is obtained from this definition by dropping condition 3.   □

Example 3.4. Let us give an example illustrating the difference between the two notions of extendible assertion functions. Consider the program P in Figure 2.

Define an assertion function I of P such that $I(entry(P)) = \top$ and $I(q) = I(exit(P)) = (i = j)$, and $I(p)$ is undefined on all program points p different from q and the entry and exit points. Then I is weakly extendible but not strongly extendible. To show that I is weakly extendible, it is enough to observe the following properties:

1. From an entry configuration, in two iterations of the loop, one reaches a configuration with the program point q in which $i = j = 1$;
2. For every $v < 100$, from a configuration with the program point q in which $i = j = v$, in two iterations of the loop, one can reach a configuration in which $i = j = v+1$;

3. For every $v \geq 100$, from a configuration with the program point q in which $\mathsf{i} = \mathsf{j} = v$, one can reach an exit configuration in which $\mathsf{i} = \mathsf{j} = v$.

To show that I is not strongly extendible, it is sufficient to note that, from any entry configuration, after one iteration of the loop, one can reach a configuration with the program point q in which $\mathsf{i} = 1$ and $\mathsf{j} = 0$ and so $\mathsf{i} = \mathsf{j}$ does not hold.   □

Weakly-extendible functions are sufficient for proving partial correctness:

Theorem 3.5. *Let I be a weakly-extendible assertion function of a program P such that $I(entry(P)) = \varphi$ and $I(exit(P)) = \psi$. Then $\{\varphi\}P\{\psi\}$, that is, P is partially correct with respect to the precondition φ and the postcondition ψ.*   □

On the other hand, strongly-extendible assertion functions serve as invariants.

Theorem 3.6. *Every strongly-extendible assertion function I of a program P is also an invariant of P.*

Proof. We have to show that, for every run $\gamma_0, \gamma_1, \ldots$ of P such that $\gamma_0 \models I$ and every I-observable configuration γ_i of this run, we have $\gamma_i \models I$. We will prove it by induction on i. When $i = 0$, the statement is trivial. Suppose $i > 0$. Take the greatest number j such that $0 \leq j < i$ and γ_j is I-observable. Such a number exists since γ_0 is I-observable. By the induction hypothesis, we have $\gamma_j \models I$. By the definition of strongly-extendible assertion function, we have that there exists an $n > 0$ and a run $\gamma_0, \ldots, \gamma_j, \ldots, \gamma_n$ such that $\gamma_n \models I$ and all configurations between γ_j and γ_n are not I-observable. Note that both γ_i and γ_n are the first I-observable configurations after γ_j in their runs. By the assumption that our programs are deterministic, we obtain $\gamma_i = \gamma_n$, so $\gamma_i \models I$.   □

We introduce other sufficient conditions on assertion functions which, on the one hand, will guarantee that an invariant is also strongly or weakly extendible, and on the other hand, make our notion of invariant similar to more traditional ones [6]. To this end, we will use paths in the program-point flow graph $\mathbf{G}_P$. Such a path is called *trivial* if it consists of a single point. To guarantee that an invariant I of a program P is strongly extendible, we require that I must be defined on certain program points such that those points break all cycles in $\mathbf{G}_P$. We introduce the notion of covering set to describe this requirement.

Definition 3.7 (Covering Set). Let P be a program and C be a set of program points in P. We say that C *covers* P if $entry(P) \in C$ and every infinite path in $\mathbf{G}_P$ contains a program point in C. An assertion function I is said to *cover* P if the set of I-observable program points covers P.   □

Any set C that covers P is often called a *cut-point set* of P.

Theorem 3.8. *Let I be an invariant of P. If I covers P, then I is strongly extendible.*

Proof. Take any run $\gamma_0, \ldots, \gamma_i$ of P such that $\gamma_0 \models I$, $\gamma_i \models I$ and γ_i is not an exit configuration. We have to extend this run to a run $\gamma_0, \ldots, \gamma_{i+n}$ satisfying the conditions of Definition 3.3. To this end, first extend this run to a complete run

$R = (\gamma_0, \ldots, \gamma_i, \gamma_{i+1}, \ldots)$. Let us show that R contains a configuration γ_{i+n} with $n > 0$ on which I is defined. Indeed, if R is finite, then the last configuration of R is an exit configuration, and then I is defined on it. If R is infinite, then the path $pp(\gamma_{i+1}), pp(\gamma_{i+2}), \ldots$ is infinite, hence contains a program point on which I is defined. Take the smallest positive n such that I is defined on γ_{i+n}. Since n is the smallest, I is undefined on all configurations between γ_i and γ_{i+n} in R. Since I is invariant, we have $\gamma_{i+n} \models I$. $\qquad\qquad\square$

The proof of the above theorem relies on one of the assumptions described in Section 2, that is, program runs can only terminate in exit states. This assumption is important since the notion of invariant does not guarantee progress due to blocking instructions. For instance, **assume** $(x > 0)$ is run in a state σ where $\sigma(x) \leq 0$. In our assumption, when the condition of **assume** does not hold, then there is a transition to the exit state, and by the requirement of assertion function, every assertion function is defined in the exit state.

Verification Conditions. Our next aim is to define a notion of verification condition as a collection of formulas and use these verification conditions to prove properties of programs. We want to define it in such a way that a verification condition guarantees certain properties of programs. To this end, we use the notions of precondition and liberal precondition for programs and paths in program-point flow graphs.

Definition 3.9 (Weakest Liberal Precondition). An assertion φ is called the *weakest liberal precondition* of a program P and an assertion ψ, if

1. $\{\varphi\}P\{\psi\}$, and
2. for every assertion φ' such that $\{\varphi'\}P\{\psi\}$, the assertion $\varphi' \Rightarrow \varphi$ is valid.

In general, the weakest liberal precondition may not exist. If it exists, we denote the weakest liberal precondition of P and ψ by $wlp_P(\psi)$.

In a similar way, we introduce the notion of a weakest liberal precondition of a path $\pi = (p_0, \ldots, p_n)$ in the flow graph. An assertion φ is called a *precondition* of the path π and an assertion ψ, if, for every state σ_0 such that $\sigma_0 \models \varphi$, there exist states $\sigma_1, \ldots, \sigma_n$ such that

$$(p_0, \sigma_0) \mapsto (p_1, \sigma_1) \mapsto \ldots \mapsto (p_n, \sigma_n)$$

and $\sigma_n \models \psi$. An assertion φ is called the *weakest precondition* of π and ψ, denoted by $wp_\pi(\psi)$, if it is a precondition of π and ψ, and, for every precondition φ' of π and ψ, the assertion $\varphi' \Rightarrow \varphi$ is valid.

An assertion φ is called a *liberal precondition* of the path π and an assertion ψ, if, for every sequence $\sigma_0, \ldots, \sigma_n$ of states such that

$$(p_0, \sigma_0) \mapsto (p_1, \sigma_1) \mapsto \ldots \mapsto (p_n, \sigma_n),$$

and $\sigma_0 \models \varphi$, we have $\sigma_n \models \psi$. An assertion φ is called the *weakest liberal precondition* of π and ψ, denoted by $wlp_\pi(\psi)$, if it is a liberal precondition of π and ψ, and, for every liberal precondition φ' of π and ψ, the assertion $\varphi' \Rightarrow \varphi$ is valid. $\qquad\square$

We have so far not imposed any restrictions on the programming languages in which programs are written. However, to provide certificates or verification conditions for program properties, we need to be able to compute the weakest and the weakest liberal precondition of a given path and an assertion.

Definition 3.10 (Weakest Precondition Property). We say that a programming language has the *weakest precondition property* if, for every assertion ψ and path π, the weakest precondition for π and ψ exists and moreover, can be effectively computed from π and ψ. □

In the sequel we assume that our programming language has the weakest precondition property. Furthermore, since for a path π and an assertion ψ, $wlp_\pi(\psi)$ is equivalent to $wp_\pi(\psi) \vee \neg wp_\pi(\top)$, one can also compute the weakest liberal precondition for π and ψ.

Next, we describe the verification conditions associated with assertion functions. Such verification conditions form *certificates* for program properties described by the assertion functions. Let I be an assertion function. A path $p_0, \ldots, p_n$ in $\mathbf{G}_P$ is called *I-simple* if $n > 0$ and I is defined on p_0 and p_n and undefined on all program points $p_1, \ldots, p_{n-1}$. We will say that the path is *between* p_0 and p_n.

Definition 3.11. Let I be an assertion function of a program P such that the domain of I covers P. The *strong verification condition* associated with I is the set of assertions

$$\{I(p_0) \Rightarrow wlp_\pi(I(p_n)) \mid \pi \text{ is an } I\text{-simple path between } p_0 \text{ and } p_n\}.$$

Note that the strong verification condition is always finite. □

Theorem 3.12. *Let I be an assertion function of a program P whose domain covers P and $\mathbb{S}$ be the strong verification condition associated with I. If every assertion in $\mathbb{S}$ is valid, then I is strongly extendible.*

Proof. Take any run $\gamma_0, \ldots, \gamma_i$ of P such that $\gamma_0 \models I$, $\gamma_i \models I$ and γ_i is not an exit configuration. Using arguments of the proof of Theorem 3.8, we extend this run to a run $\gamma_0, \ldots, \gamma_{i+n}$ such that I is defined on γ_{i+n} but undefined on $\gamma_{i+1}, \ldots, \gamma_{i+n-1}$. It remains to prove that $\gamma_{i+n} \models I$. Consider the run $\gamma_i, \ldots, \gamma_{i+n}$ and denote the program point of each configuration γ_j in this run by p_j and the state of γ_j by σ_j. Then the path $\pi = (p_i, \ldots, p_{i+n})$ is simple and we have $\sigma_i \models I(p_i)$. The assertion

$$I(p_i) \Rightarrow wlp_\pi(I(p_{i+n}))$$

belongs to the strong verification condition associated with I, hence valid, so $I(p_i)$ is a liberal precondition. By the definition of liberal precondition, we have $\sigma_{i+n} \models I(p_{i+n})$, which is equivalent to $\gamma_{i+n} \models I$. □

Note that this theorem gives us a sufficient condition for checking partial correctness of the program: given an assertion function I defined on a covering set, we can generate the strong verification condition associated with I. This condition by Theorem 3.12 guarantees that I is strongly extendible, hence also weekly extendible. Therefore, by Theorem 3.5 guarantees partial correctness. Moreover, the strong verification condition is simply a collection of assertions, so if we have a theorem prover for the assertion language, it can be used to check the strong verification condition.

One can reformulate the notion of verification condition in such a way that it will guarantee weak extendibility. For every path π, denote by $start(\pi)$ and $end(\pi)$, respectively, the first and the last point of π.

Definition 3.13. Let I be an assertion function of a program P and Π a finite set of non-trivial paths in $\mathbf{G}_P$ such that for every path π in Π both $start(\pi)$ and $end(\pi)$ are I-observable. For every program point p in P, denote by $\Pi|p$ the set of paths in Π whose first point is p.

The *weak verification condition* associated with I and Π consists of all assertions of the form

$$I(start(\pi)) \Rightarrow wlp_\pi(I(end(\pi))),$$

where $\pi \in \Pi$ and all assertions of the form

$$I(p) \Rightarrow \bigvee_{\pi \in \Pi|p} wp_\pi(\top),$$

where p is an I-observable point. □

The first kind of assertion in this definition is similar to the assertions used in the strong verification condition, but instead of all simple paths we consider all paths in Π. The second kind of assertion expresses that, whenever a configuration at a point p satisfies $I(p)$, the computation from this configuration will inevitably follow at least one path in Π. The following theorem states the sufficiency of weak verification conditions to guarantee weak extendibility.

Theorem 3.14. *Let I and Π be as in Definition 3.13 and $\mathbb{W}$ be the weak verification condition associated with I and Π. If every assertion in $\mathbb{W}$ is valid, then I is weakly extendible.*

Proof. In the proof, whenever we denote a configuration by γ_i, we use p_i for the program point and σ_i for the state of this configuration, and similarly for other indices instead of i. Take any run $\gamma_0, \ldots, \gamma_i$ of P such that $\gamma_0 \models I$, $\gamma_i \models I$ and γ_i is not an exit configuration. Since p_i is I-observable, the following assertion belongs to $\mathbb{W}$:

$$I(p_i) \Rightarrow \bigvee_{\pi \in \Pi|p_i} wp_\pi(\top),$$

and hence it is valid. Since $\gamma_i \models I$, we have $\sigma_i \models I(p_i)$, then by the validity of the above formula we have

$$\sigma_i \models \bigvee_{\pi \in \Pi|p_i} wp_\pi(\top).$$

This implies that there exists a path $\pi \in \Pi|p_i$ such that $\sigma_i \models wp_\pi(\top)$. Let the path π have the form $p_i, \ldots, p_{i+n}$. Then, by the definition of $wp_\pi(\top)$, there exist states $\sigma_{i+1}, \ldots, \sigma_{i+n}$ such that

$$(p_i, \sigma_i) \mapsto (p_{i+1}, \sigma_{i+1}) \mapsto \ldots \mapsto (p_{i+n}, \sigma_{i+n}).$$

Using that $\pi \in \Pi$ and repeating arguments of Theorem 3.12 we can prove $\sigma_{i+n} \models$ $I(p_{i+n})$.   □

Note that, in the definitions of strong and weak verification conditions, one computes the weakest precondition or the weakest liberal precondition of a path, *not* a program. Thus, there is not fix-point computation.

4   Inter-program Properties

In this section we develop further the notion of extendible assertion function so that it can be used to prove *inter-program properties*. Given a pair (P, P') of programs, we assume that they have disjoint sets of variables. A configuration is a tuple $(p, p', \hat{\sigma})$, where $p \in \mathbf{Point}_P$, $p' \in \mathbf{Point}_{P'}$, and $\hat{\sigma}$ is a state mapping from all variables of both programs to values. A state can be considered as a pair of states: one for the variables of P and one for the variables of P'. In the sequel, such a state $\hat{\sigma}$ is written as (σ, σ'), where σ is for P and σ' is for P'. Similarly, the configuration $(p, p', \hat{\sigma})$ can be written as (p, p', σ, σ').

Similar to the case of a single program, we say that a configuration $\gamma = (p, p', \sigma, \sigma')$ is called an *entry configuration for* (P, P') if $p = entry(P)$ and $p' = entry(P')$, and an *exit configuration for* (P, P') if $p = exit(P)$ and $p' = exit(P')$.

The transition relation $\mapsto$ of a pair (P, P') of programs contains two kinds of transition:

$$(p_1, p', \sigma_1, \sigma') \mapsto (p_2, p', \sigma_2, \sigma'),$$

such that $(p_1, \sigma_1) \mapsto (p_2, \sigma_2)$ is in the transition relation of P, and

$$(p, p_1', \sigma, \sigma_1') \mapsto (p, p_2', \sigma, \sigma_2'),$$

such that $(p_1, \sigma_1) \mapsto (p_2, \sigma_2)$ is in the transition relation of P'.

Having the notion of transition relation for pairs of programs, the notions of computation sequence and run can be defined in the same way as in the case of a single program.

An *assertion function* of a pair (P, P') of programs is a partial function

$$I : \mathbf{Point}_P \times \mathbf{Point}_{P'} \to \mathbf{Assertion}$$

mapping pairs of program points of P and P' to assertions such that I is defined on $(entry(P), entry(P'))$ and $(exit(P), exit(P'))$.

Given an assertion function I, we call a pair of program points (p, p') *I-observable* if $I(p, p')$ is defined. Let $\gamma = (p, p', \sigma, \sigma')$ be a configuration. Then, γ is I-observable if so is the pair of program points (p, p'). We also say that γ *satisfies* I, denoted by $\gamma \models I$, if I is defined on (p, p') and $(\sigma, \sigma') \models I(p, p')$. We will also say that I is defined on γ if it is defined on (p, p') and write $I(\gamma)$ to denote $I(p, p')$.

Unlike in the case of a single program, for a pair of programs, there are no notions of invariant and strongly-extendible assertion function. The transition relation of a pair of programs has no synchronization mechanism. For example, one program in a pair can make as many transitions as possible, while the other program in the same pair stays at some program point without making any transition. Thus, it is not useful to have the notions of invariant and strongly-extendible assertion functions.

The notion of weakly-extendible assertion function is better suited for describing inter-program properties. Weakly-extendible assertion functions for a pair of programs can be defined in the same way as in the case of a single program.

Definition 4.1. Let I be an assertion function of a pair (P, P') of programs. I is *weakly extendible* if for every run $\gamma_0, \ldots, \gamma_i$ of (P, P') such that $i \geq 0$, $\gamma_0 \models I$, $\gamma_i \models I$, and γ_i is not an exit configuration, there exists a finite computation sequence $\gamma_i, \ldots, \gamma_{i+n}$ of (P, P') such that

1. $n > 0$, and
2. $\gamma_{i+n} \models I$.   □

Example 4.2. Let us illustrate the notion of weakly-extendible assertion function for a pair of programs. Consider the two programs P and P' in Figure 2.

Define an assertion function I of (P, P') such that $I(entry(P), entry(P')) = \top$ and $I(q, q') = I(exit(P), exit(P')) = \varphi$, where where $\varphi = (\mathsf{i} = \mathsf{i}') \wedge (\mathsf{j} = \mathsf{j}') \wedge (\mathsf{i} = \mathsf{j})$. The function I is weakly extendible due to the following properties:

1. From an entry configuration of (P, P'), by taking a computation sequence consisting of two iterations of the loop of P and one iteration of the loop of P', one reaches a configuration with program points (q, q') in which φ holds.
2. For every $v < 100$, from a configuration with the program points (q, q') in which $\mathsf{i} = \mathsf{i}' = \mathsf{j} = \mathsf{j}' = v$, by taking a computation sequence consisting of two iterations of the loop of P and one iteration of the loop of P', one again reaches a configuration with program points (q, q') in which $\mathsf{i} = \mathsf{i}' = \mathsf{j} = \mathsf{j}' = v + 1$.
3. For every $v \geq 100$, from a configuration with the program points (q, q') in which $\mathsf{i} = \mathsf{i}' = \mathsf{j} = \mathsf{j}' = v$, one can reach an exit configuration in which $\mathsf{i} = \mathsf{i}' = \mathsf{j} = \mathsf{j}' = v$.   □

The notion of partial correctness for pairs of programs can be defined in the same way as that of the case of a single program. Concerning the sufficiency of weakly-extendible assertion functions for proving partial correctness, we obtain the same result as in the case of a single program.

Theorem 4.3. *Let I be an assertion function of a pair (P, P') of programs such that*

$$\varphi = I(entry(P), entry(P')) \text{ and } \psi = I(exit(P), exit(P')).$$

If the assertion function I is weakly extendible, then $\{\varphi\}(P, P')\{\psi\}$, that is, (P, P') is partially correct with respect to the precondition φ and postcondition ψ.   □

Similar to the properties of a single program, the verification conditions associated with inter-program properties use the notion of path. A path $\hat{\pi}$ of a pair (P, P') of program can be considered as a trajectory in a two dimensional space, that is, we denote such a path $\hat{\pi}$ by (π, π'), such that π and π' are the axes of the space, and π is a path of P and π' is a path of P'. Having the notion of path for a pair of programs, the notions of precondition and liberal precondition for paths of a pair of programs can be defined in the same way as in the case of a single program. In fact, the weakest precondition of a path of a pair of programs may be derived from the paths of the single programs. That is, let ψ be an assertion, we have $wp_{(\pi,\pi')}(\psi)$, $wp_\pi(wp_{\pi'}(\psi))$, and $wp_{\pi'}(wp_\pi(\psi))$ equivalent.

We can define the verification condition associated with weakly extendible assertion functions similarly to the case of a single program.

Definition 4.4. Let I be an assertion function of a pair (P, P') of programs and Π a finite set of non-trivial paths of the pair of programs such that for every path π in Π both $start(\pi)$ and $end(\pi)$ path are I-observable. For every pair (p, p') of program points, denote by $\Pi|(p, p')$ the set of paths in Π whose first pair of points is (p, p').

The *weak verification condition* associated with I and Π consists of all assertions of the form

$$I(start(\pi)) \Rightarrow wlp_\pi(I(end(\pi))),$$

where $\pi \in \Pi$ and all assertions of the form

$$I(p, p') \Rightarrow \bigvee_{\pi \in \Pi|(p,p')} wp_\pi(\top),$$

where (p, p') is an I-observable point, and (p, p') is not the exit point of (P, P').   □

Theorem 4.5. *Let I and Π be as in Definition 4.4 and $\mathbb{W}$ be the weak verification condition associated with I and Π. If every assertion in $\mathbb{W}$ is valid, then I is weakly extendible.*   □

The proof of the above theorem is similar to Theorem 3.14, and due to space limit is omitted. The notion of weak verification condition is the cornerstone of our theory of inter-program properties. It can be used as a suitable notion of certificate for properties that relate two programs.

5 Translation Validation

We have seen in the introduction an example of translation validation involving loop unrolling. In this section we discuss another example of translation validation. In particular, we will show an example that, using inter-program assertions and the notion of weak extendibility, we can prove program equivalence that cannot be proved by existing proof rules in translation validation [18,14,23,19,12].

Example 5.1. Consider the programs P and P' in Figure 3. These programs are taken from [18]. We define a notion of program equivalence as implementation correctness. A program P_1 *correctly implements* P_2 if P_1 simulates P_2 and vice versa. We say that P_1 *simulates* P_2 if for every run of P_2 that reaches an exit configuration, then there is a run of P_1 on the same input that reaches an exit configuration such that the values of return variables in these configurations coincide. We want to prove that P' correctly implements P.

In our previous work [11], we introduce the notion of basic-block (or program-point) and variable correspondence such that program equivalence can be established by finding certain program-point and variable correspondences. Intuitively, a variable x_1 at

P :

p :
g := 0;
do {
  g := g + 6;
q :
} **while** (g < 48);
return g;
r :

P' :

p' :
g' := 48
return g';
r' :

Fig. 3. Example Programs

location p_1 in a program P_1 corresponds to a variable x_2 at location p_2 in a program P_2 if they have the same values at p_1 and p_2 for all possible runs of the two programs on the same input. To establish that P' correctly implements P, one needs to prove that there is a correspondence between variables g and g' at the points r and r'. Let us call such points r and r' control points. The proof technique in [12] cannot prove the correspondence because it requires that there is at least one control point on every reachable cycle in the program-point flow graphs of P and P', and there is a one-to-one correspondence between the set of control points on reachable cycles in P and the set of control points on reachable cycles in P'. The loop in P above is reachable, but since there is no loop in P', then the requirements of the proof technique cannot be satisfied. Similarly, the rule VALIDATE in [23] is not applicable since it requires that there is a one-to-one correspondence between loop headers in P and loop headers in P'; however there is no loop in P'. The logic presented in [18] cannot prove that P simulates P' because the logic cannot prove that the loop in P terminates.

We prove that P' correctly implements P using inter-program assertions and the notion of weak extendibility. First, we define an assertion function I such that $I(p, p') = \top$, $I(q, p') = (g \le 48 \wedge \exists j.(j > 0 \wedge g = j * 6))$, and $I(r, r') = (g = g')$. Let π_{p_1, p_2} denote a path from p_1 to p_2, and π_{p_1} denote a trivial path whose only point is p_1. We argue that I is weakly extendible, which in turn proves that P' correctly implements P. For every run from a configuration satisfying $I(p, p')$, the run can follow the path $(\pi_{p,q}, \pi_{p'})$ and reach a configuration that satisfies $I(q, p')$. From this configuration, the run can be extended such that it follows either the path $(\pi_{q,q}, \pi_{p'})$ or the path $(\pi_{q,r}, \pi_{p',r'})$. If we omit the latter path from our reasoning, then I would *not* be weakly extendible. From these paths, it follows that every run of (P, P') terminates in an exit configuration satisfying $I(r, r')$, that is the values of return variables g and g' coincide in the exit configuration. Consequently, for every run of P', there is a run of P, and vice versa, such that both runs reach exit configurations, and the values of g and g' coincide in these configurations. Therefore, we proved that P' correctly implements P.

Let a set Π of paths of (P, P') consist of all the above mentioned paths, then one can prove that all assertions in the weak verification condition associated with I and Π are valid. $\qquad\qquad\qquad\square$

Using inter-program assertions and the notion of weak extendibility, we can also prove correspondence properties described by the proof techniques in [18,14,23,19,12]; a detailed description can be found in [20].

6   Related Work and Conclusion

We presented a theory for describing and proving inter-program properties. Our formalization is based on the notion of extendible assertion function. The theory deals with imperative programs represented as control-flow graphs. It defines a notion of certificate, consisting of a set of assertions obtained by calculating weakest and weakest liberal preconditions of paths in the flow graphs and postconditions.

There are many works on establishing and proving inter-program properties in various forms. Closely related is the *certifying compiler* approach to compiler verification, in particular optimizing compilers. In this approach the compiler must check that the source and the target programs are semantically equivalent and produce a proof of equivalence. The compiler can use the results of data-flow analysis to check equivalence as in credible compilation [18], or external tools for checking equivalence as in translation validation. Existing translation validation frameworks include [23,14,11,12,19]. All frameworks in certifying compilers present program analysis, notions of correspondence between two programs, and proof rules for proving the correspondences. Program equivalence is then established by finding such proofs. These frameworks use control-flow graphs, operational semantics, and simulation relations for describing correspondences. Note that unlike many other papers our paper is *not* about how to obtain a certificate. It is about the right notion of certificate. We think that our notion is in many respects unifying since the results of static analysis of any of the programs or the pair of programs obtained by other methods can be readily used as inter-program properties and contribute to a certificate.

Recently Pnueli and Zaks introduced a technique for checking equivalence by constructing a cross-product of the source and the target programs [22]. The benefit of having such a cross-product program is that existing methods of data-flow analysis of a single program are applicable to checking equivalence. In many respects their technique is similar to ours. For example, their notion of comparison graph can be considered as a special case of our transition relation for the pair of programs. Their notion of assertion network is similar to our notion of invariant. However, they assume that an invariant network is given, defined in every point and use it for checking specific observable properties. No notion of weakly extendible function is given. The construction of the cross-product program is performed by joining edges of the source and target programs such that the edges are of the same type, e.g., read, write, and call. This construction requires that there is a one-to-one correspondence between headers of reachable loops of the source and target programs, and thus is not be applicable to our Example 5.1. Unlike this paper, [22] goes beyond just the theory: it describes an implementation and also shows how one can generate intra-program invariants for some compiler optimizations

Another translation validation work by Benton [2] uses the language of types and denotational semantics to prove program equivalence. Benton's work describes a proof system for a relational version of Hoare logic with a type system describing pre- and post relations between two programs. As many other approaches to translation validation, it requires specific rules to handle loop unrolling and some other optimizations while our notion of certificate needs no modification to include them.

In our work we address neither inter-procedural optimizations nor aggressive loop optimizations, such as loop interchange and loop tiling. We can extend our formal model of programs to handle inter-procedural optimizations, like the work in [16]. Handling aggressive loop optimizations is the topic of our future work.

Another approach to compiler verification, that is weakly related to our work, is *certified compiler*. In this approach one proves that for *every* input source program, the source and the target programs are semantically equivalent. An example of development of a certified compiler using interactive prover is described in [9]. Papers [5,7,8] present languages for specifying compiler optimizations that can be proved semantics preserving. The approach of [5] is complementary to ours: they use temporal logic to certify optimizations. It will be interesting to incorporate temporal logic-based methods in our technique.

There is a vast amount of work on compiler correctness, including proving correctness of optimisations together with compiler development, e.g. [7]. Our work is *not* on proving compiler correctness so we do not overview these papers here in detail. However one can use such compilers in our framework since proofs produced by them can also be used for creating certificates in our framework. Moreover, one can use them even when correctness of some (but not all) optimisations is proved by the compiler.

Paper [1] translates certificates of original program into those of an optimised program. This technique complements ours in the sense that such techniques can also be used to transfer assertions about each of the programs into inter-program assertions.

Paper [17] introduces a technique of reasoning about inter-program properties, however in the context of functional programs.

Paper [21] defines a Hoare-style logic for a pair of programs. Although his formalisation has much in common with ours, our emphasis is different. Since we are dealing with languages satisfying the weakest precondition property and assertion functions, we do not need Hoare's logic: indeed, all reasoning we need is proofs of verification conditions that can be carried out in any proof system or by a theorem prover for the assertion language.

The notion of weakly-extendible assertion function is similar to the notion of *intermittent* assertion [10]. Intermittent assertions are of the form $sometime(\phi, p)$, which means sometime control will pass through p with assertion ϕ holds. That is, control may pass through p without satisfying ϕ, but control must pass through p at least once with ϕ satisfied. Program properties can be proved by proving theorems involving intermittent assertions. For example, "if $sometime(\phi_1, entry(P))$, then $sometime(\phi_2, exit(P))$", describes total correctness property. Proofs of program properties using intermittent invariants often require simple invariants. However, one can see that such assertions ϕ_1 and ϕ_2 can be asserted at the same point but are satisfied at different time or stage of the same computation. Thus, the proofs of intermittent assertions are rather loose with respect to the program-point flow graphs and program runs.

Our notion of an inter-program property can also be used to prove termination of one of the programs assuming that the other one terminates or given a suitable proof of termination of another program. However, treating termination is left as future work.

The theory presented here has been applied to the certification of smart-card applications in the framework of Common Criteria [13]. We also plan to apply the theory to equivalence checking between system code in the COCONUT project.

References

1. Barthe, G., Grégoire, B., Kunz, C., Rezk, T.: Certificate translation for optimizing compilers. In: Yi, K. (ed.) SAS 2006. LNCS, vol. 4134, pp. 301–317. Springer, Heidelberg (2006)
2. Benton, N.: Simple relational correctness proofs for static analyses and program transformations. In: POPL, pp. 14–25 (2004)
3. Floyd, R.W.: Assigning meaning to programs. In: Schwartz, J.T. (ed.) Proceedings of Symposium in Applied Mathematics, pp. 19–32 (1967)
4. Hoare, C.A.R.: An axiomatic basis for computer programming. CACM 12(10), 576–580 (1969)
5. Lacey, D., Jones, N.D., Van Wyk, E., Frederiksen, C.C.: Proving correctness of compiler optimizations by temporal logic. In: POPL (2002)
6. Leockx, J., Sieber, K., Stansifer, R.D.: The Foundations of Program Verification, 2nd edn. John Wiley & Sons, Inc., New York (1987)
7. Lerner, S., Millstein, T., Chambers, C.: Automatically proving the correctness of compiler optimizations. In: PLDI, pp. 220–231 (2003)
8. Lerner, S., Millstein, T., Rice, E., Chambers, C.: Automated soundness proofs for dataflow analyses and transformations via local rules. In: POPL (2005)
9. Leroy, X.: Formal certification of a compiler back-end or: programming a compiler with a proof assistant. SIGPLAN Not. 41(1), 42–54 (2006)
10. Manna, Z., Waldinger, R.: Is "sometime" sometimes better than "always"?: Intermittent assertions in proving program correctness. CACM 21(2), 159–172 (1978)
11. Narasamdya, I., Voronkov, A.: Finding basic block and variable correspondence. In: Hankin, C., Siveroni, I. (eds.) SAS 2005. LNCS, vol. 3672, pp. 251–267. Springer, Heidelberg (2005)
12. Narasamdya, I.: Establishing Program Equivalence in Translation Validation for Optimizing Compilers. PhD thesis, The University of Manchester (2007), http://www-verimag.imag.fr/~narasamd/NarasamdyaThesis.ps
13. Narasamdya, I., Périn, M.: Certification of smart-card applications in common criteria. Technical Report TR-2008-14, Verimag (September 2008)
14. Necula, G.C.: Translation validation for an optimizing compiler. In: Proceedings of the ACM SIGPLAN Conference on Principles of Programming Languages Design and Implementation (PLDI), June 2000, pp. 83–95 (2000)
15. Pnueli, A., Siegel, M., Singerman, E.: Translation validation. In: Steffen, B. (ed.) TACAS 1998. LNCS, vol. 1384, p. 151. Springer, Heidelberg (1998)
16. Pnueli, A., Zaks, A.: Translation validation of interprocedural optimizations. In: Proceedings of 4th International Workshop on Software Verification and Validation (2006)
17. Pottier, F., Simonet, V.: Information flow inference for ml. SIGPLAN Not. 37(1), 319–330 (2002)
18. Rinard, M., Marinov, D.: Credible compilation with pointers. In: Proceedings of the FLoC Workshop on Run-Time Result Verification, Trento, Italy (July 1999)
19. Rival, X.: Symbolic transfer function-based approaches to certified compilation. In: Proceedings of the 31st ACM SIGPLAN-SIGACT symposium on Principles of programming languages, pp. 1–13. ACM Press, New York (2004)
20. Voronkov, A., Narasamdya, I.: Proving inter-program properties. Technical Report TR-2008-13, Verimag (2008)
21. Yang, H.: Relational separation logic. Theor. Comput. Sci. 375(1-3), 308–334 (2007)
22. Zaks, A., Pnueli, A.: Covac: Compiler validation by program analysis of the cross-product. In: Cuellar, J., Maibaum, T., Sere, K. (eds.) FM 2008. LNCS, vol. 5014, pp. 35–51. Springer, Heidelberg (2008)
23. Zuck, L.D., Pnueli, A., Goldberg, B.: VOC: A methodology for the translation validation of optimizing compilers. J. UCS 9(3), 223–247 (2003)

Author Index